# From the classroom to the community, TEMAS engages your students in the Spanish language through active learning

With **Temas: Spanish for the Global Community**, active learning takes place not only in the classroom, but far beyond the confines of its walls. This pioneering text provides real opportunities for students to effect change in their communities through the use of their emerging linguistic skills. **Temas** prepares students for professional and social interactions with native speakers not only through its authentic language use, but also through the integration of service- and community-based learning. Authors Jorge H. Cubillos and Edwin M. Lamboy recognize that by interacting with their communities, Spanish students can use their language skills to help change the world in a positive way.

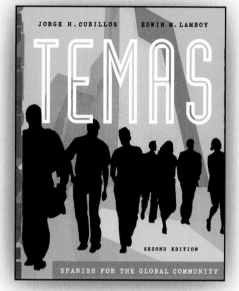

With this Second Edition the authors maintain the book's pedagogical foundations and its thematic orientation while increasing the opportunities for students to have meaningful interactions with other language learners as well as native speakers—both here and abroad. Culture permeates every chapter, giving students an appreciation of the habits, mores, and traditions of Spanish-speaking peoples in the 21st century.

Explore this Second Edition of **Temas** and discover a text that:

- ⚙ is ***structured around student-friendly themes*** (see page 2)
- ⚙ ***immerses students in the language as it is spoken today*** (see page 4)
- ⚙ engages learners with an ***abundance of real-world and community-based activities*** (see page 6)
- ⚙ supports teaching and learning with **iLrn™ Spanish** *and other interactive teaching and learning tools* (see page 7)

## NOW AVAILABLE IN THREE VOLUMES— CHOOSE THE PERFECT BOOK FOR YOUR COURSE!

**Temas: Spanish for the Global Community**
Second Edition
(Casebound; Chapters P–12)
1-4130-1049-0

**Temas: Spanish for the Global Community**
Second Edition, Volume I
(Paperbound; Chapters P–6)
1-4130-2895-0

**Temas: Spanish for the Global Community**
Second Edition, Volume II
(Paperbound; Chapters 7–12)
1-4130-2899-3

> " Temas is an exciting way to teach language because it shows students the real-life applications for what they are learning in the foreign language classroom. Temas integrates language and culture while teaching the four skills, but more importantly, it prepares students for immediate interaction with the growing Hispanic population in the United States. "
>
> MARCIE RINKA, UNIVERSITY OF SAN DIEGO

THOMSON
HEINLE™

# A carefully crafted organization that promotes student understanding of language *and* culture

Each chapter is broken down into three organizing *Temas*—content- and function-based sections that expose students to the language. With this organization students ultimately learn to manipulate and create language. Four basic sections comprise each *Tema*:

- ✺ *Vocabulario*
- ✺ *Funciones y estructuras* (two sections)
- ✺ *Perspectivas* (in *Tema 1*), *Vídeo* (in *Tema 2*), or *Lectura* (in *Tema 3*)

| | TEMA 1<br>Ésta es mi familia | TEMA 2<br>La personalidad | TEMA 3<br>Nuestra casa |
|---|---|---|---|
| Vocabulario | Los miembros de la familia | Los rasgos personales m | Los espacios y los uebles de una casa |
| Funciones y estructuras | Describing physical appearance with adjectives and the verbs **ser** and **tener**<br>Expressing possession | Talking about location, conditions, and emotional states with the verbs **estar** and **tener**<br>Talking about likes and dislikes with **gustar** | Talking about location with prepositions<br>Expressing obligation with **tener que...** and **hay que...** |
| Lecturas y vídeo | Perspectivas: La familia de José Miguel | Vídeo: Los compañeros se conocen mejor | Lectura: *La casa en Mango Street* |

The *Perspectivas, Vídeo,* or *Lectura* at the end of each *Tema* gives students the chance to explore and interact with contextualized culture-rich materials. While culturally pertinent information is provided in every section, the *Perspectivas, Vídeo,* and *Lecturas* sections focus exclusively on the acquisition and development of cultural competency.

### IV. Perspectivas: La familia de José Miguel

■ Antes de leer

Información ¿Qué información encuentran *(do you find)* en el Internet acerca de las familias? Marquen las opciones más lógicas.

| nombres de los | lugar donde | religión |
|---|---|---|
| familiares | viven | ideas |
| profesiones | fotografías | políticas |
| problemas | historia de | edades |
| médicos | la familia | |

■ A leer

#### Ésta es mi familia
La foto muestra a mi familia. De izquierda a derecha, Uds. pueden ver a mi hermana Luisa Fernanda. Ella tiene dieciséis años, estudia en el Liceo Camilo Daza y cursa el sexto año de bachillerato. Después estoy yo, José Miguel, mi mamá Angélica (lo más lindo del mundo *[the most beautiful thing in the world]*), mi papá Miguel Hernando, que es ingeniero electrónico, y finalmente mi hermana mayor, Teresa, que tiene veintitrés años y es enfermera. Yo tengo veinte años y estudio arquitectura en la Universidad Javeriana. En mi tiempo libre, toco la guitarra y navego por el Internet.

■ ¿Entendiste bien?

1. ¿Cuántas personas hay e
2. ¿Cuántas hermanas tiene
3. ¿Cuántos años tiene la h
4. ¿Cuál es la profesión de
5. ¿Cuál es la profesión de
6. ¿Qué hace José Miguel e
7. ¿Esta familia es semejant respuesta.

### IV. Vídeo: Los compañeros se conocen mejor

■ Preparación

A. Las imágenes Practice using contextual clues by answering the questions below about the brief portion of the video segment that you are about to see without audio.

1. Who is talking?
2. Where are they?
3. What are they doing?
4. What do you think they are talking about?

Now watch again, this time with audio. Were you correct?

**COMPREHENSION STRATEGY**

*Using Contextual Clues* Normal speech among natives may seem fast and difficult to follow at first. To facilitate comprehension, use all the contextual clues available to fill in the gaps with educated guesses. The more you hear authentic Spanish, the more you will get used to its speed and rhythm.

**Sugerencia A:** Play segment without audio. Only show the first 40 seconds with Sofía and Alejandra talking in their bedroom. Stop when Alejandra's testimonial begins.

**New**

Throughout each chapter, icons prompt students to access corresponding activities and exercises in **iLrn™ Spanish** for additional practice and support. For more on **iLrn™ Spanish**, turn to the inside back cover of this text.

TEMA 3

To provide additional background on the experience of Mexican immigrants in the U.S., you may want to show scenes from the PBS series *American Family* in class. The website for this series is: http://www.pbs.org/americanfamily

### IV. Lectura: *La casa en Mango Street*—Inmigrantes mexicanos en los Estados Unidos

■ Antes de leer

A. El pelo Discuss the following questions in groups of two or three students.

1. Do you think one's type of hair has anything to do with one's personality? Explain.

2. Complete the following chart with information about the members of your group.

| Nombre del (de la) compañero(a) | Tipo (o estilo) de pelo | Personalidad (dos adjetivos) |
|---|---|---|
| | | |
| | | |

have already learned the ords *corto (short)* and *largo* g). The following words are used to describe hair type: **io/lacio** *(straight)*, **rizado** *(curly)*, **ido** *(color treated)*, **calvo** *(bald)*.

**CRITICAL THINKING SKILLS**

*Analyzing* Use cognates to anticipate the content of the reading.

**READING STRATEGY**

*Skimming and Scanning* You do ot have to understand every ord. Concentrate on identifying he main points of the story and nswering the comprehension questions that follow.

B. Cognados With a partner, make a list of all the cognates you can find in the reading. Based on your findings, what do you expect this story to be about?

■ A leer

#### Sandra Cisneros

Las familias hispanas en los Estados Unidos tratan de mantener *(try to maintain)* su cultura y sus tradiciones, al mismo tiempo que *(while)* se integran a su nueva vida *(new life)* en Norteamérica. Sandra Cisneros es una autora chicana que nació en Chicago en 1954. El siguiente es un fragmento de su libro *La casa en Mango Street.*

Each chapter opener includes objectives and goals and new *Enfoque* video activities. These introductory activities help students make connections between what they've already learned and how they are going to build on that knowledge. **Temas** consistently builds on what students already know, with new material tied to existing knowledge and revisited from different perspectives.

**Temas** guides students to an appreciation of key cultural issues relevant to the communities of today's Spanish-speaking world. Each chapter focuses on a specific Spanish-speaking region or set of countries. This is highlighted in the chapter opener, and is further reinforced throughout the chapter in *Sabor regional* notes. These annotations provide students with a sense of the variety and diversity of the Spanish language as spoken in the world today.

This edition presents increased opportunities for recycling language fundamentals through *Remember* notes as well as additional readings that make the functionality of new structures more evident to students.

Activities are driven by the real-world focus of the book and expand or reinforce the chapter's theme. They are student-centered and provide a smooth progression and transition from input to meaningful output and true communication. Turn the page to learn more!

# Functional vocabulary and grammar driven by real-world interactions

Activities are organized in sets that echo the learning process and follow the vocabulary and structure sections *Asimilación, Aplicaciones,* and *Integración.* These activities are personalized, making them more relevant and motivating for your students.

The structured *Asimilación* activities focus student attention on the formal aspects of the native-speaker model provided.

Students then manipulate the language in a meaningful way with *Aplicaciones.*

Finally, open-ended *Integración* speaking and writing activities promote a unified view of the language and allow students to review and recycle familiar material, fostering a much deeper level of linguistic processing.

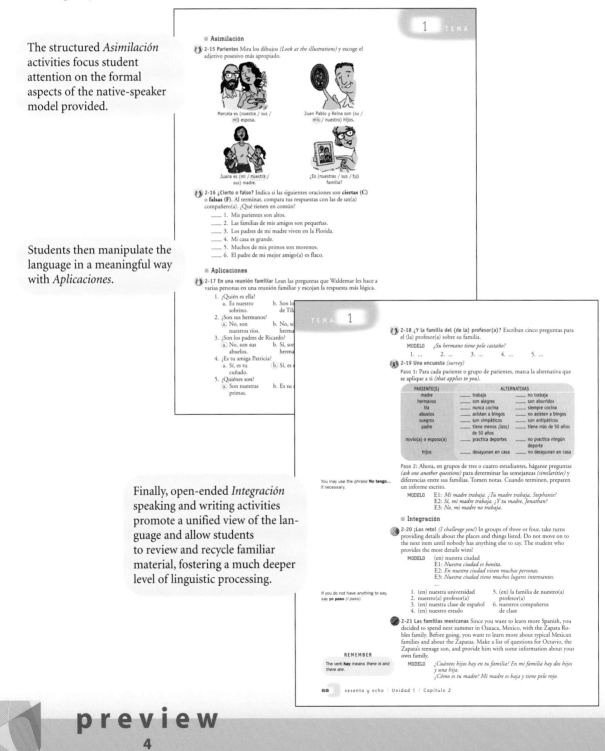

## New

The amount of vocabulary in the Second Edition was greatly reduced and carefully selected based on frequency of use and the communicative needs of today's Spanish learner. Words and terms are presented visually to appeal to both traditional and non-traditional (more mature) students. *Vocabulario práctico* sections are found throughout each chapter as well as in a complete list at the end of every chapter, making it easier for students to use for reference and study. The **Text Audio CDs** also contain vocabulary that students can listen to for correct pronunciation.

## New

Grammar explanations are streamlined in the Second Edition, making them more student-friendly and concise. Each presentation is tied to the lexical framework of the *Tema* and the chapter, and provides extensive opportunities for students to recycle previously presented vocabulary items in the activities. Learning is both an individual and a social endeavor, and effective learning often takes place when students have the chance to interact with and support one another in the process. Activities in **Temas** frequently call for pair work, group consultation, and peer feedback.

**Temas** provides opportunities for students to effect change in the world beyond the confines of their classrooms through the use of their emerging linguistic skills in real-life challenges. Learn more on the next page.

# Preparing students for the workplace and the global community

## Enhanced!

*Puesta en acción*, which occurs at the end of every unit, assigns real tasks that allow students to integrate the linguistic and cultural content of the unit. *Servicio comunitario* sections drive home the real-world focus of the entire program and require interaction with Spanish speakers in the community.

### Servicio comunitario

Go to the office of international affairs of your college or university and offer to provide one of the following services.

- Serve as conversation partner to a student from a Spanish-speaking country.
- Become a guide and offer tours of your institution to prospective foreign students.

Each *Puesta en acción* now includes a series of information-gap activities that challenge learners' oral communication abilities and allow them to use the target language creatively.

**B. ¿Dónde está Guanajuato?** Busquen *(Find)* en el mapa en la página iv la ciudad de origen de José Francisco (Guanajuato). Expliquen dónde está, usando las preposiciones de lugar **cerca de, lejos de, al lado de,** etc.

**C. El Estado de Guanajuato.** Busca información en la biblioteca o en el Internet acerca del Estado de Guanajuato.

También pueden usar las frases **al norte de** *(north of)*, **al sur de** *(south of)*, **al este de** *(east of)* y **al oeste de** *(west of)*.

**CRITICAL THINKING SKILLS**

*Researching* Find other opportunities to learn about Mexico.

| Guanajuato |
|---|
| Población |
| Industrias |
| Atracciones turísticas |
| Fiestas *(Holidays)* |
| Ciudades importantes |
| Otros datos importantes |

**D. Un artista famoso** Diego Rivera, the artist that José Francisco mentioned in his message, is one of the most famous Mexican painters of the twentieth century. To understand better why José Francisco wishes to be like him one day, find out about Diego Rivera's life and works. Complete the chart below with the information you find.

You may play the video segment on Diego Rivera and Frida Kahlo or parts of the movie *Frida* at this time.

| Biografía de Diego Rivera |
|---|
| Fecha y lugar de su nacimiento |
| Fecha y lugar de su muerte *(death)* |
| Tipo de pintura |
| Lugar donde están sus pinturas hoy |
| Temas principales de sus pinturas |
| Nombre de su esposa |
| Profesión de su esposa |

You may want to visit one of the many Diego Rivera sites on the web to find the information requested.

**E. La respuesta** Write a letter to José Francisco and provide the information he requested in his electronic message. Follow these steps.

**Paso 1:** Greet him **(Estimado José Francisco:),** identify yourself, and say how you are today.

**Paso 2:** Answer the questions José Francisco posed:
1. ¿Cuántas personas hay en su familia?
2. ¿Cómo son?
3. ¿Ustedes hablan español?
4. ¿Hay personas de mi edad *(age)* en su familia?
5. ¿La universidad está lejos de su casa?
6. ¿Cómo es mi cuarto?
7. ¿Tengo que hacer quehaceres domésticos en su casa? Si es así, ¿cuáles?

Puesta en acción | Unidad 1 | noventa y siete **97**

---

CAPÍTULOS **1 | 2** ## Puesta en acción

| | |
|---|---|
| **SITUACIÓN:** | You have decided to host a Mexican exchange student in your home. |
| **MISIÓN:** | To establish contact with this student, find out about his background, learn about his culture, and exchange information about each other's family and life. |
| **DESTREZAS *(SKILLS)*:** | Reading and responding to electronic communications, providing personal information, and researching information. |

**A. Un mensaje electrónico.** José Francisco Reyes Galindo, el estudiante de intercambio mexicano, te envía el siguiente mensaje.

| Fecha: | 27 de enero de 2006 |
|---|---|
| Para: | La familia Smith |
| De: | José Francisco Reyes Galindo |

Viaje a los Estados Unidos

Estimada Familia Smith:

Permítanme que me presente: Soy José Francisco Reyes Galindo y tengo veinte años. Aunque soy de Guanajuato, México, estudio bellas artes en la Universidad Nacional Autónoma de México, en la capital. Mi especialidad es la pintura y quiero ampliar mis conocimientos en los Estados Unidos. Mi sueño es ser un pintor famoso como Diego Rivera.

*I am planning on living* **Pienso vivir** en su casa en los Estados Unidos por seis meses. Viajo
*travel* el próximo 25 de agosto. Antes de **viajar,** quisiera hacerles varias preguntas: ¿Cuántas personas hay en su familia? ¿Cómo son? ¿Ustedes
*age* hablan español? ¿Hay personas de mi **edad** en su familia? ¿La universidad está lejos de su casa? ¿Cómo es mi cuarto? ¿Tengo que hacer quehaceres domésticos en su casa? Si es así, ¿cuáles?

*give me* También les agradecería que me **dieran** el nombre y la descripción física
*pick up* de la persona que me va a **recoger** al aeropuerto.

*welcome* Muchas gracias por su **acogida** y por la información.

Atentamente,
José Francisco Reyes Galindo

**96** noventa y seis | Unidad 1 | Puesta en acción

---

## New

**EN TU COMUNIDAD**

Research the topic of family constitution in your community or in your state. You may visit family agencies or other agencies that collect such data. Also, you can find out what the local government is doing to improve the quality of life of families. Then share the information with the class.

Every chapter contains service and community-based learning activities that give students the opportunity to use their emerging linguistic abilities to effect change in the real world. This aspect of the program is particularly highlighted in the *Enfoque comunitario* activities included in the video section of each chapter's *Tema 2. En tu comunidad* suggestions encourage students to learn from the community, thus making the experience with the target language more relevant and meaningful outside the classroom.

See the endsheets for more information about service learning and the role it plays in the **Temas** program.

# Further extend and enhance your classroom instruction with these exclusive resources

**iLrn™ Spanish** — *The all-in-one diagnostic, tutorial, assessment, assignment, and course management system that saves YOU time and saves your students money!*

References to **iLrn™ Spanish** are built into **Temas**, highlighting areas where students can turn to this online program for videos, activities, and more. Turn to the inside back cover of this book for more information about how **iLrn™ Spanish** can transform the teaching and learning experience in your course.

## INSTRUCTOR COMPONENTS

### Instructor's Resource Manual (with Test Bank CD-ROM)
1-4130-1836-X

Everything you need for streamlined course preparation! The **Instructor's Resource Manual** provides a brief introduction to the program and an explanation of its organization and content, including information on input processing and service learning. You will also find sample lesson plans, suggestions for implementing each chapter's content, as well as tips for teaching the four skills, working with technology, and teaching heritage speakers. Additional activities and ideas expand on those exercises found in the main text to address the needs of groups with differing abilities. The bound-in **Test Bank CD-ROM** offers two sample tests and three sample quizzes per chapter, that integrate vocabulary, grammar, and culture with four-skills activities. Samples of comprehensive two-semester and three-semester final exams are also included. A separate **Audio CD**, also bound-in, contains the recordings for the listening comprehension sections of the quizzes and final exams.

### Temas Video/DVD
VHS: 1-4130-1833-5 • DVD: 1-4130-1834-3

The video/DVD contains introductory segments about the landscape and history of a different Spanish-speaking country in every chapter, as well as samples of functional language with corresponding activities in the main textbook. All new video follows the lives of five students as they come together in a Spanish-speaking culture, and models the vocabulary, structures, and communicative goals of the respective chapter. The Second Edition includes all new pre-, during-, and post-viewing video activities, as well as *Enfoque comunitario* activities at the end of *Tema 2. Also available online with* **iLrn™ Spanish**.

### Juntos: Community Partnerships in Spanish and Portuguese, Volume V
0-8384-6071-2

Published in association with the American Association of Teachers of Spanish and Portuguese, **Juntos** provides a concise overview and practical guide to establishing authentic learning partnerships through service learning, promoting civic engagement.

### Spanish Transparency Bank
0-8384-0987-3

Over 100 color transparency acetates per package, identified by alpha-numeric code.

## FOR STUDENTS AND INSTRUCTORS

### Book Companion Website
**http://temas.heinle.com**

The student portion of this website includes self-correcting grammar and vocabulary quizzes, organized by *Tema*, and web exploration activities that prepare students for the book's *Puesta en acción* sections.

# Outstanding support makes **TEMAS** the most complete learning program you'll find

## Text Audio CDs
1-4130-1461-5

Included with every new copy of the text, these CDs provide the audio input for the in-text listening activities as well as the end-of-chapter vocabulary list.

## Workbook/Lab Manual
1-4130-1828-9

This helpful learning companion provides additional reading, writing, listening, and pronunciation practice outside of class. The Workbook includes process-oriented writing activities for each chapter. These activities, which are correlated to the latest version of **Atajo: Writing Assistant for Spanish**, direct students to the main points of information essential to the writing task and guide them in the writing process. An *Autoexamen* at the end of each chapter allows students to check their own mastery of each chapter's vocabulary, grammar, and cultural concepts. *Also available online with* **iLrn™ Spanish**.

## Lab Audio CDs
1-4130-1830-0

For use in conjunction with the **Workbook/Lab Manual**, these CDs provide listening comprehension reinforcement of structures and vocabulary, and also help improve pronunciation. *Also available online with* **iLrn™ Spanish**.

## Workbook/Lab Manual Answer Key with Lab Audio Script
1-4130-1829-7

This resource contains the complete script of all recorded material in the laboratory program, as well as the answers to the exercises in the **Workbook/Lab Manual**. Available for student purchase at instructor's discretion. *Also available online with* **iLrn™ Spanish**.

## Student Multimedia CD-ROM
1-4130-1832-7

The **Student Multimedia CD-ROM** provides interactive practice of the vocabulary and grammar from each *Tema*. In addition to a variety of practice activities, the CD-ROM also offers audio- and video-enhanced sections that focus on pronunciation and culture and a reading section that describes ongoing service learning projects and encourages students to think about opportunities in their own community. *Also available online with* **iLrn™ Spanish**.

## vMentor™

When you adopt this text and choose to package **vMentor™** access with every new copy at no additional cost, you give your students access to virtual office hours—live, online tutoring help from a Spanish teaching expert with a copy of the text and significant experience. In the **vMentor™** virtual classroom, students interact with the tutor and other students using two-way audio, an interactive whiteboard, and instant messaging. *Also available online with* **iLrn™ Spanish**.

## Atajo 4.0 CD-ROM: Writing Assistant for Spanish
1-4130-0060-6

This powerful program—a 2005 Codie Awards Finalist for excellence in educational technology—combines the features of a word processor with databases of language reference material, a searchable dictionary featuring the entire contents of **Merriam-Webster's® Spanish English Dictionary**, a verb conjugating reference, and audio recordings of vocabulary, example sentences, and authentic samples of the language.

## Putumayo's *Nuevo Latino* Music CD
Bundle Version: 1-4130-1877-7

*Not available separately.* In this new Latin music CD, hints of Cuban son, Argentinean tango, and Colombian cumbia can be heard alongside touches of contemporary blues, surf music, ragamuffin, trip-hop, and hip-hop.

## *Sonidos, sabores y palabras* Activity Manual*
Bundle Version: 1-4130-1875-0

The *Sonidos, sabores y palabras* Activity Manual answers the call from instructors seeking to use music as an integrated component in their Spanish class. *Sonidos* allows you to use music to increase understanding of not only the Spanish language, but also the cultural perspectives the music conveys.

*Also available for purchase as a standalone item, packaged with Putumayo's *Nuevo Latino* Music CD: 1-4130-2169-7

## Also Available:

**Merriam-Webster's® Spanish-English Dictionary**
0-87779-916-4

**Typing Accents for Spanish Bookmark**
0-7593-0659-1

---

*Due to contractual reasons, certain ancillaries described on pages 7 and 8 are available only in higher education or U.S. domestic markets. Minimum purchases may apply to receive the ancillaries at no charge. For more information, please contact your local Thomson sales representative.*

# Preface to the Instructor

In its second edition, *Temas: Spanish for the Global Community* remains committed to its goal of preparing learners of Spanish for professional and social interactions with native speakers in the global community. The pedagogical foundations of *Temas,* as well as its thematic orientation, are maintained in the second edition, while authentic language use through interactive real-world tasks remains at the core of the program.

The Second Edition of *Temas* is

- **engaging,** drawing inspiration from today's linguistic needs, with an abundance of real and community-based activities.
- **interactive,** promoting active and group-based learning.
- **user friendly,** providing teacher and students with a clear design and a consistent structure.
- **empowering,** allowing students to take more control over their learning with the support of teachers, modern technology, and one another.

## Philosophy of the authors

*Temas,* **Second Edition,** incorporates both well-established traditions and new developments in foreign language pedagogy. The program is built on four major philosophical underpinnings:

1. Language acquisition results from the systematic interaction of linguistic input and output.
2. Content-based materials, where the theme of the chapter contextualizes the presentation of grammar and vocabulary, are more meaningful and relevant to learners.
3. A student-centered approach allows students to become better, faster learners.
4. A process-oriented approach is essential for sustained learner development.

## The role of input in *Temas: Spanish for the Global Community*

- **Authentic input** Comprehension of meaningful and authentic language is the point of departure for language acquisition. The development of reading and listening skills in this context plays a pivotal role, beginning with Spanish direction lines and leading up to a wide variety of readings and video segments.
- **Input-output sequence** In *Temas,* language learning is an input-driven process.
   Structured input is required for language processing and for global comprehension of incoming messages. Structured reading and listening tasks initiate learners into the acquisition of all major grammatical topics. Target language output takes place in a progressive sequence of stages. Speaking and writing are viewed as evolving processes that begin with meaningful item manipulation and conclude with open-ended tasks and personal expression.
   Within each chapter, the input-output sequence of each **Tema** takes place in three stages.
   **Asimilación** activities are structured-input activities.
   **Aplicaciones** are structured-output activities that focus on meaningful item manipulation.
   **Integración** activities emphasize open-ended communicative tasks.

- **Evolving pedagogical focus and pacing** Content distribution in *Temas* reflects the evolving linguistic needs of beginning language learners with the overall goal of preparing them for the intermediate level. In the first part of the text **(Capítulos 1–6)** students concentrate on the acquisition of basic lexical and structural aspects of Spanish, and in the second part **(Capítulos 7–12)** they explore more complex language structures and work on the development of literacy skills (reading and writing).

- **Recycling and spiraling** Learning does not take place in a linear fashion. New material needs to be tied to existing knowledge and revisited from different perspectives to ensure deep processing. Later chapters of *Temas* present increased opportunities for recycling language fundamentals as well as additional readings that make the functionality of new structures more evident to students.

## Content-based materials

- **Content-driven, functional syllabus** In *communicatively* oriented programs, the negotiation of meaning in context is the primary organizing principle. Advancing beyond the simple presentation of a series of linguistic structures, language instruction must consider first and foremost the communicative potential (or functionality) of the language involved.

  Consistent with this approach, the presentation and sequencing of topics in *Temas* is informed by *linguistic function*. Vocabulary and grammar presentations are distributed throughout the book based on their relevance to the theme of the chapter, then practiced in highly contextualized, meaningful, and relevant activities.

- **Culture** Appreciation of other cultures (habits, mores, traditions, etc.) is at the core of this program. *Temas* guides students to an appreciation of key cultural issues relevant to the communities of today's Spanish-speaking world. Learners are regularly presented with situations and information that allow them to become aware of the similarities and differences between their own culture and those of Spanish-speaking countries.

- **Workplace and global community** Throughout the program, emphasis is placed on the workplace and everyday situations, and tasks and their goals often reflect typical interactions in these contexts. This aspect of the program is particularly highlighted in the **Enfoque comunitario** activities included in the video section of each chapter's **Tema 2,** as well as in the **En tu comunidad** annotations. **Puesta en acción** tasks at the end of each unit, especially those entitled **Servicio comunitario,** require interaction with Spanish speakers in the community.

## Student-centered approach

- **Student-centered pedagogy** The focus of the learning process is placed on the student, not on the teacher. *Temas* provides practical tools to allow students to take more responsibility for their learning and to personalize the language-learning experience, making it relevant to their lives. For this reason, students are regularly asked to express their views, opinions, needs and expectations, as well as to consider the views, opinions, needs, and expectations of others, much as we do in the real world when we interact with people.

- **Active learning** Learning is both an individual and a social endeavor, and effective learning often takes place when students have the chance to interact with and support one another in the process. Activities in *Temas* frequently call for pair work, group consultation, and peer feedback.

- **Lifelong learning** Language acquisition is a lifelong process that begins in the classroom but that ultimately transcends it. Activities in *Temas* promote the development of the independent learning skills that encourage students to become lifelong language learners.

- **Service and community-based learning** Every chapter contains service and community-based learning activities designed to give students the opportunity to use their emerging linguistic abilities to effect change in the real world. These tasks put the student in direct contact with the community, and help them develop awareness of their ability to make a difference in their immediate communities and beyond.

## Process Approach

In *Temas* the pedagogical focus shifts from the final linguistic output to the stages the speaker/writer goes through in order to organize and deliver a given message. Breaking the communicative event into its constituent parts makes real-life writing and speaking tasks less daunting and much more manageable to the student. Process pedagogy emphasizes the usefulness of *dialogue* as a teaching technique and challenges the traditional, authoritative models of teaching, in which professors (who knew everything) talked at students (who knew very little). Instead, process pedagogy empowers students by asking them to reflect on their writing and speaking at every step of the process.

## Highlights of the Second Edition

The authors have focused their efforts in revision in the following areas:

**Service and community-based learning** *Temas* provides opportunities for students to effect change in the world beyond the confines of their classrooms through the use of their emerging linguistic skills in real-life challenges. These activities can be found in the video section at the end of each **Tema 2 (Enfoque comunitario),** in the **En tu comunidad** suggestions, and in the **Puesta en acción** section at the end of each unit **(Servicio comunitario).**

**Vocabulary** Lexical items were carefully selected based on frequency of use and the communicative needs of today's Spanish learner, which significantly reduces the number of words introduced for recognition. These items are presented visually in order to appeal to both traditional and non-traditional (more mature) students. Vocabulary lists are now presented at the end of each chapter to facilitate study, review, and reference.

**Functions and structures** The scope and sequence of grammatical items were revised thoroughly. Certain topics were redistributed and simplified, and other key topics were added to prepare learners better to continue studying Spanish at the intermediate level. For example, the present tense conjugation of **-ar** verbs is now separate from that of **-er** and **-ir** verbs, and we have included sections on the uses of the relative pronouns **que/quien(es)** and the passive **se.** Furthermore, grammar explanations are more student-friendly and briefer. Special attention was given to tying each presentation to the lexical framework of the **Tema** and chapter and to providing extensive opportunities for students to recycle previously presented vocabulary items in the activities.

**Culture: *Perspectivas, Vídeo,* and *Lecturas*** At the end of each **Tema,** students have the chance to explore and interact with contextualized culture-rich materials in the form of culture capsules, video, and readings. Although culturally pertinent information is provided in every section, the **Perspectivas, Vídeo,** and **Lecturas** activities focus exclusively on the acquisition and development of cultural competency. These activities appear in **Tema 1, Tema 2,** and **Tema 3,** respectively. Special attention is given to fostering students' reflective and critical thinking skills.

**Oral Communication** Besides providing opportunities for learners to review and recycle linguistic and cultural information through real-life tasks, the **Puesta en acción** sections now include a series of information-gap activities that challenge learners' oral communication abilities and allow them to use the target language creatively.

**Writing** The *Temas* Workbook includes a process-oriented writing activity for each chapter. These activities, which are correlated to the latest version of *Atajo: Writing Assistant for Spanish,* direct students to the main points of information essential to the writing task and guide them through the writing process.

## Organization

*Temas* is divided into six units, each of which contains two chapters plus a **Puesta en acción.** Each chapter's material is organized thematically into three **Temas,** the organizing principle of this book; hence, its title.

## Chapter Features

### Chapter Opener
Each opener includes chapter objectives and goals, advance organizer activities, country focus **(Enfoque)** activities, and a new video segment that introduces the given country. Building on the chapter's advance organizer, the information students already have about the subject is activated, and interest about the new material is generated.

### Tema
Chapters are broken down into content- and function-based chunks, or themes, in whose context students are exposed to and ultimately manipulate and create language. This language is not only personalized and meaningful but is also based on ideas and concepts that reflect the theme.

Four basic sections comprise each **Tema: Vocabulario, Funciones y estructuras** (two sections) and **Perspectivas** (in **Tema 1), Vídeo** (in **Tema 2),** or **Lectura** (in **Tema 3).**

### Vocabulario
Students do not learn vocabulary in a vacuum but rather in a visual or linguistic context, followed by activities that provide opportunities to personalize content.

### Funciones y estructuras
Clear and direct presentations allow students to grasp functional and structural concepts quickly and effectively at the beginner's level.

### Vídeo
Students benefit from learning through audio and visual input, and specific learning strategies support these modalities. The native-speaker samples use the linguistic structures and functions explored in each chapter in an engaging format. Modeled after reality television, this Telly award-winning video captivates learners as they follow the lives of five strangers brought together to live and learn in a Spanish-speaking culture.

## Lectura

Students are exposed to authentic language that reflects the culture and issues relevant to the country explored in the chapter. Specific strategies (skimming, scanning, guessing from context, etc.) and extensive pre- and post-reading activities (including global and detail comprehension questions, as well as extension tasks) make the readings accessible and therefore more engaging.

## Activities

Activities are driven by the real-world focus of the book and expand or reinforce the chapter's thematic focus. They are student-centered and provide a smooth progression and transition from input to meaningful output and true communication. Since activities are personalized, they are more relevant and serve to motivate the student. In addition, direction lines are presented entirely in Spanish beginning in **Capítulo 2** to help students rely on cognate recognition and develop pattern recognition skills.

Activities are organized in sets that echo the learning process and follow the vocabulary and function/structure sections:

- **Asimilación** Structured input activities focus students' attention on the formal aspects of the native-speaker model provided. Processing instruction keeps meaning in focus, while allowing students to deal only with discrete linguistic units (a process that makes these activities more salient and memorable).

- **Aplicaciones** Meaningful manipulation of the language allows students to master the structures at hand. The guided nature of these activities permits the development of both accuracy and fluency.

- **Integración** Open-ended speaking and writing activities allow students to use the language in a creative and meaningful manner far beyond the practice of a particular structure. The global and integrative nature of the activities promotes a unified view of the language and allows students to review and recycle familiar material, fostering a much deeper level of linguistic processing.

## Puesta en acción

This section, which occurs at the end of every unit, assigns real tasks that allow students to integrate the linguistic and cultural content of the unit. This section drives home the real-world focus of the entire program.

Reviewing and recycling are important components of the learning process and important aspects of the **Puesta en acción** sections. The real-life tasks provide opportunities to reinforce the acquisition of new material and functional skills while emphasizing the practical and usefulness of language learning in today's society. Furthermore, each **Puesta en acción** includes a service learning activity (**Servicio comunitario**) that allows students to use the target language in a real-life setting and make a change in their community.

## Special chapter features

### En tu comunidad
These suggestions encourage students to learn from the community, thus making the experience with the target language more relevant and meaningful outside the classroom.

### Sabor regional
Linguistic annotations provide students with a sense of the variety and diversity of the Spanish language as spoken in the world today. They are intended to familiarize students with some of the regional variations in vocabulary they will encounter should they travel or do business internationally.

## Program components

The Second Edition of *Temas* offers a wealth of ancillary components for instructors and students alike.

In addition to the Student Edition and Annotated Instructor's Edition of the main text, each of which comes with Text Audio CDs, the following components round out the ***Temas,* Second Edition,** program.

- Workbook/Lab Manual
- Lab Audio CDs (also available IPod ready)
- Workbook/Lab Manual Answer Key with Audioscript
- iLrn™ Spanish, an all-in-one web-based diagnostic, tutorial, assessment, assignment, and course management system
- vMentor™
- iLrn™ Live!
- Instructor's Resource Manual (includes Testing Program on CD-ROM)
- Student Multimedia CD-ROM
- *Temas,* Second Edition, World Wide Website http://temas.heinle.com
- *Temas,* Second Edition, Video on VHS or DVD
- Merriam Webster's®, Spanish-English Dictionary
- Situation Cards
- Juntos: Community Partnerships in Spanish and Portuguese, Volume V
- Nuevo Latino Music CD and Sonidos Activity Manual
- Atajo 4.0
- Transparency Bank

# Instructor's support

- Extensive annotations in the **Annotated Instructor's Edition (AIE)** explain the goals and principles of classroom and homework activities and provide instructional strategies, answers for all discrete-point items, and the audio scripts for in-text listening activities.
- The **Instructor's Resource Manual** provides **additional activities** and ideas for expanding on those found in the main text in order to address the needs of groups with different abilities.
- **Audio-visual aids.** The **Text Audio CDs, Lab Audio Program**, and **Video** provide native speaker models of different ages and nationalities. Thomson-Heinle's **Spanish Transparency Bank** is available to instructors and provides a wealth of visual input to support vocabulary acquisition and stimulate class discussion.
- **Juntos: Community Partnerships in Spanish and Portuguese,** a publication in our professional series published in partnership with the American Association of Teachers of Spanish and Portuguese, provides a concise overview and practical guide to establishing authentic learning partnerships through service learning, thus promoting civic engagement.

## *Temas* and the heritage speaker

The linguistic needs of heritage speakers, particularly in the area of literacy, are very specific and deserve special consideration. Supplemental spelling, grammar and guided composition tasks are most often necessary. Nonetheless, a number of features in *Temas* will allow teachers to address heritage speakers' concerns.

**The use of authentic language** *Temas* is a program designed to sound and feel natural. Its literary excerpts and listening materials include language samples of different countries and social groups. Heritage speakers will have no problem recognizing the language they learned as children in this book.

**Country focus** The general cultural orientation of *Temas* gives heritage Spanish-speaking students an opportunity to share their background and serve as resources for the rest of the group. Many times heritage speakers are bored or seem intimidating to other students with their fluent Spanish. In *Temas,* their linguistic advantage is put to work for the benefit of the non-Hispanic students in the class.

**Sabor regional** These notes highlight the fact that Spanish has important regional variations. Heritage students can find their specific language variant recognized and validated (even if it is considered "substandard") while being encouraged to maintain an open mind (and even learn other ways of expressing the same ideas). They thus expand their own linguistic repertoires.

**Capítulo 12: La herencia hispana** This chapter should be of particular interest to heritage speakers since it validates and highlights their experience in the United States.

**Enfoque comunitario** These activities, which are part of every video task, will allow heritage speakers to learn more about (and therefore appreciate more) their own background (an important goal of any course aimed at this population).

# TEMAS

SPANISH FOR THE GLOBAL COMMUNITY

# TEMAS

## SPANISH FOR THE GLOBAL COMMUNITY

### SECOND EDITION

**JORGE H. CUBILLOS**

University of Delaware

**EDWIN M. LAMBOY**

Montclair University

**THOMSON**

**HEINLE**

Australia • Brazil • Canada • Mexico • Singapore • Spain • United Kingdom • United States

THOMSON
HEINLE

Temas
Spanish for the Global Community
Second Edition
Cubillos | Lamboy

**Executive Editor:** Carrie Brandon
**Acquisitions Editor:** Helen Alejandra Richardson
**Development Editor:** Mercedes Roffé
**Senior Project Manager, Editorial Production:** Esther Marshall
**Marketing Manager:** Lindsey Richardson
**Marketing Assistant:** Marla Nasser
**Advertising Project Manager:** Stacey Purviance
**Managing Technology Project Manager:** Sacha Laustsen
**Manufacturing Manager:** Marcia Locke
**Compositor:** Pre-Press Company, Inc.
**Project Management:** Katy Faria, Pre-Press Company, Inc.

**Photo Manager:** Sheri Blaney
**Photo Reseacher:** Jill Engebretson
**Text Permissions Editor:** Lianca Letelier
**Text Designer:** Brian Salisbury
**Senior Art Director:** Bruce Bond
**Cover Designer:** Yvo Riezebos
**Illustrator:** Dave Sullivan
**Cover Printer:** Phoenix Color
**Printer:** RR Donnelley & Sons Company

**Cover image:** ©Photodisc/GETTY IMAGES; *inside cover endpaper:* © Diana Ong/Superstock

**Thomson Higher Education**
**25 Thomson Place**
**Boston, MA 02210-1202**
**USA**

For more information about our products, contact us at:
**Thomson Learning Academic Resource Center**
**1-800-423-0563**
For permission to use material from this text or product, submit a request online at **http://www.thomsonrights.com**
Any additional questions about permissions can be submitted by e-mail to **thomsonrights@thomson.com**

Printed in the United States of America
1  2  3  4  5  6  7    09  08  07  06  05
Library of Congress Control Number: 2005931889

Student Edition ISBN 1-4130-1049-0

AIE ISBN 1-4130-1835-1

Credits appear on pages xxiii–xxv, which constitute a continuation of the copyright page.

# América del Sur

MAR CARIBE

Barranquilla
Cartagena
Maracaibo
Puerto de España
Caracas
**TRINIDAD Y TOBAGO**
R. Orinoco
Medellín
Manizales
**Bogotá**
Cali
**VENEZUELA**
Georgetown
Paramaribo
**GUYANA**
Cayenne
**SURINAM**
**GUAYANA FRANCESA**
**COLOMBIA**
OCÉANO ATLÁNTICO
ECUADOR
**Quito**
Guayaquil
**ECUADOR**
Iquitos
R. Amazo
Manaus
Belem
**PERÚ**
Cajamarca
R. Madeira
Recife
Machu Picchu
**BRASIL**
**Lima**
Ayacucho
Cuzco
L. Titicaca
**BOLIVIA**
Salvador
**Brasilia**
Arequipa
**La Paz**
Arica
Sucre
Belo Horizonte
Iquique
Potosí
São Paulo
Río de Janeiro
OCÉANO PACÍFICO
Antofagasta
**PARAGUAY**
Santos
Salta
**Asunción**
**CHILE**
Tucumán
R. Paraná
R. Uruguay
Porto Alegre
Córdoba
Mendoza
Valparaíso
Rosario
**URUGUAY**
**Santiago**
**Buenos Aires**
**Montevideo**
Concepción
La Plata
Río de la Plata
**ARGENTINA**
TRÓPICO DE CAPRICORNIO
Bahía Blanca
Puerto Montt
CORDILLERA DE LOS ANDES

| 0 | 200 | 400 | 600 | 800 millas |
|---|---|---|---|---|
| 0 | 200 | 400 | 600 | 800 kilómetros |

**ISLAS MALVINAS**

Punta Arenas
**TIERRA DEL FUEGO**
Cabo de Hornos
Estrecho de Magallanes

# México, América Central y El Caribe

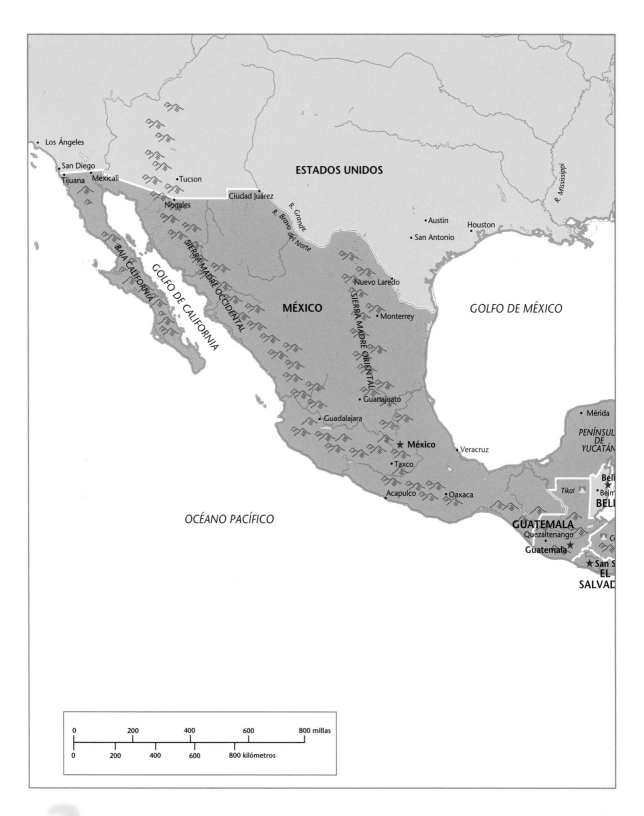

Los Ángeles

San Diego

Tijuana  Mexicali

Tucson

Nogales

Ciudad Juárez

**ESTADOS UNIDOS**

R. Grande

R. Bravo del Norte

Austin

Houston

San Antonio

R. Mississippi

BAJA CALIFORNIA

GOLFO DE CALIFORNIA

SIERRA MADRE OCCIDENTAL

**MÉXICO**

SIERRA MADRE ORIENTAL

Nuevo Laredo

Monterrey

*GOLFO DE MÉXICO*

Guanajuato

Mérida

Guadalajara

*PENÍNSUL DE YUCATÁN*

★ **México**

Veracruz

Taxco

Beli

Tikal

Belm

**BELI**

Acapulco

Oaxaca

*OCÉANO PACÍFICO*

**GUATEMALA**

Quezaltenango

**Guatemala** ★

San S

**EL SALVAD**

| 0 | 200 | 400 | 600 | 800 millas |
|---|-----|-----|-----|------------|
| 0 | 200 | 400 | 600 | 800 kilómetros |

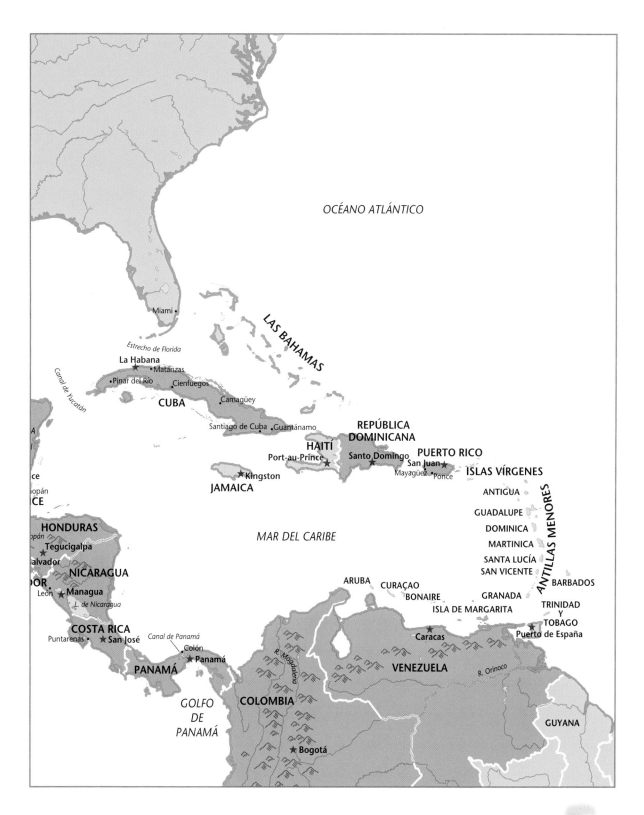

OCÉANO ATLÁNTICO

Miami •

LAS BAHAMAS

Estrecho de Florida

Canal de Yucatán

La Habana
★ • Matanzas
•Pinar del Río • Cienfuegos
CUBA
•Camagüey

Santiago de Cuba • •Guantánamo

REPÚBLICA
DOMINICANA

HAITÍ
Port-au-Prince ★ Santo Domingo
★ •San Juan ★

PUERTO RICO
Mayagüez• •Ponce

ISLAS VÍRGENES

★Kingston

JAMAICA

ANTIGUA

GUADALUPE

DOMINICA

MARTINICA

SANTA LUCÍA
SAN VICENTE

ANTILLAS MENORES

MAR DEL CARIBE

BARBADOS

HONDURAS
★Tegucigalpa
alvador

NICARAGUA

León ★Managua
L. de Nicaragua

ARUBA
CURAÇAO
BONAIRE

GRANADA

ISLA DE MARGARITA

TRINIDAD
Y
TOBAGO

COSTA RICA
Puntarenas •    ★San José

Canal de Panamá
•Colón
★Panamá

PANAMÁ

★Caracas

Puerto de España

VENEZUELA

R. Orinoco

GOLFO
DE
PANAMÁ

R. Magdalena

COLOMBIA

GUYANA

★Bogotá

opán
ce
opán
DOR

# Los hispanohablantes en los Estados Unidos

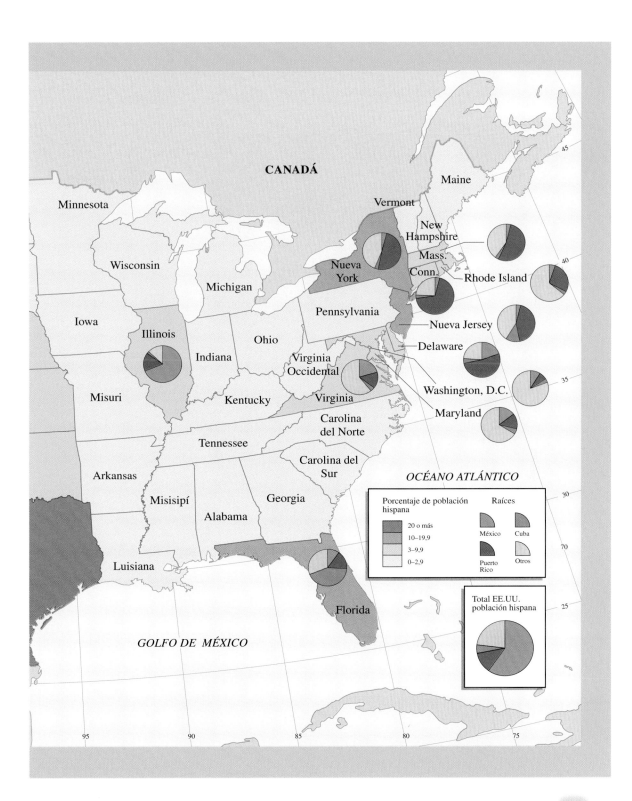

CANADÁ

Minnesota

Wisconsin

Michigan

Iowa

Illinois

Indiana

Ohio

Misuri

Kentucky

Arkansas

Tennessee

Misisipí

Alabama

Georgia

Luisiana

Maine

Vermont

New Hampshire

Mass.

Conn.

Nueva York

Rhode Island

Pennsylvania

Nueva Jersey

Delaware

Virginia Occidental

Washington, D.C.

Virginia

Maryland

Carolina del Norte

Carolina del Sur

OCÉANO ATLÁNTICO

Florida

GOLFO DE MÉXICO

Porcentaje de población hispana

Raíces

20 o más

10–19,9

3–9,9

0–2,9

México

Cuba

Puerto Rico

Otros

Total EE.UU. población hispana

# España

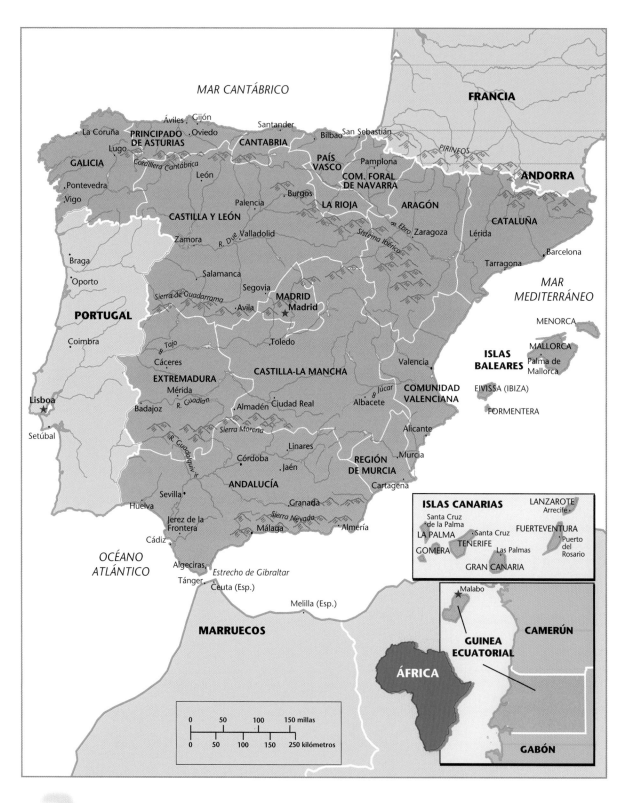

MAR CANTÁBRICO

FRANCIA

Áviles · Gijón · Santander
La Coruña · PRINCIPADO
DE ASTURIAS · Oviedo · CANTABRIA · Bilbao · San Sebastián
Lugo · León · PAÍS VASCO · Pamplona · PIRINEOS
GALICIA · Cordillera Cantábrica · COM. FORAL DE NAVARRA · ANDORRA
Pontevedra · Palencia · Burgos · LA RIOJA · ARAGÓN · CATALUÑA
Vigo · CASTILLA Y LEÓN · Valladolid · Sistema Ibérico · Ebro · Zaragoza · Lérida
Zamora · R. Due · Barcelona
Braga · Salamanca · Tarragona
Oporto · Segovia · MAR MEDITERRÁNEO
PORTUGAL · Sierra de Guadarrama · MADRID · Madrid · MENORCA
Ávila · MALLORCA
Coimbra · Toledo · ISLAS BALEARES · Palma de Mallorca
Tajo · Cáceres · Valencia · EIVISSA (IBIZA)
EXTREMADURA · CASTILLA-LA MANCHA · FORMENTERA
Mérida · Júcar · COMUNIDAD VALENCIANA
Lisboa · R. Guadian · Almadén · Ciudad Real · Albacete
Badajoz · Alicante
Setúbal · Sierra Morena · Murcia
R. Guadalquivir · Linares · REGIÓN DE MURCIA
Córdoba · Jaén · Cartagena
ANDALUCÍA
Sevilla · Granada · ISLAS CANARIAS · LANZAROTE · Arrecife
Huelva · Sierra Nevada · Santa Cruz de la Palma
Jerez de la Frontera · Málaga · Almería · LA PALMA · Santa Cruz · FUERTEVENTURA
Cádiz · GOMERA · TENERIFE · Puerto del Rosario
Algeciras · OCÉANO ATLÁNTICO · Las Palmas
Tánger · Estrecho de Gibraltar · GRAN CANARIA
Ceuta (Esp.)
Melilla (Esp.)

MARRUECOS

Malabo
GUINEA ECUATORIAL · CAMERÚN
ÁFRICA
GABÓN

0   50   100   150 millas
0   50   100   150   250 kilómetros

# Scope and Sequence

**Capítulo preparatorio**
¡A empezar!   2

**Vocabulario**

El salón de clase; Los saludos; Las despedidas y las expresiones de cortesía

Los cursos

Los días y los meses; Los números; Los colores

**Funciones y estructuras**

Personal pronouns

Gender, number, and definite articles

Indefinite articles and the invariable impersonal verbal **hay**

| | Vocabulario | Funciones y estructuras | Lecturas y vídeo |
|---|---|---|---|
| **Unidad II: La vida diaria** | | | |
| **Capítulo 3**<br>Dónde y cuándo 100 | | | **Enfoque:**<br>Puerto Rico |
| **Tema 1:**<br>Orientándonos en la ciudad 102 | Lugares de interés | Talking about location and destination with the verbs **estar** and **ir**<br>Telling time | Perspectivas: Turismo en Puerto Rico |
| **Tema 2:**<br>De compras 113 | Las compras y las formas de pago | Talking about daily activities with irregular **yo** form verbs<br>Adverbs of frequency | Vídeo: El día de la primera excursión en Puerto Rico |
| **Tema 3:** La comida 124 | Vamos a comer | Talking about daily activities with **e → i** stem-changing verbs<br>Talking about future plans | Lectura: La dieta mediterránea |
| **Capítulo 4**<br>Preferencias y prioridades 140 | | | **Enfoque:** España |
| **Tema 1:**<br>El tiempo 142 | El estado del tiempo y las estaciones | Talking about ongoing actions and events with the present progressive<br>Comparing and contrasting with comparatives and superlatives | Perspectivas: Las variaciones climáticas en el mundo hispano |
| **Tema 2:**<br>La ropa 153 | Ropa de diario y accesorios | Talking about daily activities with **e → ie** and **o → ue** stem-changing verbs<br>Talking about daily routines with reflexive verbs | Vídeo: Una charla sobre la ropa |
| **Tema 3:**<br>La diversión 163 | Los deportes | Talking about daily activities with irregular present tense verbs<br>Describing people and objects with the verbs **ser** and **estar** | Lectura: De vacaciones |
| **Puesta en acción 3/4:** Organizing a business meeting in Puerto Rico    174 | | | |

|  | Vocabulario | Funciones y estructuras | Lecturas y vídeo |
|---|---|---|---|
| **Unidad III: Ayer y hoy** | | | |
| **Capítulo 5**<br>Mi pasado 178 | | | **Enfoque:**<br>Perú, Ecuador<br>y Bolivia |
| **Tema 1:**<br>Eventos<br>importantes<br>180 | Los eventos<br>importantes y las<br>fechas | Talking about past activities with the<br>preterite tense<br>Referring to past events with<br>**hace... que** | Perspectivas: En el<br>periódico |
| **Tema 2:**<br>Buenos<br>recuerdos 192 | Los preparativos<br>para un viaje | Talking about past activities with<br>stem-changing verbs in the preterite<br>and the verbs **dar, ir, ser,** and **ver**<br>Avoiding repetition with direct ob-<br>ject pronouns | Vídeo: Otra excursión<br>en Puerto Rico |
| **Tema 3:**<br>Incidentes 205 | El cuerpo humano | Talking about past activities with<br>other stem-changing verbs<br>Talking about incidents and<br>mishaps | Lectura: Leyenda del<br>origen de los Incas |
| **Capítulo 6**<br>Recuerdos 218 | | | **Enfoque:**<br>Costa Rica,<br>Nicaragua y<br>Panamá |
| **Tema 1:**<br>La ciudad 220 | El mundo urbano | Expressing generalizations with in-<br>definite words (and review of<br>negative words)<br>Describing the past with the imper-<br>fect tense | Perspectivas: Satu-<br>ración vehicular en<br>Managua |
| **Tema 2:**<br>La naturaleza<br>232 | La vida en el<br>campo | Describing the past with irregular<br>verbs in the imperfect tense<br>Expressing knowledge and familiarity<br>with the verbs **saber** and **conocer** | Vídeo: Un baile<br>folclórico puerto-<br>rriqueño |
| **Tema 3 :** La<br>conservación<br>del medio<br>ambiente 244 | La ecología | Indicating location with demonstra-<br>tive adjectives and pronouns<br>Talking about the past with verbs<br>that change meaning in the preterite | Lectura: La leyenda<br>del Zurquí |
| **Puesta en acción 5/6:** Creating an electronic newsletter    258 | | | |

| | Vocabulario | Funciones y estructuras | Lecturas y vídeo |
|---|---|---|---|
| **Unidad IV:** Cambios y transciones | | | |
| **Capítulo 7** Cambios 264 | | | **Enfoque:** Cuba y la República Dominicana |
| **Tema 1:** Mi tierra querida 266 | Nostalgia | Discussing memories with verbs like **gustar** Expressing generalizations with the neuter article **lo** | Perspectivas: Dirección: El sur de la Florida |
| **Tema 2:** Es hora de partir 279 | Preparativos para una mudanza | Expressing purpose or reason with **por** and **para** | Vídeo: Un día triste para Valeria |
| **Tema 3:** A establecerse en una nueva casa 292 | Los bienes raíces | Referring to the beneficiary of an action using indirect object pronouns Talking about the past with the preterite and the imperfect tenses Talking about the immediate past with **acabar de** | Lectura: Soñar en cubano |
| **Capítulo 8** ¡A trabajar! 304 | | | **Enfoque:** Venezuela y Colombia |
| **Tema 1:** En busca de trabajo 306 | Los anuncios clasificados | Referring to people and things with the relative pronouns **que** and **quien(es)** Referring to past events that continue into the present with the present perfect tense | Perspectivas: Trabajos via Internet |
| **Tema 2:** Mis antecedentes y expectativas laborales 319 | La hoja de vida | Influencing others with formal commands Using pronouns and formal commands | Vídeo: El secreto de Sofía |
| **Tema 3:** El nuevo empleo 332 | Las tareas de oficina | Avoiding stating who or what is performing an action with the passive **se** Avoiding repetition using double object pronouns | Lectura: Mi amigo |
| **Puesta en acción 7/8:** Planning an international move    346 | | | |

| | Vocabulario | Funciones y estructuras | Lecturas y vídeo |
|---|---|---|---|
| **Unidad VI:** Expectativas | | | |
| **Capítulo 11**<br>Mirando hacia el futuro 442 | | | **Enfoque:**<br>Chile y Paraguay |
| **Tema 1:**<br>Proyectos personales 444 | Mis aspiraciones | Talking about aspirations (review of the future tense)<br>Expressing conjecture and probability with the conditional tense | Perspectivas: Las claves de la ilusión |
| **Tema 2:**<br>Un futuro tecnificado 456 | Las comodidades de la era electrónica | Expressing opinion, emotion, wishes, doubt, stipulation, purpose and future time frame with the subjunctive and the infinitive<br>Talking about the past using the imperfect subjunctive (regular verbs) | Vídeo: Aspiraciones y planes para el futuro |
| **Tema 3:**<br>Utopías 470 | Un mundo mejor | Talking about the past using the imperfect subjunctive (irregular verbs)<br>Expressing condition (**si** clauses) | Lectura: El albergue de las mujeres tristes |
| **Capítulo 12**<br>La herencia hispana 486 | | | **Enfoque:**<br>Los hispanos en los Estados Unidos |
| **Tema 1:**<br>Historia de la presencia hispana en los Estados Unidos 488 | | Talking about the past with the preterite, the imperfect, and the present perfect (review) | Lectura: Los antecedentes (Partes 1 y 2) |
| **Tema 2:**<br>Abriendo caminos 498 | | Giving commands, advice, and opinions (review) | Vídeo: Se les fue volando el mes |
| **Tema 3:**<br>Desafíos 504 | | Indicating probability with the future and conditional tenses (review) | Lectura: Entró y se sentó |
| **Puesta en acción 11/12:** Hispanic heritage 512 | | | |

# Preface to the Student

*¡Bienvenidos a **Temas!*** This textbook is designed to give you the opportunity to discover the Spanish language through **active learning.** Its basic philosophy is that language acquisition results from participating in **meaningful interactions** with other language learners and/or native speakers. With this program, active learning takes place through classroom and independent learning tasks with the help of multimedia and the Internet.

As you proceed through this course, keep in mind the following principles, which have helped many learners achieve proficiency in a foreign language:

- **Practice.** Seek every opportunity to use the language in and out of the classroom. Take advantage of all the human and technological resources at hand.

- **Be adventurous.** Don't be afraid to take risks. Mistakes are a natural part of the learning process.

- **Be patient.** Learning a language takes time and effort. Don't expect it to happen overnight.

- **Be flexible.** Accept that you won't always understand everything or be able to say exactly what you want to say. There are many ways to get your point across.

- **Discover.** Appreciate the uniqueness of other cultures. Bridge the gap between your culture and others.

- **Expand your horizons.** Consider studying abroad and interacting with Spanish speakers in your area.

We hope that these words of advice will help you and that your experience learning the Spanish language and exploring the diverse cultures of the Spanish-speaking world is an enriching and rewarding one.

# Acknowledgments

Writing a textbook is always a team effort, especially in the case of a project of this magnitude. For this reason, we would like to express our most sincere gratitude to Heinle Publishers for its leadership in the development of quality foreign language materials. Our deepest appreciation to Helen Alejandra Richardson (Senior Acquisitions Editor) for believing in the *Temas* program and in the promise of a second edition; to Mercedes Roffé (Developmental Editor), whose experience and pedagogical knowledge guided us toward the completion of this project; to Stasie Harrington for her incredible talent to create outstanding video activities; and to Esther Marshall (Senior Production Project Manager) for her creativity and vision. Our thanks also go to the other people at Heinle without whom we would not have successfully concluded this project: Heather Bradley (Associate Development Editor) and Caitlin McIntyre (Editorial Assistant). And finally, our thanks to all the freelancers involved with the different stages of the production and in particular, Katy Faria (Project Manager on behalf of Pre-Press Company, Inc.), Linda Beaupré (Interior Designer), Margaret Hines (Copyeditor and Proofreader), Luz Galante (Native Reader), Lucy de la Cruz Gibbs and Soledad Phelan (Proofreaders).

We wish to especially thank the authors of the *Temas,* **Second Edition,** ancillaries:

Kimberley Sallee, *University of St. Louis,* for her work on the IRM.

Jennifer Rogers, *Blue River Community College,* for her work on the Testing Program.

Andy Noverr, *University of Michigan,* for his work on the CDROM and iLrn.

Bridgette Gunnels, *State University of West Georgia,* for her work on the website.

Our deepest gratitude to all the reviewers, whose ideas and feedback oriented and shaped the development of this Second Edition in many important ways.

Lee Abraham, *Villanova University*
Joseph A. Agee, *Morehouse College*
Pilar Alcade, *University of Memphis*
Aranxta Alegre-González, *Ohio State University*
Eileen M. Angelini, *Philadelphia University*
Barbara Avila-Shah, *University at Buffalo, SUNY*
Liliana Castro, *Front Range Community College*
Ana García Chicester, *University of Mary Washington*
Sarah DeSmet, *Wesleyan College*
Conxita Domenech, *Front Range Community College*
Linda Elliott-Nelson, *Arizona Western College*
Addison Everett, *Dixie State College*
Mary Fatora-Tumbaga, *Kauai Community College*
Hector Garza, *Southern Utah University*
Donald Gibbs, *Creighton University*

Pamela Gill, *Gaston College*
Peg Haas, *Kent State University*
Denise Hatcher, *Aurora University*
Tia Huggins, *Iowa State University*
Hans Jöerg-Busch, *University of Delaware*
Herman Johnson, *Xavier University*
David Julseth, *Belmont University*
Sofia Kearns, *Furman University*
Paula Luteran, *Hutchinson Community College*
Jeffrey R. Marks, *Ohio University*
Don Miller, *California State University, Chico*
Lilijana Milojevic, *Ocean County College*
Bill Monds, *Trinity Valley Community College*
Oscar Moreno, *Georgia State University*
Denise Overfield, *University of West Georgia*
Kay E. Raymond, *Sam Houston State University*
Marcie Rinka, *University of San Diego*
Regina Roebuck, *University of Louisville*
Jennifer Rogers, *Blue River Community College*
Tara Rojas, *University of Hawaii*
Patricia Rubio, *Skidmore College*
Jacqueline Sandone, *University of Missouri-Columbia*
Carmen Schlig, *Georgia State University*
Nancy Smith, *Allegheny College*
Elizabeth Vargas Dowdy, *Manatee Community College*
Susan Villar, *University of Minnesota*
Kathleen Wheatley, *University of Wisconsin- Milwaukee*
Jonnie Wilhite, *Kalamazoo Community College*
Nancy Whitman, *Los Medanos College*

Finally, we wish to thank our family, our friends, and all the people in Latin America and Spain who offered insights about their countries and their lives. Their contributions give this book its real-life flavor.

To all, our sincere thanks.

Jorge H. Cubillos and Edwin M. Lamboy

# Student Components

**Workbook/Lab Manual:** Packaged with the Lab Audio CDs, it follows the organization of the main text, providing additional reading, writing, listening, and pronunciation pactice out of class. The writing activities, correlated to the latest version of **Atajo: Writing Assistant for Spanish,** direct you to the main points of information essential to the writing task, and guide you in the writing process.

**Lab Audio CDs:** Intended to use in conjunction with the **Workbook/Lab Manual**. These CDs provide listening comprehension reinforcement of structures and vocabulary, and also help improve pronunciation.

**Student Multimedia CD-ROM:** Provides you with fun, interactive practice of the vocabulary and grammar from each *Tema*. In addition to a variety of practice activities, the CD-ROM also offers audio- and video-enhanced sections that focus on pronunciation and culture and a reading section that describes on-going service learning projects to think about opportunities in your own community.

**Atajo 4.0 CD-ROM: Writing Assistant for Spanish:** This powerful program combines the features of a word processor with databases of language reference material, a searchable dictionary featuring the entire contents of Merriam-Webster's® Spanish English Dictionary, a verb conjugating reference, and audio recordings of vocabulary, example sentences, and authentic samples of the language. This will help you develop critical thinking skills as you learn to read, analyze, make word associations, and understand the link between language functions and linguistics structures.

# Text Credits

**pp. 424–425:** "La floreciente industria del cuerpo", reprinted by permission of *El País*, Montevideo, UY.

**pp. 453–454:** "El Tunel" by Ernesto Sabato.

**pp. 505–506:** "El albergue de las mujeres tristes" by Marcela Serrano.

**pp. 530–531:** "Entró y se sentó" by Rosaura Sanchez is reprinted with permission from the publisher of *Cuentos hispanos de los Estados Unidos* (Houston: *Arte Publico Press*–University of Houston, 1993)

**p. 93:** "La Casa en Mango Street", © 1984, Sandra Cisneros.

**pp. 134–135:** "La dieta mediterranea tambien reduce cancer y mortalidad general". Source: *EFE* 26/jun/2003, Association for the Advancement of the Mediterranean Diet.

**pp. 171–172:** "Las Vacaciones" from "La Familia no hay mas que una y al perro lo encontramos en calle". Reprinted by permission of *Gomaespuma Producciones S.L.*

**pp. 214–215:** "Historia de los incas", Pedro Sarmiento. Gamboa (1572)

**pp. 229–230:** Reprinted by permission of *El Nuevo Diario*, Martes, 18 de Marco, 2004.

**pp. 290–291:** "Dirección: el sur de la Florida", December 1997. Reprinted by permission of *Latin Trade*.

**pp. 315–316:** "Soñar en Cubano" by Christina Garcia.

**pp. 331–332:** "Encontrar trabajo vía cibernética" by Jay Dougtherty. Reprinted by permission of *El Universal Digital*, 14 de julio 1997. © dpa, 1997.

**pp. 357–358:** "Mi Amigo, Germán Cuervo", *Ediciones de la Universidad del Valle*.

**pp. 406–407:** "La hija del cannibal by Rosa Montero".

**p. 111:** Officina del Gobernador de Puerto Rico, © 1998.

# Photo Credits

All photographs not otherwise credited are owned by © The Thomson Corporation or © Thomson/Heinle Image Resource Bank.

**p. 23** left: ©Mitch Diamond/Index Stock Imagery
**p. 35:** ©Digital Vision/Getty Images
**p. 37** right: ©Spencer Grant/Photo Edit
**p. 45** left: ©SW Productions/Brand X Pictures/Getty Images
**p. 45** center: ©Lisette Le Bon/SuperStock
**p. 45** right: ©Bob Daemmrich/The Image Works
**p. 47:** ©Photodisc Green/Getty Images
**p. 72** left: ©Allen Russell/Index Stock Imagery
**p. 72** center: ©Kellie Walsh/Index Stock Imagery
**p. 72** right: ©Jim McGuire/Index Stock Imagery
**p. 76:** ©Jim Reed/Digital Vision/Getty Images
**p. 89** left: ©AP Photo/Rich Pedroncelli
**p. 89** right: ©Myrleen Cate/Index Stock Imagery
**p. 92** left: ©Mark Hunt/Index Stock Imagery
**p. 92** center: ©Mark Segal/Index Stock Imagery
**p. 97:** "The Disembarkation in Veracruz", 1951 fresco by Diego Rivera. National Palace Mexico City. ©2005 Banco de México Diego Rivera & Frida Kahlo Museums Trust.
**p. 101** left: ©Steve Dunwell/Index Stock Imagery
**p. 101** right and center: ©Wendell Metzen/Index Stock Imagery
**p. 111:** ©Jim Schwabel/Index Stock Imagery
**p. 113** top: ©Jeff Greenberg/Alamy
**p. 113** center left: ©Craig Witkowski/Index Stock Imagery
**p. 113** center right: ©Peter Ciresa/Index Stock Imagery
**p. 113** bottom left: ©Eric Kamp/Index Stock Imagery
**p. 113** bottom right: ©AbleStock/Index Stock Imagery
**p. 134:** ©Ewing Galloway/Index Stock Imagery
**p. 141** left: ©John James Wood/Index Stock Imagery
**p. 141** center: ©Peter Adams/Index Stock Imagery
**p. 141** right: ©BSIP Agency/Index Stock Imagery
**p. 142** left: ©Todd Powell/Index Stock Imagery
**p. 142** center left: ©Tim Heneghan/Index Stock Imagery
**p. 142** center right: ©James Lafayette/Index Stock Imagery
**p. 142** right: ©Peter Ciresa/Index Stock Imagery
**p. 151** bottom: ©Scott Smith/Index Stock Imagery
**p. 152:** ©MedioImages/SuperStock
**p. 154** right: ©Novastock/Index Stock Imagery
**p. 171:** ©Dennis Macdonald/Index Stock Imagery
**p. 180** top left: ©R.P. Kingston/Index Stock Imagery
**p. 180** top right: ©Ray Hendley/Index Stock Imagery
**p. 180** center left: ©Ewing Galloway/Index Stock Imagery
**p. 180** center right: ©ThinkStock LLC/Index Stock Imagery
**p. 180** bottom left: ©Ewing Galloway/Index Stock Imagery
**p. 180** bottom right: ©Spike and Ethel/Index Stock Imagery
**p. 180** bottom: ©Bill Bachmann/Index Stock Imagery
**p. 190:** ©Lindy Powers/Index Stock Imagery
**p. 191:** ©Image Source Limited/Index Stock Imagery

**p. 194:** ©Stewart Cohen/Index Stock Imagery
**p. 204** left: ©Patricia Barry Levy/Index Stock Imagery
**p. 205:** ©Robert Houser/Index Stock Imagery
**p. 207** top left: ©Big Cheese Photo/Index Stock Imagery
**p. 207** top right: ©Scott Witte/Index Stock Imagery
**p. 207** center: ©Kathy Tarantola/Index Stock Imagery
**p. 207** bottom: ©Grantpix/Index Stock Imagery
**p. 219** left: ©Inga Spence/Index Stock Imagery
**p. 229:** ©E.J. West/Index Stock Imagery
**p. 234** left: ©Timothy O'Keefe/Index Stock Imagery
**p. 234** center: ©Jacob Halaska/Index Stock Imagery
**p. 234** right: ©Timothy O'Keefe/Index Stock Imagery
**p. 236:** ©Paul Audia/Index Stock Imagery
**p. 240:** ©photolibrary.com pty. ltd./Index Open
**p. 244** top left: ©Amy and Chuck Wiley-Wales/Index Stock Imagery
**p. 244** center right: ©Ken Glaser/Index Stock Imagery
**p. 244** bottom left: ©Tony Ruta/Index Stock Imagery
**p. 246:** ©Profolio Enr./Index Stock Imagery
**p. 259** center: ©Mitch Diamond/Index Stock Imagery
**p. 260:** ©Edwin M. Lamboy
**p. 265** left: ©Francesco Venturi/CORBIS
**p. 266:** ©Sally Moskol/Index Stock Imagery
**p. 273** bottom: ©Alan Brigish/Index Stock Imagery
**p. 275:** ©age fotostock/SuperStock, Inc.
**p. 276:** ©Scott Smith/Index Stock Imagery
**p. 278** top: ©Randy Taylor/Index Stock Imagery
**p. 281:** ©AbleStock/Index Open
**p. 285:** ©Digital Vision/Getty Images
**p. 294:** ©Scott Smith/Index Stock Imagery
**p. 296:** ©John Ross, London
**p. 300:** ©Russell Illig/Photodisc Green/Getty Images
**p. 301:** ©Rudi Von Briel/Index Stock Imagery
**p. 305** left: ©Tom Carroll/Index Stock Imagery
**p. 305** right: ©Mick Roessler/Index Stock Imagery
**p. 309:** ©Eric Kamp/Index Stock Imagery
**p. 317:** ©Elisa Cicinelli/Index Stock Imagery
**p. 332** top left: ©Jon Riley/Index Stock Imagery
**p. 332** top center: ©Diaphor Agency/Index Stock Imagery
**p. 332** top right: ©Jon Riley/Index Stock Imagery
**p. 332** bottom left: ©Richard Gross/Index Stock Imagery
**p. 332** bottom center: ©Fred Slavin/Index Stock Imagery
**p. 332** bottom right: ©Lonnie Duka/Index Stock Imagery
**p. 343:** ©Wendell Metzen/Index Stock Imagery
**p. 353** left: ©Mick Roessler/Index Stock Imagery
**p. 353** center: ©Dan Gair Photography/Index Stock Imagery
**p. 353** right: ©Alyx Kellington/Index Stock Imagery
**p. 354** top left: ©Image Source Limited/Index Stock Imagery
**p. 354** top center: ©Bob Winsett/Index Stock Imagery
**p. 354** top right: ©Rubberball Productions/Index Stock Imagery

*This book is dedicated to all those who seek to learn about the cultures and people of Spanish-speaking countries and to use this knowledge and the Spanish language in the context of the global community.*

# Capítulo preparatorio

## ¡A empezar!

The following is the recommended set of instructional sequences (depending on the size of your group, this can take between two and three class periods):

Sequence 1

Levántense.                    Caminen.
Siéntense.                     Paren.

Sequence 2

Caminen a la pizarra.          Caminen a la ventana.
Caminen a la puerta.           Caminen al escritorio.

Sequence 3

Tomen el libro.                Cierren el libro.
Abran el libro.                Pongan el libro sobre el escritorio.

Sequence 4

Pongan el cuaderno enfrente del escritorio.
Pongan el cuaderno de ejercicios al lado de la mesa.
Pongan el lápiz sobre el escritorio.
Pongan el bolígrafo debajo de la mesa.

Sequence 5

Saquen un lápiz de su mochila.        Saquen una hoja de su mochila.
Guarden el lápiz en su mochila.       Guarden el libro en su mochila.

Sequence 6

Tomen la tiza.                        Tomen el borrador.
Escriban su nombre                    Borren su nombre de la pizarra.
  en la pizarra.

| | | | |
|---|---|---|---|
| **Vocabulario** | El salón de clase; Los saludos, las despedidas y las expresiones de cortesía | Los cursos | Los días y los meses; Los números; Los colores |
| **Funciones y estructuras** | Personal pronouns | Gender, number, and definite articles | Indefinite articles and the invariable impersonal verbal form **hay** |

# I. Vocabulario: El salón de clase

el profesor — la ventana — la profesora — el libro

Español 101
Buenos días

el borrador   la pizarra

la puerta

la mesa

la tiza
el cuaderno
el escritorio

el estudiante

la mochila   la estudiante

la silla   el bolígrafo

el lápiz   el cuaderno de ejercicios

## Vocabulario práctico

**Lo que dice el profesor**
Abran el libro en la página...
Cierren sus libros.
Escriban...
Lean...

*What the instructor says*
*Open your books on page . . .*
*Close your books.*
*Write . . .*
*Read . . .*

**Lo que dicen los estudiantes**
Más despacio, por favor.
¿Qué significa... ?
¿Cómo se dice... ?
Repita, por favor.
No comprendo.

*What students say*
*More slowly, please.*
*What does . . . mean?*
*How do you say . . . ?*
*Repeat, please.*
*I do not understand.*

### SABOR REGIONAL

A notebook is called a **carpeta** in Cuba and a **libreta** in the Dominican Republic and in Puerto Rico. Expect significant regional variations in the Spanish language, particularly in the area of vocabulary.

**Sugerencia:** Encourage students to create a personal vocabulary list (words that may not be part of the generic lists, but that correspond more closely to the students' particular communicative needs or interests).

**Sugerencia:** Introduce students to classroom vocabulary using Total Physical Response (TPR). Instruction should be given entirely in the target language (TL) according to the steps suggested by James Asher (1991):

1. Begin by demonstrating each command yourself.

2. Help students master each one of the commands by practicing with small groups in front of the class.

3. After a couple of modeling rounds, integrate the entire group.

4. Conclude by calling on specific individuals to test their comprehension and achievement.

**P**

**Script P-1:**

1. Escriban su nombre.
2. Muchas gracias.
3. Abran el libro en la página 25.
4. Lean el ejercicio.

CD1–2

### ■ Aplicaciones

**P-1 ¿Qué dice el (la) profesor(a)?** *(What does the instructor say?)* Match the statements made by the instructor with the following pictures.

3    1

4    2

**Answers P-2:** a. Repita, por favor./ No comprendo. b. ¿Cómo se dice… ? c. Repita, por favor. d. ¿Qué significa… ?

**P-2 ¿Qué dices?** *(What do you say?)* Provide an expression that you can use in each of the following cases.

a. When you do not understand what the instructor is saying.
b. When you do not know how to say something in Spanish.
c. When you want your instructor to repeat a key point.
d. When you do not know the meaning of a Spanish word.

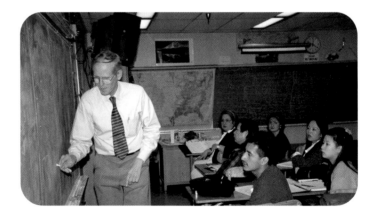

## II. Vocabulario: Los saludos, las despedidas y las expresiones de cortesía

—Buenos días, Julio.     *Good morning, Julio.*
—Buenos días, profesor Rodríguez.   *Good morning, Professor*
  ¿Cómo está Ud.?     *Rodríguez. How are you?*
—Muy bien, gracias.     *Very well, thank you.*

—Hola, Pedro.     *Hello, Pedro.*
—Buenas noches, Marta.     *Good evening, Marta.*
  ¿Cómo te va?     *How are you?*
—Muy bien, ¿y a ti?     *Very well, and you?*
—¡De maravilla!     *Wonderful!*
—Aquí está el libro.     *Here is the book.*
—Muchas gracias.     *Thanks a lot.*
—De nada.     *You're welcome.*

### SABOR REGIONAL

Other equivalent expressions used in different parts of the Spanish-speaking world for **De nada** are **A la orden, No hay de qué,** and **Con gusto.**

The following are other expressions you can use to indicate how you are doing: **más o menos/regular** *(so-so);* **mal** *(bad);* **pésimo** *(terrible).*

—Buenas tardes, ¿cómo   *Good afternoon, what is your*
  te llamas?     *name?*
—Me llamo Julián, ¿y tú?   *My name is Julián, and yours?*
—Me llamo Alicia.     *My name is Alicia. Pleased to*
  Mucho gusto.     *meet you.*
—Encantado.     *My pleasure.*

Notice that physical contact is often part of a greeting in Hispanic culture. This contact ranges from a firm handshake among men, to a kiss on the cheek for close friends. Greetings accompanied by kissing are quite common among young men and women (and among women) in both Latin America and Spain.

| | |
|---|---|
| —Adiós, Sr. Grisales. | *Good-bye, Mr. Grisales.* |
| —Bueno, hasta luego, Sr. González. | *O.K., see you later, Mr. González.* |

## Vocabulario práctico

| | |
|---|---|
| ¡Hasta pronto! *See you soon!* | Chao. *Bye.* |
| ¡Hasta la vista! *See you around!* | Nos vemos el lunes. *I'll see you on Monday.* |

### Títulos de respeto

| Títulos de respeto | **Titles of respect** |
|---|---|
| Doctor (Dr.) | *Doctor* |
| Licenciado (Lic.) | *(For various professions)* |
| Señor (Sr.) | *Sir/Mr.* |
| Señora (Sra.) | *Madam/Mrs.* |
| Señorita (Srta.) | *Miss* |

These titles are usually followed by the person's last name: **Dr. Jiménez, Sr. Gómez, Sra. Alarcón. Don** and **Doña,** which are used with older people as a sign of respect, are followed by the person's first name: **Don Juan, Doña María.**

## ▦ Aplicaciones

**P-3 Diálogos** Complete the dialogues with appropriate comments and responses.

1. La Sra. Díaz:     Buenos días, doctor.
   El Dr. Fernández:     _____
   La Sra. Díaz:     Pues no muy bien, doctor. Mire Ud.,...

2. Juan:     _____
   Ana:     Hola, Juan ¿Cómo estás?
   Juan:     _____

3. Esteban:     _____
   La profesora Ruiz:     Mucho gusto, Esteban. Yo soy la profesora Ruiz.
   Esteban:     _____

4. Julio:     _____
   Elvira:     Adiós, Julio. ¡Nos vemos el viernes!

When reporting on someone else's name, use the expression **Se llama...**

**P-4 Saluda a tus compañeros** Greet two or three of the people around you in Spanish. Learn their names and later introduce them to the rest of the class.

# III. Funciones y estructuras: Personal pronouns

| PERSON | SINGULAR | PLURAL |
|--------|----------|--------|
| **First** | **yo** *(I)* | **nosotros, nosotras** *(we*, masculine/feminine) |
| **Second** | **tú** *(you*, informal) <br> **usted** *(you*, formal) | **ustedes** *(you*, formal/informal) <br> **vosotros, vosotras** *(you*, masculine/ feminine, informal, Spain) |
| **Third** | **él** *(he)* <br> **ella** *(she)* | **ellos, ellas** *(they*, masculine/ feminine) |

As you noticed in the previous section, the distinction between formal and informal ways of addressing a person is at the essence of effective social communication. While in English the level of formality of an exchange finds its expression mainly in the tone and the type of language used, in Spanish this influence extends also to the verb forms and pronouns selected.

The informal personal pronouns in Spanish are **tú** for the singular and **ustedes** (or **vosotros** in Spain) for the plural.

Note that in Spanish there is no equivalent of the English subject pronoun *it*.

| | |
|---|---|
| Es mi escritorio. | *It is my desk.* |
| Es una clase difícil. | *It is a difficult class.* |

In Spanish there is a gender distinction when it comes to groups made exclusively of women (**nosotras, vosotras, ellas**). The masculine form is used in the case of male only or mixed groups.

| | |
|---|---|
| **Nosotras** somos profesoras. | ***We** are professors.* |
| **Vosotras** sois responsables. | ***You** are responsible.* |
| **Ellas** son mis hermanas. | ***They** are my sisters.* |

Since Spanish verbs have different endings for each person, personal pronouns are often omitted. The verb itself can indicate what the subject is.

| | |
|---|---|
| Soy estudiante. | *I am a student.* |
| Trabaja en una oficina. | *He/She works in an office.* |
| Estudiamos español. | *We study Spanish.* |

However, personal pronouns may be included in a sentence for clarification or emphasis.

| | |
|---|---|
| **Yo** soy estudiante. | *I **(myself)** am a student.* <br> (emphasis) |
| **Él** trabaja en una oficina. | *He works in an office.* <br> (clarification) |

If you will not require your students to learn the **vosotros** form, this is the time to indicate to them that this form will be covered for recognition purposes only.

P

## ■ Aplicaciones

**P-5 ¿De quién habla?** Complete the sentences with the appropriate pronoun according to the picture.

1. ___Yo___ soy Marta.

2. ___Ellas___ son mis compañeras.

3. ___Él___ es mi amigo Juan Ortega.

4. ___Nosotros___ somos estudiantes.

**P-6 Completa las frases** Make the following sentences more emphatic by adding the appropriate personal pronoun.

___Yo___ (I) soy estudiante.

___Tú___ (You, informal) eres profesora.

___Él___ (He) es Juan.

___Nosotros___ (We) somos amigos.

___Ellas___ (They, feminine) son mis hermanas.

# IV. Vocabulario: Los cursos

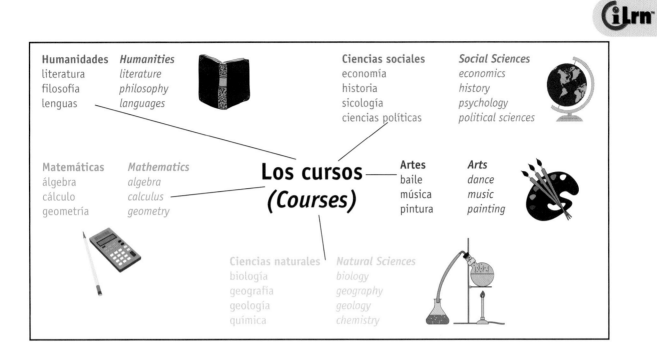

**Humanidades** *Humanities*
literatura *literature*
filosofía *philosophy*
lenguas *languages*

**Ciencias sociales** *Social Sciences*
economía *economics*
historia *history*
sicología *psychology*
ciencias políticas *political sciences*

**Matemáticas** *Mathematics*
álgebra *algebra*
cálculo *calculus*
geometría *geometry*

# Los cursos (Courses)

**Artes** *Arts*
baile *dance*
música *music*
pintura *painting*

**Ciencias naturales** *Natural Sciences*
biología *biology*
geografía *geography*
geología *geology*
química *chemistry*

## Vocabulario práctico

### Las especializaciones

administración de empresas — *business administration*
antropología — *anthropology*
comunicaciones — *communications*
derecho — *law*
educación física — *physical education*
informática — *computer science*
ingeniería — *engineering*
medicina — *medicine*
periodismo — *journalism*
fisioterapia — *physical therapy*
trabajo social — *social work*
veterinaria — *veterinary*

**Sugerencia:** Only the most common courses are introduced in this section. Encourage your students to look up the names of other relevant courses, and to include them in their **Vocabulario personal** list.

The major and minor system does not exist in Latin America or Spain. The institutions of higher education typically offer programs leading to professional degrees instead.

## ▩ Aplicaciones

**P-7 Su especialidad es...** *(His/Her concentration is . . . )* List six people you know and their concentration (major).

## V. Vocabulario: Los días y los meses

Months are not capitalized in Spanish. Dates are often expressed in the following order: day, month, year (10 de enero de 2007 = 10/01/07).

Seasons will be presented in **Capítulo 4, Tema 1.**

| lunes | martes | miércoles | jueves | viernes | sábado | domingo |
|---|---|---|---|---|---|---|
| | | | | | | |
| | | | | | | |

diciembre, enero, febrero    marzo, abril, mayo    junio, julio, agosto    septiembre, octubre, noviembre

**P-8 ¿Comprendiste bien?** Look at the following ads and answer the questions that follow.

Gran Concierto de Juanes. Coliseo Cubierto El Campín: sábado, 26 de febrero a las 6:00 p.m.

Vuele LAN a los Estados Unidos. Siempre con los mejores horarios. Santiago–Miami: dos vuelos diarios a las 10:00 y 11:00 p.m. Santiago–Nueva York: lunes, miércoles, viernes y domingos. Santiago–Los Ángeles: martes, jueves y sábados.

DE VUELTA AL COLEGIO, AHORRE EN SUS SUPERTIENDAS **MAKRO**: GRANDES DESCUENTOS EN ARTÍCULOS ESCOLARES. HORARIO ESPECIAL: LUNES A VIERNES: 7:00 A.M. A 10:00 P.M., SÁBADOS: 8:00 A.M. A 8:00 P.M., DOMINGOS: 12:00 A 6:00 P.M.

1. What days of the week is the Makro store open?
2. When does LAN fly to Miami? How about Los Angeles? And New York?
3. When is Juanes's concert?

**P-9 ¿Cuándo es... ?** Indicate in Spanish the month when the following events take place.

1. La independencia de los Estados Unidos
2. La Navidad *(Christmas)*
3. El Año Nuevo *(New Year)*
4. La Pascua *(Easter)*
5. El Día de Acción de Gracias *(Thanksgiving)*
6. El comienzo *(beginning)* de las clases
7. El examen final de la clase de español
8. El fin *(end)* del curso
9. Tu cumpleaños *(birthday)*

To find out what classes your friend is taking this semester/trimester, you can ask: **¿Qué clases tomas este (semestre/trimestre)?**

To reply you may say:
**Tomo matemáticas, inglés y español.**

**P-10 Horario** *(Schedule)* **de clases** Interview a classmate and complete his/her schedule of classes.

| | lunes | martes | miércoles | jueves | viernes | sábado | domingo |
|---|---|---|---|---|---|---|---|
| por la mañana *(in the morning)* | | | | | | | |
| por la tarde *(in the afternoon)* | | | | | | | |
| por la noche *(in the evening)* | | | | | | | |

# P

 CD1-3

**Sugerencia:** Play the text CD or demonstrate the following pronunciation guidelines, and have students repeat the following words. When necessary, point out the differences between Latin America and Spain.

**Sugerencia:** You may want to explain to students that the letters **ch**, **ll**, and **rr** are not part of the Spanish alphabet but that they should know their names.

## VI. Guía para la pronunciación: El alfabeto y las vocales

| Letra | Nombre | Ejemplos | |
|-------|--------|----------|---|
| A | a | Ana | Panamá |
| B | be | baile | Nubia |
| C | ce | casa, poco | César, Alicia |
|  | che | chévere | derecho |
| D | de | día | todo |
| E | e | enero | empresas |
| F | efe | Fernando | elefante |
| G | ge | Gabriel | elegante |
|  |  | Gertrudis | elegido |
| H | hache | hola | almohada |
| I | i | infante | estudiante |
| J | jota | junio | mejor |
| K | ka | kiosco | polka |
| L | ele | lápiz | helado |
|  | elle | lluvia | silla |
| M | eme | mamá | Guatemala |
| N | ene | nada | Honduras |
| Ñ | eñe | ñato | señor |
| O | o | Óscar | doctor |
| P | pe | Pedro | España |
| Q | cu | queso | porque |
| R | ere | arpa | pero |
|  | erre (*or* doble ere) | Ramón | perro |
| S | ese | Sandra | pasado |
| T | te | televisión | atuendo |
| U | u | uva | cuaderno |
| V | ve (*or* uve) | verano | Flavio |
| W | doble v (*or* doble uve) | Wilson | |
| X | equis | xilófono | exacto |
| Y | i griega | Yolanda | mayo |
| Z | ceta (*or* zeta) | Zapata | Mazatlán |

**Las vocales *a, e, i, o, u*** The pronunciation of vowels in Spanish does not vary.

| /a/ | /e/ | /i/ | /o/ | /u/ |
|-----|-----|-----|-----|-----|
| casa | café | tiza | sofá | uso |
| mamá | bebé | iglesia | bobo | útil |
| papá | jefe | inglés | lobo | uno |

In English there is a tendency to diphthongize words ending in vowels such as **o** or **e**. In Spanish those letters retain their original sound (/o/ or /e/).

libro     por qué

vivo     Santa Fe

amigo     porque

## VII. Vocabulario: Los números

Tiene **dos** lápices.
*She has **two** pencils.*

Éstas son mis **tres** hermanas.
*These are my **three** sisters.*

Es un edificio de **quince** pisos.
*It is a building of **fifteen** floors.*

Tengo **ochenta** dólares.
*I have **eighty** dollars.*

Hay **veinticinco** estudiantes.
*There are **twenty-five** students.*

Contiene **cincuenta** chocolates.
*It contains **fifty** chocolates.*

| | | | |
|---|---|---|---|
| cero | **0** | | |
| uno | 1 | once | 11 |
| dos | 2 | doce | 12 |
| tres | 3 | trece | 13 |
| cuatro | 4 | catorce | 14 |
| cinco | 5 | quince | 15 |
| seis | 6 | dieciséis | 16 |
| siete | 7 | diecisiete | 17 |
| ocho | 8 | dieciocho | 18 |
| nueve | 9 | diecinueve | 19 |
| diez | **10** | | |

| | | | |
|---|---|---|---|
| veinte | **20** | treinta | **30** |
| veintiuno | 21 | treinta y uno | 31 |
| veintidós | 22 | treinta y dos | 32 |
| veintitrés | 23 | cuarenta | **40** |
| veinticuatro | 24 | cincuenta | 50 |
| veinticinco | 25 | sesenta | 60 |
| veintiséis | 26 | setenta | 70 |
| veintisiete | 27 | ochenta | 80 |
| veintiocho | 28 | noventa | 90 |
| veintinueve | 29 | cien | **100** |

## P

### ■ Aplicaciones

CD1–4  **P-11 Una fiesta** Listen to a phone message someone has left in your answering machine. How many items does he/she want you to bring to the class party? Circle the correct figure in each case.

1. mesas:       2, ④, 6
2. sillas:       10, ⑳, 30
3. pizzas:      ⑤, 15, 25
4. refrescos *(soft drinks):*     11, ㉑, 31
5. platos *(dishes):*    ㊹, 74, 94
6. servilletas *(napkins):*    50, 80, ⑩⓪

**P-12 ¿Cuánto es?** In pairs, take turns completing the following calculations and expressing the results in Spanish.

Vocabulario útil: **más** = +       **menos** = −
                 **por** = ×       **dividido por** = ÷

1. $11 + 6 =$ _17_
2. $35 + 9 =$ _44_
3. $55 + 23 =$ _78_
4. $66 - 34 =$ _32_
5. $71 - 17 =$ _54_
6. $90 - 82 =$ _8_
7. $4 \times 12 =$ _48_
8. $3 \times 9 =$ _27_
9. $25 \times 3 =$ _75_
10. $20 \div 2 =$ _10_
11. $72 \div 3 =$ _24_
12. $96 \div 6 =$ _16_

Play the text CD at this time. The amount of unknown vocabulary is intentional. The idea is to help your students develop listening strategies that they are going to need when dealing with authentic listening tasks.

Script P-11: Gracias por ofrecerte a ayudarme con los arreglos para la fiesta de nuestra clase de español. Aquí está la lista de lo que necesito:

1. Primero que todo, necesito que busques *(look for)* unas **cuatro** mesas.

2. ¡Ah! Y también unas **veinte** sillas.

3. Pienso que vamos a necesitar unas **cinco** pizzas.

4. Y **veintiún** refrescos.

5. Si puedes, trae también unos **cuarenta y cuatro** platos desechables.

6. Mmm... y no te olvides de traer servilletas. Creo que **cien** serán suficientes. No sabes cómo te agradezco tu ayuda. ¡Hasta mañana!

# VIII. Vocabulario: Los colores

**Los colores**

- negro
- azul
- marrón/café
- dorado
- rojo
- gris
- verde
- anaranjado/color naranja
- rosado
- morado
- plateado
- blanco
- amarillo

Transparency I-2: Los colores

## ■ Aplicaciones

**P-13 ¿De qué color es... ?** Look at the drawing of the class on page 3 and indicate the color of each of the following items.

**Opciones:** anaranjado, azul, verde, blanco, marrón

1. la tiza _____blanco_____
2. la pizarra _____verde_____
3. la puerta _____marrón_____
4. el bolígrafo _____azul_____
5. el lápiz _____anaranjado_____

**P-14 Las banderas** *(The flags)* Indicate in Spanish the colors of the following national flags:

Colombia

México

Bolivia

España

Panamá

## IX. Funciones y estructuras: Gender, number, and definite articles

Nouns are words that designate objects, animals, or persons such as *rock*, *cat*, or *mother*. All Spanish nouns have number and gender. Number refers to quantity (singular or plural). Gender indicates whether the word is considered to be masculine or feminine.

|  | MASCULINE | FEMININE |
|---|---|---|
| Singular | **libro** | **puerta** |
| Plural | **libros** | **puertas** |

### A. Número

To form the plural of a noun, simply add **-s** to the end of the word. If it ends in a consonant, add **-es.**

cuaderno — cuaderno**s**          borrador — borrador**es**
tiza — tiza**s**                          profesor — profesor**es**

To form the plural of words ending in **-z**, change the **z** to a **c** and add **-es.**

lápi**z** — lápi**ces**                    vo**z** *(voice)* — vo**ces**

If the word ends in **-s**, then the singular and plural forms are the same.

**el** lunes *(Monday)* — **los** lunes     **el** cumpleaños *(birthday)* —
                                          **los** cumpleaños

### B. Género

Nouns that end in **-o** typically are **masculine.**

el bolígrafo                          el escritorio

Most nouns ending in **-a, -dad, -tad, -ión,** and **-sis** are **feminine.**

la mochila                            la nación *(nation)*
la crisis                             la libertad *(freedom)*

The following are notable exceptions:

la mano *(hand)*                      el sistema *(system)*
el clima *(climate/weather)*          el tema *(theme)*
el día *(day)*                        el análisis *(analysis)*
el problema *(problem)*

To help you identify the gender of all nouns, the vocabulary entries in **Temas** include the words and their corresponding *definite articles* (**el, la, los,** or **las**).

### C. Definite articles

|  | MASCULINE | FEMININE |
|---|---|---|
| Singular | **el** libro | **la** puerta |
| Plural | **los** libros | **las** puertas |

Definite articles are typically used to refer to nouns in a concrete or specific manner.

**El** juego comienza a las cinco.  *The game begins at five.*
Quiero **las** zapatillas rojas.  *I want the red sneakers.*

Definite articles are also used to refer to classes or categories.

**Los** abogados ganan mucho dinero.  *Lawyers earn a lot of money.*

**El** fútbol es un deporte muy popular.  *Soccer is a very popular sport.*

Definite articles also accompany titles of respect such as **Dr. (Dra.)** and **Sr. (Srta./Sra.).**

¿Vas al cine con **la** Sra. Gómez?  *Do you go to the movies with Mrs. Gómez?*

**El** Dr. Silva trabaja aquí en la tarde.  *Dr. Silva works here in the afternoon.*

## ■ Aplicaciones

**P-15 ¿Cuántos quiere?** *(How many do you want?)* You and your classmate are in line at a cafeteria in a Spanish-speaking country. How many of the following food items are you going to order?

This exercise reviews numbers and previews food vocabulary. More on food and ordering meals in **Capítulo 3.**

To order food you can use the following expression: **Queremos <u>dos</u> refrescos.** *We want <u>two</u> sodas.*

La comida rápida | Fast food
banana/plátano | banana
botella de agua | bottled water
café | coffee
ensalada | salad
hamburguesa | burger
helado | ice cream
manzana | apple
perro caliente | hot dog
porción de papas fritas | french fries
porción de pizza | slice of pizza
refresco | soda

**P-16 ¿Una palabra masculina o femenina?** Guess the gender of the following words and supply the corresponding definite article.

1. nacionalidad
2. inscripción
3. dirección
4. enfermera
5. secretaria
6. natación
7. atletismo
8. problema
9. mano
10. amigo

This exercise serves as a preview of **Capítulo 1** vocabulary.

## X. Funciones y estructuras: Indefinite articles and the invariable impersonal verbal form *hay*

### ■ A. Indefinite articles

In Spanish, much like in English, indefinite articles are used when referring to nouns in a general sense.

| | |
|---|---|
| Tengo **una** mesa. | *I have a table.* |
| Necesito **unos** bolígrafos rojos. | *I need some red pens.* |

Indefinite articles agree in number and gender with the nouns they refer to.

| | MASCULINE | FEMININE |
|---|---|---|
| Singular | **un** cuaderno | **una** silla |
| Plural | **unos** cuadernos | **unas** sillas |

### ■ B. The impersonal verbal form *hay*

To express *there is* and *there are*, use the impersonal verbal form **hay**. Note that this verbal form is used with both singular and plural nouns.

| | |
|---|---|
| **Hay** una estudiante que se llama Helen. | ***There is*** *a student whose name is Helen.* |
| En el escritorio **hay** diez lápices. | ***There are*** *ten pencils on the desk.* |

### ■ Aplicaciones

**P-17 ¿Qué hay** *(What is there)* **en el salón de clases?** Complete the following description of your classroom. Add other details if applicable.

En el salón hay _____ ventanas, _____ profesor(a), _____ sillas y _____ pizarra(s). También hay _____.

**P-18 ¿Qué necesitas?** *(What do you need?)* With a partner, act out the following situation.

Greet the clerk and thank him/her after the transaction. Remember that a helpful expression to indicate what you want is **Quiero...** *(I want)* . . . Look at the vocabulary you studied in this chapter to decide what you may need and the number of items you need to purchase.

Do not forget to greet the customer and to thank him/her after the transaction in a polite manner. A helpful expression to indicate price is: **Son veinte dólares.** *(It is twenty dollars.)*

**Estudiante A**
Since tomorrow is your first day of class as an exchange student in a Spanish-speaking country, you have to stop by a bookstore to get a few things for your semester. Tell the shopkeeper what you need.

**Estudiante B**
You work at a university bookstore in a Spanish-speaking country. Help this exchange student get what he/she needs.

# Vocabulario

**Objetos en el salón de clase** — *Classroom objects*

| | |
|---|---|
| el bolígrafo | *pen* |
| el borrador | *eraser* |
| el cuaderno | *notebook* |
| el cuaderno de ejercicios | *workbook* |
| el escritorio | *desk* |
| el (la) estudiante | *student* |
| el lápiz | *pencil* |
| el libro | *book* |
| la mesa | *table* |
| la mochila | *backpack* |
| la pizarra | *chalkboard* |
| el profesor | *teacher (male)* |
| la profesora | *teacher (female)* |
| la puerta | *door* |
| la silla | *chair* |
| la tiza | *chalk* |
| la ventana | *window* |

**Lo que dice el profesor** — *What the instructor says*

| | |
|---|---|
| Abran el libro en la página… | *Open your books on page . . .* |
| Cierren sus libros. | *Close your books.* |
| Escriban… | *Write . . .* |
| Lean… | *Read . . .* |

**Lo que dicen los estudiantes** — *What the students say*

| | |
|---|---|
| Más despacio, por favor. | *More slowly, please.* |
| ¿Qué significa… ? | *What does . . . mean?* |
| ¿Cómo se dice… ? | *How do you say . . . ?* |
| Repita, por favor. | *Repeat, please.* |
| No comprendo. | *I do not understand.* |

**Saludos** — *Greetings*

| | |
|---|---|
| Buenos días. | *Good morning.* |
| Buenas (tardes/noches). | *Good (afternoon/ evening).* |
| Me llamo… | *My name is . . .* |
| ¿Cómo está Ud.? | *How are you? (formal)* |
| Bien, ¿y Ud.? | *Fine, and you? (formal)* |
| Muy bien, gracias. | *Very well, thank you.* |
| Mucho gusto. Encantado(a). | *Pleased to meet you.* |
| Hola. | *Hi. Hello.* |
| ¿Cómo te va? | *How are you? (informal)* |
| Bien, ¿y a ti? | *Fine, and you? (informal)* |
| De maravilla. | *Great.* |
| De nada. | *You are welcome.* |

**Despedidas** — *Farewells*

| | |
|---|---|
| Adiós. | *Good-bye.* |
| Hasta luego. | *See you later.* |
| Hasta pronto. | *See you soon.* |
| Hasta la vista. | *See you around.* |
| Chao. | *Bye.* |
| Nos vemos el lunes. | *I'll see you on Monday.* |

**Títulos** — *Titles*

| | |
|---|---|
| Doctor(a)/Dr(a). | *Doctor* |
| Licenciado(a)/Lic(a). | *(For various professions)* |
| Señor/Sr. | *Sir/Mr.* |
| Señora/Sra. | *Madam/Mrs.* |
| Señorita/Srta. | *Miss* |

**Humanidades** — *Humanities*

| | |
|---|---|
| la literatura | *literature* |
| la filosofía | *philosophy* |
| las lenguas/los idiomas | *languages* |

**Ciencias sociales** — *Social sciences*

| | |
|---|---|
| las ciencias políticas | *political science* |
| la economía | *economics* |
| la historia | *history* |
| la sicología | *psychology* |

**Ciencias naturales** — *Natural sciences*

| | |
|---|---|
| la biología | *biology* |
| la geografía | *geography* |
| la geología | *geology* |
| la química | *chemistry* |

**Artes** — *Arts*

| | |
|---|---|
| el baile | *dance* |
| la música | *music* |
| la pintura | *painting* |

**Matemáticas** — *Mathematics*

| | |
|---|---|
| la álgebra | *algebra* |
| el cálculo | *calculus* |
| la geometría | *geometry* |

**Las especialidades** — *Majors*

| | |
|---|---|
| la administración de empresas | *business administration* |
| la antropología | *anthropology* |
| las comunicaciones | *communications* |
| el derecho | *law* |
| la educación física | *physical education* |
| la fisioterapia | *physical therapy* |
| la informática | *computer science* |
| la ingeniería | *engineering* |
| la medicina | *medicine* |
| el periodismo | *journalism* |

| el trabajo social | social work |
| la veterinaria | veterinary |

## Los días de la semana / *Days of the week*

| lunes | Monday |
| martes | Tuesday |
| miércoles | Wednesday |
| jueves | Thursday |
| viernes | Friday |
| sábado | Saturday |
| domingo | Sunday |

## *Los meses* / **Months**

| enero | January |
| febrero | February |
| marzo | March |
| abril | April |
| mayo | May |
| junio | June |
| julio | July |
| agosto | August |
| septiembre | September |
| octubre | October |
| noviembre | November |
| diciembre | December |

## Los colores / *Colors*

| amarillo | yellow |
| anaranjado/ color naranja | orange |
| azul | blue |
| blanco | white |
| dorado | gold |
| gris | gray |
| marrón/café | brown |
| morado | purple |
| negro | black |
| plateado | silver |
| rojo | red |
| rosado | pink |
| verde | green |

## Funciones y estructuras

Personal pronouns, p. 7
Gender, number, and definite articles, pp. 16–17
Indefinite articles and the invariable impersonal
   verbal form **hay**, p. 18

# Unidad 1

## El mundo hispano

In this unit you will learn how to express basic information about yourself, your family, and people you know such as occupation, personal interests, and family background. In turn, the readings and videos will introduce you to Spanish-speakers who will share similar information about themselves. You will also learn basic information about the Spanish-speaking world, its geography, and its people. At the end of the unit you will exchange emails with José Francisco Reyes Galindo from Guanajuato, Mexico, who will be an exchange student in your home. You will also be able to connect with your community through diverse service tasks such as researching Latino student organizations, employment agencies, and local government initiatives to promote positive and healthy pastimes.

# La identidad

# Capítulo 1

# Éste soy yo

**Para comenzar**

With a classmate, indicate the appropriate caption for each photograph.

- En el mundo hispano existen diversas tradiciones culturales. Foto 2
- La geografía de Latinoamérica es rica y variada. Foto 1
- Los hispanos son amables y hospitalarios. Foto 3

## In this chapter you will learn . . .

- how to exchange information
- how to describe people and objects
- how to talk about professions, daily activities, and pastimes
- how to create a personal profile
- the extent and general characteristics of the Spanish-speaking world
- about leisure time activities in the Spanish-speaking world

| | TEMA 1<br>Datos personales | TEMA 2<br>Ocupaciones | TEMA 3<br>Intereses personales |
|---|---|---|---|
| Vocabulario | Los formularios | Profesiones y ocupaciones | Los pasatiempos |
| Funciones y estructuras | Providing information with the verb **ser**<br>Describing people with adjectives | Talking about daily activities with simple present tense **-ar** verbs<br>Talking about daily activities with simple present tense **-er** and **-ir** verbs | Expressing negation<br>Exchanging information and asking questions with interrogative words |
| Lecturas y vídeo | Perspectivas: Los documentos de identificación | Vídeo: La llegada a Puerto Rico y a la Hacienda Vista Alegre | Lectura: Mi página personal en la Red |

**Foto 1**

**Foto 2**

**Foto 3**

The **Enfoque** section uses visual stimuli (video and photos) to present basic historical, geographical, and cultural information about the country (or region) explored in the chapter. The **Enfoque** section also includes **Para comenzar** activities, which are intended to introduce the general theme of the chapter and to serve as context for the presentation of chapter objectives.

# Enfoque

Transparencies A-1: España; A-2: México y la América Central; A-3: El Caribe; A-4: La América del Sur.

**A.** **¿Qué más sabes del mundo hispano?** *(What else do you know about the Spanish-speaking world?)* Before you watch the video, state what you think the following cognates (Spanish words that look like English words), taken from the video segment, mean in English.

centros administrativos    Península Ibérica    influencia africana
héroe importante    grupos indígenas    independencia

Check your answers with a partner. Then, choose **one** of the topics above and, based on what you both already know about the Spanish-speaking world, write down as much information as you can about it.

**Answers A:** administrative centers, important hero, Iberian Peninsula, indigenous groups, African influence, independence

**B.** **¿En qué orden?** *(In what order?)* As you watch the video, listen for the cognates from activity A and determine in what order they are presented in the video.

  4   centros administrativos      1   Península Ibérica
  3   influencia africana          6   héroe importante
  2   grupos indígenas            5   independencia

**C.** **¿Cierto o falso?** Watch the video one more time and, with a partner, decide if the following statements are true **(ciertos)** or false **(falsos).** (If the information is incorrect, make the necessary changes.)

  C   1. There is great cultural and ethnic variety in the Spanish-speaking world.

  C   2. The Spanish language originated in the Iberian Peninsula.

  F   3. One of the most important indigenous groups in Latin America was the Aztec, which inhabited Perú.

  C   4. Most Latin American countries became independent from Spain in the nineteenth century.

  F   5. Simón Bolívar is one of the most prominent Argentinean heroes.

**Answers C:** 3. The Aztecs lived in México. 5. Bolívar liberated Colombia, Venezuela, Ecuador, and Bolivia. He was from Venezuela.

For more info, you may want to check the **Temas** site: **http://temas.heinle.com**

# Datos personales

Transparency L-1: La hoja de inscripción

## READING STRATEGY

**Recognizing Cognates** There are many words in Spanish that resemble and have the same meaning as English words. They are called *cognates*. Even when you do not know much Spanish, you can rely on cognates to understand the general meaning of a written passage.

Find five cognates in the following application form. What are their English equivalents?

## SABOR REGIONAL

In several Spanish-speaking countries like Argentina, the Dominican Republic, Mexico, Puerto Rico and Spain, it is acceptable to use the English word **e-mail** instead of **correo electrónico**. This is also the case with many other words related to technology and science.

Notice that the words in **Vocabulario práctico** are accompanied by the masculine definite article **el** or the feminine one **la**. These articles are presented here to help you identify the gender of the noun that follows. For the sake of brevity, these definite articles are usually omitted in forms and other official documents.

**Sugerencia:** Consider the following tasks to give students an opportunity to practice stating their full names in Spanish:

1. **¿Cuál es tu nombre completo en español?** (What is your full name in Spanish?)

2. Ask a classmate about his (her) last name and get the following information. Leave any unknown information blank.

**¿Cuál es tu nombre completo en español?**

Primer nombre    Primer apellido

Segundo nombre    Segundo apellido

## I. Vocabulario: Los formularios *(application forms)*

**FORMULARIO DE INSCRIPCIÓN**

APELLIDOS: *Jones*    NOMBRES: *Susan Jane*
FECHA DE NACIMIENTO (dd-mm-aa) *23-05-72*
SEXO: *F*    PASAPORTE n° *4562339996*
DOMICILIO: *10 Savoy Road*    CIUDAD: *Chicago*
CÓDIGO POSTAL: *60681*    PAÍS: *Estados Unidos*
TELÉFONO: (312) 555-3251    FAX: (312) 555-3252
CORREO ELECTRÓNICO: *sjjones @ aol.com*
NACIONALIDAD: *estadounidense*    LENGUA MATERNA: *inglés*

**Nivel de conocimiento del español (autoevaluación):**

PRINCIPIANTE    (INTERMEDIO)    AVANZADO    SUPERIOR

**Desea inscribirse en el/los ciclo/s:**

julio (1-25)    agosto (3-28)    (septiembre (2-27))

**Alojamiento:**

• DESEA ALOJAMIENTO EN LA RESIDENCIA UNIVERSITARIA
  en habitación doble    en habitación individual
• DESEA ALOJAMIENTO CON UNA FAMILIA
• NO DESEA ALOJAMIENTO

### Vocabulario práctico

el alojamiento *lodging*
el apellido *last name*
el correo electrónico *e-mail*
desde *since*
el domicilio/la dirección *address*

la fecha de nacimiento *date of birth*
hasta *until*
la nacionalidad *nationality*
el nombre *name*
el teléfono *phone (number)*

In the Spanish-speaking world your full name often includes a first name (**primer nombre**) and a middle name (**segundo nombre**) followed by the last name of your father (**primer apellido**) and your mother's maiden name (**segundo apellido**).

Juan José Pérez Caballero
Ana María Restrepo Gómez

■ Dates are indicated in Spanish beginning with the day of the week, followed by the number and the name of the month, and ending with the year.

Hoy es jueves, 27 <u>de</u> septiembre <u>de</u> 2008 (27/09/08).
*Today is Thursday, September 27, 2008 (09/27/08).*

- Note that in Spanish the components of the date are linked by the preposition **de** *(of )*. If the day of the week is not expressed, the date begins with the definite article **el.**

  Mi madre regresa **el** diez de octubre.
  *My mother returns on October 10.*

- The first day of the month is indicated with the ordinal number **primero**. Cardinal numbers (**dos, tres, cuatro,** etc.) are used for all other days.

  Las clases comienzan el **primero** de febrero y terminan el **quince** de mayo.
  *Classes start on February first and end on May 15.*

## ■ Asimilación

**1-1 Información clave** *(Key information)* Look at the application form on page 24 and answer the following questions.

1. What is the name of the applicant?
2. Where is she from?
3. What is she applying for?
4. When does she plan to begin her course?
5. How proficient is she in Spanish already?
6. What option did she select for lodging?
   - a. with a family
   - b. at a university dorm
   - c. at a hotel
   - d. at a youth hostel
7. What do you think the form means by **lengua materna?**
   - a. her native language
   - b. her mother's maiden name
   - c. her mother's full name

## ■ Aplicaciones

**1-2 ¿Qué falta?** *(What is missing?)* Complete the form by adding the category name for each type of information supplied.

### FORMULARIO DE INSCRIPCIÓN

| | |
|---|---|
| _____ *Rodríguez* | _____ *Calle* Sol #125* |
| SEGUNDO APELLIDO: *Gil* | CIUDAD: *Málaga* |
| PRIMER NOMBRE: *Juan* | CÓDIGO POSTAL: *13421* |
| _____ *Guillermo* | PAÍS: *España* |
| _____ (dd-mm-aa) *18-02-70* | _____ *638-2311* |
| SEXO: *M* | FAX: *621-8833* |
| PASAPORTE n°: *F1-1262358* | CORREO ELECTRÓNICO: *gil12 @espa,com,es* |
| _____ *español* | LENGUA MATERNA: *español* |

## ■ Integración

**1-3 El club de español** Imagine that you have been asked to design the application form for the Spanish club in your school. With a partner, discuss what information you want the form to request from prospective applicants. Then prepare the form and submit it to your instructor for feedback.

**Sugerencia:** Ask students to state their birthday in Spanish. Provide the following model on the board as a guide:

**¿Cuándo es tu cumpleaños?** *(When is your birthday?)*

**El 28 de mayo.** *(May 28)*

The **Asimilación** sections are structured-input activities designed to provide students with opportunities to demonstrate comprehension of the discrete segments of vocabulary or grammar being presented. The overall goal of these **Asimilación** activities is to facilitate internalization of the vocabulary or the linguistic structures targeted in each segment.

**Answers 1-1:** 1. Susan Jane Jones 2. Chicago 3. to be an exchange student 4. September 5. intermediate level 6. a 7. a

The **Aplicaciones** sections contain controlled but meaningful tasks aimed at eliciting the vocabulary or grammar points explored in the **Asimilación** section.

**Answers 1-2:** Primer apellido; Segundo nombre; Fecha de nacimiento; Nacionalidad; Domicilio; Teléfono

**Extensión 1-2:** Ask students to search, print, and bring to class samples of actual study-abroad application forms found on the web (key words: **formulario cursos español**). In groups, students should underline the vocabulary words presented in this chapter and identify one or two additional vocabulary words of importance for the completion of those authentic forms.

The Spanish word **calle** means **street**.

The **Integración** sections contain open-ended tasks aimed at providing contexts for the communicative use of the targeted vocabulary or grammatical structure.

Begin the conversation by saying **¿Qué información necesitamos?** *(What information do we need?)*

## II. Funciones y estructuras: Providing personal information with the verb *ser*

The verb **ser** *(to be)* is used to talk about nationality and place of origin.

Ellos **son** dominicanos. **Son** de Santo Domingo, la capital. *They* **are** *Dominican. They* **are** *from Santo Domingo, the capital.*

Nosotros **somos** chilenos. Yo **soy** de Santiago y ella **es** de Valparaíso. *We* **are** *Chilean. I* **am** *from Santiago and she* **is** *from Valparaiso.*

Notice that the preposition **de** *(of)* is used before the name of the country or city, but not before the adjective of nationality.

Mi amigo es **de** <u>Caracas</u>. Es venezolano.

*My friend is* **from** <u>Caracas</u>. *He is Venezuelan.*

These are the forms of the verb **ser**:

| SUBJECT PRONOUN | ser | MEANING(S) |
|---|---|---|
| yo | soy | *I am* |
| tú | eres | *you (informal, singular) are* |
| él/ella/usted | es | *he/she is* |
| | | *you (formal, singular) are* |
| nosotros(as) | somos | *we are* |
| vosotros(as) | sois | *you (informal, plural, Spain) are* |
| ellos(as)/ustedes | son | *they/you (plural, Latin America) are* |

The form of **ser** changes if you wish to find out where other people are from: **¿De dónde <u>es</u> el profesor?** *(Where <u>is</u> the professor from?)* **¿De dónde <u>son</u> ellos?** *(Where <u>are</u> they from?)* etc.

To find out where someone is from, ask **¿De dónde eres?** If you want to find out someone's nationality, ask **¿Cuál es tu nacionalidad?**

—¿Cuál es tu nacionalidad, Clarisa?

*What is your nationality, Clarisa?*

—Soy uruguaya.

*I am Uruguayan.*

—Y tú, Ramón, ¿de dónde eres?

*And you, Ramón, where are you from?*

—Soy de Ecuador.

*I am from Ecuador.*

## Asimilación

**1-4 Personalidades famosas** Match the items on the left with the phrases on the right.

**Script 1-5:** ¡Hola! Me llamo Carmen Delia Martínez Sánchez. Soy de los Estados Unidos, pero mis padres son de Ecuador. Soy de California. Mis hermanos se llaman José y Ana Belén. Ellos son de los Estados Unidos también. Mi amigo Miguel Antonio Gómez Rivera es de México y, al igual que yo, vive en California. Él es estudiante de matemáticas en la Universidad de San Diego.

   _b_   Salma Hayek...

   _d_   Nicole Kidman y Russell Crowe...

   _e_   Fidel Castro: «Yo...»

   _a_   Barbara Walters a *(to)* Diane Sawyer: «Tú...»

   _c_   Derek Jeter y Alex Rodríguez: «Nosotros...»

a. eres de los Estados Unidos.

b. es de México.

c. somos de Nueva York.

d. son de Australia.

e. soy cubano.

CD1-6 **1-5 Información personal** Listen to the information provided by Carmen Delia and complete the chart below.

|  | Carmen Delia | los hermanos | el amigo |
|---|---|---|---|
| Nombre(s) | Carmen Delia | José y Ana Belén | Miguel Antonio |
| Apellidos | Martínez Sánchez | Martínez Sánchez | Gómez Rivera |
| País *(country)* de origen | Los Estados Unidos | Los Estados Unidos | México |

## Aplicaciones

**1-6 En mi clase de español** With a partner, complete the following sentences using the correct form of the verb **ser** and the information requested.

1. ¿De dónde es tu compañero(a)?
   Mi compañero(a) _____ *(nombre)* _____ de _____ *(ciudad).*

2. ¿De dónde eres tú?
   Yo _____ de _____ *(ciudad).*

3. ¿Cómo se llama tu profesor(a)? ¿De dónde es?
   Mi profesor(a) se llama _____; él/ella _____ de _____ *(country of origin).*

CD1-7 **1-7 Haciendo amigos** *(Making friends)* Listen to and practice the following dialogue. Then personalize it by substituting the underlined words with your own information.

—Hola, me llamo <u>Steve</u>. ¿Cómo te llamas?
—Me llamo <u>Lauren</u>.
—Mucho gusto, <u>Lauren</u>.
—Igualmente. ¿De dónde eres, <u>Steve</u>?
—Soy de <u>Seattle</u>, ¿y tú?
—Soy de <u>Birmingham</u>.
—<u>Encantado</u> de conocerte.
—<u>Encantada, Steve</u>.

**Script 1-7:**
—Hola, me llamo Steve. ¿Cómo te llamas?
—Me llamo Lauren.
—Mucho gusto, Lauren.
—Igualmente. ¿De dónde eres, Steve?
—Soy de Seattle, ¿y tú?
—Soy de Birmingham.
—Encantado de conocerte.
—Encantada, Steve.

Ask appropriate questions such as **¿Cómo te llamas? ¿De dónde eres? ¿Cuál es tu nacionalidad? ¿Cuál es tu especialidad?** and **¿De dónde es tu familia originalmente?**

**1-8 ¡Conózcanse mejor!** *(Get to know each other better!)* Gather the necessary information from a classmate to fill in the blanks. Then introduce him/her to the rest of the class.

Mi compañero(a) se llama _____. Es de _____ *(ciudad)*. Es estudiante de _____ *(especialidad)*. Su *(His/Her)* familia es originalmente de _____.

### ■ Integración

Sugerencia 1-9: Ask students before they begin to take a minute to think about the greeting expressions and questions they may have to use in the conversation.

**1-9 Un(a) estudiante de intercambio** *(exchange)* Act out the following situation with a classmate.

| The American student | The exchange student |
|---|---|
| There is an exchange student from Bolivia in one of your classes. He/She seems a bit overwhelmed because it is the first day of classes and you want to help. Strike up a conversation with him/her and show him/her how friendly everyone is at this institution! (Find out his/her name, where he/she is from, and his/her major). | You are an exchange student from Bolivia. This is your first day of classes at this institution and you just came across a friendly face. Greet him/her and introduce yourself. Also, find out your classmate's name, where he/she is from, and his/her major. |

**1-10 Un correo electrónico** Complete the following e-mail to tell your Spanish professor about the exchange student in one of your classes.

**Fecha:** _____

**Para:** Profesor(a) _____

**De:** _____

**Re:** Un(a) estudiante de intercambio

Estimado(a) profesor(a):

En mi clase de _____ hay un(a) estudiante de intercambio hispano(a).

Él/Ella _____ *(nombre y especialidad)*.

¡Hasta pronto!

_____ *(tu nombre)*

## III. Funciones y estructuras: Describing people with adjectives

As you learned in **Capítulo preparatorio,** Spanish nouns have gender (masculine or feminine) and number (singular or plural). When a noun is being described by an adjective, the adjective shares the same gender and number with the noun. This is called *noun-adjective agreement.*

Transparencies A-1: España; A-2: México y la América Central; A-3: El Caribe: A-4: La América del Sur.

¿Cómo es **Nina**? Ella es **buena** y **simpática**.

¿Y tus **amigos**? Ellos son **divertidos** y muy **amistosos**.

The interrogative word **cómo** followed by a form of **ser** is used to find out what someone or something is like: ¿**Cómo eres**, Rogelio? Soy inteligente. *(What are you like, Rogelio? I am intelligent.)*

■ Spanish adjectives that end in **-o** in the masculine singular form (**activo, famoso, rico,** etc.) have four endings.

|  | MASCULINE | FEMININE |
|---|---|---|
| SINGULAR | **-o**<br>José es buen**o**. | **-a**<br>Rita es buen**a**. |
| PLURAL | **-os**<br>José y Manuel son buen**os**.<br>José y Rita son buen**os**. | **-as**<br>Rita y Sara son buen**as**. |

Adjectives that describe both masculine and feminine people (or things) take the masculine plural ending: Mi **padre** y mi **madre** son **estrictos**. Mi **coche** y mi **casa** son **nuevos** *(new).*

■ Adjectives that **do not** end in **-o** in the masculine singular form (**alegre, débil, mayor,** etc.) only have two endings: singular and plural.

|  | MASCULINE | FEMININE |
|---|---|---|
| SINGULAR | Mario es inteligent**e**. | Serena es inteligent**e**. |
| PLURAL | Mario y Carlos son inteligent**es**.<br>Mario y Serena son inteligent**es**. | Serena y Lidia son inteligent**es**. |

■ If an adjective ends in a vowel, add **-s** to show agreement of number; if it ends in a consonant, add **-es.**

Los chicos son muy **diligentes.**          *The guys are very **diligent.***
Zelma y Paco son **mayores.**          *Zelma and Paco are **mature (old).***

■ Adjectives are usually placed *after* the nouns they describe.

La Sra. López es una dentista **estupenda.**          *Mrs. López is a **stupendous** dentist.*
Víctor es un escritor **prolífico.**          *Víctor is a **prolific** writer.*

The following are some common adjectives you can use to describe objects and people.

| | |
|---|---|
| activo *active* | fuerte *strong* |
| alegre *happy* | inteligente *intelligent* |
| amistoso/amigable *friendly* | joven *young* |
| antipático *unpleasant* | mayor/viejo *mature/old* |
| bueno *good* | pobre *poor* |
| débil *weak* | rico *rich* |
| diligente *diligent* | serio *serious* |
| divertido *fun* | simpático *nice* |
| estricto *strict* | tonto *foolish*, *dull* |
| famoso *famous* | trabajador *hard-working* |

Adjectives of nationality that end in a consonant in the masculine singular form add an **-a** for the feminine.

Here is a list of other nationalities:

alemán (alemana) *German*
australiano *Australian*
canadiense *Canadian*
chino *Chinese*
estadounidense *American* (USA)
francés (francesa) *French*
griego *Greek*
inglés (inglesa) *English*
irlandés (irlandesa) *Irish*
italiano *Italian*
japonés (japonesa) *Japanese*
polaco *Polish*
ruso *Russian*

Adjectives of nationality can also be used to describe people. Here is a list of nationalities of Spanish-speaking countries.

| | |
|---|---|
| argentino *Argentinean* | hondureño *Honduran* |
| boliviano *Bolivian* | mexicano *Mexican* |
| chileno *Chilean* | nicaragüense *Nicaraguan* |
| colombiano *Colombian* | panameño *Panamanian* |
| costarricense *Costa Rican* | paraguayo *Paraguayan* |
| cubano *Cuban* | peruano *Peruvian* |
| dominicano *Dominican* | puertorriqueño *Puerto Rican* |
| ecuatoriano *Ecuadorian* | salvadoreño *Salvadorian* |
| español(a) *Spanish* | uruguayo *Uruguayan* |
| guatemalteco *Guatemalan* | venezolano *Venezuelan* |

To talk about origin you can also use the expression **ser + de origen (africano/estadounidense/europeo/...).**

La familia de James **es de origen asiático.**

*James's family **is of Asian origin.***

## ■ Asimilación

CD1–8

Script 1-11: 1. Son unas muchachas simpáticas. 2. Es muy amigable. 3. Es activa e inteligente. 4. Son divertidos y un poco tontos. 5. Es rico y alegre.

**1-11 ¿Quién es?** Listen to what Minerva says about some of her friends and choose the name of the person(s) she is describing. Then compare your answers with those of a partner.

1. ____ Andrés y Lorena    ____ Felicia    _X_ Sandra y Gabriela
2. _X_ Jaime    ____ Nora y Verónica    ____ Alberto y Humberto
3. _X_ Gloria    ____ David y Jorge    ____ Rigoberto
4. ____ Marta y Linda    _X_ Pamela y Wilberto    ____ Juan
5. ____ Yolanda    ____ Vivian y Cristóbal    _X_ Felipe

**1-12 ¿Cierto o falso?** Indicate whether the following sentences are true (**cierto-C**) or false (**falso-F**).

  ___F___ 1. Sammy Sosa es de origen europeo.

  ___C___ 2. La familia Kennedy es de origen irlandés.

  ___F___ 3. Julia Roberts es inglesa.

  ___F___ 4. Gloria Estefan es de origen colombiano.

  ___C___ 5. Enrique Iglesias es español.

  ___F___ 6. Venus y Serena Williams son australianas.

## ▨ Aplicaciones

**1-13 Descripciones** Provide two logical adjectives to complete each sentence.

  1. Eminem es ____ y ____.
  2. Britney Spears y Christina Aguilera son ____ y ____.
  3. Bill Gates es ____ y ____.
  4. Oprah Winfrey es ____ y ____.
  5. Justin Timberlake y Celine Dion son ____ y ____.
  6. El Presidente y la Primera Dama *(First Lady)* son ____ y ____.

**1-14 ¿Cómo son y de dónde son?** Complete the first blank with a logical adjective. Then, complete the second blank with an adjective of nationality. Use the clues provided!

  MODELO    La Sra. Ramos no es antipática. Es *simpática*. Ella es de San Salvador. Es *salvadoreña*.

  1. Estela y Mónica no son tontas; son ___inteligentes___. Ellas son de Santo Domingo. Son ___dominicanas___.

  2. El Sr. Vega no es rico; es ___pobre___. Él es de Montevideo; por lo tanto *(therefore)*, es ___uruguayo___.

  3. Los amigos de Lupe no son mayores, sino *(but)* ___jóvenes___. Ellos son ___costarricences___; son de San José.

  4. Liliana es una niña muy mala. Ella no es ___buena___. Es de Quito. Ella es ___ecuatoriana___.

  5. Eduardo y Ángela son muy serios; no son ___amigables/amistosos___. Ellos son ___peruanos___; son de Lima.

  6. Paula y Victoria no son fuertes, sino ___débiles___. Ellas son ___mexicanas___, de la Ciudad de México.

The **En tu comunidad** annotations are expansion suggestions designed to give students the opportunity to learn something from the Spanish-speaking community on a topic that is presented and explored in the **Tema**, thus making the experience with the target language more relevant and meaningful outside the classroom. You will find that these annotations lend themselves to interesting class discussions, presentations and even special projects. They may be counted as required tasks students have to carry out or simply as optional out-of-class activities.

### EN TU COMUNIDAD

Meet with the directors of a Hispanic or Latino student organization to find out what nationalities are represented in it and the most popular fields of study of its members. If your institution does not have such an organization, perhaps you can obtain information from the office of international affairs. Then, share with the class or write a short summary about your findings.

**Sugerencia 1-15, Paso 2:** Change **tus amigos(as)** to **los (las) amigos(as) de** *(name)*, **tus padres** to **los padres de** *(name)*, and **tu profesor(a) de español** to **el (la) profesor(a) de español de** *(name)*.

**1-15 Firma aquí, por favor** *(Sign here, please)*

**Paso 1:** Use the given clues to form questions and find six classmates who answer affirmatively. Pay attention to the endings of the adjectives and to the forms of the verb **ser!**

MODELO  tú - activo
E1: *¿Eres activo(a)?*
E2: *Sí, soy activo(a).*
E1: *Firma aquí, por favor. Gracias.*
o...
E2: *No, no soy activo(a).*
E1: *Gracias. Hasta luego.*

**Firma**

1. tus amigos(as)—joven      _____
2. tú—trabajador(a)          _____
3. tus padres—estricto       _____
4. tu profesor(a) de español—amistoso  _____
5. tú—de origen...           _____

**Paso 2:** Now share the information with the rest of the class.

MODELO  *Chris es activo. | Jennifer es activa.*

### Integración

**Activity 1-16** recycles vocabulary on subjects and fields of study.

**1-16 Los profesores de mi compañero(a)** Find out what classes your partner is taking this semester and ask him/her to describe his/her professors.

MODELO  E1: *¿Qué cursos tienes* (do you have) *este semestre?*
E2: *Matemáticas, sociología, ...*
E1: *¿Cómo es el profesor o la profesora de matemáticas?*
E2: *La profesora es...*

**1-17 Un resumen** *(summary)* Write a summary of the answers you provided in activity 1-16. When you finish, hand it in to your professor for feedback.

## IV. Perspectivas. Los documentos de identificación

### ▓ Antes de leer

**Su identificación, por favor** What forms of identification are commonly used in the United States? What information do they provide? (Make a list in Spanish of the pieces of information typically found on an American ID.)

### ▓ A leer

Look now at the following national IDs from Colombia and Spain. List the similarities and differences between those pieces of ID and the one you have in your wallet.

### ▓ ¿Entendiste bien?

Indicate which country's ID . . .

1. includes information about the owner's blood type ___Colombia___
2. includes the owner's home address ___España___
3. provides information about the owner's place of birth ___Colombia/España___
4. includes the names of the owner's parents ___España___
5. provides information about the owner's height ___Colombia___

# Ocupaciones

## I. Vocabulario: Profesiones y ocupaciones

Transparency D-3:
Las profesiones

✳ The masculine
form is **el hombre
de negocios.**

**la cocinera**

**el ingeniero**

**el policía**

**la mujer
de negocios***

**la peluquera**

**el enfermero**

**la mesera**

**el abogado**

**el obrero**

Many professions in Spanish have
English cognates: **el (la) profesor(a)**,
**el (la) secretario(a)**, **el (la) dentista**,
**el (la) científico(a)**, **el (la) doctor(a)**,
**el actor/la actriz**, **el (la) músico(a)**,
**el (la) director(a)**, **el (la) atleta**,
**el (la) veterinario(a)**, **el (la) bió-
logo(a)**, **el (la) recepcionista**, etc.

### SABOR REGIONAL

As you may expect, names of
occupations vary. For example,
*hairdresser* is **estilista** in Mexico
and Panama, while *waiter/wait-
ress* is **mozo(a)** in Argentina,
Bolivia, Costa Rica, the Dominican Republic, and Uruguay.

### Vocabulario práctico

el ama de casa *housewife*
el (la) arquitecto(a) *architect*
el (la) contable *accountant*
el (la) chofer *driver*
el (la) empleado(a) doméstico(a) *maid*
el (la) gerente *manager*
el (la) periodista *journalist*
el (la) programador(a) de computadoras *computer programmer*
el (la) vendedor(a) *salesperson*

### ■ Asimilación

**1-18 Herramientas de trabajo** *(Work tools)* Working with a classmate,
indicate the name of the profession that requires the following work tools.

**OPCIONES:** recepcionista   mujer de negocios   empleada doméstica   obrero

**Answers 1-18:** 1. empleada doméstica 2. mujer de negocios 3. obrero
4. recepcionista

**1**   **2**   **3**   **4**

**CD1-9** 🔊 **1-19 ¿De qué profesión se trata?** *(What occupation are we talking about?)*
Indicate the name of the profession or occupation described.

1. obrero, ingeniero, empleada doméstica
2. profesora, abogado, arquitecto
3. artista, recepcionista, peluquera
4. policía, enfermera, periodista

**LISTENING STRATEGY**

Don't be upset if you do not understand every word you hear. Efficient listeners often guess the meaning of unfamiliar terms based on information provided by other contextual clues (words or phrases coming before or after unknown/unfamiliar words).

### ■ Aplicaciones

**1-20 ¿Quién trabaja aquí?** *(Who works here?)* Indicate the profession of at least two people who work in each of the following places.

1. una oficina
2. una estación de televisión
3. un hospital
4. un restaurante
5. una universidad

MODELO    *Una recepcionista y un gerente trabajan en un hotel.*

**Script 1-19:** 1. Trabaja en la casa. Ordena las habitaciones y prepara la comida. 2. Trabaja en una escuela o universidad. Enseña a los estudiantes. 3. Trabaja en una oficina. Escribe cartas y contesta el teléfono. 4. Trabaja en un hospital. Cuida y atiende a los pacientes enfermos.

**Extensión 1-20:** Ask students to describe the personal attributes of each of the professions in activity 1-19.

**1-21 Intereses**

**Paso 1:** Complete the chart with a list of at least four professions or occupations that appeal to you (on the left) and four that are of little or no interest to you (on the right).

| Profesiones y ocupaciones que me interesan | Profesiones y ocupaciones que <u>no</u> me interesan |
|---|---|
| | |

**Sugerencia 1-21, Paso 2:** Use the following model:

**Preguntas para la discusión:** ¿Qué profesiones te interesan más? ¿Qué profesiones no te interesan?

**Informe *(Report)*:** Las profesiones más populares son ____. Las profesiones menos populares son ____.

**Paso 2:** When finished, compare your list with that of other members of your group. What are the most popular professions in your group? What are the least popular? Present a summary of your findings to the rest of the class.

**1-22 ¿Qué ocupación recomiendan?** *(What occupation do you recommend?)* Complete the chart with the ideal profession or occupation for the following people.

| Nombre | Descripción | Cursos o actividades favoritos | Ocupación ideal |
|--------|-------------|-------------------------------|-----------------|
| María | inteligente | la física y las matemáticas | |
| Julio | fuerte, honesto | los deportes | |
| Esteban | creativo | visitar los museos de arte | |
| Josefina | diligente | la biología y la anatomía | |
| Antonio | independiente | los idiomas | |

MODELO  E1: *María es inteligente. Ella estudia física y matemáticas. ¿Cuál es una profesión ideal para ella?*
E2: *Una profesión ideal para ella es...*

### ■ Integración

This activity offers a preview of family vocabulary, which will be fully covered in **Capítulo 2.**

**1-23 ¡Adivina!** *(Guess!)* Take turns describing a profession or an occupation to one of your classmates by creating short sentences or by listing words and phrases that could be associated with that profession. Have him/her guess what profession or occupation you are talking about. Use only Spanish!

MODELO  E1: *Hospital, no es un doctor.*
E2: *¡Enfermera! Pizarra, tiza.*
E1: *¡Profesor!*

**1-24 Mi familia** Write a brief report about the profession or occupation of at least five members of your immediate family.

MODELO  *Mi padre es vendedor y mi madre es abogada. Mi tío John es abogado y mis tías Juana y Raquel son estudiantes. Mi hermana...*

# II. Funciones y estructuras: Talking about daily activities with simple present tense -*ar* verbs

Los cocineros **preparan** la comida en un restaurante.
*Cooks **prepare** food at a restaurant.*

La enfermera **cuida** a las personas enfermas.
*The nurse **takes care of** the sick.*

Spanish verbs belong to one of three groups: those that end in **-ar** (es-**cuchar**), those that end in **-er** (**comprender**), and those that end in **-ir** (**escrib<u>ir</u>**). This form of the verb is called the *infinitive*. The first part of the infinitive, which carries the meaning of the verb (**escuch-, comprend-, escrib-**), is called the *stem* of the verb.

When we want to say that someone is actually carrying out a particular action, the ending of the verb changes to agree with the subject. This is called *conjugating a verb*.

> Ella **trabaj<u>a</u>** en una oficina, pero yo **trabaj<u>o</u>** en un hospital.
> Los arquitectos **diseñan** casas.

> *She **works** in an office, but I **work** in a hospital.*
> *Architects **design** houses.*

Verbs ending in **-ar** are conjugated by dropping the **-ar** from the infinitive and attaching the appropriate ending to the stem of the verb. These are the endings to be used with **-ar** verbs.

Think of this classification of verbs as "families" (**-ar** family, **-er** family, and **-ir** family) that sometimes behave differently and sometimes behave similarly.

Do not confuse noun-adjective agreement (agreement of gender and number) with subject-verb agreement (agreement of person [first, second, or third] and number).

| SUBJECT | -ar VERBS ENDING | escuchar *(to listen)* |
|---|---|---|
| yo | **-o** | escuch**o** |
| tú | **-as** | escuch**as** |
| él/ella/usted | **-a** | escuch**a** |
| nosotros(as) | **-amos** | escuch**amos** |
| vosotros(as) | **-áis** | escuch**áis** |
| ellos(as)/ustedes | **-an** | escuch**an** |

Here are some **-ar** verbs that can be used to talk about daily activities.

| | |
|---|---|
| administrar *to administer, to manage* | informar *to inform* |
| bailar *to dance* | investigar *to investigate* |
| caminar *to walk* | limpiar *to clean* |
| cantar *to sing* | manejar *to drive* |
| cenar *to have dinner* | mirar *to look at, to see, to watch* |
| cocinar *to cook* | organizar *to organize* |
| comprar *to buy* | pintar *to paint* |
| contestar *to answer* | practicar *to practice* |
| cuidar *to take care of* | preparar *to prepare* |
| desayunar *to have breakfast* | programar *to program* |
| diseñar *to design* | representar *to represent* |
| enseñar *to teach* | tocar *to touch, to play an instrument* |
| escuchar *to listen* | tomar *to take, to drink* |
| estudiar *to study* | trabajar *to work* |
| hablar *to speak* | viajar *to travel* |

**SABOR REGIONAL**

The verb **conducir** is the preferred term for *to drive* in Chile, Colombia, Panama, and Spain. In Puerto Rico people use **guiar**.

The present tense is used to talk about actions that:

- are happening at the present time
  **Estudio** para un examen.                *I am studying for a test.*

- happen on a regular basis
  Simón **camina** por el parque todos los días.       *Simon walks in the park every day.*

- will happen in the near future
  **Viajamos** a España el jueves.           *We are traveling to Spain on Thursday.*

Here are some expressions that will help you indicate how frequently an action takes place.

| | |
|---|---|
| casi nunca *almost never* | nunca *never* |
| casi siempre *almost always* | siempre *always* |
| los... *on (day[s] of the week)* | todos los días *every day* |

## ■ Asimilación

**1-25 Las responsabilidades laborales** *(work responsibilities)* Match the professions listed on the left with the responsibilities listed on the right. Then, compare your answers with those of a classmate.

_b_ 1. el (la) policía     a. contesta el teléfono
_c_ 2. el (la) cocinero(a)     b. investiga crímenes
_d_ 3. el (la) gerente     c. prepara la comida en un restaurante
_e_ 4. el (la) periodista     d. administra una compañía
_a_ 5. el (la) secretario(a)     e. informa a las personas
_f_ 6. el (la) chofer     f. maneja un autobús o un taxi

D1–10   **1-26 La profesora Gutiérrez** Listen to a series of sentences about Professor Gutiérrez and write their numbers below the correct pictures. Careful! There is an extra picture!

**Script 1-26:** 1. La profesora Gutiérrez enseña matemáticas. 2. Ella siempre cena con su familia en su casa. 3. La profesora Gutiérrez trabaja en una escuela secundaria. 4. Ella y su esposo casi siempre preparan la comida juntos.

A _____  B _3_  C _1_  D _4_  E _2_

## ■ Aplicaciones

### 1-27 Actividades rutinarias

**Paso 1:** Fill in the blanks with different activities that you do.

Regularmente, yo _____ y _____ por la mañana. Por la tarde, (yo) _____ y _____. Por la noche, (yo) _____ y _____.

**Paso 2:** Now share the information with the rest of the class. What are the most popular and least popular activities?

**1-28 ¿Con qué frecuencia?** Form complete sentences about the people listed on the left. Include an expression of frequency and a different activity in each sentence. Conjugate the verbs correctly.

MODELO    nosotros    casi siempre    hablar español en clase
         *Nosotros casi siempre hablamos español en clase.*

1. nosotros(as)     | siempre     cenar en restaurantes caros (*expensive*)
2. los estudiantes típicos    | casi siempre    viajar a países de habla española
3. nuestros amigos    | casi nunca    hablar por teléfono
4. el (la) profesor(a)             escuchar la música de los Rolling Stones
         | nunca     limpiar la casa los sábados
                     comprar en Banana Republic
                     tomar café de Starbucks
                     usar productos biodegradables

**1-29 Los fines de semana**

**Paso 1:** Find out if two of your classmates do some of these activities on weekends. Keep track of the answers.

MODELO    E1: *Mary Anne, ¿estudias español los fines de semana?*
          E2: *Sí, estudio español los fines de semana. (o No, no estudio...)*
          E1: *Y tú, Roger, ¿estudias... ?*
          ...

estudiar español
desayunar en un café
bailar en un club
escuchar música
hablar por teléfono

limpiar la casa
mirar la televisión
trabajar en una oficina
practicar un deporte

To make your writing flow naturally you can use connectors such as **pero** *(but)*, **y** *(and)*, **también** *(also)*, **por otro lado** *(on the other hand)*, and **finalmente** *(finally)* in **Paso 2**.

**Paso 2:** Use the information you gathered in **Paso 1** to prepare a brief summary and share it with the class.

MODELO    *Mary Anne y Roger estudian español los fines de semana, pero yo no estudio. Por otro lado, ...*

## ■ Integración

**1-30 El estilo de vida** *(lifestyles)* **de los famosos** Act out the following situation with a partner. When you are finished, switch roles.

| **El (La) periodista** | **La persona famosa** |
|---|---|
| You are a journalist interested in finding out what a famous person does on a regular basis. Take into consideration this person's occupation and what you know about his/her life (or what you would like to know!) when asking questions. Be creative! | You are a famous person being interviewed by a journalist. (Your partner and you must decide who you are first [a singer, an actor/actress, a scientist, a TV personality, a well-known business mogul, etc.].) He/She wants to know what you do on a regular basis. Be creative in your answers! |

The journalist may ask direct questions like **¿Usted desayuna con amigos los sábados? ¿Usted siempre cena en...? ¿Usted maneja un carro...?** etc.

**1-31 Un día en la vida de...** Now write a summary about the lifestyle of the famous person you interviewed in activity 1-30. When you are ready, read your summary to the class without mentioning the person's name. Can your classmates guess the name of the celebrity you interviewed?

# III. Funciones y estructuras: Talking about daily activities with simple present tense *-er* and *-ir* verbs

Transparencies M-1: La rutina diaria(1); M-2: La rutina diaria(2); M-3: El fin de semana

Somos atletas y **corremos** cinco millas todos los días.
*We are athletes and we **run** five miles every day.*

Soy periodista. Yo **escribo** artículos para un periódico.
*I am a journalist. I **write** articles for a newspaper.*

Verbs ending in **-er** and **-ir** are conjugated by dropping the **-er/-ir** from the infinitive and attaching the appropriate ending to the stem of the verb. These are the endings to be used with these verbs.

| SUBJECT | ENDING | correr *(to run)* | escribir *(to write)* |
|---------|--------|-------------------|----------------------|
| | | **-er/-ir** verbs | |
| yo | **-o** | corr**o** | escrib**o** |
| tú | **-es** | corr**es** | escrib**es** |
| él/ella/usted | **-e** | corr**e** | escrib**e** |
| nosotros(as) | **-emos/-imos\*** | corr**emos\*** | escrib**imos\*** |
| vosotros(as) | **-éis/-ís\*** | corr**éis\*** | escrib**ís\*** |
| ellos(as)/ustedes | **-en** | corr**en** | escrib**en** |

*Note that the only differences between the present tense conjugation of **-er** and **-ir** verbs are in the **nosotros(as)** and **vosotros(as)** forms.

Here are some common **-er** and **-ir** verbs that can be used to talk about daily activities.

**-er** VERBS
aprender *to learn*
beber *to drink*
comer *to eat*
comprender *to understand*
correr *to run*
creer (que) *to think/believe (that)*
deber *should, must* (do something)
leer *to read*
responder *to respond*
vender *to sell*

**-ir** VERBS
abrir *to open*
asistir (a) *to attend*
compartir *to share, to spend time*
discutir *to discuss*
escribir *to write*
recibir *to receive*
vivir *to live*

**SABOR REGIONAL**

Another Spanish word for **beber** is **tomar**.

The verb **creer** is commonly used in sentences that require the use of a second conjugated verb: Yo **creo** que su madre **es** ama de casa. (*I **think** [that] her mother **is** a housewife.*) While the use of *that* is optional in English, the use of **que** is obligatory in Spanish.

**Deber** is followed by a verb in the infinitive form: **Debes visitar** a María el sábado. (*You **should visit** María on Saturday.*) As you can see, **deber** is the verb that agrees with the subject.

## ■ Asimilación

**1-32 ¿Lógica o ilógica?** First, match the occupations on the left with the phrases on the right. Then, indicate whether the sentences you created are **lógicas (L)** or **ilógicas (I).** When you finish, compare your answers with those of your partner.

<u>c</u> 1. Los buenos actores...

<u>a</u> 2. Los escritores...

<u>e</u> 3. Los buenos ingenieros...

<u>f</u> 4. Las recepcionistas...

<u>b</u> 5. Los vendedores...

<u>d</u> 6. Los atletas...

a. escriben novelas de ciencia ficción. <u>L</u>

b. venden productos a los consumidores. <u>L</u>

c. creen que Al Pacino es mediocre. <u>I</u>

d. no corren frecuentemente. <u>I</u>

e. deben aprender a diseñar. <u>L</u>

f. responden al teléfono. <u>L</u>

Script 1-33: Mi día típico es muy complicado. Generalmente, leo el periódico por la mañana y después me preparo para ir a la universidad. A veces escribo algunos informes antes de salir. Generalmente, cuando estoy en mi oficina, preparo las lecciones y respondo a los mensajes del correo electrónico. Por la tarde, después de enseñar mis clases, siempre bebo café con mis colegas y, por lo general, asisto a reuniones importantes. Finalmente, cuando regreso a mi casa, como con mi familia y miro algún programa de televisión.

CD1–11

**1-33 ¿Cómo es un día típico de tu profesor(a)?** Mark the activities that you think make up a typical day in the life of your professor. Then listen to the description to see which ones you guessed right.

<u>X</u> asiste a reuniones

<u>X</u> escribe informes

\_\_\_\_ vende libros por el Internet

<u>X</u> come con su familia

\_\_\_\_ bebe refrescos *(soft drinks)*

\_\_\_\_ comparte la computadora con sus hijos

<u>X</u> lee el periódico

<u>X</u> responde a los mensajes *(messages)* electrónicos

## ■ Aplicaciones

**1-34 Por lo general...** *(Generally . . . )*

**Paso 1:** Indicate whether or not the following phrases apply to you. If they do not, change the underlined words to make the sentence correct.

MODELO    aprender mucho en la clase de <u>biología</u>
*Por lo general, (yo) aprendo mucho en la clase de biología.* o
*Por lo general, (yo) aprendo mucho en la clase de español.*

1. escribir <u>buenas</u> monografías *(papers)*
2. creer que esta universidad es <u>buena</u>
3. comprender a las personas <u>mayores</u>

4. asistir a conciertos de música <u>popular</u>
5. comer en restaurantes <u>chinos</u>
6. discutir <u>mis problemas</u> con mis amigos

**Paso 2:** Turn the phrases in **Paso 1** into questions and find out if they apply to a partner. How similar or different are you?

MODELO    E1: *Noreen, ¿aprendes mucho en la clase de biología?*
E2: *Sí, aprendo mucho en la clase de biología.*
o    *No, aprendo mucho en la clase de cálculo.*

**1-35 Creemos que...** With a partner, choose two classmates and write five sentences about different things you think they do and do not do. Use some of the verbs on page 41 and follow the model. When you are ready, read the sentences and have the two classmates you chose react by saying **cierto** or **falso.** How well do you know them?

> MODELO    *Creemos que... y ...*

**1-36 ¿Con qué frecuencia?** Write sentences about the people listed on the left. Include an expression of frequency and a different activity in each sentence. Conjugate the verbs correctly and follow the model.

> MODELO    nosotros    casi nunca    comprender las decisiones del
>                                     gobierno
> *Nosotros casi nunca comprendemos las decisiones del gobierno.*

| | | |
|---|---|---|
| 1. nosotros(as) | siempre | vender los libros al final *(end)* del semestre |
| 2. ustedes (la clase) | casi siempre | responder a comentarios tontos |
| 3. el (la) profesor(a) | casi nunca | beber vino *(wine)* con la cena |
| 4. nuestra familia | | comer vegetales |
| | nunca | leer novelas románticas |
| | | escribir poemas de amor *(love)* |

## ■ Integración

**1-37 Conociéndonos mejor** *(Getting to know each other better)* Take a few minutes to think about the questions you need to ask to talk about the topics listed below. Then, in groups of two or three students, interview each other. Take notes.

- when, where, and how often you drink . . . /eat . . . /read . . .
- where you live
- whether or not you run, where and how often
- whether or not you believe certain things (*que el [la] profesor[a] es... , que la clase de español es... , que... , etc.*)

**1-38 Una persona admirable** Think about a person you would like to emulate (a friend, a relative, a celebrity, etc.). What is this person like? What does he/she do and not do that makes you like him/her so much? Write a short paragraph about this person beginning with the following phrase: **Creo que** *(name)* **es una persona admirable.** When you finish, share it with your professor.

**Sugerencia:** You may wish to brainstorm the questions that have to be used in this activity with the entire class before breaking it into groups.

You may have to use the following interrogative words and phrases: **cuándo** *(when)*, **dónde** *(where)*, and **con qué frecuencia** *(how often)*.

### VÍDEO

**Retratos del mundo hispano** As you complete **Tema 2,** you will get to know five Spanish speakers who share a unique intercultural experience in San Juan, Puerto Rico. Pre-viewing activities **(Preparación)** incorporate specific strategies to help you better comprehend what you will see and hear. Post-viewing activities **(¿Entendiste bien?)** will allow you to demonstrate both your comprehension and ability to actively use vocabulary, linguistic structures, and functions presented in each video segment.

### COMPREHENSION STRATEGY

**Anticipating** Trying to guess the content of a message based on what we know about its context (who is involved, why, etc.) is a very helpful strategy to deal with authentic, native-speaker speech.

## IV. Vídeo: La llegada a Puerto Rico y a la Hacienda Vista Alegre

### ■ Preparación

**A. Expectativas** What type of personal information do you think that the new roommates will share as they meet each other for the first time?

1. Place an X next to the **three** topics you expect to hear discussed.
   - __X__ a. sus nombres y apellidos
   - ____ b. su edad
   - ____ c. su fecha de nacimiento
   - __X__ d. su nacionalidad/país de origen
   - ____ e. sus actividades rutinarias
   - __X__ f. sus estudios/especialidades

2. Compare your selections with those of a classmate. For each topic that you have chosen in common, write questions and responses that you expect to hear used in the video segment, for example: —¿Cómo te llamas? —Me llamo...

3. Watch the video and check your predictions. Were you correct? Did you hear any of the questions and responses you wrote?

### ■ ¿Entendiste bien?

**B. Más detalles sobre los compañeros** Complete the table below with information about the roommates. First, complete the first row with the three correct topics from activity A. Then, watch the video again and fill in the information for each roommate.

| | NOMBRE | NACIONALIDAD | INTERESES |
|---|---|---|---|
| | | | |
| | | | |
| | | | |
| | | | |
| | | | |

**C. ¿Cómo son los compañeros?** Write a brief description of each roommate using descriptive adjectives. Compare your descriptions with those of a classmate. Are your initial impressions of each person similar or different?

**D. Enfoque comunitario** In the video you saw how Spanish speakers introduce themselves and ask questions in order to get to know each other. Imagine that you meet a Spanish-speaking visitor in your town. How would you introduce yourself? How would you find out his/her name, country of origin, or profession? With a partner, create a brief self-introduction and a couple of questions you would ask the new aquaintance. Consider practicing this new language skill by actually introducing yourself to a native Spanish-speaking person in your community.

# Intereses personales

## I. Vocabulario: Los pasatiempos

Juliana **charla** constantemente **por teléfono** con sus amigas.

David **escucha música** mientras estudia.

Pancho **navega por la Red** todas las tardes.

Paco **toca la guitarra** frecuentemente.

Los Merino **ven televisión** por la noche después de cenar.

### Vocabulario práctico

charlar por teléfono *to chat on the phone*

escuchar música *to listen to music*

leer un libro *to read a book*

(mirar/ver) televisión *to watch TV*

navegar por (la Red/el Internet) *to surf the Net*

pasear *to take a short trip, to go for a walk*

pasar (tiempo libre/los ratos libres) *to spend free time*

tocar un instrumento *to play an instrument*

Transparencies G-5: Pasatiempos; G-6: Deportes(1); G-7: Deportes(2); G-8: En el lago; G-9: En la playa

The verbs **mirar** and **ver** are used in different parts of the Spanish-speaking world to refer to the act of watching TV. Both verbs are understood by all Spanish-speakers, and the rationale for selecting one or the other is mostly regional (or national).

## ▨ Asimilación

**1-39 Los pasatiempos de los españoles** Look at the charts below and answer the questions that follow, on page 46.

**ACTIVIDADES DENTRO DE CASA (JÓVENES DE 15 A 29 AÑOS)**

- Leer libros 12%
- Ver televisión 31.4%
- Oír música 22.8%
- Trabajar en los quehaceres (chores) del hogar 3.3%
- Jugar videojuegos 3%
- Dormir, descansar, no hacer nada 11%
- Estudiar 3.6%
- Usar la computadora 6.2%

**ACTIVIDADES FUERA DE CASA**

- Ir al cine 2.4%
- Ir a conciertos 2.4%
- Salir con amigos 4.9%
- Beber, ir de copas 17.7%
- Leer libros 17.2%
- Bailar 13.9%
- Viajar 13.7%
- Hacer deporte 20.5%

**Fuente:** INJUVE, Calidad de vida de los jóvenes, 1998

1. ¿Cuál es el pasatiempo favorito de los jóvenes españoles dentro *(inside)* de casa?
2. ¿Cuál es el pasatiempo favorito de los jóvenes españoles fuera *(outside)* de casa?
3. ¿Son similares o diferentes los pasatiempos de los jóvenes españoles y los pasatiempos de los estadounidenses?
4. Selecciona dos actividades que haces dentro de casa y dos actividades que haces fuera de casa.

CD1-12

**1-40 ¿Cómo pasa el (la) profesor(a) su tiempo libre?** Listen and check your professor's pastimes. When finished, compare your answers with those of a classmate.

_____ Charla por teléfono.
__X__ Escucha música.
__X__ Lee un libro.
__X__ Mira televisión.
_____ Navega por la Red.
_____ Toca un instrumento.
__X__ Pasea.
_____ Escribe cartas.

### Aplicaciones

**1-41 En mis ratos libres...** Complete the paragraph with the correct form of the verb in parentheses.

Me llamo Rosa. Trabajo en una oficina de abogados y también estudio en la universidad. En mis pocos ratos libres, ____leo____ (leer). Casi nunca ____miro____ (mirar) televisión. A veces mi esposo *(husband)* y yo __escuchamos__ (escuchar) música o __paseamos__ (pasear). Los fines de semana (yo) ____charlo____ (charlar) con mis amigas, mientras mi esposo y sus amigos ____miran____ (mirar) los partidos de fútbol por televisión.

**1-42 ¿Cómo pasan sus ratos libres?** List three likely pastime activities of the following personalities. Use your imagination!

1. la reina de Inglaterra
2. Bill Gates
3. el Papa
4. Martha Stewart
5. Fidel Castro
6. Donald Trump
7. Brad Pitt y Antonio Banderas
8. Michael Jordan
9. Paris Hilton
10. Tiger Woods

**1-43 ¡A dibujar y a adivinar!** *(Let's draw and guess!)* Think of a pastime and then draw on a piece of paper something related to that activity (the equipment used, the place where it is carried out, etc.). Your classmate must guess in 20 seconds or less.

Sugerencia 1-43: Call time at 20-second intervals, and then instruct students to switch roles.

## ■ Integración

**1-44 Tus pasatiempos favoritos** Talk to your partner about his/her pastimes and write down the answers.

- ¿Cuándo tienes tiempo libre? (los fines de semana, por las noches, un día en particular,...)
- ¿Lees mucho? ¿Cuál es tu autor(a) favorito(a)?
- ¿Miras la televisión? ¿Qué programas? ¿Cuál es tu actor/actriz favorito(a)?

**1-45 Los pasatiempos de mi compañero(a)** Based on the previous conversation, prepare a brief report about your classmate's pastimes.

**Paso 1:** Begin your report by writing the name of the person you interviewed and one statement that describes the person based on how he/she spends his/her free time.

**Paso 2:** List the main activities he/she does in his/her spare time. Remember to use connectors such as **y** *(and),* **pero** *(but),* and **también** *(also).*

**Paso 3:** Close your report with an additional summary statement about your classmate or your personal opinion about his/her pastimes. Introduce this statement with one of the following expressions: **en conclusión** *(in conclusion),* **en resumen** *(in summary),* or **en mi opinión** *(in my opinion).*

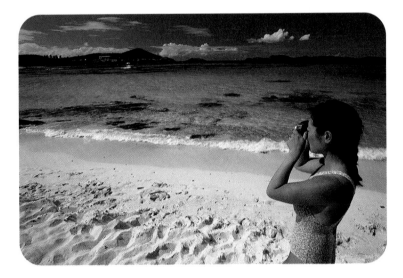

## II. Funciones y estructuras: Expressing negation

To make a negative statement, place the word **no** before the conjugated verb.

| | |
|---|---|
| Matilde **no** ve televisión por la noche. | *Matilde does **not** watch TV at night.* |
| Nosotros **no** escuchamos música rap. | *We do **not** listen to rap music.* |

There are other Spanish words you can use to express negation.

| | |
|---|---|
| nada *nothing* | ni... ni *neither . . . nor* |
| nadie *nobody* | nunca *never* |
| ningún/ninguno(a) *no, none, any* | tampoco *either, neither* |

| | |
|---|---|
| **Nadie** pasea durante la semana. | ***Nobody** goes for a walk during the week.* |
| Clara **nunca** charla por teléfono por la noche. | *Clara **never** talks on the phone at night.* |

As you can see in the previous examples, these negative words can be used before the conjugated verb. However, if they are used after the conjugated verb, the word **no** must precede the verb. The result is a double-negative statement, which is correct and quite frequent in Spanish.

| | |
|---|---|
| **No** pasea **nadie** durante la semana. | ***Nobody** goes for a walk during the week.* |
| Carla **no** charla **nunca** por teléfono por la noche. | *Clara **never** talks on the phone at night.* |

The word **ninguno** becomes **ningún** before masculine singular nouns, while **ninguna** is used before feminine singular nouns.

| | |
|---|---|
| Esmeralda no toca **ningún** instrumento. | *Esmeralda does not play **any** instrument.* |

The words **ninguno, ninguna,** and **ningún** normally function as adjectives and agree in gender (masculine/feminine) and number (singular/plural) with the noun to which they refer. Since they literally mean *not one*, they are usually used in the singular.

| | |
|---|---|
| Mi primo no tiene **ningún** pasatiempo. | My cousin does not have **any** pastimes. |
| **Ninguna** de mis hermanas toca el piano. | **None** of my sisters plays the piano. |

The expression **ni... ni** can be used with nouns and with verbs. Nouns: *Mi madre no toca **ni** la guitarra **ni** la flauta.* Verbs: *Mi padre **ni** navega por la Red **ni** pasea.*

## ■ Asimilación

**1-46 Mis fines de semana** Think about the things you normally do and not do during the weekend and indicate whether or not the following statements apply to you. When you finish, compare your answers with those provided by your partner. Do you have similar routines?

\_\_\_\_ 1. No navego por la Red los fines de semana.

\_\_\_\_ 2. Nunca miro la televisión por la mañana.

\_\_\_\_ 3. No escucho música ni el sábado ni el domingo.

\_\_\_\_ 4. Nunca toco un instrumento.

\_\_\_\_ 5. Tampoco paseo con mi familia.

\_\_\_\_ 6. No leo ningún libro los domingos.

\_\_\_\_ 7. No charlo por teléfono con nadie.

\_\_\_\_ 8. No paso mi tiempo libre ni en mi casa ni en la universidad.

CD1–13 **1-47 ¿Y Sabrina?** Now listen to what Sabrina says about her weekends. Write **sí** next to the activities she does and **no** next to the activities she does not do.

\_\_sí\_\_ charlar por teléfono

\_\_no\_\_ pasear

\_\_no\_\_ escuchar música

\_\_no\_\_ tocar un instrumento

\_\_no\_\_ leer libros

\_\_sí\_\_ mirar la televisión

**Script 1-47:** Por lo general, yo no hago muchas cosas los fines de semana. No soy una persona muy activa. Por ejemplo, ni leo libros ni escucho música. A veces charlo por teléfono con mis amigas o miro la televisión, pero no paseo nunca y no toco un instrumento tampoco. Así son mis fines de semana. ¡Aburridos!

## ■ Aplicaciones

**1-48 Situaciones** Use the given negative words to complete the blanks. Pay attention to the use of double negatives!

1. Bianca \_\_\_no\_\_\_ desea pasear y \_\_ni (no)\_\_ desea ver televisión \_\_tampoco\_\_. ¡Ella \_\_nunca\_\_ es así *(like that)*! (no, nunca, tampoco, ni)

2. \_\_Ni\_\_ Paco \_\_ni\_\_ Valentín escuchan música popular. En realidad, creo que ellos \_\_no\_\_ escuchan \_\_ningún\_\_ tipo de música. (no, ni, ningún, ni)

3. Nosotras \_\_no/nunca\_\_ leemos libros de Danielle Steel. \_\_nunca/no\_\_ leemos libros de John Grisham \_\_tampoco\_\_. ¡\_\_Ninguno\_\_ de mis amigos lee esos libros! (tampoco, no, nunca, ninguno)

**Answers 1-49:** 1. Ni (Sonia/Nancy) ni (Nancy/Sonia) toca el piano. 2. ¿Tú no navegas por la Red los fines de semana? 3. Nadie mira los programas de Nickelodium. 4. Nosotros no (miramos la televisión/paseamos) y tampoco (paseamos/miramos la televisión) los lunes. 5. Ellos nunca charlan por teléfono durante la semana.

**1-49 Sopa de palabras** *(Word soup)* Put the given words and phrases in logical order.

1. toca / ni Sonia / el piano / ni Nancy
2. ¿navegas / no / por la Red / los fines de semana / tú?
3. los programas / nadie / de Nickelodium / mira
4. miramos / no / los lunes / nosotros / la televisión / y / paseamos / tampoco
5. nunca / por teléfono / ellos / charlan / durante / la semana

**1-50 Comparaciones** First, make a list of four activities you do on a regular basis and four activities you never do. Then, take turns with your partner to read your activities and react by saying whether you do or do not do the same things. Do you have anything in common?

MODELOS    E1: *Yo practico fútbol y fútbol americano.*
           E2: *Pues* (Well) *yo nunca practico ni fútbol ni fútbol americano.*

                 o...
                 *Yo también practico fútbol y fútbol americano.*

           E1: *Yo nunca desayuno en la universidad.*
           E2: *Yo tampoco desayuno en la universidad.*

■ **Integración**

**1-51 Manteniendo las apariencias con** *(keeping up appearances with)* **los Jones** Your partner and you are very rich. You are always competing for the title of the most spoiled millionaire in the world. Talk about the things you do not do using negative words (**no, nunca, ni... ni..., tampoco, nada, nadie,** etc.) and try to outdo each other! Be creative!

**1-52 Los buenos amigos** What do good friends do and not do? Think about the answer to this question and write a paragraph using most of the negative words you just learned.

## III. Funciones y estructuras: Exchanging information and asking questions with interrogative words

In Spanish, to ask a *yes/no* question you can (1) raise your voice at the end of a sentence, (2) invert the position of the subject and the verb in the sentence, or (3) add the tag question **¿verdad?**, **¿cierto?**, or **¿no?** at the end of the sentence.

(1) ¿Gustavo lee libros de historia?

(2) ¿Lee Gustavo libros de historia?　　(Sí,/No, no) lee libros de historia.

(3) Gustavo lee libros de historia,
　　　¿verdad?

Note that Spanish questions do not include an equivalent for the auxiliary verbs *do* and *does*. You may simply use a conjugated form of the main verb: ¿José **toca** la guitarra? (***Does*** *José* ***play*** *the guitar?*)

To ask questions that request specific information and require more than a *yes* or *no* answer, you may use the following interrogative words.

| INTERROGATIVE WORDS | EXAMPLES |
|---|---|
| **¿cómo?** *(how?/what . . . like?)* | **¿Cómo** estás, Lola? **¿Cómo** es este libro? |
| **¿cuál(es)?** *(what?/which?)* <br><br> Note that **cuál** is singular and **cuáles** is plural. | **¿Cuál** es tu artista favorito? **¿Cuáles** son tus discos? |
| **¿cuándo?** *(when?)* | **¿Cuándo** es la clase de música? |
| **¿cuánto(a)?** *(how much?)* <br><br> **¿cuántos(as)?** *(how many?)* <br><br> **Cuánto(s)** refers to masculine nouns and **cuánta(s)** to feminine nouns. | **¿Cuanto** tiempo toma el paseo? **¿Cuánta** agua hay? <br><br> **¿Cuántos** instrumentos toca ella? <br> **¿Cuántas** sillas hay? |
| **¿dónde?** *(where?)* | **¿Dónde** está la biblioteca? ¿De **dónde** son tus padres? |
| **¿por qué?** *(why?)* <br> Questions that contain **por qué** are generally answered with **porque** *(because).* | **¿Por qué** estudias español? **Porque** es la lengua de mis abuelos. |
| **¿qué?** *(what?)* | **¿Qué** es el Internet? |
| **¿quién(es)?** *(who?)* <br> **Quién** is used to inquire about one person while **quiénes** is used to inquire about more than one person. | **¿Quién** es el Dr. Suárez? **¿Quiénes** son esas señoras? |

### ▪ Asimilación

01-14 **1-53 Preguntas personales** Answer the questions you will hear in complete sentences.

1. ...　　　4. ...

2. ...　　　5. ...

3. ...

**Script 1-53:** 1. Tú eres de los Estados Unidos, ¿verdad? 2. Tus amigos son simpáticos, ¿no? 3. La clase de español es interesante, ¿cierto? 4. Los estudiantes miran la televisión frecuentemente, ¿no? 5. Tú tocas un instrumento, ¿verdad?

**1-54 ¡Y más preguntas personales!** For each question, choose the appropriate interrogative word. When you finish, compare your answers with the answers provided by your partner.

1. —¿(Cuántos/Cuánto) cursos tomas por semestre?
   —Tomo cinco cursos.
2. —¿(Qué/Cuál) es tu curso favorito?
   —Mi favorito es el curso de historia medieval.
3. —¿(Cuándo/Dónde) vives?
   —Vivo en la casa de mis padres, en los suburbios.
4. —¿(Cómo/Qué) son tus padres?
   —Mis padres son estrictos, pero son muy buenos.
5. —¿(Por qué/Quién) es tu mejor amiga?
   —Mi mejor amiga es Moraima.

■ **Aplicaciones**

**Answers 1-55:** 1. ¿Quién es ella? 2. ¿De dónde es (ella)? 3. ¿Cómo es (ella)? 4. ¿Cuál es su pasatiempo favorito? 5. ¿Ella es amiga de Norberto?/Ella es amiga de Norberto, ¿no? 6. ¿Qué estudia? 7. ¿Por qué estudia comunicaciones? 8. Ella es atractiva, ¿no?

**1-55 Al revés** *(Backwards)* Make up the questions you would have to ask to get the following answers.

MODELO    Es mi prima. → ¿*Quién es?*

1. Ella es Lisa.
2. Ella es de Miami.
3. Es inteligente y un poco antipática.
4. Su pasatiempo favorito es leer.
5. No, ella no es amiga de Norberto.
6. Estudia comunicaciones.
7. Porque desea ser reportera de televisión.
8. Sí, ella es muy atractiva.

**1-56 ¡Más detalles, por favor!** Your partner and you always ask people to provide more details. React to the following statements by asking at least one logical question. Take turns asking and reacting to the statements.

MODELO    Anita no escucha música clásica.
          *¿Por qué no escucha música clásica? ¿Qué música escucha?*
          *¿Cuál es su música favorita?*

1. Alejandro es muy joven.
2. La familia de Margarita es grande.
3. Ni Petra ni Gisela estudian filosofía.
4. Nunca como en la cafetería universitaria.
5. Raúl es muy activo los fines de semana.
6. Vivimos en un apartamento precioso.
7. Mi horario es muy ajetreado *(busy)*.
8. Mi amigo se llama Federico.

## 1-57 En su tiempo libre...

**Paso 1:** Take a few minutes to write at least six questions you want to ask a classmate to find out more information about what he/she does in his/her free time. Use a different interrogative word in each question. Then, ask the questions and take notes.

**Paso 2:** Share the information with the rest of the class. Does he/she enjoy doing the things you thought he/she would enjoy? How similar or different are you?

### ■ Integración

**1-58 Un nuevo miembro del club** Act out the following situation in groups of three or four.

| Los miembros de la comisión directiva | El nuevo miembro | El (La) amigo(a) |
|---|---|---|
| You are members of the board of directors of a club in your school. A new member brought one of his/her friends to a meeting because the friend is interested in joining the club as well. You want to find out as much as possible about him/her. Take turns asking questions related to his/her life, interests, studies/work, family, home, etc. | You have brought a friend to a meeting of a school club you recently joined because he/she wants to become a member too. Two of the members of the board of directors want to talk to him/her. As you expected, they will ask many questions to get to know him/her better. Try to help him/her make a good impression! | You are at a meeting of a school club your friend recently joined because you want to join as well. Two of the members of the board of directors want to meet you and they have many questions for you. They want to get to know as much as possible about you before accepting you as a new member of the club. Make a good impression! You may ask them questions as well. |

**1-59 En busca de un(a) nuevo(a) empleado(a)** *(In search of a new employee)* You are the director of an after-school program for adolescents and you need to hire a new employee. This person must be dynamic, reliable, and very special. Create the application form you will use to get as much information as possible about potential candidates for this position. Include varied and pertinent questions. Be creative!

## IV. Lectura: Mi página personal en la Red

### ■ Antes de leer

**A. Para conversar en grupos** What information do you expect to find on a personal home page on the World Wide Web? Make a list of those items in Spanish.

**B. Cognados** Circle the cognates you find on this home page.

**C. Vocabulario nuevo** Connect each word with its definition. Use your dictionary if necessary.

_b_ 1. la derecha     a. historia, antecedentes

_c_ 2. disfrutar     b. el lado opuesto al del corazón (usualmente las personas escriben con esta mano)

_d_ 3. la izquierda     c. pasar un buen rato, pasarlo bien

_e_ 4. novia     d. lo opuesto de la derecha

_a_ 5. trayectoria     e. amiga especial con quien se tiene una relación romántica

**VOCABULARIO PRÁCTICO**

nombre, información personal, fotografías, conexiones favoritas

**READING STRATEGY**

**Skimming** Remember that when you skim a reading the first time, you are looking for cognates and the main ideas of the text.

### Mi página en la Red

#### Fabián Pérez León

overview

I enjoy

¡Hola y bienvenido! Mi nombre es Fabián Pérez León. Soy de Medellín, Colombia. A continuación te presento mi **trayectoria** académica y personal, así como algunas de las actividades que **disfruto** hacer. Mi domicilio permanente es Calle 45 #20-31, Barrio Caldas, Medellín, Colombia. ¡Espero que disfrutes con la visita! ¡Gracias!

**Datos personales** Éste soy yo. Tengo veintitrés años y vivo en Medellín. Aquí incluyo fotos de mi familia y de Nubia, mi novia.

**Trayectoria académica y laboral** Soy ingeniero de sistemas y trabajo para IBM en esta ciudad.

equipment
weightlifting

I love

**Pasatiempos** Me interesa todo lo referente a **equipo** y programas de PCs. También practico **levantamiento de pesas** y, desde luego, fútbol. En el cine **me encanta** la trilogía de «Star Wars» y las películas de Steven Spielberg, de Arnold Schwarzenegger y Sylvester Stallone.

With regard to

eagles

**En cuanto a** la música, me gusta especialmente la música romántica. Para leer siempre busco revistas sobre deportes y ciencia y también me gustan algunas novelas. ¿Escribir? En ocasiones. Mis animales favoritos son los leones, los tigres y las **águilas**.

## ■ A leer

**D. ¿Qué dice?** *(What does it say?)* Answer the following questions in Spanish about this home page. Use the glossary and cognate recognition to make associations for meaning.

1. ¿De dónde es Fabián?
2. ¿Cuál es su profesión?
3. ¿Dónde trabaja?
4. ¿Cuáles son sus pasatiempos favoritos?

____ charlar por teléfono

____ navegar por la Red

____ escuchar música

____ tocar un instrumento

____ leer libros

____ pasear

____ mirar la televisión

____ otro(s): ____

**E. Para conversar** What information is missing in this home page? Prepare a list with your ideas and share it with the rest of the class.

**F. Mi propia página web** Imagine how you would like to represent yourself on a web page. Start by writing information that characterizes you. Prepare your own home page in Spanish for the web.

# Vocabulario

| **Formulario** | **Application form** |
| --- | --- |
| el alojamiento | *lodging* |
| el apellido | *last name* |
| desde | *since* |
| el domicilio/la dirección | *address* |
| la fecha de nacimiento | *date of birth* |
| hasta | *until* |
| la nacionalidad | *nationality* |
| el nombre | *name* |
| el teléfono | *phone number* |
| el correo electrónico | *e-mail* |

| **Características** | |
| --- | --- |
| activo | *active* |
| alegre | *happy* |
| amistoso/amigable | *friendly* |
| antipático | *unpleasant* |
| bueno | *good* |
| débil | *weak* |
| diligente | *diligent* |
| divertido | *fun* |
| estricto | *strict* |
| famoso | *famous* |
| fuerte | *strong* |
| inteligente | *intelligent* |
| joven | *young* |
| mayor | *mature, old* |
| pobre | *poor* |
| rico | *rich* |
| serio | *serious* |
| simpático | *nice* |
| tonto | *foolish, dull* |
| trabajador(a) | *hardworking* |
| viejo | *old* |

| **Nacionalidades** | **Nationalities** |
| --- | --- |
| argentino | *Argentinean* |
| boliviano | *Bolivian* |
| chileno | *Chilean* |
| colombiano | *Colombian* |
| costarricense | *Costa Rican* |
| cubano | *Cuban* |
| dominicano | *Dominican* |
| ecuatoriano | *Ecuadorian* |
| español | *Spanish* |
| estadounidense | *American (from the U.S.)* |
| guatemalteco | *Guatemalan* |
| hondureño | *Honduran* |
| mexicano | *Mexican* |
| nicaragüense | *Nicaraguan* |

| | |
| --- | --- |
| panameño | *Panamanian* |
| paraguayo | *Paraguayan* |
| puertorriqueño | *Puerto Rican* |
| salvadoreño | *Salvadorian* |
| uruguayo | *Uruguayan* |
| venezolano | *Venezuelan* |

| **Mi familia es de origen...** | |
| --- | --- |
| africano | *African* |
| asiático | *Asian* |
| europeo | *European* |

| **Expresiones de frecuencia** | |
| --- | --- |
| casi nunca | *almost never* |
| casi siempre | *almost always* |
| los... | *on (day[s] of the week)* |
| nunca | *never* |
| siempre | *always* |
| todos los días | *every day* |

| **Conectores** | |
| --- | --- |
| en (conclusión/mi opinión/resumen) | *in (conclusion/my opinion/summary)* |
| finalmente | *finally* |
| pero | *but* |
| por otro lado | *on the other hand* |
| también | *also* |
| tampoco | *either, neither* |
| y | *and* |

| **Profesiones** | |
| --- | --- |
| el (la) abogado(a) | *attorney, lawyer* |
| el (la) gerente | *manager* |
| el ama de casa | *housewife* |
| el (la) arquitecto(a) | *architect* |
| el (la) cocinero(a) | *cook* |
| el (la) contable | *accountant* |
| el (la) chofer | *driver* |
| el (la) empleado(a) doméstico(a) | *maid* |
| el (la) enfermero(a) | *nurse* |
| el hombre/la mujer de negocios | *businessman (woman)* |
| el (la) ingeniero(a) | *engineer* |
| el (la) obrero(a) | *construction worker* |
| el (la) peluquero(a) | *hairdresser* |
| el (la) periodista | *journalist* |
| el (la) policía | *policeman/woman* |
| el (la) programador(a) de computadoras | *computer programmer* |
| el (la) vendedor(a) | *salesperson* |

## Pasatiempos

charlar por teléfono
escuchar música
leer un libro
(mirar/ver) televisión
navegar por (la Red/el
    Internet)
pasear

pasar tiempo libre/los
    ratos libres
tocar un instrumento

## *Leisure time*

*to chat on the phone*
*to listen to music*
*to read a book*
*to watch TV*
*to surf the Net*


*to take a short trip;*
    *to go for a walk*
*to spend free time*


*to play an instrument*

## Funciones y estructuras

Verbos que terminan en **-ar**, p. 37
Verbos que terminan en **-er**, p. 41
Verbos que terminan en **-ir**, p. 41
Palabras negativas, p. 48
Palabras interrogativas, p. 51

# Capítulo 2

# En familia

## Para comenzar

- ¿Quiénes son? *(Who are these people?)*
- ¿Dónde están? *(Where are they?)*
- ¿Qué hacen? *(What are they doing?)*

## In this chapter you will learn . . .

- how to describe individuals
- how to describe a person's emotional state or condition
- how to talk about your home
- how to express possession and obligation
- how to talk about likes and dislikes
- about Spanish-speaking family values

| | **TEMA 1**<br>Ésta es mi familia | **TEMA 2**<br>La personalidad | **TEMA 3**<br>Nuestra casa |
|---|---|---|---|
| Vocabulario | Los miembros de la familia | Los rasgos personales | Los espacios y los muebles de una casa |
| Funciones y estructuras | Describing physical appearance with adjectives and the verbs **ser** and **tener**<br>Expressing possession | Talking about location, conditions, and emotional states with the verbs **estar** and **tener**<br>Talking about likes and dislikes with **gustar** | Talking about location with prepositions<br>Expressing obligation with **tener que...** and **hay que...** |
| Lecturas y vídeo | Perspectivas: La familia de José Miguel | Vídeo: Los compañeros se conocen mejor | Lectura: *La casa en Mango Street* |

Foto 1

Foto 2

Foto 3

# Enfoque

**A.** **¿Qué sabes ya de México?** Before you watch the video, look at the phrases below and decide if they refer to Mexico's economy, government, tourism, or capital city. Write the letter of the corresponding category in the space provided. When you finish, check your answers with a partner.

**E** = la economía   **G** = el gobierno   **T** = el turismo   **C** = la capital

<u>G</u> 1. una república federal

<u>E</u> 2. la producción industrial y agrícola

<u>T</u> 3. playas famosas

<u>C</u> 4. la Ciudad de México

<u>E</u> 5. el petróleo

<u>T</u> 6. los sitios arqueológicos y pueblos coloniales

**B.** **¿Dónde está... ?** As you watch the video for the first time, focus your attention on the video images and identify the places on the map on page vi.

<u>4</u> el Océano Pacífico   <u>1</u> los Estados Unidos   <u>3</u> Belice   <u>7</u> Veracruz

<u>5</u> la Ciudad de México   <u>2</u> Guatemala   <u>6</u> Teotihuacán

**C.** **Un viaje para dos a México** As you are reading a travel magazine, you come across the following sweepstakes that is offering all-inclusive getaway packages to Mexico. Read the description and follow the instructions to enter the contest.

**Los encantos de México** Tenemos tres paquetes de vacaciones «todo incluido» diferentes para Ud.:

1. Celebre **El Día de la Independencia de México**, 16 de septiembre, visitando tres famosos sitios arqueológicos: Uxmal, Tula y Teotihuacán (14–19 de septiembre).
2. Celebre **El Día de Nuestra Señora de Guadalupe**, el 12 de diciembre, en el Distrito Federal (10–15 de diciembre).
3. Celebre el **Carnaval** en Veracruz (22–27 de febrero).

For more info, you may want to check the **Temas** site:
**http://temas.heinle.com**

# Ésta es mi familia

## I. Vocabulario: Los miembros de la familia

Transparency
E-1: La familia
(1); E-2: La familia (2)

La **abuela** de Pedro se llama Berta. Tiene 63 años y es ama de casa.

La **madre** de Pedro se llama Marta. Tiene 46 años y es enfermera.

El **padre** de Pedro se llama Juan. Tiene 47 años y es electricista.

El **hermano mayor** de Pedro se llama Esteban. Tiene 26 años y es psicólogo.

Pedro tiene 18 años y es estudiante.

**Pedro**

La **hermana** de Pedro se llama Gabriela. Tiene 15 años y es estudiante.

### Vocabulario práctico

**La familia inmediata**

el (la) abuelo(a) *grandfather/ grandmother*

el (la) esposo(a) *husband/wife*

el (la) hermano(a) *brother/sister*

el (la) hijo(a) *son/daughter*

la madre/mamá *mother*

el (la) nieto(a) *grandson/ granddaughter*

el padre/papá *father*

**Otros parientes (*relatives*)**

el (la) cuñado(a) *brother-in-law/ sister-in-law*

el (la) hermanastro(a) *stepbrother/ stepsister*

la madrastra *stepmother*

el padrastro *stepfather*

el (la) primo(a) *cousin*

el (la) sobrino(a) *nephew/niece*

el (la) suegro(a) *father-in-law/ mother-in-law*

el (la) tío(a) *uncle/aunt*

- Notice that **parientes** *(relatives)* is a false cognate. The Spanish word for *parents* is **padres.** Similarly, **parentesco** means *relationship.*

- Masculine plural terms (**padres, abuelos,** etc.) are often used in Spanish to refer to entire categories. For instance, the word **tíos** can be used to designate either *uncles* or both *uncles and aunts;* the word **sobrinos** can refer to *nephews* or to both *nephews and nieces,* etc.

- Use **mayor(es)** to talk about *older* siblings or children and **menor(es)** to talk about *younger* siblings or children.

- A negative statement such as **No tengo hermanas** *(I don't have any sisters)* can be used to indicate your lack of family members under a given category.

- If a family member has already passed away, you can say **falleció** *(passed away).* Use **fallecieron** if two or more family members have passed away (e.g., **Mis abuelos fallecieron.**).

- **Don** and **doña** are titles of respect often used when referring to older people. These titles are used only with first names and are not capitalized unless they begin a sentence (e.g., **Don Jorge es muy simpático. Él y doña María son los padres de Graciela.**).

## ■ Asimilación

**2-1 ¿Cierto o falso?** Indica si las oraciones *(sentences)* son **ciertas (C)** o **falsas (F)** según *(according to)* el gráfico en la página 60. Luego *(Then),* compara tus respuestas con las de un(a) compañero(a).

F  1. Pedro tiene dos hermanas.

F  2. La madre de Pedro se llama Matilde.

C  3. El esposo de Marta es electricista.

C  4. La nieta de Berta se llama Gabriela.

F  5. La abuela de Pedro es dentista.

C  6. La hija de Marta se llama Gabriela.

C  7. Doña Berta es la suegra de Juan.

F  8. Esteban es el sobrino de doña Berta.

F  9. Esteban y Gabriela son primos.

F  10. Gabriela es la cuñada de doña Berta.

**Script 2-2:** El profesor Vargas tiene una familia muy simpática. Su esposa se llama Irene, tiene 35 años y es profesora de inglés. Sus hijos se llaman Andrés y Rebeca y tienen 8 y 12 años respectivamente. Doña Juana, la madre del profesor, vive con él desde que su padre, don Guillermo, falleció. No conozco a los hermanos del profesor, pero tengo entendido que se llaman Francisco y Mercedes. Mercedes vive en la capital con su esposo y sus dos niñas.

**Sugerencia 2-2:** As a listening challenge, you can ask students to write down at least one additional piece of information about each family member. A good variation on this activity would be a personalized narrative about their own family.

CD1-16 **2-2 La familia del profesor Vargas** Escucha *(Listen to)* la descripción de la familia del profesor Vargas. Luego, copia el siguiente *(the following)* árbol genealógico *(family tree)* y complétalo con **los nombres** de sus familiares *(family members)*.

### La familia del profesor Vargas

This activity recycles professions from **Capítulo 1**.

## ■ Aplicaciones

**2-3 Información personal** Completa las oraciones con el nombre y la ocupación de los familiares indicados. Indica también *(also)* una de sus características personales.

MODELO    Mi padre *se llama Thomas y es abogado. Él es muy simpático.*

1. Mi madre _____.
2. Mi padre _____.
3. Mi primo(a) _____.
4. Mi hermano(a) menor _____.
5. Mi abuelo(a) _____.

**2-4 La familia de Raúl** Completa el párrafo con la palabra *(word)* más apropiada según el contexto.

Raúl es mexicano, tiene 36 años *(is 36 years old)* y vive en Veracruz. Su _____ (esposa / hija) se llama Alicia, tiene 32 años y trabaja en el puerto. Esteban es su _____ (padre / hijo mayor) y está en sexto grado *(sixth grade)*. Gonzalo es su _____ (hermano mayor / hijo menor) y va al jardín infantil *(kindergarten)*. Raúl tiene solamente un _____ (hijo menor / hermano) que es ingeniero y vive en la capital. Doña Teresa, la _____ (madre / hija menor), es ama de casa y vive con su hijo y sus nietos en Veracruz.

**2-5 Entrevista** Hazle preguntas *(Ask questions)* a tu compañero(a) y elabora *(draw)* su árbol genealógico. **Nota:** Recuerda *(Remember)* que puedes dar información real o imaginaria.

MODELO    *¿Cómo se llama tu padre?*

**REMEMBER**

Use question words such as **qué** *(what)*, **cómo** *(how)*, **cuánto/s** *(how much/how many)*, **cuándo** *(when)*, **dónde** *(where)*, etc.
- ¿**Cómo** se llama tu madre?
- ¿**Cuál** es la profesión de tu padre?
- ¿**Cómo** es él?

## ■ Integración

**2-6 Entrevista** Representa la siguiente situación con un(a) compañero(a).

| Estudiante A | Estudiante B |
|---|---|
| Imagine that you have decided to host a Mexican exchange student in your home. He/She is calling you from his/her home in Puebla. Find out as much information as possible about his/her family (their names, profession, personality, etc.). Be prepared to answer questions about your family. | You are a student from Puebla, Mexico, who is planning to participate in an exchange program in the U.S. Your host family is on the phone and they would like to have more information about you and your family. Be prepared to answer their questions, and ask some questions of your own (names of the different family members, profession, personality, etc.). |

**EN TU COMUNIDAD**

Research the topic of family constitution in your community or in your state. You may visit family agencies or other agencies that collect such data. Also, you can find out what the local government is doing to improve the quality of life of families. Then share the information with the class.

This activity recycles vocabulary on professions from **Capítulo 1**. The family description that your students are writing in this activity will be further expanded and refined in the following sections of **Temas.**

**2-7 Mi familia** Prepare a description of your family (include pictures, if possible). Be sure to provide information about the age, profession, place of residence, and personality of your closest relatives. Keep in mind that you will be exchanging compositions with other class members.

## II. Funciones y estructuras: Describing physical appearance with adjectives and the verbs *ser* and *tener*

Mi tío Felipe es **gordo,** pero mi primo José es **delgado.**

Mi cuñada Beatriz es **rubia,** pero mi cuñada Ligia **tiene pelo negro.**

Transparency J-1: Las descripciones; J-3: La gente

The verb **ser** is used to describe physical appearance. Following is a list of adjectives you can use to describe yourself and others, as well as objects.

| | |
|---|---|
| alto *tall* | flaco *skinny* |
| bajo *short* (in height) | gordo *fat, overweight* |
| bonito *pretty* | grande *big* |
| calvo *bald* | guapo *handsome* |
| corto *short* (in length) | largo *long* |
| delgado *thin* | moreno *dark-haired* |
| difícil *difficult* | nuevo *new* |
| fácil *easy* | pequeño *small* |
| feo *ugly, unattractive* | rubio *blond(e)* |

These adjectives, like other adjectives you have already learned, must agree in number and gender with the noun(s) they describe.

Mi **esposa** es **morena** y yo soy **rubio.**
*My **wife** is **dark-haired** and I am **blond(e).***

Los **exámenes** de filosofía son **difíciles.**
*Philosophy **exams** are **difficult.***

The verb **tener** *(to have)* can also be used in descriptions. Like **ser**, **tener** is an irregular verb.

| | |
|---|---|
| yo **tengo** | nosotros(as) **tenemos** |
| tú **tienes** | vosotros(as) **tenéis** |
| él/ella/usted **tiene** | ellos(as)/ustedes **tienen** |

**Tener** can be used to talk about:

- hair color

 Mis parientes **tienen pelo rojo,** pero yo **tengo pelo negro.**
 *My relatives **have red hair**, but I have **black hair**.*

### REMEMBER

**Ser** is also used to describe objects and people and to talk about someone's nationality and origin.

**Sugerencia:** You may wish to mention that the adjectives **corto**, **largo,** and **nuevo** are not used to describe people and that **grande** is often used to refer to growth, not weight (**Tu niño está grande.** *Your child **has grown**.*)

### SABOR REGIONAL

Other words for *dark-haired* are **morocho(a)** (Argentina and Uruguay) and **trigueño(a)** (Colombia, Cuba, and the Dominican Republic). The adjective **moreno(a)**, on the other hand, refers to skin color in places like Puerto Rico. Finally, other words for *blond* are **güero(a)** (Mexico) and **catire(a)** (Venezuela).

To describe a good-looking man, use the adjective **guapo** instead of **bonito.**

When talking about hair color (**tener pelo...**), you may use the following words: **blanco** *(gray)*, **castaño** *(brown)*, **negro** *(black)*, **rojo** *(red)*, and **rubio** *(blond)*.

- features of different body parts

Mi cuñada Tatiana **tiene** ojos azules.

*My sister-in-law Tatiana **has** blue eyes.*

- age

—**¿Cuántos años tiene** tu hermano?
—Mi hermano menor **tiene** quince años.

*How old is your brother?*
*My younger brother **is** fifteen years old.*

## ■ Asimilación

Script 2-8: 1. Los padres tienen un hijo y una hija. 2. La madre es rubia. 3. El padre es alto. 4. El hijo tiene pelo castaño. 5. La hija no es gorda. 6. La madre tiene pelo corto.

CD1–17

**2-8 ¿Qué familia es?** La familia Roldán Mercado y la familia Vera Cintrón viven en Guadalajara, México. Escucha las descripciones e indica a cuál de las dos familas se refieren. **¡OJO!** Las descripciones pueden *(may)* referirse a ambas *(both)* familias.

**Familia Roldán Mercado**

**Familia Vera Cintrón**

| | | |
|---|---|---|
| 1. ___ Familia Roldán Mercado | ___ Familia Vera Cintrón | X ambas familias |
| 2. X Familia Roldán Mercado | ___ Familia Vera Cintrón | ___ ambas familias |
| 3. ___ Familia Roldán Mercado | X Familia Vera Cintrón | ___ ambas familias |
| 4. ___ Familia Roldán Mercado | X Familia Vera Cintrón | ___ ambas familias |
| 5. ___ Familia Roldán Mercado | ___ Familia Vera Cintrón | X ambas familias |

**2-9 ¿Quiénes son así** *(like that)*? Completen las oraciones con el nombre de personas famosas que cumplan con *(fit)* las descripciones.

1. ____ y ____ son morenos.
2. ____ tiene pelo gris.
3. ____ y ____ son bajas.
4. ____ es guapo.
5. ____ no es vieja.
6. ____ tiene ojos verdes.
7. ____ y ____ son bonitas.
8. ____ tiene aproximadamente veinte años.

## ■ Aplicaciones

**2-10 Descripciones** Completa las oraciones con una palabra lógica.

> MODELO La Sra. Bermúdez no es baja. Ella es muy _alta_.

1. Mis hermanas no tienen pelo corto. Ellas tienen pelo ___largo___.
2. La casa *(house)* de Nicolás no es ___nueva___; es vieja.
3. Carlota y Doris son ___feas___. Ellas no son bonitas.
4. El primo de Mauricio sólo *(only)* tiene doce años. Él es ___joven___.
5. Mi familia es muy ___pequeña___; no es nada grande.
6. Mi sobrina no es rubia. Ella tiene pelo ___castaño/negro/...___.

**2-11 Una persona de la clase** Escojan *(Choose)* a una persona de la clase y descríbanla. Escriban cinco oraciones diferentes y usen los verbos **ser** y **tener** correctamente. Cuando terminen *(When finished)*, léanle *(read to)* las oraciones a la clase. ¿Sus compañeros pueden adivinar *(guess)* quién es?

| | | |
|---|---|---|
| 1. ... | 3. ... | 5. ... |
| 2. ... | 4. ... | |

**2-12 La familia de...**

Paso 1: Entrevista a un(a) compañero(a) y completa el siguiente cuadro *(table)*.

*This activity recycles vocabulary related to daily activities. You may ask students to review **Capítulo 1**.*

| PARIENTE(S) | NOMBRE(S) | EDAD(ES) | DESCRIPCIÓN(-ONES) | ACTIVIDADES FAVORITAS |
|---|---|---|---|---|
| padre | | | | |
| madre | | | | |
| hermano(a/os/as) | | | | |
| abuelos | | | | |
| tíos | | | | |
| primos | | | | |

Paso 2: Preséntenle al resto de la clase la información sobre dos o tres de los miembros de la familia del (de la) compañero(a). ¿Quisieran conocer *(Would you like to know)* a estas personas?

*Sugerencia 2-12, Paso 1: Have students take a few minutes to think about the questions they have to ask to get the information they need. For a complete list of interrogative words, have them look at **Capítulo 1, Tema 3**.*

## ■ Integración

**2-13 Una familia de la televisión** Túrnense *(Take turns)* para describir a los miembros de la familia de algún *(any)* programa de televisión. ¿Tu compañero(a) puede adivinar *(guess)* quiénes son?

> MODELO E1: *Es una familia muy interesante. El padre es gordo, alto y calvo. La madre tiene mucho pelo y es alta. Ellos tienen tres hijos: un hijo y dos hijas. El hijo es bajo y...*
> E2: *¡Los Simpson!*

**2-14 Mi familia** Usa la descripción de tu familia de la actividad 2-7 e *(and)* incluye *(include)* una descripción física de tus parientes inmediatos. Recuerda que algunos de tus compañeros van a leer *(will read)* tu trabajo.

## III. Funciones y estructuras: Expressing possession

Éste es **mi** primo favorito, Dixon. Ella es Paloma, **su** novia. *This is **my** favorite cousin, Dixon. She is Paloma, **his** girlfriend.*

Y éstas son **mis** sobrinas Laura, Cristina y Sheila. *And these are **my** nieces Laura, Cristina and Sheila.*

To express possession you may use the following adjectives.

| ONE OWNER OR POSSESSOR | MORE THAN ONE OWNER OR POSSESSOR |
|---|---|
| **mi(s)** *my* | **nuestro(a/os/as)** *our* |
| **tu(s)** *your* (informal) | **vuestro(a/os/as)** *your* (informal in Spain) |
| **su(s)** *his/her/your* (formal) | **su(s)** *their/your* (Latin America) |

Possessive adjectives have more than one form because, like other adjectives, they agree in gender and number with the noun they describe. Notice though that possessive adjectives do not reflect the gender of the possessor or owner. Thus, when we say **nuestras clases**, **nuestras** is feminine plural because **clases** is a feminine plural noun, regardless of the gender of the people whose classes we are talking about.

| | |
|---|---|
| ¡Son **mis cosas**, no **nuestras cosas**! | *These are **my things**, not **our things**!* |
| **Sus hijos** son amigos de **vuestros hijos**. | ***Their children** are friends with **your** (pl.) **children**.* |

Although context provides clarity, using the adjectives **su** and **sus** may lead to ambiguity because they have multiple meanings (i.e., *his/her/your* [sing, formal], *their,* and *your* [pl.]). In these cases you may use the following structure with the preposition **de**:

(noun) + **de** + (possessor or owner)

| | |
|---|---|
| Lobo es el perro **de** ella. | *Lobo is **her** dog.* |
| Ésa es la esposa **de** él. | *That is **his** wife.* |

The same structure is used in cases in which we would use an apostrophe to indicate possession in English. Apostrophes are not used in Spanish.

When the preposition **de** is followed by the article **el**, they contract to **del**. The use of this contraction is obligatory in Spanish.

| | |
|---|---|
| Charo es la nieta **de** Teresa. | *Charo is Teresa's granddaughter.* |
| Mota es la gata **del** Sr. Vizcaíno. | *Mota is Mr. Vizcaíno's cat.* |

## Asimilación

**2-15 Parientes** Mira los dibujos *(Look at the illustrations)* y escoge el adjetivo posesivo más apropiado.

Marcela es (nuestra / sus / (mi)) esposa.

Juan Pablo y Reina son (su / (mis) / nuestro) hijos.

Juana es (mi / (nuestra) / sus) madre.

¿Es (nuestras / sus / (tu)) familia?

**2-16 ¿Cierto o falso?** Indica si las siguientes oraciones son **ciertas (C)** o **falsas (F)**. Al terminar, compara tus respuestas con las de un(a) compañero(a). ¿Qué tienen en común?

_____ 1. Mis parientes son altos.

_____ 2. Las familias de mis amigos son pequeñas.

_____ 3. Los padres de mi madre viven en la Florida.

_____ 4. Mi casa es grande.

_____ 5. Muchos de mis primos son morenos.

_____ 6. El padre de mi mejor amigo(a) es flaco.

## Aplicaciones

**2-17 En una reunión familiar** Lean las preguntas que Waldemar les hace a varias personas en una reunión familiar y escojan la respuesta más lógica.

1. ¿Quién es ella?
   a. Es nuestro sobrino.
   b. Son los nietos de Tila.
   (c.) Es mi abuela.

2. ¿Son sus hermanos?
   (a.) No, son nuestros tíos.
   b. No, son tus hermanos.
   c. Sí, es mi cuñada.

3. ¿Son los padres de Ricardo?
   (a.) No, son sus abuelos.
   b. Sí, son mis hermanastros.
   c. Sí, es mi yerno.

4. ¿Es tu amiga Patricia?
   a. Sí, es tu cuñado.
   (b.) Sí, es mi amiga.
   c. Sí, es la amiga de Patricia.

5. ¿Quiénes son?
   (a.) Son nuestras primas.
   b. Es su nieta.
   c. Es el padre de ellos.

**2-18 ¿Y la familia del (de la) profesor(a)?** Escriban cinco preguntas para el (la) profesor(a) sobre su familia.

> MODELO    *¿Su hermano tiene pelo castaño?*
>
> 1. ...      2. ...      3. ...      4. ...      5. ...

**2-19 Una encuesta** *(survey)*

**Paso 1:** Para cada pariente o grupo de parientes, marca la alternativa que se aplique a ti *(that applies to you).*

| PARIENTE(S) | ALTERNATIVAS | |
| --- | --- | --- |
| madre | _____ trabaja | _____ no trabaja |
| hermanos | _____ son alegres | _____ son aburridos |
| tía | _____ nunca cocina | _____ siempre cocina |
| abuelos | _____ asisten a bingos | _____ no asisten a bingos |
| suegros | _____ son simpáticos | _____ son antipáticos |
| padre | _____ tiene menos *(less)* de 50 años | _____ tiene más de 50 años |
| novio(a) o esposo(a) | _____ practica deportes | _____ no practica ningún deporte |
| hijos | _____ desayunan en casa | _____ no desayunan en casa |

**Paso 2:** Ahora, en grupos de tres o cuatro estudiantes, háganse preguntas *(ask one another questions)* para determinar las semejanzas *(similarities)* y diferencias entre sus familias. Tomen notas. Cuando terminen, preparen un informe escrito.

You may use the phrase **No tengo...** if necessary.

> MODELO    E1: *Mi madre trabaja. ¿Tu madre trabaja, Stephanie?*
> E2: *Sí, mi madre trabaja. ¿Y tu madre, Jonathan?*
> E3: *No, mi madre no trabaja.*

## ■ Integración

**2-20 ¡Los reto!** *(I challenge you!)* In groups of three or four, take turns providing details about the places and things listed. Do not move on to the next item until nobody has anything else to say. The student who provides the most details wins!

> MODELO    (en) nuestra ciudad
> E1: *Nuestra ciudad es bonita.*
> E2: *En nuestra ciudad viven muchas personas.*
> E3: *Nuestra ciudad tiene muchos lugares interesantes.*
> ...

If you do not have anything to say, say **yo paso** *(I pass).*

1. (en) nuestra universidad
2. nuestro(a) profesor(a)
3. (en) nuestra clase de español
4. (en) nuestro estado
5. (en) la familia de nuestro(a) profesor(a)
6. nuestros compañeros de clase

**2-21 Las familias mexicanas** Since you want to learn more Spanish, you decided to spend next summer in Oaxaca, Mexico, with the Zapata Robles family. Before going, you want to learn more about typical Mexican families and about the Zapatas. Make a list of questions for Octavio, the Zapata's teenage son, and provide him with some information about your own family.

**REMEMBER**

The verb **hay** means *there is* and *there are*.

> MODELO    *¿Cuántos hijos hay en tu familia? En mi familia hay dos hijos y una hija.*
> *¿Cómo es tu madre? Mi madre es baja y tiene pelo rojo.*

# IV. Perspectivas: La familia de José Miguel

## ■ Antes de leer

**Información** ¿Qué información encuentran *(do you find)* en el Internet acerca de las familias? Marquen las opciones más lógicas.

| | | |
|---|---|---|
| ____ nombres de los familiares | ____ lugar donde viven | ____ religión |
| ____ profesiones | ____ fotografías | ____ ideas políticas |
| ____ problemas médicos | ____ historia de la familia | ____ edades |

## ■ A leer

**Ésta es mi familia**

La foto muestra a mi familia. De izquierda a derecha, Uds. pueden ver a mi hermana Luisa Fernanda. Ella tiene dieciséis años, estudia en el Liceo Camilo Daza y cursa el sexto año de bachillerato. Después estoy yo, José Miguel, mi mamá Angélica (lo mas lindo del mundo *[the most beautiful thing in the world]*), mi papá Miguel Hernando, que es ingeniero electrónico, y finalmente mi hermana mayor, Teresa, que tiene veintitrés años y es enfermera. Yo tengo veinte años y estudio arquitectura en la Universidad Javeriana. En mi tiempo libre, toco la guitarra y navego por el Internet.

## ■ ¿Entendiste bien?

1. ¿Cuántas personas hay en la familia?
2. ¿Cuántas hermanas tiene este joven?
3. ¿Cuántos años tiene la hermana menor de José Miguel?
4. ¿Cuál es la profesión de su padre?
5. ¿Cuál es la profesión de su hermana mayor?
6. ¿Qué hace José Miguel en su tiempo libre?
7. ¿Esta familia es semejante o diferente a tu familia? Explica tu respuesta.

**Answers:** 1. cinco 2. dos 3. dieciséis años 4. ingeniero electrónico 5. enfermera 6. toca la guitarra y navega por la Red 7. *Answers will vary.*

# La personalidad

## I. Vocabulario: Los rasgos personales

Mi hermana Mercedes es **simpática.**

Mi abuelo Juan es **gracioso.**

Mi hermano Joaquín es un poco *(somewhat)* **serio.**

**tonto**

inteligente

**malo**

**bueno**

**perezoso**

**diligente**

**tímido**

**extrovertido**

### Vocabulario práctico

| | |
|---|---|
| alegre *cheerful* | honrado *honest* |
| amable *kind* | ingenioso *resourceful* |
| antipático *unfriendly* | responsable *responsible* |
| egoísta *selfish* | sincero *sincere* |
| generoso *generous* | talentoso *talented* |
| grosero *rude* | voluble *fickle* |

Transparencies J-1: Las descripciones, J-2: ¿Qué piensas?; J-4 E1 carácter

## ■ Asimilación

**2-22 ¿Quién es?** Indica el número de la oración *(sentence)* que describe cada dibujo *(each drawing)*.

**a. Elsa**

**b. Marcela**

**c. Laura**

1. __c__ es simpática.
2. __b__ es graciosa.
3. __a__ es inteligente.

**2-23 Tu familia** Completa las oraciones con el nombre de la persona de tu familia que corresponda a la descripción.

1. Mi _____ es cómico(a).
2. Mis _____ son simpáticos.
3. Mi _____ es un poco perezoso(a).
4. Mis _____ son muy inteligentes.
5. Mi _____ es muy generoso(a).

## ■ Aplicaciones

**2-24 ¿Cómo son?** Expresa tu opinión según las opciones. Luego, compara tus respuestas con las de un(a) compañero(a). ¿Están de acuerdo? *(Do you agree?)*

1. Tom Hanks es...
   a. simpático.          c. tonto.
   b. tímido.             d. otra descripción

2. Jay Leno y Conan O'Brien son...
   a. graciosos.          c. materialistas.
   b. serios.             d. otra descripción

3. Gloria Estefan y Shakira son...
   a. diligentes.         c. graciosas.
   b. pesimistas.         d. otra descripción

4. El presidente de los Estados Unidos es...
   a. materialista.       c. tímido.
   b. inteligente.        d. otra descripción

5. _____ *(tu personaje favorito)* es...
   a. idealista.          c. sincero(a).
   b. generoso(a).        d. otra descripción

**Sugerencia 2-24:** Feel free to substitute the names of these characters with names of individuals who are more familiar or relevant to your class. Encourage discussion and support of opinions.

**REMEMBER**

Most adjective endings indicate the gender of the person being described.

**2-25 Opuestos** Completen la descripción de los miembros de la familia Jiménez.

**OPCIONES:** diligente, sincero, optimista, tímido, seria, generoso

Los Jiménez son muy diferentes entre sí *(among themselves)*. El señor Jiménez es un abogado ___tímido___. Por el contrario, la señora Jiménez es una pintora alegre y extrovertida. Guillermo, el hijo mayor, es ___diligente___, pero su hermanito Pedro es perezoso. Las niñas también son distintas: Cristina es graciosa; en cambio *(however)*, Marcela es ___seria___. A pesar de sus diferencias, todos se llevan bien.

**Sugerencia 2-26:** Consider extending this activity beyond the three photographs provided to include all students in the class or specific domains: movie stars, TV characters, politicians, etc.

**2-26 ¿Quién es?** Pick one of the following pictures and have your classmate guess your selection by describing in Spanish the personality traits you would associate with such an individual.

**Foto 1**

**Foto 2**

**Foto 3**

**Sugerencia 2-26:** You may have students use the text in activity 2-25 as a model for their reports.

### ■ Integración

**2-27 Entrevista** Túrnense para hacer y responder a las preguntas. Al terminar, preséntenle un informe al resto de la clase.

1. ¿Cómo son tus padres? ¿Cuál es su profesión? ¿Qué hacen en su tiempo libre?
2. ¿Cuántos hermanos(as) tienes? ¿Cómo son? ¿Dónde trabajan o estudian tus hermanos(as)?
3. ¿Tienes novio(a) o esposo(a)? ¿Cómo es?
4. ¿Tienes sobrinos? ¿Cómo son?
5. Y tú, ¿cómo eres? ¿Qué haces los fines de semana o durante tu tiempo libre?

**2-28 Mi familia** Añádele *(Add)* información sobre la personalidad de los miembros de tu familia a la descripción que empezaste *(you began)* en el **Tema 1.**

## II. Funciones y estructuras: Talking about location, conditions, and emotional states with the verbs *estar* and *tener*

Nelda y Cuca **están** en el parque. Ellas **están** contentas. *Nelda and Cuca **are** at the park. They **are** happy.*

El Sr. Delgado **tiene sueño**. **Está** muy cansado. *Mr. Delgado **is sleepy**. He **is** very tired.*

There are two ways of saying *to be* in Spanish: **ser** and **estar**. The verb **estar**, like **ser**, is irregular.

> **REMEMBER**
>
> **Ser** is used to talk about professions and occupations, place of origin, physical description and personality description.

| | |
|---|---|
| yo **estoy** | nosotros(as) **estamos** |
| tú **estás** | vosotros(as) **estáis** |
| él/ella/usted **está** | ellos(as)/ustedes **están** |

**Estar** is used to talk about:

- location

    ¡Mis hermanos **están** en el aeropuerto y yo todavía **estoy** aquí!

    *My siblings **are** at the airport and I **am** still here!*

- conditions and emotional states

    Nora, ¿**estás** enojada? ¡Yo **estoy** feliz!

    *Nora, **are you** angry? I **am** happy!*

The following are common adjectives of condition and emotion used with **estar**.

| | |
|---|---|
| aburrido *bored* | enojado *angry* |
| alegre/contento/feliz *happy* | listo *ready* |
| cansado *tired* | nervioso *nervous* |
| deprimido *depressed* | ocupado *busy* |
| emocionado *excited* | preocupado *worried* |
| enfermo *sick* | triste *sad* |

These adjectives must also agree in gender and number with the noun described.

The verb **tener** *(to have)* can also be used to talk about certain states and conditions. Here are some expressions that require using this verb.

| | |
|---|---|
| tener calor *to be hot* | tener prisa *to be in a hurry* |
| tener éxito *to be successful* | tener rabia *to be mad* |
| tener frío *to be cold* | tener sed *to be thirsty* |
| tener hambre *to be hungry* | tener sueño *to be sleepy* |
| tener miedo *to be afraid* | |

To express degree of intensity, say **mucho(a)** *(very, much)* or **un poco de** *(a little bit [of])* after **tener.** Keep in mind that **hambre**, **prisa,** and **sed** are feminine nouns and are used with **mucha.**

Tengo (**mucha** / **un poco de**) hambre.

*I am (**very** / **a little bit**) hungry.*

Jaime, ¿tienes (**mucho** / **un poco de**) calor?

*James, are you (**very** / **a little bit**) hot?*

### ▓ Asimilación

**2-29 ¿Dónde está Ignacio?** Escucha las oraciones sobre Ignacio e indica a qué dibujo se refieren.

CD1–18

a. __2__   b. __3__   c. __5__   d. __1__   e. __4__

**2-30 Reacciones** Lean las siguientes situaciones y escojan el adjetivo más lógico.

1. Tengo un examen de economía esta tarde. El material es muy difícil y debo estudiar mucho. Estoy (alegre / preocupado / cansado).

2. Los amigos de Estela están de vacaciones. Ella está en su casa y no hay programas buenos en la televisión. Ella está (aburrida / lista / enferma).

3. Nina y tú tienen una fiesta esta noche. Deben ir al supermercado, limpiar la casa y preparar la comida. Tienen muchas cosas que hacer *(to do)* y poco tiempo. Ustedes están (contentas / deprimidas / ocupadas).

4. Mi novia y yo estamos en la Pirámide del Sol en México. Es un lugar espectacular y muy impresionante. Nosotros estamos (emocionados / listos / tristes).

5. Verónica no puede ir *(cannot go)* a Acapulco con su familia porque está muy ocupada. Ella trabaja para una compañía internacional y debe escribir varios informes. Ella está (feliz / cansada / enojada).

## ■ Aplicaciones

**2-31 Conocimientos** *(knowledge)* **geográficos** Túrnense para hacer preguntas sobre la localización de los siguientes lugares de interés *(landmarks)* del mundo.

> MODELO  la Estatua de la Libertad
> E1: *¿Dónde está la Estatua de la Libertad?*
> E2: *Está en Nueva York.*

1. el Coliseo Romano
2. Cancún y Cozumel
3. el Partenón
4. Hollywood
5. la Torre Eiffel y el Arco del Triunfo
6. las ciudades de Sydney y Melbourne

**2-32 ¿Dónde? ¿Cómo?** Describan los siguiente dibujos. Indiquen dónde están las personas y cómo están.

> MODELO  Francisco *está en su oficina y está cansado.*

Here are some useful words: **aeropuerto** *(airport)*, **habitación** *(bedroom)*, and **restaurante** *(restaurant)*.

**Dolores y yo...**

**Aníbal...**

**Yo...**

**Ellas...**

Nota: This activity recycles the conjugation of **-ar**, **-er**, and **-ir** verbs.

Pay attention to the conjugation of the underlined verbs included in these phrases.

**2-33 ¿Cómo te sientes** (you feel) **cuando... ?** Túrnense para hacer preguntas con la siguiente información. Usen expresiones con **estar** y **tener** en las respuestas.

> MODELO    <u>caminar</u> por el desierto
> E1: *¿Cómo te sientes cuando caminas por el desierto?*
> E2: *Cuando camino por el desierto, tengo sed y estoy cansado(a).*

1. no <u>tener</u> tiempo para almorzar en la cafetería
2. <u>recibir</u> una nota mala en una clase
3. la temperatura es de 110º F en el verano
4. <u>tener</u> un examen en dos minutos y no <u>estar</u> listo(a)
5. <u>mirar</u> una película (movie) de horror
6. la temperatura es de 20º F en el invierno
7. son las 3:00 P.M. y no has comido (have not eaten) nada
8. <u>tener</u> tarea de todas las clases

### ■ Integración

**2-34 Terapia grupal** ¿Cómo estás? ¿Por qué? En grupos de tres o cuatro, túrnense para contestar estas preguntas. ¡Usen la imaginación! Además, reaccionen (react) a los comentarios de sus compañeros con sugerencias.

> MODELO    E1: *Hoy estoy... porque... También estoy... porque...*
> E2: *Pues debes... porque...*

**2-35 La historia más original** Escribe un resumen (summary) de las respuestas y reacciones más originales de la actividad 2-34.

> MODELO    *Deborah está... hoy porque... Charlie opina que ella debe...,*
> *pero Lisa opina que ella...*

## III. Funciones y estructuras: Talking about likes and dislikes with *gustar*

A nosotras **nos gusta** hablar por teléfono. *We like to talk on the phone.*

A Romualdo **le gusta** leer en su tiempo libre. *Romualdo likes to read in his spare time.*

Spanish does not have a verb that is used exactly like the English verb *to like*. The verb used to talk about likes and dislikes is **gustar**, which works very much like the English *to be pleasing*.

<u>Me gusta</u> <u>estudiar español.</u>

<u>*To study Spanish*</u> <u>*is pleasing*</u> <u>*to me.*</u>

(= *I like to study Spanish.*)

In this example, **estudiar español** is the subject of the sentence (what is pleasing) and **me** is an indirect object pronoun that indicates the person to whom the subject is pleasing.

Sentences with **gustar** follow this pattern:

| INDIRECT OBJECT PRONOUN | gustar | SUBJECT |
|---|---|---|
| **me** *(to me)*<br>**te** *(to you,* informal)<br>**le** *(to him/her/you,* formal)<br>**nos** *(to us)*<br>**os** *(to you,* informal, pl.)<br>**les** *(to them/you,* formal and informal, pl.) | **gusta**<br><br>**gustan** | + { singular noun / verb(s) (in the infinitive)<br>+ { plural noun |

Notice that in the table above **gusta** is used when what is pleasing is a singular noun or an action (or series of actions) expressed in the infinitive form while **gustan** is used when what is pleasing is a plural noun.

| | |
|---|---|
| A ella le **gusta la biología**, pero no le **gustan las matemáticas**. | *She likes **biology**, but she does not like **mathematics**.* |
| ¿Te **gusta navegar** por el Internet en tu casa o en la biblioteca? | *Do you like **to surf** the Internet at home or at the library?* |

If you want to clarify or emphasize the person(s) to whom something is pleasing, you may add a phrase introduced by the preposition **a** at the beginning of the sentence, especially if the indirect object pronoun may refer to several people as **le** and **les** do.

| | |
|---|---|
| **A Carolina** le gustan las artes, pero **a Iván** le gustan los idiomas. | *Carolina likes the arts, but Iván likes languages.* |
| **A ellos** les gusta visitar a la familia, pero **a ustedes** no les gusta. | *They like to visit their family, but you do not like to do that.* |

To specify to what degree you like something, say **mucho** *(a lot)* or **un poco** *(a little bit)* after **gusta(n)**. On the other hand, to express that you do not like something at all, say **nada** after **gusta(n)**.

| | |
|---|---|
| Me gusta **mucho** la música clásica. | *I like classical music **a lot**.* |
| No me gusta **nada** la música rock. | *I do not like rock music **at all**.* |

## ▪ Asimilación

**2-36 ¿Cuánto te gusta(n)?** Indica cuánto te gustan las siguientes cosas y actividades. Al terminar, compara tus respuestas con las de un(a) compañero(a). ¿Tienen gustos *(likes)* semejantes o diferentes?

| | ME GUSTA(N) MUCHO | ME GUSTA(N) | ME GUSTA(N) UN POCO | NO ME GUSTA(N) | NO ME GUSTA(N) NADA |
|---|---|---|---|---|---|
| 1. el color amarillo | _____ | _____ | _____ | _____ | _____ |
| 2. el otoño | _____ | _____ | _____ | _____ | _____ |
| 3. mi hermano(a) | _____ | _____ | _____ | _____ | _____ |
| 4. tomar clases de noche | _____ | _____ | _____ | _____ | _____ |
| 5. los lunes | _____ | _____ | _____ | _____ | _____ |
| 6. el español | _____ | _____ | _____ | _____ | _____ |
| 7. mis profesores | _____ | _____ | _____ | _____ | _____ |
| 8. usar el Internet | _____ | _____ | _____ | _____ | _____ |

**CD1-19** **2-37 Los gustos de Tere y los de sus padres** Escucha a Tere hablar de sus gustos y de los gustos de sus padres, y completa la tabla que sigue.

| A Tere... | le gusta(an) la literatura, las ciencias, leer, pasear | no le gusta(n) la pasta |
|---|---|---|
| A sus padres... | les gusta(n) las comidas italianas, leer | no les gusta(n) las humanidades, la biología, la química |

**Script 2-37:** Mis padres y yo somos semejantes en algunas cosas y muy diferentes en otras. Por ejemplo, a mí me gusta mucho la literatura, pero a mis padres no les gustan nada las humanidades. Además, a mí me gustan las ciencias y a mis padres no les gusta ni la biología ni la química. A la hora de comer, a mí no me gusta la pasta, mientras que a mis padres les gustan mucho las comidas italianas. Finalmente, a mis padres les gusta hacer ejercicio *(exercise)* en su tiempo libre. Yo prefiero otras cosas: me gusta leer y pasear.

## ■ Aplicaciones

**2-38 ¡Qué difícil de complacer** *(to please)*! Lean la conversación entre Daniel, Paca y Silvia, y llenen los espacios en blanco con el pronombre de objeto indirecto (**me**, **te**, **le**, etc.) y la forma correcta de **gustar.**

Silvia: ¿Quieren ir al Museo de Arte Moderno esta tarde?

Daniel: No, Silvia. A nosotros no ____nos____ ____gusta____ el arte. Personalmente, a mí no ____me____ ____gustan____ nada las pinturas ni las esculturas modernas.

Paca: ¡No es cierto, Daniel! ¡A ti ____te____ ____gustan____ las pinturas de Frida Kahlo! Además, a mí ____me____ ____gusta____ mucho Picasso.

Daniel: ¿Qué dices? A Camilo y a Rosa sí que ____les____ ____gusta____ otras cosas, como Frida Kahlo, pero a mí no. A mí ____me____ ____gustan____ las actividades al aire libre *(outdoors)*.

Paca: Silvia, en realidad, a Daniel no ____le____ ____gusta____ hacer *(to do)* nada. En cambio, a mí ____me____ ____gusta____ tu idea. Vamos al museo.

Silvia: ¡Ay, Daniel! ¡Qué difícil de complacer eres!

**2-39 Los gustos del (de la) profesor(a)** De acuerdo con *(according to)* lo que saben *(you know)* sobre su profesor(a), escriban cinco oraciones sobre sus gustos. Incluyan oraciones afirmativas y negativas. Cuando terminen, lean las oraciones. El (La) profesor(a) debe decir si son **ciertas** o **falsas**.

MODELO    Profesor(a), a usted..., ¿verdad?

1. …
2. …
3. …
4. …
5. …

Tema 2 | setenta y nueve **79**

**2-40 Entre** *(Between)* **tú y yo**

**Paso 1:** Escoge dos elementos de cada columna e indica si te gustan o no te gustan, en oraciones diferentes.

MODELO     el azul

*No me gusta el azul.*

| A | B | C |
|---|---|---|
| la química | los viernes | tener prisa |
| el básquetbol | los cantantes hispanos | estudiar en esta universidad |
| la primavera | las personas perezosas | vivir en este estado |
| la música rap | las hamburguesas | beber cerveza |

**Paso 2:** Túrnense para averiguar *(find out)* si al otro le gustan o no le gustan las cosas que escogieron. Tomen notas. Cuando terminen, preparen un informe escrito y preséntenlo a la clase.

MODELO     E1: *Betsy, ¿te gusta el azul?*
                   E2: *Sí, me gusta mucho el azul.*

In your written report you may use connectors such as **y** *(and)*, **pero** *(but)*, **sin embargo** *(however)*, and **por otro lado** *(on the other hand)*.

**EN TU COMUNIDAD**

Interview at least ten members of the community to find out how they feel about a particular person (a politician, a local leader, a person who has been in the news a lot, etc.) or thing (a product, a new plan, a new measure, etc.) and present your findings to the class.

■ **Integración**

**2-41 El (La) nuevo(a) empleado(a)** *(employee)* Representa la siguiente situación con un(a) compañero(a).

You may talk about different topics you are familiar with such as leisure time activities, family, and routines.

| **El (La) nuevo(a) empleado(a)** | **El (La) empleado(a) con experiencia** |
|---|---|
| This is your first day of work at a big company in a big city and you do not know anybody yet. A co-worker approaches you and strikes up a conversation.<br>■ Greet him/her.<br>■ Say your name and where you come from.<br>■ Find out about his/her likes and dislikes. | There is a new employee who does not know anybody in the company. Start a conversation with him/her and try to make a very good impression.<br>■ Greet him/her and introduce yourself.<br>■ Find out his/her name and where he/she comes from.<br>■ Find out about his/her likes and dislikes. |

Review the list of adjectives used with **estar** and the expressions with **tener** you learned in the previous **Funciones y estructuras** section.

**2-42 Reflexionando sobre tu comportamiento** *(behavior)* ¿Qué te gusta hacer cuando te sientes de cierta manera *(you feel a certain way)*? ¿Y qué no te gusta hacer? Escribe una auto-reflexión sobre tu comportamiento.

MODELO     *Cuando estoy enojado(a), me gusta... , pero no me gusta... Sin embargo, cuando tengo hambre me gusta..., pero no me gusta...*

## IV. Vídeo: Los compañeros se conocen mejor

### ■ Preparación

**A. Las imágenes** Practice using contextual clues by answering the questions below about the brief portion of the video segment that you are about to see without audio.

1. Who is talking?
2. Where are they?
3. What are they doing?
4. What do you think they are talking about?

Now watch again, this time with audio. Were you correct?

**COMPREHENSION STRATEGY**

*Using Contextual Clues* Normal speech among natives may seem fast and difficult to follow at first. To facilitate comprehension, use all the contextual clues available to fill in the gaps with educated guesses. The more you hear authentic Spanish, the more you will get used to its speed and rhythm.

**Sugerencia A:** Play segment without audio. Only show the first 40 seconds with Sofía and Alejandra talking in their bedroom. Stop when Alejandra´s testimonial begins.

**B. ¿Qué compañero(a)?** In this video segment the roommates reveal information about themselves and their first impressions of their new housemates.

**Paso 1:** As you watch the video, indicate who provides the following information about himself/herself: Alejandra (A), Antonio (T), Javier (J), Sofía (S) or Valeria (V).

___A___ a. «Me gusta escuchar música y salir con amigas... ¡y con amigos!»

___S___ b. «Me gusta leer y escribir. Quiero ser escritora.»

___J___ c. «Tengo un hermano mayor. Tiene 29 años y es médico.»

___J___ d. «A mí me gusta la naturaleza, las actividades al aire libre.»

___V___ e. «Mi mamá es una modelo jubilada. Y mis dos hermanas practican el modelaje, como yo.»

**Paso 2:** Watch the video again and this time pay attention to what the roommates have to say about each other. Indicate WHO says the following about WHOM.

| | | ¿QUIÉN? | ¿SOBRE QUIÉN? |
|---|---|---|---|
| a. | «...tu madre es blanca de pelo negro, y bajita como tú. Te pareces mucho a ella.» | Sofía | Alejandra |
| b. | «Él cree que es muy gracioso, pero a mí me parece muy pesado.» | Valeria | Antonio |
| c. | «...ya somos amigos y compartimos el mismo cuarto.» | Antonio | Javier |
| d. | «Creo que a nadie le gusta —aunque a mí no me disgusta del todo.» | Antonio | Valeria |
| e. | «Es una muchacha inteligente. Además, le gustan mis fotos.» | Alejandra | Sofía |
| f. | «...es una chica muy guapa... pero es insoportable.» | Sofía | Valeria |
| g. | «Yo creo que a él no le gusta su carrera para nada.» | Sofía | Javier |

**C. Un retrato más detallado de los compañeros** After watching this video segment, you have learned more about each roommate. Now describe each one of them in detail, starting with his/her physical appearance and continuing with his/her personal traits. Do not forget to review the use of adjectives with **ser** and **tener**. When you finish, share your descriptions with a classmate.

**D. Enfoque comunitario** Get in touch with the office of international students in your school and interview one of their Spanish-speaking students. Ask him/her to describe his/her family and prepare for your instructor a brief summary of your findings in Spanish. If possible, invite the student to visit your class.

# Nuestro hogar *(Our home)*

## I. Vocabulario: Los espacios y los muebles de una casa *(house)*

Transparencies C-2: En los cuartos; C-4: La sala/El dormitorio; C-5: El cuarto de baño/La cocina; L-6: Buscar un apartamento

iLrn

### Los espacios de una casa

el techo
el ático
la recámara/ la habitación/ el dormitorio
la ventana
la puerta
el baño
el garaje
la pared
la escalera
la sala
el comedor
la cocina
el jardín
el sótano

el primer piso

la planta baja

### Los muebles de una casa

las cortinas
el espejo
el estéreo
la mesa
la silla
el estante/ el librero
la mesita/ mesa de centro
el sofá
la alfombra
el teléfono
la estufa
el refrigerador/ la nevera
el horno microondas
la lámpara
el clóset / el armario
el cuadro
el despertador
la cama
la mesita/ mesa de noche/ mesa de luz
la computadora/ el ordenador
el sillón
el escritorio
la silla
el televisor

## ■ Asimilación

**2-43 ¿Qué casa les conviene?** Lee los anuncios *(ads)* y escoge la mejor opción para cada familia. Compara luego tus respuestas con las de un(a) compañero(a). ¿Están de acuerdo?

| | | |
|---|---|---|
| **CASAS EN VENTA** **1. ABASTOS** UNA RECÁMARA, 2 BAÑOS, FACILIDADES 349.000 TEL. 684 5889 | **2. BOSQUES** LOMAS, EXCELENTE, 3 RECÁMARAS, OPCIÓN 4, PISCINA, 4 BAÑOS, SALÓN JUEGOS, 1,900,000.00, OTRA EN LOMAS 1.600.000 TEL. 905 412 6818 Y 359 1333 CLAVE 19024 | **3. RESIDENCIA** EN ZONA SUR, LAS ÁGUILAS, TORRENTES 127, ACABADOS DE LUJO, TODOS LOS SERVICIOS, CON PUERTA AUTOMÁTICA, COCINA EQUIPADA, ESTACIONAMIENTO PARA TRES AUTOS, TEL. 601 0494 |
| **4. ÁGUILAS** AXOMIATLA, PRECIOSA RESIDENCIA, VIGILANCIA, VISTA PANORÁMICA, $ 2.200.000 TEL. 635 1952 | **5. BOSQUES** LOMAS «LISTA PARA HABITARSE» TRES RECÁMARAS, ESTUDIO, 3 BAÑOS, $ 2.850.000 TEL. 540 3501 «DATO»] | |

1. Marcela tiene muchos amigos y necesita espacio para sus fiestas. Busca la casa más grande posible. Debe considerar el anuncio número ___2___.
2. El señor Gómez, su esposa y su hijo Fernando trabajan fuera de casa y tienen tres coches. Deben considerar el anuncio número ___3___.
3. Doña Mercedes recibe solamente una pensión y necesita comprar una casa económica. Debe considerar el anuncio número ___1___.

**Script 2-44: Mi sala es** CD1–20 pequeña pero muy acogedora. En ella tengo un sofá y dos sillas pequeñas. En las paredes tengo unos cuadros de algunos amigos artistas y en el centro tengo una mesita con algunos adornos y revistas.

**2-44 La sala del (de la) profesor(a)** Tu profesor(a) va a describir lo que hay en su sala. Identifica los artículos que escuches.

| | | |
|---|---|---|
| __X__ sofá | ___ lámparas | ___ alfombras |
| __X__ sillas | ___ mesas | __X__ cuadros |
| ___ sillones | ___ espejos | ___ estantes |

## ■ Aplicaciones

**2-45 ¿Qué parte es?** Túrnense para describir y adivinar los nombres de los diferentes espacios de una casa. **¡OJO!** ¡Tienen sólo dos oportunidades!

The following are some of the verbs you can use in this activity: **cocinar, charlar, estudiar, descansar, guardar** *(to keep, put away)* **el auto, comer, escuchar música, ver televisión, hablar por teléfono.**

**MODELO**  E1: *Es el lugar* (place) *donde come la familia.*
E2: *¿La cocina?*
E1: *No exactamente. La familia come, pero **no** prepara la comida ahí* (there).
E2: *Entonces* (Then, what about), *¿el comedor?*
E1: *¡Exactamente!*

**2-46 Una casa a todo dar** *(A really neat home)* Tu profesor(a) ha terminado de decorar su casa. Completa la descripción.

**OPCIONES:**  sillas  sillones  cuadros  lámparas  estante

Su sala-comedor es muy bonita. En las paredes hay varios _____cuadros_____ grandes. El comedor es moderno, con una mesa grande y varias _____sillas_____ de color negro. Hay dos _____lámparas_____, una sobre una mesa y otra colgada *(hung)* del techo. Tiene también un par de plantas y un _____estante_____ grande. Los _____sillones_____ en la sala son grandes y cómodos.

**2-47 ¿Cómo es tu casa?** Averigua *(Find out)* cómo es la casa (o el apartamento) de tu compañero(a). Al terminar, preséntale un pequeño informe al resto de la clase.

Remember to use questions such as: **¿Cuántos pisos tiene? ¿Cuántas habitaciones tiene? ¿Tiene garaje?** etc.

### ■ Integración

**2-48 Mi casa ideal** Representa la siguiente situación con un(a) compañero(a).

| Agente de bienes raíces *(Real estate agent)* | Cliente |
|---|---|
| A customer is looking for a new home. Describe for him/her the house in the next activity and convince him/her that it is the best house on the market. | You and your spouse are looking for your first home. At this point you would like to buy a house with enough room for the children you expect to have in the near future. Find out what this agent has to offer. Don't rush into anything! |
| **Vocabulario opcional** To express admiration you may use expressions such as: **¡Es fantástico(a)! ¡Es perfecto(a)! ¡Es ideal! ¡Es maravilloso(a)!** *(It's wonderful!)* To urge your client to buy the house you may say: **Cómprela ahora mismo.** *(Buy it right now.)* or **No deje pasar esta oportunidad.** *(Don't let this opportunity pass you by.)* | **Vocabulario opcional** To express what you are interested in, use **Quisiera** *(I would like)* or **Necesito** *(I need)*. To express doubt you may use expressions such as: **No sé** *(I don't know)*; **Necesito consultarlo con mi esposo(a).** *(I have to consult with my husband/wife.)*; **Tengo que pensarlo.** *(I have to think about it.)* |

**2-49 Anuncio clasificado** Esta casa en Acapulco está para la venta *(for sale)*. Usando la información de la foto (y la imaginación), prepara un anuncio clasificado *(classified ad)*.

**SABOR REGIONAL**

**Padrísimo(a)** is a colloquial term used in Mexico to describe something exceptionally nice or convenient (like the word *cool* in American English). In other countries, you can expect to find different words to refer to the same concept, for instance, **chévere** in Venezuela, Colombia, and Puerto Rico, **bárbaro** in Argentina, and **guay** in Spain.

**EN TU COMUNIDAD**

Find out about housing in your community. You can consider issues such as cost, affordability, availability, construction, and public versus private. Visit real estate agencies as well as government offices and then share your findings with the class.

## II. Funciones y estructuras: Talking about location with prepositions

Transparencies C-2: En los cuartos; C-4: La sala/El dormitorio; C-5: El cuarto de baño/ La cocina

La lámpara está **sobre** el escritorio. *The lamp is **on** the desk.*
La ventana está **detrás de** la cama. *The window is **behind** the bed.*
El libro está **al lado de** la silla. *The book is **next to** the chair.*

**REMEMBER**

**Estar** *(to be)* is an irregular verb used to talk about location, conditions and emotional states. Its conjugation is: (yo) **estoy**, (tú) **estás**, (él/ella/usted) **está**, (nosotros[as]) **estamos**, (vosotros[as]) **estáis** and (ellos[as]/ustedes) **están**.

To talk about the specific location of things, people, or places, you may use the verb **estar** and the following prepositions.

### Vocabulario práctico

| | |
|---|---|
| al lado de *next to* | en *at, in, on* |
| arriba de *above* | enfrente de *in front of* |
| cerca de *close to* | entre *between* |
| debajo de *under* | fuera de *outside of* |
| dentro de *inside of* | lejos de *far from* |
| detrás de *behind* | sobre/encima de *on, over, above* |

As you have seen before, when one of the prepositions that end in **de** is followed by the masculine singular definite article **el**, it contracts to **del**. Remember that this contraction is obligatory in Spanish.

La cocina está cerca **del** comedor. *The kitchen is close **to the** dining room.*
La estufa está enfrente **del** refrigerador. *The stove is in front **of the** refrigerator.*

## ■ Asimilación

CD1-21 **2-50 ¿Cuál de los dos dormitorios?** Escucha las oraciones e indica si se refieren al dormitorio A, al dormitorio B, o a los dos.

**Script 2-50:** 1. La mesa de noche está entre la cama y el clóset. 2. El televisor está al lado del sillón. 3. La planta está enfrente de la ventana. 4. La lámpara está sobre la mesa de noche. 5. La ventana está detrás de la cama. 6. El televisor no está al lado del sillón. 7. La cama está cerca del clóset. 8. El televisor está arriba de la cama.

**dormitorio A**

**dormitorio B**

1. ... _los dos_
2. ... _A_
3. ... _B_
4. ... _A_
5. ... _A_
6. ... _B_
7. ... _los dos_
8. ... _B_

 **2-51 ¿Qué está... ?** Miren el segundo dibujo *(Look at the second drawing)* de la página 83 y completen las siguientes oraciones.

Pay attention to the use of **de la** and **del**.

MODELO   La lámpara está al lado _del sillón_.

1. La mesa de centro está entre ___el sofá___ y ___el escritorio___.
2. La computadora está encima ___del escritorio___.
3. Los libros están en ___el estante/librero___.
4. En la cocina, la mesa está enfrente ___del refrigerador/de la nevera___.
5. El teléfono está al lado ___del sofá___.
6. El despertador está lejos ___de la cocina___.
7. La lámpara está detrás ___del sillón___.
8. En el dormitorio, el cuadro está encima ___de la cama___.

**Answer:** 6. *Answer will vary.*

## ■ Aplicaciones

**2-52 En la clase de español** Escriban seis oraciones sobre la localización de algunos compañeros con relación a otros compañeros o a los muebles del salón de clase. Escriban oraciones ciertas y oraciones falsas. Luego, lean las oraciones y pídanle *(ask)* a un(a) compañero(a) que diga si son ciertas o falsas.

MODELO   E1: *Michael está detrás de JoAnne.*
         E2: *Falso.*

**2-53 ¡Ésta es mi universidad!** Usen la siguiente información para hacer preguntas sobre los diferentes edificios de su universidad y sobre su localización. Túrnense para hacer las preguntas.

> MODELO   Administración de Empresas
> E1: *¿Cuál es el edificio de Administración de Empresas?*
> E2: *Es Partridge Hall.*
> E1: *¿Dónde está Partridge Hall?*
> E2: *Está al lado de Calcia Hall.*

1. Artes
2. Ciencias Naturales
3. Humanidades
4. Ingeniería
5. Matemáticas
6. Ciencias Sociales
7. Comunicaciones
8. Educación
9. Derecho
10. Educación Física

**2-54 La habitación de mi compañero(a)**

The following expressions may help you talk about the specific location of your room furniture: **a la izquierda de** *(to the left of)* y **a la derecha de** *(to the right of).*

**Paso 1:** Averigua qué muebles tiene tu compañero(a) en su habitación y dónde están localizados. Toma notas.

> MODELO   E1: *¿Tienes una computadora en tu habitación?*
> E2: *Sí, tengo una computadora.*
> E1: *¿Dónde está?*
> E2: *Está al lado de mi cama, sobre el escritorio.*

**Extensión 2-54, Paso 2:** You may ask students to present their drawings and describe them.

**Paso 2:** Ahora, trata de dibujar un plano de la habitación de tu compañero(a). ¿Qué opina él/ella de tu representación artística?

## ■ Integración

**2-55 La universidad** Túrnense para hacer preguntas sobre la localización de algunos edificios en su universidad. Sean *(Be)* lo más específicos que puedan.

> MODELO   E1: *¿Dónde está el edificio... ?*
> E2: *Está entre... y... , detrás de...*

**2-56 Mi ciudad o pueblo** ¿Recuerdas a Octavio, el hijo de la familia Zapata Robles de Oaxaca, México, con la cual *(with which)* vas a vivir este verano? Él quiere saber más sobre tu ciudad o pueblo porque le interesa visitarte en el futuro. Escribe una breve descripción siguiendo el modelo.

> MODELO   *Octavio, yo vivo en... , en el estado de... Mi pueblo está al lado de la ciudad de...*

## III. Funciones y estructuras: Expressing obligation with *tener que*... and *hay que*...

Este fin de semana...

Arminda **tiene que** lavar la ropa...
*Arminda **has to** do laundry...*

y **hay que** limpiar la casa.
*and my house **has to be** cleaned.*

The verb **tener** can also be used to talk about obligations and things people have to do. To express this, use the following structure: a form of **tener** + **que** + a verb in the infinitive.

Celia **tiene que** cocinar y nosotras **tenemos que** aspirar.
*Celia **has to** cook and we **have to** vacuum.*

Mi padre **tiene que** cortar el césped y yo **tengo que** lavar el carro.
*My father **has to** cut the grass and I **have to** wash the car.*

Here are some household chores you can use to talk about obligations.

### Vocabulario práctico

arreglar la casa *to tidy up the house*

aspirar *to vacuum*

cocinar *to cook*

cortar el césped *to cut the grass*

hacer la cama *to make the bed*

lavar el carro/coche *to wash the car*

lavar los platos *to do the dishes*

lavar la ropa *to do laundry*

limpiar la casa *to clean the house*

sacar la basura *to take out the garbage*

Another verb that can be used to talk about obligations is **hay**. It is used in the following structure: **hay que** + verb in the infinitive. Unlike the structure **tener** + **que** + infinitive, this structure is used when the speaker does not want to or cannot specify who is in charge of doing the action. It is equivalent to the English expressions *has/have to be* + past participle and *it is necessary to*.

¡Chicos, **hay que** limpiar el apartamento antes de la fiesta!

*Guys, the apartment **has to be** cleaned before the party!*

**Hay que** cortar el césped hoy.

*It is necessary to cut the grass today.*

When you use this structure, only the verb **tener** changes endings. The other verb remains in the infinitive form. You have learned other structures that work similarly: **deber** *(should, must)* + infinitive and **gustar** *(to be pleasing)* + infinitive.

### SABOR REGIONAL

Other words for *grass* are **pasto** (Argentina, Chile, Colombia, Mexico, and Peru), **yerba** (Cuba), and **grama** (El Salvador, Guatemala, Honduras, Puerto Rico, and Venezuela).

### REMEMBER

In **Capítulo preparatorio** you learned that **hay** *(there is, there are)* is an impersonal form of the verb **haber** that is invariable when used to express existence and to talk about quantities: **En mi casa hay dos televisores.** *In my house **there are** two television sets.*

### SABOR REGIONAL

The word **carro** is more commonly used in Latin America whereas **coche** is more commonly used in Spain.

## Asimilación

**2-57 Recomendaciones** Escucha lo que dicen varios de tus amigos y
escoge la recomendación más lógica que les puedes dar. Luego compara
tus respuestas con las de un(a) compañero(a).

__5__ a. Tienes que cortar el
césped.

__2__ b. Tienes que cocinar.

__4__ c. Tienes que limpiar la casa.

__1__ d. Tienes que arreglar la
casa.

__6__ e. Tienes que lavar los
platos.

__3__ f. Tienes que lavar la ropa.

**2-58 Un estudiante universitario exitoso** *(successful)* ¿Qué hay que hacer
para ser un estudiante universitario exitoso? Indica si las siguientes
sugerencias son lógicas o no. Escribe **sí** o **no.**

Para ser un estudiante universitario exitoso, hay que...

__sí__ estudiar regularmente.

__no__ tener mucho dinero.

__sí__ saber usar una computadora.

__sí__ ser disciplinado.

__sí__ tomar buenas notas en clase.

__no__ comprar un buen carro.

## Aplicaciones

**2-59 La agenda de Josefina** Túrnense para hacer y responder a preguntas
sobre la agenda de Josefina para esta semana. También traten de
mencionar otras cosas relacionadas que ella tiene que hacer.

| lunes | a.m. | ir a la cita con el doctor |
| | p.m. | cenar con los Vélez Fernández |
| martes | a.m. | |
| | p.m. | limpiar la casa |
| miércoles | a.m. | confirmar la reservación en el hotel en Cozumel |
| | p.m. | asistir a la clase de administración y supervisión |
| jueves | a.m. | desayunar con Adalberto |
| | p.m. | |
| viernes | a.m. | escribir el informe para la clase |
| | p.m. | lavar la ropa |
| sábado | a.m. | visitar a mis padres |
| | p.m. | comprar el sillón |
| domingo | a.m. | llamar a la hermana de Adalberto |
| | p.m. | ¡descansar! |

As in English, the verb **hacer** *(to do)*
is not used in most answers to
questions that include this verb:
**¿Qué tienes que *hacer*? Tengo que
estudiar** para un examen. *What do
you have to do? I have to study for
a test.*

**REMEMBER**

To indicate on what day an
action takes place, use the
definite article **el** before the day
of the week: **el lunes**, **el martes**,
**el miércoles**, etc.

MODELO    E1: *¿Qué tiene que hacer Josefina el lunes por la mañana?*
E2: *Ella tiene que ir a la cita con el doctor. Ella está enferma.*

**2-60 Las responsabilidades profesionales** Piensen en las cosas que hacen las personas que tienen las siguientes profesiones y completen las oraciones. Luego, indiquen qué cosas son necesarias para tener estas profesiones. Al terminar, preséntenle sus respuestas al resto de la clase.

MODELO   Los profesores *tienen que enseñar varias clases, corregir exámenes y preparar lecciones.* Para ser profesor *hay que comprender a los estudiantes.*

1. Los actores...
   Para ser actor o actriz...
2. Los médicos...
   Para ser médico...
3. Los cocineros...
   Para ser cocinero...
4. Los vendedores...
   Para ser vendedor(a)...
5. Los enfermeros...
   Para ser enfermero(a)...
6. Los periodistas...
   Para ser periodista...

**2-61 Este fin de semana**

**Paso 1:** Haz una lista de seis cosas que tienes que hacer este fin de semana.

MODELO   *Tengo que ir a la biblioteca.*

1. ...   3. ...   5. ...
2. ...   4. ...   6. ...

**Paso 2:** Ahora, averigua si tu compañero(a) tiene que hacer las mismas *(same)* cosas. Toma notas. Cuando termines, prepara un informe y preséntalo a la clase. ¿Los estudiantes tienen obligaciones semejantes o diferentes?

MODELO:   E1: *Zach, ¿tienes que ir a la biblioteca este fin de semana?*
          E2: *Sí, tengo que ir a la biblioteca este fin de semana.*
          o   *No, no tengo que ir a la biblioteca.*

## ■ Integración

**2-62 Consejos prácticos** *(Practical pieces of advice)*

**Paso 1:** Individualmente, inventa *(make up)* una situación un poco trágica. ¡Incluye muchos detalles!

MODELO   *Soy una persona muy tímida. No me gusta hablar con las personas y soy introvertido. Nunca voy a lugares públicos.*

**Paso 2:** En grupos de tres o cuatro estudiantes, túrnense para leer las situaciones y reaccionar con consejos prácticos.

MODELO   E1: *...*
         E2: *Tienes que hablar con más personas e ir a muchos lugares. También tienes que ver a un sicólogo.*
         E3: *Pues yo creo que tienes que...*

**2-63 Las obligaciones de mi familia** Escribe un párrafo sobre las obligaciones que tienen algunos miembros de tu familia la próxima semana.

MODELO   *El lunes por la mañana tengo que asistir a mi clase de economía. Por la tarde tengo que... Por otro lado, el lunes por la mañana mi padre tiene que...*

Use connectors such as **por otro lado** (on the other hand), **en contraste** (in contrast), **por el contrario** (on the contrary), and **sin embargo** (however).

**iLrn™**

## IV. Lectura: *La casa en Mango Street*—Inmigrantes mexicanos en los Estados Unidos

### ■ Antes de leer

To provide additional background on the experience of Mexican immigrants in the U.S., you may want to show scenes from the PBS series *American Family* in class. The website for this series is: http://www.pbs.org/americanfamily

**A. El pelo** Discuss the following questions in groups of two or three students.

1. Do you think one's type of hair has anything to do with one's personality? Explain.

You have already learned the words **corto** (*short*) and **largo** (*long*). The following words are also used to describe hair type: **liso/lacio** (*straight*), **rizado** (*curly*), **teñido** (*color treated*), **calvo** (*bald*).

2. Complete the following chart with information about the members of your group.

| Nombre del (de la) compañero(a) | Tipo (o estilo) de pelo | Personalidad (dos adjetivos) |
|---|---|---|
| | | |
| | | |
| | | |

**CRITICAL THINKING SKILLS**

***Analyzing*** Use cognates to anticipate the content of the reading.

**READING STRATEGY**

***Skimming and Scanning*** You do not have to understand every word. Concentrate on identifying the main points of the story and answering the comprehension questions that follow.

**B. Cognados** With a partner, make a list of all the cognates you can find in the reading. Based on your findings, what do you expect this story to be about?

### ■ A leer

### Sandra Cisneros

Las familias hispanas en los Estados Unidos tratan de mantener *(try to maintain)* su cultura y sus tradiciones, al mismo tiempo que *(while)* se integran a su nueva vida *(new life)* en Norteamérica. Sandra Cisneros es una autora chicana que nació en Chicago en 1954. El siguiente es un fragmento de su libro *La casa en Mango Street*.

## La casa en Mango Street (fragmento)

### Pelos

Cada uno en mi familia tiene pelo diferente. El de mi papá **se para** en el aire como escoba. Y yo, el mío es **flojo.** Nunca **hace caso de** broches o diademas. El pelo de Carlos es grueso y derechito, no necesita **peinárselo.** El de Nenny es **resbaloso,** se escurre de tu mano, y Kiki, que es el menor, tiene pelo de **peluche.** Pero el pelo de mi madre, el pelo de mi madre, es de rositas en botón, como **rueditas** de caramelo todo rizado y bonito porque **se hizo anchoas todo el día,** fragante para meter en él la nariz cuando ella está **abrazándote** y te sientes **segura,** es el **olor** cálido del pan antes de **hornearlo,** es el olor de cuando ella te **hace un campito** en su cama aún tibia de su piel, y una duerme a su lado, cae la lluvia afuera y papá **ronca.** El ronquido, la lluvia y el pelo de mamá oloroso a pan.

*sticks up*
*loose / pays attention to*

*to comb it / slippery*
*plush*
*little wheels*
*made anchovies the whole day*
*hugging you*
*safe / smell / baking it*
*makes some space*
*snores*

### ■ ¿Entendiste bien?

**C. Ideas principales** Complete the following chart with the information found in the text.

| Personajes (Characters) | Tipo de pelo |
|---|---|
| Papá | *se para en el aire* |
| Narradora (Narrator) | |
| Carlos | |
| Nenny | |
| Kiki | *de peluche* |
| Mamá | |

**D. Inferencias** In groups of three or four students, complete the following chart describing the personalities of the different characters introduced in the previous novel fragment.

| Personajes | Personalidad |
|---|---|
| Papá | *serio* |
| Narradora | |
| Carlos | |
| Nenny | |
| Kiki | *simpática* |
| Mamá | |

**E. Actividad de extensión** Following Sandra Cisneros' model, write a description of the personalities of different members of your family based on the type of hair they have.

### CRITICAL THINKING SKILLS

**Making Associations and Creating** Use the author's idea by applying it in an imaginative way.

# Vocabulario

## La familia

| | |
|---|---|
| el (la) abuelo(a) | *grandfather/ grandmother* |
| el (la) cuñado(a) | *brother-in-law/ sister-in-law* |
| el (la) esposo(a) | *husband/wife* |
| el (la) hermanastro(a) | *stepbrother/stepsister* |
| el (la) hermano(a) (mayor/menor) | *(older/younger) brother/sister* |
| el (la) hijo(a) (mayor/menor) | *(older/younger) son/ daughter* |
| la madrastra | *stepmother* |
| la madre/mamá | *mother* |
| el (la) nieto(a) | *grandson/granddaughter* |
| el padrastro | *stepfather* |
| el padre/papá | *father* |
| el (la) pariente | *relative* |
| el (la) primo(a) | *cousin* |
| el (la) sobrino(a) | *nephew/niece* |
| el (la) suegro(a) | *father-in-law/ mother-in-law* |
| el (la) tío(a) | *uncle/aunt* |

## Descripciones

| | |
|---|---|
| alto | *tall* |
| bajo | *short (height)* |
| bonito | *pretty, beautiful* |
| corto | *short (length)* |
| delgado | *thin* |
| difícil | *difficult* |
| fácil | *easy* |
| feo | *ugly* |
| flaco(a) | *skinny* |
| gordo | *fat* |
| grande | *big* |
| guapo | *handsome* |
| largo | *long* |
| moreno | *dark-haired* |
| nuevo | *new* |
| pequeño | *small* |
| rubio | *blond(e)* |
| el pelo blanco | *gray hair* |
| el pelo castaño | *brown hair* |
| el pelo negro | *black hair* |
| el pelo rojo | *red hair* |
| el pelo rubio | *blond hair* |

## Rasgos personales — *Personal traits*

| | |
|---|---|
| bueno | *good* |
| diligente | *diligent* |
| cómico/gracioso/de buen humor | *funny* |

| | |
|---|---|
| extrovertido | *extroverted* |
| inteligente | *intelligent* |
| listo | *smart* |
| malo | *bad, mean* |
| perezoso | *lazy* |
| tímido | *shy* |
| tonto/estúpido | *foolish, stupid* |
| trabajador(a) | *hardworking* |
| serio | *serious* |
| simpático | *nice* |

## ¿Cómo estás? — *How are you?*

| | |
|---|---|
| aburrido | *bored* |
| alegre/contento/feliz | *happy* |
| cansado | *tired* |
| deprimido | *depressed* |
| emocionado | *excited* |
| enfermo | *sick* |
| enojado | *angry* |
| listo | *ready* |
| nervioso | *nervous* |
| ocupado | *busy* |
| preocupado | *worried* |
| triste | *sad* |

## Más conectores

| | |
|---|---|
| en cambio | *instead* |
| mientras que | *while, whereas* |

## La casa — *House*

| | |
|---|---|
| el ático | *attic* |
| el baño | *bathroom* |
| la cocina | *kitchen* |
| el comedor | *dining room* |
| la escalera | *stairs* |
| el garaje | *garage* |
| el jardín | *garden* |
| la pared | *wall* |
| la planta baja | *first floor* |
| el primer piso | *second floor* |
| la puerta | *door* |
| la recámara / la habitación / el dormitorio | *bedroom* |
| la sala | *living room* |
| el sótano | *basement* |
| el techo | *roof* |
| la ventana | *window* |

## Los muebles — *Furniture*

| | |
|---|---|
| la alfombra | *carpet* |
| el armario / clóset | *closet* |
| la cama | *bed* |
| la computadora / el ordenador | *computer* |

| | |
|---|---|
| las cortinas | *curtains* |
| el cuadro | *painting* |
| el despertador | *alarm clock* |
| el escritorio | *desk* |
| el espejo | *mirror* |
| el estante | *bookcase* |
| el estéreo | *stereo* |
| la estufa | *stove* |
| el horno microondas | *microwave oven* |
| la lámpara | *lamp* |
| la mesa | *table* |
| la mesa de centro | *coffee table* |
| la mesa de noche / mesa de luz | *bedside table* |
| el refrigerador / la nevera | *refrigerator* |
| la silla | *chair* |
| el sillón | *armchair* |
| el sofá | *sofa* |
| el teléfono | *telephone* |
| el televisor | *TV* |

## Exclamaciones

¡Es fantástico! \
¡Es ideal! \
¡Es maravilloso!      *It's wonderful!* \
¡Es perfecto!

## Los quehaceres del hogar — *Household chores*

| | |
|---|---|
| arreglar la casa | *to tidy up the house* |
| aspirar | *to vacuum* |
| cocinar | *to cook* |
| cortar el césped | *to cut the grass* |
| hacer la cama | *to make the bed* |
| lavar el carro/coche | *to wash the car* |
| lavar los platos | *to do the dishes* |
| lavar la ropa | *to do laundry* |
| limpiar la casa | *to clean the house* |
| sacar la basura | *to take out the garbage* |

## Funciones y estructuras

Expresiones con **tener**, p. 73
Preposiciones de lugar, p. 86

# Puesta en acción

| | |
|---|---|
| **SITUACIÓN:** | You have decided to host a Mexican exchange student in your home. |
| **MISIÓN:** | To establish contact with this student, find out about his background, learn about his culture, and exchange information about each other's family and life. |
| **DESTREZAS** *(SKILLS):* | Reading and responding to electronic communications, providing personal information, and researching information. |

**A. Un mensaje electrónico.** José Francisco Reyes Galindo, el estudiante de intercambio mexicano, te envía el siguiente mensaje.

| Fecha: | 27 de enero de 2006 |
|---|---|
| Para: | La familia Smith |
| De: | José Francisco Reyes Galindo |

Viaje a los Estados Unidos

Estimada Familia Smith:

Permítanme que me presente: Soy José Francisco Reyes Galindo y tengo veinte años. Aunque soy de Guanajuato, México, estudio bellas artes en la Universidad Nacional Autónoma de México, en la capital. Mi especialidad es la pintura y quiero ampliar mis conocimientos en los Estados Unidos. Mi sueño es ser un pintor famoso como Diego Rivera.

*I am planning on living*
*travel*

**Pienso vivir** en su casa en los Estados Unidos por seis meses. Viajo el próximo 25 de agosto. Antes de **viajar**, quisiera hacerles varias preguntas: ¿Cuántas personas hay en su familia? ¿Cómo son? ¿Ustedes hablan español? ¿Hay personas de mi **edad** en su familia? ¿La universidad está lejos de su casa? ¿Cómo es mi cuarto? ¿Tengo que hacer quehaceres domésticos en su casa? Si es así, ¿cuáles?

*age*

*give me*
*pick up*

También les agradecería que me **dieran** el nombre y la descripción física de la persona que me va a **recoger** en el aeropuerto.

*welcome*

Muchas gracias por su **acogida** y por la información.

Atentamente,
José Francisco Reyes Galindo

**B. ¿Dónde está Guanajuato?** Busquen *(Find)* en el mapa en la página vi la ciudad de origen de José Francisco (Guanajuato). Expliquen dónde está, usando las preposiciones de lugar **cerca de**, **lejos de**, **al lado de**, etc.

También pueden usar las frases **al norte de** *(north of)*, **al sur de** *(south of)*, **al este de** *(east of)* y **al oeste de** *(west of)*.

**C. El Estado de Guanajuato.** Busca información en la biblioteca o en el Internet acerca del Estado de Guanajuato.

**CRITICAL THINKING SKILLS**

*Researching* Find other opportunities to learn about Mexico.

| Guanajuato | |
|---|---|
| Población | |
| Industrias | |
| Atracciones turísticas | |
| Fiestas *(Holidays)* | |
| Ciudades importantes | |
| Otros datos importantes | |

**D. Un artista famoso** Diego Rivera, the artist that José Francisco mentioned in his message, is one of the most famous Mexican painters of the twentieth century. To understand better why José Francisco wishes to be like him one day, find out about Diego Rivera's life and works. Complete the chart below with the information you find.

You may play the video segment on Diego Rivera and Frida Kahlo or parts of the movie *Frida* at this time.

| Biografía de Diego Rivera | |
|---|---|
| Fecha y lugar de su nacimiento | |
| Fecha y lugar de su muerte *(death)* | |
| Tipo de pintura | |
| Lugar donde están sus pinturas hoy | |
| Temas principales de sus pinturas | |
| Nombre de su esposa | |
| Profesión de su esposa | |

You may want to visit one of the many Diego Rivera sites on the web to find the information requested.

**E. La respuesta** Write a letter to José Francisco and provide the information he requested in his electronic message. Follow these steps.

**Paso 1:** Greet him **(Estimado José Francisco:)**, identify yourself, and say how you are today.

**Paso 2:** Answer the questions José Francisco posed:
1. ¿Cuántas personas hay en su familia?
2. ¿Cómo son?
3. ¿Ustedes hablan español?
4. ¿Hay personas de mi edad *(age)* en su familia?
5. ¿La universidad está lejos de su casa?
6. ¿Cómo es mi cuarto?
7. ¿Tengo que hacer quehaceres domésticos en su casa? Si es así, ¿cuáles?

The person who is going to pick you up at the airport = **la persona que te va a recoger en el aeropuerto**

**Paso 3:** Now describe the person who is going to pick him up at the airport: yourself. Give as many details as possible. Then, finish the letter with the appropriate expressions (**Esperamos conocerte pronto. Atentamente** [your name]).

**Paso 4:** Reread the letter and make sure you use connectors such as **y** *(and)*, **también** *(also)*, **pero** *(but)*, **sin embargo** *(however)*, **por otro lado** *(on the other hand)*, and **finalmente** *(finally)*. When you have your first draft ready, exchange drafts with a classmate. Use the following checklist as a guide to correct his or her work.

- Did your partner answer all of José Francisco's questions?
- Is the letter clear and well organized?
- Underline all the adjectives. Do they agree in number and gender with the noun they describe? Then, circle all the verbs. Are they properly conjugated?

When you get the first draft back from your classmate, make all the necessary revisions and give the second draft to your instructor for additional feedback.

**F. El árbol genealógico** *(family tree)* **de José Francisco.** You just opened the attachment with José Francisco's family tree. You printed it out and, unfortunately, ended up with half of the tree on one sheet and the other half on another. Have one of your classmates describe one of the halves to you and complete the illustration. Then do the same so your classmate can complete his/her part of the illustration. Look at the model to know how to ask for and provide clues. One of you must turn the book upside-down. Do not let your classmate see your part of the family tree!

MODELO   E1: *¿Cómo se llama el abuelo paterno de José Francisco?*
E2: *Se llama Alberto Reyes Gómez.*
E1: *¿Cuántos años tiene?*
E2: *Él tiene setenta y ocho años.*

## Servicio comunitario

Go to the office of international affairs of your college or university and offer to provide one of the following services.

- Serve as conversation partner to a student from a Spanish-speaking country.
- Become a guide and offer tours of your institution to prospective foreign students.

**Estudiante 1**

**Estudiante 2**

# Unidad 2

## La vida diaria

### Puerto Rico y España

In this unit you will learn how to plan a vacation in Spanish, to find your way around a Spanish-speaking city, and to get access to goods and services. Also, you will talk about daily routines and express your preferences with regard to clothing, food, and leisure activities. The readings will give you a taste of everyday life in Puerto Rico and Spain, and the videos will show you people giving directions and shopping for clothing in these countries. At the end of the unit you will plan the logistics of a business meeting in Puerto Rico. You will also be able to connect with your community by researching services available to Spanish speakers at local businesses and government agencies.

# Capítulo 3

## ¿Dónde y cuándo?

### Para comenzar

- Observa las fotografías de Puerto Rico y completa la siguiente oración.
- Puerto Rico es un lugar ideal para..., ... y...

### In this chapter you will learn ...

- how to talk about location and destination
- how to tell time and express frequency
- how to shop
- how to talk about food and order in a restaurant
- how to talk about future plans
- about tourism opportunities in Puerto Rico

**Las playas de Isla Verde**  **Las tiendas de artesanías**  **El Viejo San Juan**

# Enfoque

Transparency A-10: Country Profile: Puerto Rico

**A. ¿Qué sabes ya de Puerto Rico?** Antes de ver el vídeo, empareja los siguientes lugares con sus descripciones. Cuando termines *(When you finish)*, compara tus respuestas con las de otro(a) estudiante(a).

Answers A: 2. un bosque tropical 3. una ciudad 4. una fortaleza 5. la capital del país

| **Lugar** | **¿Qué es?** |
|---|---|
| 1. Puerto Rico | la capital del país |
| 2. El Yunque | una ciudad |
| 3. Ponce | una fortaleza |
| 4. San Felipe del Morro | un bosque tropical |
| 5. San Juan | una isla |

**B. Puerto Rico con más detalle** Lee las siguientes frases sobre los lugares de la actividad anterior. Luego, mira el vídeo y escribe el número del lugar (1–5) que corresponde a cada frase. **¡OJO!** Tienes que usar uno de los números dos veces *(twice)*.

___2___ a. un refugio de muchas especies de animales raros

___1___ b. Isla del Encanto

___5___ c. un importante destino turístico debido a sus monumentos históricos y atractivas playas

___3___ d. La Perla del Sur

___5___ e. una de las ciudades españolas más antiguas de las Américas

___4___ f. construida en el siglo XVI por los españoles

**C. Mis preferencias y las de la clase** Sigue los siguientes pasos para determinar tus preferencias y las de tus compañeros de clase sobre lugares de interés en Puerto Rico.

**Paso 1:** Pon en orden los lugares mencionados en el vídeo según el interés que tienes en visitarlos. (1 = de mayor interés; 5 = de menor interés)

_____ San Juan          _____ El Yunque

_____ Ponce             _____ las playas puertorriqueñas

_____ San Felipe del Morro

For more info, you may want to check the **Temas** site: **http://temas.heinle.com**

**Paso 2:** En grupos de cuatro o cinco estudiantes, comparen sus preferencias. Determinen cuál es el lugar favorito de su grupo y escojan a un(a) representante.

# Orientándonos en la ciudad

## I. Vocabulario: Lugares de interés

**Sugerencia:** You may point out to students that **lugares de interés** refers not only to places one may find interesting, but also to places one may need or want to know about.

Transparencies F-1 Los Lugares públicos; F-2 Un pueblo; F-3 ¿Dónde está?; F4: La ciudad; F-6: Mapas de Madrid, San Juan y México, D.F.

### SABOR REGIONAL

Other Spanish words for *parking lot* are **el aparcamiento** (Spain) and **el parqueadero** (Colombia and Panama).

el aeropuerto · el banco · la biblioteca · la farmacia · el centro comercial · el cine · el gimnasio · el estacionamiento · el hospital · el hotel · la iglesia · el museo · la oficina de correos · el supermercado · el restaurante · el parque

### Vocabulario práctico

**Puntos de referencia**
*(Reference points)*

el bar / la barra *bar*
el cajero automático *automatic teller machine*
el centro *downtown*
la cuadra/manzana *city block*
el edificio *building*
la esquina *corner*
la estación de (trenes/autobús/metro) *(train/bus/subway) station*
la lavandería *laundromat*
la librería *bookstore*
la parada de (autobús/tren/metro) *(bus/train/subway) stop*
la peluquería / el salón de belleza *barber shop, beauty parlor*
el semáforo *traffic light*
la tienda / el almacén *store*
la tintorería *dry cleaners*

## ■ Asimilación

**3-1 ¿Dónde?** Indiquen dónde ustedes pueden *(where you can)* obtener los siguientes servicios.

**Sugerencia:** Encourage your students to work in groups to go over these structured input activities. For best results, try to maintain all classroom interactions in the target language.

_h_ 1. Como platos deliciosos en...  a. el gimnasio

_g_ 2. Recibo atención médica en...  b. la biblioteca

_a_ 3. Hago ejercicios aeróbicos en...  c. la iglesia

_b_ 4. Leo libros y estudio en...  d. el centro comercial

_f_ 5. Reservo una habitación en...  e. el cine

_c_ 6. Asisto a un servicio religioso en...  f. el hotel

_e_ 7. Miro una película de acción en...  g. el hospital

_d_ 8. Compro ropa *(clothes)* en...  h. el restaurante

**3-2 ¿Adónde tiene que ir** *(to go)***?** Tu profesor(a) tiene mucho que hacer hoy. Indica los lugares adonde tiene que ir.

_x_ cajero automático     _x_ restaurante

____ hotel     _x_ supermercado

____ lavandería     ____ hospital

____ cine     _x_ peluquería

____ iglesia

**Script 3-2:** Tengo un día muy agitado hoy. Primero tengo que sacar dinero de un cajero automático. Después tengo que comprar comida para mi familia en el supermercado. A las tres tengo una cita en la peluquería y a las cinco tengo que encontrarme con mi esposo en el restaurante de la calle Washington.

**Sugerencia 3-2:** You may personalize the passage.

## ■ Aplicaciones

**3-3 ¿Dónde...?** Túrnense para hacer y para responder a las preguntas.

MODELO     nadar
           E1: *¿Dónde nadas?*
           E2: *Nado en el gimnasio High Energy.*

1. ver películas
2. buscar un libro
3. estudiar
4. hacer compras
5. recibir servicios médicos
6. rezar *(to pray)*

**3-4 Puntos de referencia** Completen las oraciones con el punto de referencia más apropiado. **¡OJO!** En algunos casos deben usar la forma plural de la palabra.

OPCIONES:  centro  edificio  iglesia  cuadra  parque  esquina
           plaza  estacionamiento

Hola, me llamo Martín Díaz. Vivo más o menos a diez ___cuadras___ de la escuela, en un ___edifico___ de diez pisos, y trabajo en el supermercado que está en la ___esquina___ de la avenida San Mateo y la calle Toribio. Me gusta mi barrio porque tiene muchos ___parques___ y porque está cerca del ___centro___.

**3-5 En San Juan** Observen el mapa del Viejo San Juan (zona histórica) y contesten las preguntas.

> MODELO  E1: *¿Dónde puedo* (Where can I) *comer platos típicos de Puerto Rico?*
> E2: *En el restaurante El Patio de Sam.*

1. ¿Dónde puedo ver *(to see)* una exposición de arte?
2. ¿Dónde puedo hacer unas compras?
3. ¿Dónde puedo comprar unas aspirinas?
4. ¿Dónde puedo cambiar un cheque?
5. ¿Dónde puedo obtener información acerca de Puerto Rico?

Ahora, observen el mapa otra vez y completen la siguiente tarjeta postal *(postcard)*.

---

¡Hola a todos!

Estamos felices en Puerto Rico. Todo aquí es muy bonito. Hay muchos lugares históricos como ___ y ___. También hay muchas tiendas como ___ y, desde luego, excelentes restaurantes como ___, donde sirven la deliciosa comida de este país.

Un abrazo,

Juan Carlos

---

## ■ Integración

**3-6 ¿Qué lugares de interés hay en esta ciudad?** En parejas, discutan y decidan cuáles son los **cinco** lugares más importantes de su ciudad.

> MODELO  E1: *El museo de arte moderno es un lugar de interés para los turistas, ¿no?*
> E2: *Sí, estoy de acuerdo.*

**EN TU COMUNIDAD**

Prepare a brief report on the services available for Spanish speakers at prominent historical landmarks in your town or region.

**3-7 Lugares de interés** Preparen un folleto *(pamphlet)* para los turistas hispanos de su ciudad con las siguientes recomendaciones e información general. ¡El diseño *(design)* del folleto debe ser atractivo! Incluyan un título, un mapa del centro de la ciudad y una lista de los lugares de interés con indicaciones *(directions)* generales.

> MODELO  *Lugares de interés en Boston*
> *Algunos lugares de interés en esta ciudad son:*
> ■ *La iglesia Old North. Está en la calle Salem cerca del puerto.*
> ■ *El Museo de Arte de Boston está en la calle Huntington cerca de la Universidad Northeastern.*

# II. Funciones y estructuras: Talking about location and destination with the verbs *estar* and *ir*

Transparencies F-1: Los lugares públicos; F-2: Un pueblo; F-3: ¿Dónde está?; F-4: La ciudad

¿Dónde **está** Inés? Ella **está** en el salón de belleza?
*Where is Ines? She is at the beauty parlor.*

As you learned in **Capítulo 2, Tema 2**, one of the uses of the verb **estar** is to talk about the location of people and things.

| | |
|---|---|
| Mis primas **están** en la iglesia. | *My cousins **are** at church.* |
| La pintura **está** en el Museo de Arte de Ponce. | *The painting **is** at the Museum of Art of Ponce.* |

**REMEMBER**

Do you recall how to conjugate the irregular verb **estar**? Its six forms are: (yo) **estoy**, (tú) **estás**, (él/ella/usted) **está**, (nosotros[as]) **estamos**, (vosotros[as]) **estáis**, and (ellos[as]/ustedes) **están**.

Ellos **van** al parque por la tarde.
*They **go** to the park in the afternoon.*

The verb **ir** *(to go)*, on the other hand, is used to express movement and destination. Like **estar**, this verb has an irregular conjugation.

Note that the irregular **yo** form of **ir** (**voy**) ends in **-oy**, like the **yo** forms of **ser** (**soy**) and **estar** (**estoy**).

**Sugerencia:** You may want to point out that, to form questions, **estar** is used with ¿**dónde**? *(where?)* while **ir** is used with ¿**adónde**? *(where . . . to?)*.

| | |
|---|---|
| yo **voy** | nosotros(as) **vamos** |
| tú **vas** | vosotros(as) **vais** |
| él/ella/usted **va** | ellos(as)/ustedes **van** |

| | |
|---|---|
| ¿Adónde **vas** los sábados, Milagros? | *Where do you **go** on Saturdays, Milagros?* |
| Siempre **voy** al centro con mi madre. | *I always **go** downtown with my mother.* |

When making a statement, the verb **ir** is used in the following structure.

**ir** + **a** + article + name of place

| | |
|---|---|
| Hoy **vamos a la biblioteca** y mañana **vamos al cine**. | *Today we **go to the library** and tomorrow we **go to the movie theater**.* |

Note that when the preposition **a** is followed by the masculine singular article **el**, it is necessary to form the contraction **al**. As you may remember, the same applies to **de** + **el** (= **del**).

## ■ Asimilación

**3-8 En el Viejo San Juan** Mira el mapa del Viejo San Juan de la página 104 y determina si las siguientes oraciones son ciertas (**C**) o falsas (**F**).

_C_ 1. La Tienda el Artesano está en la calle Tetuán.

_F_ 2. La Iglesia de San Francisco está en la esquina de la calle San Francisco y la calle Tanca.

_F_ 3. La Fortaleza está cerca del Hard Rock Café.

_C_ 4. La Catedral de San Juan está entre las calles Cristo y San José.

_C_ 5. El Paseo de la Princesa no está lejos de los muelles de barcos de crucero.

_F_ 6. El Patio de Sam está al este *(east)* del Museo Pablo Casals.

CD1–25

**3-9 Un día normal** Escucha la descripción que da Noel sobre un día normal en la vida de su familia. Luego, indica si las siguientes acciones se refieren a Noel, a su madre, a su padre o a su hermana.

_su madre_ 1. Va al gimnasio.

_su padre_ 2. Va al hospital por la tarde.

_su hermana_ 3. Va a la escuela.

_su madre_ 4. Va a la casa de una amiga.

_Noel_ 5. Va a la universidad.

_su hermana_ 6. Va a la escuela de baile.

_su padre_ 7. Va a la oficina.

_su madre_ 8. Va al supermercado

**Script 3-9:** En un día normal nosotros hacemos muchas cosas. Por ejemplo, mi padre va a la oficina y por la tarde va al hospital a visitar pacientes. Él es médico. Mi madre, como trabaja en la casa, va al gimnasio por la mañana y luego va al supermercado. En cambio, mi hermana va al colegio y yo voy a la universidad. Por las noches, yo voy a la biblioteca, mi hermana va a la escuela de baile y mi madre va a la casa de alguna amiga.

## ■ Aplicaciones

**3-10 ¿Dónde estamos?** Túrnense para leer las claves y decir dónde están las personas indicadas. Usen el verbo **estar** correctamente.

MODELO   E1: *Ramiro tiene hambre y desea comer.*
E2: *Ramiro está en el restaurante.*

1. Sara y Penélope tienen que enviarle un paquete a su amigo de Puerto Rico.

2. Nosotros tenemos que depositar dinero en nuestra cuenta de ahorros.

3. Argelio está de vacaciones en San Juan de Puerto Rico y tiene sueño.

4. Yo estoy enfermo y necesito comprar una medicina.

5. Ellas necesitan lavar la ropa lo antes posible.

6. Tú tienes que tomar el autobús para llegar a tu trabajo.

**Answers 3-10:** 1. Sara y Penélope están en la oficina de correos. 2. (Nosotros estamos/Ustedes están) en el banco. 3. Argelio está en el hotel. 4. Tú estás en la farmacia. 5. Ellas están en la lavandería. 6. Yo estoy en la parada del autobús.

### 3-11 Los fines de semana

**Paso 1:** Escribe por lo menos seis oraciones sobre los lugares a los que generalmente vas durante los fines de semana.

1. …        4. …
2. …        5. …
3. …        6. …

**Paso 2:** Ahora, entrevista a tu compañero(a) para saber si él/ella va a los mismos lugares. Tomen notas. Cuando terminen, preparen un informe y preséntenlo a la clase.

MODELO    E1: *Martín, ¿vas a las tiendas los fines de semana?*
             E2: *Sí, voy a las tiendas los fines de semana.*
             o   *No, no voy a las tiendas los fines de semana.*

### 3-12 ¿Dónde están o adónde van?

Túrnense para decir en dónde están ustedes o adónde van en los momentos que se mencionan a continuación.

MODELO    E1: *Los lunes a las ocho de la mañana estoy en la clase de*
                 *biología.*
             E2: *Y yo voy al trabajo los lunes por la mañana.*

1. el Día de Año Nuevo
2. los viernes a las nueve de la noche
3. el 4 de julio
4. el día de mi cumpleaños
5. en julio y en agosto
6. el Día de San Valentín
7. los miércoles a las tres de la tarde
8. en el receso *(break)* de primavera

### ■ Integración

**3-13 Un día perfecto** Imagínate que estás viviendo *(you are living)* un día perfecto y descríbeles a tus compañeros de grupo dónde estás y adónde vas. Da *(Give)* todos los detalles que puedas. **¡OJO!** Debes estar preparado(a) para responder a las preguntas de tus compañeros.

You may use some of the connectors (**primero, después, luego, finalmente**, etc.) and time expressions (**por la mañana, por la tarde, por la noche**).

**3-14 El día perfecto de...** Ahora, escribe dónde está y adónde va en su día perfecto uno de tus compañeros de grupo de la actividad 3–13. Incluye todos los detalles *(details)* que recuerdes. Al terminar, entrégale *(turn in)* el trabajo a tu profesor(a) para que lo corrija.

## III. Funciones y estructuras: Telling time

To ask for the time in Spanish, say **¿Qué hora es?** When the time is between the hour and the half hour, use the following expression.

You may want to review the list of numbers presented in **Capítulo preparatorio**.

**ser** + article + hour (+ **y** + minutes)

Son las doce y media.

Son las cuatro en punto.

Son las nueve y veinticinco.

Es la una y cuarto.

Note that **es la** is used when the hour is one while **son las** is used for all other hours. Also, note the use of **en punto** (o'clock), **cuarto** (quarter of an hour = 15 minutes) and **media** (half an hour = 30 minutes).

■ Use **Es mediodía** for *It's noon* and **Es medianoche** for *It's midnight.*

When the time is between the half hour and the hour, use the following expression.

**ser** + article + next hour + **menos** + minutes to the hour

Es la una menos cuarto.

Son las siete menos veinte.

As a general rule, use **de la tarde** until 6:30 p.m.

■ To specify the time of the day, add the expression **de la mañana** (*in the morning*), **de la tarde** (*in the afternoon*), or **de la noche** (*in the evening / at night*).

To find out at what time an action takes place, say **¿A qué hora... ?** To answer this question, use the preposition **a** instead of **es** or **son**.

—¿**A qué hora** vas a la universidad? **At what time** *do you go to school?*

—Voy **a** las siete y media de la mañana. *I go* **at** *7:30 a.m.*

## ■ Asimilación

**3-15 La hora** Empareja *(Match)* las horas de la izquierda con las oraciones de la derecha. Cuando termines, compara tus respuestas con las de un(a) compañero(a).

| | | | |
|---|---|---|---|
| _d_ | 1. 6:00 p.m. | a. | Son las cinco y doce de la mañana. |
| _b_ | 2. 4:15 a.m. | b. | Son las cuatro y cuarto de la mañana. |
| _f_ | 3. 6:54 p.m. | c. | Son las cuatro menos cuarto de la tarde. |
| _h_ | 4. 6:30 a.m. | d. | Son las seis en punto de la tarde. |
| _g_ | 5. 1:00 p.m. | e. | Es la una menos veinte de la mañana. |
| _c_ | 6. 3:45 p.m. | f. | Son las siete menos seis de la noche. |
| _a_ | 7. 5:12 a.m. | g. | Es la una en punto de la tarde. |
| _e_ | 8. 12:40 a.m. | h. | Son las seis y media de la mañana. |

D1–26

**3-16 La agenda de Elsa** Escucha la descripción que da Elsa de sus actividades para el día de hoy. Luego, completa la agenda a continuación, escribiendo la acción correcta al lado de la hora correspondiente.

**OPCIONES:** cenar con Betty   estudiar para el examen de historia   almorzar con Pedro   ir a la clase de física   trabajar   buscar a Andrés   ir al laboratorio de química

> **miércoles, 8 de febrero**
>
> 8:00 a.m. — ir a la clase de física
> 10:30 a.m. — ir al laboratorio de química
> 12:00 p.m. — almorzar con Pedro
> 1:30 p.m. — trabajar
> 4:45 p.m. — buscar a Andrés
> 7:00 p.m. — cenar con Betty
> 9:00 p.m. — estudiar para el examen de historia

**Script 3-16:** Tengo muchas cosas que hacer hoy. A las ocho de la mañana tengo mi clase de física y a las diez y media tengo mi laboratorio de química. Al mediodía voy a almorzar con Pedro para hablar del proyecto de la clase de estadística. Por la tarde tengo que trabajar, a la una y media. Después, como a las cinco menos cuarto, tengo que buscar a mi hermano Andrés en la escuela de karate. Luego, a las siete de la noche, voy a cenar con Betty en un restaurante francés. Finalmente, a eso de las nueve de la noche, quiero estudiar para el examen de historia.

## ■ Aplicaciones

**3-17 ¿Qué hora es?** Túrnense para decir qué hora es (en oraciones completas). Especifiquen el momento del día.

MODELO   10:00 p.m.
E1: *¿Qué hora es?*
E2: *Son las diez en punto de la noche.*

| | | | |
|---|---|---|---|
| 1. 3:05 p.m. | 3. 8:00 p.m. | 5. 10:50 p.m. | 7. 9:00 a.m. |
| 2. 12:35 a.m. | 4. 2:15 p.m. | 6. 4:30 p.m. | 8. 9:45 a.m. |

**Answers 3-17:** 1. Son las tres y cinco de la tarde. 2. Es la una menos veinticinco de la mañana. 3. Son las ocho en punto de la noche. 4. Son las dos y cuarto de la tarde. 5. Son las once menos diez de la noche. 6. Son las cuatro y media de la tarde. 7. Son las nueve en punto de la mañana. 8. Son las diez menos cuarto de la mañana.

**3-18 Programas de televisión** Túrnense para hacer y responder a preguntas sobre varios programas de televisión.

MODELO   E1: *¿A qué hora es el programa 20/20?*
E2: *Es a las diez en punto de la noche los viernes.*

**3-19 Preferencias diferentes** Formen oraciones diferentes usando elementos de cada columna. Conjuguen los verbos correctamente *(correctly)* y terminen cada oración con una hora lógica. Pueden añadir información adicional.

MODELO:  nosotros(as)  desayunar
*Nosotros desayunamos en casa a las siete en punto de la mañana.*

| nosotros(as) | | descansar | |
| los estudiantes típicos | | ir a la universidad | |
| el (la) profesor(a) | | tener la clase de español | |
| un(a) estudiante de la clase | + | regresar a casa | + ... |
| nuestros amigos | | ir a la biblioteca | |
| | | comer | |
| | | hablar por teléfono | |
| | | cocinar | |

## ▣ Integración

**3-20 Mis compañeros de clase y yo**

**Paso 1:** Toma unos minutos para completar la primera columna de la tabla que sigue con cinco actividades cotidianas *(daily)* diferentes. Puedes usar verbos en el infinitivo. Luego, escribe la hora a la que generalmente haces *(you do)* esa actividad en la segunda columna.

| Actividades | Yo | Nombre: _____ | Nombre: _____ |
|---|---|---|---|
| | | | |
| | | | |
| | | | |
| | | | |

**Paso 2:** Ahora, entrevista a dos compañeros de clase para saber a qué hora generalmente hacen esas actividades. Tomen notas.

MODELO  E1: *Laura, ¿a qué hora estudias para la clase de español?*
E2: *Generalmente estudio a las dos en punto de la tarde.*
E1: *Y tú, Brandon, ¿a qué hora... ?*
E3: ...

**3-21 ¿Diferentes o semejantes?** De acuerdo con la información de la actividad 3-20, ¿tus compañeros de clase y tú son diferentes o semejantes? Escribe un breve informe y entrégaselo a tu profesor(a).

## IV. Perspectivas: Turismo en Puerto Rico

### ■ Antes de leer

**A. ¿Qué sabes de Puerto Rico?** La lectura siguiente es sobre Puerto Rico. Escribe una lista de palabras que asocias con esta isla.

**B. Expectativas** Ahora, lee el artículo. ¿Cuáles de las palabras de tu lista aparecen en la lectura?

### ■ A leer

#### Turismo en Puerto Rico

Si lo que busca es descansar... esta isla es pura tranquilidad... Si lo que desea es acción... las noches no duermen en esta isla de música y color. Puerto Rico le ofrece todo un continente de variedad del que nunca se cansará y que querrá visitar una y otra vez. Si lo que busca es hoteles, los hay de todos los precios y para todos los gustos... cerca de la playa... con hermosas vistas y fascinantes posibilidades... o arriba en la montaña o cerca de los **campos**... con diferentes estilos y entretenimientos diversos... o si desea, rodeados de campos de golf, canchas de tenis, caminos para **pasear a caballo** o simplemente... espacios amplios donde olvidar todo... Las zonas turísticas del Viejo San Juan, Condado e Isla Verde le ofrecen toda una serie de hoteles, donde encuentra desde el mejor servicio hasta las mejores tiendas con excelentes precios... Por la noche, los casinos están **dispuestos** para que Ud. pruebe su suerte... los restaurantes están listos para sorprender el gusto más exigente... y las mejores orquestas y artistas están preparados para hacerle pasar una noche **inolvidable**...

Si desea, puede escaparse en excursiones que lo lleven a visitar el Yunque, el único **bosque tropical** bajo el cuidado del Servicio Nacional de Parques de los Estados Unidos... o las **cuevas** de Camuy, extraordinarias cavernas naturales con formas caprichosas que tomaron cientos de años en formarse... o visitar una vieja hacienda de café... o de **caña**... y si desea, puede pasar la noche en una casa hacienda del **siglo** pasado... o puede pasear de noche en una de nuestras bahías **fosforescentes**, donde la luna y la naturaleza le juegan una **broma** curiosa a su imaginación... o puede visitar el futuro... en el radio-observatorio de Arecibo, el más grande del mundo... Si lo que quiere es ver algo substancialmente distinto... pruebe las villas al este de la isla... o los hoteles espectaculares que incluyen hasta una isla propia... Por la noche, el tiempo parece detenerse en los **adoquines** del Viejo San Juan... mientras jóvenes y adultos disfrutan de las múltiples actividades en los alrededores de la ciudad capital... Si la historia le llama la atención, una visita a las fortificaciones que dejaron los conquistadores españoles lo hará comprender por qué San Juan es la capital más antigua bajo la bandera estrellada.

*fields*

*ride horseback*

*ready*

*unforgettable*

*rain forest*
*caves*

*sugar cane*
*century*
*fluorescent / joke*

*cobblestones*

## ■ ¿Entendiste bien?

**C. Temas** Indica si se mencionan los siguientes aspectos de la vida en Puerto Rico.

_x_ el descanso

_x_ la historia

_x_ los deportes

____ la gente

_x_ las montañas

____ la política

_x_ la comida

_x_ la diversión

_x_ las compras

_x_ las playas

**D. Aspectos lingüísticos** Identifica en el texto los verbos de acción y completa el cuadro.

**Extensión D:** You may extend this activity by asking students to create new sentences about a tropical vacation by using those verbs.

| Verbos *-ar* | Verbos *-er* | Verbos *-ir* |
|---|---|---|
| descansar, visitar, pasear, probar, escapar, disfrutar | ver, recorrer | dormir |

**E. Para conversar en grupos** ¿Qué aspecto de la isla les parece más interesante? Expliquen por qué.

**F. Actividad de extensión** Imagínense que trabajan para la corporación de turismo de su región. Preparen un artículo semejante al artículo «Turismo en Puerto Rico» de la página 111 acerca de su ciudad, su región o su estado.

# De compras

## I. Vocabulario: Las compras y las formas de pago

Transparencies I-1: La ropa;
I-10 Comprar un regalo

| | |
|---|---|
| DEPENDIENTE: | ¿En qué puedo servirle, señor? |
| CLIENTE: | Busco un libro de García Márquez que se titula *Crónica de un secuestro*. |
| DEPENDIENTE: | Sí, señor, tenemos ese libro. Lo puede encontrar en la sección de autores colombianos. |
| CLIENTE: | De acuerdo, muchas gracias. |

**Más tarde...**

| | |
|---|---|
| DEPENDIENTE: | El siguiente, por favor... Son 20 dólares, señor. |
| CLIENTE: | ¿Aceptan tarjetas de crédito? |
| DEPENDIENTE: | Sí, todas, excepto American Express. |
| CLIENTE: | Aquí tiene mi tarjeta. Muchas gracias. |
| DEPENDIENTE: | De nada. Vuelva pronto. |

la tarjeta de crédito

el cheque

el efectivo

el cambio

## ■ Asimilación

**3-22 ¿El cliente o el dependiente?** Indica quién dice cada frase.

1. De nada. dependiente
2. ¿Aceptan tarjetas de crédito? cliente
3. Busco un libro. cliente
4. ¿En qué puedo servirle, señor? dependiente
5. Son 20 dólares. dependiente

CD1–28

**Script 3-23:** Hoy en día uso mi tarjeta de crédito para casi todo: La uso cuando voy de compras al centro comercial, cuando salgo a cenar con amigos, cuando salgo de vacaciones… aún cuando voy de compras al supermercado. En realidad, es una forma de pago muy cómoda. Claro que hay ocasiones en que prefiero…

**Sugerencia:** You may personalize the passage in the audio script.

**3-23 ¿Cómo prefieres pagar?** Escucha la descripción de cómo paga usualmente sus cuentas esta persona. Selecciona la opción (o las opciones) que corresponda(n).

|  | Lleva efectivo | Usa una tarjeta de crédito | Paga con cheque |
|---|---|---|---|
| cuando *(when)* va de compras al supermercado |  | X |  |
| cuando va de compras al centro comercial |  | X |  |
| cuando sale a almorzar |  |  |  |
| cuando sale a cenar con amigos |  | X |  |
| cuando sale de vacaciones |  | X |  |
| cuando paga los servicios públicos (agua, electricidad, teléfono) |  |  |  |

## ■ Aplicaciones

**Answers 3-24:** *Answers may vary slightly.*

**3-24 De compras** Ordenen la siguiente conversación.

- _4_ Azul o negro, por favor.
- _1_ Buenos días, ¿en qué puedo servirle?
- _7_ No, señor. Solamente aceptamos pagos en efectivo.
- _5_ Aquí tiene. Son 18 dólares.
- _3_ ¿Qué color prefiere?
- _6_ ¿Aceptan tarjetas de crédito?
- _2_ Busco una camiseta.
- _8_ Bueno, entonces tengo que pasar por un cajero automático primero.

**3-25 Normalmente...** Indica la forma de pago más común de los siguientes artículos. Compara tus respuestas con las de otros compañeros.

1. el alquiler de un apartamento
2. un boleto de avión
3. una camiseta (*T-shirt*)
4. chicle (*chewing gum*)
5. tus libros
6. el almuerzo
7. el estacionamiento
8. un taxi
9. tu cuenta de teléfono
10. tu matrícula (*tuition*)

**3-26 Necesito enviar un fax** Escojan la oración más apropiada para completar el diálogo.

1. DEPENDIENTE: __c__
   a. ¿Qué desea comer esta noche?
   b. ¿Cuántos quiere?
   c. ¿En qué puedo servirle?

2. DEPENDIENTE: __c__
   a. ¿Cuántas personas?
   b. ¿Qué color prefiere?
   c. ¿Cuál es el número?

   TÚ: Es el 212-555-1234.

3. DEPENDIENTE: __b__
   a. Aquí tiene.
   b. ¿Algo más?
   c. Éste es el número.

   TÚ: No, gracias. Nada más.

4. TÚ: Quiero este cuaderno. ¿Cuánto es?
   DEPENDIENTE: __a__
   a. Son 3 dólares.
   b. Necesita otra talla.
   c. Sí, de nada.

5. TÚ: ¿Aceptan tarjetas de crédito?
   DEPENDIENTE: __a__
   a. No, sólo efectivo.
   b. Vuelva pronto.
   c. Hasta mañana.

6. TÚ: Muy bien. Aquí tiene.
   DEPENDIENTE: __a__
   a. Gracias y vuelva pronto.
   b. Está al fondo a la derecha.
   c. Sí, voy a llamar un taxi.

**Sugerencia:** Upon completion of the task, encourage students to practice reading the dialogue out loud.

## Integración

**3-27 De compras** Representa la siguiente situación con un(a) compañero(a).

| Turista | Dependiente |
|---|---|
| During your trip to Puerto Rico you discovered a great salsa group and you want to buy one of their CDs. Make sure to a) tell the clerk what you are looking for; b) indicate the type of music you want; c) ask any pertinent questions (price, accepted forms of payment, etc.); and d) pay for your CD. | You are the clerk in a store in San Juan. A tourist wants to make a purchase. Wait on him/her appropriately. Make sure to a) greet your client; b) inquire about his/her needs; c) tell him/her what section (type of music) to look for; d) answer any questions he/she may have; and e) ring up the purchase. |

**Sugerencia 3-27:** Suggest other situations to your students for additional role-play practice (shopping for other products, having different reasons for wanting a refund, switching roles, etc.).

**3-28 Devoluciones** *(Refunds)* Representa la siguiente situación con un(a) compañero(a).

| Turista | Dependiente |
|---|---|
| Your CD does not have the songs you wanted. Ask for a refund. You may want to use some of the following expressions in this conversation: **Quiero otro** *(I want another one)*, **Me gustaría cambiarlo** *(I would like to exchange it)*, and **Quiero mi dinero** *(I want my money back)*. | This customer has changed his/her mind and wants a refund. Explain that you usually do not accept exchanges or returns. You may want to use some of the following expressions in this conversation: **Imposible** *(Impossible)*, **No puedo** *(I can't)*, **Lo siento** *(I'm sorry)*, **No me está permitido** *(I'm not allowed)*, and **¿Tiene el recibo?** *(Do you have your receipt?)*. |

### EN TU COMUNIDAD

Interview a local Spanish-speaking store owner to find out: 1) if his/her business has a significant immigrant clientele (and if so, from what countries or continents); 2) if he/she can speak a foreign language; and 3) if he/she thinks that speaking a foreign language helps (or would help) his/her business. Then, discuss your findings in small groups and present a general conclusion.

## II. Funciones y estructuras: Talking about daily activities with irregular *yo* form verbs

Todas las mañanas, cuando **salgo** para el trabajo, le **doy** un abrazo a mi esposo.

So far you have learned how to use several irregular verbs like **ser, estar, tener,** and **ir.** Spanish also has a number of verbs that are irregular only in the **yo** form (much like **estar**). The following is a list of some of these verbs.

Your students will learn more about the difference between the verbs **conocer** and **saber** in **Capítulo 6.**

| VERB | MEANING | CONJUGATION |
|---|---|---|
| dar | to give | **doy**, das, da, damos, dais, dan |
| conocer | to know (to be acquainted or familiar with somebody or something) | **conozco**, conoces, conoce, conocemos, conocéis, conocen |
| hacer | to do, to make | **hago**, haces, hace, hacemos, hacéis, hacen |
| poner | to put | **pongo**, pones, pone, ponemos, ponéis, ponen |
| saber | to know (information or how to do something) | **sé**, sabes, sabe, sabemos, sabéis, saben |
| salir | to go out, to leave | **salgo**, sales, sale, salimos, salís, salen |
| traer | to bring | **traigo**, traes, trae, traemos, traéis, traen |

Most questions that include the verb **hacer** are answered with sentences that have a different verb.

¿Qué **haces** los domingos por la mañana?  
**Voy** a la iglesia con mis hijos.

*What do **you do** on Sunday mornings?*  
***I go** to church with my children.*

These are some common idioms with the verb **hacer.**

hacer cola/fila *to stand in line*  
hacer la comida *to cook*  
hacer compras *to shop*  
hacer ejercicio *to work out*  

hacer mandados/diligencias *to run errands*  
hacer una pregunta *to ask a question*  
hacer tareas *to do homework*  
hacer un viaje *to go on a trip*

## ■ Asimilación

**3-29 Acciones rutinarias** Lee las siguientes oraciones e indica si son ciertas (**C**) o falsas (**F**). Al terminar, compara las respuestas con las de un(a) compañero(a). ¿Son diferentes o semejantes?

_____ 1. Doy fiestas en mi casa los fines de semana.

_____ 2. Hago ejercicio por lo menos tres veces por semana.

_____ 3. Conozco bien a todos mis profesores.

_____ 4. Siempre salgo de mi casa con una tarjeta de crédito.

_____ 5. Sé hablar más de una lengua.

_____ 6. Traigo muchos libros a la universidad.

_____ 7. Cuando llego a casa, pongo mis libros sobre el escritorio.

_____ 8. Hago por lo menos un viaje todos los años.

D1-29 **3-30 De compras** Escucha la rutina de compras de Alisa y escoge las oraciones correctas.

__X__ Conoce bien las tiendas del centro comercial.

_____ Lleva _(Takes)_ cheques para hacer sus compras.

_____ Sale de compras los viernes por la tarde.

__X__ Sabe que puede encontrar buenas ofertas _(sales)_.

__X__ Les da regalos a sus padres.

_____ Su madre hace la comida.

_____ No va a las tiendas del centro.

__X__ Sale de su casa muy temprano.

**Script 3-30:** Siempre salgo de compras los sábados por la mañana. Llevo una tarjeta de crédito y dinero en efectivo para estar bien preparada. Normalmente salgo muy temprano, compro un té en el café de la esquina y tomo el autobús hasta el centro comercial. Allí hago algunas compras. Conozco muy bien todas las tiendas y sé que siempre puedo encontrar buenas ofertas. Luego como cualquier cosa y tomo el autobús para ir a las tiendas del centro. Por la tarde voy a casa de mis padres y les doy algunos regalos. Después voy a casa y hago la comida.

## ■ Aplicaciones

**3-31 Causa y consecuencia** Para cada situación, escojan una consecuencia lógica de la lista. Cambien los verbos a la forma **yo**.

MODELO   Quiero estar en buena condición física. → _Hago ejercicio regularmente._

OPCIONES:   traer una fruta de casa    dar dinero a la Cruz _(Cross)_ Roja
poner todo en su lugar    saber que debo estudiar todos los días
hacer muchas preguntas    salir con mis amigos

1. No me gusta estar solo en casa. →   Salgo con mis amigos.

2. Soy una persona muy organizada. →   Pongo todo en su lugar.

3. No quiero gastar dinero para comer. →   Traigo una fruta de casa.

4. Me gusta ayudar a otras personas. →   Doy dinero a la Cruz Roja.

5. Necesito sacar buenas notas este semestre. →   Sé que debo estudiar todos los días.

6. Me gusta participar en las clases. →   Hago muchas preguntas.

**3-32 ¡Adivina, adivinador!** Túrnense para darse _(give each other)_ claves _(clues)_ relacionadas con las expresiones con el verbo **hacer**.

MODELO   E1: _Los sábados, hacer compras, ir al banco, ir a la tintorería._
E2: _Hacer mandados o diligencias._
E1: _¡Sí!_

**3-33 Firma aquí** *(Sign here)*, **por favor** Usa las siguientes frases para hacerles preguntas a tus compañeros de clase. Si alguien responde negativamente, di *(say)* **Gracias** y pregúntale a otra persona. Si alguien responde afirmativamente, di **Firma aquí, por favor.** Debes obtener una firma para cada frase. Cuando termines, prepara un informe para la clase.

MODELO    salir todos los viernes por la noche
E1: *¿Sales todos los viernes por la noche?*
E2: *No, no salgo los viernes.*
E1: *Gracias.*
o
E2: *Sí, salgo todos los viernes por la noche.*
E1: *Firma aquí, por favor.*

**Firma**

1. conocer a alguien de España _____
2. dar regalos *(gifts)* a tus amigos _____
3. hacer tareas en la biblioteca _____
4. saber cuál es la capital de
   Puerto Rico _____
5. traer lápices a clase _____
6. poner los libros en una mochila _____

### ■ Integración

**3-34 La Oficina de Asuntos Estudiantiles** *(Student Affairs)* Representa la siguiente situación con un(a) compañero(a). Al terminar, cambien de papel *(exchange roles)*.

Here are some questions the Office of Student Affairs employee may ask:
**¿Qué haces después de clase? Regularmente, ¿haces tareas? ¿Traes una computadora portátil a la universidad? ¿Conoces a tu consejero** *(advisor)***? ¿Pones la radio para estudiar? ¿Con quién sales?** etc.

| **Empleado(a) de la Oficina de Asuntos Estudiantiles** | **Estudiante** |
|---|---|
| You work for the Office of Student Affairs of your university and are conducting an informal survey about some of the things students do, bring to school, and know. You also want to know what they do when they go out. Be prepared to ask as many follow-up questions as you can. | An employee of the Office of Student Affairs of your university is calling you as part of a survey. He/She wants general information about what you do, bring to school and know, as well as information about what you do when you go out. Provide as many details as possible. |

**3-35 Cuestionario** El empleado de la Oficina de Asuntos Estudiantiles de la actividad 3-34 te ha pedido que hagas *(has asked you to create)* un cuestionario de veinte preguntas para dárselo a los estudiantes de tu universidad. Este funcionario *(official)* desea obtener más información sobre las acciones rutinarias de los estudiantes. ¡Sé creativo(a) *(Be creative)* y original! Usa los verbos en la forma **yo** e incluye todos los verbos que aprendiste en esta sección. Al terminar, dale el cuestionario a un(a) compañero(a) para que lo conteste indicando **sí** o **no**.

## III. Funciones y estructuras: Adverbs of frequency

**Nunca** llego a la oficina a las siete de la mañana.

**A menudo** almuerzo con clientes.

**Siempre** tengo que escribir informes hasta después de las ocho de la noche.

In this section you will review some adverbs of frequency you already know and will learn some new ones. Here is a complete list.

| nunca | casi nunca | a veces | a menudo | normalmente | casi siempre | siempre |

| | |
|---|---|
| nunca / jamás | *never* |
| casi nunca / rara vez | *hardly ever, rarely* |
| a veces / de vez en cuando | *sometimes* |
| a menudo / con frecuencia | *often, frequently* |
| normalmente / usualmente / por lo general | *usually* |
| casi siempre | *almost always* |
| siempre | *always* |

### ■ Asimilación

**3-36 ¿Con qué frecuencia…?** Indica con qué frecuencia haces las siguientes cosas. Al terminar, compara tus respuestas con las de un(a) compañero(a). ¿Qué cosas tienen en común?

| ACTIVIDAD | jamás | rara vez | de vez en cuando | usualmente | casi siempre | siempre |
|---|---|---|---|---|---|---|
| Hago la comida. | | | | | | |
| Pago con cheque. | | | | | | |
| Leo el correo electrónico. | | | | | | |
| Voy a un museo. | | | | | | |
| Trabajo los fines de semana. | | | | | | |
| Hablo español en clase. | | | | | | |
| Salgo a un bar. | | | | | | |
| No tengo que hacer tareas. | | | | | | |

CD1-30

**3-37 Los cumpleaños de Mauricio** Mauricio va a decir cómo pasa el día de su cumpleaños. Escucha su descripción y luego determina si las siguientes oraciones son ciertas (**C**) o falsas (**F**).

_C_ 1. La esposa de Mauricio rara vez le prepara desayuno.

_F_ 2. Sus hijos nunca le cantan «Feliz cumpleaños».

_C_ 3. Mauricio a veces va a un parque con su familia.

_F_ 4. Sus padres siempre lo visitan.

_F_ 5. De vez en cuando, él sale con sus amigos por la noche.

_C_ 6. Los cumpleaños de Mauricio nunca son aburridos.

## ■ Aplicaciones

**3-38 Situaciones diversas** Completen las siguientes oraciones con un adverbio de frecuencia lógico.

1. _____ compramos una Coca-Cola con tarjeta de crédito.

2. Los profesores _____ tienen horas de oficina.

3. La gente (*people*)_____ come pasta en un restaurante italiano.

4. Los buenos amigos _____ hablan por teléfono por más de media hora.

5. Los niños _____ comen en la sala mientras miran la televisión.

6. Los periodistas _____ son personas introvertidas.

7. En los supermercados _____ hay mucha gente.

8. Los estudiantes _____ vienen preparados a clase.

**3-39 Los famosos** Formen oraciones sobre las siguientes personas famosas. Escojan un adverbio de la segunda columna y completen las oraciones con actividades diferentes.

MODELO      Regis Philbin          nunca
            *Regis Philbin nunca usa ropa de The Gap.*

Las gemelas Olson

Tiger Woods

La familia Simpson

Julia Roberts          +

El presidente

…

nunca

casi nunca

de vez en cuando

con frecuencia          +      …

usualmente

casi siempre

siempre

**3-40 Preguntas para el (la) profesor(a)** Escriban por lo menos seis preguntas para su profesor(a) sobre la frecuencia con que él/ella hace ciertas actividades.

> MODELO *¿Usted enseña clases de noche normalmente?*

## ■ Integración

### 3-41 El (La) estudiante ejemplar

**Paso 1:** Primero, piensen en las características de un(a) estudiante ejemplar. ¿Qué cosas hace siempre o usualmente? ¿Y qué cosas no hace nunca? Luego, en grupos de tres o cuatro estudiantes, háganse preguntas para determinar quién es el (la) estudiante ejemplar del grupo. Tomen notas.

**Paso 2:** Compartan su opinión con el resto de la clase. ¿Quién es el (la) estudiante ejemplar? ¿Por qué?

### 3-42 ¿Y el (la) profesor(a) ejemplar? ¡Ahora tienes la oportunidad de describir las características de un(a) profesor(a) ejemplar! Explica qué cosas hace siempre, casi siempre, por lo general, a menudo y de vez en cuando. También, explica qué cosas no hace nunca o casi nunca. Al terminar, comparte lo que escribiste con un(a) compañero(a) para que te dé su opinión.

You may ask your professor about the following actions: **manejar a la universidad, beber café por la mañana, asistir a conciertos de rock, cortar el césped, ser diligente, estar cansado(a), tener que corregir algún trabajo, gustarle sus clases, ir al laboratorio de lenguas.**

These are some of the questions you may ask: **¿Con frecuencia estudias mucho antes de un examen? ¿De vez en cuando hablas con los profesores después de clase? ¿Siempre haces muchas preguntas? ¿Casi siempre llegas temprano a tus clases?**

# IV. Vídeo: El día de la primera excursión en Puerto Rico

## ■ Preparación

**A. ¿Qué hacen los compañeros hoy?** Antes de ver el vídeo, emparejen las horas con las actividades de los compañeros.

___3___ A las ocho y treinta y cinco de la mañana.

___1___ A las nueve en punto de la mañana.

___5___ A la una en punto de la tarde.

___4___ A las cuatro en punto de la tarde.

___2___ A las cinco en punto de la tarde.

1. Los compañeros tienen que salir de la casa.
2. Todos los compañeros tienen que volver a La Plaza de la Rogativa para luego ir todos juntos a casa.
3. Los compañeros hacen cola para usar el baño.
4. Sofía y Javier tienen que regresar al centro.
5. Como los compañeros no quieren hacer las mismas cosas, deciden separarse.

**COMPREHENSION STRATEGY**

**Listening for Details** As you watch the video and do the following listening comprehension activities, keep in mind that you are listening for recognition of specific pieces of information about what the roommates do during their first full day together in Puerto Rico.

## ■ ¿Entendiste bien?

**B. Un día lleno de actividades** Mientras miras el vídeo, comprueba tus respuestas para la actividad A. Luego, indica la respuesta correcta para las siguientes preguntas.

1. ¿Cuánto tiempo lleva Valeria en el baño?
   a. unos quince minutos
   b. una media hora *(marcada)*
   c. una hora

2. ¿Qué compañero(a) dice que le gusta levantarse temprano por la mañana, tomar un café y luego tomar una ducha?
   a. Javier
   b. Alejandra
   c. Sofía *(marcada)*

3. ¿Adónde van Sofía y Javier?
   a. de compras a tiendas
   b. a un mercado
   c. al Castillo de San Felipe del Morro *(marcada)*

4. ¿Qué hacen Antonio y Alejandra?
   a. van al Paseo de la Princesa *(marcada)*
   b. almuerzan comida típica
   c. se pierden en las calles del Viejo San Juan

5. Completa las direcciones sobre cómo llegar a la Plaza de la Rogativa que le da la mujer a Valeria: «De esta ___esquina___, caminas ___tres___ cuadras. Tomas la izquierda *(left),* tres ___cuadras___ más y la tienes justo frente a ti».

**C. Su rutina diaria** Describe un día típico de los compañeros de la Hacienda Vista Alegre. Enlaza tus ideas con palabras como **primero, después, luego, finalmente,** etc., y usa expresiones de tiempo como **por la mañana** y **por la tarde.** Usa la información del vídeo y también la imaginación.

**D. Enfoque comunitario** Preparen un panfleto en español para la oficina de estudiantes internacionales de su escuela con una descripción detallada sobre la localización de los siguientes lugares:

1. de interés histórico: un monumento, una plaza, etc.
2. de interés comercial: una zona de compras, un centro comercial, una zona de negocios, etc.
3. de interés turístico: un parque, un museo, un restaurante famoso, etc.

# La comida

## I. Vocabulario: Vamos a comer

**el pan tostado**

**el cereal**

**el jugo/ el zumo de naranja**

**el panqueque**

**el café**

Desayuno

**la hamburguesa**

**las patatas/ las papas fritas**

**el emparedado/ el sándwich/ el bocadillo**

**el refresco**

**la ensalada**

**la pizza**

**la sopa**

Almuerzo/Comida

**la carne**

**el pescado**

**las legumbres/ las verduras**

**el vino**

**las papas/ las patatas**

**el agua/ el agua mineral**

**el pollo**

**la pasta**

**el arroz**

Cena

**las galletas**

**la torta**

**el helado**

**el flan**

Postres

Transparencies B-1:   CD1–31
Bebidas calientes y frías;
B-2: El desayuno y la merienda;
B-3: Tapas (1); B-4: Tapas (2);
B-5: Comida mexicana; I-7: En el
mercado; I-8: En el supermercado,
N-1: Menú: Restaurante La Barraca;
N-2: Los cubiertos; N-3: En un restau-
rante; N-5: La guía del ocio

**Sugerencia:** You may play the text CD
at this time. After playing the CD a
couple of times, you may want to
have students practice reading the
dialogue out loud in groups of three.

| | |
|---|---|
| RECEPCIONISTA: | Buenas noches, ¿en qué puedo servirle? |
| CLIENTE: | Tengo una reservación a nombre de José Luis García. |
| RECEPCIONISTA: | Sí, señor. Sígame, por favor. |

**Más tarde...**

| | |
|---|---|
| MESERO: | ¿Desea ordenar algo de tomar? |
| CLIENTE: | Sí. Tráigame una botella de vino tinto de la casa, por favor. |
| MESERO: | Con mucho gusto. |
| MESERO: | ¿Está listo para pedir? |
| CLIENTE: | Sí. De entrada, una sopa de ajo. |
| MESERO: | ¿Y de plato principal? |
| CLIENTE: | Un filete de ternera con patatas. |

**Más tarde...**

MESERO:   ¿Desea algún postre? ¿O quizás un café?

CLIENTE:   No, gracias. La cuenta, por favor.

MESERO:   Aquí tiene, señor.

CLIENTE:   Muchas gracias.

la lechuga  el tomate  la banana/el plátano

la manzana

la cebolla  el ajo

la uva  la naranja

Verduras  Frutas

el bistec  la langosta

el tocino

la chuleta (de cerdo)  los camarones/ las gambas

el filete de salmón

la salchicha  el cangrejo

Carnes  Pescado y mariscos

## Vocabulario práctico

**Condimentos (Seasonings)**

el aceite *oil*
el aderezo *dressing*
el azúcar *sugar*
la mayonesa *mayonnaise*
la miel *honey*
la mostaza *mustard*
la pimienta *pepper*
la sal *salt*
la salsa de tomate *catsup*
el vinagre *vinegar*

**Platos y cubiertos (China and silverware)**

la copa *wine glass*
la cuchara *spoon*
la cucharita *teaspoon*
el cuchillo *knife*
el mantel *tablecloth*
el plato *plate (dish)*
la servilleta *napkin*
la taza *cup*
el tenedor *fork*
el vaso *glass*

**En el restaurante**

el aperitivo *before-dinner drink*
la carta *menu*
la cuenta *check*
la entrada / el entremés *appetizer*
el plato principal *entrée, main course*
la propina *tip*
la sección de no fumar *nonsmoking section*

■ **Asimilación**

**3-43 ¿Cuál no corresponde?** Identifiquen el alimento *(food item)* que no pertenece *(belongs)* al grupo. Expliquen por qué.

1. el café, el vino, (el ajo)
2. el bistec, el tocino, (el café)
3. la uva, (el cereal,) la manzana
4. las galletas, las tortas, (las carnes)
5. las gambas, la langosta, (la cebolla)
6. la sal, el aderezo, (el agua mineral)
7. el tenedor, (el azúcar,) el cuchillo
8. (la servilleta,) la cuenta, la propina

CD1-32

**3-44 ¿Qué va a comer?** Escucha la siguiente conversación e indica los alimentos que pide el cliente.

**Script 3-44:**
Mesero: ¿Desea ordenar?
Cliente: Sí. Por favor, tráigame una ensalada mixta y una sopa minestrone.
Mesero: ¿Algo para tomar?
Cliente: Un agua mineral sin gas.
Mesero: Con gusto.
----
Mesero: ¿Quiere algo de postre, un flan, un helado?
Cliente: No, gracias.

__x__ un agua mineral     ____ una naranja

____ un bocadillo     ____ unas legumbres

____ pollo     ____ un helado

____ un jugo     ____ un café

__x__ una ensalada     ____ pescado

__x__ una sopa

■ **Aplicaciones**

CD1-33

**3-45 En la cafetería** Escuchen y practiquen la siguiente conversación entre dos amigos.

**Sugerencia 3-45:** As you play the audio, encourage your students to replace the underlined information in the dialogue with choices that reflect their personal preferences.

**Script 3-45:**
A: ¿Qué vas a comer?
B: Yo quisiera un emparedado, ¿y tú?
A: ¿Qué me sugieres?
B: Pues, aquí venden unas ensaladas deliciosas.
A: Bueno, entonces, para mí, una ensalada.
B: ¿Y qué vas a tomar?
A: Un refresco.
B: Y yo voy a tomar un café.

A: ¿Qué vas a comer?

B: Yo quisiera <u>un emparedado</u>, ¿y tú? (**otras opciones:** ensalada, sopa, pizza)

A: ¿Qué me sugieres?

B: Pues aquí venden <u>unas ensaladas</u> deliciosas. (**otras opciones:** pastas, patatas fritas, hamburguesas)

A: Bueno, entonces, para mí, <u>una ensalada</u>.

B: ¿Y qué vas a tomar?

A: <u>Un refresco</u>. (**otras opciones:** café, agua mineral, jugo de naranja)

B: Y yo voy a tomar <u>un café</u>. (**otras opciones:** leche, limonada, té)

**3-46 ¿Qué falta?** Completa las siguientes comidas de una manera lógica. Al terminar, compara tus respuestas con las de un(a) compañero(a). ¿En qué están de acuerdo?

OPCIONES: cereal  café  pan tostado  hamburguesa  ensalada sopa  agua mineral  legumbres  helado  huevos jugo de naranja

1. ensalada, pasta y ____
2. café, jugo de naranja y ____
3. patatas, carne y ____
4. pan tostado, café y ____
5. pollo, arroz y ____

**3-47 Costumbres** Entrevista a tu compañero(a) para saber más acerca de sus hábitos alimenticios *(eating habits)*. Luego, preséntale un resumen de sus respuestas al resto de la clase.

You may use questions like:
**1. ¿Desayunas? ¿Normalmente dónde desayunas? ¿A qué hora? ¿Qué (no) comes? (¿Por qué sí o por qué no?)**
**2. ¿Almuerzas? ¿Usualmente dónde almuerzas? ¿A qué hora? ¿Qué (no) comes? (¿Por qué sí o por qué no?)**
**3. ¿Cenas? ¿Por lo general dónde cenas? ¿A qué hora? ¿Qué (no) comes? (¿Por qué sí o por qué no?)**

## ■ Integración

**3-48 En el restaurante** Representa la siguiente situación con un(a) compañero(a).

| **Cliente(a) vegetariano(a)** | **Mesero(a)** |
|---|---|
| Imagine that you are in a restaurant and want to order a vegetarian meal. (Refer to the list of foods on pages 124 and 125.) Make sure to: a) greet the waiter; b) tell him/her about your diet restrictions; c) ask for recommendations **(¿Qué me recomienda?)**; d) place your order; and e) ask for the check. | Help this vegetarian client order his/her meal. Make sure to: a) greet the client; b) offer him/her a drink before ordering; c) suggest some vegetarian alternatives **(Le recomiendo...)**; d) offer him/her dessert; and e) give him/her the check. |

You may want to extend this activity to include clients with other dietary needs or restrictions: **un jugador de fútbol, una modelo, una persona diabética, etc.**

**3-49 Nutricionistas** Imagínense que tienen invitados en su casa este fin de semana. Preparen el menú de cada día *(each day)*. **¡OJO!** ¡No olviden planear una dieta bien balanceada!

## II. Funciones y estructuras: Talking about daily activities with *e→i* stem-changing verbs

FERNANDA: Darío, este restaurante es muy bonito. ¿Qué tipo de comida **sirven** aquí?

DARÍO: **Sirven** platos caribeños. Su especialidad es la cocina puertorriqueña.

FERNANDA: ¿Y qué **pides** cuando vienes?

DARÍO: Generalmente **pido** algún plato con arroz y frijoles.

FERNANDA: ¡Mmm! ¡Me suena bien! *(It sounds good to me!)*

You have already learned how to use verbs that undergo stem changes in their conjugation, like the verb **tener**. You will now learn about a group of verbs whose stem vowel **e** changes to **i** in the present tense. One of these verbs is **pedir** *(to order* [in a restaurant], *to ask for, to request).*

| | |
|---|---|
| yo p**i**do | nosotros(as) **pedimos** |
| tú p**i**des | vosotros(as) **pedís** |
| él/ella/usted p**i**de | ellos(as)/ustedes p**i**den |

✳ Notice that the stem vowel **e** does not change to **i** in the **nosotros(as)** and **vosotros(as)** forms.

The **yo** form of **seguir** is **sigo** (similar to **hago**, **salgo**, **traigo**, etc.).

From now on, when you learn new **e→i** stem-changing verbs, they will have the letter **i** in parentheses next to the infinitive: **servir (i).**

The following is a list of other **e→i** stem-changing verbs.

| | |
|---|---|
| competir *to compete* | seguir *to continue, to follow* |
| conseguir *to get, to find* | servir *to serve* |
| repetir *to repeat, to have seconds* | vestir *to dress, to wear* |

## ■ Asimilación

**3-50 ¿Siempre, a veces o nunca?** Indica si haces las siguientes actividades **siempre**, **a veces** o **nunca**. Cuando termines, compara tus respuestas con las de un(a) compañero(a). ¿Son semejantes o diferentes?

_____ 1. Aunque no tengo hambre, sigo comiendo.

_____ 2. Me visto con ropa elegante para ir a los restaurantes.

_____ 3. Pido el mismo plato en mi restaurante favorito.

_____ 4. Compito con mis amigos para ver quién come más.

_____ 5. Consigo frutas frescas en mi supermercado favorito.

_____ 6. Si me gusta mucho la comida, repito.

_____ 7. Sirvo frutas y verduras en mis fiestas.

_____ 8. Sigo las instrucciones de las recetas *(recipes)* cuando cocino.

D1–34 **3-51 Tomás, Blanca y Herminio** Escucha las descripciones que hacen Tomás, Blanca y Herminio de sus restaurantes favoritos. Luego, completa la tabla que sigue con la información correcta. **¡OJO!** Escribe una **X** si no se provee la información.

|  | **Tomás** | **Blanca** | **Herminio** |
|---|---|---|---|
| Restaurante favorito | Del Mar | Planeta Verde | La Parrillada |
| ¿Qué sirven? | mariscos y pescados | comida vegetariana | carnes |
| ¿Qué piden? | langosta y flan | ensalada rusa y sopa de tomate | bistec con papa asada |
| ¿Y de postre? | flan | X | torta |

## ■ Aplicaciones

### 3-52 Categorías

**Paso 1:** Escribe por lo menos dos palabras o frases que se relacionen con cada uno de los verbos de la tabla.

| **repetir** | **servir** | **conseguir** |
|---|---|---|
| *una materia* | *comida internacional* | *un buen restaurante* |
| **competir** | **vestir** | **pedir** |
| *partido de fútbol* | *informal* | *la cuenta* |

**Paso 2:** Ahora, escribe por lo menos cuatro oraciones sobre ti mismo(a) *(yourself)* usando cuatro de estos verbos y frases de la tabla.

MODELO     *Generalmente no voy a restaurantes que sirven comida internacional.*

Script 3-51:
Tomás: ¿Adónde vamos a comer?
Blanca: No sé, Tomás. ¿Cuál es tu restaurante favorito?
Tomás: Me gusta mucho Del Mar, que está en la avenida Ponce de León. El menú es variado y sirven buenos mariscos y pescados muy frescos. Mi plato favorito es la langosta; siempre pido langosta. De postre pido flan; es delicioso. ¿Qué opinas, Blanca?
Blanca: Preferiría ir a mi restaurante favorito, Planeta Verde, que está en la avenida Muñoz Rivera. Sirven comida vegetariana y hacen muy buenas ensaladas. Cuando voy, pido una ensalada rusa y una sopa de tomate que vale la pena. ¿Qué te parece, Herminio?
Herminio: Mmm… ¿Por qué no vamos a mi restaurante favorito, La Parrillada? Sirven buenísimas carnes. Les va a gustar. Miren, yo siempre pido bistec con papa asada. Y tienen tortas excelentes: son para chuparse los dedos. ¿Entonces?
Blanca: ¡Creo que por esta indecisión vamos a terminar en el mismo lugar de siempre!

**3-53 En los restaurantes de mi ciudad** Comenten los platos que sirven y que ustedes piden en algunos de los restaurantes de su ciudad.

MODELO    E1: *¿Qué sirven en China Garden?*
E2: *En China Garden sirven comida china, como* (like) *arroz, carnes, pollo y fideos* (noodles).
E1: *¿Qué pides en China Garden?*
E2: *Pido sopa de huevo y pollo con verduras.*

**3-54 Entrevista**

**Paso 1:** Escoge la alternativa que, en tu opinión, mejor complete cada oración. Puedes incluir una alternativa diferente.

1. Nunca pido (ensalada/pasta/carne/_____) en mi restaurante favorito.
2. En mis fiestas, casi siempre sirvo (papas y salsa/galletas/queso/_____).
3. Casi siempre visto ropa (ligera/formal/festiva/_____) para ir a un restaurante.
4. La comida del día en la que posiblemente repito es (el desayuno/el almuerzo/la cena/_____).
5. A veces compito con (mi hermano[a]/mi primo[a]/mi amigo[a]/_____).
6. Por lo general, consigo buenos precios en (el supermercado/la tienda de ropa/la librería de la universidad/_____).

**Paso 2:** Convierte las oraciones del **Paso 1** en preguntas para tu compañero(a). Haz los cambios necesarios y toma notas. Cuando termines, prepara un informe para la clase.

MODELO    E1: *Marisa, ¿nunca pides ensalada en tu restaurante favorito?*
E2: *No, nunca pido ensalada.*
o   *Sí, pido ensalada, pero nunca pido postre.*

### ■ Integración

**3-55 Una cena especial** Averigua qué hacen tres de tus compañeros de clase para tener una cena especial con uno de sus seres queridos *(loved ones)*. Primero, piensa en las preguntas que tienes que hacer para obtener la siguiente información. Toma notas durante las entrevistas.

With whom they go, What restaurant they go to and why, What they serve at this restaurant, What they order and why, How they dress and why

*You may want to brainstorm the questions with the entire class before breaking into groups.*

**3-56 ¡El (La) ganador(a)** *(winner)* **es... !** Decide cuál de las descripciones de tus compañeros de clase en la actividad 3-55 te parece más original y escribe un resumen. Además, compara algunas de las cosas que hace esta persona para tener una cena especial con algunas de las cosas que tú haces.

## III. Funciones y estructuras: Talking about future plans

En Puerto Rico, **voy a visitar** las playas de Cabo Rojo. **Espero tomar** muchas fotos.

When you want to talk about actions that will take place in the immediate future, use the following Spanish structure.

**ir** + **a** + verb in the infinitive

**Voy a desayunar** con Ana.  *I am going to have breakfast with Ana.*

**Vamos a pedir** cuentas separadas.  *We are going to ask for separate checks.*

In this structure, **ir** is the auxiliary verb, while the infinitive is the main verb. The auxiliary verb is the one that agrees with the subject, not the main verb.

You can use other verbs and phrases to imply general intention, wish or desire, and obligation. They are also followed by infinitives.

| GENERAL INTENTION | WISH OR DESIRE | OBLIGATION |
|---|---|---|
| pensar *(to think)* | querer *(to want)* | tener que *(to have to)* |
| planear *(to plan)* | desear *(to wish, to desire)* | deber *(should)* |
|  | esperar *(to hope)* |  |

Your students will study verbs with stem changes in more detail in **Capítulo 4**.

Carmelo **planea abrir** un restaurante.  *Carmelo is planning to open a restaurant.*

¿**Deseas tomar** algo?  *Do you wish to drink anything?*

Ustedes **deben comer** comida más saludable.  *You should eat healthier food.*

Here is a list of time expressions you can use to talk about the future:

| | |
|---|---|
| esta tarde | *this afternoon* |
| esta noche | *tonight* |
| mañana | *tomorrow* |
| este lunes (martes/etc.) | *this Monday (Tuesday/etc.)* |
| el lunes (martes/etc.) | *on Monday (Tuesday/etc.)* |
| la próxima semana | *next week* |
| el próximo mes (año) | *next month (year)* |

### ■ Asimilación

**3-57 ¿Posible o imposible?** ¿Qué piensas que tu profesor(a) va a hacer mañana? Lee las siguientes oraciones e indica si esas acciones son probables (**P**) o improbables (**I**). Luego, compara tus respuestas con las de un(a) compañero(a). ¿Están de acuerdo?

_____ 1. Va a hacer ejercicio.

_____ 2. Tiene que trabajar todo el día.

_____ 3. Planea corregir exámenes.

_____ 4. Debe ir al médico.

_____ 5. Va a tomar una clase de yoga.

_____ 6. Debe dormir muchas horas mañana.

_____ 7. Desea ir a una discoteca.

_____ 8. Va a ir al cine.

_____ 9. Espera salir por la noche.

_____ 10. Va a hacer un viaje.

Script 3-58: 1. ¿Esperas pasar tiempo con tus amigos esta noche? 2. ¿Vas a estudiar para un examen? 3. ¿Tienes que limpiar la casa? 4. ¿Esperas ver televisión toda la noche? 5. ¿Vas a ir al teatro? 6. ¿Deseas cenar con mariscos? 7. ¿Vas a trabajar en el cuaderno de ejercicios de *Temas*? 8. ¿Debes llamar a algún pariente?

CD1-35

**3-58 Preguntas personales** Piensa en lo que vas a hacer esta noche. Luego, contesta las preguntas personales que vas a escuchar con **sí** o **no**.

1. sí / no  3. sí / no  5. sí / no  7. sí / no
2. sí / no  4. sí / no  6. sí / no  8. sí / no

### ■ Aplicaciones

**3-59 La próxima semana** ¿Qué van a hacer las siguientes personas la próxima semana? En parejas, completen las oraciones con por lo menos una actividad lógica.

MODELO  Jennifer López
*Jennifer López va a dar un concierto y va a salir a bailar.*

1. Lance Armstrong
2. muchos estudiantes <u>no</u>
3. Goldie Hawn y Kurt Russell
4. mi compañero(a) y yo <u>no</u>
5. (compañero[a] de clase)
6. Bill Gates y su esposa <u>no</u>
7. el/la rector(a) *(president)* de la universidad
8. nuestra familia y nosotros

**3-60 Reacciones** Escriban una reacción lógica para cada situación.

> MODELO   ¡Tengo mucha hambre! Yo _voy a comer_.

1. Estamos muy aburridos. No tenemos nada que hacer. Nosotros

   _____.

2. Hay elecciones este año. El presidente de los Estados Unidos

   _____.

3. Leonor planea perder peso, pero no le gustan las verduras. Ella

   _____.

4. Tú eres muy buena para las matemáticas. (Tú) _____.

5. Mis padres trabajan mucho y finalmente tienen vacaciones. Ellos

   _____.

6. Estoy muy enferma desde esta mañana. Yo _____.

7. A mi familia y a mí nos gusta el arte contemporáneo. Nosotros

   _____.

8. Froilán y tú son amantes de los deportes acuáticos. Ustedes

   _____.

**3-61 Este fin de semana**

**Paso 1:** Haz una lista de por lo menos seis actividades que deseas hacer este fin de semana.

| | | |
|---|---|---|
| 1. … | 3. … | 5. … |
| 2. … | 4. … | 6. … |

**Paso 2:** Ahora, averigua si tu compañero(a) va a hacer las mismas cosas. Al terminar, compartan la información con el resto de la clase.

> MODELO   _Este fin de semana, mi compañero y yo vamos a trabajar. Además, yo espero ir a una fiesta, pero mi compañero espera visitar a sus tíos en…_

## ■ Integración

**3-62 ¡Unas vacaciones!** Tu compañero(a) y tú ya son tan buenos(as) amigos(as) que desean ir de vacaciones juntos(as). Hagan planes y preparen un itinerario de actividades. Incluyan los siguientes temas en su conversación.

- lugar de vacaciones
- actividades
- lugares para visitar
- comidas típicas
- regalos para sus familiares
- preparativos para el viaje

You may use these connectors to help the reader create a better picture of what you want to do during this vacation: **primero** (first), **segundo** (second), **tercero** (third), **luego** (then), **después** (afterwards), **más tarde** (later), **además** (also), and **finalmente** (finally). In addition, make sure you are using the verb structure **auxiliary verb** + **a** + **infinitive** correctly.

 **3-63 El itinerario de las vacaciones** Ahora, prepara el itinerario del viaje que planeaste _(you planned)_ con tu compañero(a). Cuando termines, dale una copia a él/ella para ver si olvidaste _(you forgot)_ algún detalle importante. Finalmente, dale una copia a tu profesor(a).

## IV. Lectura: La dieta mediterránea

### ■ Antes de leer

**A. Para conversar** En grupos, contesten las siguientes preguntas.

1. ¿Cuáles son las dietas más populares en este momento?
2. ¿Cuáles son los ingredientes básicos de una de esas dietas?
3. ¿Es fácil o difícil para un estudiante universitario seguir una dieta? ¿Por qué?

**B. Vocabulario y conceptos** Empareja cada palabra con la definición correspondiente.

| | | |
|---|---|---|
| _c_ 1. dieta | a. bueno |
| _a_ 2. saludable | b. hacer menor una cantidad |
| _e_ 3. seguir | c. la comida de todos los días |
| _b_ 4. reducir | d. cantidad (su símbolo es % [por ciento]) |
| _d_ 5. porcentaje | e. adherirse, llevar hasta el fin |

### ■ A leer

## La dieta mediterránea también reduce el cáncer y la mortalidad en general

Un nuevo estudio indica que la dieta mediterránea no solamente beneficia el sistema cardiovascular, sino que también reduce el número de casos de cáncer y la mortalidad en general.

La dieta mediterránea, a base de frutas, verduras, pescado, legumbres y aceite de oliva, es en realidad la forma de alimentación tradicional de los países del sur de Europa y norte de África.

*risks* — La mayor investigación realizada hasta ahora sobre los efectos beneficiosos de esa forma de alimentación señala que esta dieta reduce en un 33 por ciento los **riesgos** de mortalidad por problemas cardiovasculares y en un 24 por ciento los de cáncer.

*Greece* — El estudio, publicado en la revista *New England Journal of Medicine,* fue realizado en **Grecia** por científicos de la Facultad de Medicina de las universidades de Atenas y Harvard (Massachusetts) en un total de 22.043 adultos sanos de entre 20 y 86 años de edad.

*underwent / exhausting interview* — Cada persona **fue sometida** a una **entrevista agotadora** para determinar sus hábitos de alimentación, y se le asignaron puntos en función de cuánto seguía la dieta mediterránea.

Este régimen alimenticio incluye también el consumo casi a diario de yogur, cereales integrales y frutos secos, así como de vino en dosis moderadas, con una reducida cantidad de carnes rojas.

Los sujetos que participaron en el estudio fueron sometidos a un **seguimiento** medio de 44 meses, durante los cuales se determinó que aquéllos **que siguieron** la dieta mediterránea presentaron una menor mortalidad por cáncer y problemas cardiovasculares.

*follow up*
*who followed*

Diversos estudios científicos **realizados** en los últimos años habían confirmado las virtudes de esta dieta en el sistema cardiovascular, pero los efectos tan favorables en la prevención del cáncer son una auténtica **novedad.**

*carried out*

*novelty/news*

«**Cuanto más se sigue la dieta mediterránea,** menor es la mortalidad por enfermedades cardiovasculares y cáncer», dice Frank Hu, profesor de nutrición de la Escuela de Salud Pública de la Universidad de Harvard, quien admite que las nuevas **ventajas** sobre el cáncer «son muy intrigantes».

*The more the Mediterranean diet is followed*

*advantages*

Un factor interesante es que los beneficios de la dieta se producen cuando esta forma de alimentación se sigue en su totalidad, sin excluir ninguno de sus elementos, y los científicos se preguntan por qué.

Hu indica que ello puede deberse a dos posibilidades: que los efectos de cada grupo alimentario **scan demasiado pequeños** como para tener un impacto considerable de forma individual o que hay efectos sinérgicos entre los componentes de la dieta.

*may be / too small*

En los hábitos de alimentación mediterráneos, aproximadamente el 40 por ciento de las calorías **procede de** grasas consideradas «saludables», como el aceite de oliva y el pescado, y el restante 50 por ciento de carbohidratos **complejos,** procedentes de cereales integrales, frutas y legumbres.

*come from*

*complex*

Otro factor muy importante es el ejercicio físico. La investigación también determinó que la realización de una hora de ejercicio intenso diario —fuera en el trabajo o por diversión— contribuye a aumentar aún más los beneficios de la dieta mediterránea, ya que el riesgo de mortalidad que presentaron los participantes **fue** un 28 por ciento menor.

*was*

## ¿Entendiste bien?

**C. Ingredientes** Indiquen cuáles de los siguientes ingredientes forman parte de la dieta mediterránea:

| | | |
|---|---|---|
| _x_ pescado | _x_ vino | ___ arroz |
| _x_ bananas | ___ carnes | _x_ tomates |
| ___ refrescos | _x_ manzanas | ___ helado |
| ___ pollo | _x_ lechuga | |
| ___ pizza | _x_ aceite de oliva | |

**D. ¿Cierto o falso?** Indiquen si las oraciones son ciertas (**C**) o falsas (**F**).

___F___ 1. El artículo presenta los resultados de investigaciones de científicos españoles.

___C___ 2. La dieta mediterránea reduce la incidencia de problemas cardiovasculares.

___F___ 3. La dieta mediterránea no reduce la incidencia de cáncer.

___C___ 4. La dieta mediterránea es efectiva solamente cuando se sigue en su totalidad.

___C___ 5. El ejercicio físico incrementa la efectividad de la dieta mediterránea.

*This comprehension task targets scanning skills specifically.*

**E. Datos y resultados** Completen las frases con la información del artículo.

1. Número total de participantes en el estudio: 22.043
2. Duración del estudio: 44 meses
3. Edad de los participantes en el estudio: entre 20 y 86 años
4. Porcentaje de reducción de problemas cardiovasculares: 33%
5. Porcentaje de reducción del cáncer: 24%
6. Porcentaje de calorías que proceden de grasas saludables en la dieta mediterránea: 40%
7. Porcentaje de calorías que proceden de carbohidratos complejos en la dieta mediterránea: 50%
8. Cantidad de ejercicio diario recomendado: una hora

**EN TU COMUNIDAD**

Prepare a brief report or share with the class information about the types of services that are available in your community to assist Spanish-speaking immigrants dealing with weight concerns.

**F. Para conversar** ¿Qué es mejor, la dieta mediterránea o la dieta de Atkins (mucha proteína y muy pocos carbohidratos)? ¿Por qué?

**G. Enfoque comunitario** ¿Dónde puedes encontrar *(can you find)* la dieta mediterránea? Prepara una lista de lugares en (o cerca de) tu universidad que ofrecen comidas de la dieta mediterránea.

|  | Lugar | Menú |
|---|---|---|
| Desayuno |  |  |
| Almuerzo |  |  |
| Cena |  |  |

## Lugares de interés / *Landmarks*

| | |
|---|---|
| el aeropuerto | *airport* |
| el banco | *bank* |
| el bar / la barra | *bar* |
| la biblioteca | *library* |
| el cajero automático | *ATM* |
| la calle | *street* |
| el centro comercial | *shopping mall* |
| el cine | *movie theater* |
| la cuadra/manzana | *city block* |
| el edificio | *building* |
| la esquina | *street corner* |
| la estación de policía | *police station* |
| la estación de (trenes/ autobús/metro) | *(train/bus/subway) station* |
| el estacionamiento/ parqueadero/ aparcamiento | *parking lot* |
| la farmacia | *pharmacy* |
| el gimnasio | *gym* |
| el hospital | *hospital* |
| el hotel | *hotel* |
| la iglesia | *church* |
| la lavandería | *laundromat* |
| la librería | *bookstore* |
| el museo | *museum* |
| la oficina de correos | *post office* |
| la oficina de turismo | *tourist office* |
| la parada de (autobús/ tren/metro) | *(bus/train/ subway) stop* |
| el parque | *park* |
| la peluquería / el salón de belleza | *barber shop, beauty parlor* |
| la plaza | *town square* |
| el restaurante | *restaurant* |
| el semáforo | *traffic light* |
| el supermercado | *supermarket* |
| la tienda / el almacén | *store* |
| la tienda de ropa | *clothing store* |
| la tintorería | *dry cleaners* |

## Formas de pago

| | |
|---|---|
| el cambio | *change* |
| el cheque | *check* |
| el efectivo | *cash* |
| la tarjeta de crédito | *credit card* |

## Expresiones para ir de compras

| | |
|---|---|
| ¿En qué puedo servirle, señor? | *How can I help you, sir?* |
| Busco... | *I am looking for . . .* |
| Aquí tiene. | *Here you are.* |
| ¿Aceptan tarjetas de crédito? | *Do you take credit cards?* |
| De nada. / A sus órdenes. / A su servicio. / Con mucho gusto. | *You are welcome.* |
| Vuelva pronto. | *Come back soon.* |

## Desayuno / *Breakfast*

| | |
|---|---|
| el café | *coffee* |
| el cereal | *cereal* |
| los huevos | *eggs* |
| revueltos | *scrambled* |
| fritos | *fried* |
| el jugo/el zumo de naranja | *orange juice* |
| la leche | *milk* |
| la mantequilla | *butter* |
| la mermelada | *marmalade, jam, jelly* |
| el pan tostado | *toast* |
| el té | *tea* |

## Almuerzo/Comida / *Lunch*

| | |
|---|---|
| el emparedado/sándwich/ bocadillo | *sandwich* |
| de jamón | *ham* |
| de atún | *tuna* |
| de queso | *cheese* |
| de pavo | *turkey* |
| la ensalada | *salad* |
| la hamburguesa | *hamburger* |
| la limonada | *lemonade* |
| las patatas/las papas fritas | *French fries* |
| la pizza | *pizza* |
| el refresco | *soda* |
| la sopa | *soup* |

## Cena — Dinner

| | |
|---|---|
| el agua mineral | *mineral water* |
| el arroz | *rice* |
| la carne | *meat* |
| las legumbres / los vegetales | *vegetables* |
| la pasta | *pasta* |
| las patatas/las papas | *potatoes* |
| el pescado | *fish* |
| el pollo | *chicken* |
| el vino | *wine* |

## Postres — Desserts

| | |
|---|---|
| las galletas | *cookies* |
| el helado | *ice cream* |
| la torta / el pastel | *cake, pie* |

## Verduras — Vegetables

| | |
|---|---|
| el ajo | *garlic* |
| las arvejas / los chícharos | *peas* |
| el brócoli | *broccoli* |
| la cebolla | *onion* |
| el champiñón | *mushroom* |
| los espárragos | *asparagus* |
| los frijoles / las judías verdes | *string beans* |
| la lechuga | *lettuce* |
| el maíz | *corn* |
| el plátano | *plantain* |
| el tomate | *tomato* |
| la zanahoria | *carrot* |

## Frutas — Fruits

| | |
|---|---|
| la banana / el plátano | *banana* |
| la fresa | *strawberry* |
| el mango | *mango* |
| la manzana | *apple* |
| el melón | *melon* |
| la naranja | *orange* |
| la pera | *pear* |
| la piña | *pineapple* |
| la sandía | *watermelon* |
| la uva | *grape* |

## Carnes — Meats

| | |
|---|---|
| el bistec | *beef steak* |
| la chuleta (de cerdo) | *(pork) chop* |
| el filete de res | *beef filet* |
| la salchicha | *sausage (hot dog)* |
| la ternera | *veal* |
| el tocino | *bacon* |

## Pescado y mariscos — Fish and seafood

| | |
|---|---|
| las almejas | *clams* |
| los camarones / las gambas | *shrimp* |
| el cangrejo | *crab* |
| el filete de salmón | *salmon filet* |
| la langosta | *lobster* |
| los mejillones | *mussels* |
| el róbalo | *bass* |
| la trucha | *trout* |

## Condimentos

| | |
|---|---|
| el aceite | *oil* |
| el aderezo | *dressing* |
| el azúcar | *sugar* |
| la mostaza | *mustard* |
| la miel | *honey* |
| la pimienta | *pepper* |
| la sal | *salt* |
| la salsa de tomate | *tomato sauce* |
| el vinagre | *vinegar* |

## Los cubiertos — Tableware

| | |
|---|---|
| la copa | *wine glass* |
| la cuchara | *spoon* |
| la cucharita | *teaspoon* |
| el cuchillo | *knife* |
| el individual | *placemat* |
| el mantel | *tablecloth* |
| el platillo | *saucer* |
| el plato | *plate (dish)* |
| la servilleta | *napkin* |
| la taza | *cup* |
| el tenedor | *fork* |
| el vaso | *glass* |

## En el restaurante

| | |
|---|---|
| el aperitivo | *before-dinner drink* |
| la carta | *menu* |
| la cuenta | *check* |
| la entrada / el entremés | *appetizer* |
| el mesero | *waiter* |
| el plato principal | *entrée (main course)* |
| la propina | *tip* |
| la sección de no fumar | *nonsmoking section* |

## Expresiones en el restaurante

| | |
|---|---|
| ¿Algo más? | *Anything else?* |
| Bienvenidos. | *Welcome.* |
| ¿Desean ordenar algo de tomar? | *Anything to drink?* |
| Están/Son como para chuparse los dedos. | *They are finger licking good.* |
| ¿Están listos para pedir? | *Are you ready to order?* |
| ¿Me podría traer... ? | *Could you bring me . . . ?* |
| Tenemos una reservación a nombre de... | *We have a reservation. The name is . . .* |

## Funciones y estructuras

# 4

## Para comenzar

Para cada foto de España, escoge la descripción que le corresponde.

- España es un país rico en historia y tradiciones. Foto 1
- Tiene industrias modernas. Foto 3
- También es famosa por sus ciudades cosmopolitas. Foto 2

# Preferencias y prioridades

## In this chapter you will learn . . .

- how to describe weather conditions
- how to talk about clothing preferences
- how to make comparisons
- how to express what is happening at the moment
- how to talk about sports and one's daily routine
- about vacation customs in Spain

|  | **TEMA 1**<br>El tiempo | **TEMA 2**<br>La ropa | **TEMA 3**<br>La diversión |
|---|---|---|---|
| Vocabulario | El estado del tiempo y las estaciones | Ropa de diario y accesorios | Los deportes |
| Funciones y estructuras | Talking about ongoing actions and events with the present progressive<br>Comparing and contrasting with comparatives and superlatives | Talking about daily activities with **e→ie** and **o→ue** stem-changing verbs<br>Talking about daily routines with reflexive verbs | Talking about daily activities with irregular present tense verbs<br>Describing people and objects with the verbs **ser** and **estar** |
| Lecturas y vídeo | Perspectivas: Las variaciones climáticas en el mundo hispano | Vídeo: Una charla sobre la ropa | Lectura: De vacaciones |

**Foto 1**  **Foto 2**  **Foto 3**

Transparency A-5: Country Profile: España

Answers A, #3: Besides 17 autonomous communities, Spain has two autonomous cities (Ceuta and Melilla).

# Enfoque

**A. ¿Qué sabes ya de España?** Antes de ver el vídeo, decide si las siguientes oraciones son ciertas **(C)** o falsas **(F)** y después compara tus respuestas con las de un(a) compañero(a).

<u> C </u> 1. España se encuentra en el suroeste de Europa, en la Península Ibérica, al oeste de Portugal.

<u> F </u> 2. La capital de España es Barcelona, una de las grandes ciudades europeas.

<u> C </u> 3. España está formada por 17 comunidades autónomas.

**B. La diversidad dentro de España** El vídeo te va a presentar con más detalle **seis** comunidades autónomas. Indica con qué comunidad autónoma se relaciona cada ciudad, lengua o característica.

**OPCIONES:** Andalucía (A)   Cataluña (C)
la Comunidad Valenciana (V)   Galicia (G)
El País Vasco (PV)   Castilla-La Mancha (CM)

<u> A </u> 1. Sevilla
<u> PV </u> 2. Vitoria
<u> CM </u> 3. un terreno llano
<u> G </u> 4. el gallego

<u> C </u> 5. un centro financiero
<u> CM </u> 6. Toledo
<u> C </u> 7. el catalán
<u> PV </u> 8. el euskera

<u> A </u> 9. el flamenco
<u> V </u> 10. un antiguo reino moro
<u> G </u> 11. Santiago de Compostela
<u> V </u> 12. el valenciano

**C. Nuestra comunidad autónoma** Ahora, divídanse en seis grupos (un grupo para cada comunidad autónoma descrita en el vídeo) y hagan las siguientes actividades:

1. Mientras ven el vídeo por segunda vez, presten atención a la información (**hablada y visual**) sobre **su** comunidad autónoma: la geografía (¿dónde se encuentra? ¿es una zona montañosa, llana, costera? etc.); la capital; ciudades importantes; idiomas (¿se habla otro idioma además del castellano, o sea, el español?) y otras características.

2. Compartan su información y escriban juntos una descripción de su comunidad autónoma para presentarla a la clase.

3. Después de escuchar las presentaciones de las seis comunidades autónomas, infórmenles a sus compañeros de grupo a qué comunidad irían *(you would go)* durante un viaje a España y explíquenles por qué.

For more info, you may want to check the **Temas** site:
**http://temas.heinle.com**

# El tiempo

## I. Vocabulario: El estado del tiempo y las estaciones

| invierno (diciembre, enero, febrero) | primavera (marzo, abril, mayo) | verano (junio, julio, agosto) | otoño (septiembre, octubre, noviembre) |
|---|---|---|---|

Nos gusta el **invierno** porque **nieva** y **hace** mucho **frío**.

Yo prefiero la **primavera** porque **llueve** y **hace fresco**.

Nos gusta el **verano** porque **hace sol** y mucho **calor**.

Bueno, a mí me gusta mucho el **otoño** porque casi siempre **está nublado** y **hace viento**.

Transparencies H-1: Las estaciones del año; H-3: El tiempo; H-4: El tiempo en España

The verb **hacer** *(to do, to make)* is used to talk about several weather conditions.

| ¿Qué tiempo **hace**? | *What is the weather like?* |
|---|---|
| **Hace** viento. | *It's windy.* |
| **Hace** (buen/mal) tiempo. | *The weather is (good/bad).* |

The words **un poco de** *(a bit, somewhat)* and **mucho** *(very, quite a bit)* can be used to indicate the degree of a given weather condition.

| Hace **mucho** frío hoy. | *It's **very** cold today.* |
|---|---|
| Hace **un poco de** viento esta mañana. | *It's **a bit** windy this morning.* |
| Llueve **mucho** en esta ciudad. | *It rains **a lot** in this city.* |

### ■ Asimilación

**4-1 En los Estados Unidos...** Completa la oración con la información más apropiada, de acuerdo con el contexto.

1. En los Estados Unidos hace calor durante los meses de __a__.
   - a. junio, julio y agosto
   - b. diciembre, enero y febrero
   - c. marzo, abril y mayo
2. Por lo general, en este país hace fresco durante los meses de __c__.
   - a. diciembre y enero
   - b. junio y julio
   - c. abril y octubre
3. Aquí siempre hace frío en __a__.
   - a. diciembre y enero
   - b. junio y julio
   - c. abril y octubre
4. Llueve mucho en __c__.
   - a. diciembre y enero
   - b. junio y julio
   - c. abril y octubre
5. Casi siempre nieva durante los meses de __a__.
   - a. diciembre y enero
   - b. junio y julio
   - c. abril y octubre

**4-2 Informe meteorológico** Escucha el siguiente informe del tiempo y escoge la respuesta apropiada para cada ciudad.

    **a** 1. En Madrid...
        a. hace sol.     b. hace frío.     c. hace viento.

    **a** 2. En Bilbao...
        a. está nublado.   b. nieva.      c. llueve.

    **c** 3. En Valencia...
        a. hace sol.     b. está nublado.  c. hace viento.

    **c** 4. En Málaga...
        a. está nublado.   b. nieva.      c. hace sol.

    **b** 5. En Barcelona...
        a. hace sol.     b. llueve.      c. hace calor.

**iLrn**

Script 4-2: En Madrid hoy hace sol y tenemos una temperatura máxima de 28 grados centígrados, mientras que en Bilbao el cielo se encuentra nublado, con una temperatura máxima de sólo 14 grados centígrados. En Valencia tendremos vientos fuertes, pero en Málaga se puede esperar un día caluroso y despejado, perfecto para ir a la playa. Los habitantes de Barcelona deberán sacar el paraguas y la chaqueta, pues llueve y el día está fresco.

**SABOR REGIONAL**

In Spain the word **previsión** is often used to refer to a weather forecast.

## Aplicaciones

**4-3 ¿Qué tiempo hace?** Describan el tiempo en cada una de las siguientes imágenes.

MODELO    *Hace frío. Parece que* (it seems like) *hace un poco de viento y no hace sol,...*

Imagen 1                Imagen 2

Imagen 3

**4-4 El tiempo hoy** Con un(a) compañero(a), describan el estado del tiempo el día de hoy.

MODELO    *Hoy hace sol y hace un poco de calor. También...*

**4-5 El estado del tiempo en España** Completen el pronóstico del tiempo *(weather forecast)* para España, de acuerdo con el siguiente mapa.

En el norte, en las regiones de Galicia, la Cordillera Cantábrica, Castilla y León, Navarra, La Rioja, Aragón y el norte de Cataluña, _____llueve_____. En el sur de Cataluña y en el norte de La Mancha, de Extremadura y de Valencia _____está nublado_____. En el sur, en Extremadura, Andalucía y las Islas Canarias, _____hace sol_____. Finalmente, en Galicia, Asturias y el Estrecho de Gibraltar _____hace viento_____.

### ■ Integración

**4-6 ¿Cuál es tu estación favorita?** Prepara varias preguntas para determinar cuál es la estación favorita de uno(a) de tus compañeros y por qué. Luego, preséntale un breve informe de sus respuestas al resto de la clase.

**4-7 El tiempo en los Estados Unidos** Completen la siguiente tabla con el estado del tiempo y las actividades más recomendables para el día de hoy en las diferentes regiones de los Estados Unidos.

| | Previsión del tiempo | Actividades recomendadas |
|---|---|---|
| El noreste | | |
| El sureste | | |
| El centro | | |
| Las montañas | | |
| El noroeste | | |
| El suroeste | | |

## II. Funciones y estructuras: Talking about ongoing actions and events with the present progressive

Hoy hace muy buen tiempo. Por eso **estamos nadando** en la piscina.

When you want to emphasize that an action is taking place right at this moment, you may use the present progressive tense, the equivalent of the English structure *to be + -ing*. This tense is formed with the verb **estar** followed by the present participle form (**gerundio** in Spanish) of the main verb.

| | |
|---|---|
| Como **está lloviendo, estamos mirando** una película en casa. Raquel y David **están estudiando** en Madrid. | Since ***it is raining, we are watching*** a movie at home. *Raquel and David **are studying** in Madrid.* |

The present participle of **-ar** verbs is formed by attaching the **-ando** ending to the stem of the verb while the present participle of **-er** and **-ir** verbs is formed by attaching the **-iendo** ending to the stem.

| VERB | STEM | PRESENT PARTICIPLE |
|---|---|---|
| **-ar:** tomar | tom- | tom**ando** |
| **-er:** comer | com- | com**iendo** |
| **-ir:** escribir | escrib- | escrib**iendo** |

When the stem of an **-er** or **-ir** verb ends in a vowel, the ending **-iendo** is changed to **-yendo**.

| VERB | STEM | PRESENT PARTICIPLE |
|---|---|---|
| leer | le- | le**yendo** |
| oír | o- | o**yendo** |
| ir | X | **yendo** |

**-ir** verbs that undergo stem changes in the present tense also have stem changes in the present participle.

| | |
|---|---|
| pedir (i, **i**) | pidiendo |
| preferir (ie, **i**) | prefiriendo |
| dormir (ue, **u**) | durmiendo |

As you learned in **Capítulo 3, Tema 3**, stem changes are indicated in parentheses. For example, the verb **pedir** has a change **e→i** in both the present tense and the present participle.

Stem-changing verbs with **e→ie** (**pref**e**rir→pref**ie**ro**) and **o→ue** (**d**o**rmir→d**ue**rmo**) changes will be presented in **Tema 2**.

## ■ Asimilación

**4-8 El tiempo, las estaciones y nuestras acciones** Para cada situación, indica si la actividad es lógica (**L**) o ilógica (**I**).

___I___ 1. Es invierno. Nosotros estamos nadando en la playa.

___I___ 2. Está lloviendo mucho. Yo estoy caminando por el parque.

___L___ 3. Es verano. Estás mirando un partido de béisbol en la televisión.

___I___ 4. Hace calor. Ricardo y José Luis están esquiando en las montañas.

___I___ 5. Es otoño. Dora está celebrando el Día de San Valentín con su novio.

___L___ 6. Hace buen tiempo. Tú estás jugando en el patio de tu casa.

Script 4-9: Hola, mamá. CD1–38 Soy Tere. Te llamo para decirte que estamos en la casa y que todo está bien. Consuelo está leyendo un libro en la sala y Marta está preparando unos bocadillos para el almuerzo. El bebé está durmiendo en la cuna. Y Miguelito está escuchando música y jugando con los vecinos. Papá está lavando el carro antes de salir para el trabajo. ¡Ah! Y yo estoy haciendo tareas para tener tiempo para ir al centro comercial esta noche. ¿Qué te parece? ¡Besos! ¡Adiós!

**4-9 ¿Quién?** Escucha el mensaje que Tere le deja a su madre en el contestador *(answering machine)*. Luego, contesta las preguntas que siguen.

**OPCIONES:**   Tere   Miguelito   Consuelo   el bebé   el padre   Marta

1. ¿Quién está lavando el carro? ____el padre____
2. ¿Quién está escuchando música? ____Miguelito____
3. ¿Quién está preparando el almuerzo? ____Marta____
4. ¿Quién está leyendo un libro? ____Consuelo____
5. ¿Quién está durmiendo? ____el bebé____
6. ¿Quién está haciendo tareas? ____Tere____

## ■ Aplicaciones

**4-10 ¿Qué hacen aquí?** Indiquen qué están haciendo las siguientes personas en estos lugares.

**MODELO**   Ellos están en el supermercado. Ellos *están comprando alimentos.*

1. Yo estoy en la lavandería. Yo...
2. Gladis está en el museo. Ella...
3. Nosotros estamos en la parada de metro. Nosotros...
4. Vosotros estáis en el centro. Vosotros...
5. El Sr. Nogueras y la Sra. Guzmán están en la oficina. Ellos...
6. Tú estás en el aeropuerto. Tú...

Sugerencia 4-10, #4: If you do not want your students to use the vosotros form, change the pronoun to ustedes.

Since the cultural focus of this chapter is Spain, you will get the chance to use and practice the vosotros(as) form of the verb. Remember that this pronoun, which means all of you (informal), is used in the northern and central part of Spain.

Answers 4-10: Answers will vary: 1. estoy lavando ropa. 2. está mirando cuadros. 3. estamos esperando el metro. 4. estáis haciendo compras... 5. están trabajando. 6. estás (saliendo de vacaciones/ esperando a una persona).

**4-11 Un día en el Parque del Retiro** Digan qué está haciendo la gente que está en el Parque del Retiro en este momento.

**4-12 Tu ambiente y tú** Tu compañero(a) quiere saber cómo reaccionas a ciertos estímulos relacionados con el ambiente, particularmente con el tiempo y las estaciones. Escucha la clave e indica dónde estás y qué estás haciendo. ¡Usa la imaginación! Al terminar, cambien de papel.

MODELO     E1: *Es verano y hace mucho sol.*
                E2: *Estoy en una playa de Málaga, España. Estoy tomando el sol, nadando en el mar y bebiendo zumo.*

### ■ Integración

**4-13 Un miércoles como cualquier otro** *(as any other)* Averigua qué hace tu compañero(a) a diferentes horas los miércoles. Hagan preguntas específicas y reaccionen a lo que el otro dice.

MODELO     E1: *Lorraine, generalmente, ¿qué estás haciendo los miércoles a las diez en punto de la mañana?*
                E2: *Generalmente estoy estudiando en la biblioteca.*
                E1: *¿Con qué frecuencia estudias en la biblioteca? ¡No me gusta estudiar ahí!*
                E2: *Pues yo usualmente estudio en la biblioteca.*
                E1: *¿Y qué estás haciendo los miércoles al mediodía?*
                E2: *...*

**4-14 Una tarjeta postal** Imagínate que estás de vacaciones viajando por diferentes partes de España y escríbele una tarjeta postal a tu mejor amigo(a). Dile qué cosas estás haciendo. ¡Usa la imaginación! Al terminar, intercambia *(exchange)* tu tarjeta con la de un(a) compañero(a) de clase. Háganse preguntas y digan qué cosas están haciendo diariamente en sus vacaciones.

**Answers 4-11:** *Answers may vary slightly*: Sergio y Mara están jugando. Joaquín está escuchando / oyendo música. Don Paco está leyendo el periódico. Rosita y Doris están jugando. Augusto y Fiona están comiendo (hamburguesas). La Sra. Toledo está caminando. Lucas está pintando. Edelmira está hablando por teléfono.

**Sugerencia 4-14:** Encourage students to use the vocabulary, structures, and cultural information they have learned in this and other chapters. Here is a list of some of the activities they may include: **comer tapas, ir a la playa, practicar español, conocer a personas interesantes, aprender mucho sobre la historia del país,** and **visitar diferentes ciudades como...**

## III. Funciones y estructuras: Comparing and contrasting with comparatives and superlatives

—En España, ¿la primavera es **más lluviosa que** el invierno?
—No, el invierno es **la estación más lluviosa**. El invierno es **tan lluvioso como** la primavera en los Estados Unidos.

■ To make comparisons of equality, use the following structures.

**tan** + (adjective/adverb) + **como**

Julio es **tan caluroso como** agosto.
Hoy llueve **tan intensamente como** ayer.

*July is **as hot as** August.*
*Today it is raining **as intensely as** yesterday.*

Notice that the adjective (**caluroso**) must agree in gender and number with the noun it describes (**julio**).

**tanto/a/os/as** + noun + **como**

En Seattle no hay **tantos días soleados como** en Miami.

*In Seattle there are not **as many sunny days as** in Miami.*

Notice that the form of **tanto** (**tantos**) must agree in number and gender with the noun (**días**).

**verb** + **tanto como**

En Boston **llueve tanto como** en Nueva York.

*In Boston **it rains as much as** in New York.*

To express equality among nouns you may also use the expression **el/la/los/las** + **mismo/a/os/as** + noun + **que**: *Esta semana tenemos **la misma temperatura que** la semana pasada.*

■ To make comparisons of inequality, use the following structures.

**más/menos** + (adjective/adverb/noun) + **que**

La primavera es **menos fría que** el invierno.
Enero tiene **más días que** febrero.

*Spring is **less cold than** winter.*
*January has **more days than** February.*

■ The Spanish superlative is formed using the following structure.

**el/la/los/las** + noun + **más/menos** + adjective + **de...**

El otoño es **la estación más aburrida**.
Julio y agosto son **los meses menos agradables del año**.

*Fall is **the most boring season**.*
*July and August are **the least pleasant months of the year**.*

The ending **de...** is only used when the speaker wants to mention the group to which the noun belongs. The preposition **de** must be followed by a definite article **(el/la/los/las).** Keep in mind that **de + el = del.**

The following adjectives have irregular comparative and superlative forms.

| ADJECTIVE | COMPARATIVE | SUPERLATIVE |
|---|---|---|
| **bueno** *(good)* | **mejor(es)** *(better)* <br> El verano es **mejor** que el invierno. | **(el/la/los/las) mejor(es)** *(the best)* <br> El verano es **la mejor** estación. |
| **malo** *(bad)* | **peor(es)** *(worse)* <br> El calor es **peor** que el frío. | **(el/la/los/las) peor(es)** *(the worst)* <br> El calor es **el peor** tipo de clima. |
| **grande, viejo** *(big/old)* | **mayor(es)** *(bigger/older)* <br> Sara es **mayor** que ustedes. | **(el/la/los/las) mayor(es)** *(the biggest/oldest)* <br> Sara es **la mayor** de su familia. |
| **pequeño, joven** *(small/young)* | **menor(es)** *(smaller/younger)* <br> Nosotros somos **menores** que Lucas. | **(el/la/los/las) menor(es)** *(the smallest/youngest)* <br> Somos **los menores** de todos los hijos. |

## ■ Asimilación

**4-15 El tiempo** Completen las oraciones que siguen con las alternativas más lógicas.

1. Quebec es tan fría como ___b___ .
   a. Madrid          b. Montreal          c. California
2. En ___c___ hace más calor que en el otoño.
   a. la primavera          b. el invierno          c. el verano
3. En Albuquerque llueve menos frecuentemente que en ___c___ .
   a. Phoenix          b. Las Vegas          c. Seattle
4. ___b___ es uno de los lugares del mundo donde más nieva.
   a. La selva del Amazonas          b. Siberia          c. El Caribe
5. En San Juan hace tanto calor como en ___a___ .
   a. Santo Domingo          b. París          c. Buenos Aires
6. ___c___ es una de las ciudades donde hace más viento.
   a. Atlanta          b. San Luis          c. Chicago

D1–39 **4-16 ¿Qué opinas de los alimentos?** Escucha las preguntas sobre los alimentos y selecciona la alternativa más lógica. Luego, compara tus respuestas con las de un(a) compañero(a). ¿Están de acuerdo?

1. los refrescos / el vino
2. la lechuga / el brócoli
3. los camarones / la pizza
4. el pan / el pollo
5. las papas / la langosta
6. el helado / el tomate

**Script 4-16:** 1. ¿Cuál es la bebida más popular? 2. ¿Cuál es la verdura más nutritiva? 3. ¿Cuál es la comida más famosa entre los estudiantes? 4. ¿Cuál es el alimento menos nutritivo? 5. ¿Cuál es el alimento más caro? 6. ¿Cuál es el alimento más sabroso?

This activity recycles vocabulary related to foods and beverages. You may want to ask students to review these words before listening to the text CD.

**Answers: 4-16:** *Answers may vary in some cases:* 1. los refrescos 2. el brócoli 3. la pizza 4. el pan 5. la langosta 6. el helado

## ■ Aplicaciones

**4-17 El mundo de las estrellas** Completen las siguientes oraciones con los nombres de personas famosas. ¡Cuidado con la concordancia!

MODELO     _Cindy Lauper_ es menos popular que _Madonna_.

1. _____ es el mejor cantante del mundo.
2. _____ y _____ tienen menos talento que _____.
3. _____ es la peor actriz de los Estados Unidos.
4. _____ es tan presumido _(conceited)_ como _____.
5. _____ y _____ son más simpáticas que _____.
6. _____ es el/la animador(a) _(host/hostess)_ más cómico(a) de la televisión.

**4-18 Las personas de la clase** Formen oraciones para comparar a las personas de la clase.

You may use some of these options:

ADJETIVOS: **alto, bueno, interesante, guapo, atractivo, responsable, simpático**

SUSTANTIVOS: **interés en la clase, cuadernos, libros**

VERBOS: **hablar español, llegar tarde a clase, salir al baño**

MODELO     _Warren es más estudioso que Mike._
           _Kate y Joseph son los estudiantes menos altos de la clase._

**4-19 Guía turística de Barcelona** Completen el siguiente párrafo con las frases de la lista.

OPCIONES:     los museos más importantes    la zona más antigua
              la mejor vista _(view)_    los mejores restaurantes
              el almacén más popular    la temporada más turística

Barcelona es una ciudad fascinante. ___La zona más antigua___ se llama Barrio Gótico y tiene muchas iglesias y monumentos medievales. ___Los mejores restaurantes___ están en La Ribera y ofrecen gran variedad de comidas y precios. ___El almacén más popular___ es El Corte Inglés y está en la Plaza Catalunya. ___Los museos más importantes___ son los de Picasso y Miró, los cuales están abiertos de martes a domingo. ___La mejor vista___ es desde Montjuïc, al suroeste de la ciudad. Desde allí se puede ver el puerto y toda Barcelona. El verano es ___la temporada más turística___ de esta ciudad; por eso es preciso hacer reservaciones con tiempo.

### EN TU COMUNIDAD

Compile a list of restaurants in the community that specialize in Spanish or Latin American food. Besides providing their names and location, you should investigate their schedules, prices, and most popular dishes to create a basic restaurant directory to be posted at the Office of International Students.

## ■ Integración

**4-20 Así es la familia** Túrnense para hacer y responder a preguntas sobre su familia. Cubran temas diversos y den _(provide)_ detalles.

**4-21 Apreciación culinaria** Escribe tu propia crítica sobre los restaurantes de tu ciudad o tu región. ¡Debes tratar de convencer a tu profesor(a) con tus argumentos! Usa algunas de los siguientes frases.

You may ask questions such as the following: **¿Eres tan alto(a) como tus hermanos? ¿Tu madre es más estricta que tu padre? ¿Cuál es tu tío más hablador? ¿Eres mayor que tus primos? ¿Tus parientes saben tanto como tú?**

...tiene los precios más económicos, ...es más/menos caro, en... sirven los mejores/peores..., ...es el más bonito, en... tienen el mejor/peor servicio, en... el menú es más/menos variado.

# IV. Perspectivas: Las variaciones climáticas en el mundo hispano

## ■ Antes de leer

En grupos, contesten y expliquen su respuesta a la siguiente pregunta:

> ¿Es el clima en el mundo hispano similar o diferente al de los Estados Unidos?

Transparencies H-2: La hora y la temperatura; H-5: El tiempo en América Latina

## ■ A leer

### Variaciones climáticas

La mayoría de los países hispanos están en la zona tropical y no tienen fluctuaciones térmicas significativas durante el año. En estos países se habla, en cambio, de períodos secos y períodos lluviosos. Un factor muy importante en el clima de algunos de los países de habla hispana es la altura *(elevation);* siempre hace frío o fresco en las regiones altas y calor en las bajas, o sea, al nivel del mar *(sea level)*. Las estaciones en países como Argentina y Chile son opuestas a las de España (o los Estados Unidos) debido a su ubicación en el hemisferio sur.

### Diferencias en las escalas de temperatura

En España y Latinoamérica se usa la escala Celsius para medir la temperatura. Para la conversión de temperaturas entre el sistema centígrado y el Fahrenheit, usa la siguiente fórmula:

$$°C = 0.55 \times (°F - 32).$$

## ■ ¿Entendiste bien?

**A. ¡Qué variación!** Clasifica los siguientes países de acuerdo con la información dada en la nota anterior.

OPCIONES:   No tiene estaciones.
En enero es verano.
En enero es invierno.

1. Argentina
2. Chile
3. Colombia
4. España
5. Costa Rica
6. Estados Unidos

Answers A: 1. En enero es verano. 2. En enero es verano. 3. No tiene estaciones. 4. En enero es invierno. 5. No tiene estaciones. 6. En enero es invierno.

**B. Conversiones** Convierte las siguientes temperaturas de la escala Celsius a la escala Fahrenheit.

| Las temperaturas en Madrid | | |
|---|---|---|
| **Mes** | **Escala Celsius** | **Escala Fahrenheit** |
| diciembre y enero | Entre 2 y 11 °C | Entre ____ y ____ °F |
| marzo y octubre | Entre 5 y 18 °C | Entre ____ y ____ °F |
| julio y agosto | Entre 17 y 31 °C | Entre ____ y ____ °F |

**C. ¿Cierto o falso?** Indica si las siguientes oraciones acerca de la temperatura en Madrid corresponden o no con la información de la tabla.

_F_ 1. En enero hace mucho calor en Madrid.

_F_ 2. Julio es un mes fresco.

_C_ 3. En octubre la temperatura es de más o menos 15 grados centígrados.

_F_ 4. Las temperaturas durante el mes de abril en Madrid oscilan entre los 50 y los 70 grados Fahrenheit.

El invierno en Madrid

# La ropa

## I. Vocabulario: Ropa de diario y accesorios

### Vocabulario práctico

**Materiales**

el algodón *cotton*
el cuero *leather*
de fantasía *costume jewelry*
la lana *wool*
el material sintético (acrílico,
   poliéster) *synthetic material
   (acrylic, polyester)*
el metal *metal*
el oro *gold*
la pana *corduroy*
la plata *silver*
la seda *silk*
la tela *fabric*

**Diseños *(Designs)***

a cuadros *checked*
a rayas *striped*
de puntos/lunares *polka-dots*
estampado *print*
liso / de un solo tono *solid color*

**Otras prendas *(Other garments)***

las sandalias *sandals*
los tejanos / los vaqueros *jeans*
el traje de baño / el bañador
   *bathing suit*
las zapatillas *slippers*
los zapatos de tenis / las zapatillas
   *tennis shoes / sneakers*

Transparencies I-3 La ropa de
hombre; I-4: La ropa de mujer;
C-3: Artículos personales

### SABOR REGIONAL

Sneakers are called **zapatillas** in
Argentina, Chile, Panama, Peru,
and Uruguay.

To describe what something is made of, use the expression **ser** + **de** followed by the material.

El chaleco **es de cuero.**        *The vest is made of leather.*
Estos abrigos **son de lana.**        *These coats are made of wool.*

You may describe articles of clothing with colors or by using the expression **de color** followed by the masculine singular form of the color.

Mis medias son **amarillas.**        *My socks are yellow.*
Tus pantalones son **verdes/negros.**        *Your pants are green/black.*
El cinturón es **de color** blanco.        *The belt is white (in color).*

## ■ Asimilación

**4-22 ¿Qué prenda es?** Empareja las prendas con sus descripciones.

___e___ 1. la falda
___c___ 2. los pantalones
___a___ 3. el abrigo
___b___ 4. los zapatos
___d___ 5. la camisa

a. Es una prenda que usas cuando hace frío.
b. Los llevas en los pies para caminar.
c. Generalmente son cortos en el verano.
d. Los hombres de negocios las prefieren blancas.
e. La llevan solamente las mujeres.

CD1-40  **4-23 ¿Quién es?** Identifica la persona que se describe a continuación.

Foto 1

Foto 2

## ■ Aplicaciones

**4-24 Recomendaciones** Un(a) amigo(a) está preparándose para ir a esquiar a las montañas. ¿Qué ropa creen que debe (o no debe) llevar? Preparen una lista.

**4-25 Los materiales** Normalmente, ¿de qué material son las siguientes prendas? Indica tus respuestas y, al terminar, compáralas con las de un(a) compañero(a).

OPCIONES:    seda   oro   lana   algodón   cuero   material sintético

1. los cinturones: _____cuero_____
2. los impermeables: _____material sintético_____
3. las blusas: _____seda_____
4. los aretes: _____oro_____
5. los tejanos: _____algodón_____

**4-26 Variaciones de acuerdo con la estación** Clasifica los siguientes artículos según la estación. **¡OJO!** Algunas prendas y accesorios se pueden usar en más de una época del año.

**Extensión 4-26:** For an additional challenge, you may give your students the following task:

**¿Qué falta?** (What's missing?) Ahora, en parejas, comparen sus respuestas y traten de completar el cuadro de la actividad 4-26 con otros artículos indispensables (absolutely necessary) para cada estación.

**Sugerencia 4-26:** To encourage answers that are more detailed, consider dividing the class into small groups (3–4 students maximum) and assigning a season to each one. At the time of the presentation, the rest of the class could be asked to react to the completeness of their answers.

| chaqueta | lentes de sol | abrigo | tejanos |
| gorra | camiseta | aretes | bermudas |
| zapatillas | corbata | sandalias | guantes |
| blusa | impermeable | bañador/traje de baño | cinturón |
| botas | vestido | | |

| | |
|---|---|
| primavera | |
| verano | |
| otoño | |
| invierno | |

## ■ Integración

**4-27 De compras** Representa la siguiente conversación con un(a) compañero(a).

### Comprador(a)

Imagine that you are in Spain and are buying clothes for a special occasion. Tell the clerk what you are looking for, explore your options (different colors, materials, designs, etc.), and complete the transaction. Remember: This is not a shopping spree! You are traveling on a budget.

You may want to use expressions such as: **Busco...** (I'm looking for . . . ) **¿Dónde está el vestidor?** (Where is your fitting room?) **¿Tiene otros colores/materiales/diseños?** (Do you have any other colors/materials/ designs?) **¿Tiene una talla más grande/chica?** (Do you carry bigger/smaller sizes?) **¿Cuánto cuesta?** (How much is it?) **¿Aceptan tarjetas de crédito?** (Do you take credit cards?)

### Vendedor(a)

Imagine that you are a clerk at a department store in Spain. Help this customer with his/her purchase. Remember: You work on commission, so you want to encourage this client to buy as many items of clothing and accessories as possible!

You may want to use expressions such as: **¿Le puedo ayudar en algo?** (How may I help you?) **Le queda muy bien.** (It looks great on you.) **Está en rebaja.** (It is on sale.) **Le recomiendo también este cinturón que va muy bien con esos pantalones.** (I also recommend this belt that goes well with those pants.)

**4-28 Desfile de modas** (Fashion show) Formen grupos de cuatro estudiantes. Su misión es presentar las modas de los estudiantes universitarios de los Estados Unidos. Dos estudiantes van a actuar como modelos y los otros dos van a describir los colores, materiales y diseños de sus prendas de vestir.

1. Decidan qué prendas van a llevar los modelos.
2. Escriban lo que van a decir los anfitriones (presenters) y cómo van a presentar a los modelos.

### EN TU COMUNIDAD

Visit a local department store and locate garments made in Spain or Latin America. In your reports, you should compare the price, quality, and style of these garments with those made in Asia and/or the United States.

## II. Funciones y estructuras: Talking about daily activities with *e→ie* and *o→ue* stem-changing verbs

NELLY: ¿Qué **piensas** de estos zapatos?
PALOMA: ¡Son preciosos! ¿Cuánto **cuestan**?
NELLY: Sólo veinticinco dólares.
PALOMA: ¡**Quiero** unos para mí también! ¿**Puedo** verlos?

As you learned in **Capítulo 3, Tema 3**, the stem of some Spanish verbs changes when the verb is conjugated (**pedir: pido, pides, pide**, etc.). In this section you will learn about two more stem changes: **e → ie** and **o → ue**. Look at the conjugations of the verbs **pensar** *(to think)* and **poder** *(to be able to)*.

| pensar (e→ie) | poder (o→ue) |
| --- | --- |
| yo **pienso** | yo **puedo** |
| tú **piensas** | tú **puedes** |
| él/ella/usted **piensa** | él/ella/usted **puede** |
| nosotros(as) **pensamos** | nosotros(as) **podemos** |
| vosotros(as) **pensáis** | vosotros(as) **podéis** |
| ellos(as)/ustedes **piensan** | ellos(as)/ustedes **pueden** |

*Notice that the stem in the **nosotros(as)** and **vosotros(as)** forms does not change, as with the **e→i** stem-changing verbs.

Here is a list of some common **e→ie** and **o→ue** stem-changing verbs.

**e→ie**
cerrar *to close*
comenzar *to begin*
despertar *to wake*
empezar *to begin*
mentir *to lie*
pensar *to think*
perder *to lose*
preferir *to prefer*
querer *to want*
sentir *to feel*

**o→ue**
acostar *to put to bed*
almorzar *to have lunch*
contar (con) *to count (on)*
costar *to cost*
demostrar *to demonstrate*
devolver *to return*
dormir *to sleep*
encontrar *to find*
llover *to rain*
morir *to die*
mostrar *to show*
mover *to move*
poder *to be able to*
probar *to taste, to try*
recordar *to remember*
soñar *to dream*
volar *to fly*
volver *to return*

Even though the verb **jugar** *(to play a sport or game)* does not have an **o** in its stem, it behaves like any **o→ue** stem-changing verb: **juego, juegas, juega, jugamos, jugáis, juegan.**

The stem of those **-ir** verbs that have the **e→ie** change uses an **i** in the present participle: **mentir → mintiendo**. On the other hand, the stem of those **-ir** vebs that have the **o → ue** change uses a **u**: **dormir → durmiendo**.

## ■ Asimilación

**4-29 ¿Con qué frecuencia?** Indica con qué frecuencia haces las siguientes actividades. Cuando termines, compara tus respuestas con las de un(a) compañero(a). ¿Qué cosas tienen en común?

| ACTIVIDAD | FRECUENCIA |
|---|---|
| 1. Sueño con monstruos y fantasmas. | |
| 2. Pierdo prendas de vestir. | |
| 3. Almuerzo en la cafetería de la universidad. | |
| 4. Comienzo a celebrar mi cumpleaños el día anterior. | |
| 5. No recuerdo fechas importantes. | |
| 6. Prefiero vestir con tejanos y camiseta. | |
| 7. Me pruebo la ropa antes de comprarla. | |
| 8. Devuelvo las cosas que les pido a mis amigos. | |

CD1–41 **4-30 Los estudiantes de tu universidad** Escucha las oraciones e indica si se aplican o no se aplican a los estudiantes de tu universidad.

1. se aplica / no se aplica
2. se aplica / no se aplica
3. se aplica / no se aplica
4. se aplica / no se aplica
5. se aplica / no se aplica
6. se aplica / no se aplica

Script 4-30: 1. Usan ropa que cuesta mucho dinero. 2. Piensan que estudian en una buena universidad. 3. Se acuestan muy tarde y se despiertan muy temprano. 4. Quieren hacer estudios de postgrado. 5. Pueden mantener un promedio general de 3.50. 6. Recuerdan las fechas de los exámenes finales.

## ■ Aplicaciones

**4-31 Categorías** Escriban cada palabra o frase de la lista al lado del verbo con el que se relaciona.

Answers 4-31: *Answers may vary.*

OPCIONES: una identificación   un aniversario   mucho dinero
el aeropuerto   la billetera   el cementerio   la puerta
la ventana   una bebida   una oportunidad   la licencia
una blusa   un viaje   la tarea   la funeraria   un diploma

querer: mucho dinero, un diploma   morir: el cementerio, la funeraria
recordar: un aniversario, la tarea   mostrar: una identificación, la licencia
perder: la billetera, una oportunidad   probar: una bebida, una blusa
cerrar: la puerta, la ventana   volar: el aeropuerto, un viaje

**4-32 Dependiendo del tiempo...** Escribe las palabras y frases de la lista al lado de la expresión de tiempo (en el cuadro en la página 158) con la que más las relaciones para formar oraciones. Puedes usar algunas frases más de una vez *(more than once)*. Cuando termines, comparte la información con el resto de la clase.

The expression **empezar + a** *(to begin to)* is always followed by a verb in the infinitive, much like **ir + a**: **Ella empieza a trabajar el lunes.** *She begins to work on Monday.*

OPCIONES: preferir...   (no) querer...   (no) poder...   dormir...
(no) pensar que...   preferir llevar...   (no) querer llevar...
recordar...   sentir que...   empezar a...

| Cuando... | ACTIVIDADES |
|-----------|-------------|
| hace calor | *No quiero trabajar.* |
| hace mucho frío | |
| llueve | |
| hace mucho viento | |

**4-33 Mi hija la distraída** *(absent-minded)* Completen el siguiente párrafo con los verbos de la lista. Conjúguenlos correctamente.

volver   tener   querer   perder   poder   encontrar   despertar recordar

Mi hija es muy distraída. Por las mañanas, ella nunca __encuentra__ la ropa que (ella) __quiere__ llevar para el colegio. Por eso, siempre llego tarde al trabajo, a pesar de que (yo) me __despierto__ dos horas antes que ella. Por otro lado, ella nunca __recuerda__ dónde están sus libros o sus cuadernos. Yo le pido que busque con cuidado, pero (ella) siempre __vuelve__ y me dice: «¡Mamá, no sé dónde están!» Para colmo *(on top of that)*, (ella) siempre __pierde__ el dinero que le doy para el almuerzo. ¡(Yo) No __puedo__ tolerar más esta situación! ¡Mi hija __tiene__ que cambiar!

### ■ Integración

**4-34 Una invitación** Representa la siguiente situación con un(a) compañero(a),

Here are some expressions student B may use to refuse student A's invitation: **Lo siento, No puedo porque tengo que..., No quiero...,** and **Prefiero...**

| Estudiante A | Estudiante B |
|---|---|
| The weather is perfect and you would like to spend the day with your friend. Tell him/her all the details of what you prefer, want, and/or are able to do today. Try to convince him/her! | Although the weather is perfect today, you do not feel like doing the things your friend wants to do today. Try to convince him/her to do the activities you prefer, want, and/or are able to do today. |

**4-35 La ropa apropiada** Describe la ropa que prefieres llevar y qué cosas no quieres llevar a por lo menos tres eventos o lugares de la lista. Además, explica por qué. Cuando termines, entrégale una copia a tu profesor(a).

OPCIONES:   a la iglesia
a un picnic en el parque   al cine   a la universidad
a una cena formal en un hotel lujoso

MODELO   *Para ir a..., yo PREFERIR llevar..., ... y ... porque...*
*Por otro lado, no QUERER llevar... porque... Si llevo...,*
*yo (no) PODER...*

## III. Funciones y estructuras: Talking about daily routines with reflexive verbs

Transparency M-1: La rutina diaria (1)

Julia **se despierta** a las seis y media de la mañana, ...

**se cepilla** los dientes, ...

**se viste** rápidamente ...

y **se va** para el trabajo.

In the previous examples, **Julia** is doing something to or for herself. These actions in which the doer (subject) and recipient (object) are the same require the use of reflexive pronouns. Here is the list of Spanish reflexive pronouns.

Notice that, for a reflexive structure to be constructed correctly, the subject, the reflexive pronoun, and the verb must refer to the same person. For example, in the sentence **Mirna se maquilla mucho**, **Mirna** (subject), **se** (pronoun), and **maquilla** (verb) are all in the third person singular.

| REFLEXIVE PRONOUNS | | | |
|---|---|---|---|
| **me** | *myself* | **nos** | *ourselves* |
| **te** | *yourself* (informal) | **os** | *yourselves* (Spain) |
| **se** | *himself, herself, yourself* (formal) | **se** | *themselves, yourselves* |

Reflexive pronouns are placed before the conjugated verb. When they are used in a verb phrase that includes an infinitive or a past participle, they may be placed before the auxiliary verb or attached to the main verb.

Nosotras no **nos maquillamos.**
**Me voy a vestir / Voy a vestirme** de negro.
Carlos **se está afeitando / está afeitándose.**

*We do not **wear make-up.***
*I am going to dress in black.*
*Carlos **is shaving.***

Past participles with a pronoun attached to them take a written accent mark in the third-to-the-last syllable as in **afeitándose.**

*Notice that the infinitive form of re-flexive verbs ends in **-se**.

The meaning of many of these reflex-ive verbs varies significantly from their nonreflexive form: **dormir** *(to sleep)* – **dormirse** *(to fall asleep)*, **ir** *(to go)* – **irse** *(to leave)*, **poner** *(to put)* – **ponerse** *(to put on [clothing])*, etc.

The following is a list of some common Spanish reflexive verbs.

| | | | |
|---|---|---|---|
| acostarse (ue) | *to go to bed* | levantarse | *to get up* |
| afeitarse | *to shave* | llamarse | *to be called* |
| arreglarse | *to fix up, get ready* | llevarse | *to take away, to get along* |
| arrepentirse | *to regret* | maquillarse | *to put on make-up* |
| bañarse | *to bathe* | peinarse | *to comb (one's hair)* |
| cepillarse | *to brush* | perfumarse | *to put on perfume* |
| despertarse (ie) | *to wake up* | ponerse | *to put on (clothing)* |
| divertirse (ie) | *to have fun* | prepararse | *to get ready* |
| dormirse (ue) | *to fall asleep* | probarse (ue) | *to try on (clothing)* |
| ducharse | *to shower* | quedarse | *to stay* |
| graduarse | *to graduate* | quitarse | *to take off (clothing)* |
| irse | *to leave* | sentarse (ie) | *to sit down* |
| lavarse | *to wash up* | vestirse (i) | *to get dressed* |

## ■ Asimilación

**4-36 Con frecuencia...** Indica cuáles de estas acciones haces con frecuen-cia. Luego, compara tus respuestas con las de un(a) compañero(a). ¿Qué actividades tienen en común?

\_\_\_\_\_ Me maquillo para ir a la universidad.

\_\_\_\_\_ Me pruebo la ropa antes de comprarla.

\_\_\_\_\_ Me ducho antes de desayunar.

\_\_\_\_\_ Me voy a casa después de la clase de español.

\_\_\_\_\_ Me levanto tan pronto *(as soon as)* suena *(goes off)* el despertador.

\_\_\_\_\_ Me quedo en casa los viernes por la noche.

\_\_\_\_\_ Me lavo el pelo todos los días.

Script 4-37: ¿Qué cuál es mi rutina matutina? Generalmente me despierto temprano, a eso de las siete de la mañana. Siempre me quedo un rato en la cama y me levanto como a las ocho. Luego me cepillo los dientes y desayuno mien-tras miro las noticias en la televisión. Después me baño y me visto. Final-mente, me voy para la oficina y allí me maquillo. ¡Y estoy lista para mi día!

CD1–42 **4-37 La rutina matutina de Pilar** Escucha la descripción de la rutina matutina de Pilar y selecciona las oraciones que sean ciertas.

\_\_\_\_\_ Se maquilla en casa.     \_\_\_\_\_ No desayuna.

\_\_X\_\_ Se despierta temprano.     \_\_\_\_\_ Se cepilla los dientes después

\_\_X\_\_ Se queda en la cama           de mirar las noticias.

      un rato.              \_\_X\_\_ Se baña por la mañana.

## ■ Aplicaciones

Answers 4-38: *Answers may vary.* 1. ...nos ponemos la ropa, ...nos divertimos en la fiesta y... nos quitamos la ropa. 2. ...nos bañamos, ...nos vestimos elegantemente y... nos cepillamos el pelo. 3. ...nos acostamos tarde, ...nos dormimos inmediata-mente y... nos despertamos por la mañana. 4. ...nos afeitamos, ...nos duchamos rápidamente y... nos probamos diferentes camisas. 5. ...nos vamos para la universidad, ...nos sen-tamos en la sala de clase y... nos preparamos para tomar el examen.

**4-38 En orden lógico** Pongan las siguientes actividades en orden.

MODELO     irse para el trabajo    levantarse temprano    prepararse
                *Primero nos levantamos temprano, luego nos preparamos y finalmente nos vamos para el trabajo.*

1. divertirse en la fiesta, ponerse la ropa, quitarse la ropa

2. bañarse, peinarse, vestirse elegantemente

3. dormirse temprano, despertarse por la mañana, acostarse tarde

4. afeitarse, ducharse rápidamente, probarse diferentes camisas

5. prepararse para tomar el examen, sentarse en la sala de clase, irse para la universidad

**4-39 Los Padilla** Completen el siguiente párrafo con los verbos de la lista. Conjúguenlos correctamente.

**OPCIONES:** acostarse  levantarse  arrepentirse  llamarse  afeitarse
llevarse  bañarse  sentarse

Las mañanas en mi casa son un poco locas. Yo _____ me levanto _____ tempranо, pero mi esposo y mis hijos no. Mi esposo siempre usa el baño primero. Él _____ se afeita/se baña _____ y _____ se baña/se afeita _____, y después me ayuda a preparar el desayuno. Mi hija mayor, que _____ se llama _____ Mónica, es la más problemática. Ella _____ se acuesta _____ muy tarde mirando la televisión y por la mañana no quiere ir a la escuela. Mónica y mi hija menor, Lily, no _____ se llevan _____ bien y discuten *(argue)* constantemente, hasta cuando (nosotros) _____ nos sentamos _____ a la mesa a desayunar. Mi casa puede ser un caos por las mañanas, pero (yo) no _____ me arrepiento _____ de tener una familia tan particular.

**4-40 Gustos** *(likes and dislikes)* **diferentes**

**Paso 1:** Completa las siguientes frases de manera lógica y de acuerdo con tus propios gustos.

MODELO     PERFUMARSE para ir a *una cita*

1. PONERSE _____ para ir a un baile
2. DESPERTARSE tarde los _____ (día[s])
3. ACOSTARSE a la(s) _____ los lunes por la noche
4. VESTIRSE con ropa _____ para venir a la universidad
5. LLEVARSE mal con _____
6. GRADUARSE de la universidad en el año _____

**Paso 2:** Ahora, usa la información del **Paso 1** para hacerle preguntas a un(a) compañero(a). Toma notas. Cuando termines, prepara un informe para el resto de la clase.

MODELO     E1: *Mary, ¿te perfumas para ir a una cita?*
E2: *Sí, me perfumo para ir a una cita y también me perfumo para ir a mi trabajo.*

■ **Integración**

**4-41 Una entrevista de trabajo (I)** Imagínate que tienes una entrevista de trabajo muy importante mañana por la mañana. Explícale a tu compañero(a) las cosas que vas a hacer antes de ir a la entrevista. ¡Debes estar preparado(a) para las preguntas de tu compañero(a)! Toma notas cuando tu compañero(a) explique lo que él/ella va a hacer.

**4-42 Una entrevista de trabajo (II)** Ahora, haz un resumen de las cosas que tu compañero(a) va a hacer antes de ir a su entrevista de trabajo. Cuando termines, dale una copia a él/ella para ver si tienes todos los detalles necesarios.

**REMEMBER**

In this activity you have to use the structure **ir + a +** infinitive and other expressions you learned in **Capítulo 3, Tema 3**. Remember that in these structures the reflexive pronoun may be placed before the auxiliary (conjugated) verb or attached to the infinitive.

You can use the following connectors for activities 4-41 and 4-42: **primero** *(first)*, **antes de...** *(before . . .),* **después** *(afterward),* **luego** *(then),* **entonces** *(then),* and **finalmente** *(finally).*

## IV. Vídeo: Una charla sobre la ropa

### ▨ Preparación

**A. La ropa de Sofía** En el vídeo, Sofía le va a enseñar a Alejandra su ropa. Antes de ver el vídeo, indica cuáles de las siguientes prendas crees que Sofía tiene en su armario. **¡OJO!** No olvides *(Do not forget)* que ella está en Puerto Rico y hace buen tiempo.

| | | |
|---|---|---|
| _____ abrigo | _____ guantes | __X__ vestido de playa |
| _____ blusa | _____ impermeable | __X__ vaqueros |
| _____ calcetines | __X__ pantalones | __X__ zapatos |
| __X__ camisetas | __X__ sandalias | __X__ chaqueta |
| _____ falda | __X__ traje de baño | _____ corbata |

 Ahora, mira el vídeo y revisa tus respuestas de la actividad A. Luego, compara tus respuestas con las de un(a) compañero(a).

### ▨ ¿Entendiste bien?

**B. Gustos diferentes** Mira el vídeo por segunda vez. Como ves, Sofía y Alejandra tienen gustos y opiniones muy diferentes sobre la ropa. Completa cada oración con el nombre de la chica correspondiente.

1. A _____ le gusta tener mucha ropa y accesorios como bolsos y aretes. Le gusta comprar cosas nuevas y siempre estar a la moda.

2. _____ no tiene mucha ropa y piensa que la moda no es tan importante. No le gusta la ropa muy colorida ni demasiado atrevida *(daring, risqué)*.

**C. ¿Mejor o peor?** Miren las fotos de Sofía (la «de antes» y la «de después») y contesten las siguientes preguntas.

- ¿Prefieren las prendas originales de Sofía o las que Alejandra le prestó *(loaned)*? ¿Por qué?
- ¿Creen que Alejandra está realmente a la moda? Comparen su estilo con la moda actual de los estudiantes universitarios de los Estados Unidos.

**D. Enfoque comunitario** Imaginen que son dependientes en una tienda local. Preparen una lista de expresiones que deben usar para atender a clientes hispanos que no hablen bien inglés. Incluyan expresiones para averiguar *(to ascertain)* sus preferencias (color, material, precio, etc.) y también para responder a sus dudas o sus quejas *(complaints)*.

# La diversión

## I. Vocabulario: Los deportes

Margarita **hace aeróbicos** tres veces por semana.

Lucho y sus amigos **juegan baloncesto** en la cancha de su barrio.

Doña Gabriela lleva a sus hijas a la práctica de **fútbol** los jueves por la tarde.

Esteban **patina sobre hielo** durante el invierno.

### Vocabulario práctico

el árbitro *referee*
el equipo *team*
el jugador *player*

### Otros deportes *(Other sports)*

el atletismo *track and field*
el béisbol *baseball*
el esquí *ski*
el fútbol americano *football*
la gimnasia *gymnastics*
el levantamiento de pesas
    *weight lifting*
la lucha libre *wrestling*
la natación *swimming*
el tenis *tennis*
el vóleibol *volleyball*

### Verbos

hacer (ejercicio/deporte) *to work
    out, to exercise*
hacer (aeróbicos/gimnasia) *to do
    (aerobics/gymnastics)*
levantar pesas *to lift weights*
patinar (sobre hielo) *to (ice) skate*
practicar (baloncesto/béisbol/
    fútbol/vóleibol/tenis) *to play
    (basketball/baseball/soccer/
    volleyball/tennis)*
practicar (atletismo/natación/lucha
    libre) *to do track and field/
    to swim/to wrestle*

Transparencies G-6: Deportes (1); G-7: Deportes (2); G-9: En la playa

### ■ Asimilación

**4-43 ¿Se necesita un balón?** *(Do you need a ball?)* Indica si los siguientes deportes requieren el uso de un balón (o pelota). Al terminar, compara tus respuestas con las de otros compañeros.

**¿Sí o no?**

1. baloncesto __sí__
2. fútbol __sí__
3. natación __no__
4. gimnasia __no__
5. lucha libre __no__
6. esquí __no__
7. vóleibol __sí__
8. ciclismo __no__
9. patinaje __no__

CD1-43

**Script 4-44:** El equipo olímpico de los Estados Unidos ha tenido una participación destacada en los juegos olímpicos de este año. Hasta el momento, ha obtenido tres medallas de oro en atletismo, dos en lucha libre y cinco en natación. Las competencias de gimnasia y levantamiento de pesas tendrán lugar mañana y se espera que el equipo estadounidense coseche aún más triunfos.

**4-44 Medallas de oro** (*Gold medals*) Escucha el siguiente informe deportivo y completa el cuadro con el número de medallas obtenidas por el Equipo Olímpico (*Olympic Team*) de los Estados Unidos.

| Deporte | Número de medallas de oro |
|---|---|
| El atletismo | 3 |
| La gimnasia | 0 |
| La lucha libre | 2 |
| La natación | 5 |
| El levantamiento de pesas | 0 |

## Aplicaciones

**4-45 ¿Cuándo se practican estos deportes?** Escriban algunos de los deportes típicos de cada estación (primavera, verano, otoño, invierno) en los Estados Unidos.

This activity recycles comparatives and superlatives previously presented in **Tema 1.**

**4-46 Comparaciones** Formen oraciones para comparar los deportes que se mencionan.

MODELO    el béisbol – la natación
                 *El béisbol es más popular que la natación en los Estados Unidos.*

> **REMEMBER**
>
> To complete this activity, you can use a variety of expressions: **más... que, menos... que, tan... como, el más..., el menos...,** etc.

1. el fútbol – el fútbol americano
2. la lucha libre – el atletismo
3. el ciclismo – el vóleibol – la natación
4. el baloncesto – el béisbol – el fútbol americano
5. la gimnasia – los aeróbicos

**Sugerencia 4-47:** Call time at 20-second intervals, and then instruct students to switch roles.

**4-47 ¡A dibujar y a adivinar!** (*Let's draw and guess!*) Túrnense para seleccionar un deporte y luego dibujar en un papel algo relacionado con ese deporte (una persona que practica el deporte, el equipo necesario, dónde se practica el deporte, etc.). El otro (La otra) estudiante debe adivinar de qué deporte se trata. **¡OJO!** Sólo tienen 20 segundos.

## Integración

**4-48 Entrevista** Túrnense para hacer y responder a las siguientes preguntas. **Importante:** Tomen notas de las respuestas de su compañero(a).

1. ¿Te interesa algún deporte en particular? ¿Cuál?
2. ¿Practicas ese deporte?
3. ¿Cuál es tu equipo (o jugador) favorito? ¿Por qué?
4. ¿Qué opinión tienes de los equipos de tu universidad? (¿Son buenos, mediocres, malos... ?)
5. ¿Cuál consideras que es el deporte más representativo de los Estados Unidos? ¿Por qué?

**4-49 Los intereses deportivos de mi compañero(a)** Usa las notas de la conversación anterior para escribir un informe acerca de los intereses deportivos de tu compañero(a).

MODELO    *A mi compañero(a) le gusta mucho el fútbol americano. Él (Ella) practica fútbol todos los fines de semana con sus amigos. Su equipo favorito es los Eagles. A mi compañero(a) no le gusta el golf ni la natación. Con respecto a los deportes en la universidad, mi compañero(a) prefiere...*

## II. Funciones y estructuras: Talking about daily activities with irregular present tense verbs

**Pertenezco** al equipo de fútbol de mi universidad. **Vengo** a práctica tres veces por semana. Me gusta mucho porque me **mantengo** en excelente condición física y me **río** mucho con mis compañeros.

You have already learned how to use many irregular verbs, including the verbs **ser, estar,** and **ir** and other verbs with stem changes. In this section you will learn how to use verbs with orthographic changes and other irregularities.

To maintain the sound of certain letters included in their stems, some **-er** and **-ir** Spanish verbs suffer changes in the first person singular (**yo**) conjugation. Here is a list of those changes.

| CHANGES | EXAMPLES | OTHER VERBS |
|---------|----------|-------------|
| c→z | vencer *(to win)* <br> (yo) **venzo,** (tú) **vences,** ... | cocer (ue) *(to cook)* <br> convencer *(to convince)* <br> torcer (ue) *(to twist)* |
| c→zc | conocer *(to know)* <br> (yo) **conozco,** (tú) **conoces,** ... | conducir *(to drive)* <br> introducir *(to introduce)* <br> merecer *(to deserve)* <br> parecer *(to seem)* <br> pertenecer a *(to belong to)* <br> producir *(to produce)* <br> reconocer *(to recognize)* |
| g→j | proteger *(to protect)* <br> (yo) **protejo,** (tú) **proteges,** ... | coger *(to grab)* <br> corregir (i) *(to correct)* <br> dirigir *(to direct)* <br> escoger *(to select)* <br> recoger *(to pick up)* |

Notice that some of these verbs have other stem changes (**cocer, torcer,** and **corregir**). Remember that these changes do not affect the **nosotros(as)** and **vosotros(as)** forms.

| | |
|---|---|
| Voy al médico cuando me **tuerzo** un tobillo. | *I go to the doctor when **I twist** my ankle.* |
| Creo que **merezco** la medalla de oro este año. | *I think **I deserve** the gold medal this year.* |
| Muchachos, yo **recojo** el equipo. | *Guys, **I will pick up** the equipment.* |

The following are other verbs with irregular present tense conjugations. Irregularities are highlighted in bold.

| VERBS | CONJUGATIONS |
|---|---|
| decir *(to say)* | **dig**o, **dic**es, **dic**e, decimos, decís, **dic**en |
| mantener *(to maintain)* | mante**ng**o, mant**ie**nes, mant**ie**ne, mantenemos, mantenéis, mant**ie**nen |
| oír *(to hear)* | **oig**o, o**y**es, o**y**e, oímos, oís, o**y**en |
| reír *(to laugh)* | **rí**o, **rí**es, **rí**e, reímos, reís, **rí**en |
| venir *(to come)* | ve**ng**o, v**ie**nes, v**ie**ne, venimos, venís, v**ie**nen |
| ver *(to see)* | **ve**o, ves, ve, vemos, veis, ven |

Other derived verbs that end in **-tener** (e.g., **mantener**) are also irregular and are conjugated like **tener**: **contener** *(to contain)*, **detener** *(to detain)*, **entretener** *(to entertain)*, and **obtener** *(to obtain)*.

Cuando **oigo** o **veo** a mi jugador favorito, me **río**.

*When **I hear** or **see** my favorite player, **I laugh**.*

### ■ Asimilación

**4-50 ¿Sí o no?** Indica si las siguientes oraciones se aplican a tu vida diaria o no. Al terminar, compara tus respuestas con las de un(a) compañero(a). ¿Qué tienen en común?

_____ 1. Oigo música *country*.

_____ 2. Veo partidos de béisbol por televisión.

_____ 3. Escojo las mejores clases todos los semestres.

_____ 4. Cuezo bien las carnes cuando cocino.

_____ 5. Merezco una A en la clase de español.

_____ 6. Me río con personas que no conozco.

**4-51 ¿Qué hace el (la) profesor(a)?** El (La) profesor(a) va a decirte qué hace normalmente en la universidad. Marca con **X** las actividades que menciona.

__X__ Dirige varios clubes.

_____ Recoge la oficina.

__X__ Se ríe con las historias de sus colegas.

_____ Escoge libros en la biblioteca.

__X__ Conoce a sus colegas en la universidad.

_____ Ayuda al estudiante que lo merece.

__X__ Corrige trabajos.

__X__ Oye las cintas que hacen sus estudiantes.

CD1–44

Script 4-51: Cuando estoy en la universidad, corrijo los trabajos de mis estudiantes y escojo los materiales que voy a usar en las lecciones. También voy al comedor de profesores y conozco a mis colegas. ¡Me río mucho cuando escucho las historias de sus estudiantes! A veces oigo las cintas que hacen mis estudiantes de español y les doy consejos para mejorar su pronunciación. Lo más importante es que dedico tiempo para ver a mis estudiantes. Los veo en mi oficina o en las reuniones de los clubes. Como me gusta compartir mi tiempo con ellos, dirijo varios clubes estudiantiles.

### ■ Aplicaciones

**4-52 Asociaciones** Escriban las frases de la lista bajo el verbo con el que más se relacionen.

**OPCIONES:**   el equipo opuesto   una orquesta   una fiesta
lugares de interés   exámenes   música   los invitados
un partido de vóleibol   una persona famosa
una compañía   tareas   la radio

| conocer | dirigir | entretener |
|---|---|---|
| lugares de interés | una orquesta | una fiesta |
| una persona famosa | una compañía | los invitados |
| **vencer** | **oír** | **corregir** |
| el equipo opuesto | música | exámenes |
| un partido de vóleibol | la radio | tareas |

**4-53 Las cualidades** *(qualities)* ¿Cuál es tu mejor cualidad? Las siguientes personas están dando su respuesta para esta pregunta. Para saber qué responden, combinen las palabras y conjuguen los verbos correctamente.

1. SELENA:  Yo / reconocer / mis errores.
2. JUAN:    Yo / proteger / a mi familia y a mis amigos.
3. GABY:    Yo / contener / mis emociones negativas.
4. BERTO:   Yo siempre / decir / la verdad.
5. KARINA:  Yo / mantener / buenas relaciones con los demás.
6. FRANK:   Yo / escoger / buenas amistades.

**Answers 4-53:** 1. Yo reconozco mis errores. 2. Yo protejo a mi familia y a mis amigos. 3. Yo contengo mis emociones negativas. 4. Yo siempre digo la verdad. 5. Yo mantengo buenas relaciones con los demás. 6. Yo escojo buenas amistades.

**4-54 Tú y yo**

**Paso 1:** Lee otra vez las oraciones que escribiste en la actividad 4-53 e indica si tú también tienes esas cualidades o no.

1. ...    3. ...    5. ...
2. ...    4. ...    6. ...

**Paso 2:** Ahora, averigua si tu compañero(a) tiene las mismas cualidades. Al terminar, prepara un resumen y preséntalo al resto de la clase.

MODELO    E1: *Desirée, ¿reconoces tus errores?*
          E2: *Sí, reconozco mis errores.*
          o   *No, no reconozco mis errores.*

## ■ Integración

**4-55 Entrevista** Túrnense para hacer y responder a las siguientes preguntas. Tomen notas.

1. ¿Oyes la radio? ¿Qué tipo de programa (musical, de noticias, de comentarios, de deportes) oyes? ¿Y qué música oyes regularmente?

2. ¿Ves programas de deportes en la televisión? ¿Qué otros programas ves?

3. ¿Conduces a la universidad? Si no, ¿cómo vienes (en autobús, en tren, en metro o a pie)?

4. ¿Perteneces a alguna organización estudiantil? ¿A cuál?

5. Generalmente, ¿obtienes las cosas que deseas en la vida? ¿Puedes dar ejemplos?

**4-56 Mi compañero(a)** Ahora, usa la información de la actividad 4-55 para escribir una breve descripción de tu compañero(a) de clase.

**EN TU COMUNIDAD**

Interview a student from Spain or Latin America about his/her daily routine here in the United States. You must include in your reports information about the most significant adjustments that your interviewee had to make to his/her daily routine upon arriving in America.

## III. Funciones y estructuras: Describing people and objects with the verbs *ser* and *estar*

Aníbal **es** muy buen ciclista. Él **es** de Valencia. **Está** practicando para una competencia.

Kim y Rosita **son** jugadoras de vóleibol de playa. **Están** en perfecta condición física. **Son** muy simpáticas.

As you know, the verbs **ser** and **estar** mean *to be*. Although they have the same meaning, they are used in different contexts.

Other expressions with **estar** are **¡Está bien!** *(All right!)* and **¡Está de más!** *(It is not necessary!)*.

| ser is used . . . | estar is used . . . |
|---|---|
| • to describe inherent characteristics: *Sammy Sosa es muy talentoso.* <br>• to talk about origin and nationality: *Él no es de España. Es dominicano.* <br>• to talk about professions and occupations: *Sammy es jugador de béisbol.* <br>• to tell the time: *Son las dos de la tarde. El partido es en una hora.* <br>• to express possession: *Los boletos para el partido son de mi hermano.* | • to talk about location: *El estadio está en la ciudad de Chicago.* <br>• to talk about condition: *Mi hermano está enfermo hoy y no puede venir.* <br>• to talk about emotional state: *Está muy enojado por eso.* <br>• as part of the progressive tense: *Estoy esperando a mi amigo Sancho para salir.* <br>• as part of certain expressions: *¡Estoy de acuerdo! ¡El partido va a estar estupendo!* |

A number of adjectives change in meaning when used with either **ser** or **estar**.

| ADJECTIVE | ser | estar |
|---|---|---|
| aburrido | to be boring | to be bored |
| listo | to be smart | to be ready |
| rico | to be rich | to be delicious |
| verde | to be green | to be unripe |

**Eres aburrida. / Estás aburrida.** Estas manzanas **son verdes.** / Estas manzanas **están verdes.**

*You **are boring.** / You **are bored.** These apples **are green.** / These apples **are unripe.***

Some adjectives, including **bonito** *(pretty)*, **guapo** *(handsome)*, **callado** *(quiet)*, and **frío** *(cold)*, can be used with either **ser** or **estar**. Although the verb choice depends on what the speaker wants to emphasize, in general, the use of **estar** implies that the characteristic is not permanent (the equivalent of the English verbs *to feel, to look,* or *to seem*).

| | |
|---|---|
| Nela **es** bonita. | *Nela **is** pretty.* |
| Lupe **está** bonita (hoy). | *Lupe **looks** pretty (today).* |
| Daniel **es** callado. | *Daniel **is** a quiet person.* |
| Chucho **está** callado (ahora). | *Chucho **seems** quiet (now).* |

## ▥ Asimilación

**4-57 Yo estoy...** Selecciona las frases que se apliquen a ti en este momento. Al terminar, compara tus respuestas con las de un(a) compañero(a). ¿Qué tienen en común?

En este momento, yo estoy...

| | | |
|---|---|---|
| ____ enfermo(a). | ____ nervioso(a). | ____ tomando café. |
| ____ en la biblioteca. | ____ en mi habitación. | ____ cansado(a). |
| ____ muy contento(a). | ____ relajado(a). | ____ en el salón de clase. |
| ____ estudiando. | ____ aburrido(a). | ____ triste. |
| ____ en mi casa. | ____ mascando chicle *(chewing gum)*. | ____ listo para trabajar. |

1-45 **4-58 ¿Cómo soy?** Escucha cómo las siguientes personas se describen a sí mismas. Luego, selecciona la alternativa que mejor conteste la pregunta **¿Cómo soy?**

1. (a.) Eres antipático.    b. Eres diligente.    c. Eres alto.
2. a. Eres pesimista.    b. Eres paciente.    (c.) Eres optimista.
3. a. Eres bajo.    b. Eres mayor.    (c.) Eres joven.
4. a. Eres alegre.    (b.) Eres activa.    c. Eres sincera.
5. a. Eres rico.    (b.) Eres inteligente.    c. Eres entusiasta.
6. (a.) Eres morena.    b. Eres pelirroja.    c. Eres rubia.

**Script 4-58:** 1. No me gusta estar con otras personas. Prefiero estar solo en mi casa. Tampoco me gusta hablar con nadie. ¿Cómo soy? 2. Creo que el mundo es bueno y que las personas son buenas. ¡La vida es hermosa! ¿Cómo soy? 3. Tengo dieciocho años y estoy lleno de energía. Soy estudiante universitario. ¿Cómo soy? 4. Practico muchos deportes. Me gusta mucho la natación y el tenis. También practico yoga y golf. ¡Ah! ¡Y también me encanta bailar! ¿Cómo soy? 5. Saco muy buenas notas en todas mis clases. Estudio todos los días, pero, en realidad, creo que todas las materias son fáciles. ¿Cómo soy? 6. Tengo pelo negro y largo. No me veo bien con pelo rubio. ¿Cómo soy?

## ▥ Aplicaciones

**4-59 Mi amigo Nelson** Completen las oraciones con la forma correcta del verbo **ser** o **estar**.

Éste ____es____ mi amigo Nelson. Él ____es____ de Sevilla, España. ____Está____ estudiando computación en un instituto técnico. ____Está____ muy contento con sus estudios. Él ____es____ extrovertido y muy alegre. Sus padres ____son____ madrileños. Ellos ____están____ de vacaciones en Almería, al sureste del país. (Ellos) ____Son____ profesores de matemática en el mismo instituto técnico. Nelson también ____es____ un excelente jugador de tenis. Creo que (él) ya ____está____ listo para formar parte del equipo olímpico de tenis de España.

**4-60 En el restaurante** Describan la escena que ven en el dibujo. Usen los verbos **ser** y **estar** correctamente.

MODELO  *Las personas están en un restaurante. El señor de la camisa azul está...*

**4-61 ¡Soy más preguntón(-ona) que tú!** Primero, decidan quién va a hacer preguntas con **ser** y quién va a hacer preguntas con **estar**. Luego, túrnense para hacer y responder a sus preguntas sin parar. ¡Sean creativos! ¿Cuál de los dos puede hacer más preguntas?

MODELO  E1: *¿**Eres** simpático(a)?*
E2: *Sí, **soy** simpático(a). ¿**Estás** en la librería?*
E1: *No, no **estoy** en la librería. **Estoy** en la clase de español. ¿...?*
E2: *...*

### ■ Integración

**4-62 Con el consejero(a)** *(advisor)* Representa la siguiente situación con un(a) compañero(a). Al terminar, cambien de papel.

| El (La) consejero(a) | El (La) estudiante |
|---|---|
| You are meeting one of your advisees for the first time. Ask him/her as many questions as you can to get to know him/her better. Some of the questions may include the following: where the student is from, his/her major, his/her personal traits, how he/she feels at this institution. | You have been assigned a new advisor and decided to stop by his/her office to get to know him/her. Be prepared to answer his/her questions and to ask him/her questions of your own. |

**4-63 Una descripción personal** El (La) consejero(a) de la actividad 4-62 quiere que escribas un breve resumen sobre tu origen, tu personalidad y tus metas *(goals)* académicas para ponerlo en tu expediente *(file)*. Piensa en los temas que discutieron *(you talked about)* en la conversación. Cuando termines, dale una copia a tu profesor(a) para que la corrija.

## IV. Lectura: De vacaciones

### ■ Antes de leer

**A. Las vacaciones de los norteamericanos** Contesten las siguientes preguntas.

1. ¿Les gusta a ustedes salir de vacaciones con su familia?
2. ¿Cómo son las vacaciones de una familia típicamente norteamericana? Describe el comportamiento *(behavior)* típico de cada una de las siguientes personas:
   - el padre (la madre) planea el viaje/maneja el coche...
   - los hijos pelean/discuten/juegan...
   - los abuelos leen/duermen/caminan...

**B. Vocabulario y conceptos** Las siguientes palabras son importantes para la comprensión del texto. Lean sus definiciones y completen las oraciones.

**amueblado:** que tiene muebles (sillas, camas, mesas, etc.)

**descolorido:** que no tiene color, pálido

**quemado:** de color oscuro por el efecto del sol

**triste:** lo opuesto de alegre

Completa las oraciones con el adjetivo más apropiado.

1. Siempre me siento ___triste___ cuando terminan las vacaciones.
2. Este pantalón está ___descolorido___.
3. Después de tres días en el sol estoy ___quemado___.
4. Quiero pasar mis vacaciones en un apartamento bien ___amueblado___.

### «Las vacaciones»

Gomaespuma

Gomaespuma es un dúo español nuevo, formado por los periodistas Guillermo Fesser y Juan Luis Cano, que nació en 1982 en la estación de televisión Antena 3. Debido al éxito *(success)* de su trabajo en televisión, en 1986 fundaron *(founded)* Gomaespuma Producciones, una empresa dedicada a la creatividad en el mundo de los medios de comunicación. Desde entonces, Gomaespuma ha producido *(has produced)* varios libros humorísticos sobre la vida diaria de los españoles, entre ellos *Marchando una de mili, Navidad con orejas, Pasando olímpicamente* y *Familia no hay más que una.*

Suele ser el período de descanso en el verano.

Por fin se llega al apartamento. Es un **cuchitril** mal amueblado, porque los propietarios prefieren tener muebles viejos y feos ya que todos los veranos queda **destrozado**.

Se asignan las habitaciones y aquí siempre hay problemas. Al final la mejor es para la hija, mientras los chicos toman la pequeña. La abuela duerme con la chica en una **cama-mueble**.

dilapidated dwelling

destroyed

sofa-bed

| | |
|---|---|
| *skin* | El primer día de la playa todo es estupendo, excepto el color de la **piel.** |
| *ghost* | Mientras todo el mundo presenta un moreno maravilloso, la familia |
| *tight / knee* | está más pálida que alguien que ha visto un **fantasma.** El hijo mayor |
| *that is driving the father crazy* | lleva un bañador **ajustado,** el pequeño uno de dibujos hasta la **rodilla,** |

El primer día de la playa todo es estupendo, excepto el color de la **piel.** Mientras todo el mundo presenta un moreno maravilloso, la familia está más pálida que alguien que ha visto un **fantasma.** El hijo mayor lleva un bañador **ajustado,** el pequeño uno de dibujos hasta la **rodilla,** la chica un bikini **que trae al padre por la calle de la amargura** porque se transparenta todo, la madre un bañador estampado y un gorro de baño de flores que se pone en la cabeza cada vez que se mete en el agua, el padre lleva un bañador azul descolorido por el efecto del tiempo, y la abuela va vestida completamente, excepto los pies, que los lleva desnudos.

*pick up*

A las dos, la madre, el padre y la abuela **recogen** sus sillitas y sus toallas y se suben al apartamento.

*a short while*
*flunked / to cram*
*drowsiness*

Después de comer todos duermen un **ratito** de siesta, excepto la chica que ha **cateado** latín y se tiene que quedar a **empollar** con todo el **sopor** de después de la comida.

*to go hang out*
*board game*
*late*
*gets mad / reprimands*

Por la noche los chicos piden permiso para **salir por ahí.** El pequeño se queda en casa jugando **al cinquillo** con la madre y la abuela y el chico mayor y la chica salen a tomar algo. Regresan **a las tantas.** El padre **se cabrea** y los **regaña** desde la cama y al día siguiente cuando desayunan, pero se vuelve a repetir la historia durante todo el mes.

*madly*
*muy triste*

La hija se enamora **perdidamente** de un chico de Valencia y cuando se acaba el verano se va **tristísima** porque deja a su amor, aunque han quedado en escribirse y en ir a visitarse.

### ■ ¿Entendiste bien?

**C. Un día típico en la playa** ¿Cómo es un día típico de vacaciones en España, según Gomaespuma? Organicen los siguientes eventos.

    <u>3</u>  Duermen la siesta.

    <u>1</u>  Todos se ponen sus bañadores y van a la playa.

    <u>4</u>  Los chicos salen por ahí.

    <u>2</u>  Los padres recogen las sillas y regresan al apartamento.

    <u>5</u>  Los chicos regresan tarde.

**Answers D:** 1. porque los propietarios saben que la gente daña sus muebles 2. porque tiene que estudiar para su examen de latín 3. porque los chicos llegan tarde por la noche

**D. ¿Por qué?** Respondan a las siguientes preguntas.

1. ¿Por qué está el apartamento mal amueblado?
2. ¿Por qué no duerme la siesta la hija?
3. ¿Por qué se disgusta el padre?

**Answers E:** llega, asignan, toman, duerme, lleva, se pone, va, recogen, suben, comer, empollar, pedir permiso, salir por ahí, se queda, salen, regresan, se cabrea, regaña, desayunan, se enamora, se va, deja

**E. Enfoque lingüístico** Identifiquen cinco verbos referentes a las actividades típicas de una familia española durante las vacaciones de verano.

**F. Para conversar** ¿Qué opinan Uds.? ¿Las vacaciones de las familias españolas son semejantes o diferentes a las vacaciones familiares de los norteamericanos? Presenten algunos puntos concretos.

**G. Actividad de extensión** Usa las notas de la actividad A en la página 171 para escribir una descripción cómica de unas vacaciones en familia, semejante a la de Gomaespuma.

## Las estaciones / Seasons

| | |
|---|---|
| la primavera | spring |
| el verano | summer |
| el otoño | fall |
| el invierno | winter |

## El tiempo / The weather

| | |
|---|---|
| estar (parcialmente) nublado | to be (partly) cloudy |
| hacer buen/mal tiempo | to be good/bad weather |
| hacer calor | to be hot |
| hacer fresco | to be cool |
| hacer frío | to be cold |
| hacer sol | to be sunny |
| hacer viento | to be windy |
| llover (ue) | to rain |
| nevar (ie) | to snow |
| ¿Qué tiempo hace? | What is the weather like? |

## Las prendas de vestir

| | |
|---|---|
| el abrigo | coat |
| la blusa | blouse |
| las botas | boots |
| la camisa | shirt |
| la camiseta | T-shirt |
| el chaleco | vest |
| la chaqueta (americana) | jacket |
| la falda | skirt |
| la gorra | cap |
| el impermeable | raincoat |
| la minifalda | mini-skirt |
| los pantalones | pants |
| los pantalones cortos | shorts |
| la ropa | clothing items |
| la ropa interior | underwear |
| las sandalias | sandals |
| el sombrero de sol | sun hat |
| el suéter | sweater |
| los tejanos/vaqueros | blue jeans |
| el traje | suit |
| el traje de baño / el bañador | swimsuit |
| el vestido | dress |
| los zapatos | shoes |
| los zapatos altos/de tacones | high heel shoes |
| los zapatos de tenis | sneakers |
| las zapatillas | slippers |
| llevar/usar | to wear |

## Accesorios

| | |
|---|---|
| los aretes/pendientes | earrings |
| los calcetines / las medias | socks |
| el cinturón | belt |
| el collar | necklace |
| la corbata | tie |
| los guantes | gloves |
| los lentes de sol | sunglasses |
| las medias | stockings |
| la pulsera | bracelet |
| el reloj | watch |

## Materiales

| | |
|---|---|
| el algodón | cotton |
| el cuero | leather |
| de fantasía | costume (jewelry) |
| la lana | wool |
| el material sintético, acrílico, poliéster | synthetic material, acrylic, polyester |
| el metal | metal |
| el oro | gold |
| la pana | corduroy |
| la plata | silver |
| la seda | silk |
| la tela | fabric |

## Diseños / Designs

| | |
|---|---|
| a cuadros | plaid, checked |
| a rayas | striped |
| de puntos/lunares | polka-dots |
| de un solo tono/liso | solid color |
| estampado | print |

## Los deportes / Sports

| | |
|---|---|
| los aeróbicos | aerobics |
| el árbitro | referee |
| el atletismo | track and field |
| el baloncesto | basketball |
| el béisbol | baseball |
| el equipo | team |
| el esquí | ski |
| el fútbol | soccer |
| el fútbol americano | football |
| la gimnasia | gymnastics |
| el jugador | player |
| el levantamiento de pesas | weight lifting |
| la lucha libre | wrestling |
| la natación | swimming |
| el patinaje (sobre hielo) | (ice) skating |
| el tenis | tennis |
| el vóleibol | volleyball |

## Funciones y estructuras

Comparaciones de adjetivos, p. 148
Verbos con cambio del radical **e → ie**, p. 156
Verbos con cambio del radical **o → ue**, p. 156
Verbos reflexivos, p. 159
**Ser** y **estar**, p. 168
Otros verbos, p. 165

# Puesta en acción

| | |
|---|---|
| **SITUACIÓN:** | You are working for a company with business interests in Latin America. Between April 12 and 14, there will be a shareholders' meeting in Puerto Rico. About 100 people from Latin America, Spain, and the United States will meet in San Juan for this event. Since you know some Spanish, your company has asked you to participate in planning the logistics of this important meeting. |
| **MISIÓN:** | To make all the strategic plans for this meeting and to organize and communicate the meeting agenda to all the participants. |
| **DESTREZAS:** | Organizing a business meeting; organizing and communicating the agenda for a business meeting; and informing participants about meeting conditions, plans, and requirements. |

Include as many verbs from the following list as possible: **cerrar, comenzar, conseguir, convencer, encontrar, escoger, ir, mover, obtener, oír, ver, volar, volver**.

**A. La agenda** Preparen la agenda de la reunión para enviársela *(send it)* a los participantes. Incluyan actividades de negocios, actividades turísticas y de descanso o recreación.

| HORA | 12 de abril | 13 de abril | 14 de abril |
|---|---|---|---|
| 8:00 a.m. | Desayunan en el hotel. | | |
| 10:00 a.m. | Comienza la reunión en la sala #3. | | |
| 12:00 a.m. | | Almuerzan en el restaurante del hotel. | |
| 2:00 p.m. | | | |
| 4:00 p.m. | | | |
| 6:00 p.m. | | | Vuelan a... |
| 8:00 p.m. | | | |

**B. Reservaciones** Representen la siguiente situación.

### Organizador(a) de la reunión

As organizer of this important meeting, you have to make hotel reservations for the company's shareholders. Call the hotel in San Juan and find out if they have adequate facilities. If that is the case, make the necessary reservations for 100 people.

You may use some of the following expressions: **¿Me podría decir si su hotel tiene... ?** (Could you tell me if your hotel has . . . ?) **¿Hay buenos restaurantes cerca del hotel?** (Are there good restaurants near the hotel?) **¿Qué lugares de interés hay en el área?** (What places of interest are there in the area?) **Me gustaría hacer una reservación para...** (I would like to make a reservation for . . .)

### Recepcionista del hotel

An important client is calling to find out about the services at your hotel. Provide this client with all the information he/she needs about the hotel amenities and services and use the chart below to write down the information you need to process the reservation.

You may use some of the following expressions: **Desde luego. / Por supuesto.** (Of course.) **Con mucho gusto.** (My pleasure.) **¿Cuántas habitaciones necesita?** (How many rooms do you need?) **Necesito algunos datos.** (I need some information.)

---

### Hotel El Convento
### Reservas

Nombre:  
Fecha de llegada:  
Fecha de partida:  
Tipo(s) de habitación(-ones):  

Servicios requeridos:  
Número de teléfono:  
Correo electrónico:  
Tarjeta de crédito:  

---

**C. Un memo** Escríbele un memo a tu supervisor, el Sr. Tomasini, para describirle el hotel que reservaste para la reunión. Incluye detalles sobre la localización, el costo y los servicios.

**D. El tiempo en San Juan, la ropa y las comidas** Preparen un volante *(flyer)* para enviarles a los participantes de la reunión. Incluyan información sobre las condiciones del tiempo en San Juan en el mes de abril y recomendaciones acerca de la ropa y los accesorios que deben traer para asistir a las reuniones y para hacer turismo. Además, incluyan una lista de platos típicos puertorriqueños que desean sugerir para los desayunos, los almuerzos y las cenas. Incluyan algunos platos vegetarianos.

| Estado del tiempo | Ropa y accesorios | Menú |
|---|---|---|
|  |  |  |

To find out what the weather is like in Puerto Rico during the month of April, go to **www.weather.com**.

## Servicio comunitario

Visit the public relations office of your local government and offer to provide one of the following services.

- Organize and coordinate a clothes drive.
- Organize and coordinate a food drive.
- Translate brochures about local attractions into Spanish.

**E. Información de interés general** Tu asistente y tú desean preparar una lista de lugares de interés para los participantes de la reunión. Túrnense para hacer preguntas sobre los lugares donde pueden hacer las actividades de su lista y para responder usando la información de sus mapas.

MODELO    E1: *¿Adónde puede ir una persona que quiere comprar una medicina?*
                 E2: *Puede ir a la Farmacia El Amal.*

### Estudiante 1

| Actividad | Nombre del lugar |
|---|---|
| comprar una medicina | *Farmacia El Amal* |
| ir a un concierto | Coliseo José Miguel Agrelot |
| comer un sándwich criollo | El Hipopótamo |
| correr o caminar | Parque Luis Muñoz Marín |
| comprar algo para comer en el hotel | Supermercado Pueblo Xtra |
| leer un libro sobre historia de Puerto Rico | Biblioteca de la Universidad de Puerto Rico |
| sacar dinero | Banco Popular |

San Juan, Puerto Rico

San Juan, Puerto Rico

### Estudiante 2

| Actividad | Nombre del lugar |
|---|---|
| ver arte religioso | Catedral de San Juan |
| comprar un libro de recetas puertorriqueñas | Librería La Tertulia |
| hacerse un estudio médico | Hospital Pavía |
| nadar o tomar un poco de sol | Playa del Condado |
| apreciar pinturas de artistas locales | Museo de Arte de Puerto Rico |
| hacer unas compras | Plaza Las Américas |

# Unidad 3

## Ayer y hoy

## Perú, Ecuador, Bolivia, Nicaragua y Costa Rica

In this unit you will talk about past events and describe how things used to be. The readings will introduce you to life in the rural and urban areas of the Spanish-speaking world. In turn, the videos will introduce you to people from Central and South America who will talk about their backgrounds and their memories as they were growing up in their homelands. At the end of the unit you will create a newsletter in Spanish to be posted on the web. You will also be able to connect with your community by educating others about the importance of recycling and taking care of the environment, solving some of the problems that affect your area, and informing Spanish speakers about available health services.

# Capítulo 5

## Mi pasado

### Para comenzar

¿A qué foto se refiere la siguiente información?

- Quito    Foto 2
- Las culturas indígenas    Foto 3
- Las Islas Galápagos    Foto 1

### In this chapter you will learn . . .

- how to talk about landmark events in your life
- how to describe how things used to be
- how to avoid redundancy
- about legends and traditions of the Spanish-speaking people

|  | **TEMA 1**<br>Eventos importantes | **TEMA 2**<br>Buenos recuerdos | **TEMA 3**<br>Incidentes |
|---|---|---|---|
| Vocabulario | Los eventos importantes y las fechas | Los preparativos para un viaje | El cuerpo humano |
| Funciones y estructuras | Talking about past activities with the preterite tense<br>Referring to past events with **hace... que** | Talking about past activities with stem-changing verbs in the preterite and the verbs **dar, ir, ser,** and **ver**<br>Avoiding repetition with direct object pronouns | Talking about past activities with other stem-changing verbs<br>Talking about incidents and mishaps |
| Lecturas y vídeo | Perspectivas: En el periódico | Vídeo: Otra excursión en Puerto Rico | Lectura: Leyenda del origen de los Incas |

**Foto 1**　　　　　　　**Foto 2**　　　　　　　**Foto 3**

# Enfoque

Transparencies A-12: Country Profile: Perú, Ecuador; A-13: Country Profile: Bolivia, Chile

**iLrn**

**A. ¿Qué sabes ya de Ecuador?** Antes de ver el vídeo, completa las siguientes oraciones con la información que aparece en **Para comenzar** e indica a qué foto se refiere cada oración. Después, compara tus respuestas con las de otro(a) compañero(a).

1. _____Quito_____, la capital de Ecuador, está situada al pie del volcán Pichicha.　Foto 2

2. Hoy en día __las culturas indígenas__ siguen manteniendo sus tradiciones.　Foto 3

3. __Las Islas Galápagos__ están situadas a unas 650 millas de distancia del continente y ofrecen una experiencia inolvidable para los visitantes interesados en la historia natural.　Foto 1

**B. Ecuador, continente e islas** Miren el vídeo y emparejen las siguientes frases sobre Ecuador. Luego, indiquen con qué foto se asocia la frase: las Islas Galápagos (I), Quito (Q) o las culturas indígenas (C).

__b-C__ 1. Los habitantes del pueblo de Otabal...

__c-I__ 2. Este archipiélago es de origen volcánico...

__a-Q__ 3. Esta capital es una ciudad en donde...

a. la arquitectura colonial y las construcciones modernas se complementan.

b. son famosos por sus textiles y su música.

c. y está formado por trece islas grandes, seis islas pequeñas y cuarenta y dos islotes.

**C. ¡Descubran las Islas Galápagos!** Lean las siguientes descripciones de distintos tipos de excursiones que pueden hacer en las Islas Galápagos. Luego, en grupos, escojan **una** excursión y prepárense para explicarle a la clase por qué prefieren esa excursión.

**Opción #1: *Trekking*** Hagan *trekking* en el Parque Nacional. A las personas deportistas esta excursión les permite explorar el interior de las islas y ver sitios diferentes a los de los cruceros. Las caminatas van desde tres hasta seis horas, pero no son de mucha distancia, y les da tiempo suficiente para observar la riqueza de la flora y la fauna de las Galápagos.

**Opción #2: Buceo** Vengan a la Reserva Marina de Galápagos para un día de buceo. Descubran la belleza del fondo marino del archipiélago. Buceen rodeados de espectaculares arrecifes de coral e impactante fauna marina: tortugas, lobos marinos, pingüinos, peces espada, delfines e incluso ballenas. ¡Una experiencia inolvidable!

For more info, you may want to check the **Temas** site: **http://temas.heinle.com**

# Eventos importantes

## I. Vocabulario: Los eventos importantes y las fechas

Nacimiento (1946)

Bautizo (1947)

Cumpleaños (1948)

Graduación (1968)

### SABOR REGIONAL

In some Spanish-speaking countries, the words **la boda** and **el casamiento** are synonyms of **el matrimonio.** In other countries, they refer specifically to the wedding ceremony.

Matrimonio (1970)

Aniversario (1995)

Jubilación (2000)

## Los números después de 100

| | | | | | |
|---|---|---|---|---|---|
| cien | 100 | seiscientos(as) | 600 | diez mil dos | 10.002 |
| ciento uno(a) | 101 | setecientos(as) | 700 | cien mil | 100.000 |
| ciento dos | 102 | ochocientos(as) | 800 | cien mil uno(a) | 100.001 |
| ciento tres | 103 | novecientos(as) | 900 | cien mil dos | 100.002 |
| doscientos(as) | 200 | mil | 1.000 | novecientos mil | 900.000 |
| doscientos uno(a) | 201 | mil uno(a) | 1.001 | novecientos | 999.000 |
| doscientos dos | 202 | mil dos | 1.002 | noventa y nueve mil | |
| doscientos tres | 203 | dos mil | 2.000 | un millón | 1.000.000 |
| trescientos(as) | 300 | tres mil | 3.000 | dos millones | 2.000.000 |
| cuatrocientos(as) | 400 | diez mil | 10.000 | | |
| quinientos(as) | 500 | diez mil uno(a) | 10.001 | | |

The word **cien** is used before nouns.

> Los padres del Sr. Jones llegaron a América hace más de **cien** años.
> *Mr. Jones's parents arrived in America more than **one hundred** years ago.*

> Su casa está a unas **cien** millas de Boston.
> *His house is about **one hundred** miles from Boston.*

**Ciento** is used to express quantities from 101 to 199. Notice that there is no **y** following the word **ciento.**

> El Sr. Jones vive en el número **ciento** quince de la calle Main.
> *Mr. Jones lives at 115 Main Street.*

> Su casa tiene más de **ciento** ochenta y cinco años.
> *His house is more than **one hundred** eighty-five years old.*

The ending **-cientos** changes to **-cientas** before feminine nouns.

> Su casa cuesta ahora unos ocho**cientos** mil dólares.
> *His house is worth now about eight **hundred** thousand dollars.*

> Su casa está a unas dos**cientas** millas de la playa.
> *His house is about two **hundred** miles from the beach.*

Dates after the year 2000 are expressed as follows:

> La graduación de su hijo fue en 2003 (**dos mil tres**).
> *His son's graduation was in **two thousand three.***

When expressing exact quantities, the word **mil** does not have a plural form, but **millón** does (**millones**).

> El Sr. Jones gana ochenta y cinco **mil** dólares al año.
> *Mr. Jones makes eighty-five **thousand** dollars a year.*

> El presupuesto de su compañía es de ocho **millones** de dólares.
> *His company's budget is eight **million** dollars.*

✳ Notice that the word **millón(-ones)** is followed by **de** before nouns.

## ■ Asimilación

 **5-1 ¿Cuándo ocurrió?** *(When did it happen?)* Identifiquen el año de los siguientes eventos históricos.

<u>e</u> 1. Los ingleses establecen su primera colonia en América (Jamestown)

<u>a</u> 2. La Declaración de Independencia

<u>f</u> 3. Lincoln pronuncia el discurso de Gettysburg

<u>c</u> 4. Los hermanos Wright vuelan por primera vez

<u>b</u> 5. Los autobuses son desegregados en Alabama gracias al boycot organizado por Martin Luther King, Jr.

<u>d</u> 6. Los astronautas Armstrong y Aldrin caminan en la Luna

a. mil setecientos setenta y seis
b. mil novecientos cincuenta y seis
c. mil novecientos tres
d. mil novecientos sesenta y nueve
e. mil seiscientos siete
f. mil ochocientos sesenta y tres

---

**Script 5-2:** El profesor Martínez ha tenido una vida muy interesante. Él nació en México, el 3 de mayo de 1970. Terminó la escuela secundaria en 1988 y en 1989 ingresó a la universidad para estudiar literatura española. El profesor Martínez se graduó en 1993 y empezó a trabajar en esta universidad en 1995, después de terminar su maestría. En 1998 se casó con Matilde Suárez y en 2001 nació su primer hijo. Hoy tiene tres hijos y el mayor va a ingresar a la escuela este año.

CD1–47

**5-2 Eventos importantes en la vida del profesor Martínez** Escucha la información e indica cuál es la fecha correcta. Al terminar, compara tus respuestas con las de a un(a) compañero(a).

1. Fecha de su graduación:
   a. 1983
   b. 1993
   c. 1973
2. Fecha de su matrimonio:
   a. 1978
   b. 1968
   c. 1998
3. Fecha del nacimiento de su primer hijo:
   a. 2002
   b. 2001
   c. 2000

---

## ■ Aplicaciones

**Sugerencia 5-2:** You may also personalize the activity and refer to important dates in your life.

**Extensión 5-3:** You may want to extend this activity by asking students to continue this circumlocution task with other events from the vocabulary in this section.

**5-3 ¿De qué evento se trata?** Identifiquen el evento según la descripción.

1. Es una celebración que tiene lugar todos los años. La gente usualmente recibe tarjetas o regalos en este día.   **cumpleaños**
2. Es la celebración del fin de un curso de estudios. Los estudiantes por lo general reciben un diploma.   **graduación**
3. Es una ceremonia religiosa. Los padres usualmente llevan a sus hijos pequeños a la iglesia y les asignan un nombre.   **bautizo**
4. Es la unión de dos personas que quieren formar una familia. Puede ser una ceremonia religiosa o civil.   **matrimonio**

**5-4 ¿Cuánto es?** Túrnense para leer y resolver los siguientes problemas:

1. $100 + 200 =$   300
2. $350 + 500 =$   850
3. $550 + 1 =$   551
4. $1.000 - 1 =$   999
5. $5.000 - 2.000 =$   3.000
6. $900.000 - 10.000 =$   890.000

7. $400 \times 10 =$   4.000
8. $30 \times 50 =$   1.500
9. $200 \times 200 =$   40.000
10. $10.000 \div 2 =$   5.000
11. $200.000 \div 5 =$   40.000
12. $700 \div 7 =$   100

**REMEMBER**

To ask the question use one of the following expressions.
**¿Cuántos son *cien más trescientos*?** $(100 + 300)$
**¿Cuántos son *trescientos menos cien*?** $(300 - 100)$
**¿Cuántos son *trescientos por cien*?** $(300 \times 100)$
**¿Cuántos son *trescientos dividido por cien*?** $(300 \div 100)$

**5-5 ¿Cuándo fue?** *(When did it take place?)* Indica la fecha de los siguientes eventos y luego intercambia información con un(a) compañero(a). Al terminar, preséntenle un informe breve al resto de la clase.

MODELO    E1: *¿Cuándo fue tu <u>graduación de la escuela secundaria</u>?*
E2: *Mi <u>graduación</u> fue en <u>dos mil cinco</u>.*

1. nacimiento
2. graduación de la escuela primaria
3. graduación de la escuela secundaria
4. cumpleaños número quince
5. inicio de los estudios universitarios

## ■ Integración

**5-6 Investigacion** Un amigo quiere estudiar *(wants to study)* en los Estados Unidos. Indica el costo de las siguientes cosas.

1. la matrícula *(tuition)* en tu universidad
2. los libros cada semestre
3. un coche nuevo
4. el alquiler *(rent)* de un apartmento
5. comida para un mes

*Sugerencia 5-6: You may want to point out to your students that they will need this information to carry out the following conversation activity.*

**5-7 El costo de vida** *(cost of living)* Representa la siguiente situación con un(a) compañero(a).

### Estudiante extranjero(a)

Tú deseas estudiar en los Estados Unidos, pero necesitas más información acerca del costo de vida en ese país. Pregúntale a tu amigo(a) estadounidense el precio de algunas cosas básicas (como, por ejemplo, el hospedaje, la comida, los libros, etc.). También, pregúntale si hay trabajos para estudiantes dentro o fuera de la universidad. Averigua dónde pueden trabajar los estudiantes, qué tienen que hacer, cuánto les pagan, etc.

### Estudiante estadounidense

Responde a las preguntas de este(a) estudiante internacional acerca del costo de vida en los Estados Unidos. Háblale del costo del hospedaje, de la comida, de los libros, etc. También, dale información sobre las oportunidades de trabajo que existen dentro y fuera de la universidad.

**EN TU COMUNIDAD**

Interview an international student (preferably, but not necessarily, from a Spanish-speaking country) and prepare a brief report on the cost of living in his/her home country. To help you focus your interview, concentrate on investigating the cost of housing, food, transportation, and clothing. In groups, discuss your findings and present a summary.

## II. Funciones y estructuras: Talking about past activities with the preterite tense

Mi sobrina Alanita **nació** en 2004.
*My niece Alanita **was born** in 2004.*

Sus padres **celebraron** su quinto aniversario en 2005. *Her parents **celebrated** their fifth anniversary in 2005.*

You may wish to inform your students that in **Capítulo 6** they will learn about another past tense *(the imperfect tense)* that is used to talk about actions, states, and events that are not perceived as completed.

The preterite tense is used to talk about actions, states, or events that were completed in the past, regardless of how long it took to complete them.

Ayer por la noche **cené** con Meche, **estudié** y **me acosté** tarde.

*Last night **I had dinner** with Meche, **I studied,** and **I went to bed** late.*

The following is a list of the endings used to conjugate regular verbs in the preterite.

Notice that the conjugation of regular **-er** and **-ir** verbs is the same in the preterite. Also, notice that the **nosotros(as)** forms of **-ar** and **-ir** verbs are identical in the present and preterite tenses. Context will generally allow you to figure out what tense is being used.

| **-ar** verbs | **-er** verbs | **-ir** verbs |
|---|---|---|
| **estudiar** *(to study)* | **beber** *(to drink)* | **vivir** *(to live)* |
| estudié | bebí | viví |
| estudiaste | bebiste | viviste |
| estudió | bebió | vivió |
| estudiamos | bebimos | vivimos |
| estudiasteis | bebisteis | vivisteis |
| estudiaron | bebieron | vivieron |

There is a group of verbs that suffer orthographic changes in the **yo** form in order to maintain the sound of the last letter in the verb stem. These changes affect verbs that end in **-car, -gar,** and **-zar** in the infinitive.

| c→qu | g→gu | z→c |
|---|---|---|
| **sacar** *(to take out)* | **llegar** *(to arrive)* | **empezar** *(to begin)* |
| sa**qu**é | lle**gu**é | empe**c**é |
| sacaste | llegaste | empezaste |
| sacó | llegó | empezó |
| ... | ... | ... |
| Other verbs: **buscar** *(to look for)* and **tocar** *(to touch, to play [an instrument])* | Other verbs: **conjugar** *(to conjugate),* **entregar** *(to deliver, to hand [in/over]),* **jugar** *(to play [a sport or game]),* and **pagar** *(to pay)* | Other verbs: **almorzar** *(to have lunch),* **comenzar** *(to begin),* **organizar** *(to organize),* and **realizar** *(to do, to carry out)* |

Here is a list of common expressions you can use to indicate when a past action, state, or event took place.

| | |
|---|---|
| anoche | *last night* |
| ayer | *yesterday* |
| el (jueves/mes/verano/ año/...) pasado | *last (Thursday/month/summer/ year/ . . .)* |
| esta mañana/tarde | *this morning/afternoon* |
| hace (dos semanas/cuatro meses/un año/...) | *(two weeks/four months/ a year/. . .) ago* |

## ■ Asimilación

**5-8 Ayer** Piensa en las cosas que hiciste *(you did)* ayer y escoge la alternativa que mejor complete cada oración. Luego, compara tus respuestas con las de un(a) compañero(a). ¿Qué tienen en común?

1. Me levanté...    a. temprano.    b. tarde.
2. Estudié... horas.    a. menos de dos    b. más de dos
3. Almorcé...    a. en la cafetería.    b. en otro lugar.
4. Bebí... en la cena.    a. un refresco    b. otra cosa
5. Asistí a... clases.    a. menos de cuatro    b. más de tres
6. Miré televisión...    a. por la tarde.    b. por la noche.

CD1–48 **5-9 ¿Cuándo?** Escucha la descripción del día que tuvo Pablo ayer e indica en qué momento hizo las siguientes actividades.

| Actividad | Por la mañana | Por la tarde | Por la noche |
|---|:---:|:---:|:---:|
| Entregó una monografía de sociología. | | x | |
| Bailó música de todo tipo. | | | x |
| Limpió su habitación. | x | | |
| Visitó a unos amigos. | | x | |
| Compró un pastel para un cumpleaños. | x | | |
| Se preparó para ir a una fiesta. | | x | |

**Script 5-9:** Ayer hice muchas cosas. Por la mañana, limpié mi habitación y ayudé a mi padre a cortar el césped. También compré un pastel para el cumpleaños de Paula. Después, por la tarde, le entregué una monografía a la profesora de sociología y visité a unos amigos. Además, busqué a mi madre al aeropuerto y me preparé para ir a la fiesta de Paula. Por la noche, en la fiesta, hablé con muchos de mis parientes, bailé todo tipo de música y conocí al novio de Paula. ¡Y también conocí a la mujer de mi vida, mi futura esposa!

## Aplicaciones

**5-10 La semana pasada** Para saber qué hicieron *(they did)* estas personas la semana pasada, escojan el verbo lógico y conjúguenlo en el pretérito.

> MODELO   Leticia (estudiar/comer/patinar) sobre hielo con su familia.
> *patinar → patinó*

1. Yo (levantarse/salir/organizar) una reunión en mi trabajo.
2. Fermín y Verónica (quedarse/perder/traer) en un hotel lujoso.
3. Mi jefe y yo (salir/hablar/anunciar) de viaje para Quito, Ecuador.
4. La Sra. Montalbán (tomar/jugar/vender) su apartamento.
5. Yo (cocinar/sacar/vencer) vídeos de películas extranjeras.
6. Yo (nadar/jugar/hacer) fútbol en el parque de mi pueblo.
7. Doña Fela (comprar/asistir/pasar) tiempo con su familia.

**Answers 5-10:** 1. organicé 2. se quedaron 3. salimos 4. vendió 5. saqué 6. jugué 7. pasó

**5-11 ¿Qué hizo el (la) profesor(a)?** ¿Qué creen que hizo el (la) profesor(a) esta mañana? Escriban por lo menos seis preguntas para él/ella usando la forma **usted** de los verbos.

> MODELO   *Profesor(a), ¿usted desayunó esta mañana?*

Here is a list of phrases you may use to form your questions: **levantarse temprano, manejar a la universidad, hablar con sus colegas, comer pan tostado, responder a los mensajes de correo electrónico, tomar té, escribir un informe, recibir buenas noticias, pagar algunas cuentas.**

**5-12 ¿Qué tenemos en común?**

**Paso 1:** Completa la siguiente tabla con algunas actividades que hiciste en los momentos indicados. Escribe por lo menos una actividad en cada espacio.

| anoche | el fin de semana pasado | hace dos meses | el verano pasado |
|--------|-------------------------|----------------|------------------|
|        |                         |                |                  |

**Paso 2:** Hazle preguntas a tu compañero(a) para saber si hizo *(he/she did)* las mismas actividades que tú. Toma notas. Cuando termines, prepara un resumen y compártelo con la clase.

> MODELO   E1: *James, ¿trabajaste anoche?*
> E1: *Sí, trabajé anoche.*   o   *No, no trabajé anoche.*

Notice that these verbs are derived from nouns you already know: **nacer** *(to be born)*, from **nacimiento** *(birth)*; **bautizarse** *(to be baptized)*, from **bautizo** *(baptism)*; etc. If they are reflexive, they are conjugated like any other reflexive verb.

**REMEMBER**

You will have to ask questions with interrogative words such as **¿cuándo? ¿dónde? ¿por qué? ¿quién? ¿cómo?**

## Integración

**5-13 Los eventos importantes** Entrevista a tu compañero(a) para averiguar cuándo celebró los eventos importantes de la lista. Además, trata de averiguar todos los detalles que puedas.

| | | |
|---|---|---|
| **nacer**\* | **casarse**\* | **celebrar su** |
| **bautizarse**\* | **jubilarse**\* | **cumpleaños** |
| **graduarse**\* **de la escuela** | **celebrar su aniversario** | **número...** |
| **(primaria/intermedia/** | **número...** | |
| **secundaria)** | | |

You may connect your ideas by using expressions such as **entonces, después, de pronto** *(suddenly)*, **inmediatamente, un poco más tarde,** and **finalmente.**

**5-14 Una experiencia personal** Cuéntale *(Tell)* a tu profesor(a) qué ocurrió en un evento importante o especial de tu vida. Puedes escribir sobre un evento trágico, cómico o interesante (¡o puedes usar la imaginación!). Cuando termines, entrégale una copia a tu profesor(a) para que te dé *(so that he/she gives you)* su opinión.

## III. Funciones y estructuras: Referring to past events with *hace... que*

—¿**Cuánto tiempo hace que** te jubilaste, Olga?     *How long ago did you retire, Olga?*

—**Hace dos años que** me jubilé.     *I retired **two years ago.***

To find out how long ago an action or event took place, use the following question.

> **¿Cuánto (tiempo) hace que** + verb in the preterite tense?

The use of the word **tiempo** in this question is optional.

And to answer these questions, use one of the following structures.

> **Hace** + length of time + **que** + verb in the preterite tense
> Verb in the preterite tense + **hace** + length of time

—¿**Cuánto hace que** te graduaste de la escuela secundaria?     *How long ago did you graduate from high school?*

—**Hace seis meses que** me gradué. / Me gradué **hace seis meses.**     *I graduated **six months ago.***

If the action of the verb started in the past and continues in the present, the present tense is used instead of the preterite.

—¿Cuánto hace que Tito **vive** en Bolivia?     *How long **has** Tito **been living** in Bolivia?*

—Hace un año y medio que **vive** ahí. / **Vive** ahí hace un año y medio.     *He **has been living** there for a year and a half.*

When the action continues in the present, you can also use the question: ¿**Desde cuándo** + verb in the present tense? ¿**Desde cuándo estudian** en esta universidad? (***How long have you been studying** at this university?*)

### ■ Asimilación

**5-15 El pasado** Escoge las oraciones que sean ciertas. Cuando termines, compara tus respuestas con las de un(a) compañero(a). Comenten las diferencias.

_____ Comí una hamburguesa hace más de veinticuatro horas.

_____ Hace más de un año que tomé una clase de matemáticas.

_____ Hace menos de seis horas que me levanté.

_____ Limpié mi habitación hace más de una semana.

_____ Hace solamente unas horas que estudié en la biblioteca.

_____ Nací hace más de veinticinco años.

_____ Me afeité hace más de dos días.

_____ Hace más de un año que me casé.

> **REMEMBER**
>
> **Más de** means *more than* and **menos de** means *less than.*

CD1-49

**5-16 Los Hernández** Escucha a la Sra. Hernández hablar de algunos de los eventos en la vida de su esposo y de ella. Luego, escoge las alternativas que mejor completen las siguientes oraciones. **¡OJO!** Imagínate que estamos en el año 2000.

1. Los Hernández se casaron...
   a. hace 45 años.　　b. hace 40 años.　　c. hace 50 años.

2. ...que el Sr. Hernández se graduó de la universidad.
   a. Hace 40 años　　b. Hace 42 años　　c. Hace 38 años

3. ...que ellos celebraron su vigésimo quinto (twenty-fifth) aniversario de boda.
   a. Hace 30 años　　b. Hace 25 años　　c. Hace 20 años

4. Ellos se jubilaron...
   a. hace 5 años.　　b. hace 10 años.　　c. hace 15 años.

5. Su primer bisnieto (great-grandchild) nació...
   a. hace 10 años.　　b. hace 15 años.　　c. hace 20 años.

■ **Aplicaciones**

**5-17 ¿Cuánto tiempo hace que... ?** Túrnense para hacer y responder a preguntas usando los siguientes datos.

> MODELO　　Noelia / tomar unas vacaciones / cuatro años
> E1: *¿Cuánto hace que Noelia tomó unas vacaciones?*
> E2: *Hace cuatro años que Noelia tomó unas vacaciones.*
> o　*Noelia tomó unas vacaciones hace cuatro años.*

1. Andrés y Luis / conocerse / un año
2. doña Gabriela / preparar unas tortillas / seis horas
3. el Sr. Bonilla / salir del trabajo / unos minutos
4. los niños / enfermarse / dos semanas
5. Mariel y Anneris / empezar a estudiar / dos horas
6. tus amigos / reunirse / tres meses

**5-18 ¿Cuánto saben de mí?** Toma unos minutos para escribir por lo menos cinco preguntas sobre ti. Luego, hazles las preguntas a tus compañeros de clase para ver quién puede dar la respuesta correcta. Guíalos (Guide them) respondiendo **más** o **menos** si no te dan la respuesta correcta.

> MODELO　　E1: *¿Cuánto tiempo hace que cumplí cinco años?*
> E2: *Hace trece años que cumpliste cinco años.*
> E1: *Más.*
> E3: *Hace quince años que cumpliste cinco años.*
> E1: *¡Correcto!*

**Script 5-16:** Mi esposo y yo hemos compartido muchos momentos importantes en nuestra vida. Nosotros nos casamos en 1955 en Ecuador. Yo me gradué de la universidad en 1960 y mi esposo se graduó en 1962. Trabajamos juntos en una compañía de turismo. Los dos nos jubilamos en 1990. También celebramos nuestro vigésimo quinto aniversario de bodas en 1980 con todos nuestros hijos y nietos. Por otro lado, celebramos el nacimiento de nuestro primer bisnieto en 1985. ¡Ha sido una vida muy feliz!

**Answers 5-17:** 1. ¿... se conocieron? Hace un año que Andrés y Luis se conocieron. / Andrés y Luis se conocieron hace un año. 2. ¿... preparó unas tortillas? Hace seis horas que doña Gabriela preparó unas tortillas. / Doña Gabriela preparó unas tortillas hace seis horas. 3. ¿... salió del trabajo? Hace unos minutos que el Sr. Bonilla salió del trabajo. / El Sr. Bonilla salió del trabajo hace unos minutos. 4. ¿... se enfermaron? Hace dos semanas que los niños se enfermaron. / Los niños se enfermaron hace dos semanas. 5. ¿... empezaron a estudiar? Hace dos horas que Mariel y Anneris empezaron a estudiar. / Mariel y Anneris empezaron a estudiar hace dos horas. 6. ¿... se reunieron? Hace tres meses que mis amigos se reunieron. / Mis amigos se reunieron hace tres meses.

## 5-19 Tú y yo

**Paso 1:** Toma unos minutos para indicar cuánto tiempo hace que hiciste las siguientes actividades.

1. comenzar a aprender español
2. graduarse de la escuela secundaria
3. conocer a mi mejor amigo(a)
4. bañarse
5. recibir una visita inesperada *(unexpected)*
6. comprar unos tejanos nuevos

**Paso 2:** Ahora, usa la misma lista de actividades para entrevistar a tu compañero(a). Toma notas y, al terminar, prepara un resumen.

MODELO   E1: *¿Cuánto tiempo hace que comenzaste a aprender español?*
E2: ...

## ■ Integración

### 5-20 Buscando un(a) compañero(a) de apartamento Representa la siguiente situación con un(a) compañero(a).

| **Estudiante A** | **Estudiante B** |
|---|---|
| Imagínate que estás buscando a la persona apropiada para compartir un nuevo apartamento. Quieres que esta persona sea responsable, tranquila, que no tenga vicios *(addictions)* y que te ayude con la limpieza. Entrevista a tu compañero(a) y averigua cómo es, cuáles son algunos de sus hábitos y actividades favoritas y cuánto tiempo hace que hace esas actividades. | Necesitas encontrar un lugar donde vivir y vas a una entrevista con una persona que está buscando un(a) compañero(a) de apartamento. Él/Ella quiere saber cómo eres, cuáles son algunos de tus hábitos y actividades favoritas y cuánto tiempo hace que haces esas actividades. Para ti la honestidad es muy importante y quieres que él/ella sepa que eres una persona de espíritu libre *(free spirit)* y aventurera. |

Para que la interacción sea interesante y controvertida, pueden hablar de temas como **fumar** *(to smoke)*, **tomar bebidas alcohólicas, dar fiestas todos los fines de semana, escuchar música a todo volumen, limpiar (la cocina/el baño/...), lavar los platos, no graduarse de la escuela secundaria, no creer en el matrimonio**, etc.

#### REMEMBER

You must use the present tense in questions and answers with **hace... que** if the action began in the past and continues in the present. Otherwise, use the preterite.

### 5-21 Una persona admirable ¿A qué persona admiras por sus logros *(achievements)*? Haz una lista de algunas de las cosas que esta persona ha logrado en su vida y compártela con tu profesor(a). Puedes escribir sobre algún pariente, amigo o persona famosa.

MODELO   *Mi madre nació hace cuarenta años, en el año 1966.*
*Ella se graduó de... hace... años... y trabaja en...*
*hace... años.*

## IV. Perspectivas: En el periódico

### ■ Antes de leer

**A. El periódico** Observen el periódico local e identifiquen las siguientes secciones.

Noticias *(news)* internacionales     Cultura

Noticias nacionales     Eventos sociales

Noticias locales     Clasificados

Deportes

**Sugerencia:** Provide or ask students to bring local newspapers for the pre-reading tasks.

**B. ¿Qué sección recibe más cobertura** *(coverage)*? Identifiquen la sección que tiene más cobertura.

**C. La sección social** ¿Qué eventos se mencionan en esta sección? (Mencionen los tres más importantes.)

### ■ A leer

Observa ahora esta sección de eventos sociales tomada del periódico peruano *El Comercio.*

If you have access to the Internet, you may want to provide a more recent edition of this newspaper by visiting: http://www.elcomercioperu. com.pe/ sociales/html/EventosAzulIndex.html

### Cóctel en el Marriott

*corporate bonds*

Con motivo de la presentación de la primera emisión de **bonos corporativos,** el Banco Financiero del Perú organizó un cóctel en el Salón San Martín del Hotel Marriott. Ramón Anaya, gerente general de esta **entidad,** fue el **encargado** de la presentación.

*entity, corporation*
*person in charge*

#### La despedida de Juan Diego

En San Isidro, Octavio y Teresa Fernández ofrecieron una cena en honor del tenor peruano Juan Diego Flórez. Después de la última función de *La Figlia del Regimento,* el sábado en el Teatro Segura, el invitado especial llegó para compartir un simpático momento junto a los invitados. Ellos y sus **anfitriones** disfrutaron una noche de baile que se **prolongó** por varias horas.

*hosts*
*lasted*

*evening party*

#### Velada musical en la embajada rusa

En el marco de las celebraciones por el trigésimo quinto (treinta y cinco) aniversario del restablecimiento de las relaciones diplomáticas ruso-peruanas, el embajador de dicho país, Anatoly Moltchanov, ofreció una velada musical con la participación de la maestra rusa Larissa Petrovski y el maestro peruano Fernando de Luna.

### Salcedo - Asturias

En ceremonia llevada a cabo en su casa de Totoritas, al sur de Lima, Liliana Asturias Botero contrajo matrimonio con Luis Salcedo Triviño. La novia es hija de Luis Asturias Carmona y de Anita Botero de Asturias. El novio es hijo de Eduardo Salcedo Meléndez y de Maruja Triviño de Salcedo. La pareja partió en viaje de bodas al Brasil.

### Benavides - Cárdenas

En ceremonia llevada a cabo en la iglesia Nuestra Señora del Carmen, de San Miguel, contrajeron matrimonio César Antonio Benavides Galindo y Claudia Patricia Cárdenas Medina. La novia es hija de Pedro Alfonso Cárdenas Valenzuela y de María Gabriela Medina de Cárdenas. El novio es hijo de César Antonio Benavides Oviedo y de Ana María Galindo de Benavides.

## ■ ¿Entendiste bien?

**D. Eventos importantes** ¿Cuáles de los siguientes eventos se presentan en esta sección? Marca los que correspondan.

\_\_\_\_ nacimientos

\_\_\_\_ bautizos

\_\_\_\_ cumpleaños

\_\_\_\_ graduaciones

\_X\_ matrimonios

\_\_\_\_ aniversarios

\_X\_ otros: \_\_cóctel, cena, velada musical\_\_

**E. ¿Cierto o falso?** Indiquen si las siguientes oraciones son ciertas (**C**) o falsas (**F**) según el artículo.

\_C\_ El padre de Claudia Patricia Cárdenas se llama Pedro.

\_F\_ El suegro de Liliana Asturias se llama Alberto.

\_F\_ Perú restableció relaciones diplomáticas con Rusia en 1995.

\_F\_ Ramón Anaya es el gerente del hotel Marriott de Lima.

\_C\_ Juan Diego Flórez es un famoso cantante peruano.

\_F\_ César Benavides y su esposa Claudia viajaron a Francia después de su boda *(wedding)*.

**F. Actividad de extensión** Preparen una pequeña reseña en español para informar acerca de los eventos sociales más importantes de esta semana en su universidad.

# Buenos recuerdos

Transparencies O-2: En la agencia de viajes; O-3: En el aeropuerto; O-4: En el avión; O-5: El horario de tren; L-5: La Guia Michelin

## I. Vocabulario: Los preparativos para un viaje

### Los documentos de viaje

| el boleto/ billete | la tarjeta de embarque | el pasaporte | la visa | los cheques de viajero |

### El equipaje

| el maletín | la maleta | la mochila | la cartera | la billetera |

---

**SABOR REGIONAL**

In Mexico the word for suitcase is **la valija,** and in Spain the word for visa is **el visado.**

**Vocabulario práctico**

el asiento *seat*

el equipaje de mano *carry on luggage*

el pasillo *aisle*

la sala de espera *boarding area*

el terminal internacional *international departures terminal*

la ventanilla *window*

**Verbos**

abordar *to board*

cambiar *to exchange*

empacar *to pack*

mostrar(ue) *to show*

sacar *to get, obtain*

## ■ Asimilación

**5-22 ¿En qué orden?** Organiza los siguientes eventos de una manera lógica.

Answers 5-22: Answers may vary slightly.

 6  Abordo el avión.

 1  Saco el pasaporte.

 5  Presento la tarjeta de embarque.

 4  Empaco la maleta.

 2  Compro el boleto.

 3  Compro los cheques de viajero.

D1-50 **5-23 ¿Qué es?** Identifica el objeto basándote en las descripciones que vas a escuchar.

1. (a.) los cheques de viajero
   b. el maletín de mano
   c. cl pasaporte
2. a. la tarjeta de embarque
   b. la visa
   (c.) el pasaporte
3. a. el boleto
   b. la ventanilla
   (c.) la maleta
4. (a.) la tarjeta de embarque
   b. los cheques de viajero
   c. el boleto

Script 5-23: 1. Es una forma de dinero que llevan por lo general los turistas cuando van de vacaciones a otro país o a otra ciudad. 2. Es un documento oficial de identidad. 3. Es grande y se usa para transportar ropa y otros objetos. 4. Es un documento que necesitas para entrar al avión.

Expansión 5-23: You may want to expand this circumlocution activity by asking students to prepare and read their own descriptions.

## ■ Aplicaciones

**5-24 Preparativos de viaje** Completen las oraciones con la palabra o frase del vocabulario más apropiada.

**OPCIONES:**   pasaporte   boleto   tarjeta de embarque
cheques de viajero   maletas

1. Necesito llamar a la agencia de viajes para comprar un
   ___boleto___ de ida y vuelta a La Paz, Bolivia.
2. Tengo que tomarme una fotografía para mi ___pasaporte___.
3. Me gustaría pasar por el banco esta tarde para comprar unos
   ___cheques de viajero___.
4. Sólo permiten dos ___maletas___ en vuelos internacionales.
5. Mi ___tarjeta de embarque___ indica que mi asiento es el 10L.

**5-25 Prioridades** Imagínense que están preparando un viaje a un país de habla hispana. ¿Adónde quieren ir? ¿Por qué? ¿Qué necesitan para el viaje? Preparen una lista.

CD1-51 **5-26 En el aeropuerto** Túrnense para hacer el papel de la empleada y el papel del viajero en la siguiente conversación.

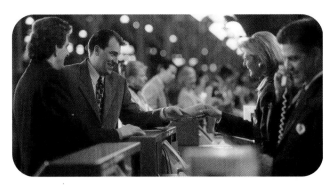

EMPLEADA: Buenos días, señor. Su pasaporte y su boleto, por favor.
VIAJERO: Aquí los tiene.
EMPLEADA: ¿Cuántas maletas lleva?
VIAJERO: Dos y un maletín de mano.
EMPLEADA: ¿Prefiere pasillo o ventanilla?
VIAJERO: Ventanilla, por favor.
EMPLEADA: Muy bien. Su asiento es el 6A. Aquí tiene su tarjeta de embarque, su boleto y su pasaporte. Pase inmediatamente a la sala de espera 5.
VIAJERO: Muchas gracias.
EMPLEADA: Con gusto. Que tenga un buen viaje.

## Integración

**5-27 Quiero viajar al extranjero** Representa la siguiente situación con un(a) compañero(a).

Ask your friend questions to make sure he/she has what is needed. Use the vocabulary list as a checklist and point of departure. Also suggest clothing depending on your partner's destination.

Use Internet resources to investigate the travel documents required for the different Spanish-speaking countries (they vary considerably), and also the baggage allowances and restrictions of an American carrier of your choice.

| **Estudiante A** | **Estudiante B** |
|---|---|
| Tú eres un(a) viajero(a) muy experimentado(a) (has viajado por todo el mundo), pero tu amigo(a) nunca ha viajado fuera del país. Ayúdale a decidir adónde puede ir y explícale lo que tiene que hacer para preparar su viaje. | Tú quieres ir de viaje a un lugar diferente y exótico, pero no sabes adónde ir o cómo prepararte para el viaje. Pídele información a tu amigo(a); él/ella ha viajado mucho y sabe mucho sobre este tema. |

### EN TU COMUNIDAD

Visit a travel agency and obtain brochures on vacation packages to Spain and/or Latin America. In small groups, select and briefly describe the most attractive vacation package. Then, share with the class the reasons for your selection.

**5-28 Antes de venir a los Estados Unidos...** Imagínate que trabajas para la revista de una aerolínea estadounidense. Escribe un artículo breve para ayudar a los visitantes hispanos a prepararse para su viaje a los Estados Unidos.

## II. Funciones y estructuras: Talking about past activities with stem-changing verbs in the preterite and the verbs *dar, ir, ser,* and *ver*

Nathan y Jenny **se fueron** para Perú esta mañana. Ellos **pidieron** asiento de ventanilla. Durante el vuelo, **leyeron** revistas sobre lugares de interés en el centro de Lima y **durmieron** un poco. **Fue** un vuelo muy bueno.

You are already familiarized with stem changes in the present tense. You will find it interesting that **-ar** and **-er** verbs that undergo stem changes in the present tense do not undergo such changes in the preterite tense.

| | |
|---|---|
| **Encontré** la maleta en el ático. | **I found** the suitcase in the attic. |
| La Sra. Estrada **perdió** el vuelo ayer. | Mrs. Estrada **missed** her flight yesterday. |

On the other hand, many **-ir** verbs that suffer stem changes in the present tense also suffer stem changes in the preterite. These changes only affect the **él/ella/usted** and **ellos(as)/ustedes** forms.

| e→i | | o→u | |
|---|---|---|---|
| **sentir** *(to feel)* | | **dormir** *(to sleep)* | |
| sentí | sentimos | dormí | dormimos |
| sentiste | sentisteis | dormiste | dormisteis |
| sintió | sintieron | durmió | durmieron |

Other similar verbs:
**competir** *(to compete)*, **conseguir** *(to find)*, **despedirse** *(to say good-bye)*, **divertirse** *(to have fun)*, **mentir** *(to lie)*, **preferir** *(to prefer)*, **reírse** *(to laugh)*, **repetir** *(to repeat)*, **seguir** *(to follow)*, **servir** *(to serve)*, **sonreír** *(to smile)*, **sugerir** *(to suggest)*, **vestirse** *(to get dressed)*

Other similar verbs: **morir** *(to die)*

| | |
|---|---|
| Mi madre **se vistió** cómoda para el viaje. | My mother **dressed** comfortably for the trip. |
| Ellos **prefirieron** llevar cheques de viajero, no efectivo. | They **preferred** to take traveler's checks, not cash. |

Verbs whose stems end in a vowel also suffer changes in the **él/ella/usted** and **ellos(as)/ustedes** forms of the preterite tense. These verbs take a **y** in these forms.

| **leer** *(to read)* | |
|---|---|
| leí | leímos |
| leíste | leísteis |
| leyó | leyeron |
| Other similar verbs: **caer(se)** *(to fall)*, **construir** *(to build)*, **creer** *(to believe)*, **distribuir** *(to distribute)*, **incluir** *(to include)*, **oír** *(to hear)* | |

Notice that the forms that take a **y** also lose the **i** of the regular ending (-**i**ó→**yó** and -**i**eron→**yeron**).

Samuel **oyó** el anuncio, salió corriendo y se **cayó**.

*Samuel **heard** the announcement, left running, and **fell**.*

The following is a group of verbs with different irregularities and changes.

| **dar** *(to give)* | **ir** *(to go)* / **ser** *(to be)* | **ver** *(to see)* |
|---|---|---|
| di | fui | vi |
| diste | fuiste | viste |
| dio | fue | vio |
| dimos | fuimos | vimos |
| disteis | fuisteis | visteis |
| dieron | fueron | vieron |

As you may have noticed, the preterite endings of **dar** and **ver** do not have accent marks. Also, the verbs **ir** and **ser** have exactly the same forms in the preterite tense. In this case, context will help you identify which verb is used.

Cuando **fuimos** a Guayaquil, **vimos** muchas artesanías indígenas.

*When **we went** to Guayaquil we saw a lot of indigenous crafts.*

■ **Asimilación**

**5-29 De viaje** ¿En qué orden hicieron Tatiana y Lázaro las siguientes cosas? Ponlas *(Put them)* en orden y compara tus respuestas con las de un(a) compañero(a).

  __6__   El empleado de la aerolínea les dio la tarjeta de embarque.

  __2__   Se vistieron.

  __3__   Prefirieron tomar un taxi para ir al aeropuerto.

  __1__   Durmieron hasta las seis en punto de la mañana.

  __5__   Pidieron asiento de pasillo.

  __8__   Oyeron el llamado *(call)* para abordar.

  __4__   Cuando llegaron al aeropuerto, fueron a la ventanilla de la aerolínea.

  __7__   Se despidieron del empleado de la aerolínea.

D1-52 🎧 **5-30 ¿Qué hizo Lázaro?** Primero, empareja las frases de la izquierda con las frases de la derecha. Luego, escucha lo que dice Lázaro sobre las cosas que hizo ayer e indica si las oraciones que formaste son ciertas **(C)** o falsas **(F)**.

<table>
<tr><td>_b_ 1. Lázaro fue...</td><td>a. el periódico. _F_</td></tr>
<tr><td>_e_ 2. Él construyó...<br>para su hija.</td><td>b. a la playa. _C_</td></tr>
<tr><td></td><td>c. muy enojado. _F_</td></tr>
<tr><td>_a_ 3. Leyó...</td><td>d. a varios colegas del trabajo. _F_</td></tr>
<tr><td>_d_ 4. Allí vio...</td><td>e. un castillo de arena (sand castle). _C_</td></tr>
<tr><td>_c_ 5. Él se sintió...</td><td></td></tr>
</table>

**Script 5-30:** Ayer por la tarde fui a la playa con mi hija y pasamos un día fantástico. Allí le construí un castillo de arena y ella jugó en el agua con otros niños. Yo aproveché el tiempo y leí una novela de Vargas Llosa hasta que vi a unos amigos y hablé con ellos un rato. Al final del día me sentí muy contento de haber compartido esas horas con mi hija.

■ **Aplicaciones**

🎭 **5-31 Situaciones** Completen las siguientes oraciones con los verbos que se proveen y conjúguenlos correctamente. **¡OJO!** Hay un verbo adicional en cada grupo.

reírse    ir    morir    ver

**En el cine:** Jesús y yo ___vimos___ una película en el cine anoche. En esta película, una mujer ___se murió___ de amor porque su novio la abandonó. Jesús ___se rió___ muchísimo porque la historia le pareció ridícula.

oír    vestirse    servir    despedirse

**¡Tremenda fiesta!:** Romualdo fue a una fiesta muy elegante el miércoles. Él ___se vistió___ elegantemente con un traje negro muy fino. En la fiesta (ellos) ___sirvieron___ caviar, camarones y langosta. A la medianoche, Romualdo ___se despidió___ de toda la gente porque tenía que trabajar el jueves por la mañana.

creer    dormir    preferir    ser

**Mis compañeras de cuarto:** Ayer ___fue___ un día muy raro para mis compañeras de cuarto. ¡El día empezó muy mal para ellas! (Ellas) ___durmieron___ sólo hasta las cinco de la mañana porque (ellas) ___creyeron___ que el examen de física era (was) ayer. ¡Pero ayer era domingo!

🎭 **5-32 Preguntas indiscretas** Usen la siguiente información para hacerle preguntas a su profesor(a) usando la forma **usted** del verbo. Añadan información adicional y expresiones de tiempo.

MODELO    repetir un curso
           *¿Ud. repitió un curso en la universidad alguna vez?*

1. leer el libro... de...
2. caerse en...
3. ser...
4. vestirse... para ir a...
5. preferir estudiar...
6. pedir... cuando ir a...
7. dar dinero a...
8. sentirse... en ...

**5-33 Las mejores vacaciones** Hazle las siguientes preguntas a tu compañero(a) para saber cómo fueron sus mejores vacaciones. Toma notas. Cuando terminen, cambien de papel.

**Sugerencia 5-33:** Encourage students to take good notes because they will need them to complete activity **5-35.**

1. ¿Adónde fuiste en tus últimas vacaciones? ¿Cuándo fuiste? ¿Con quién fuiste?
2. ¿Conseguiste un buen paquete vacacional? ¿Qué incluyó el paquete?
3. ¿Cómo fuiste (en avión/en carro/en tren/...)? ¿Cuántas maletas llevaste?
4. ¿Te divertiste? ¿Qué hiciste? ¿Dormiste mucho?
5. ¿Cómo te vestiste para viajar? ¿Por qué?
6. ¿Qué cosas viste? ¿Qué lugares visitaste?
7. ¿Compraste muchas cosas? ¿Conseguiste buenos precios?
8. ¿Cómo te sentiste cuando regresaste?

You can use questions like **¿Dónde fue la fiesta? ¿Cuántas personas fueron? ¿Qué sirvieron? ¿Cómo se sintieron los invitados? ¿Cómo se vistieron? ¿Algunas personas se durmieron? ¿Qué tipo de música oyeron?** Come up with other original questions and be creative in your answers!

## ■ Integración

**5-34 La última fiesta** Tu compañero(a) y tú van a describir cómo fue la última fiesta a la que fueron. Háganse preguntas y respondan de acuerdo con el dibujo que les corresponde. El estudiante B debe voltear su libro al revés *(turn his/her book upside down)*.

**Estudiante A**

**Estudiante B**

REMEMBER

You may use expressions you already know such as **en primer lugar, por otro lado, además, luego, después,** and **finalmente.**

**5-35 Unas vacaciones inolvidables** Usa la información que recopilaste en la actividad 5-33 y prepara un resumen sobre las mejores vacaciones de tu compañero(a). Cuando termines, dale una copia a él/ella para que te dé más información. Cuando añadas esta información, dale una copia del resumen a tu profesor(a).

## III. Funciones y estructuras: Avoiding repetition with direct object pronouns

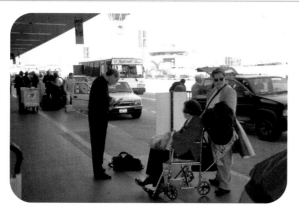

iLrn

| | |
|---|---|
| —Efraín, ¿tienes los billetes? | *Efraín, do you have the tickets?* |
| —Sí, aquí **los** tengo. | *Yes, I have **them** here.* |
| —¿Y mi cartera? | *And my purse?* |
| —Gustavo **la** tiene. | *Gustavo has **it**.* |

The direct object is the part of the sentence that refers to the person or thing that receives or is directly affected by the action of the verb. For example, in the following examples, **una mochila** receives the action of the verb **comprar** (it is the thing that is bought) and **mi agente de viajes** is the person affected by the verb **llamar** (the person who is called).

| | |
|---|---|
| Matilde compró **una mochila nueva.** | *Matilde bought **a new backpack.*** |
| Tengo que llamar a **mi agente de viajes.** | *I have to call **my travel agent.*** |

The preposition **a** is used before direct objects that are human beings or pets. It is known as the *personal a.*

When the direct object has already been mentioned in the conversation, we can use direct object pronouns instead. In the third person singular and the third person plural, Spanish direct object pronouns must agree in number (singular or plural) and gender (masculine or feminine) with the noun to which they refer.

| DIRECT OBJECT PRONOUNS | |
|---|---|
| **me** *me* | **nos** *us* |
| **te** *you* (informal sing.) | **os** *you* (informal plural, in Spain) |
| **lo** *you* (formal sing., m.), *him, it* (m.) | **los** *you* (formal plural), *them* (m., m.+f.) |
| **la** *you* (formal sing., f.), *her, it* (f.) | **las** *you* (formal plural), *them* (f.) |

| | |
|---|---|
| —¿Conseguiste **los pasaportes?** | *Did you get **the passport?*** |
| —Sí, **los** conseguí. | *Yes, I got **them**.* |
| —¿Marcos **te** conoce? | *Does Marcos know **you?*** |
| —No, él no **me** conoce. | *No, he does not know **me**.* |

As you may have noticed, direct object pronouns are placed before the conjugated verb and after **no.** When they are used in sentences with verb phrases (phrases that consist of an auxiliary verb and a main verb), these pronouns can be placed either before the auxiliary verb or attached to the main verb (which could be an infinitive or a present participle).

| | |
|---|---|
| ¿Los libros? Yo **los** voy a traer. / Yo voy a traer**los.** | The books. I am going to bring **them.** |
| ¿Ricardo? **Lo** tengo que visitar. / Tengo que visitar**lo.** | Ricardo? I have to visit **him.** |
| Nina **me** está ayudando. / Nina está ayudándo**me.** | Nina is helping **me.** |

Most of the verbs you have been using with reflexive pronouns can also be used with direct object pronouns. Notice how the meanings change in these two examples.

| | |
|---|---|
| Mi madre **se despierta** temprano. | My mother wakes (herself) up early. |
| Mi madre **nos despierta** temprano. | My mother wakes us up early. |

## ■ Asimilación

**5-36 ¿Cierto o falso?** Indica si las siguientes alternativas son ciertas **(C)** o falsas **(F).** Al terminar, compara tus respuestas con las de un(a) compañero(a). ¿Tienen mucho en común?

_____ 1. ¿La comida? Mi madre la prepara.

_____ 2. ¿El libro de español? Lo detesto.

_____ 3. ¿A mí? Mis amigos no me invitan a fiestas.

_____ 4. ¿Mis vacaciones? Las voy a tomar en el verano.

_____ 5. ¿El presidente de los Estados Unidos? No lo tolero.

_____ 6. ¿La clase de español? El (La) profesor(a) la hace muy interesante.

**Script 5-37:** 1. Elena la compró en un almacén. 2. Los tengo que lavar hoy mismo. 3. Mi hermano lo escucha en la radio todas las mañanas. 4. Yo la preparo con tomates y pimientos. 5. Estoy mirándolas en este momento.

CD1–53

**5-37 ¿A qué se refieren?** Escucha las oraciones y selecciona a qué se refieren los pronombres de complemento directo.

1. a. el bolso      b. la maleta      c. los sombreros
2. a. las gafas     b. el vestido     c. los pantalones
3. a. a Delia       b. los anuncios   c. el programa
4. a. el sándwich   b. las pastas     c. la tortilla de huevos
5. a. a María y a Silvia  b. a Silvia y a Berto  c. a María

## ■ Aplicaciones

**5-38 ¡Ya hicimos todo!** Imagínense que la clase va de viaje a Perú para visitar Machu Picchu. El (La) profesor(a) quiere estar seguro(a) de que ustedes están listos(as) y les hace las siguientes preguntas. Respóndanle afirmativamente.

> MODELO     ¿Solicitaron la visa?
> *Sí, ya la solicitamos.*

1. ¿Recibieron sus pasaportes?    Sí, ya los recibimos.
2. ¿Leyeron las regulaciones sobre el equipaje?    Sí, ya las leímos.
3. ¿Fueron a comprar las maletas?    Sí, ya (las) fuimos a comprar(las).
4. ¿Llamaron al agente de viajes?    Sí, ya lo llamamos.
5. ¿Buscaron los cheques de viajero?    Sí, ya los buscamos.
6. ¿Pidieron asiento de ventanilla?    Sí, ya lo pedimos.

**5-39 Preguntas y más preguntas** Túrnense para hacer y responder a preguntas con la información dada. Deben incluir un pronombre de objeto directo en cada pregunta y respuesta.

> MODELO     las películas de Tom Cruise / ver (Uds. / no)
> E1: *¿Las ven?*
> E2: *No, no las vemos.*

1. a Clotilde y a Juan / tener que invitar al baile (nosotros / sí)
2. a mí / llamar con frecuencia (tú / no)
3. a mi amigo y a mí / comprender cuando hablamos español (el [la] profesor[a] / sí)
4. la lección / estudiar antes de la clase (Elín y Patricia / sí)
5. el periódico / ir a leer ahora (ella / no)
6. los músicos sudamericanos / conocer bien (tú / no)

Answers 5-39: 1. ¿(Los) tenemos que invitar(los) al baile? Sí, (los) tenemos que invitar(los). 2. ¿Me llamas con frecuencia? No, no te llamo con frecuencia. 3. ¿Nos comprende cuando hablamos español? Sí, nos comprende. 4. ¿La estudian antes de la clase? Sí, la estudian antes de la clase. 5. ¿(Lo) va a leer(lo) ahora? No, no (lo) va a leer(lo) ahora. 6. ¿Los conoces bien? No, no los conozco bien.

**5-40 ¡Firma aquí, por favor!**

**Paso 1:** Busca compañeros de clase que respondan afirmativamente a las siguientes preguntas. Cuando encuentres a alguien, dile **Firma aquí, por favor.** Si alguien responde negativamente, dile **gracias** y pregúntale a otra persona.

**Firma**

_____ 1. ¿Tus amigos te invitan a salir todos los fines de semana?

_____ 2. ¿Tus compañeros te ayudan con la tarea de español?

_____ 3. ¿Tu familia te apoya en tus decisiones?

_____ 4. ¿Tus compañeros de clase te conocen bien?

_____ 5. ¿Tus parientes te ven regularmente?

_____ 6. ¿Tu consejero(a) académico(a) te escucha con atención?

**Paso 2:** Comparte la información con la clase y da tu opinión personal. Haz los cambios necesarios.

> MODELO     *La madre de Angeline la despierta por la mañana y mi madre me despierta por la mañana también.*
> o ..., *pero mi madre no me despierta por la mañana.*

Some of the verbs you can use to talk about relatives with whom you do not have a good relationship are **detestar** *(to detest)*, **no querer** *(do/does not love)*, **no tolerar** *(cannot tolerate)*, and **no soportar** *(cannot stand).*

*will be in effect*

### SUGERENCIAS

You may follow these steps:
**Paso 1:** Underline the nouns you find.
**Paso 2:** Determine which nouns are repeated in each section and may be replaced with direct object pronouns.
**Paso 3:** Determine what pronouns you have to use.
**Paso 4:** Rewrite the sign. Be careful where you place the pronouns!

## ■ Integración

 **5-41 En familia** ¿Qué cosas hacen diferentes miembros de tu familia por ti? ¿Y qué sienten ellos verdaderamente hacia ti? Comenta estas cosas con tu compañero(a). Puedes hablar de temas como: **ayudar con (los problemas personales / los quehaceres del hogar / el cuidado de los niños / las cuentas / ...), apoyar en (mis decisiones / mis estudios / mi relación con... / ...), aconsejar con relación a (mis estudios / mis problemas personales / mis finanzas / ...), admirar por (mis logros / mi personalidad / mis notas / mi sentido de responsabilidad / ...)** y **mantener económicamente.**

**5-42 Aviso a nuestros pasajeros** *(passengers)* Lee el siguiente aviso que una aerolínea fijó *(posted)* para todos sus pasajeros y reescríbelo incluyendo pronombres de objeto directo cuando sea posible.

---

### AVISO A NUESTROS PASAJEROS

Queremos avisarle que las siguientes reglas van a entrar en vigor* el 1° de enero:

- Ud. sólo va a poder registrar dos maletas. Debe registrar las maletas en nuestra ventanilla y nuestros asistentes le van a dar un recibo. Ud. tiene que mostrar el recibo para recoger sus maletas.

- Ud. sólo podrá llevar una pieza de equipaje de mano. Debe poner el equipaje de mano debajo del asiento delantero. También puede poner el equipaje de mano en el compartimiento de arriba.

- Ud. puede obtener su tarjeta de embarque en una de nuestras estaciones de computadora. Debe obtener la tarjeta de embarque antes de abordar y tiene que mostrar la tarjeta de embarque a uno de nuestros asistentes.

- Ud. debe mostrar una tarjeta de identificación reciente en la ventanilla. También debe tener disponible la tarjeta de identificación para abordar y para recoger su equipaje.

---

## IV. Vídeo: Otra excursión en Puerto Rico

### ■ Preparación

**A. Hacer esnórkeling** En su próxima excursión, los compañeros van a hacer esnórkeling. Antes de ver el vídeo, lean el resumen de lo que van a ver e intenten adivinar *(guess)* el significado de las palabras en negrita *(bold)*.

Al llegar los compañeros, Edwin, su guía, ya está esperándolos a bordo del bote. Suben al bote y Edwin les pregunta si están listos para (1) **zarpar.** Todos menos Valeria responden: «¡Sí! ¡Vámonos! ¡Vamos!». Navegan en el bote y llegan al sitio donde van a hacer esnórkeling. Sofía, Alejandra, Javier y Antonio se ponen el equipo de esnórkeling: las (2) **aletas** para ayudarles a nadar, (3) la **máscara** para poder ver bajo el agua y el tubo para poder respirar. Luego, desde el lado del bote, ellos (4) **brincan** al agua. Valeria los mira desde el bote porque ella no quiere hacer esnórkeling. Sofía, Alejandra, Javier y Antonio se divierten mucho. Bajo el agua ven (5) **peces** de colores, corales preciosos y algas marinas.

1. a. anchor b. change course c. set sail
2. a. mask b. fins c. esnórkel
3. a. mask b. fins c. esnórkel
4. a. swim b. sunbathe c. jump
5. a. fish b. reefs c. algae

### ■ ¿Entendiste bien?

**B. ¿Qué hicieron?** Primero, lee los siguientes eventos del día de esnórkeling. Luego, mira el vídeo y ponlos en orden cronológico. Finalmente, compara tus respuestas con las de un(a) compañero(a).

___4___ Sofía, Alejandra, Javier y Antonio se vistieron para hacer esnórkeling.

___2___ Edwin, su guía, les dio la bienvenida a los compañeros a bordo del bote.

___1___ Los cinco compañeros fueron en coche al puerto.

___5___ Bajo el agua vieron peces de colores, corales preciosos y algas marinas.

___3___ Como no sabe nadar, Valeria se sintió avergonzada *(embarrassed)* y les mintió a los compañeros. Dijo que le da miedo hacer esnórkeling.

___6___ Los compañeros se fueron a casa.

**C. ¿Hacerlo o no hacerlo?** Piensa en **una** de las siguientes situaciones y cuéntales a los otros miembros del grupo qué ocurrió.

**Situación #1:** Algo que hice por primera vez en mi vida y me gustó mucho.
- ¿Qué fue? (practicar un deporte, tocar un instrumento, ir a un evento de un club, etc.)
- ¿Cuándo?
- ¿Por qué te gustó?
- ¿Sigues haciéndolo? ¿Por qué sí o por qué no?

**Situación #2:** Algo que no hice.
- ¿Qué fue?
- ¿Por qué no lo hiciste? (posibles razones: te dio miedo, te contaron algo negativo, etc.)
- ¿Cuándo?
- ¿Te arrepientes de *(regret)* tu decisión? ¿Por qué sí o por qué no?

**D. Enfoque comunitario** Preparen la descripción de algunos eventos o festividades importantes que tienen lugar en su escuela o comunidad todos los años para incluirlas en un panfleto informativo para estudiantes internacionales. Para cada evento, incluyan la fecha, el lugar, el precio de la entrada y las actividades que se realizan.

# Incidentes

## I. Vocabulario: El cuerpo humano

Transparencies K-1: El cuerpo;
K-4: Una vista al médico

El cuerpo humano

el pelo — la cabeza
las orejas — los ojos
la boca — la nariz — la cara
la garganta — los dientes
el cuello
el brazo
el codo
los pulmones
el corazón
la espalda
el estómago
la mano
los dedos
las piernas
las rodillas
el oído
los tobillos
los pies
la piel
los dedos del pie

### Vocabulario práctico

las cejas *eyebrows*          el hueso *bone*
la cintura *waist*            las uñas *fingernails*
el hombro *shoulder*

### ■ Asimilación

**5-43 ¿Cómo es Ana María?** Observa la foto de esta muchacha y escoge la palabra más apropiada para completar la descripción. Al terminar, compara tus respuestas con las de un(a) compañero(a).

Ana María es (gorda / joven / vieja). Tiene el pelo (castaño / bajo / negro), las piernas (altas / cortas / largas) y los brazos son (delgados / bajos / pequeños). A ella le gusta hacer ejercicio; por eso tiene un abdomen muy (grande / firme / corto).

CD1-54

**5-44 En la sala de emergencias** Escucha la siguiente conversación entre un paciente y un médico y marca en los diagramas con una **X** las partes del cuerpo que menciona el paciente. (Observa el modelo.)

**Script 5-44:**

Doctor: ¿Cómo se siente, señor?

Paciente: Pues me duele la pierna derecha, desde el tobillo hasta la rodilla y también me duele el brazo y la mano derecha.

Doctor: ¿Y el cuello, qué tal?

Paciente: Sí, doctor. Me duele el cuello y la cabeza un poco.

Doctor: ¿Y la espalda?

Paciente: También, doctor... Me duele mucho la espalda y me duele un poco el estómago.

This activity previews the use of the verb **doler.** Although students have not studied this verb yet, the context will be sufficient for them to understand the conversation and complete the assigned task.

**Answers 5-44:** rodilla, tobillo, brazo derecho, mano derecha, cuello, cabeza, espalda, estómago

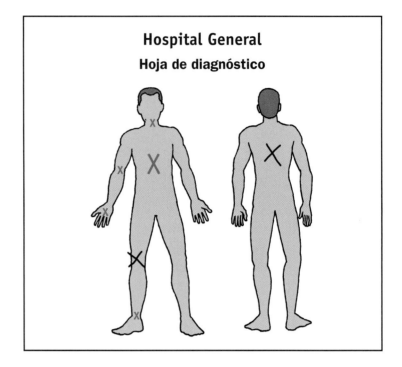

**Hospital General**

**Hoja de diagnóstico**

### EN TU COMUNIDAD

Visit the Emergency Room in a local hospital to investigate the accommodations available to speakers of languages other than English (particularly Spanish). Prepare a brief report on the level of demand for hospital services from non-English speakers, and the hospital's ability to attend to their needs.

**Sugerencia 5-46:** You may want to challenge students to come up with additional groupings to test the rest of the class.

### ▓ Aplicaciones

**5-45 ¿Qué partes del cuerpo usas para...?** Indica las partes del cuerpo que asocias con las siguientes actividades: **nadar, cantar, estudiar, bailar** y **escribir.**

**5-46 Relaciones** Indica la palabra que no se relaciona con las demás.

1. ojos, orejas, rodillas
2. rodillas, hombros, cuello
3. pecho, espalda, estómago
4. pelo, nariz, dedos
5. codo, pulmones, corazón

**5-47 ¿Cómo es?** Preparen una breve descripción de la apariencia física de este hombre. Incluyan por lo menos cinco de las siguientes palabras: **pelo, ojos, orejas, nariz, brazos, manos, cuello.**

## ■ Integración

**5-48 ¿Dónde está?** Un(a) estudiante debe describir la apariencia física de una de las personas en estas fotos. El (La) otro(a) estudiante debe adivinar en cuál de las tres fotos está esa persona.

You may use the description in activity 5-43 as a model.

Nota: Limiten las descripciones a la apariencia física de la persona. No incluyan información acerca de su ropa.

**Foto 1**

**Foto 2**

**Foto 3**

**5-49 ¡Ayúdenme a encontrarlo!** Mientras hacías compras con tu familia, tu primito de cuatro años se perdió *(got lost)*. Escribe una descripción detallada de su apariencia física para dársela al departamento de seguridad.

## II. Funciones y estructuras: Talking about past activities with other stem-changing verbs

Luisito **estuvo** enfermo anoche y su mamá lo **trajo** al hospital. El doctor le **dijo** que tenía *(he had)* un virus estomacal.

Mi hija **vino** enferma de la escuela ayer y **tuve** que cuidarla. Le **hice** una sopa y se sintió mejor.

In **Tema 2** you learned about a group of verbs that have stem changes in the third person forms of the preterite. Now you will learn about verbs that have stem changes in all of their preterite forms. These verbs can be grouped into four categories: verbs that take an **i,** verbs that take a **u,** verbs that take **uv** and verbs that take a **j.**

| i | u | uv | j |
|---|---|---|---|
| **hacer** *(to do/make)* | **poder** *(to be able to)* | **estar** *(to be)* | **traer** *(to bring)* |
| hice | pude | estuve | traje |
| hiciste | pudiste | estuviste | trajiste |
| hizo* | pudo | estuvo | trajo |
| hicimos | pudimos | estuvimos | trajimos |
| hicisteis | pudisteis | estuvisteis | trajisteis |
| hicieron | pudieron | estuvieron | trajeron |
| Other similar verbs: **decir→dij- querer→quis- venir→vin-** | Other similar verbs: **haber→hub- poner→pus- saber→sup-** | Other similar verbs: **andar→anduv- tener→tuv-** | Other similar verbs: **conducir→conduj- introducir→introduj- producir→produj- traducir→traduj-** |

*Notice that the **él/ella/usted** preterite form of **hacer (hizo)** has a **c→z** change in order to maintain the sound of the letter **c** in the infinitive.

Verbs that take a **j** in the stem (including **decir,** which also takes an **i**) end in **-eron** (not **-ieron**) in the third person plural preterite form: **condujeron, dijeron, introdujeron,** etc.

As you may have noticed, these verbs are also irregular because they take a different set of endings, regardless of whether they are -**ar,** -**er,** or -**ir** verbs.

| ENDINGS | |
|---|---|
| -e | -imos |
| -iste | -isteis |
| -o | -ieron |

—Diana, ¿te **pusiste** la bolsa de hielo en la rodilla?

*Diana, **did you put** the ice bag on your knee?*

—**Quise** hacerlo, pero no **pude.**

*I **wanted** to do it, but **I was** not able to.*

—¡**Anduvimos** desde casa y nos duelen los pies!

*We **walked** from home and our feet hurt!*

—¿Por qué no **vinieron** en autobús?

*Why **didn't you come** by bus?*

**REMEMBER**

The verb **haber** is only used in the third person singular: **hay** (present tense)—*there is/are;* **hubo** (preterite tense)—*there was/were.*

## ■ Asimilación

**5-50 ¿Quién de la clase?** Piensa en las cosas que pasaron en la clase la semana pasada y completa las oraciones con el nombre de la(s) persona(s) que hizo/hicieron estas cosas. Al terminar, compara tus respuestas con las de un(a) compañero(a). ¿Coincidieron en muchas cosas?

1. _____ estuvo enfermo(a).
2. _____ trajo comida a la clase.
3. _____ no dijo nada en clase.
4. _____ y _____ hicieron toda la tarea.
5. _____ y _____ vinieron tarde.
6. _____ tuvo que irse temprano un día.

**5-51 ¿Qué hizo ayer?** Escucha la información acerca de las actividades de tu profesor(a) el día de ayer y completa las oraciones.

1. Tuvo que ir a __la biblioteca__.
2. Pudo hacer todo __el trabajo__ porque llegó temprano.
3. Después hizo __unas compras__ en el supermercado.
4. Estuvo en el supermercado por __treinta__ minutos.
5. Cuando llegó a casa, puso la comida en __el refrigerador__.

**Script 5-51:** Ayer, después de mis clases, tuve que ir a la biblioteca para buscar un artículo y para trabajar un poco. Llegué temprano, así que pude hacer todo mi trabajo sin problemas y sin tener que esperar. Cuando salí de la biblioteca, hice unas compras en el supermercado. Estuve ahí como treinta minutos. Después me fui a casa, puse la comida en el refrigerador y me acosté un rato.

## ■ Aplicaciones

**5-52 En el consultorio del médico otra vez** *(again)* Lee el diálogo entre Rómulo y su doctor, y complétalo con los verbos de la lista para saber qué ocurrió. Conjuga los verbos correctamente. **¡OJO!** Hay un verbo adicional.

**OPCIONES:** hacer  venir  traer  decir  poder  ponerse  tener

DOCTOR:    ¡Rómulo, aquí otra vez! ¿Qué te ocurrió?

PACIENTE:  Doctor, (yo) ___vine___ a verlo otra vez porque el brazo me duele mucho todavía. (Yo) ___Tuve___ que faltar al trabajo, pero fue necesario.

DOCTOR:    ¿___Hiciste___ (tú) las cosas que te (yo) ___dije___ para mejorar la condición de tu brazo?

PACIENTE:  Sí, doctor, todo.

DOCTOR:    A ver. ¿Te tomaste las medicinas y (tú) ___te pusiste___ la crema para aliviar el dolor?

PACIENTE:  Pues no, doctor. (Yo) No ___pude___ comprar las medicinas ni la crema porque son muy caras.

DOCTOR:    ¡Me lo imaginé! *(That's what I thought!)*

**5-53 Causa y efecto** Usen los verbos entre paréntesis para indicar una causa lógica para cada efecto.

MODELO    Carol *no trajo su libro.* → Carol tiene que usar el libro de su
(no traer...)            compañero.

1. Nosotros _____ → Nosotros ahora estamos en perfecto
(hacer...).            estado de salud.
2. Tú _____ → Tú tienes un horario de clases
(poder...).            perfecto.
3. Nelson _____ → Él vio a muchos actores y actrices
(estar en...).            famosos.
4. Yo _____ → Afortunadamente, ahora me siento
(tener que...).            muy bien.
5. Paulina y Leonardo _____ → Ahora tenemos los documen-
(traducir...).                tos en español y en inglés.
6. Tú _____ → Nosotros no podemos encontrar
(poner...).            los cubiertos.

**5-54 El invierno pasado** Combinen elementos de las dos columnas para formar oraciones sobre lo que estas personas hicieron durante el invierno pasado. ¡Sean creativos!

MODELO    mi familia y yo + (no) poder...
*Mi familia y yo no pudimos ir a esquiar a Colorado el invierno pasado.*

| mi familia y yo | (no) poder... |
| yo | (no) decir... |
| mi mejor amigo(a) | (no) hacer... |
| el (la) profesor(a)         + | (no) estar... |
| los estudiantes de la clase | (no) querer... |
| | (no) conducir a... |
| | (no) andar... |
| | (no) tener que... |

## ■ Integración

**5-55 ¿Qué hicieron?** Cuéntales a tres de tus compañeros lo que hiciste para prepararte para tu vida de estudiante universitario(a). Trata de usar por lo menos ocho de los siguientes verbos: **decir, estar, hacer, poder, poner, querer, tener (que), traducir, traer** y **venir.** Toma notas sobre las cosas que ellos dicen.

**REMEMBER**

Some of the expressions you can use to organize your summary are **sin embargo, por otro lado, por ejemplo, en cambio,** and **finalmente.**

**5-56 ¡No pensé en eso!** Escribe un resumen de las cosas que tus compañeros mencionaron en la actividad 5-55 y que tú no hiciste para prepararte para tu vida de estudiante universitario(a). Cuando termines, dale una copia a tu profesor(a) para que te dé su opinión.

## III. Funciones y estructuras: Talking about incidents and mishaps

 Transparency K-3: Las enfermedades

El año pasado fue bastante trágico.

Simón tuvo un accidente de carro y **se rompió** el cuello,... *Simon had a car accident and **broke** his neck, . . .*

mi abuela **se cayó** y **se lastimó** un brazo y... *my grandmother **fell** and **hurt** her arm, and . . .*

Mario **se torció** un tobillo y se lo **enyesaron**. *Mario **twisted** an ankle and they **put it in a cast**.*

There are many reflexive verbs that can be used to talk about mishaps, incidents and accidents.

caerse *to fall*
contagiarse *to get infected*
cortarse *to get cut*
darse (en/con)* *to hit (a body part), to bump into*
desmayarse *to faint*
enfermarse *to get sick*
fracturarse *to fracture (a body part)*

hacerse daño *to hurt oneself*
hincharse *to swell*
lastimarse *to injure oneself, to get hurt*
quemarse *to burn oneself*
resfriarse *to get a cold*
romperse *to break (a body part)*
torcerse *to twist (a body part)*

 Use **darse en** before the body part that got hit and **darse con** before the object into which the person bumped.

Cuando **me caí, me fracturé** una rodilla.
Jacinta **se quemó** en la cocina de su casa.
Mi hermana **se dio con** la mesa y **se cortó**.

*When **I fell**, **I fractured** my knee.*
*Jacinta **got burned** in the kitchen of her house.*
*My sister **bumped into** the table and **got cut**.*

Note that body parts are generally used with definite articles, not with possessive adjectives. The reflexive pronoun indicates whose body part it is.

Here is a list of other verbs and expressions you can use to talk about negative events.

| | |
|---|---|
| **doler (ue)** *to hurt* | **tener dolor de garganta** *to have* |
| **enyesar** *to put in a cast* | *a sore throat* |
| **internar** *to check into* | **tener (fiebre/tos)** *to have* |
| *(a hospital)* | *a (fever/cough)* |
| **tener dolor de...** *to have* | **tropezar** *to trip* |
| *a . . . ache* | **vomitar** *to vomit* |

**¿Tienes dolor de cabeza?** Yo **tengo dolor de estómago.**
**Internaron** a don Juancho en el hospital.

***Do you have a headache?*** ***I have a stomachache.***
*Don Juancho was **checked into** the hospital.*

You may wish to inform your students that the verbs **doler** and **enyesar** are normally used with indirect object pronouns, which they will study in **Capítulo 7, Tema 2.**

### ▓ Asimilación

**5-57 Una vez...** *(One time . . .)* Lee las siguientes oraciones e indica si son ciertas (**C**) o falsas (**F**). Cuando termines, compara tus respuestas con las de un(a) compañero(a). ¿Qué cosas tienen en común?

Una vez...

_____ 1. me rompí una pierna.
_____ 2. me desmayé en el gimnasio.
_____ 3. me dio dolor de cabeza en clase.
_____ 4. me internaron en el hospital.
_____ 5. me quemé la mano cocinando.

_____ 6. me caí frente a muchas personas.
_____ 7. me enfermé el día de un examen.
_____ 8. me corté afeitándome.
_____ 9. me fracturé un dedo jugando.
_____ 10. me di con un espejo.

Script 5-58: Necesito una ambulancia inmediatamente. Mi hijo se cayó de la bicicleta y parece que se rompió un brazo. Está vomitando y dice que tiene dolor de estómago, así que se dio en el pecho también. El brazo está demasiado hinchado. Por favor, dense prisa. Estamos en la calle Jiménez número 45.

CD1-56 **5-58 Una llamada al 911** Escucha la llamada que una madre hizo al 911 y escoge las oraciones correctas.

_____ El niño se dio en la rodilla.
_____ Él se desmayó.
__X__ Tiene dolor de estómago.
__X__ Se rompió el brazo.

__X__ Se cayó de la bicicleta.
_____ Se torció una muñeca.
__X__ Un brazo se hinchó.
_____ Tiene un poco de fiebre.

### ▓ Aplicaciones

**5-59 Uno, dos y tres** Organicen los eventos de cada grupo en orden lógico.

1. __3__ La pierna se hinchó.
   __1__ Me caí.
   __2__ Me lastimé una pierna.
2. __1__ Tropecé.
   __3__ Me corté un dedo.
   __2__ Me di con la puerta.

3. __1__ Me desmayé y me caí.
   __2__ Me di en la cabeza.
   __3__ Me duele la cabeza.
4. __2__ Me dolió mucho.
   __3__ Lo enyesaron.
   __1__ Me fracturé un brazo.

**5-60 ¿Qué pasó?** Completen las siguientes oraciones de forma lógica.

> **MODELO**   Comí mucho en la cena y ahora _tengo dolor de estómago_.

1. Santiago corrió diez millas esta tarde y _____ las piernas.
2. Nosotros estamos deshidratados; por eso _____.
3. Me di en una rodilla con el escritorio y la rodilla _____.
4. Ellas tropezaron con una silla y _____.
5. Tú no tuviste cuidado y _____ con el cuchillo.
6. Mara se dio con la cama y _____ un dedo del pie.

**Answers 5-60:** *Answers may vary.*
1. se (lastimó / hizo daño en / ...),
2. nos desmayamos / tenemos dolor de cabeza/..., 3. se (hinchó/ lastimó/...), 4. se (cayeron/ rompieron.../...), 5. te (cortaste/ hiciste daño/...), 6. se (lastimó/ rompió/fracturó/...)

**5-61 ¡A actuar!** Adivinen cuál es la acción que otro(a) compañero(a) va a dramatizar. Túrnense para actuar y adivinar.

> **MODELO**   If your classmate acts as if he/she trips, falls, and hurts his/her foot, you say: *Tropezaste, te caíste y te lastimaste un pie.*

### ■ Integración

 **5-62 Accidentes y enfermedades** Representa la siguiente situación con un(a) compañero(a). Cuando terminen, cambien de papel.

| **Estudiante A** | **Estudiante B** |
|---|---|
| Descríbele a tu compañero(a) qué te pasó y cómo te sentías *(how you felt)* la última vez que fuiste al doctor o a la sala de emergencias de un hospital. Debes mencionar todos los detalles pertinentes. | Tu compañero(a) va a narrar qué le pasó y cómo se sentía la última vez que fue al doctor o a la sala de emergencias. Como eres muy curioso(a), trata de averiguar todos los detalles pertinentes. |

**5-63 La peor experiencia** Compara la experiencia que tu compañero(a) te narró en la actividad 5-62 con la experiencia que tú le narraste. ¿Cuál fue peor? ¿Quién recibió mejor atención médica? ¿Quién esperó más tiempo para ser atendido *(to be helped)*? Piensa en esto y escribe un párrafo breve. Al terminar, dale una copia a tu profesor(a) para que lo corrija.

**ESTUDIANTE A**

To talk about what the doctor(s) did, you may use these expressions: **me (recetó/recetaron) unas medicinas** *(prescribed some medicine for me)*, **me (puso/pusieron) una inyección** *(gave me a shot)*, **me (puso/ pusieron) suero** *(gave me an IV)*, or **me (enyesó/enyesaron)** *(put me in a cast)*.

**ESTUDIANTE B**

Use the interrogative words that you already know: **cuándo, cómo, dónde, por qué, cuánto/os/as,** y **quién.**

**REMEMBER**

Some of the expressions you have to use to make comparisons are **tan... como, más/menos... que** and **tanto como.** Please refer to **Capítulo 4, Tema 1** to see a complete list.

## IV. Lectura: Leyenda del origen de los Incas

### Antes de leer

**A.** ¿Cuál es el origen del ser humano? ¿Cómo explican la ciencia y la religión el origen del ser humano? En dos o tres oraciones, presenten las ideas básicas de cada perspectiva.

- Explicación científica
- Explicación religiosa (identifiquen la religión correspondiente)

**B. Vocabulario y conceptos** Las siguientes palabras son importantes para comprender la leyenda. Empáréjalas con las definiciones de la derecha.

| | | | |
|---|---|---|---|
| _d_ | crear | a. | que no tiene luz o claridad |
| _b_ | vicio | b. | mala costumbre o hábito |
| _f_ | castigar | c. | lluvia muy fuerte y prolongada |
| _a_ | oscuridad | d. | hacer algo nuevo |
| _c_ | diluvio | e. | tener hijos |
| _e_ | procrear | f. | imponer una penalidad física o moral a quien ha cometido una falta o delito |
| _g_ | mandar | g. | ordenar, dar instrucciones o indicaciones |

### A leer

#### Leyenda del origen de los Incas

*there was*
*sun / moon / stars*

En el principio, **había** uno que llamaban Viracocha, el cual creó el mundo oscuro y sin **sol** ni **luna** ni **estrellas;** y por esta creación le llamaron Viracocha Pachayachachi, que quiere decir Creador de todas las cosas. Y después de creado el mundo formó unos gigantes deformes,

*if it would be*

para ver **si sería** bueno hacer los hombres de aquel tamaño. Y como le parecieron de muy mayor

*his own*
*to be (subjunctive) / large / to be (future) / resemblance*
*to live (imperfect tense)*

proporción que la **suya,** dijo: «No está bien que las gentes **sean** tan **crecidas;** mejor **será** que sean de mi tamaño». Y así creó a los hombres, a su **semejanza** como los que ahora son. Y **vivían** en oscuridad.

*fights*
*under penalty*
*But / pride / greed*

A éstos les mandó Viracocha vivir sin **desavenencias,** y conocerlo y servirlo; y les puso este precepto **so pena** de castigo. Guardaron este precepto algún tiempo. **Mas** como entre ellos nacieron vicios de **soberbia** y **codicia** y olvidaron el precepto de Viracocha Pachayachachi, éste se enojó y los

*to curse (preterite)*
*to swallow (preterite)*

**maldijo.** Unos fueron convertidos en piedras y otros en otras formas, a otros los **tragó** la tierra y a otros el mar, y sobre todos les mandó un diluvio general, al cual ellos llaman *uno pachacuti,* que quiere decir

*to alter (preterite) / earth*
*to flood (preterite)*

«agua que **trastornó** la **tierra**». Y dicen que llovió sesenta días y sesenta noches, y que **anegó** todo lo creado, y que sólo quedaron algunas señales de los que se convirtieron en piedras para memoria del hecho y para ejemplo de las futuras generaciones en los edificios de Pucara, que

*league (measure)*

está a sesenta **leguas** de Cuzco.

Viracocha guardó **consigo** tres hombres, el uno de los cuales se llamó Taguapacac, para servirle y ayudarle a crear las nuevas gentes que había de hacer en la segunda edad después del diluvio, lo cual hizo de esta manera: Pasado el diluvio y seca la tierra, determinó el Viracocha **poblar**la por segunda vez, y para hacerlo con más perfección determinó crear **luminarias** que diesen claridad. Y para **conseguir**lo se fue

*to himself*

*to populate*
*light sources*
*to achieve*

con sus criados a una gran laguna que está en el Collao, y en la laguna hay una isla llamada Titicaca, que quiere decir montes de **plomo.** Viracocha fue a esa isla y mandó salir el sol, la luna y las estrellas y que fueran al cielo para dar **luz** al mundo, y así fue hecho.

*lead*

*light*

Viracocha lcs mandó algunas cosas a sus **criados,** pero el Taguapaca fue desobediente. El Viracocha, indignado, mandó a los otros dos criados que tomasen a Taguapaca, y **atado de pies y manos,** así lo echaron en una **balsa** a la laguna. El Taguapaca, ofendido, **amenazó** con volver a tomar **venganza.** Los criados lo llevaron entonces por el **desaguadero** de la laguna, y nadie volvió a ver al Taguapaca por mucho tiempo. Hecho esto, Viracocha fabricó en aquel lugar un altar en **señal** de lo que allí había hecho y creado.

*servants*

*tied by hands and feet*
*raft / to threaten (preterite)*
*revenge*
*drain, outlet*

*sign*

Viracocha dejó entonces la isla con sus dos criados y fue a un lugar que ahora llaman Tiaguanaco y en este lugar **esculpió** y **dibujó** en unas rocas grandes todas las naciones que **pensaba** crear. Entonces, les ordenó a sus dos criados memorizar los nombres que él les **decía** de aquellas **gentes** que allí **había pintado,** y de los valles y provincias y lugares de donde las tales **habían de salir,** que eran los de toda la

*to carve (preterite)*
*to draw (preterite)*
*to think, plan (imperfect tense)*

*decir (imperfect tense) / peoples /*
*had painted*

*were to emerge*

**tierra.** Y a cada uno de ellos mandó ir por diferente **camino,** llamando las tales gentes, y mandándolas salir, procrear y **henchir** la tierra. Y los dichos criados suyos obedecieron el mandato de Viracocha, y el uno se fue por la sierra hacia el Mar del Sur, y el otro en dirección a las montañas que decimos de los Andes, al **levante** del dicho mar. Por estas sierras **iban caminando** y a altas voces diciendo: «¡Oh, gentes y naciones! **¡Oíd y obedeced** el **mandato** del Tici Viracocha Pachayachachi, el cual **os manda** salir, multiplicar y henchir la tierra!» Y el mismo Viracocha **iba haciendo** lo mismo por las tierras intermedias de sus dos criados, nombrando todas las naciones y provincias por donde **pasaba.** Y a las **voces** que daban todo lugar obedeció y así salieron unos de lagos, otros de **fuentes,** valles, **cuevas,** árboles, cavernas, peñas y montes, e hinchieron las tierras y multiplicaron las naciones que son hoy el Perú.

*earth / road*
*to populate*

*east*
*they were walking*
*listen and heed / command*
*commands you to*
*was doing*

*to pass by (imperfect tense) / loud*
*cries / springs / caves*

Pedro Sarmiento de Gamboa. *Historia de los Incas.* 1572. (adaptado)

■ **¿Entendiste bien?**

**C. Orden de la creación** Organicen los siguientes eventos de la creación del mundo, según las tradiciones de los Incas.

<u>5</u>  Viracocha creó el sol, la luna y las estrellas.

<u>1</u>  Viracocha creó unos gigantes.

<u>2</u>  Viracocha creó los hombres a su imagen y semejanza.

<u>4</u>  Viracocha ordenó un diluvio.

<u>6</u>  Viracocha creó las diferentes naciones.

<u>3</u>  Los primeros hombres desobedecieron los preceptos de Viracocha.

<u>7</u>  Viracocha y sus criados ordenaron a las naciones multiplicarse y poblar la tierra.

**D. Semejanzas** Busque dos semejanzas entre la historia del origen del hombre en la tradición judeocristiana y la de los Incas.

**E. Las diferentes caras del dios Viracocha** Busquen en el texto referencias acerca de las diferentes manifestaciones del dios inca.

dios creador
dios destructor
dios administrador
dios artista

**F. Enfoque lingüístico** Identifiquen las formas del pretérito de los verbos en el primer párrafo y en el último párrafo. Luego, escriban las formas correspondientes del infinitivo.

**G. Actividad de extensión: ¿Qué hizo después?** Escribe un párrafo sobre lo que imaginas que el dios Viracocha realizó después de crear los pueblos y las naciones de la Tierra.

**Answers D:** Students may comment on the creation of the human being in the image of God, the deluge in response to human sin, the naming of things as part of the divine creative process, the fall from grace of one of God's assistants and his promise of revenge, God as a sculptor (creating people from natural elements), light as a special aspect of creation, etc.

**Answers E:** *Answers may vary.* dios creador: paragraph 1 ("El cual creó el mundo obscuro y sin sol ni luna ni estrellas"); dios destructor: paragraph 2 ("y sobre todos les mandó un diluvio general, al cual ellos llaman *uno pachacuti,* que quiere decir «agua que trastornó la tierra»"), dios administrador, paragraph 5 ("Entonces, ordenó a sus dos criados memorizar los nombres que él les decía de aquellas gentes"), dios artista: paragraph 5 ("en este lugar esculpió y dibujó en unas rocas grandes todas las naciones que pensaba crear").

**Answers F:** párrafo 1 (crear, llamar, formar, parecer, decir), párrafo 5 (dejar, ir, esculpir, dibujar, ordenar, mandar, obedecer, salir, henchir, multiplicar).

You may want to point out to students that the verb **henchir** is an **e→i** verb.

# Vocabulario

CD1-57

## Eventos importantes

| | |
|---|---|
| aniversario | *anniversary* |
| bautizo | *baptism* |
| cumpleaños | *birthday* |
| graduación | *graduation* |
| jubilación | *retirement* |
| matrimonio/boda/ casamiento | *wedding* |
| nacimiento | *birth* |

## Los números después de 100

| | |
|---|---|
| cien | 100 |
| ciento uno/a | 101 |
| ciento dos | 102 |
| ciento tres | 103 |
| doscientos/as | 200 |
| doscientos uno/a | 201 |
| doscientos dos | 202 |
| doscientos tres | 203 |
| trescientos/as | 300 |
| cuatrocientos/as | 400 |
| quinientos/as | 500 |
| seiscientos/as | 600 |
| setecientos/as | 700 |
| ochocientos/as | 800 |
| novecientos/as | 900 |
| mil | 1.000 |
| mil uno/a | 1.001 |
| mil dos | 1.002 |
| diez mil | 10.000 |
| diez mil uno/a | 10.001 |
| diez mil dos | 10.002 |
| cien mil | 100.000 |
| cien mil uno/a | 100.001 |
| cien mil dos | 100.002 |
| novecientos mil | 900.000 |
| novecientos noventa y nueve mil | 999.000 |
| un millón | 1.000.000 |
| dos millones | 2.000.000 |

## Preparativos para un viaje

| | |
|---|---|
| el asiento | *the seat* |
| la billetera | *wallet* |
| el boleto/billete | *airline ticket* |
| la cartera | *handbag* |
| los cheques de viajero | *traveler's checks* |
| el equipaje | *luggage* |
| el equipaje de mano | *carry on luggage* |
| la maleta | *suitcase* |
| el maletín | *briefcase* |
| la mochila | *backpack* |
| el terminal internacional | *international departures terminal* |
| el pasaporte | *passport* |
| el pasillo | *aisle* |
| la sala de espera | *boarding area* |
| la tarjeta de embarque | *boarding pass* |
| la ventanilla | *window* |
| abordar | *to board* |
| cambiar | *to exchange* |
| empacar | *to pack* |
| mostrar (ue) | *to show* |
| sacar | *to get, obtain* |

## El cuerpo humano

| | |
|---|---|
| el abdomen | *abdomen* |
| la boca | *mouth* |
| los brazos | *arms* |
| la cabeza | *head* |
| la cara | *face* |
| las cejas | *eyebrows* |
| la cintura | *waist* |
| los codos | *elbows* |
| el corazón | *heart* |
| el cuello | *neck* |
| los dedos | *fingers* |
| los dedos del pie | *toes* |
| los dientes | *teeth* |
| la espalda | *back* |
| el estómago | *stomach* |
| la garganta | *throat* |
| el hombro | *shoulder* |
| el hueso | *bone* |
| las manos | *hands* |
| la nariz | *nose* |
| el oído | *inner ear* |
| los ojos | *eyes* |
| las orejas | *ears* |
| el pelo | *hair* |
| la piel | *skin* |
| las piernas | *legs* |
| los pies | *feet* |
| los pulmones | *lungs* |
| las rodillas | *knees* |
| los tobillos | *ankles* |
| las uñas | *fingernails* |

## Funciones y estructuras

Verbos con cambios ortográficos, p. 184
Verbos irregulares, pp. 195, 196
Verbos con terminaciones especiales, p. 208
Verbos para hablar de incidentes y accidentes, p. 211

Vocabulario | doscientos diecisiete **217**

# Capítulo

# 6

## Para comenzar

- ¿Qué diferencias o semejanzas hay entre San José y tu localidad?
- ¿Cuáles son algunas de las ventajas de vivir en una ciudad como San José?
- ¿Hay algunas desventajas?
- ¿Qué prefieres tú?

# Recuerdos

## In this chapter you will learn . . .

- how to talk about the differences between urban and rural life
- how to talk about the environment
- how to express generalizations
- how to describe in the past
- how to talk about one's life in the past
- about some of the environmental issues that affect Latin America today

|  | TEMA 1<br>La ciudad | TEMA 2<br>La naturaleza | TEMA 3<br>La conservación del medio ambiente |
|---|---|---|---|
| Vocabulario | El mundo urbano | La vida en el campo | La ecología |
| Funciones y estructuras | Expressing generalizations with indefinite words (and review of negative words)<br>Describing the past with the imperfect tense | Describing the past with irregular verbs in the imperfect tense<br>Expressing knowledge and familiarity with the verbs **saber** and **conocer** | Indicating location with demonstrative adjectives and pronouns<br>Talking about the past with verbs that change meaning in the preterite |
| Lecturas y vídeo | Perspectivas: Saturación vehicular en Managua | Vídeo: Un baile folclórico puertorriqueño | Lectura: La leyenda del Zurquí |

**Vista aérea de la ciudad
de San José**

**El centro de la ciudad**

**Un barrio residencial**

# Enfoque

Transparencies A-15: Country Profiles: Costa Rica, Panamá;
A-17: Country Profiles: Honduras, Nicaragua

iLrn

**A. ¿Qué sabes ya de Costa Rica?** Antes de ver el vídeo, completa las siguientes oraciones. Luego, compara tus respuestas con las de un(a) compañero(a).

1. Costa Rica comparte frontera con dos países: con _____ al norte y con _____ al sur.
   a. Honduras, Nicaragua      (b.) Nicaragua, Panamá      c. Panamá, Colombia
2. La divisa o moneda del país es el _____ costarricense.
   (a.) colón            b. peso            c. sol
3. Aunque *(Even though)* la cultura costarricense es el reflejo de la mezcla de razas que coexisten en el país, la influencia principal es la _____.
   (a.) europea          b. indígena          c. asiática
4. Desde 1948, Costa Rica no tiene _____. El dinero que se ahorra
   *(saves)* el país lo invierte en mejorar el nivel de vida de los costarricenses.
   a. iglesia oficial      (b.) ejército          c. gobierno central

**B. Costa Rica – «Pura vida»** Lee las siguientes oraciones sobre Costa Rica. Luego, marca con una **X** las que escuches en el vídeo. **¡OJO!** En el vídeo no se mencionan todas las oraciones.

_X_ 1. Costa Rica es un pequeño país centroamericano con más de tres millones de habitantes.

_X_ 2. En el Museo de Oro se puede ver artículos precolombinos, es decir, los artículos que los indígenas hicieron antes de la llegada de los españoles al continente americano.

_X_ 3. La economía de Costa Rica es principalmente agrícola; algunos productos importantes son las bananas y el café.

____ 4. Más o menos un 18% de Costa Rica está formado por reservas y parques nacionales, dos de los cuales fueron declarados Patrimonio de la Humanidad por la UNESCO.

_X_ 5. San José es la capital de Costa Rica; es el centro de la población, de la cultura y de la industria.

The sentences that are not mentioned in the video are facts about Costa Rica that could be explored in class.

**C. El ecoturismo** Como vieron en el vídeo, los costarricenses son muy conscientes de la riqueza natural de su país y hacen esfuerzos para protegerla. ¿Cuánto saben del ecoturismo?

1. ¿Qué es y qué opinan del ecoturismo?
2. ¿Les gustaría *(would you like)* hacer ecoturismo? ¿Por qué sí o por qué no?
3. ¿Dónde se puede hacer ecoturismo en los Estados Unidos? ¿Hay un sitio en tu comunidad o cerca de ahí?

For more info, you may want to check the **Temas** site:
**http://temas.heinle.com**

Capítulo 6 | doscientos diecinueve    **219**

# La ciudad

## I. Vocabulario: El mundo urbano

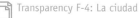 Transparency F-4: La ciudad

**Voy a mudarme a un nuevo apartamento, así que necesito conectar varios servicios.**

el agua — el alcantarillado — el cable — la conexión a Internet — el gas — la luz (la electricidad) — el teléfono

## Los problemas de la vida urbana

la contaminación — el ruido — la congestión — el costo de vida — la delincuencia — la basura

## Vocabulario práctico

el barrio *neighborhood*

el centro *downtown*

**Los servicios sociales** *(Social services)*

la educación *education*

la salud *health*

el transporte *transportation*

**Los funcionarios públicos** *(Public officials)*

el (la) alcalde (alcaldesa) *mayor*

los basureros *garbage haulers*

los bomberos *fire department (firefighters)*

los paramédicos *paramedics*

la policía *police*

la policía vial/de tránsito *traffic police*

## ■ Asimilación

**6-1 ¿Corresponde o no?** En cada uno de los siguientes grupos hay un elemento que no corresponde. Determinen cuál es y expliquen por qué no es parte del grupo.

1. educación, transporte, salud, (agua)
2. hospital, (gas), escuela, metro
3. transporte, (cable), tráfico, ruido
4. agua, luz, (museo), teléfono
5. (camarero), alcalde, bombero, médico

1–58 **6-2 Su nuevo hogar en Managua** Un amigo tuyo viajó recientemente a Nicaragua para trabajar. Escucha su mensaje en el contestador.

1. Lo que más le gusta de Managua es...
   a. los museos.   (b.) el centro.   c. el parque.
2. Encontró en la ciudad...
   a. una casa.   (b.) un apartamento.   c. una oficina.
3. Ahora necesita instalar...
   (a.) el teléfono.   b. la luz.   c. el agua.

**Script 6-2:** Hola. ¿Cómo estás? ¿Adivina quién es? Sí, es tu amigo Frank. Te llamo desde Nicaragua. Me gusta mucho este país, ¿sabes? Especialmente el centro de Managua, con tanta actividad y alegría. Encontré ayer un apartamento muy agradable. Te voy a enviar una postal con la dirección. Ahora sólo me falta instalar el teléfono. Cuando lo instalen te llamo de nuevo. Espero encontrarte... ¿dónde estás? Es tarde ya... Pues nada, un abrazo y que continúes estudiando español. Es muy útil. Chao.

## ■ Aplicaciones

**6-3 ¿Qué se requiere?** Muchas de nuestras actividades cotidianas *(daily)* que parecen simples en realidad requieren la confluencia de muchos y complejos servicios. Indica cuáles se requieren para **tomar una ducha de agua caliente** *(to take a hot shower)*. Compara luego tus respuestas con las de otros compañeros.

_____ gas

_____ alcantarillado

_____ teléfono

_____ transporte

_____ electricidad

_____ salud

_____ agua

_____ educación

**Answers 6-3:** *Answers may vary.* Encourage students to express and support their opinions.

**6-4 La vida en Managua** Completa la siguiente carta de Marisa, tu *e-mail–pal* nicaragüense, sobre la vida en su ciudad.

Managua es una ciudad grande, con muchos lugares bonitos para visitar. El ___centro___ es un poco congestionado, pero los ___barrios___ periféricos son tranquilos. El sistema de ___transporte___ es eficiente y económico. Hay autobuses y taxis, pero no hay metro. Como aumenta el número de automóviles particulares, el problema de la ___contaminación___ y la congestión nos preocupa mucho ahora en la ciudad. Pero bueno, ¿y cómo es tu ciudad?

**EN TU COMUNIDAD**

Interview a real estate agent and write a report about recent trends in the housing market in your community (Are there more buyers or sellers at this time? What is the average sale price of a home? Are interest rates favorable?). Also, investigate the type of support available to non-English speakers in this agent's real estate firm.

**6-5 ¿Sabes?** Describan la vida urbana.

1. Nombren tres cosas que debemos instalar en una casa nueva.
2. Nombren tres tipos de servicios sociales que se encuentran *(are found)* en una ciudad.
3. Nombren tres lugares donde trabaja la gente de la ciudad.
4. Nombren tres lugares donde la gente de la ciudad se divierte.
5. Nombren tres problemas que **no** tiene tu pueblo o tu ciudad.

**SUGERENCIAS**

**Step 1:** Make a list of the things that make your city or town unique and a list of some of its problems.
**Step 2:** Select the information that you will include in your composition and link related ideas with connectors such as **como** *(since)*, **además** *(in addition)*, **lo peor** *(the worst thing)*, **lo mejor** *(the best thing)*.
**Step 3:** Exchange compositions with a classmate and check the following aspects:
**a. content** (is the description of the town complete and fair?);
**b. organization** (is it easy to read? Are there any unclear segments?); **c. vocabulary** (did your classmate include a variety of words from this chapter?);
**d. grammar** (do you find any agreement problems?).

■ **Integración**

**6-6 Entrevista** Trabajando en parejas, hagan y respondan a las siguientes preguntas. Al terminar, preparen un breve informe sobre las respuestas del (de la) compañero(a).

1. ¿Tienes suficiente luz natural en tu apartamento o en tu casa?
2. ¿Hay demasiado ruido en tu apartamento o en tu casa?
3. ¿Dónde tiras la basura?
4. ¿Quién saca la basura en tu casa?
5. ¿Hay mucha delincuencia en tu barrio?
6. ¿Hay mucho tráfico donde vives?
7. ¿Es alto el costo de vida en tu comunidad?

**6-7 La vida en tu pueblo o en tu ciudad** Escribe una breve descripción de tu ciudad para responder a la pregunta que Marisa hizo en el mensaje de la actividad 6-4.

This writing exercise will be recycled in activity **6-14**. Ask students to keep a copy.

## II. Funciones y estructuras: Expressing generalizations with indefinite words (and review of negative words)

SERGIO: Hay **algo** que me preocupa: hay mucha basura en las calles. ¿Conoces a **alguna** persona que trabaje en la oficina del alcalde?

ANABEL: No, no conozco a **nadie**, pero podemos ir **algún día** para hablar con **alguien.**

In **Capítulo 1, Tema 3,** you learned how to use negative words such as **nada, nadie, ni… ni, ningún/ninguno(a), nunca,** and **tampoco.** As you may recall, these words are placed either before the verb or after a verb that is preceded by **no.**

**No** tenemos **ni** cable **ni** teléfono.

**Nadie** puede encontrar **ninguna** solución al problema de la delincuencia.

*We have **neither** cable **nor** phone.*

***Nobody** can find **any** solution for the delinquency problem.*

> **REMEMBER**
>
> Double negatives are correct in Spanish. See the examples provided.

The affirmative counterparts of these negative words are the indefinite words, which refer to people and objects in a generic and unspecified way. Here is a list of these words.

| | |
|---|---|
| algo *something* | alguna vez/una vez *sometime, ever/once* |
| alguien *someone, somebody* | o… o…/ y *either . . . or . . . / and* |
| algún/alguno(a/os/as) *a/an, some, any* | siempre *always* |
| algún día *some day* | también *also* |

To say *everybody*, use the expression **todo el mundo.**

The expressions **alguna vez** and **una vez** usually refer to actions in the past while **algún día** refers to actions in the future.

El ruido es **algo** que no tolero.

**Alguien** me dijo que los basureros están en huelga.

*Noise is **something** that I do not tolerate.*

***Somebody** told me that garbage haulers are on strike.*

The word **alguno** changes to **algún** when it is used before a masculine singular noun.

¿Hay **algún** funcionario en esta oficina?

¿Tienes **algún** problema con el transporte?

*Is there **any** public official in this office?*

*Do you have **any** transportation problem?*

## ■ Asimilación

**6-8 Los estudiantes de mi clase** Escoge las oraciones que describan a los estudiantes de tu clase. Al terminar, compara tus respuestas con las de un(a) compañero(a). ¿Están de acuerdo?

_____ Siempre quieren tomar clases por la mañana.

_____ Toman algunas clases fáciles para mejorar el promedio *(grade point average)*.

_____ Quieren ir a algún país de habla hispana algún día.

_____ Alguna vez hicieron trampa *(cheated)* en un examen.

_____ Cuando están enojados con el (la) profesor(a), dicen algo.

_____ Buscan a alguien semejante a ellos para trabajar en grupos.

_____ Todo el mundo llega a clase temprano.

_____ Sacan A o sacan B en todos los trabajos.

**Script 6-9:** Creo que todo el mundo debe asumir su responsabilidad cívica para que podamos vivir bien en nuestra ciudad. Aunque yo nunca participo en manifestaciones públicas, hago otras cosas. Por ejemplo, yo siempre divido la basura y la reciclo. También, siempre evito el ruido excesivo y hablo con los jóvenes para prevenir la delincuencia. Además, a veces camino al centro para ayudar con la congestión en las calles. ¡Y así hago ejercicio!

CD1-59

**6-9 La responsabiliad cívica** Escucha lo que dice Beatriz sobre la responsabilidad cívica e indica la frecuencia con la que ella hace las actividades de la lista.

| Actividad | siempre | algunas veces | nunca |
|---|---|---|---|
| 1. Evita el ruido excesivo. | X | | |
| 2. Participa en manifestaciones públicas. | | | X |
| 3. Camina al centro para ayudar con la congestión. | | X | |
| 4. Divide y recicla la basura. | X | | |
| 5. Habla con los jóvenes para prevenir la delincuencia. | X | | |

## ■ Aplicaciones

**6-10 En este barrio** Lean lo que dice Adolfo sobre su barrio y escojan las palabras correctas.

Me gusta mucho mi barrio porque (alguien / nadie) tira la basura a la calle y porque (siempre / nunca) hay mucho ruido. Además, es un barrio donde no hay delincuencia y (también / tampoco) hay contaminación (o / y / ni) congestión. Pero hay (algo / nada) que no es bueno: el costo de vida es muy alto. (Algunos / Ningún) funcionarios públicos prometen que esto va a mejorar, pero no lo creo. (También / Tampoco), desafortunadamente, hay (algunas / ningunas) personas que no se preocupan por la educación ni por los servicios públicos.

**6-11 ¡Qué contradictorio(a)!** Túrnense para leer y reaccionar a las siguientes oraciones en forma opuesta.

MODELO  E1: *Siempre me pongo ropa de colores oscuros.*
E2: *Pues yo nunca me pongo ropa de colores oscuros.*
o *Pues yo no me pongo nunca ropa de colores oscuros.*

1. Creo que no hay ninguna película interesante en el cine.
2. Pienso que no hay nadie aburrido en esta clase.
3. Algún día espero tomar clases de acupuntura.
4. En mi casa cenamos juntos todos los días.
5. Una vez fui de vacaciones a Costa Rica.
6. Creo que alguien aquí se puso mucho perfume.

**6-12 En nuestras familias**

**Paso 1:** Piensa en las personas de tu familia y completa las siguientes oraciones.

1. En mi familia nadie _____.
2. Mis parientes siempre _____ y _____.
3. Ellos nunca _____ ni _____.
4. Algún día, nosotros vamos a _____.
5. Algo cómico en mi familia es que nosotros _____.
6. Ninguno de mis parientes es _____.

**Paso 2:** Convierte las oraciones del **Paso 1** en preguntas para tu compañero(a). Escribe las respuestas que él/ella dé y prepara un breve informe.

A simple way of turning these sentences into questions is by asking what is called an *echo question*, which consists of placing an interrogative word in the place where the answer would go, for example, **¿En tu familia nadie qué?**

## Integración

**6-13 ¿Qué opinan?** En grupos de tres o cuatro estudiantes, describan cómo es la vida y cuáles son algunos aspectos positivos y negativos de alguna ciudad famosa de los Estados Unidos. Incorporen el vocabulario que se presentó al principio de este **Tema.**

You can use expressions such as **algo (interesante/aburrido/ridículo/que [no] me gusta) de esta ciudad es que...; aquí (siempre/nunca/nadie/todo el mundo)...; cuando alguien visita esta ciudad,...; en esta ciudad, (algunas personas/nadie)...; aquí hay (algún/os/as)...; aquí... y... también y aquí ni... ni... tampoco.**

**6-14 La vida en tu pueblo o en tu ciudad** Vuelve a leer *(Read again)* la descripción de tu ciudad que escribiste en la actividad 6-7 y añade más detalles. Usa las palabras y frases que aprendiste en esta sección. Cuando termines, dale una copia a tu profesor(a) para que la corrija.

You may want to use some of the expressions that were presented in activity 6-13.

## III. Funciones y estructuras: Describing the past with the imperfect tense

En el barrio donde yo crecí **había** muchas casas y la playa **estaba** muy cerca.

Cuando era niño, yo **jugaba** con mis amigos todos los días. **Nos divertíamos** muchísimo.

As you may have noticed, the previous examples include verbs in a past tense that is not the preterite. This tense is called the imperfect. Here is a list of the basic uses of this tense.

- To talk about habitual actions in the past (the equivalent of *used to . . .*).

  Yo **visitaba** a mis abuelos todas las tardes.

  *I **used to visit** my grandparents every afternoon.*

- To provide descriptions.

  Su casa **tenía** un jardín muy grande.

  *Their house **had** a very big garden.*

You will learn more about the difference between the preterite and the imperfect tenses in **Capítulo 7, Tema 3.**

- To talk about an event that was in progress while another action was taking place. The action that takes place while another action is in progress is reported in the preterite.

  Yo **estaba** en la escuela primaria cuando nos mudamos a otro barrio.

  *I **was** in elementary school when we moved to another neighborhood.*

- To provide descriptions of the participants who carry out the main events of a story, including age, physical appearance, conditions and emotions.

  **Tenía** diez años y **era** un chico muy bueno.

  *I **was** ten years old and **was** a very good boy.*

Students will learn how to conjugate **ser** and other irregular verbs in the imperfect in **Capítulo 6, Tema 2.**

- To provide background information of past events, including time and weather conditions.

  Cuando salimos de la casa, **eran** como las tres de la tarde y **llovía.**

  *When we left the house, **it was** around three o'clock in the afternoon, and **it was raining.***

The endings of the imperfect tense are the following.

| tomar (to take, to drink) | correr (to run) | vivir (to live) |
|---|---|---|
| tomaba | corría | vivía |
| tomabas | corrías | vivías |
| tomaba | corría | vivía |
| tomábamos | corríamos | vivíamos |
| tomabais | corríais | vivíais |
| tomaban | corrían | vivían |

*Notice that the endings for **-er** and **-ir** verbs are identical. Also, notice that only the endings for **-ar** verbs have the letter **b**.

Unlike in the preterite, there are not any stem-changing verbs in the imperfect tense.

Yo **pensaba** que **tenía** los mejores padres del mundo.
Y **soñaba** con ser policía.

*I **used to think** that **I had** the best parents in in the world.*
*And **I used to dream** about being a police officer.*

The imperfect tense form of the verb **haber** is **había** *(there used to be, there was/were)*.

En mi pueblo **había** muchas tiendas de antigüedades.

***There were** many antique shops in my town.*

## ■ Asimilación

**6-15 Tu pueblo** Escoge las oraciones que describan el pueblo en que creciste y sus habitantes. Luego, compara tus respuestas con las de un(a) compañero(a). ¿Eran pueblos semejantes o diferentes?

_____ No tenía alcalde ni policía municipal.
_____ Había muchos parques.
_____ Tenía muchos habitantes.
_____ Tenía muchas calles.
_____ Estaba cerca de una ciudad.

_____ Había mucha contaminación.
_____ Mucha gente usaba transporte público.
_____ No había un centro comercial.
_____ Estaba lejos de esta universidad.
_____ La gente se comunicaba bien.

-60 **6-16 ¿Cuándo?** Abraham va a hablar de algunas de las cosas que hacía antes. Escucha lo que dice e indica si él hacía estas actividades cuando era niño o cuando estaba en la escuela secundaria. **¡OJO!** Hay actividades que Abraham no hacía.

**Clave:** a = cuando era niño     b = cuando estaba en la escuela secundaria

_a_ 1. Tomaba clases de karate.
_____ 2. Miraba la televisión.
_a_ 3. Jugaba béisbol.
_b_ 4. Estaba en el club de teatro.
_b_ 5. Estudiaba más.
_____ 6. Leía mucho.
_a_ 7. Patinaba.
_b_ 8. Trabajaba en el museo del pueblo.

Script 6-16: ¿Qué cosas hacía? Bueno, cuando era niño, patinaba en el parque, tomaba clases de karate y jugaba béisbol. Como era un niño muy activo, no leía mucho ni tampoco miraba la televisión. Después, en la escuela secundaria, estudiaba más y tocaba el clarinete. También estaba en el club de teatro y a veces trabajaba en el museo de mi pueblo.

## ■ Aplicaciones

**6-17 ¿Qué hacían?** Mencionen por lo menos dos actividades que las siguientes personas posiblemente hacían cuando tenían diez años. ¡Sean originales!

> MODELO   Donald Trump *tenía muchas novias y leía la revista* Forbes.

1. David Letterman
2. Venus y Serena Williams
3. el (la) gobernador(a) del estado
4. Madonna
5. Howard Stern
6. Halle Berry
7. el presidente de los Estados Unidos
8. otra persona: _____

**6-18 Mini-situaciones** Completen las siguientes situaciones con detalles interesantes y cómicos.

> MODELO   Cuando mi mejor amigo(a) llegó a su clase de español, <u>no había nadie en la sala de clase. El profesor lo esperaba con un examen y él/ella no estaba preparado(a)</u>.

1. Cuando el (la) profesor(a) entró a su casa anoche,...
2. Cuando me mudé a la casa donde vivo ahora,...
3. Cuando nosotros comenzamos a estudiar español,...
4. Cuando tenía cinco años, yo...
5. Cuando los estudiantes de la clase de 1985 se graduaron,...

**6-19 La niñez** *(Childhood)*

**Paso 1:** Escribe seis oraciones sobre las cosas que hacías y que no hacías en tu niñez.

> MODELO   *No regresaba a casa antes de las ocho de la noche.*

1. ...
2. ...
3. ...
4. ...
5. ...
6. ...

**Paso 2:** Usa las oraciones del **Paso 1** para formar preguntas para tus compañeros de clase. Debes buscar a seis personas diferentes que respondan afirmativamente a una de las preguntas. Cuando las encuentres, escribe los nombres. Al terminar, prepara un informe para la clase.

> MODELO   *En tu niñez, ¿no regresabas a casa antes de las ocho de la noche?*

## ■ Integración

You may talk about clothing and colors, hair styles, the role of men and women in society, things children used to do, music, TV shows, food, etc.

You may use the following connectors to compare both decades: **primero** *(first),* **segundo** *(second),* **tercero** *(third),* **en cambio** *(instead, on the other hand),* **por el contrario** *(on the contrary),* **sin embargo** *(however),* **por ejemplo** *(for example),* **además** *(in addition),* and **finalmente** *(finally).*

**6-20 ¡Cómo han cambiado las cosas!** Descríbele a tu compañero(a) cómo era la vida en una década específica (los cincuenta, los sesenta, los setenta, los ochenta, los noventa, etc.). Luego, tu compañero(a) va a describir una década diferente. Si es necesario, busquen información sobre esto en el Internet.

**6-21 La mejor década** De acuerdo con la discusión que tuviste con tu compañero(a) en la actividad 6-20, ¿cuál fue la mejor década, la que tú describiste o la que él/ella describió? Escribe una composición corta para exponerle tu punto de vista *(point of view)* a tu profesor(a). Cuando termines, intercambia tu composición con un(a) compañero(a) para ver si te faltan *(if you are missing)* algunos detalles. Cuando hagas las correcciones, dale una copia a tu profesor(a). ¿Crees que lo/la vas a poder convencer?

# IV. Perspectivas: Saturación vehicular en Managua

## ▪ Antes de leer

**A. ¿Qué opinan de esta declaración** *(statement)*? Hay demasiados coches en este país.

**B. ¿Eres un(a) conductor(a) responsable?** Marca tus respuestas y compáralas con las de tu compañero(a).

| | |
|---|---|
| Excedo el límite de velocidad. | Siempre / A veces / Nunca |
| Uso el cinturón de seguridad. | Siempre / A veces / Nunca |
| Respeto las leyes de tránsito. | Siempre / A veces / Nunca |
| Bebo antes de conducir. | Siempre / A veces / Nunca |
| Pongo a los niños en sillas especiales. | Siempre / A veces / Nunca |

## ▪ A leer

### Sesenta y cuatro carros nuevos por día en las calles de Managua

Minsa y OPS expresan preocupación y piden endurecer sanciones a conductores irresponsables.

—Lucía Navas—

**Cada día,** la dirección de Tránsito de la Policía inscribe 64 nuevos vehículos para que circulen en Managua, lo cual está aumentando la saturación vehicular y potenciando más la accidentalidad.

*Each day*

Autoridades del **Minsa** y representantes de la Organización Panamericana de la Salud (OPS) dijeron que por ser los traumatismos causados por accidentes de tránsito «una epidemia», se debe aplicar mayores sanciones en contra de conductores que violenten las leyes.

*Ministerio de Salud*

Se insiste en que los conductores **ebrios,** la alta velocidad en las **carreteras,** el desuso de protectores (**cascos** y cinturones) y el irrespeto a las señales de tránsito por conductores y peatones provocan que las lesiones por accidentalidad en Nicaragua estén entre las primeras causas de muerte en grupos de 5 a 49 años.

*drunk*
*highways/roads / helmets*

«El sistema de vigilancia en hospitales en Nicaragua reporta que el 18 por ciento de las emergencias son por lesiones de tránsito y el 28 por ciento están relacionadas con el exceso de alcohol», dijo Montesano, de OPS.

| | |
|---|---|
| *rollovers / hit* | Las muertes se dan por **volcones** de los carros, **atropellamiento** y por |
| *falls* | **caídas** de pasajeros del transporte público. |

Se planteó la suspensión de licencia de conducir por seis meses para

*intoxication* quienes manejen en estado de **ebriedad,** y de por vida a quienes

reincidan. La actual Ley de Tránsito permite que hasta la cuarta vez de

*regulation* reincidencia se aplique la **medida.**

**Más accidentes... más carros**

El comisionado Gilberto Solís, de la Dirección de Tránsito Nacional,

*número de autos* indicó que el **parque vehicular** de Managua crece cada semana al

darse 450 nuevas inscripciones de carros.

Dijo que los accidentes también ocurren por mala programación de los

*weakness* semáforos y la **debilidad** de la infraestructura de las carreteras.

«También hay mucha intolerancia e impaciencia en las carreteras, lo

que provoca mayores niveles de estrés en los conductores, y ello genera

más accidentes e infartos en los ciudadanos», explicó la comisionada

Vilma Rosa Rosales, directora del Centro de Educación Vial.

*Ministerio de Educación, Cultura y* La Policía se coordina con el **MECD** para implementar la educación

*Deportes / pertaining to roads and* **vial** permanente en los centros escolares. Y con la creación del Consejo

*highways* de Seguridad Vial pretenden «formar, educar y corregir a los

conductores y peatones». El obstáculo actual es que, físicamente, el

centro como tal no existe, y que para subsanar la debilidad están

aplicando mayores exigencias.

Entre lo recomendado por OPS está una campaña masiva de

*speedometers* educación vial en el país, y que haya más **velocímetros** controlando las

carreteras. Además, que los carros particulares utilicen sillas especiales

*back seat* para llevar niños en el **asiento trasero,** que se mejore la visibilidad de

vehículos y peatones en la vía pública por las noches, y se insista en el

*adherence to* **cumplimiento de** las medidas de seguridad vial.

Source: *El nuevo diario.* Martes, 18 de mayo de 2004 (adaptado)
(http://www.elnuevodiario.com.ni/archivo/2004/mayo/18-mayo-
2004/nacional/nacional18.html)

## ¿Entendiste bien?

**C. Ideas principales** Escoge la opción más apropiada según el texto.

These questions target skimming and scanning skills.

1. ¿Cuántos nuevos autos inscribe la policía de Managua cada mes?
   a. más de 60
   b. más de 400
   c. más de 1900

2. Las autoridades nicaragüenses están preocupadas porque un aumento de autos resulta en...
   a. más contaminación.
   b. más accidentes.
   c. más tráfico.

3. En Managua, más de un cuarto de las emergencias por lesiones de tránsito están relacionadas con...
   a. la velocidad.
   b. el estrés.
   c. el alcohol.

4. Según el artículo, en Nicaragua **no** son causa principal de fatalidades de tránsito...
   a. los choques de autos.
   b. las caídas de pasajeros del transporte público.
   c. los atropellamientos.

5. La solución propuesta por el gobierno incluye...
   a. sanciones y nuevos semáforos.
   b. educación y una nueva infraestructura vial.
   c. sanciones y educación vial.

**D. Detalles importantes** Busquen la siguiente información.

These questions target scanning skills.

1. Identifiquen los cuatro factores que provocan los accidentes de tránsito en Nicaragua.

2. Identifiquen las cinco propuestas presentadas por el gobierno nicaragüense para solucionar el problema de tránsito.

**Answers D:** 1. conductores ebrios, alta velocidad, desuso de protectores, irrespeto de señales de tránsito 2. campaña masiva de educación, más velocímetros, uso de sillas especiales para niños en el asiento trasero, mejorar la visibilidad de vehículos y peatones, insistir en cumplimiento de las medidas de seguridad

**E. Para conversar** ¿Qué otras soluciones debería considerar el gobierno nicaragüense para reducir la saturación vehicular y los accidentes en su país?

# La naturaleza

## I. Vocabulario: La vida en el campo

la isla

la playa

el valle

la montaña

el lago

el volcán

el mar

la arena

el árbol

la selva

el río

el ganado

el cultivo

el toro

la vaca

el pato

el agricultor

la gallina

el perro

la finca /
la hacienda

el caballo

el cerdo/
puerco

el gato

el pavo

la cosecha

El campo y los animales domésticos *(the countryside and farm animals)*

**Vocabulario práctico**

los campesinos/trabajadores
   *workers*
el campo *countryside (field)*
el suelo *soil*

**Trabajo**
alimentar *to feed*
cosechar *to harvest*
criar *to raise*
cultivar *to cultivate*
recoger *to pick*
sembrar (ie) *to sow*

**Diversión**
acampar *to camp*
bucear *to dive*
escalar *to climb, to hike*
esquiar *to ski*
esquiar en el agua *to waterski*
hacer surf *to surf*
montar a caballo *to horseback
   ride*
nadar *to swim*

## ■ Asimilación

**6-22 El campo en los Estados Unidos** Indiquen si las siguientes oraciones son ciertas (**C**) o falsas (**F**).

   _C_   1. Crían mucho ganado en Texas.

   _F_   2. Todas las fincas están en el centro del país.

   _C_   3. Hay plantaciones de tabaco en Carolina del Sur.

   _C_   4. Los cultivos de cereales en Kansas están muy tecnificados.

   _F_   5. Las cosechas de naranjas son excelentes en Massachusetts.

   _C_   6. Muchos inmigrantes hispanos recogen las cosechas en California.

**6-23 ¿Adónde fueron?** Escucha las descripciones de diferentes vacaciones que ha tomado el Sr. Espinoza e identifica el destino de sus viajes.

1. En 2001, los Espinoza fueron a...
   a. una finca.
   b. una ciudad.
   c. una playa.
2. En 2002 fueron a...
   a. un desierto.
   b. una selva.
   c. un río.
3. En 2004 fueron a...
   a. una finca.
   b. un desierto.
   c. una playa.
4. En 2005 fueron a...
   a. una finca.
   b. una selva.
   c. una ciudad.

**Script 6-23:** A nosotros nos gusta tomar vacaciones en diferentes partes de Panamá todos los años. Por ejemplo, en 2001 estuvimos en Chiriquí y vimos muchos cultivos y ganado en una finca. En 2002, en cambio, fuimos al parque Nacional de Darién, en donde disfrutamos de los ríos y de la gran variedad de árboles y animales. En 2004 visitamos las Islas de San Blas y nos alojamos en una cabaña al lado del mar. Finalmente, en 2005 nos quedamos en Ciudad de Panamá, hicimos compras y fuimos a los museos y al teatro.

## ■ Aplicaciones

**6-24 Tres animales** Mencionen tres animales con cada una de las siguientes características.

1. Tienen pelo.
2. Tienen plumas (*feathers*).
3. Son famosos por las películas.
4. Viven con los humanos en las ciudades.
5. Su nombre empieza con «p».

**EN TU COMUNIDAD**

Visit a farm and provide a report on property size, type of production (crops, animals, etc.), and number of employees required. Also, determine if this farm uses migrant workers in any aspect of production.

**6-25 Adivina dónde** Una persona tiene que pensar en un lugar y describir las actividades que se pueden hacer allí. La otra persona tiene que adivinar de qué lugar se trata.

MODELO    E1: *Puedes esquiar y escalar.*
                E2: *Las montañas.*

**6-26 ¿Qué hicieron?** Imaginen que Uds. pasaron sus vacaciones en Panamá. Mencionen por lo menos tres actividades que hicieron en cada uno de los siguientes lugares.

MODELO     *En la Ciudad de Panamá fuimos a varios museos, asistimos a un concierto y salimos a cenar en unos restaurantes muy buenos.*

1. Las islas de San Blas          2. La playa Río Mar          3. Parque Nacional de Darién

## ■ Integración

 **6-27 En la agencia de viajes** Representa la siguiente situación con un(a) compañero(a).

| Estudiante A | Estudiante B |
| --- | --- |
| Eres agente de viajes. Puedes ganar una comisión mayor si convences a tu cliente de tomar varias excursiones durante su visita a Panamá. Explícale qué puede ver en diferentes lugares de este país centroamericano. Sé *(Be)* persistente. | Vas a viajar a Panamá este invierno, pero no tienes mucho dinero. Te gustaría hacer alguna excursión, pero no sabes qué vale la pena visitar. Pide información sobre los destinos más interesantes en este país, pero no permitas que te vendan excursiones caras. |

**6-28 La belleza natural de mi país** A Marisa, tu *e-mail-pal* nicaragüense, le fascina la naturaleza. Completa el siguiente mensaje electrónico con la descripción de tu sitio natural favorito en los Estados Unidos.

**SUGERENCIAS**

Mention the name of the place and its location, describe the landscape, list some of the activities you can carry out there, and indicate the approximate cost of food and lodging in the area.

De:          _____ (your e-mail address)
Fecha:       _____ (today's date)
Para:        Marisa@sol.racsa.co.ni
Asunto:      La naturaleza en mi país

Marisa:
En los Estados Unidos hay muchas oportunidades para disfrutar de unas vacaciones en medio de la naturaleza. Mi lugar favorito es...
Un abrazo,

_____ (tu nombre)

## II. Funciones y estructuras: Describing the past with irregular verbs in the imperfect tense

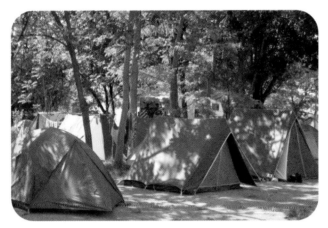

Cuando niños, **íbamos** al campo a acampar. **Era** divertido porque siempre **veíamos** muchos animales diferentes.

There are only three irregular verbs in the imperfect tense: **ir, ser,** and **ver.**

| ir | ser | ver |
|---|---|---|
| iba | era | veía |
| ibas | eras | veías |
| iba | era | veía |
| íbamos | éramos | veíamos |
| ibais | erais | veíais |
| iban | eran | veían |

Notice that the **yo** and **él/ella/usted** forms of each of these verbs are identical.

### ▥ Asimilación

**6-29 En el campo** Piensa en las vacaciones que tomabas cuando eras niño(a) y escoge las alternativas que sean correctas. Cuando termines, compara tus respuestas con las de un(a) compañero(a). ¿Qué cosas eran diferentes?

_____ Iba al campo todos los veranos.

_____ Montar a caballo era mi actividad favorita.

_____ Veía muchos animales salvajes.

_____ Iba con toda mi familia.

_____ Nosotros veíamos a las mismas personas todos los años.

_____ Y también íbamos al mismo lugar todos los años.

_____ Era un(a) niño(a) aventurero(a) y hacía muchas cosas como bucear y escalar montañas.

_____ Nunca iba al campo de vacaciones.

CD1–62 **6-30 Las vacaciones de Iraida** Escucha lo que dice Iraida sobre las vacaciones que tomaba su familia cuando ella era niña y escoge la alternativa correcta para cada pregunta.

**Script 6-30:** Cuando era niña, mi familia y yo siempre íbamos a un lago a pasar las vacaciones. El lago estaba muy lejos de mi casa y mi padre tenía que manejar por muchas horas. Nos quedábamos en una cabaña a la orilla del lago. La cabaña era de madera, muy bonita y grande. Estas vacaciones eran especiales porque veía a mis primos que vivían en los Estados Unidos. Nosotros éramos muy felices porque podíamos esquiar, nadar en el lago y disfrutar de la naturaleza.

1. Iraida iba de vacaciones a...
   a. una selva.    b. un río.    c. un lago.
2. Este lugar estaba... de su casa.
   a. lejos    b. cerca    c. al lado
3. La cabaña *(cabin)* de madera era...
   a. pequeña.    b. cómoda.    c. grande.
4. Durante las vacaciones, Iraida veía a sus...
   a. abuelos.    b. tíos.    c. primos.
5. Ella... con ellos.
   a. hacía surf    b. escalaba    c. esquiaba

■ **Aplicaciones**

**6-31 La casa de mi infancia** Completen los espacios en blanco con las formas correctas de los verbos **ir**, **ser** y **ver**.

La casa de mi infancia ___era___ muy acogedora (cozy). Tenía sólo dos habitaciones, pero (las habitaciones) ___eran___ bastante grandes. Desde el balcón de la casa, (nosotros) ___veíamos___ las montañas y el río. Todos los sábados, mientras mi padre ___iba___ a pescar, mis hermanos y yo ___íbamos___ a jugar con los animales de la granja. A veces (nosotros) ___veíamos___ a algunos turistas que estaban de vacaciones y jugábamos con los niños. ¡Vivir tan cerca de la naturaleza ___era___ magnífico!

**6-32 ¿Cómo? ¿Adónde? ¿Qué?**

**Paso 1:** Completa las siguientes oraciones para indicar cómo eras, adónde ibas en tu tiempo libre y qué programas de televisión veías cuando estabas en la escuela secundaria.

Yo era _____ y _____.

Yo iba a _____ y a _____.

Yo veía _____ y _____.

**Paso 2:** Usa la información del **Paso 1** para hacerle preguntas a tu compañero(a). Toma notas de sus respuestas.

MODELO
E1: *Leonard, ¿eras introvertido?*
E2: *No, yo era extrovertido. También era...*
E1: *¿Ibas al cine con tus amigos?*
E2: *...*

**Paso 3:** Usa la información que recopilaste en el **Paso 2** para escribir un breve informe.

MODELO
*Cuando estaba en la escuela secundaria, yo era introvertido; pero Leonard era extrovertido y... Nosotros íbamos al cine y a...*

**6-33 Creemos que...** Ahora, usen los modelos de la actividad 6-32 para describir los hábitos que dos personas de la clase tenían cuando estaban en la escuela secundaria. Escojan a dos personas que tengan personalidades similares. Al terminar, compartan la información con el resto de la clase. ¿Los demás estudiantes pueden adivinar de quiénes están hablando?

## Integración

**6-34 Una persona entrañable** *(dear)* Descríbele a tu compañero(a) una persona que tuvo un efecto positivo en tu vida. ¿Cómo era esta persona? ¿Qué hacían juntos? ¿Adónde iban?

You may talk about one of your elementary, middle or high school teachers, a relative who passed away, a childhood friend, etc.

**6-35 Preguntas para un(a) compañero(a) de clase** Prepara una serie de preguntas para saber un poco más de la vida en el pasado de un(a) compañero(a) de clase. Cuando termines, entrégale las preguntas a él/ella para que las conteste por escrito *(in writing)*. ¡Debes estar preparado(a) para que él/ella te haga preguntas también!

You may write questions related to his/her personality, his/her favorite activities, his/her favorite TV shows, his/her relatives, places he/she used to visit, etc.

## III. Funciones y estructuras: Expressing knowledge and familiarity with the verbs *saber* and *conocer*

—¿**Conoces** al agricultor que vende verduras en el mercado?
—Sí, lo **conozco**. Se llama Arturo.
—¿**Sabes** dónde está su finca?
—Creo que está en Villa Hermosa.

As you already know, the verbs **saber** and **conocer** have the same meaning: *to know*. Nevertheless, these verbs are used in completely different contexts. Here is a list of their uses.

| The verb **saber** is used to talk about knowing . . . | |
|---|---|
| ■ facts and information. | |
| Yo **sé** dónde está Nicaragua. | *I **know** where Nicaragua is.* |
| ¿**Sabías** que Panamá está al este de Costa Rica? | *Did you **know** that Panama is to the east of Costa Rica?* |
| ■ how to do something. | |
| Mi abuela **sabe** cocinar muy bien. | *My grandmother **knows** how to cook very well.* |
| Ellas **saben** hablar inglés y francés. | *They **know** how to speak English and French.* |

| The verb **conocer** is used to talk about knowing . . . | |
|---|---|
| ■ people and places (being familiar or acquainted). | |
| **Conozco** a los dueños de esta finca. | *I **know** the owners of this land.* |
| ¿**Conoces** el Canal de Panamá? | *Do you **know** (are you familiar with) the Panama Canal?* |

Notice that **conocer** requires the use of the personal **a** when the direct object is a person or pet.

## ■ Asimilación

**6-36 ¿Cierto o falso?** Indica si las siguientes oraciones son ciertas (**C**) o falsas (**F**) y compara tus respuestas con las de un(a) compañero(a). ¿Qué cosas tienen en común?

_____  1. No sé montar a caballo.

_____  2. Sé esquiar en el agua.

_____  3. No sé nadar.

_____  4. Sé los nombres científicos de muchos animales.

_____  5. Sé cultivar y cuidar plantas exóticas.

_____  6. Conozco a muchos campesinos.

_____  7. No conozco tiendas de productos agrícolas.

_____  8. Conozco las Montañas Apalaches.

_____  9. Conozco por lo menos uno de los grandes lagos.

_____ 10. No conozco al / a la secretario(a) de agricultura.

**6-37 Un mensaje telefónico** Escucha el mensaje que el Sr. Hidalgo dejó en el contestador de la Sra. Sánchez, que necesita un asistente para su agencia de turismo en Nicaragua. Escribe las cosas que él sabe y conoce bajo la columna correcta.

| Sabe... | Conoce... |
|---|---|
| hablar inglés y alemán, y un poco de francés; usar varios programas de computadora, y comunicarse bien con personas de diferentes culturas. | todos los lugares de interés turístico en Nicaragua, Costa Rica y Panamá; y a los directores de todos los parques nacionales. |

**Script 6-37:** Buenas tardes, señora Sánchez. Soy el señor Eleuterio Hidalgo y la llamo porque estoy interesado en el puesto de asistente en su agencia. Yo sé hablar inglés y alemán, y un poco de francés. También sé usar varios programas de computadora y comunicarme bien con personas de diferentes culturas. Además, conozco todos los lugares de interés turístico de Nicaragua, Costa Rica y Panamá. ¡Ah! Y conozco a los directores de todos los parques nacionales. Por favor, llámeme tan pronto como pueda al 24-56-98-17. Muchas gracias y que tenga un buen día.

## ■ Aplicaciones

**6-38 La respuesta** La Sra. Sánchez escuchó el mensaje del Sr. Hidalgo, lo llamó y dejó este mensaje en su contestador. Lean la transcripción del mensaje y escojan el verbo correcto.

Buenas tardes, Sr. Hidalgo. Es la Sra. Sánchez, de la Agencia Turismo Centroamericano. Por lo que mencionó, (sé / conozco) que Ud. está muy bien cualificado para el puesto. Además, Ud. (sabe / conoce) los lugares turísticos de los que nosotros les hablamos a los turistas y (sabe / conoce) usar bien la computadora. Yo (sé / conozco) a su prima Deborah y ella le dio una excelente recomendación. (Sé / Conozco) que Ud. es el candidato perfecto. Llámeme mañana para hablar un poco más de las responsabilidades que el puesto exige. Gracias y hasta luego.

**6-39 ¿Cuánto tiempo hace que...?** Averigüen cuánto tiempo hace que su compañero(a) sabe o conoce las siguientes cosas, personas y lugares.

MODELO    manejar un carro
E1: *¿Cuánto tiempo hace que sabes manejar un carro?*
E2: *Hace cuatro años que sé manejar un carro. ¿Y tú?*
E1: *Yo no sé manejar. Tomo el autobús.*

1. esta universidad
2. a tu mejor amigo(a)
3. usar el Internet
4. al / a la profesor(a)
5. tu restaurante favorito
6. tu lugar de vacaciones favorito
7. nadar
8. a tu novio(a) o esposo(a)

**6-40 Talentos y conocimiento**

**Paso 1:** Toma unos minutos para completar la siguiente tabla con información que los demás estudiantes no saben de ti. Escribe por lo menos tres oraciones en cada columna.

| Yo sé... | Yo conozco... |
|---|---|
|  |  |
|  |  |

**Paso 2:** Usa la información del **Paso 1** para hacerles preguntas a varios compañeros de clase. Toma notas de sus respuestas. Al terminar, prepara un resumen y preséntaselo a la clase.

MODELO    E1: *Patricia, yo sé jugar tenis muy bien. Y tú, ¿sabes jugar tenis?*
E2: *Sí, yo sé jugar tenis también.*
o *No, yo no sé jugar tenis.*

## ■ Integración

**6-41 Una entrevista de empleo** Representa la siguiente situación con un(a) compañero(a). Al terminar, intercambien papeles.

| El (La) entrevistador(a) | El (La) entrevistado(a) |
|---|---|
| Tú eres el (la) gerente de personal de Mundo Acción, una agencia que organiza excursiones turísticas para personas a quienes les gusta hacer actividades al aire libre *(outdoors)* en los Estados Unidos. Vas a entrevistar a una persona para un puesto y quieres que esta persona conozca lugares interesantes y atractivos y que sepa *(knows)* hacer las actividades que va a promocionar *(advertise)*. ¡Sé creativo(a) al hacer las preguntas! | Te interesa mucho trabajar para Mundo Acción, una agencia que organiza excursiones turísticas para personas a quienes les gusta hacer actividades al aire libre *(outdoors)* en los Estados Unidos. Crees que eres la persona ideal para este puesto porque conoces muchos lugares interesantes y atractivos y porque sabes hacer muchas actividades que generalmente se hacen al aire libre. ¡Impresiona al / a la entrevistador(a) con tu experiencia y conocimiento! |

You may use vocabulary words that were presented in this **Tema** as well as expressions such as **saber jugar (béisbol/golf/...)**, **saber dónde es posible...**, **saber qué es necesario para...**, **conocer (el lago/el bosque/el río/la playa/las montañas)...**, and **saber qué se puede hacer en (el lago/el bosque/el río/la playa/las montañas)...**

**6-42 Recomendado(a) o no recomendado(a)** Imagínate que tu profesor(a) es el (la) dueño(a) de la agencia Mundo Acción y que tienes que enviarle un correo electrónico para recomendarle o no al / a la candidato(a) que entrevistaste en la actividad 6-41. De acuerdo con las respuestas que esta persona te dio, ¿le darías *(would you give him/her)* el puesto? Para justificar tu decisión, menciona las cosas que esta persona (no) sabe y (no) conoce.

**De:** _____ (your e-mail address)
**Fecha:** _____ (today's date)
**Para:** el (la) dueño(a)@mundoacción.com
**Asunto:** Entrevista a _____ (your partner's name)

Estimado(a) _____ (your professor's name):
Le escribo este mensaje para informarle que hoy entrevisté a _____
_____ y mi opinión es que (sí/no) debemos contratarlo(la) por las siguientes razones:

Cordialmente,
_____ (your name)

# IV. Vídeo: Un baile folclórico puertorriqueño

## ▣ Preparación

### A. Bailes típicos

1. Basándose en el título y en la foto de arriba, ¿qué creen que va a pasar en el vídeo?
2. ¿Conocen alguno de estos bailes puertorriqueños: la plena, la bomba, la danza? Descríbanlos si pueden.

## ▣ ¿Entendiste bien?

**B. La lección de baile folclórico** Mira el vídeo y decide si las siguientes oraciones son ciertas (**C**) o falsas (**F**).

_C_ 1. Valeria no quería bailar.

_F_ 2. El baile que los compañeros estaban aprendiendo se llama la plena puertorriqueña.  la bomba

_C_ 3. Mientras bailaba, Alejandra se lastimó el tobillo.

_F_ 4. Hace un año, Alejandra se rompió el pie y se lo enyesaron.  la pierna

_F_ 5. Sofía quería salir por la noche con Víctor, el instructor de baile.  Alejandra

Compara tus respuestas con las de un(a) compañero(a) y juntos corrijan las oraciones falsas.

**C. ¡Bailar!** Descríbele a un(a) compañero(a) la última vez que bailaste o viste a otras personas que estaban bailando.

- ¿Dónde estabas? (en la escuela, en una boda, en una discoteca, etc.)
- ¿Con quién estabas?
- ¿Qué tipo de música tocaban?
- Cuando tocaban la música, ¿bailabas, mirabas a la gente bailar o ambas cosas?
- Mientras los otros bailaban, ¿te divertías? Y las demás personas, ¿qué hacían?

**D. Enfoque comunitario** La música y los bailes son parte de nuestra cultura y evolucionan con los años (los estilos de música, los tipos de bailes, la manera de bailar, la ropa que lleva la gente, etc.). Entrevista a una persona mayor de tu comunidad sobre cómo eran la música y los bailes cuando él/ella tenía tu edad y presenta un informe oral en clase sobre sus respuestas.

# TEMA 3

# La conservación del medio ambiente

## I. Vocabulario

**Rápidos del Río Reventazón**
- Disfrute de naturaleza, belleza y aventura
- Ideal para principiantes y aventureros
- Excursión de rápidos más popular del país

## Costa Rica
### Su Mejor Destino

**Volcán Arenal y aguas termales**
- El volcán más activo del país
- Exuberante vegetación
- Aguas termales

**Parque Nacional Tortuguero**
- Sitio de la tortuga verde y tortuga baula
- Observación de aves y especies de fauna acuática
- Hospedaje en albergue rústico

### Vocabulario práctico

**El medio ambiente**
**(The environment)**
la ecología *ecology*
el ecólogo *ecologist*
el ecosistema *ecosystem*
las especies *species*
la extinción *extinction*
la fauna *fauna, wildlife*
la flora *flora*
el guardaparques *park ranger*
la investigación *research*
el naturalista *naturalist*
los recursos naturales *natural resources*

el refugio natural/silvestre *wildlife reserve*
la reserva biológica *biological reserve*
la variedad *variety*

**Verbos**
conservar/preservar *to preserve*
extinguirse *to become extinct*
investigar *to research*
mantener (ie) *to maintain, to support*
proteger *to protect*
reciclar *to recycle*
reforestar *to reforest*

## ▓ Asimilación

**6-43 Asociaciones** ¿Qué palabras asocian con los siguientes conceptos? En dos minutos, escriban todas las palabras posibles. El grupo con las listas más largas gana.

| ecólogo | *parque nacional* | *ecoturismo* |
|---|---|---|
| investigación | | |
| científico | | |
| estudiar | | |
| observar | | |
| plantas | | |
| etc. | | |

01–64 **6-44 Excursión al Volcán Poás y a Sarchí** Escucha el siguiente itinerario e indica las actividades principales de la excursión.

  X   conocer una ciudad     ____ nadar en un río

____ bucear en el mar     X  observar plantas y animales

 X  observar el paisaje     X  visitar dos cráteres de un volcán

 X  comprar artesanías

## ▓ Aplicaciones

**6-45 Adivina** Un(a) estudiante piensa en una palabra relacionada con la conservación del medio ambiente y da su definición. El (La) compañero(a) tiene que adivinar de qué palabra se trata.

MODELO    E1: *Es una persona que investiga los ecosistemas.*
             E2: *Un ecólogo.*

**6-46 Una excursión ecológica** Completa las oraciones con la palabra o frase más lógica.

OPCIONES:  especies  ecosistema  reforestación  ecólogo
           fauna  flora  reserva biológica

1. El siguiente es el itinerario de nuestra excursión a una __reserva biológica__ .
2. Durante el recorrido, todos pueden admirar la ___flora___ y la ___fauna___ locales.
3. En el parque podemos estudiar un ___ecosistema___ fascinante.
4. Antes del almuerzo vamos a hacer una caminata por el bosque para apreciar las diversas ___especies___ de plantas que existen en la reserva.
5. Después del almuerzo vamos a escuchar la charla de un famoso ___ecólogo___ y luego vamos a disfrutar una aventura de dos horas por el río.
6. Antes de regresar vamos a plantar un árbol para colaborar con los programas de ___reforestación___ de este parque.

This activity recycles countryside vocabulary introduced in the previous **Tema.** Have students generate as many words as possible and have the winning team read its list to the class. The other students can debate whether or not the answers are legitimate.

Script 6-44: Señores turistas: La excursión sale de San José en dirección al volcán Poás a las ocho de la mañana. En la ruta, vamos primero a conocer la ciudad de Alajuela y a aprender un poco de su historia. En el camino, vamos también a observar un hermoso paisaje compuesto por plantaciones de café, fresas y plantas ornamentales. Hacia el mediodía, vamos a llegar al volcán y vamos a recorrer sus dos cráteres. Luego de visitar el volcán y de observar su flora y fauna, vamos a dirigirnos hacia Sarchí, donde vamos a poder comprar artesanías directamente de las fábricas. La duración del viaje es de ocho horas e incluye transporte, entrada, almuerzo y, desde luego, la guía turística.

This activity recycles travel vocabulary. While students are working, walk around the room and encourage them to keep their plans centered around the ecotourism theme. After they have had sufficient time to prepare, ask for volunteers (one or two pairs are enough) to read their answers to the class. The rest of the class should help supplement their itinerary (give ideas for additional destinations, activities or items required).

**6-47 ¡Vamos a Costa Rica!** Imagínense que se han ganado un viaje ecológico a Costa Rica con todos los gastos pagados. Completen el cuadro con los lugares que piensan visitar, las actividades que pueden hacer y las cosas que van a necesitar.

| Lugares que quieren ver | Actividades que quieren realizar | Cosas que van a necesitar |
|---|---|---|
| | | |

## ▪ Integración

**6-48 Vacaciones ecológicas** Representa la siguiente situación con un(a) compañero(a).

Useful expressions: **¿Me podría dar información acerca de...?** *(Could you give me information about . . .?)* **Me interesa...** *(I am interested in . . .)*

Useful expressions: **Tengo el plan perfecto para Ud.** *(I have the perfect plan for you.)* **No se preocupe.** *(Don't worry.)*

| **Turista hispano(a)** |
|---|
| Eres un(a) turista hispano(a) que quiere disfrutar de la naturaleza durante tu visita a este país. Habla con este(a) guía para averiguar tus opciones. |

| **Guía** |
|---|
| Como guía turístico(a), tienes que ayudarle a la gente a organizar sus viajes. Ayúdale a este(a) viajero(a) hispano(a) a organizar una serie de actividades ecológicas en tu región. Usa la información de la actividad anterior como guía. |

EN TU COMUNIDAD

Investigate if there are any conservation efforts being carried out in your community (recycling, ecotourism, environmental protection projects, etc.). In your report, you need to include the location and importance of the site, as well as a brief summary of the conservation efforts under deployment.

**6-49 Ruta ecológica** Imagínense que trabajan para la corporación de turismo de su estado. Preparen un itinerario en español para promover la conservación y la apreciación de la naturaleza en su región.

1. Preparen una lista de los sitios naturales en el área.
2. Piensen en las actividades ecológicas que pueden hacer allí.

# II. Funciones y estructuras: Indicating location with demonstrative adjectives and pronouns

— Liana, ¿te gusta más **esta** excursión o **ésa**?
— Me gusta más **ésta** porque uno visita parques ecológicos. **Aquella** excursión sólo incluye visitas a lugares históricos.

Demonstratives are used to indicate the location (in space or in time) of people and things in relation to the speakers. They agree in number and gender with the noun they modify or refer to.

| DEMONSTRATIVE ADJECTIVES | DEMONSTRATIVE PRONOUNS | MEANING | LOCATION |
|---|---|---|---|
| este, esta | éste, ésta | *this (one)* | **aquí** *(here)* |
| estos, estas | éstos, éstas | *these* | |
| ese, esa | ése, ésa | *that (one)* | **ahí** *(there)* |
| esos, esas | ésos, ésas | *those* | |
| aquel, aquella | aquél, aquélla | *that (over there)* | **allá/allí** *(over there)* |
| aquellos, aquellas | aquéllos, aquéllas | *those (over there)* | |

In general, the forms of **este**/**éste** are used to refer to people or things that are close to the speaker while the forms of **ese**/**ése** are used to refer to people or things that are close to the listener. The forms of **aquel**/**aquél**, on the other hand, are used by both the speaker and the listener to refer to people or things that are far from both of them.

Demonstrative pronouns, which are used to refer to nouns that have already been mentioned in the discourse, are distinguished from their adjectival counterparts by accent marks.

¿Te gustan **estas** variedades de plantas o **éstas**?

*Do you like **these** varieties of plants or **these**?*

¿Vamos a reciclar **ese** recipiente o **ése**?

*Are we going to recycle **that** container or **that one**?*

Demonstrative pronouns also have a neuter form: **esto, eso,** and **aquello.** They are used when objects have not been identified yet or to refer to ideas, concepts, and situations.

¿Qué es **esto**? ¿Es una flor silvestre?
¿La extinción de animales? ¡**Eso** es inaceptable!
**Aquello** no se podía creer.

*What is **this**? Is it a wild flower?*
*Animal extinction? **That's** unacceptable!*
***That** was hard to believe.*

### ■ Asimilación

**6-50 En la sala de clase** Imagínate que estás en la sala de clase, en el lugar donde normalmente te sientas. Luego, lee las oraciones que siguen e indica si podrías *(if you could)* decir estas cosas o no. Ten en cuenta *(keep in mind)* cuán *(how)* cerca o lejos estás de las personas y objetos que se mencionan.

_____ 1. Esta silla es muy cómoda.

_____ 2. Aquella ventana es grande.

_____ 3. Esta sala de clase tiene aire acondicionado.

_____ 4. Casi siempre trabajo con ese(a) compañero(a) de clase, no con éste(a).

_____ 5. Siempre pongo mis libros y cuadernos en esa silla.

_____ 6. El (La) mejor estudiante de la clase es aquél/aquélla.

CD1-65 **6-51 En mi antiguo** *(former)* **barrio** Escucha lo que Gabriel le dice a su amigo Rubén cuando le está mostrando su antiguo barrio. Escribe el número de la descripción debajo del dibujo correcto.

2

3

1

## ▪ Aplicaciones

**6-52 De compras** Hoy es sábado y tu compañero(a) y tú están de compras en un centro comercial. Escojan el demostrativo que usarían en las siguientes oraciones. **¡OJO!** Usen los adverbios **aquí, ahí** y **allá/allí** como claves (clues).

1. Estas faldas están a buen precio, pero (éstas / ésas / aquéllas) que están ahí son un poco caras.

2. Aquellos vestidos son de seda y (estos / esos / aquellos) pantalones de aquí son de algodón.

3. Me gusta esta camiseta, pero (ésta / ésa / aquélla) que está allá me gusta más.

4. ¿Sabes cuánto cuestan (estos / esos / aquellos) sombreros que están ahí?

5. Esa tienda de artículos para el hogar no tiene mucha variedad. Vamos para (ésta / ésa / aquélla) de allí.

6. Aquellas lámparas son bonitas, pero (ésta / ésa / aquélla) que está aquí combina (matches) con los muebles de mi sala.

7. ¿Qué opinas de (estos / esos / aquellos) sillones que están ahí?

8. Creo que voy a comprar (estas / esas / aquellas) cortinas que están allá.

**6-53 En el supermercado** Luego de hacer compras en el centro comercial, Uds. deciden ir al supermercado para comprar los ingredientes que necesitan para preparar la cena. Completen las oraciones con el adjetivo o el pronombre demostrativo correcto.

1. Estos tomates están frescos, pero ___estos___ (these) pimientos están aún más frescos.

2. Me gustan mucho las gambas, pero ___ésas___ (those) que están ahí son muy pequeñas, ¿no?

3. ¿Quieres comprar arroz de esa marca (brand) o de ___ésta___ (this one)?

4. ¡No hay frijoles negros! ¡___Eso___ (That) es increíble!

5. Creo que debemos llevar jugo de naranja. ___Aquél___ (That one) que está allá es el mejor.

6. ¿Quieres llevar de este pan o de ___ése___ (that one)?

7. ¿Qué es ___esto___ (this)? ¿No hay lechuga para la ensalada?

8. ¿Llevamos estas tortas o ___aquéllas___ (those) de allá?

**6-54 La vida en este estado** Túrnense para hacer y responder a las siguientes preguntas sobre el estado donde viven.

1. ¿Te gusta vivir en este estado?

2. ¿Qué cosas (no) hay en otros estados que (no) hay en éste?

3. ¿Qué piensan las personas de otros estados sobre éste? ¿Crees que tienen razón o no? ¿Algunas de esas cosas te molestan (bother you)?

4. ¿Tienes parientes en otros estados? ¿Visitas a esos parientes?

5. ¿Piensas vivir en otro estado cuando te gradúes? ¿Por qué te interesa hacer esto?

## ■ Integración

**6-55 Guardaparques** Tu compañero(a) y tú trabajan como guardaparques en un parque nacional y están con un grupo de visitantes. Túrnense para describir el paisaje del dibujo de abajo. **¡OJO!** Imaginen que los visitantes están al lado de Uds. ¡Sean creativos y traten de captar la atención y el interés de los visitantes con su descripción!

You may describe the following:
**árboles, bosque, caballos, centro de visitantes, flores, hombre que está escalando la montaña, montañas, pájaros, pavos, plantas exóticas, recursos naturales, refugio natural, río, turistas, zona de acampar.**

MODELO    *Estos pavos son nativos de esta región. Hay muchos en este parque.*

**6-56 Visitantes** Imagínate que estás visitando la reserva natural del dibujo de arriba. Como eres una persona muy curiosa y te interesa mucho la naturaleza, escribe una lista de preguntas que les quieres hacer a los guardaparques. Usa la lista de sugerencias de la actividad 6-55 e imagina que estás al lado de los guardaparques.

MODELO    *¿Qué comen estos pavos?*
          *¿De qué especie son aquellos pájaros?*
          *¿Y ésos?...*

## III. Funciones y estructuras: Talking about the past with verbs that change meaning in the preterite

Ayer **conocí** algunas de las bellezas naturales de Costa Rica. Siempre **quise** venir aquí porque sabía que era un país espectacular. También **pude** probar la comida costarricense. ¡Es deliciosa!

The verbs **conocer** *(to know)*, **poder** *(to be able to)*, **querer** *(to want, to love)*, and **saber** *(to know)* change meanings when they are used in the preterite tense. Here is a summary of those changes.

Notice that **poder** and **querer** have different meanings when they are used with the adverb **no**.

| VERB | MEANING IN THE PRETERITE |
|---|---|
| **conocer** | *to meet; to visit, to get to see a place (for the first time)*<br>■ Ayer **conocí** a una ecóloga panameña.<br>*Yesterday **I met** a Panamanian ecologist.*<br>■ Mi hermana **conoció** la ciudad de San José el mes pasado.<br>*My sister **visited** the city of San José for the first time last month.* |
| **poder** | *to succeed (**no poder** = to fail)*<br>■ El Dr. Loveras **pudo** descubrir la causa de la epidemia.<br>*Dr. Loveras **was able to (succeeded at)** discover the cause of the epidemic.*<br>■ Los científicos no **pudieron** prevenir la extinción de esas especies.<br>*Scientists **could not (did not succeed at, were not able to, failed at)** prevent the extinction of those species.* |
| **querer** | *to try, to make an effort, to attempt (**no querer** = to refuse)*<br>■ Los funcionarios **quisieron** preservar el medio ambiente, pero la gente **no quiso** cooperar.<br>*Public officials **tried (made an effort, attempted to)** preserve the environment, but people **refused** to cooperate.* |
| **saber** | *to find out, to hear*<br>■ **Supimos** que hay una cura naturalista para esta enfermedad.<br>***We found out (heard)** that there is a naturalistic cure for this illness.* |

## ■ Asimilación

**6-57 En los últimos meses** ¿Qué cosas han pasado en los últimos meses? Empareja cada verbo de la izquierda con una frase lógica de la derecha e indica si cada oración que formas es cierta **(C)** o falsa **(F).** Cuando termines, compara tus respuestas con las de un(a) compañero(a). ¿Qué tienen en común?

<u>d</u> 1. Pude sacar...

<u>e</u> 2. No quise trabajar...

<u>f</u> 3. Supe que (yo)...

<u>a</u> 4. Conocí a...

<u>c</u> 5. Quise levantarme...

<u>b</u> 6. No pude ir...

a. mi novio(a). ____

b. de vacaciones a ningún lugar. ____

c. temprano todos los días para hacer ejercicio, pero no pude. ____

d. A en todos los exámenes que tomé. ____

e. mientras estudio. ____

f. no me puedo graduar este año. ____

**Script 6-58:** La semana pasada, Paco y yo fuimos al Parque Nacional Tortuguero. Pudimos ver muchos pájaros exóticos y nadar en el lago, y también conocimos a varias personas muy simpáticas de los Estados Unidos. Quisimos quedarnos en el hotel del parque, pero no pudimos. Supimos que no había habitaciones disponibles porque había un grupo muy grande de turistas europeos.

**Answers 6-58:** ver muchos pájaros exóticos; nadar en el lago; varias personas muy simpáticas de los Estados Unidos; quedarse en el hotel del parque; habitaciones disponibles

CD1-66

**6-58 En el Parque Nacional Tortuguero** Sofía va a hablar de lo que Paco y ella hicieron en el Parque Nacional Tortuguero la semana pasada. Escúchala y completa el siguiente párrafo.

En el parque Nacional Tortuguero, Sofía y Paco pudieron _____ y _____. Ellos conocieron a _____. Quisieron _____, pero no pudieron. Supieron que no había _____.

## ■ Aplicaciones

**6-59 Problemitas durante las vacaciones** ¿Qué problemitas tuvieron los Vizcaíno durante sus vacaciones en el área del Río Reventazón? Para saber cómo responde esta pregunta el Sr. Vizcaíno, completen los siguientes párrafos con la forma correcta de los verbos de la lista.

**Opciones:** poder   saber   no querer   no poder   querer   conocer

   Éstas fueron unas vacaciones magníficas, pero tuvimos varios problemitas. Por ejemplo, yo __quise__ bañarme en el río, pero no pude porque el agua estaba muy turbulenta y casi me ahogo *(I almost drowned)*. Además, mis hijas se enojaron mucho cuando (ellas) __supieron__ que eran demasiado pequeñas *(too young)* para ir a la excursión de los rápidos. Lo peor de todo fue que *(The worst thing of all was that)*, mi hijo Jaime __no pudo__ hacer nada porque el primer día se cayó y se lastimó una pierna.

   A pesar de todo lo que pasó *(that happened)*, éstas fueron unas vacaciones magníficas. (Nosotros) __pudimos__ disfrutar de la naturaleza de Costa Rica. También (nosotros) __conocimos__ las bellezas naturales de este hermoso país. A mi esposa le gustó tanto que (ella) __no quiso__ regresar a casa el día que teníamos previsto *(that we had planned)* y extendimos la estadía una semana más.

**6-60 El año pasado...** Formen oraciones lógicas sobre algunas de las cosas que pasaron en la vida de estas personas el año pasado. ¡Sean originales y añadan detalles interesantes!

> MODELO   nosotros(as)   (no) poder
> *Nosotros no pudimos ir a la Florida en las vacaciones de primavera porque los profesores nos dieron mucha tarea.*

nosotros(as)
yo
nuestros hermanos          +      (no) conocer      +   ...
[un(a) estudiante de la clase]     (no) poder
[una persona famosa]               (no) querer
                                   (no) saber

**6-61 La vida ajetreada** *(busy)* **del / de la profesor(a)** Como Uds. saben, el (la) profesor(a) tiene una vida muy ajetreada. Escriban por lo menos cinco preguntas para saber cómo fue su día de ayer. Usen los verbos **conocer, (no) poder, (no) querer** y **saber.**

> MODELO   *Profesor(a), ¿Ud. no quiso corregir nada ayer?*

### ■ Integración

**6-62 Trabajo, estudio y diversión** Los estudiantes típicos tienen un dilema todos los veranos: dedicarse a trabajar, a estudiar o a divertirse. Piensen en las cosas que hicieron el verano pasado para balancear estas tres cosas y explíquenle a su compañero(a) qué pudieron y no pudieron hacer, qué quisieron y no quisieron hacer, qué cosas supieron y a qué personas y lugares conocieron. ¿Fue un verano bueno o malo?

**6-63 Un recuento de mis logros** *(achievements)* Tu profesor(a) quiere saber un poco sobre algunas de las cosas que has logrado en tu vida. Haz un recuento de tus logros y entrégale una copia a él/ella.

Answer the following questions before you begin the writing process: **¿Qué cosas pudiste hacer? ¿Y qué cosas no pudiste hacer? ¿Conociste a alguien a quien querías conocer? ¿Qué piensan tus parientes y amigos sobre estos logros?**

## IV. Lectura: La leyenda del Zurquí

**A. El formato** Observa el título y los dibujos que acompañan el cuento. De acuerdo con esto, identifica:

- los personajes principales
- los lugares donde sucede la acción

**B. Vocabulario y conceptos** Escriban delante de cada palabra la letra correspondiente a su definición.

| | | |
|---|---|---|
| _c_ 1. cacique | a. espíritu |
| _f_ 2. guerrero | b. transformarse, hacerse |
| _d_ 3. tribu | c. el líder de una tribu indígena |
| _e_ 4. perseguir | d. grupo de indígenas |
| _b_ 5. convertirse | e. buscar, acosar |
| _a_ 6. alma | f. soldado, luchador |

### READING STRATEGY

**Analyzing Format Clues** Look at how the story is illustrated and broken down into segments. Use that information to identify the characters and the location of the story.

The student should be able to recognize from observing these format clues that a young indigenous woman and a warrior are the central characters and that a mountainous and forested area is where the story takes place.

### ■ A leer

### Elías Zeledón (1953– )

Es un bibliotecólogo costarricense. Como investigador, se ha preocupado por recuperar los valores folclóricos de su país. Ha trabajado como editor de las revistas *El Rualdo*, *La Edad de Oro* y *Turí Guá* (las dos últimas dedicadas a los niños). Su libro *Leyendas costarricenses* es una compilación de cuentos e historias tradicionales escritas por diversos autores, muchas de las cuales pertenecen a la tradición oral.

### La leyenda del Zurquí

Cerca de la ciudad de San José se encuentran los valles del volcán Barva.

Hace muchísimos años vivió allí una princesa térraba llamada Turi Uha.

Turi Uha vivía tranquila en el poblado en donde gobernaba su padre, el cacique. Pero un día, un guerrero fuerte y valiente cruzó los bosques del Zurquí para llegar a la tribu térraba.

—— ✿ ——

amar, *imperfect tense*

Él guerrero buscaba a Turi Uha, la mujer a quien **amaba**, la mujer más bella de la región. La princesa también amaba al guerrero, pero no podía casarse con él, ya que las tribus de sus padres eran enemigas y no permitirían su unión.

El amor no puede crecer en el territorio de guerra, y por eso Turi Uha huyó por la montaña con el guerrero. Sólo la acompañaron algunas amigas.

Cuando el cacique padre de Turi Uha **se dio cuenta** de que su hija había escapado con el guerrero de la tribu enemiga, se enfureció y salió con sus guerreros en busca de los fugitivos. El **retumbar** de los **pasos y** el **chasquido** de las **ramas rotas** al correr se oyeron por toda la montaña. Y el enamorado guerrero cayó **muerto** por sus perseguidores.

*realized*

*echo / steps*
*snapping / broken twigs*
*dead*

— ❀ —

El alma del valiente guerrero subió a la **cima del cerro**, allí donde, según la creencia de su gente, **habitaban** los muertos, en la **morada** del dios Sibú.

*hilltop*

*vivían / casa*

La princesa y sus amigas continuaron huyendo a través de la selva. Turi Uha **quería alcanzar** la cima, para habitar allí con el alma de su amado. Pero mientras la princesa y sus amigas huían de sus perseguidores, ocurrió algo maravilloso: poco a poco sus cuerpos se volvieron **ágiles**, su piel se transformó en **sedosas alas**…y convertidas en mariposas, alzaron vuelo para alcanzar el cielo.

*wanted to reach*

*rápidos / silky wings*

Es por eso que es común ver hermosas mariposas en grandes cantidades por las mágicas **cumbres** del Zurquí.

*mountaintops*

## ▦ ¿Entendiste bien?

**C. Primera aproximación a la lectura** Sigue las instrucciones para entender mejor la lectura.

1. Lee rápidamente las primeras cuatro oraciones. Resume brevemente la idea principal.
2. Ahora, lee rápidamente el segundo segmento del texto. ¿Qué le pasó al guerrero? ¿Por qué?
3. Termina de leer el texto. ¿Qué les pasó a la princesa y a sus amigas?

**D. A leer otra vez** Lean el cuento una vez más y respondan a las siguientes preguntas:

1. **¿En qué orden?** Organicen los eventos de la historia.

   __3__ El guerrero y la princesa huyeron de sus respectivas tribus.

   __2__ Un guerrero se enamoró de la princesa.

   __4__ El cacique persiguió y mató al guerrero.

   __1__ La princesa Turi Uha vivía tranquila en su poblado.

   __5__ La princesa y sus amigas se convirtieron en mariposas.

The questions will help students complete the first reading of the text. Each question looks at one segment of the story and enables them to discover progressively the different characters and events of the plot. You may want to do this as a group activity so that the more advanced readers can help those who are less proficient.

**Answers:** 1. *Answers will vary.* 2. He was killed by the father of the princess because he did not approve of their relationship. 3. They turned into butterflies and fled to the top of the mountain.

### READING STRATEGY

***Skimming*** Find out the general theme of the story.

### READING STRATEGY

***Scanning*** Keeping in mind the characters and context, look for facts about the story line.

2. **¿Qué pasó?** Respondan a las preguntas.
   a. ¿Por qué quería matar el cacique al guerrero?
   b. ¿Por qué quería alcanzar la cima del cerro la princesa?
   c. ¿Qué fenómenos naturales representa y explica esta leyenda?

**Answers 2:** a. porque las tribus del cacique y del guerrero eran enemigas b. porque quería estar con el alma de su amado c. las mariposas que vuelan por el cerro Zurquí

**E. Enfoque lingüístico** Busquen ejemplos de usos del imperfecto en la lectura.

| Para hablar de acciones habituales en el pasado | vivía, buscaba, habitaban, amaba |
|---|---|
| Para hacer descripciones físicas, emocionales o psicológicas | tenía, eran |

**F. Actividad de extensión** ¿Conocen alguna leyenda de su cultura o de otra cultura? ¿Qué fenómeno de la naturaleza explica o qué lección enseña? Comenten estas leyendas.

## Los servicios públicos — *Utilities*
| | |
|---|---|
| el agua | *water* |
| el alcantarillado | *sewage system* |
| el cable | *cable* |
| la conexión a Internet | *Internet connection* |
| el gas | *natural gas* |
| la luz/la electricidad | *electricity* |
| el teléfono | *telephone* |

## Los servicios sociales
| | |
|---|---|
| la educación | *education* |
| la salud | *health* |
| el transporte | *transportation* |

## Los problemas urbanos
| | |
|---|---|
| la basura | *garbage* |
| la congestión | *traffic congestion* |
| la contaminación | *pollution* |
| el costo de la vida | *cost of living* |
| la delincuencia (juvenil) | *(youth) crime* |
| el ruido | *noise* |

## Los funcionarios públicos — *Public officials*
| | |
|---|---|
| el alcalde | *mayor* |
| los basureros | *garbage haulers* |
| los bomberos | *firefighters* |
| los paramédicos | *paramedics* |
| la policía | *police* |
| la policía vial/de tránsito | *traffic police* |

## La vida en el campo — *Life in the countryside*
| | |
|---|---|
| el árbol | *tree* |
| la arena | *sand* |
| la isla | *island* |
| el lago | *lake* |
| el mar | *sea* |
| la montaña | *mountain* |
| la playa | *beach* |
| el río | *river* |
| la selva | *jungle* |
| el valle | *valley* |
| el volcán | *volcano* |

## La finca y los animales domésticos — *The farm and farm animals*
| | |
|---|---|
| el agricultor | *farmer* |
| el caballo | *horse* |
| el cerdo/puerco | *pig* |
| la cosecha | *harvest* |
| el cultivo | *crop* |
| la gallina | *hen* |
| el ganado | *livestock* |
| el gato | *cat* |
| el pato | *duck* |
| el pavo | *turkey* |
| el perro | *dog* |
| el toro | *bull* |
| la vaca | *cow* |

## La producción agrícola
| | |
|---|---|
| el campo | *countryside (field)* |
| el suelo | *soil* |
| los trabajadores/campesinos | *workers* |

## Trabajo
| | |
|---|---|
| alimentar | *to feed* |
| cosechar | *to harvest* |
| criar | *to raise* |
| cultivar | *to cultivate* |
| recoger | *to pick* |
| sembrar (ie) | *to sow* |

## Diversión
| | |
|---|---|
| acampar | *to camp* |
| bucear | *to dive* |
| escalar | *to climb* |
| esquiar | *to ski* |
| esquiar en el agua | *to waterski* |
| hacer surf | *to surf* |
| montar a caballo | *to horseback ride* |
| nadar | *to swim* |

## El medio ambiente — *The environment*
| | |
|---|---|
| la ecología | *ecology* |
| el ecólogo | *ecologist* |
| el ecosistema | *ecosystem* |
| las especies | *species* |
| la extinción | *extinction* |
| la fauna | *fauna, wildlife* |
| la flora | *flora* |
| el guardaparques | *park ranger* |
| la investigación | *research* |
| el naturalista | *naturalist* |
| los recursos naturales | *natural resources* |
| el refugio natural/silvestre | *wildlife reserve* |
| la reserva biológica | *biological reserve* |
| la variedad | *variety* |

## Acciones relacionadas con el medio ambiente
| | |
|---|---|
| conservar/preservar | *to preserve* |
| extinguirse | *to become extinct* |
| investigar | *to research* |
| mantener (ie) | *to maintain, to support* |
| proteger | *to protect* |
| reciclar | *to recycle* |
| reforestar | *to reforest* |

## Funciones y estructuras
Palabras negativas e indefinidas, p. 223
Adjetivos y pronombres demostrativos, p. 247

# Puesta en acción

| | |
|---|---|
| **SITUACIÓN:** | Tu universidad está interesada en tener una versión en español de su periódico para publicarla electrónicamente a través del Internet y de esta manera atraer a más estudiantes de habla hispana. |
| **MISIÓN:** | Publicar una edición completa del periódico universitario, incluyendo las secciones de eventos sociales, de turismo, de medio ambiente y de la vida diaria. |
| **DESTREZAS:** | Coordinar la publicación de un periódico, escoger temas de interés para los lectores, resumir y comunicar efectivamente la información relacionada con esos temas y publicar el periódico. |

**A. Noticias sobre el medio ambiente** Antes de preparar tu artículo, sería bueno *(it would be good)* hacer un repaso del vocabulario y las estructuras gramaticales que vas a usar. Completa el siguiente párrafo con las palabras de la lista.

**OPCIONES:**   fauna   fincas   reservas naturales
contaminación   medio ambiente

El gobierno nacional acaba de anunciar un plan para la conservación del ___medio ambiente___ en la zona oriental del país. Debido al *(Due to)* aumento de las ___fincas___ ganaderas en la zona, el nivel de deforestación y de ___contaminación___ de las aguas de los ríos locales, se ha puesto en peligro *(danger)* el futuro del frágil ecosistema de la región. Para evitar la desaparición de las especies nativas y para rescatar *(rescue)* el equilibrio ecológico de la región, se van a crear varias ___reservas naturales___. De esta manera, la ___fauna___ y la flora locales van a tener la oportunidad de regenerarse y prosperar como siempre lo han hecho en esta hermosa zona del país.

**B. Noticias económicas** Completa el siguiente artículo con la forma correcta del pretérito de los verbos entre paréntesis.

En una reunión auspiciada por la Cámara de Comercio local, el alcalde de la ciudad ___habló___ (hablar) de su nuevo programa económico. El líder ___dijo___ (decir) que el problema principal de la ciudad era el desempleo y ___prometió___ (prometer) crear nuevos puestos en las áreas de manufactura y construcción. Por otro lado, su asistente ___se concentró___ (concentrase) en probar que se ha superado la crisis de la inflación e ___indicó___ (indicar) que la presente administración va a reducir los impuestos. Tanto *(Both)* el alcalde como su asistente ___mencionaron___ (mencionar) que, de acuerdo con sus proyecciones, el déficit bajará un 10% en el próximo año fiscal y ___se refirieron___ (referirse) a la situación precaria que se vive en otras ciudades del país. Finalmente, cuando los periodistas ___preguntaron___ (preguntar) sobre el problema de salud pública, el alcalde ___prefirió___ (preferir) no hacer ningún comentario.

**C. Noticias internacionales** Organicen las siguientes oraciones para formar un artículo con un orden lógico.

____ Varios científicos nicaragüenses lo esperaban.

____ Sus compañeros del Frente de Oposición a la minería se quedaron en Costa Rica. Están trabajando en otros proyectos.

____ Habló con los periodistas en el Aeropuerto Internacional de Managua.

____ Hoy se preparó todo el día para su participación en el Congreso sobre el medio ambiente.

____ Sale en dos días para Honduras.

_1_ Llegó ayer a Nicaragua Marco Tulio Araya Barboza, periodista y ambientalista costarricense.

____ Manifestó que se sentía muy contento de estar en la capital nicaragüense.

____ Estaba un poco cansado por el viaje.

____ Piensa pasar sólo unos días allí.

____ Su discurso fue muy positivo. Sirvió de inspiración para los que asistieron.

To write a coherent article, you may use the following connectors: **así que** *(therefore)*, **aunque** *(even though)*, **como** *(since)*, **después** *(afterward)*, **luego** *(then, later)*, **más tarde** *(later)*, **porque** *(because)*, **y** *(and)*, **sin embargo** *(however)*.

**Answers C:** Answers will vary.

**D. Eventos sociales** Usen la información que se provee para escribir las notas sobre eventos sociales en su comunidad. Añadan *(Add)* los detalles necesarios (tipo de evento, lugar, personas que celebraron el acontecimiento, etc.).

**Answers D:** Answers will vary.

**15 de febrero**

Lorena Suárez Nogueras y David Escobar Negrón

**20 de diciembre**

Nidia María Agosto Toledo

**6 de enero**

Maximino Calderón Acevedo

**Paso 1:** Busquen información sobre la isla hondureña de Roatán y completen el cuadro que sigue. Luego, usen la información para escribir un artículo de interés turístico sobre este lugar.

| | |
|---|---|
| Localización | |
| Tamaño | |
| Población | |
| Atractivos | |
| Actividades | |
| Otra información importante | |

**Paso 2:** Tu compañero(a) y tú entrevistaron por separado a una persona que fue de vacaciones a la isla de Roatán recientemente. Imaginen que él/ella y tú tienen una conversación telefónica para obtener todos los datos sobre las vacaciones de esta persona. Túrnense para hacerse preguntas y para responderlas. Cuando terminen, usen la información para ampliar el artículo que escribieron en el **Paso 1.**

## Estudiante 1

*Fecha de llegada:* 5 de junio
*Fecha de salida:* _11 de junio_
*Aerolínea:* KAGY
*Hotel:* Mango Creek Lodge
*Comidas favoritas:* _camarones, mariscos, ensaladas_
*Bebidas favoritas:* _jugos de frutas_
*Artesanías favoritas:* cerámicas, joyería de plata, pinturas
*Actividades favoritas:* _nadar, tomar el sol y hablar con la gente de la isla_
*Información adicional:* la gente de Roatán es muy simpática y hospitalaria,
_es posible ir a Roatán en barco crucero_

**F. Proyecto final** Traigan a clase un periódico reciente y sigan los siguientes pasos.

**Paso 1: Decisión y discusión** Escojan la sección sobre la cual quieren escribir (política, economía, vida social, salud pública, turismo, etc.) y reúnanse *(get together)* con los demás estudiantes que escogieron la misma sección. (Es preferible trabajar en grupos pequeños.) Comenten los posibles temas que van a incluir en su sección. (Decidan qué noticias van a cubrir.)

**Paso 2: Investigación** Consulten el periódico local y busquen noticias relacionadas con la sección que escogieron en el **Paso 1.** (También pueden consultar otras fuentes de información.)

**Paso 3: Vocabulario y gramática** Hagan una lista de las palabras del vocabulario que van a necesitar. Luego, hagan una lista de los eventos principales usando el pretérito. Finalmente, hagan una lista de frases descriptivas y de trasfondo *(background information)* sobre estos eventos usando el imperfecto.

**CRITICAL THINKING SKILLS**

***Researching*** Find information on the topics you have selected. Use all the sources at your disposal (local newspapers, the Internet, TV, personal interviews, etc.).

## Servicio comunitario

Contact someone from the university or from the local government and offer to provide one of the following services:

- Educate others about the importance of recycling and taking care of the environment.
- Organize groups to help solve problems that affect your community.
- Inform Spanish-speaking students (or members of the community) about available health services.

**Para hacer en casa**

**Paso 4: Primer borrador** *(draft)* Preparen una versión inicial de su informe. Incluyan fotos o dibujos para que el artículo tenga más interés visual.

- Seleccionen una noticia que tenga mucha cobertura *(coverage)*.
- Identifiquen a las personas y entidades involucradas *(involved)*.
- Capten la idea principal *(gist)* de la noticia y preparen un resumen.
- Parafraseen la noticia usando el vocabulario y las estructuras que saben. Presenten los hechos *(facts)* lo más claramente posible.
- Incluyan fotos o dibujos apropiados.

**Para hacer en clase**

**Paso 5: Correcciones** Intercambien este primer borrador con el de otro grupo y corrijan el borrador que ellos prepararon. Usen la siguiente guía.

- **Tema.** ¿Les parece que vale la pena incluir este tema en el periódico? Si la respuesta es negativa, expliquen brevemente por qué.
- **Contenido.** ¿Está toda la información necesaria? Si no es así, ¿qué otros aspectos importantes de la noticia se deben incluir?
- **Organización.** ¿Está claro de qué se trata el artículo? ¿Cuántos párrafos hay? ¿Cuál es la idea principal de cada párrafo? ¿Está clara la presentación?
- **Gramática.** ¿Se usó bien el pretérito (para hablar de los eventos importantes) y el imperfecto (para las descripciones y para la información de trasfondo)?
- **Formato y presentación.** ¿Hay elementos visuales y de diseño (fotos, diagramas, dibujos, etc.) interesantes y atractivos?

**Para hacer en casa**

**Paso 6: Versión final y publicación** Hagan las correcciones y cambios pertinentes. ¿Está listo el artículo para publicar en el Internet? Denle una copia al / a la profesor(a).

# Unidad 4

## Cambios y transiciones

### Cuba, la República Dominicana, Venezuela y Colombia

In this unit you will discuss issues pertaining to moving and relocating, such as finding a home, conducting financial and real estate transactions, and finding a new job. Also, you will discuss job-related topics such as experience, qualifications, and aspirations. The readings will give you insights into the experience of Cuban immigrants in the United States, while the videos will introduce you to the life of Cuban and Venezuelan professionals. At the end of the unit you will make all the necessary arrangements for an international job transfer.

# Capítulo 7

# Cambios

**In this chapter you will learn . . .**

- how to talk about moving and relocating
- how to talk about financial and real estate transactions
- how to talk about past events
- how to talk about the immediate past
- how to express likes and dislikes
- how to refer to abstract notions
- about Cuban immigration to the U.S.

## Para comenzar

Compara las fotos de La Habana, Cuba, con las fotos de La Pequeña Habana de Miami.

- ¿Qué aspectos comunes existen entre las dos ciudades?
- ¿Encuentras algunas diferencias?

| | TEMA 1<br>Mi tierra querida | TEMA 2<br>Es hora de partir | TEMA 3<br>A establecerse en una nueva casa |
|---|---|---|---|
| Vocabulario | Nostalgia | Preparativos para una mudanza | Los bienes raíces |
| Funciones y estructuras | Discussing memories with verbs like **gustar**<br>Expressing generalizations with the neuter article **lo** | Expressing purpose or reason with **por** and **para**<br>Referring to the beneficiary of an action using indirect object pronouns | Talking about the past with the preterite and the imperfect tenses<br>Talking about the immediate past with **acabar de** |
| Lecturas y vídeo | Perspectivas: Dirección: El sur de la Florida | Vídeo: Un día triste para Valeria | Lectura: Soñar en cubano |

La ciudad de La Habana, Cuba

La Pequeña Habana en Miami

# Enfoque

Transparency A-11: Country Profile: Cuba, La República Dominicana

**A. ¿Qué sabes ya de Cuba?** Antes de ver el vídeo, empareja las siguientes frases para formar oraciones verdaderas sobre Cuba. Luego, escribe en el espacio en blanco la letra de la categoría correspondiente.

**OPCIONES:**  A = la agricultura    C = la capital    P = la política

___P___ 1. Como la República de Cuba es un estado socialista,...

___A___ 2. Por su clima tropical, Cuba es un país rico de una exuberante vegetación...

___C___ 3. Con más de 2.000.000 de personas,...

___P___ 4. El Partido Comunista de Cuba (el PCC)...

...todo el poder pertenece al pueblo trabajador.

...es la fuerza superior que gobierna la sociedad.

...es la ciudad más populosa del país y es el centro del gobierno.

...donde abundan el tabaco y el azúcar, y las frutas tropicales como la piña, el mango y el coco.

Answers A: 1. ...todo el poder... 2. ...donde abundan...
3. ...es la ciudad más... 4. ...es la fuerza...

Compara tus respuestas con las de un(a) compañero(a).

**B. Un recorrido** El vídeo te lleva a recorrer varias áreas y atracciones turísticas de La Habana incluyendo los pequeños comercios (C), el Vedado (V), el Malecón (M), La Rampa (R) y La Plaza de la Revolución (P). Mientras ves el vídeo, indica dónde se encuentran las cosas que se mencionan a continuación. Escribe la letra correspondiente en el espacio en blanco.

___C___ 1. cintas de música afrocaribeña

___P___ 2. la mayoría de las organizaciones políticas y sociales

___V___ 3. el barrio más popular de La Habana

___M___ 4. un popular mercado de artesanías

Compara tus respuestas con las de un(a) compañero(a).

**C. Nuestro recorrido por La Habana** Según el vídeo: «Recorrer La Habana es volver a tiempos antiguos y a la vez volver a los años cincuenta y sesenta.» Si tuvieran sólo un día para recorrer La Habana y ver esta mezcla de lo antiguo y lo moderno, ¿adónde irían *(would you go)* y qué verían *(would you see)*? Planeen juntos su recorrido y contesten las siguientes preguntas. ¡Recuerden que no es posible hacerlo y verlo todo en un día!

■ ¿Qué sitios mencionados en el vídeo van a visitar, cuándo (por la mañana, tarde o noche) y por qué?

■ Si deciden ir de compras a los pequeños comercios, ¿qué recuerdos les gustaría comprar, para quién(es) y por qué?

For more info, you may want to check the **Temas** site:
http://temas.heinle.com

# Mi tierra querida

## I. Vocabulario: Nostalgia

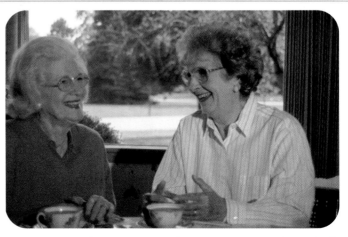

CD2–2

MARTA: Amalia, supe que tu hermana te visitó el pasado fin de semana. ¿Lo pasaron bien?

AMALIA: Sí. Las dos somos muy unidas *(close)* y nos gusta reunirnos para hablar de los viejos tiempos.

MARTA: ¿Extrañan mucho Cuba?

AMALIA: Claro. Ya hace bastante tiempo que salimos de nuestra isla, pero todavía la recordamos con mucha nostalgia.

MARTA: Pero, pueden ir a Miami. Allí encuentran de todo lo cubano... ¡hasta una pequeña Habana!

AMALIA: Ay, chica, pero no es lo mismo...

MARTA: ¿Y qué es lo que más extrañas de tu tierra?

AMALIA: Pues todo, su clima tropical, su mar, sus montañas, la alegría de la gente, la comida...

MARTA: Me gustaría regresar a Cuba. ¿Y a ti?

AMALIA: Sí. La verdad es que yo no pierdo la esperanza de volver algún día.

### Vocabulario práctico

**Los recuerdos *(Memories)***
la tierra/patria *homeland*

**Verbos**
añorar *to long for*
extrañar/echar de menos *to miss*
irse *to leave*
mudarse *to move*
olvidar *to forget*
olvidarse de *to forget about*
regresar *to return*

## ■ Asimilación

**7-1 ¿Entendiste bien?** Indica si las siguientes oraciones son ciertas (**C**) o falsas (**F**) según la conversación anterior. Al terminar, compara tus respuestas con las de un(a) compañero(a).

__C__ 1. Amalia y Marta son cubanas.

__F__ 2. La hermana de Amalia vive en Miami.

__C__ 3. Amalia recuerda y extraña Cuba.

__C__ 4. Amalia quiere regresar algún día a Cuba.

**7-2 Mi primer trabajo** Escoge la opción más apropiada según la narración de un profesor acerca de su primer trabajo.

1. Su primer trabajo fue en...
   a. una escuela primaria.     c. una universidad.
   (b.) una escuela secundaria.     d. otro: _____

2. El profesor recuerda especialmente...
   a. el nombre del libro que usó.     (c.) el nombre de su supervisor.
   b. el nombre de todos sus estudiantes.     d. otra cosa: _____

3. El profesor...
   a. nunca regresó a esa escuela.     c. aún trabaja en esa escuela.
   (b.) recuerda y visita con regularidad esa escuela.

**Script 7-2:** Mi primer trabajo fue en una escuela secundaria. Enseñaba español en los grados noveno y décimo. Recuerdo especialmente a mi supervisor, el señor Martínez. Él era un profesor de mucha experiencia que me ayudó mucho durante esos primeros años. De vez en cuando voy a visitarlo y a ver a mis otros colegas que todavía trabajan allí.

## ■ Aplicaciones

**7-3 Recuerdos** ¿Qué extrañas de la escuela secundaria? Después de indicar tus respuestas, compáralas con las de otros estudiantes. Presenten un informe acerca de lo que tienen en común.

Students should work individually first and then in groups of three or four in order to compare answers and create a brief summary. Insist on the use of Spanish throughout the activity.

____ los profesores     ____ las actividades extra-curriculares
____ los amigos     ____ tu novio(a)
____ las clases     ____ otro: _____
____ la comida de la cafetería

**Informe:** *En nuestro grupo, todos extrañamos..., algunos extrañan... y otros extrañan... Nadie extraña...*

### ESTRATEGIA DE COMPRENSIÓN

*Anticipating* Read the questions before you listen to the passage.

**7-4 Un cubano en Nueva York** Escucha el diálogo y completa las oraciones con las palabras más apropiadas.

**Opciones:** salgo   echo de menos   tierra   se mudó

ANA: ¿A quién le escribes?

BETO: A **Manuel.** ___Se mudó___ a **Nueva York** hace **dos meses** y lo ___echo de menos___ .

ANA: ¿Cuándo va a regresar a su ___tierra___?

BETO: No sé. Creo que se va a quedar a vivir allá.

ANA: Bueno, entonces vas a tener que ir a visitar**lo**...

BETO: Sí. ___Salgo___ para **Nueva York a fin de mes.**

**Script 7-4:**
Ana: ¿A quién le escribes?
Beto: A Manuel. Se mudó a Nueva York hace dos meses y lo echo de menos.
Ana: ¿Cuándo va a regresar a su tierra?
Beto: No sé. Creo que se va a quedar a vivir allá.
Ana: Bueno, entonces vas a tener que ir a visitarlo...
Beto: Sí. Salgo para Nueva York a fin de mes.

**7-5 Su primer amor** Hazle las siguientes preguntas a un(a) compañero(a) y prepara un breve resumen de sus respuestas.

1. ¿Cuántos años tenías cuando tuviste tu primer(a) novio(a)?
2. ¿Qué recuerdas de esa persona? Menciona por lo menos tres características.
3. ¿Lo/La extrañas?
4. ¿Son amigos todavía?

## ■ Integración

**7-6 Entrevista** Hazle las siguientes preguntas a un(a) compañero(a) y prepara un breve resumen de sus respuestas.

1. ¿Se ha mudado alguno de tus familiares de una región de los Estados Unidos a otra (o quizás de un país a otro)?
2. ¿De dónde se mudó? ¿Adónde fue?
3. ¿Cuándo se mudó a esa región o a ese país?
4. ¿Le gusta?
5. ¿Qué extraña de su antigua región o de su país?
6. ¿Crees que va a regresar algún día?

**7-7 La vida de Ana** Ana es una mujer cubana que vive ahora en Tampa. Haz las actividades con un(a) compañero(a) y, al terminar, usen sus respuestas para escribir una composición sobre la vida de Ana.

**Paso 1:** Escriban oraciones con las palabras indicadas. No se olviden de usar la forma correcta de los verbos y de añadir las palabras necesarias.

1. Ana / mudarse / 1999
2. Ana / encontrar / trabajo / Tampa
3. Ana / casarse / 2003
4. esposo / ser / español
5. Ana / echar de menos / familia
6. Ana y su esposo / extrañar / tierra

**Paso 2:** Respondan a las siguientes preguntas. ¡Usen la imaginación!

1. ¿Cómo era la vida de Ana en Cuba?
2. ¿Cómo era su familia?
3. ¿Qué extraña ella de su vida en Cuba?

**Paso 3:** Combinen sus respuestas para formar una composición coherente.

## II. Funciones y estructuras: Discussing memories with verbs like *gustar*

En una cafetería cubana en La Pequeña Habana...

MAURICIO: **¡Me encanta** esta cafetería! Preparan unos sándwiches cubanos que **me fascinan.**

DÉBORA: ¿Y qué más **te gusta**?

MAURICIO: ¡La carne frita! A mis padres **les parece** que es el mejor plato de este lugar.

DÉBORA: Pues la voy a probar.

As you may have noticed, the verbs in bold in the previous dialogue are accompanied by pronouns. These verbs work like the verb **gustar,** which you learned in **Capítulo 2, Tema 2,** in that they are used in the following structure.

| INDIRECT OBJECT PRONOUN | VERB (IN THE THIRD PERSON) | SUBJECT |
|---|---|---|
| me *(to me)* <br> te *(to you)* <br> le *(to him/her/you)* <br> nos *(to us)* <br> os *(to you)* <br> les *(to them/you)* | gusta/encanta/... + <br><br> gustan/encantan/... + | esta tierra <br> (noun in singular) <br> recordar (infinitive) <br><br> los cubanos <br> (noun in plural) |

Notice that, according to this structure, the subject in the Spanish sentence is the direct object in its English equivalent. On the contrary, the person(s) to whom the indirect object pronoun refers in the Spanish sentence is the subject in its English equivalent.

The third person singular form of these verbs is used when the subject is a noun in the singular form or an infinitive. The third person plural form, on the other hand, is used when the subject is a noun in the plural form.

| | |
|---|---|
| Nos **importa la familia.** | *Family is **important** to us.* |
| ¿Te **hace falta ir** a tu patria? | *Do you **need to go** to your homeland?* |
| Le **molestan los recuerdos** desagradables. | *Unpleasant **memories bother** him/her/you.* |

The indirect object may be further specified by adding a phrase introduced by the preposition **a.** Although this would be redundant in English, it adds clarity in Spanish, especially when the speaker uses the pronouns **le** and **les.**

| | |
|---|---|
| **A María** le preocupan las cuentas. | *Bills worry her (María) = She (María) is worried about bills.* |
| **A Paco y a Sila** les falta dinero. | *Paco and Sila lack (need) money.* |

Here is a list of verbs that work just like **gustar.**

convenir (ie, i) *to suit, to be suitable*

disgustar *to displease*

doler (ue) *to hurt, to ache*

encantar *to love, to like very much*

faltar *to lack, to need, to be missing*

fascinar *to love, to be fascinated*

hacer falta *to lack, to need, to be missing*

importar *to matter, to be important*

interesar *to interest, to be interested*

molestar *to bother*

parecer *to seem (like), to appear*

preocupar *to worry, to be worried about*

quedar *to remain, to be left*

tocar *to be one's turn, to be obligated*

The verb **tocar** does not work like **gustar** when it means *to touch* or *to play (an instrument).*

### ■ Asimilación

 **7-8 De vacaciones** Completa las actividades relacionadas con las siguientes ofertas vacacionales.

**Paso 1:** Busca los verbos como **gustar** en los siguientes anuncios.

**¿Le encantan las aventuras bajo el sol?**

**¡Venga a Varadero!**

Sol Club Las Sirenas
**Avenida de las Américas y Calle K**
**Reparto La Torre,**
**Varadero, Matanzas, Cuba**
**Tel. (53-5) 667080**
**Fax (53-3) 667085**

*¿Le preocupa el dinero? Tranquilo, porque todo está incluido.*

*Tenemos programas para toda la familia y a los mejores precios del Caribe.*

**SUPERCLUBS – CUBA**
¡Un resort con sabor latino para cada estilo de vida!
Club Varadero – Sierra Mar – Los Galeones

Si le hace falta un descanso...

Disfrute de unas vacaciones tranquilas en nuestros hoteles de cinco estrellas frente a las playas más bellas del mundo.

***PLAYA ESMERALDA RESORT***
Playa Esmeralda
Carretera de Guardalavaca,
Apartado Postal 007
Holguín, Cuba
Tel. (53-24) 30300
Fax (53-24) 30305

**Paso 2:** Completa las siguientes oraciones. Cuando termines, compara tus respuestas con las de un(a) compañero(a). ¿Están de acuerdo?

*Me encanta la oferta... porque...*
*No me gusta para nada la oferta... porque...*

**7-9 Una nueva vida** Escucha lo que dice Armando sobre su nueva vida en los Estados Unidos y escoge la palabra o frase que mejor complete cada una de las siguientes oraciones.

1. A Armando le encanta la vida en...
   - ⓐ los Estados Unidos.
   - b. Cuba.

2. Le fascinan...
   - ⓐ las oportunidades de trabajo.
   - b. las diferentes personas.

3. No le gusta...
   - a. ir de vacaciones.
   - ⓑ el ritmo de vida acelerado.

4. A él le molesta...
   - ⓐ el frío.
   - b. el verano.

5. A Armando le parece que es cuestión de...
   - ⓐ acostumbrarse.
   - b. resignarse.

Script 7-9: Me llamo Armando. Soy cubano y llegué a los Estados Unidos hace poco más de un año. Me encanta la vida en este país. Me fascinan las oportunidades de trabajo que hay y me gusta mucho poder viajar a estados diferentes cuando tengo vacaciones. Pero no me gusta nada el ritmo de vida tan acelerado. Aquí el tiempo es un problema. Siempre me falta tiempo para hacer ciertas cosas por el problema del tráfico. También me molesta el frío del invierno. En ese sentido, me hace falta mi país. Me parece que es cuestión de acostumbrarme.

■ **Aplicaciones**

**7-10 ¿Qué piensan?** Digan qué piensan sobre los siguientes temas. Usen verbos como **gustar** y presten atención al uso de la forma singular y la forma plural de los verbos.

1. las ciencias naturales
2. la drogadicción
3. los chismosos (gossipers)
4. manejar con precaución
5. el (la) profesor(a) de español
6. tomar clases por la noche
7. tiempo para dormir
8. los meses de invierno

**7-11 Situaciones** Completen las siguientes situaciones con la forma correcta del presente de los verbos de cada lista. **¡OJO!** Hay un verbo adicional en cada grupo.

*parecer   fascinar   convenir   quedar*

1. A mi consejero __le parece__ que no voy a poder graduarme este año. Yo creo que sí porque (a mí) sólo __me quedan__ cuatro cursos y los voy a tomar el próximo semestre. (A mí) __me conviene__ mucho graduarme pronto porque necesito empezar a ganar dinero.

*hacer falta   importar   doler   gustar*

2. Jaime está en el hospital porque __le duele__ mucho el estómago. Creo que comió muchas cosas fritas en la fiesta de Nelia. Le dije que tuviera cuidado, pero ya sabes que a él no __le importa__ su salud. ¡Y ahora está en el hospital, un lugar que no __le gusta__ nada!

*molestar   preocupar   tocar   encantar*

3. Señora, queremos decirle que a nosotras __nos molestan__ los ruidos en su apartamento. Somos estudiantes universitarias y __nos preocupa__ no poder estudiar en silencio en nuestro propio apartamento. A Ud. __le toca__ hacer algo al respecto (about it) o vamos a llamar al administrador del edificio.

**7-12 La vida en sociedad**

Puedes repasar el vocabulario sobre este tema en **Capítulo 6, Tema 1.**

**Paso 1:** Piensa en los problemas de la vida urbana y completa la siguiente tabla.

| Me importa(n) mucho... | Me preocupa(n)... | Creo que me toca... |
|---|---|---|
| | | |
| Me conviene(n)... | Me molesta(n)... | Me hace(n) falta... |
| | | |

**Paso 2:** Comparte la información del **Paso 1** con dos compañeros y averigua qué piensan. Al terminar, preparen un informe breve.

MODELO     *A nosotros nos importa(n)... y nos preocupa(n)... Creemos que nos toca... y que nos conviene...*

### EN TU COMUNIDAD

Interview someone who recently moved to your town or city (preferably, but not necessarily from a Spanish-speaking country) and find out what they think about their new living conditions and their new neighborhood. You may discuss your findings in small groups, prepare a brief report, and share it with the rest of the class.

## ■ Integración

**7-13 Los inmigrantes** ¿Alguna vez Uds. se han puesto en la situación *(have put yourself in the situation)* de un(a) inmigrante en los Estados Unidos? Piensen en esto y traten de explicar su situación.

**7-14 ¡Así soy!** Aunque ya tu profesor(a) te conoce bastante bien, él/ella quiere saber un poco más sobre las cosas y actividades que te gustan, te fascinan, te interesan, te molestan, te disgustan, te hacen falta, etc. Escribe una breve composición sobre estos temas y entrégasela cuando termines.

### SUGERENCIAS

Usen las siguientes preguntas como guía:
1. ¿Qué cosa(s) les preocupa(n)?
2. ¿Qué cosa(s) de primera necesidad les hace(n) falta?
3. ¿Qué (no) les importa?
4. ¿Qué cosas les toca hacer para mejorar su calidad de vida?
5. ¿Qué cosa(s) les encanta(n)/ molesta(n)/disgusta(n) a Uds. de su experiencia como inmigrantes en los Estados Unidos?

# III. Funciones y estructuras: Expressing generalizations with the neuter article *lo*

**Lo hermoso** de Cuba es el paisaje,...

¡pero **lo que más me gusta** es su gente!

In the previous sentences, the neuter article **lo** was used to refer to specific characteristics of things and to express an opinion. This article can be used:

The English translation of phrases with **lo** and an adjective include words such as *thing, part, aspect,* and *nature.*

- followed by an adjective in the masculine singular form.

| | |
|---|---|
| Para mí, **lo difícil** fue dejar a mi familia. | *For me, **the difficult thing (part)** was to leave my family behind.* |
| Me encanta **lo tranquilo** de esta ciudad. | *I love the **tranquil nature** of this city.* |

- followed by a clause introduced by **que.**

| | |
|---|---|
| Esto es **lo que** menos me interesa del curso. | *This is **what** interests me the least about the course.* |
| **Lo que** queremos es regresar a nuestra patria. | ***What** we want is to go back to our homeland.* |

## ■ Asimilación

**7-15 Lo mejor y lo peor de ti** Escoge las frases de la lista para indicar qué es lo mejor y lo peor de ti. Luego, compara tus respuestas con las de un(a) compañero(a). ¿Son parecidos?

| Lo mejor de mí es/son... | Lo peor de mí es/son... |
| --- | --- |
| ____ mi personalidad | ____ mi temperamento |
| ____ mi simpatía | ____ mi hábito de fumar |
| ____ mis hábitos de estudio | ____ mis cualidades físicas |
| ____ mi compasión | ____ mis hábitos de estudio |
| ____ mi sentido del humor | ____ mi personalidad |
| ____ mis sentimientos | ____ mis valores |
| ____ mis cualidades físicas | ____ mi falta de metas |
| ____ mi ética | ____ mi forma de gastar dinero |
| ____ mis valores religiosos | ____ mi falta de carácter |
| ____ otro aspecto | ____ otro aspecto |

**Script 7-16:** Para mí, lo importante en la vida es la familia y tener buenos amigos. Creo que el dinero, la apariencia física y las cosas materiales no son importantes porque pasan y se van. En cambio, el amor, la amistad *(friendship)*, la salud, vivir en un lugar que me gusta y hacer lo que me gusta sí son importantes porque me hacen sentir feliz y me permiten disfrutar de la vida. Para otras personas, lo importante viene de afuera; para mí, lo importante de la vida viene de adentro.

**Answers 7-16:** la familia, tener buenos amigos, la salud, vivir en un lugar que te gusta, hacer lo que le gusta, las cosas que vienen de adentro

CD2-6 **7-16 Lo importante en la vida** Escucha lo que dice Matilde sobre lo que es importante en la vida y escribe por lo menos cuatro de las cosas que ella menciona.

1. ...  3. ...
2. ...  4. ...

## ■ Aplicaciones

**7-17 Esta universidad** Describan algunos aspectos de esta universidad. Pueden escribir sobre **lo más interesante, lo más aburrido, lo mejor, lo peor,** etc.

MODELO *Lo más difícil de esta universidad es conseguir todas las clases que uno quiere. Por otro lado, lo más interesante es...*

**7-18 La vida pasada de tu profesor(a)** Preparen una lista de por lo menos ocho preguntas para saber un poco sobre el pasado del / de la profesor(a). ¡Usen adjetivos que sirvan para formar preguntas interesantes (**raro, desagradable, vergonzoso, tonto,** etc.)!

MODELO *¿Qué fue lo más absurdo que le pasó en la escuela secundaria? ¿Qué fue lo más inesperado que le pasó en la universidad?*

## 7-19 Los estudiantes universitarios

**Paso 1:** Piensen en el (la) estudiante universitario(a) típico(a) y completen las siguientes oraciones con dos cosas o actividades.

1. Lo que menos le gusta(n) es/son _____.
2. Lo que prefiere hacer es _____.
3. Lo que nunca hace es _____.
4. Lo que le preocupa(n) es/son _____.
5. Lo que come regularmente es _____.
6. Lo que siempre trae a la universidad es _____.

**Paso 2:** Comparen sus respuestas con las de dos grupos más y tomen notas. Luego, preparen un resumen de todas las respuestas y preséntenlo en clase.

MODELO   *Nosotros pensamos que lo que menos le gusta al estudiante universitario típico es/son... Por otro lado, lo que el estudiante típico prefiere hacer es...*

### ■ Integración

**7-20 Vivir en este pueblo o en esta ciudad** En parejas, comenten qué piensan sobre el pueblo o sobre la ciudad donde viven. Por ejemplo, pueden dar su opinión sobre lo mejor, lo peor, lo más gracioso, lo más curioso, lo que más les gusta y lo que más les disgusta de vivir ahí. Tomen notas.

**7-21 Un *e-mail pal* cubano** Imagínate que tu *e-mail pal* cubano quiere saber qué opinas de tu pueblo o de tu ciudad. Escríbele un mensaje e incorpora la información que intercambiaste con tu compañero(a) en la actividad 7-20. Como quieres impresionar a tu amigo(a) con tu dominio del español, dale una copia del mensaje a tu compañero(a) para que lo corrija antes de que lo envíes *(send it).*

**SUGERENCIAS**

Usen palabras y frases como **por otro lado** (on the other hand), **sin embargo** (however), **además/también** (also) y **finalmente** (finally) para conectar sus ideas de forma coherente.

Ask students to take good notes because they will need this information to complete activity **7-21.**

**Sugerencias 7-20:** This is a good activity to recycle a lot of vocabulary that students have previously learned. You may want to do a brainstorming exercise first.

**SUGERENCIAS**

Éstos son algunos de los temas que pueden comentar: la localización, los lugares de interés (las tiendas, las bibliotecas, los parques, etc.), la diversión (cafés, restaurantes, clubes, bares, museos, etc.), los servicios públicos (la electricidad, el agua, el cable, etc.), el sistema educativo, el sistema de salud pública, la diversidad étnica, los centros deportivos, los problemas urbanos, el clima y el costo de vida.

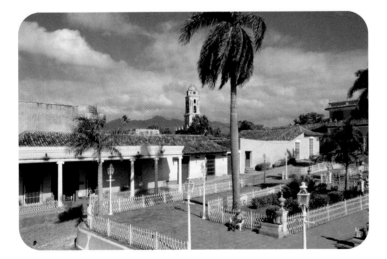

## IV. Perspectivas: Dirección: El sur de la Florida

### ■ Antes de leer

This reading serves as a preview of the vocabulary and themes of **Tema 3**.

**A. Para conversar** Respondan a las siguientes preguntas.

1. ¿Hay vecindades o barrios bien definidos en su ciudad? Si es así, ¿cuál es su vecindad favorita? (Expliquen por qué.)
2. ¿Cuáles son las características de una vecindad ideal? Preparen una lista (por ejemplo: seguridad, accesibilidad, servicios, etc.). Usen el diccionario si es necesario.

**B. Vocabulario y conceptos** Escriban junto a cada palabra la letra que corresponde a su definición.

| | | |
|---|---|---|
| _e_ 1. bienes raíces | a. barato |
| _b_ 2. segunda vivienda familiar | b. una casa para pasar las vacaciones |
| _a_ 3. precio asequible | c. mucho tiempo para pagar |
| _f_ 4. financiamiento | d. costumbres, actividades, preferencias |
| _c_ 5. largo plazo | e. propiedades como casas y edificios |
| _d_ 6. estilo de vida | f. crédito, pago diferido con intereses |

### ■ A leer

### Dirección: El sur de la Florida
**Los compradores internacionales alimentan la bonanza en bienes raíces de la Costa de Oro de la Florida**

por Phyllis Apple

¿Por qué tanta gente quiere vivir en el sur de la Florida?

*county*

*monopolize*

En la zona metropolitana de Miami, en el **Condado** de Dade, aproximadamente el 25% de todas las compras de bienes raíces las realizan personas de otros países, quienes **acaparan** casi el 55% de todas las ventas de condominios destinados a usarse como segunda vivienda familiar.

Los latinoamericanos representan un 60% de estas ventas.

Los precios asequibles del sur de la Florida, especialmente cuando se comparan con los de propiedades situadas frente al mar en América del Sur y Europa, así como la disponibilidad de un financiamiento a largo plazo y a bajo interés, son algunas de las razones principales de la fiebre de compras. Otros factores que influyen en este mercado son la seguridad, la accesibilidad y la gama de servicios modernos que los estadounidenses **dan por sentados.**

*take for granted*

«Llegar acá es fácil», observa Alicia Cervera, una de las principales agentes de bienes raíces de Miami, «pero vivir acá es más fácil todavía. Es preciso viajar al país latinoamericano más refinado para apreciar todo lo que tenemos aquí en términos de comodidad, seguridad, carreteras, así como servicios confiables. Estas cosas hacen que el clima y las playas del sur de Florida sean aún más llamativos para los latinoamericanos».

Con el objeto de satisfacer la demanda, los urbanistas entregan nuevos productos para satisfacer toda una gama de **presupuestos** y de estilos de vida. Desde las comunidades country club, donde la vida **gira alrededor** del tenis y del golf, hasta las propiedades frente al mar, diseñadas para los **amantes** de la playa y el **yatismo,** las opciones y los destinos son tan amplios como los compradores mismos. En virtud de la diversidad de opciones y la fuerte demanda, invertir en una residencia de lujo en la Costa de Oro del sur de la Florida representa hoy en día una decisión sólida y **provechosa.**

*budgets*
*revolves around*

*lovers / yachting*

*advantageous*

■ **¿Entendiste bien?**

**C. En resumen...** En dos o tres oraciones, sintetiza la idea principal de este texto.

*Answers C: Answers may vary, but they should all present in one way or another the following two ideas: Muchos hispanoamericanos están comprando propiedades en el sur de la Florida. Los latinoamericanos invierten en la Florida por los beneficios económicos y personales de vivir en los Estados Unidos.*

**D. ¿Cierto o falso?** Indica si las siguientes oraciones son ciertas (**C**) o falsas (**F**).

- _F_ 1. Un 55% de todos los latinoamericanos tienen una segunda vivienda en la Florida.
- _F_ 2. Un 60% de los compradores de bienes raíces en la Florida son extranjeros.
- _C_ 3. Las propiedades frente al mar en Latinoamérica son más costosas que en la Florida.
- _C_ 4. Según la autora, los términos de crédito son muy favorables en los Estados Unidos.
- _C_ 5. Alicia Cervera sugiere que la vida en Estados Unidos es más fácil que en Latinoamérica.

**E. Aspectos lingüísticos** Adivina, según el contexto, el significado de las palabras en negrilla *(boldface).*

1. «Apreciar todo lo que tenemos aquí en términos de comodidad, seguridad, carreteras, así como servicios **confiables.**»
   a. feeble          b. funny          c. reliable
2. «Estas cosas hacen que el clima y las playas del sur de Florida sean aún más **llamativos** para los latinoamericanos.»
   a. expensive          b. appealing          c. modern
3. «Los urbanistas entregan nuevos productos para satisfacer toda una **gama** de presupuestos y de estilos de vida.»
   a. game          b. range          c. gold

**ESTRATEGIA DE LECTURA**

**Scanning** You do not have to understand every word. Concentrate on identifying the main points of the story and completing the following comprehension activity.

**F. ¿Lo recuerdan?**

1. Mencionen cuatro razones por las cuales los latinoamericanos están invirtiendo en el sur de la Florida.
2. Mencionen dos ejemplos del tipo de vivienda que les ofrecen los urbanistas a los compradores latinoamericanos.

**G. Para conversar** ¿Creen Uds. que la autora tiene una visión positiva o negativa acerca de la inversión en bienes raíces en el sur de la Florida por parte de los latinoamericanos? Justifiquen su respuesta.

**H. Enfoque comunitario** Imagínate que tienes que promover la inversión *(promote the investment)* de los latinoamericanos en casas de vacaciones en tu área. Escribe un folleto sobre las ventajas de hacer este tipo de inversión.

En el sur de la Florida

# Es hora de partir

## I. Vocabulario: Preparativos para una mudanza

Primero llamaron a la **compañía de mudanzas** para obtener una **cotización.**

Luego **empacaron** todo cuidadosamente en **cajas de cartón.**

**Envolvieron** los objetos delicados en **plástico de burbujas.**

El día de la **mudanza,** los **empacadores** llegaron temprano y **cargaron** todo el **embalaje** en el **camión** en menos de dos horas.

Ahora los González ya están en su nueva casa y sólo tienen que **desempacar** y **acomodar** su **menaje.**

### Vocabulario práctico

la caja (de cartón) *(cardboard) box*

el camión de mudanzas *moving truck*

la cinta *tape*

la cotización / el estimado *price estimation*

el embalaje *packing*

los empacadores *packing staff*

el guardamuebles *storage*

la manta *blanket*

el marcador *marker*

el menaje *household goods, belongings*

la mudanza *move*

el plástico de burbujas *bubblewrap*

las tijeras *scissors*

el transporte *transportation*

el traslado *relocation, transfer*

### Verbos

acomodar *to accommodate, to arrange*

alquilar *to rent*

cargar *to load*

desempacar *to unpack*

envolver (ue) *to wrap*

guardar *to store*

marcar *to label*

trasladarse *to relocate*

## Asimilación

**7-22 Preparativos** Pon *(Put)* los siguientes preparativos en orden lógico. Al terminar, compara tus respuestas con las de un(a) compañero(a). ¿Están de acuerdo?

<u>7</u> acomodar el menaje en las diferentes habitaciones

<u>2</u> alquilar un camión de mudanzas

<u>3</u> envolver los objetos delicados en mantas o plástico de burbujas

<u>1</u> llamar a la compañía de mudanzas para pedir una cotización

<u>8</u> desempacar las cajas

<u>4</u> empacar todo cuidadosamente

<u>5</u> marcar las cajas con el nombre de la habitación correspondiente

<u>6</u> cargar el menaje en el camión

CD2–7 **7-23 ¿Qué le falta?** Escucha la siguiente narración y marca con una **X** los preparativos que faltan.

____ conseguir más cajas de cartón

____ reservar un camión <u>X</u>

____ comprar cinta

<u>X</u> comprar unos marcadores

<u>X</u> recoger unas mantas

____ comprar plástico de burbujas

## Aplicaciones

**7-24 Adivina** Túrnense para describir y adivinar objetos o actividades relacionados con las mudanzas.

MODELO    E1: *Es un objeto que usas para guardar o transportar la ropa o las cosas de la casa.*
E2: *¿Una caja?*
E1: *¡Eso es!*

**7-25 Preguntas** Un(a) amigo(a) hispano(a) está ayudándote con tu mudanza. Prepara varias preguntas para asegurarte de que todo está listo.

MODELO    las cajas de cartón / comprar
*¿Compraste las cajas de cartón en la compañía de mudanzas?*

1. la cinta y las tijeras / traer
2. las cajas / marcar
3. los objetos delicados / envolver
4. la cotización / pedir
5. la nueva dirección / dejar en el correo
6. el embalaje / cargar
7. la reservación del camión / hacer
8. los empacadores / llamar

**7-26 Entrevista** Túrnense para hacerse y para responder a las siguientes preguntas. Al terminar, preparen un breve informe.

1. ¿Cuándo fue la última vez que te mudaste?
2. ¿Contrataste una compañía de mudanzas o hiciste la mudanza tú mismo(a) *(by yourself)*?
3. ¿Qué fue lo mejor de esa mudanza?
4. ¿Qué fue lo más difícil?

MODELO  *Mi compañero(a) se mudó el año pasado. Sus amigos lo ayudaron a mudarse...*

## ▥ Integración

**7-27 Un traslado** Representa la siguiente situación con un(a) compañero(a).

| Estudiante A | Estudiante B |
|---|---|
| La empresa donde trabajas te va a trasladar a otra ciudad. Llama a una compañía de mudanzas para hacer los arreglos pertinentes. | Tú trabajas para una compañía de mudanzas. Un(a) cliente está preparando su traslado a otra ciudad. Ayúdalo(la) a hacer los preparativos pertinentes. |

**SUGERENCIAS**

Recuerden que tienen que decidir los siguientes aspectos:
- materiales para la mudanza (cajas, cinta, marcadores, etc.)
- reservaciones (del camión, de avión, de hotel, etc.)
- empacar y desempacar
- cargar el menaje en el camión
- notificar del cambio de dirección

**7-28 ¿Qué tengo que hacer?** Imagínense que tienen que ayudar a unos amigos a mudarse a otra ciudad. Hagan una lista de los preparativos necesarios para una mudanza de este tipo.

## II. Funciones y estructuras: Expressing purpose or reason with the prepositions *por* and *para*

| | |
|---|---|
| CARMEN: | Ligia, ¿**para** dónde te mudas? |
| LIGIA: | **Para** los suburbios. Son más tranquilos. |
| CARMEN: | ¿Y cuánto pagaste **por** la casa? |
| LIGIA: | Menos de trescientos mil dólares. |

The most common use of the prepositions **por** and **para** is to convey the meaning of *for*. However, they have other very important uses. Here is a summary.

**Por** is used:

■ to express reason or cause (*because of, due to*).

| | |
|---|---|
| Nos mudamos **por** el tráfico de la ciudad. | *We moved **because of (due to)** the traffic in the city.* |

■ to express *by means of (by, on)*.

| | |
|---|---|
| Voy a Miami **por** avión. | *I am going to Miami **by** plane.* |
| Hablé **por** teléfono con los empacadores. | *I talked **on** the phone with the packing staff.* |

■ to express movement in space (*along, through, throughout, by*).

| | |
|---|---|
| El camion de mudanzas cruzó **por** tu pueblo. | *The moving truck crossed **through** your town.* |
| Voy a pasar **por** la bodega hoy. | *I am stopping **by** the warehouse today.* |

■ to express duration of time (*for, in, during*).

| | |
|---|---|
| Vamos a estar desempacando **por** muchas horas. | *We will be unpacking **for** many hours.* |

■ to express *on behalf of*.

| | |
|---|---|
| ¿Puedes velar el menaje **por** mí? | *Can you watch the household goods **on my behalf (for me)**?* |

■ to express general location (*around*).

| | |
|---|---|
| ¿Viste la cinta **por** aquí? | *Did you see the tape **around** here?* |

■ to express that there was an exchange or purchase (*in exchange for*).

| | |
|---|---|
| No tuve que pagar nada **por** la cotización. | *I did not have to pay anything **(in exchange) for** the price estimation.* |

■ in some fixed expressions.

> por ciento *percent*  por fin *finally*
> por cierto *by the way*  por la mañana *in the morning*
> por ejemplo *for example*  por lo menos *at least*
> por (ello/eso) *because of that*  por si acaso *just in case*
> por esto *because of this*  por supuesto *of course*
> por favor *please*  por todas partes *everywhere*

**Para** is used:

■ to express purpose or motive *(in order to)*.

> Se mudaron **para** criar a sus  *They moved **(in order) to** raise*
> hijos en otro ambiente.  *their kids in a different*
> *environment.*

■ to express who the recipient of something is *(for)*.

> Este cheque es **para** su empleado.  *This check is **for** your employee.*

■ to express destination *(for)*.

> ¿Ya salieron **para** California?  *Did they leave **for** California*
> *already?*

■ to express the time or day by which an action must be completed *(for, by)*.

> Esperamos estar allá **para** el sábado.  *We hope to be there **by** Saturday.*

## ■ Asimilación

**7-29 Un lunes como cualquier otro** *(like any other)* Piensa en las actividades que normalmente haces los lunes y escoge las oraciones correctas. Al terminar, compara tus respuestas con las de un(a) compañero(a). ¿Tienen rutinas semejantes o diferentes?

_____ Voy a la universidad por la mañana.

_____ Llego temprano para estudiar en la biblioteca.

_____ Salgo para casa a eso de las seis de la tarde.

_____ Tomo por lo menos cuatro clases.

_____ Casi nunca paso por el centro de estudiantes.

_____ No almuerzo por falta de tiempo.

_____ Trabajo por más de cinco horas.

_____ Por fin, me acuesto como a las once de la noche.

CD2-8  **7-30 ¡A completar!** Completa las oraciones que vas a escuchar con la frase más apropiada.

1. _b_     3. _d_     5. _g_     7. _e_
2. _f_     4. _h_     6. _a_     8. _c_

a. para mi esposo.
b. para terminar de empacar.
c. por eso no pudo venir a clase.
d. por tren.
e. por esta silla?

f. por la tarde.
g. por el supermercado?
h. para conseguir un mejor empleo

Script 7-30: 1. Necesito más cajas de cartón... 2. Generalmente miro la televisión... 3. Enviamos el menaje a Chicago... 4. Quiero graduarme de la universidad... 5. ¿Piensas pasar... 6. Compré esta camisa... 7. ¿Olivia pagó doscientos dólares... 8. Leonel está enfermo...

■ **Aplicaciones**

**7-31 Planificando un viaje** Completen el diálogo con las palabras y frases de la lista. Préstenle atención al uso de las preposiciones **por** y **para.**

OPCIONES:  estudiar italiano   Venezuela   cierto   mañana
quinientos dólares   avión   mi hermano   la noche

ELENA:  ¿Adónde vas este verano?

OMAR:  Quisiera salir para _____Venezuela_____ en junio.

ELENA:  ¿Vas en barco crucero?

OMAR:  No, en _____avión_____. Conseguí una oferta buenísima por sólo _____quinientos dólares_____. ¿Quieres venir conmigo?

ELENA:  Mmm... Me encantaría, pero no puedo. Tengo que trabajar por _____mi hermano_____ en la tienda de mis padres. Él quiere ir a Roma para _____estudiar italiano_____.

OMAR:  ¿Por qué no lo piensas y me das una respuesta definitiva mañana por _____la noche_____?

ELENA:  Está bien. Voy a hablar con mis padres y ya tendré la respuesta para _____mañana_____. Por _____cierto_____, ¿se necesita pasaporte?

OMAR:  Creo que no, pero luego hablamos de eso.

**7-32 ¡Lista!** Completen el siguiente mensaje telefónico con **por** o **para.**

¡Hola, Héctor! ¡Soy Norma! ¡Creo que estoy lista ___para___ la mudanza! Ya tengo las cajas de cartón y la cinta que necesito ___para___ empacar. Mi familia viene ___para___ ayudarme hoy ___por___ la tarde. Aunque *(Even though)* mi padre no puede venir, mi cuñado viene ___por___ él. También me comuniqué con el gerente de la compañía de mudanzas ___por___ correo electrónico ___para___ pedirle que los empacadores estén aquí ___para___ las siete de la mañana el viernes. ___Por___ supuesto, también le pedí que trajeran algunas mantas. Si puedes y tienes tiempo, ven ___por___ aquí y charlamos. Chao. Un beso.

**SUGERENCIAS**

La historia puede ser sobre una cena en un restaurante, una reunión familiar, un evento deportivo o unas vacaciones. Pueden consultar la lista de temas que ya han estudiado en el índice *(table of contents)*.

**7-33 Una historia interesante** Inventen una historia interesante relacionada con un tema que escojan entre los dos. Incorporen las preposiciones **por** y **para** y las expresiones **por cierto, por ejemplo, por (eso/ello/esto), por la (mañana/tarde/noche), por si acaso, por supuesto, por todas partes** y **por fin.** ¡Sean creativos!

## Integración

**7-34 El proceso de mudarse** Imagínate que vas a mudarte en las próximas semanas y explícale a tu compañero(a) en qué consiste este proceso. Considera las siguientes preguntas antes de empezar.

- Where are you moving?
- When are you moving?
- How are you getting there?
- What towns or cities do you have to drive through to get there?
- What steps did you have to take to get ready to move and why?
- Who is going to help you and do things for you?

**7-35 Tu comportamiento** *(behavior)* ¿Sabes por qué y para qué haces algunas de las cosas que haces en tu vida? Piensa en esto y escribe un breve resumen. Cuando termines, entrégaselo a tu profesor(a) para que te dé su opinión.

## III. Funciones y estructuras: Referring to the beneficiary of an action by using indirect object pronouns

LARA: ¿**Le** enviaste los documentos al gerente de la compañía de mudanzas?

NORBERTO: Sí, ya lo hice. ¿Y él **te** envió la cotización?

LARA: **Me** la envió por fax esta mañana.

Notice that some of these pronouns also function as direct object pronouns, which you studied in **Capítulo 5, Tema 2.** Context, as well as the meaning of the verb, will always help you figure out the specific function of these pronouns.

The pronouns in bold in the preceding dialogue are indirect object pronouns. The indirect object is the person or thing that benefits from the action of the verb. For example, the pronoun **le** refers to the manager of the moving company, the person who benefited from the action of the verb *to send* and received the documents. To identify the indirect object you may ask **¿a quién?** *(to whom?)* or **¿para quién?** *(for whom?)* to the verb.

Here is a list of the indirect object pronouns in Spanish.

### REMEMBER

These pronouns are also used with verbs like **gustar** (**encantar, fascinar, faltar,** etc.).

| INDIRECT OBJECT PRONOUNS | |
| --- | --- |
| **me** *(to or for me)* | **nos** *(to or for us)* |
| **te** *(to or for you,* familiar singular) | **os** *(to or for you,* familiar plural in Spain) |
| **le** *(to or for him/her/it/you,* formal singular) | **les** *(to or for them/you,* formal plural) |

The verbs **aconsejar** *(to give advice),* **dar, decir (i), doler, enviar, escribir, explicar, hablar de, llevar, ofrecer** *(irreg.),* **pedir (i), preguntar, prestar** *(to lend),* **prometer que, recomendar (ie), regalar** *(to give a gift),* **responder,** and **sugerir (ie)** *(to suggest)* are often used with indirect object pronouns because they imply doing something to or for a beneficiary.

Estela **me** dijo que necesitaba más plástico de burbujas.

¿**Les** preguntaste si venían a las ocho?

*Estela told **me** that she needed more bubblewrap.*

*Did you ask **them** if they were coming at eight?*

As you may have noticed, indirect object pronouns are placed before the conjugated verb. When you use a verb phrase, they can be placed before the auxiliary verb or attached to the main verb (an infinitive or a present participle).

**Te** van a traer / Van a traer**te** un buen marcador.

¿**Me** estás empacando / Estás empacando**me** la vajilla?

*They are going to bring **you** a good marker.*

*Are you packing the china **for me**?*

Besides using an indirect object pronoun, you may also use a phrase introduced by the preposition **a** to add clarity and emphasis. This is particularly helpful in the case of **le** and **les,** which may refer to different people. Although this would be redundant in English, it is perfectly correct in Spanish.

**Les** di las gracias **a los empacadores.**

*I thanked **them (the packing staff)**.*

**Le** prometí **a mi madre** que iba a ayudar.

*I promised **her (my mother)** that I was going to help.*

## ■ Asimilación

**7-36 ¿Cierto o falso?** Lee cada oración e indica si es cierta (**C**) o falsa (**F**). Luego, compara tus respuestas con las de un(a) compañero(a). ¿Qué tienen en común?

_____ 1. Mis padres me dan dinero.

_____ 2. Mi profesor(a) de español me hace muchas preguntas en clase.

_____ 3. Mis amigos me dicen siempre la verdad.

_____ 4. Mi novio(a) o esposo(a) me da regalos caros.

_____ 5. Mis hermanos me piden que los ayude con la tarea.

_____ 6. Mi mejor amigo(a) me habla por teléfono diariamente.

_____ 7. Mis compañeros me dicen «hola» cuando entro al salón de clase.

_____ 8. Mi madre me prepara mi plato favorito todos los fines de semana.

**02-9** **7-37 Anuncios** Escucha los tres anuncios e indica a qué se refiere el pronombre **le** o **les** en cada caso.

1. _X_ los clientes      _____ las tiendas      _____ las compras

2. _____ la película      _____ las bebidas      _X_ al público

3. _____ la aerolínea      _____ el tiempo      _X_ los pasajeros

**Script 7-37:** Número 1: Estimados clientes, les informamos que nuestras tiendas van a estar cerradas el próximo lunes por ser un día feriado. Les recomendamos que hagan todas sus compras hoy y les aconsejamos que aprovechen las ofertas que tenemos en todos los departamentos. Número 2: Le pedimos, querido público, que no tire la basura en el piso. También le pedimos que no use su teléfono celular y que se abstenga de hablar y de fumar. También le recordamos que en nuestro concesionario puede comprar bebidas muy frías y palomitas de maíz calientitas y frescas. ¡Que disfrute de la película! Número 3: Estimados pasajeros, les notificamos que el vuelo 763 con destino a la ciudad de La Habana fue atrasado por las condiciones del tiempo. Les pedimos que permanezcan en el área de espera. En nombre de Cubana de Aviación, les damos las gracias por su paciencia y comprensión.

## Aplicaciones

**7-38 Un correo electrónico** Completen el siguiente mensaje de correo electrónico con los pronombres de complemento indirecto correctos.

**De:** Marta
**Fecha:** 16 de septiembre
**Para:** Mateo
**Asunto:** ¡Estamos en nuestra nueva casa!

Querido Mateo:

___Te___ escribo para decirte que todo salió bien en la mudanza. ¡Ya estamos en nuestra nueva casa! La compañía ___nos___ entregó todo en muy buenas condiciones (a nosotros) y no ___les___ tuvimos que pagar más de lo que decía la cotización (a ellos). Estamos muy contentos, pero tenemos mucho que hacer.

Los nuevos vecinos son magníficos. Tan pronto llegamos, ___nos___ dieron la bienvenida y ___nos___ ofrecieron algo de comer (a nosotros).

Necesito un favor: ¿___Me___ puedes enviar la dirección de Ligia (a mí)? Tengo que enviar___le___ una tarjeta de agradecimiento (a ella) por ayudarnos tanto.

Un abrazo,

Marta

*This activity recycles the use of the imperfect tense. You may want to have students review this verb form first.*

**7-39 A ti y a mí**

**Paso 1:** Usa la siguiente información para formar oraciones sobre las cosas que otras personas te hacían cuando eras niño(a).

MODELO   amigos / prestar dinero
*Mis amigos (no) me prestaban dinero.*

1. padres / dar sermones *(lectures)* con frecuencia
2. abuelos / comprar dulces
3. compañeros de clase / hacer preguntas en los exámenes
4. madre / llevar la comida a la cama cuando estaba enfermo(a)
5. profesores / dar muchas tareas
6. hermanos / leer libros

**Paso 2:** Ahora, convierte las oraciones del **Paso 1** en preguntas para tu compañero(a). Toma notas y, al terminar, prepara un breve informe comparando tus respuestas y las respuestas de él/ella.

MODELO   *¿Tus amigos te prestaban dinero?*

**7-40 ¿Y a otras personas?** Formen oraciones con elementos de cada columna. Reemplacen los puntos suspensivos (...) por información original. Usen los pronombres **le** y **les** correctamente. ¡Sean creativos!

MODELO    nosotros   causar...  a...
*Nosotros les causamos problemas a nuestros padres.*

| | |
|---|---|
| nosotros | causar... |
| el (la) profesor(a) | dar... |
| el presidente | escribir...    a... |
| nuestros hermanos | decir... |
| los estudiantes de la clase | ofrecer... |
| ... | recomendar... |
| | pedir... |
| | preguntar... |
| | prestar... |
| | regalar... |

## ■ Integración

### 7-41 Reciprocidad

**SUGERENCIAS**

Pueden usar los verbos que se mencionan en la anotación de la página 286.

**Paso 1:** Escriban los nombres de cinco personas importantes en sus vidas y su relación con ellas. Luego, intercambien sus notas.

**Paso 2:** Averigüen qué hace su compañero(a) para expresar su afecto por esas personas y ellas por él/ella.

MODELO    E1: *Chris, ¿le regalas perfumes caros a Nancy, tu novia?*
                 E2: *Sí, le regalo perfumes caros.*
                 E1: *¿Qué perfumes le regalas?*
                 E2: *...*
                 E1: *¿Y ella te regala perfumes caros a ti?*
                 E2: *...*

**7-42 Una compañía de mudanzas internacionales** Escribe un anuncio comercial para una compañía de mudanzas internacionales. Menciona los servicios que ofrece y los países en los que tiene oficinas.

## IV. Vídeo: Un día triste para Valeria

iLrn

**ESTRATEGIA DE COMPRENSIÓN**

*Anticipating* Consider the context of a birthday party and the similarities and differences between how we celebrate our birthdays as children and as adults.

**A. Los cumpleaños de antes y los de ahora** Antes de ver el vídeo, piensen en cómo son las fiestas de cumpleaños y completen el siguiente cuadro.

|  | Los cumpleaños de niños | Los cumpleaños de adultos |
|---|---|---|
| ¿Dónde se celebran? |  |  |
| ¿Quiénes asisten? |  |  |
| ¿Qué se come y se bebe? |  |  |
| ¿Qué se hace durante la celebración? (por ejemplo, jugar, bailar, etc.) |  |  |
| ¿Cómo se siente la persona que cumple años? ¿Por qué? |  |  |

### ¿Entendiste bien?

**B. Valeria y Alejandra se ponen nostálgicas**

1. Lee las siguientes preguntas y luego mira el vídeo para poder contestarlas.

   - ¿Cuántos años cumple Valeria hoy?
   - ¿Por qué está triste?
   - ¿Quiénes se olvidaron del cumpleaños de Valeria?

**Answers 1:** 24 años; porque ninguno de sus amigos se acordó de su cumpleaños (nadie le escribió para felicitarla); los amigos de Valeria

2. Completa lo que le dice Alejandra a Valeria para intentar animarla *(cheer her up)*:

   «*Ay, bueno, pero no lo tomes tan a pecho. Quizás tus* ___amigos___ *piensan que estás muy* ___ocupada___ *aquí en Puerto Rico y no tienes tiempo para revisar tu* ___correo electrónico___ . *Es cierto, ¿no? Casi nunca estamos en* ___casa___ *desde que llegamos a Puerto Rico.*»

3. ¿Se asocian las siguientes cosas con los cumpleaños de Valeria (**V**) o los de Alejandra (**A**)?

    _A_  a. una fiesta de cumpleaños con los compañeros de escuela

    _V_  b. su comida favorita

    _A_  c. un pastel de cumpleaños, refrescos y helados

    _A_  d. la piñata

    _V_  e. fiestas de cumpleaños muy grandes

    _V_  f. un ramo de flores

    _A_  g. bolsitas con confites

Compara tus respuestas con las de un(a) compañero(a).

**C. ¿Es mejor ser niño(a) o adulto(a)?** Entrevista a un(a) compañero(a) sobre los cambios en su vida al crecer *(grow up)* y si le parece mejor ser niño(a) o adulto(a).

1. ¿Cuáles de estas cosas extrañas de tu niñez? ¿Por qué?

    _____ los amigos

    _____ vivir en la casa de tus padres

    _____ la escuela (primaria y secundaria)

    _____ las celebraciones (cumpleaños, días festivos, etc.)

    _____ las actividades, juegos, deportes, etc.

    _____ la falta de preocupaciones

    _____ otra: _____

2. ¿Cuáles de las siguientes cosas son ventajas de ser adulto(a)?

    _____ la independencia

    _____ los amigos

    _____ el poder tener hijos

    _____ el poder casarse

    _____ tener una casa propia

    _____ otra: _____

3. ¿Te hace falta algo que tenías de niño(a)?

4. ¿Qué te tocaba hacer cuando eras niño(a) que no haces ahora y viceversa?

5. ¿Puedes pensar en algunas cosas que ahora te importan, pero que no te importaban cuando eras niño(a) y viceversa?

6. Si tuvieras *(you had)* la posibilidad, ¿te interesaría revivir tu niñez? ¿Por qué sí o no?

Ahora, basándote en las respuestas de tu compañero(a), ¿crees que a él/ella le gusta más ser niño(a) o adulto(a)? ¿Por qué? Explícale a tu compañero(a) tu opinión y averigua si él/ella está de acuerdo contigo o no.

**D. Enfoque comunitario** ¿Hay muchos estudiantes cubanos en tu universidad? Investiga y trata de localizar a algún estudiante que sea de origen cubano. Invítalo(la) a la clase para que hable de su país, sus tradiciones o costumbres familiares (cumpleaños, bodas, etc.) y sobre sus experiencias en los Estados Unidos.

# A establecerse en una nueva casa

## I. Vocabulario: Los bienes raíces

¿Cuánto es la cuota inicial?

Queremos una hipoteca a 20 años.

### Vocabulario práctico

los bienes raíces *real estate*
el contrato *contract*
la cuota inicial / el anticipo
   *down payment*
la hipoteca *mortgage*
la inmobiliaria / agencia de
   bienes raíces *real estate agency*

los planos *blueprints*
el préstamo *loan*
la propiedad *property*
los términos de financiamiento
   *credit terms*
la ubicación *location*

## ■ Asimilación

**7-43 Atractivos** Indica cuáles son los principales atractivos de estos
condominios.

  _X_  la cuota inicial          _X_  los términos de la hipoteca
  _X_  la ubicación              _X_  las facilidades para obtener préstamos

---

# Key Biscayne

### Una comunidad exclusiva y segura en la Isla de Key Biscayne, Florida.
### Con excelentes términos de financiamiento disponibles.
### Perfecto para un ambiente familiar.

THE OCEAN CLUB
*Key Biscayne*

The Ocean Club, en la Isla de Key Biscayne, en la Florida, a minutos de Miami, le ofrece lujosos condominios en una comunidad
privada. Con vistas al Océano Atlántico, la Bahía de Biscayne, los
rascacielos de Miami y un lago privado. 300 metros de playa; Un
club de tenis con canchas de arcilla; Un Club de Playa donde se
puede cenar formalmente o al aire libre; Gimnasio y spa; Cabañas
privadas en la playa; Piscinas; Parques para los niños; Y mucho más.

   Todo esto a sólo un puente de Miami y a 20 minutos del Aeropuerto Internacional de Miami.

The Ocean Club puede recomendarle a excelentes entidades
bancarias para facilitarle el financiamiento, el cual tiene una cuota
inicial del 30% e hipotecas de 15 a 30 años.

   Si usted busca una residencia a orillas del mar en la Florida, no
tiene que ir más allá de Key Biscayne y The Ocean Club.

   Apresúrese. Las residencias se están vendiendo muy rápido.
   Con precios desde los $300.000 a los $2.100.000.
   Para recibir un folleto y vídeo gratis, llame a nuestra oficina en
Key Biscayne.

---

**CD2-10** 🎧 **7-44 ¿Sí o no?** Indica si las oraciones que vas a escuchar corresponden o no a la información del anuncio.

1. ...  no
2. ...  no
3. ...  no
4. ...  sí
5. ...  sí

**Script 7-44:** 1. La cuota inicial de estos condominios es del 10 por ciento. 2. Están ubicados (located) en el centro de Miami. 3. El nombre de la inmobiliaria es Key Biscayne. 4. La compañía ofrece hipotecas a 20 años. 5. La inmobiliaria ayuda a sus clientes a obtener préstamos bancarios.

## ■ Aplicaciones

**7-45 Busco un condominio** Completa la carta con el vocabulario más apropiado.

OPCIONES:  hipoteca   bienes raíces   ubicación   financiamiento

Inmobiliaria Punto Norte

Estimados señores:

Me dirijo a Uds. para solicitar los servicios de uno de sus agentes de ____bienes raíces____ . Estoy buscando un condominio de dos o tres habitaciones, preferiblemente en el sur de la ciudad, con buena ____ubicación____ (tal vez cerca de un supermercado o de una línea del metro). Les agradecería también información acerca de oportunidades de ____financiamiento____ a través de bancos locales. (Necesito una ____hipoteca____ a 30 años.)

Les agradecería que me enviaran la información a la siguiente dirección: 2315 S.W. 8th Street. Miami, FL 33135. Tel: 305-642-1788.

Atentamente,

Juanita Martínez

**7-46 Tengo algo para Ud.** Organicen las siguientes frases y luego reconstruyan el texto de la carta que le envió el agente de bienes raíces a Juanita.

- Alberto Jaramillo
- Atentamente,
- nuestros / sólo / ofrecen / Desgraciadamente / financiamiento /entre / 15 y 25 años / bancos
- condominio / un / encontré / ideal / para / Ud.
- recuerdo / le / que / la / del 20% / es / cuota inicial
- si es posible, / esta semana / hablar / con Ud. / me gustaría
- Srta. Martínez / Estimada
- Tiene / estación del metro / a dos cuadras / tres habitaciones y dos baños / y / está / tres cuadras /de / una

**Answers 7-46:** Estimada Srta. Martínez: Encontré el condominio ideal para Ud. Tiene tres habitaciones y dos baños y está a dos cuadras de una estación de metro. Desgraciadamente, nuestros bancos sólo ofrecen financiamiento entre 15 y 25 años. Le recuerdo que la cuota inicial es del 20%. Si es posible, me gustaría (I would like to) hablar con Ud. esta semana. Atentamente, Alberto Jaramillo

**7-47 Preguntas** Preparen cuatro preguntas que Juanita debería hacerle al agente de bienes raíces acerca del condominio.

## ■ Integración

**7-48 Necesito...** Representa la siguiente situación con un(a) compañero(a).

| Comprador(a) | Agente de bienes raíces |
|---|---|
| Deseas mudarte a una nueva casa o a un nuevo apartamento. Llama al / a la agente de bienes raíces para averiguar qué tiene disponible *(available)*. Pregúntale también acerca de sus planes de financiamiento. | Tú eres agente de bienes raíces. Recibe la llamada de este(a) cliente y escribe toda la información que necesitas para empezar tu búsqueda *(search)*. Infórmale también acerca de los planes de financiamiento que puedes ofrecerle. |

**7-49 Condominios en Miami** Imagina que trabajas como agente de bienes raíces en el sur de la Florida. Escribe una carta para un cliente latinoamericano y descríbele un condominio en Miami.

## II. Funciones y estructuras: Talking about the past with the preterite and the imperfect tenses

**Llamé** a la inmobiliaria y el agente me **dijo** que el contrato **estaba** listo y que **tenía** que pasar por allá para discutir algunos términos de financiamiento. **Fui** inmediatamente.

The previous caption includes verbs conjugated in the preterite tense and verbs conjugated in the imperfect tense. Can you identify them? If you said that **llamé, dijo,** and **fui** are in the preterite and **estaba** and **tenía** are in the imperfect, you were right! Now, can you explain why these verbs are used in these tenses? This may be somewhat more difficult. To help you, here is a summary of the uses of these two past tenses.

The **preterite** tense is used to talk about:

- the beginning or the end of an action that took place in the past.

  La reunión **empezó** a las diez y **terminó** al mediodía.

  *The meeting **began** at ten and **ended** at noon.*

- actions that took place at specific moments in the past (usually accompanied by expressions such as **ayer, anoche, una vez** *[once]*, **el** [day/mes/año] **pasado, la semana pasada,** and **a la[s]** [time]).

  El martes pasado me **aprobaron** el préstamo.

  *Last Tuesday they **approved** my loan.*

  Ayer **firmamos** el contrato.

  *Yesterday we **signed** the contract.*

- actions that are perceived as completed.

  El cierre **fue** en noviembre.

  *The closing **was** in November.*

- a series of actions thet were completed in the past.

  Ella **vio** la casa, le **gustó** e **hizo** una oferta, todo el mismo día.

  *She **saw** the house, **liked** it and **made** an offer, all in the same day.*

The **imperfect** tense is used to talk about:

- habitual actions in the past (usually accompanied by the expressions **todos los días/años** *[every day/year]* **todas las semanas** *[every week]*, **siempre,** or **frecuentemente**).

  Cuando niña, siempre **jugaba** en el patio de mi casa.

  *When I was a child, I always **used to play** in my house's yard.*

**REMEMBER**

The verbs **conocer, poder, querer,** and **saber** have different meanings in the preterite and in the imperfect. You may review this in **Capítulo 6, Tema 3.**

■ descriptions.

El patio **era** grande y **tenía** una piscina.

*The yard **was** big and it **had** a pool.*

■ events that were in progress while other actions were taking place (usually introduced by the word **mientras** [*while*]).

Cuando emigramos a los Estados Unidos, yo **estaba** en la escuela primaria.

*When we emigrated to the United States, I **was** in elementary school.*

Mientras mis padres **buscaban** casa, **vivíamos** con mi tío Luis.

*While my parents **looked for** a house, we **were living** with my uncle Luis.*

■ descriptions of the participants who carry out the main events of a story (including age, physical appearance, conditions, and emotions).

Luna, la primera persona que conocí, **tenía** diez años y **era** muy graciosa.

*Luna, the first person I met, **was** ten years old and **was** very funny.*

■ background information of past events (including time and weather conditions).

Recuerdo que, cuando la conocí, **hacía** mucho sol y **eran** como las dos.

*I remember that, when I met her, it **was** sunny and it **was** about two.*

## ▓ Asimilación

**7-50 Acciones y reacciones** Empareja las acciones de la izquierda con las reacciones de la derecha. Luego, organiza las oraciones que formes en orden lógico usando números. Cuando termines, compara tus respuestas con las de un(a) compañero(a). ¿Están de acuerdo?

| | | | |
|---|---|---|---|
| _c_ _3_ | El agente de la inmobiliaria quería ayudarla... | a. | se mudó en sólo dos meses. |
| _e_ _1_ | A Delia no le gustaba su vecindario... | b. | pero escogió una casa cerca de sus padres |
| _a_ _5_ | Aunque no le parecía que iba a ser tan fácil,... | c. | y le mostró fotos de diferentes casas |
| _d_ _2_ | Ella quería buscar información... | d. | y fue a una inmobiliaria |
| _b_ _4_ | Delia estaba indecisa,... | e. | y decidió hacer algo para mudarse |

CD2-11 **7-51 Carlos Acosta** Escucha la historia de Carlos Acosta, un bailarín cubano, y clasifica los verbos que escuches usando la siguiente tabla.

| PRETÉRITO | IMPERFECTO | |
|---|---|---|
| nació, comenzó, se | **Descripción** | tenía |
| entusiasmó, fue, ganó, | **Acciones o estados** | quería |
| ingresó | **habituales** | |

**Carlos Acosta**

## Aplicaciones

**7-52 ¡Qué vergüenza!** *(How embarrassing!)* Seleccionen la forma verbal correcta para completar la siguiente narración.

Anoche, mientras (miré / miraba) la televisión, (escuché / escuchaba) un ruido en la cocina. (Salí / Salía) corriendo y (fui / iba) a la casa de mi vecino. Aunque (fueron / eran) más de las once de la noche y él (estuvo / estaba) durmiendo, lo (desperté / despertaba). Le (pedí / pedía) que viniera a ver qué (hubo / había) en la cocina y (entramos / entrábamos) juntos. Cuando él (encendió / encendía) la luz, (vimos / veíamos) que mi gato (estuvo / estaba) comiéndose tranquilamente el pastel que yo había dejado *(I had left)* sobre la mesa. ¡Qué vergüenza! ¡No (supe / sabía) qué decir! ¡Tanta conmoción por un triste gato!

**7-53 Una historia aburrida** La siguiente historia sólo incluye las acciones principales. Vuelvan a escribirla y añadan los detalles que consideren necesarios (descripciones [edad, apariencia física, estados y emociones], acciones simultáneas, trasfondo [tiempo y hora], etc.). ¡El resultado debe ser una historia interesante y original! Tengan en cuenta las reglas de uso del pretérito y del imperfecto.

Mario se levantó temprano. Se afeitó y después tomó café. Se vistió y se fue para el trabajo. En el autobús conoció a una chica preciosa. Hablaron un rato y le pidió su número de teléfono. Él pensó en ella todo el día. Cuando llegó a su casa por la tarde, la llamó. La invitó a cenar y ella aceptó. Fueron a un restaurante francés. Mario regresó a casa muy contento e ilusionado.

**7-54 La vida pasada del / de la profesor(a)** Escriban por lo menos seis preguntas que quieran hacerle al / a la profesor(a) para saber un poco más sobre su vida pasada. Usen el pretérito y el imperfecto correctamente.

## Integración

**7-55 ¡Invéntala!** En grupos de cuatro o cinco estudiantes, túrnense para añadirle algo a una historia curiosa que van a inventar. Cada estudiante debe prestar atención a lo que dicen los demás para poder decir algo pertinente e interesante. El (La) estudiante que tarde más de cinco segundos en hablar, queda eliminado(a). ¿Quién gana al final?

**7-56 Un cuento** *(story)* **infantil** ¿Recuerdas algunos de los cuentos infantiles que te gustaban cuando eras niño(a) (como «La Cenicienta» [*Cinderella*] o «Hansel y Gretel»)? Escribe un resumen del cuento que más te gustaba y dale una copia a un(a) compañero(a) para que lo corrija usando los criterios de la lista de sugerencias. Haz las correcciones y dale una copia a tu profesor(a). Repasa los usos del pretérito y del imperfecto antes de comenzar.

> **SUGERENCIAS**
>
> Usen conectores como **érase una vez** *(once upon a time)*, **de pronto** *(suddenly)*, **además** *(also)*, **por otro lado** *(on the other hand)*, **sin embargo** *(however)*, **por el contrario** *(on the contrary)*, **por ejemplo** *(for example)*, y **finalmente** *(finally)*.

> **SUGERENCIAS**
>
> Para corregir el resumen de tu compañero(a), presta atención a los siguientes elementos:
> **Contenido:** ¿La información del cuento infantil es correcta? ¿Falta algún detalle importante?
> **Organización:** ¿El resumen sigue una secuencia lógica? ¿Es necesario usar frases conectoras?
> **Vocabulario:** ¿La selección de vocabulario es apropiada? ¿Hay algún término usado de forma incorrecta?
> **Lenguaje:** ¿El uso del pretérito y del imperfecto sigue las reglas? ¿Los verbos están bien conjugados?

## III. Funciones y estructuras: Talking about the immediate past with *acabar de*

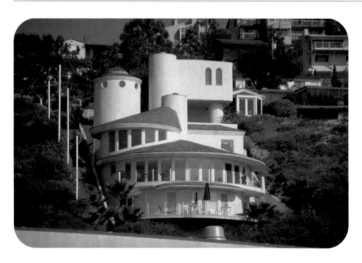

CELIA: ¡Leo, **acabo de comprar** la casa de mis sueños!
LEO: ¡Felicidades! ¡Pues vamos a celebrar!

The expression **acabar de** + infinitive is used to talk about actions that took place in the immediate past.

Maite **acaba de regresar** de Cuba.     *Maite **just came back** from Cuba.*
Nosotros **acabamos de firmar** el       *We **just signed** the contract.*
   contrato.

When you have to use a direct object, indirect object, or reflexive pronoun, it may be placed either before the form of **acabar** or attached to the main verb.

**Lo** acabo de llamar. / Acabo de llamar**lo**.     *I just called **him**.*
**Le** acabo de decir que no. /     *I just told **him/her** no.*
   Acabo de decir**le** que no.
**Me** acabo de bañar. / Acabo de bañar**me**.     *I just took a bath
                          (bathed **myself**).*

Here is a list of other verbs that require the use of the preposition **de** followed by a verb in the infinitive form.

> acordarse (ue) de  *to remember*
> asegurarse de *to make sure*
> dejar de *to stop doing something*
> ocuparse de *to take care of*
> olvidarse de *to forget*
> tener ganas de *to feel like doing something*
> tratar de *to try*

## ■ Asimilación

**7-57 Acaba de...** ¿Conoces bien a tus compañeros de clase? Completa las siguientes oraciones con el nombre de un(a) compañero(a) que, en tu opinión, acaba de hacer estas actividades. Luego, compara tus respuestas con las de un(a) compañero(a). ¿En qué coincidieron?

1. _____ acaba de tomar café.
2. _____ acaba de despertarse.
3. _____ acaba de comer algo.
4. _____ acaba de salir de una clase.
5. _____ acaba de venir de la biblioteca.
6. _____ acaba de abrir el libro.
7. _____ acaba de decirle algo al / a la profesor(a).
8. _____ acaba de entrar al salón de clase.

02–12 **7-58 Buenas y malas noticias** Escucha la conversación entre Moisés y Daniel e indica qué actividades acaban de hacer. Escribe algunos de los detalles que recuerdes.

| Moisés acaba de... hablar con su profesor de química |
| --- |
| DETALLES: Moisés sacó la nota más alta en un examen que tomó ayer. |
| Daniel acaba de... tener un accidente |
| DETALLES: Daniel está bien, pero está un poco nervioso. Su coche fue pérdida total. |

## ■ Aplicaciones

**7-59 Actividades** Escriban por lo menos dos cosas que las personas con las siguientes profesiones posiblemente acaban de hacer: **un cocinero, una secretaria, un agente de bienes raíces, una enfermera, un arquitecto.**

MODELO   *Una periodista posiblemente acaba de entrevistar a un político y de escribir un artículo para un periódico.*

**7-60 Comparaciones**

**Paso 1:** Haz una lista de cinco cosas que acabas de hacer.

1. ...              4. ...
2. ...              5. ...
3. ...

**Paso 2.** Busca a otros compañeros que acaban de hacer las mismas cosas que tú. Apunta sus nombres.

Script 7-58:
Moisés: ¡Daniel, tengo muy buenas noticias!
Daniel: Cuéntame. ¿Por qué estás tan emocionado, Moisés?
Moisés: Acabo de hablar con mi profesor de química y me dijo que había sacado la nota más alta de toda la clase en el examen de ayer. ¿Qué te parece?
Daniel: Qué bueno, Moisés...
Moisés: ¿Qué te pasa, hombre? ¿Por qué estás así?
Daniel: Si supieras... Acabo de tener un accidente y mi coche fue pérdida total.
Moisés: ¡Caramba, Daniel! ¿Pero estás bien?
Daniel: Sí, no me hice nada, pero estoy un poco nervioso todavía.
Moisés: Ven, vamos a tomarnos un refresco y a hablar.
Daniel: Gracias. Lo necesito.

You may want to ask students to review the vocabulary on places and landmarks in **Capítulo 3, Tema 1.**

**7-61 Pues estabas en...** Túrnense para describir cosas que acaban de hacer y para adivinar dónde estaban haciendo esas cosas.

MODELO    E1: *Acabo de enviarle un paquete a mi mejor amiga, de comprar sellos y de buscar mis cartas. ¿Dónde estaba?*
E2: *Pues estabas en la oficina de correos.*
E1: *¡Correcto!*

### ■ Integración

**7-62 ¿Y ahora qué?** Representa la siguiente situación con un(a) compañero(a).

**SUGERENCIAS**

Puedes usar estas expresiones para pedir consejo: **¿Qué sugieres?** *(What do you suggest?)* **¿Qué recomiendas?** *(What do you recommend?)* **¿Qué debo hacer?** *(What should I do?)*

| Estudiante A | Estudiante B |
|---|---|
| Imagínate que acabas de graduarte de la universidad y, de pronto *(suddenly)*, no sabes qué hacer para prepararte para tu vida profesional. Llama a tu mejor amigo(a), háblale de tu preocupación y pídele un consejo *(advice)*. | Tu mejor amigo(a) acaba de graduarse de la universidad y necesita tu consejo sobre qué debe hacer para prepararse para su vida profesional. Cuando te llame, escúchalo(a) y dale tu consejo *(advice)*. |

**SUGERENCIAS**

Para dar consejos, puedes usar estas expresiones: **Creo/ Pienso/Me parece que debes...** *(I think you should . . .)* También, puedes usar algunas de las frases verbales presentadas en esta sección: **acuérdate de..., asegúrate de..., deja de..., olvídate de..., ocúpate de...,** y **trata de...** Estas frases verbales están en forma de mandatos, un tema que estudiarás en el **Capítulo 10, Tema 1.** Por ahora, úsalos por lo que significan y no te preocupes por la forma.

**7-63 En la clase de hoy** Imagínate que uno de tus compañeros no pudo venir a clase hoy. Mándale un correo electrónico para informarle lo que pasó en la clase. Puedes usar oraciones con **acabar de** y las expresiones **acuérdate de..., asegúrate de..., deja de..., olvídate de..., ocúpate de...** y **trata de...**

# IV. Lectura: Soñar en cubano

## ■ Antes de leer

**A. Para conversar** En grupos de cuatro o cinco estudiantes, intercambien opiniones sobre las siguientes preguntas.

1. ¿Qué aspectos de la vida en los Estados Unidos creen que pueden sorprender a un inmigrante hispanoamericano que viene de la zona del Caribe?

2. En general, ¿quién creen que se va a adaptar más rápidamente a este nuevo país: un niño o un adulto? Expliquen por qué.

**B. Vocabulario y conceptos** Las siguientes palabras son importantes para la comprensión del texto que vas a leer a continuación. Para cada una, escribe la letra de su definición. (Consulta el diccionario si es necesario.)

<u>c</u> 1. el fracaso      a. bajar mucho la temperatura, formar hielo

<u>d</u> 2. la intervención      b. hacer sonidos semejantes a algo que se

<u>a</u> 3. helar               quiebra o se fragmenta

<u>b</u> 4. crujir           c. la ruina, la destrucción, el fin

                             d. intromisión, participación arbitraria en

                                 un asunto ajeno

## ■ A leer

### Cristina García

Nació en La Habana, Cuba, en 1958, y creció en Nueva York. Asistió a Barnard College y a la Escuela de Estudios Internacionales Avanzados de la Universidad Johns Hopkins. Cristina García ha trabajado como corresponsal para la revista *Time* en San Francisco, Miami y Los Ángeles, donde vive con su esposo. *Soñar en cubano* es su primera novela.

### Soñar en cubano (fragmento)

Recuerdo cuando llegamos a Nueva York. Vivimos durante cinco meses en un hotel de Manhattan, mientras mis padres esperaban el fracaso de la revolución o la intervención de los norteamericanos en Cuba. Mi madre me sacaba a pasear por Central Park.

Una vez, uno de los agentes del **espectáculo** de Art Linkletter nos **detuvo** en el zoo infantil y le preguntó a mi madre si yo podía formar parte en el show. Pero yo todavía no sabía hablar inglés, y mi madre **siguió** caminando. Mamá me vestía con un abriguito de lana rojo oscuro con el cuello y los **puños** de **terciopelo** negro. El aire era distinto al de Cuba. Tenía un olor a frío, a **humo**, que helaba mis **pulmones.** El cielo y los árboles

*Note that the word* **abriguito** *is derived from the word* **abrigo.** *The colloquial endings* **-ito** *and* **-cito** *are used to indicate small size or affection. Examples: Ana:* **Anita** *casa:* **casita** *papá:* **papito** *Pepe:* **Pepito** *libros:* **libritos** *hijos:* **hijitos** *carro:* **carrito** *mamá:* **mamita** *corazón:* **corazoncito**

*show*
*to stop (preterite)*

*to continue (preterite)*

*cuffs / velvet*
*smoke / lungs*

*dry leaves piled up*
*palm trees*
*naked branches*

también eran diferentes. Yo me ponía a correr sobre las **hojas secas amontonadas** para escucharlas crujir como las **palmeras** de Cuba durante los huracanes. Pero luego me sentía triste al ver las **ramas desnudas** y pensaba en abuela Celia. Me pregunto cómo sería mi vida con ella en Cuba.

■ **¿Entendiste bien?**

**C. Preguntas y respuestas** Respondan a las siguientes preguntas.

**Answers C:** 1. a Nueva York 2. porque esperaban el fracaso de la revolución o la intervención de los Estados Unidos 3. los paseos que daba con su madre por Central Park
4. tristes: el clima y el paisaje eran muy diferentes a los de su Cuba tropical

1. ¿Adónde se mudó la familia de la narradora después de salir de Cuba?
2. ¿Por qué vivían en un hotel? (¿No tenían dinero para alquilar *[rent]* o comprar una casa?)
3. ¿Qué recuerda especialmente la narradora acerca de esa época?
4. ¿Sus recuerdos son alegres o tristes? Explica por qué.
5. Dibuja la escena de la narradora en el Central Park.

**D. Conjeturas** Al final del fragmento, la niña dice: «Me pregunto cómo sería mi vida con ella en Cuba». Usando la imaginación, describan la vida de esta niña en la isla. (¿Cómo es su casa y su vecindad? ¿A qué se dedica? ¿Es feliz?, etc.)

**E. Enfoque lingüístico** Clasifiquen los verbos en pretérito o imperfecto que encuentren en la lectura usando la siguiente tabla.

| PRETÉRITO | IMPERFECTO | |
|---|---|---|
| llegamos, vivimos, nos detuvo, preguntó, siguió | **Descripción** | me sentía, era, tenía |
| | **Acciones habituales** | esperaba, sacaba, sabía, vestía, helaba, me ponía, pensaba |

**F. Enfoque comunitario** Entrevisten a un(a) estudiante extranjero(a) de cualquier nacionalidad y averigüen qué le gusta de los Estados Unidos, qué extraña de su país natal y qué ajustes ha tenido que hacer para vivir en este país. Presenten un informe oral sobre sus respuestas.

# Vocabulario

**Los recuerdos** — *Memories*

la tierra/patria — *homeland*

**Verbos para hablar de los recuerdos**

añorar — *to long for*
extrañar/echar de menos — *to miss*
irse — *to leave*
mudarse — *to move*
olvidar — *to forget*
olvidarse de — *to forget about*
regresar — *to return*

**Preparativos para una mudanza** — *Preparations for a move*

la caja (de cartón) — *(cardboard) box*
el camión de mudanzas — *moving truck*
la cinta — *tape*
la cotización / el estimado — *price estimation*
el embalaje — *packing*
los empacadores — *packing staff*
el guardamuebles — *storage*
la manta — *blanket*
el marcador — *marker*
el menaje — *household goods, belongings*
la mudanza — *move*
el plástico de burbujas — *bubblewrap*
las tijeras — *scissors*
el transporte — *transportation*
el traslado — *relocation, transfer*

**Verbos para hablar de mudanzas**

acomodar — *to accommodate, to arrange*
alquilar — *to rent*
cargar — *to load*
desempacar — *to unpack*
envolver (ue) — *to wrap*
guardar — *to store*
marcar — *to label*
trasladarse — *to relocate*

**Los bienes raíces** — *Real estate*

el contrato — *contract*
la cuota inicial / el anticipo — *down payment*
la hipoteca — *mortgage*
la inmobiliaria/agencia de bienes raíces — *real estate agency*
los planos — *blueprints*
el préstamo — *loan*
la propiedad — *property*
los términos de financiamiento — *credit terms*
la ubicación — *location*

**Funciones y estructuras**

Verbos como **gustar,** p. 269
Expresiones con **por,** p. 282
Verbos que requieren **de,** p. 298

# Capítulo 8

## ¡A trabajar!

**Para comenzar**

- Túrnense para describir estas fotografías y adivinar de qué lugar se trata. **¡OJO!** ¡Sólo tienen **dos** oportunidades para adivinar!
- ¿Conocen algunos lugares similares a éstos en los Estados Unidos? ¿Dónde están?

**In this chapter you will learn . . .**

- how to talk about jobs, salary, and benefits
- how to express work experience and qualifications
- how to make a business call
- how to give instructions
- about job opportunities and conditions in Latin America and Spain today

|  | **TEMA 1**<br>En busca de trabajo | **TEMA 2**<br>Mis antecedentes y expectativas laborales | **TEMA 3**<br>El nuevo empleo |
|---|---|---|---|
| **Vocabulario** | Los anuncios clasificados | La hoja de vida | Las tareas de oficina |
| **Funciones y estructuras** | Referring to people and things with the relative pronouns **que** and **quien(es)**<br>Referring to past events that continue into the present with the present perfect tense | Influencing others with formal commands<br>Using pronouns and formal commands | Avoiding stating who or what is performing an action with the passive **se**<br>Avoiding repetition using double object pronouns |
| **Lecturas y vídeo** | Perspectivas: Trabajos vía Internet | Vídeo: El secreto de Sofía | Lectura: Mi amigo |

Venezuela es uno de los principales productores mundiales de petróleo.

La ciudad de Caracas tiene una población aproximada de 4 millones de habitantes.

Cartagena, Colombia, es un importante puerto caribeño desde la época colonial.

# Enfoque

Transparencies A-14: Country Profile: Venezuela; A-18: Country Profile: Colombia

**A. ¿Qué sabes ya de Venezuela?** Antes de ver el vídeo, intenta contestar las siguientes preguntas.

1. ¿Quién es Simón Bolívar y dónde nació?
2. ¿Qué porcentaje de gente vive en los centros urbanos de Venezuela?
   a. el 40%    b. el 60%    c. el 90%
3. En Venezuela, ¿hasta qué edad es gratuita y obligatoria la educación?
   a. los 14 años  b. los 16 años  c. los 18 años

4. ¿Qué porcentaje de la población sabe leer y escribir?
   a. el 65%    b. el 77%    c. el 91%

**Answer A-1:** Llamado «el Libertador», fue un militar y político de América del Sur y se considera el padre de la independencia. Nació en Caracas, Venezuela, el 24 de julio de 1783.

Compara tus respuestas con las de un(a) compañero(a).

**B. Vivir y trabajar en Venezuela** Imagínense que tienen la oportunidad de vivir y trabajar en Venezuela. Busquen en el Internet información acerca de estas ciudades: Maracaibo, Caracas y Maturín. Decidan qué ciudad escogerían *(you would choose)* para vivir y trabajar. Comenten con la clase su elección y las razones por las que escogieron esa ciudad.

**C. Venezuela, un país encantador** Mientras ves el vídeo, indica si las siguientes oraciones son ciertas **(C)** o falsas **(F)**.

___C___ 1. Caracas, la capital, tiene un buen sistema de metro que la gente usa con frecuencia por su gran eficiencia.

___C___ 2. Los centros comerciales de Caracas también son centros sociales donde los jóvenes se reúnen para divertirse y para ir de compras.

___F___ 3. En Caracas se pueden ver varios ejemplos de la arquitectura modernista, como la hermosa catedral y el impresionante Panteón Nacional.

___F___ 4. Entre semana, después del trabajo, la gente sale mucho.

For more info, you may want to check the **Temas** site: http://temas.heinle.com

Compara tus respuestas con las de un(a) compañero(a) y corrijan las frases falsas.

# En busca de trabajo

## I. Vocabulario: Los anuncios clasificados

Transparency M-4: Buscar trabajo

This section recycles basic vocabulary on professions introduced in **Capítulo 1, Tema 2.**

Un buen abogado debe tener mucha **experiencia** para **defender** apropiadamente a sus clientes.

Esta ingeniera tiene excelentes **referencias** y una gran **facilidad de expresión.**

Los técnicos **se encargan de manejar** y **reparar** los equipos.

### Vocabulario práctico

la buena presencia *good personal appearance*
la facilidad de expresión *ease of expression, ability to speak*
la hoja de vida / el currículum *résumé*
el técnico *technician*
el trabajador no calificado *unqualified worker*

### Verbos

arreglar/reparar *to fix*
colaborar *to collaborate*
cuidar *to care for, to watch over*
defender (ie) *to defend*
encargarse de + infinitive *to be responsible for doing something*
entretener (ie) *to entertain*
manejar *to operate, to handle*
presentarse *to present oneself, to appear*
solicitar *to request*

## ■ Asimilación

### 8-1 Clasificados

**Paso 1:** Lean los siguientes anuncios clasificados.

---

(1)
Solicitamos varios técnicos en fotocopiadoras, fax, máquinas de escribir, sumadoras, microondas, televisores, equipos electrónicos, impresoras, CPU, fuentes de energía. 541.5946, 541.6809.

(2)
Se solicita secretaria recepcionista, mínimo 5 años experiencia, excelentes referencias, manejo de Word y Excel, para oficina de ingeniería en Chacaíto. Telf. 261.3559, 261.3549, fax 263.7827, Sra. Elena.

(3)
Importante empresa solicita vendedores con buena presencia. Facilidad de expresión y trato con el público. Traer hoja de vida a la Avenida Libertador. Centro Comercial Sambil nivel Feria, local FR-20. Telf. 0149-233697, 0149-233916.

(4)
Seguridad Berna requiere para vinculación inmediata veinte supervisores de vigilancia, experiencia, libreta militar, de primera, 30–45 años. Presentarse lunes a viernes horas de oficina en la Avenida Urdaneta, entre Veroes y Santa Capilla, edificio Cipriano Morales, piso 1, oficina B.

(5)
Solicitamos mensajeros a pie, motorizados, bachilleres, experiencia Caracas, ciudades vecinas, dirección: Av. Las Palmas, Boleíta Sur, Centro Inoesa, piso dos.

(6)
Solicitamos asistente técnico en reparaciones, mantenimientos computadoras, impresoras, monitores. Empresa Celedatos 763.2115, 763.0841. Entrevista lunes a viernes.

---

**Paso 2: ¿Qué tipo de trabajo es?** Clasifiquen las ofertas de empleo según las siguientes categorías. Escriban los números de los anuncios correspondientes.

| Trabajo técnico | Relaciones públicas | Seguridad | Trabajo no calificado |
|---|---|---|---|
| 1, 6 | 2, 3 | 4 | 5 |

**Paso 3: A mí (no) me gusta...** ¿Te interesa alguno de esos trabajos? Conversa con tu compañero(a) sobre el trabajo (o los trabajos) de la lista que más (o menos) te gustaría desempeñar. Explica tus razones.

2–14 **8-2 ¿Reconoces estas profesiones?** Identifica la profesión que corresponde a cada descripción que vas a escuchar.

<u> 5 </u> médico       <u> 1 </u> policía

<u> 2 </u> ingeniero de sistemas       <u> 4 </u> cantante

<u> 3 </u> periodista

**Script 8-2:** Número 1: Usualmente trabaja en las calles. Se encarga de cuidar y proteger a los ciudadanos de los delincuentes y criminales. Número 2: Participa en el diseño de programas y de sistemas computacionales. Maneja equipos electrónicos sofisticados. Número 3: Se encarga de mantener al público informado de las últimas noticias nacionales e internacionales. En ocasiones, colabora con la investigación de sucesos importantes. Número 4: Participa en la creación y divulgación de la música popular. Entretiene al público con sus canciones. Número 5: Cuida a sus pacientes. Se encarga de diagnosticar sus problemas y de darles un tratamiento apropiado.

## ■ Aplicaciones

**8-3 ¿Qué hacen y dónde trabajan?** Describe las actividades de una de estas personas para que tu compañero(a) adivine de qué ocupación se trata. **¡OJO!** Tienen sólo cinco segundos para contestar.

> ingeniero    enfermera    gerente    científico
> artista    programador de computadoras

MODELO  E1: *Atiende a pacientes como un médico, pero sólo les examina los dientes.*
E2: *¿El dentista?*
E1: *¡Sí!*

**8-4 Buscamos...** Imaginen que están en Venezuela y que necesitan algunos colaboradores *(helpers)*. Preparen los anuncios clasificados para enviarlos al periódico *El Universal.* (Usen como guía los anuncios de la actividad 8-1 de la sección **Asimilación.**)

1. un(a) enfermero(a)
2. una nana (niñera)
3. una criada
4. un chofer

**8-5 Superación personal** *(Self-improvement)* Lean la siguiente descripción de un curso por Internet que se ofrece en Caracas.

---

**Instituto Tecnológico, Universidad Central de Venezuela, Aplicaciones instrumentales de Internet en Humanidades, Ciencias Sociales y afines**

**Qué ofrece:** Dirigido más hacia el «¿cómo se hace?» que al «¿por qué ocurre?», este curso busca entrenar a usuarios calificados en el manejo de Internet y no formar expertos en el área técnica.

**Dirigido a:** Profesionales de las áreas de Humanidades, Ciencias Sociales y afines, quienes por formación y experiencia suelen desconocer los recursos adecuados para el manejo de Internet.

**Duración:** 20 horas.

**Costo:** 70 mil bolívares. Incluye material de apoyo, refrigerios y certificado de asistencia.

**Inicio:** Comienzan cursos mensualmente, en horario vespertino, jueves y viernes.

**Información: Instituto Tecnológico, segundo piso, edificio del Decanato, Facultad de Ingeniería, Universidad Central de Venezuela. E-mail: mendezn@fiucv.ing.ucv.ve**

Los técnicos **se encargan de manejar** y **reparar** los equipos.

---

1. Este curso es para profesionales especializados en _____.
2. Los participantes aprenden a usar _____.
3. Los cursos comienzan cada _____.

## ■ Integración

**8-6 ¿Qué debo estudiar?** Representa la siguiente situación con un(a) compañero(a).

| **Consejero(a)** | **Estudiante** |
|---|---|
| Imagina que eres consejero(a) estudiantil y que a tu oficina llega un(a) estudiante que no sabe en qué especializarse. | Tú eres un(a) estudiante indeciso(a). Tu consejero(a) quiere ayudarte a escoger una buena carrera para el futuro. Pídele toda la información posible acerca de la carrera que te va a recomendar. |
| ■ Averigua sus intereses y recomiéndale una carrera apropiada. | ■ ¿Dónde puedes estudiarla? |
| ■ Indícale dónde puede estudiar esa carrera. | ■ ¿Qué requisitos se necesitan? |
| ■ Indica qué requisitos se necesitan. | ■ ¿Dónde puedes trabajar al terminar tus estudios? |
| ■ Recomiéndale dónde puede trabajar al terminar sus estudios. | |

**8-7 ¿Qué hace mi compañero(a)?** Descríbele tu carrera o tu especialización al / a la compañero(a). (Mientras una persona habla, la otra toma notas.) Después, presenta un informe al resto de la clase acerca de las respuestas del / de la compañero(a).

Asegúrense de incluir la siguiente información:

■ ¿Cuál es la carrera del / de la compañero(a)? ¿Qué áreas o materias incluye?

■ ¿Por qué escogió esa carrera?

■ ¿Cuáles son sus objetivos en la vida?

■ ¿Cuál es la importancia de esa carrera para el futuro del país?

■ ¿Qué contribución piensa hacer tu compañero(a) en beneficio de la sociedad?

## II. Funciones y estructuras: Referring to people and things with the relative pronouns *que* and *quien(es)*

---

(1)
Prestigiosa universidad privada solicita tutores **que** puedan trabajar durante los fines de semana. Los candidatos a **quienes** vamos a considerar deben tener una maestría en su área de especialización. Llamar a la Dra. Bermúdez. 248.9953.

(2)
Empresa **que** presta servicios a hospitales solicita técnicos de computadoras con experiencia. **Quien** esté interesado debe enviar su hoja de vida. Fax: 249.0611.

---

Relative pronouns are pronouns that refer to an entity that has already been mentioned in the discourse. This entity is called *the antecedent*. For example, in the first ad, **que** refers to **tutores** (its antecedent) and **quienes** refers to **candidatos** (its antecedent).

While English has four main relative pronouns *(who, whom, that,* and *which),* Spanish has two (**que** and **quien**[**es**]).

> **Quienes** is used when the antecedent is plural.

The pronoun **que** is used to refer to:

■ people *(who)*

| | |
|---|---|
| El gerente **que** contrató a mi hermana renunció. | *The manager **who** hired my sister resigned.* |

■ things *(that, which)*

| | |
|---|---|
| ¿Ya recibió el currículum **que** le envié? | *Did you receive the résumé **that** I sent you?* |
| Estos trabajos, **que** no me gustan, pagan muy poco. | *These jobs, **which** I do not like, pay very little.* |

The pronoun **quien(es)** is used to refer to:

■ people *(who, whom)*—when **quien** comes after a preposition or when it is the first word in a nonrestrictive clause (a phrase that is enclosed in commas)

> The speaker has the choice of using either **quien(es)** or **que** in nonrestrictive clauses. However, only **que** can be used in restrictive clauses.

| | |
|---|---|
| Los hombres con **quienes** hablé tenían buena presencia. | *The men with **whom** I spoke had good personal appearance.* |
| La Sra. Mercado, **quien** se encarga de los archivos, es muy simpática. | *Mrs. Mercado, **who** is responsible for filing, is very pleasant.* |

### ▓ Asimilación

**8-8 ¿Qué o quién?** Escribe el nombre de la cosa o de la(s) persona(s) que cumple(n) con cada descripción.

1. El (La) profesor(a) con quien mejor me llevo.  _____
2. La clase que más me gusta.  _____
3. Los compañeros de clase a quienes casi no les hablo.  _____
4. La prenda de vestir que menos me gusta.  _____
5. La persona a quien menos tolero.  _____
6. Las cosas que siempre traigo a la universidad.  _____

**D2–15** **8-9 Después de una entrevista de empleo** Escucha lo que dice Blanca y selecciona las frases que mejor completen las siguientes oraciones.

1. Blanca cree que... en la entrevista.
   a. le fue mal          (b.) le fue bien          c. no actuó bien
2. La mujer con quien se entrevistó...
   (a.) era muy paciente.     b. era antipática.     c. no tenía interés.
3. Habló con otras personas, quienes se impresionaron con...
   a. su facilidad de     b. su presencia.     (c.) su experiencia.
   expresión.
4. El trabajo que más le interesa...
   a. es con          b. no está          (c.) está cerca
   computadoras.          disponible.          de la casa.

■ **Aplicaciones**

**8-10 El mundo del trabajo** Completen las oraciones con **que, quien** o **quienes.**

1. El jefe o la jefa, ___que/quien___ toma las decisiones en una empresa, debe tener buena comunicación con sus empleados.
2. La característica de un administrador ___que___ más admiran sus compañeros de trabajo es la honestidad.
3. La persona ___que___ se encarga de contabilizar el dinero de una empresa tiene una responsabilidad muy grande.
4. Los supervisores con ___quienes___ uno trabaja deben dar el ejemplo de puntualidad y buena presencia.
5. El currículum ___que___ uno le entrega a un posible empleador *(employer)* cuando solicita un trabajo es un documento confidencial.
6. Un técnico ___que___ no repara bien las cosas no debe permanecer en un trabajo.

**8-11 Opiniones personales** Primero, seleccionen el pronombre correcto. Luego, escriban los datos necesarios para completar las oraciones.

1. Las personas con (que / quien / (quienes)) quiero trabajar deben ser _____ y _____.
2. La hoja de vida ((que)/ quien / quienes) voy a preparar para solicitar mi trabajo ideal va a ser _____ y _____.
3. Una persona ((que)/ quien / quienes) busca trabajo debe estar preparada para _____ y para _____.
4. Antes de contratar a un trabajador ((que)/ quien / quienes) no está calificado, un empleador debe pensar en _____ y en _____.
5. Alguien con experiencia, ((que)/ (quien)/ quienes) tiene ventaja sobre otras personas, sólo tiene que preocuparse de _____ y de _____.

**Script 8-9:** Acabo de llegar de una entrevista en una agencia de empleos. Creo que me fue bastante bien. La mujer encargada de hacer las entrevistas era muy paciente y comprensiva. Le gustó mucho la hoja de vida y la carta de presentación que le di. También hablé con otras personas, quienes me dijeron que estaban impresionadas con mi experiencia. El trabajo que más me interesa, que está cerca de casa, es en una agencia de publicidad internacional, pero también me interesa un trabajo en una compañía de computadoras.

**EN TU COMUNIDAD**

You may wish to go to an employment agency or a career training agency and find out about the interview techniques their clients have considered most successful. Afterward, discuss your findings in groups and present an oral report on the most common techniques.

Both **que** and **quien** can be used in number 5.

## 8-12 Preguntas

**Paso 1:** Completa las preguntas que le vas a hacer a un(a) compañero(a) con frases que empiecen con **que, quien** o **quienes.**

> MODELO  ¿Cuál es la persona con *quien más hablas de tu familia*?
> ¿Dónde está el restaurante *que visitas con más frecuencia*?

1. ¿Cómo se llama el (la) amigo(a) para _____?
2. ¿Cuál es la comida _____?
3. ¿Dónde compras los libros _____?
4. ¿Cómo es tu madre, _____?
5. ¿Te gusta estudiar en esta universidad, _____?

**Paso 2:** Hazle las preguntas a tu compañero(a) y toma notas. Después, informa al resto de la clase sobre sus respuestas.

### ■ Integración

**8-13 Problemas** Representa la siguiente situación con un(a) compañero(a). Cuando terminen, intercambien papeles.

This activity recycles the use of the invariable **lo.** You may want to review the expression **lo que...** with your students.

**SUGERENCIAS**

Un posible problema sería: «Éste es mi último semestre en la universidad y no sé qué voy a hacer después de graduarme. No tengo trabajo y necesito ganar dinero para pagar los préstamos estudiantiles.»

**SUGERENCIAS**

Algunas frases que puedes usar son: **El problema que tienes es...**, **Opino que...**, **La(s) persona(s) con quien(es) debes hablar es/son...**, **La(s) persona(s) a quien(es) debes visitar es/son...** y **Lo que debes hacer es...**

**SUGERENCIAS**

Algunas de las cosas que debes considerar son: **las personas a quienes quiero apelar, los logros que quiero resaltar** (stand out) y **el tipo de trabajo que quiero conseguir.** ¿En cuántas cosas más puedes pensar?

**Estudiante A**

Toma unos minutos para inventar tres problemas. Luego, cuéntale a tu compañero(a) estos problemas y pídele que te dé su opinión. Como eres una persona testaruda *(stubborn)*, no aceptes sus consejos tan fácilmente.

**Estudiante B**

Tu compañero(a) tiene varios problemas. Como buen(a) amigo(a), escúchalo(a) y dale tu opinión. ¡Debes estar listo(a) para defender tu punto de vista!

**8-14 Antes de escribir** Más adelante en este capítulo vas a escribir una carta de presentación *(cover letter)*. Antes de hacer esto, es importante pensar en las características de este tipo de carta y en las personas que van a leerla (los lectores). Usa la siguiente tabla para hacer una lista de las cosas que debes considerar antes de empezar a escribir (primera columna) y anota las ideas importantes que te vengan a la mente *(come to mind)*.

| Cosas que debo considerar | Ideas importantes |
|---|---|
| 1. | |
| 2. | |
| 3. | |
| 4. | |
| 5. | |

## III. Funciones y estructuras: Referring to past events that continue into the present with the present perfect tense

—¿Usted **ha trabajado** en una tienda de ropa antes?
—Sí, **he trabajado** en varias tiendas de ropa.

The present perfect (known as **pretérito perfecto** in Spanish) is used to talk about actions that began in the past and continue in the present. In English, it is formed with the auxiliary verb *has* or *have* followed by the past participle of the main verb (*I have studied, Anne has visited,* etc.).

To form the present perfect in Spanish, use the present tense of the auxiliary verb **haber** and the past participle of the main verb. The past participle ending of **-ar** verbs is **-ado** while the past participle ending of **-er** and **-ir** verbs is **-ido.**

| PRESENT PERFECT | | |
|---|---|---|
| AUXILIARY VERB **haber** | PAST PARTICPLE OF THE MAIN VERB | |
| | **-ar** verbs | **-er/-ir** verbs |
| he has ha hemos habéis han | estudiar → estudi**ado** cantar → cant**ado** | beber → beb**ido** salir → sal**ido** |

Susana **ha completado** todos los formularios.

*Susan **has filled in** all the forms.*

Ellos **han defendido** a muchos criminales.

*They **have defended** many criminals.*

Several verbs have irregular past participle forms.

| | | | | |
|---|---|---|---|---|
| abrir → abierto | *opened* | morir → muerto | *died* |
| cubrir → cubierto | *covered* | poner → puesto | *put, set* |
| decir → dicho | *said* | resolver → resuelto | *solved* |
| describir → descrito | *described* | romper → roto | *broken* |
| escribir → escrito | *written* | satisfacer → satisfecho | *satisfied* |
| freír → frito | *fried* | ver → visto | *seen* |
| hacer → hecho | *done, made* | volver → vuelto | *returned* |

In Spanish, the unity of the auxiliary verb **haber** and the past participle may not be broken by negative words or pronouns: **Él nunca <u>ha colaborado</u> en ningún proyecto.** (He <u>has</u> never <u>collaborated</u> in any project.) **<u>¿Has visto</u> al Dr. Pérez?** (<u>Have</u> you <u>seen</u> Dr. Pérez?)

**He hecho** varios cambios en la empresa.
Nosotros **hemos resuelto** ese problema.

*I have made* several changes in the company.
We *have solved* that problem.

Here is a list of time expressions normally used with verbs conjugated in the present perfect.

| | |
|---|---|
| desde el lunes / el mes pasado / la semana pasada /... | *since Monday / last month / last week / . . .* |
| hasta ahora / el momento | *up until now* |
| por una semana / un mes / un año /... | *for a week / a month / a year / . . .* |
| todavía/aún | *yet* |

To find out if something has *ever* happened, use the expression **alguna vez**: **¿Alguna vez han trabajado Uds. en California?** (Have you ever worked in California?)

## ■ Asimilación

**8-15 ¿Qué has hecho hasta ahora?** Piensa en las cosas que has hecho hasta ahora en el día de hoy y selecciona las oraciones que se apliquen a ti. Al terminar, compara tus respuestas con las de un(a) compañero(a). ¿Han hecho las mismas cosas?

_____ He visto televisión.
_____ He almorzado.
_____ He asistido a más de dos clases.
_____ He escrito una monografía.
_____ He ido al trabajo.

_____ He hablado por teléfono.
_____ He leído el periódico.
_____ Me he afeitado/ maquillado.
_____ He comprado una bebida.
_____ He roto algo.

Script 8-16: Mis compañeros de trabajo y yo somos muy eficientes. Son sólo las once de la mañana y ya hemos hecho muchas cosas. Por ejemplo, hemos llamado a muchos clientes y hemos cancelado varias citas. También hemos organizado el archivo y nos hemos reunido para hablar de algunos casos. ¡Pero no todo es trabajo! También hemos desayunado juntos y hemos hablado de lo que hicimos en el fin de semana. ¡Ah! Y hemos hecho todo esto a pesar de que hemos abierto la oficina a las nueve de la mañana. ¡Somos tan productivos!

Answers 8-16: llamar, cancelar, organizar, reunirse, desayunar, hablar, abrir

CD2–16

**8-16 Empleados muy eficientes** Son sólo las once de la mañana y los empleados de la firma legal Ramírez y Asociados ya han hecho muchas cosas. Escucha al Lic. Ramírez y escribe por lo menos cinco de las actividades que han hecho. Escribe la forma del infinitivo de los verbos.

1. ...
2. ...

3. ...
4. ...

5. ...

## ■ Aplicaciones

**8-17 ¿Qué han hecho?** Den un ejemplo de algo que seguramente han hecho esta semana los siguientes profesionales. Pueden seleccionar verbos de la lista o usar otros.

> MODELO    un cocinero
> *Un cocinero ha preparado una cena espectacular para un cliente importante.*

OPCIONES:  descubrir  completar  romper  describir  defender resolver  preparar  decir

1. un juez
2. un científico
3. un policía
4. un periodista
5. un atleta
6. un ingeniero

**8-18 Mini-situaciones** Completen las siguientes mini-situaciones con la forma correcta del pretérito perfecto de los verbos de cada lista. **¡OJO!** Hay verbos adicionales.

> *decidir    escribir    poner    tener    salir    decir*

1. Yo no <u>he escrito</u> la monografía para la clase de historia porque no <u>he tenido</u> tiempo. Pero el profesor nos <u>ha dicho</u> que podemos entregarla tarde. Un amigo de la clase y yo <u>hemos decidido</u> que vamos a trabajar juntos hoy, pero él no <u>ha salido</u> del trabajo todavía.

> *poner    presentarse    tomar    satisfacer    hacer    ofrecer*

2. El Sr. Nieves y yo <u>hemos tomado</u> una decisión: vamos a despedir *(fire)* a la Sra. Jiménez. Desafortunadamente, ella no <u>ha hecho</u> su trabajo como es debido. Por otro lado, (ella) no <u>se ha presentado</u> a ninguno de los talleres *(training sessions)* que la compañía <u>ha ofrecido</u>. Lamentablemente, su desempeño *(performance)* no nos <u>ha satisfecho</u>.

**8-19 Desde que empecé a estudiar en esta universidad...**

**Paso 1:** Escribe por lo menos cinco cosas que has hecho o logrado *(accomplished)* desde que empezaste a estudiar en esta universidad.

> MODELO    *He aprendido a hablar español.*

1. ...
2. ...
3. ...
4. ...
5. ...

**Paso 2:** Convierte las oraciones del **Paso 1** en preguntas, y entrevista a tres o cuatro de tus compañeros de clase. Toma notas y, cuando termines, prepara un informe y preséntalo al resto de la clase.

> MODELO    *¿Has aprendido a hablar español?*

## ■ Integración

**8-20 Presidente(a) de la Asociación de Estudiantes** Representa la siguiente situación con un(a) compañero(a).

| Aspirante a Presidente(a) de la Asociación de Estudiantes | Delegado(a) de la Asociación de Estudiantes |
|---|---|
| Tú eres uno(a) de los candidatos a la presidencia de la Asociación de Estudiantes de tu universidad. Estás reunido(a) con uno(a) de los delegados de esta asociación, quien quiere saber más sobre tu experiencia en diversas áreas importantes para este puesto. Habla con este(a) estudiante y convéncelo(a) de que eres el (la) mejor candidato(a). | Tú eres el (la) delegado(a) de tu facultad *(college)* en la Asociación de Estudiantes de tu universidad. Estás reunido(a) con uno(a) de los candidatos a la presidencia de esta organización estudiantil. Quieres conocerlo(la) mejor y saber qué tipo de experiencia tiene en diferentes áreas importantes. También debes darle tu opinión sobre estos temas. Entrevista a esta persona para determinar si le vas a dar tu voto o no. |

**8-21 Mi carta de presentación** En la actividad 8-14 tuviste la oportunidad de pensar en las cosas que debes tomar en cuenta antes de escribir tu carta de presentación. Ahora vas a comenzar a escribir la carta. Sigue estos pasos:

1. Haz una lista de actividades recientes relacionadas con tu trabajo y con tu preparación académica y personal («He asistido a dos congresos sobre...», «He participado en un proyecto de investigación con el Dr. / la Dra...», etc.).

2. Organiza estas actividades en dos o tres categorías: experiencia académica, experiencia laboral, experiencia de investigación, etc.

3. Prepara un bosquejo *(outline)* usando las categorías que creaste.

## IV. Perspectivas: Trabajos vía Internet

### ■ Antes de leer

**A. Para conversar** ¿Cómo puede uno encontrar un empleo? Hagan una lista de las maneras en las que una persona puede informarse acerca de oportunidades laborales. De la lista que prepararon, ¿cuál creen que es la manera más efectiva? Expliquen por qué.

> MODELO    La radio, la televisión...
> *Creemos que la radio es más efectiva porque...*

**B. Vocabulario y conceptos** Escribe junto a cada palabra la letra de la definición más apropiada. (Usa el diccionario si es necesario.)

   <u>c</u> 1. la búsqueda
   <u>f</u> 2. la solicitud
   <u>a</u> 3. odioso(a)
   <u>b</u> 4. hallar
   <u>d</u> 5. tentador(a)
   <u>e</u> 6. la Red

a. que molesta, que no es agradable
b. encontrar, descubrir
c. proceso para encontrar algo
d. muy atractivo(a)
e. espacio cibernético que contiene mucha información
f. un documento con información personal que enviamos cuando queremos un empleo

### ■ A leer

Dale una lectura rápida al texto y contesta las preguntas.

### Encontrar trabajo vía cibernética, una alternativa poco explorada

Jay Dougherty DPA / *El Universal*

**Caracas** ¿Busca usted un nuevo empleo o quiere cambiar de carrera?

Para la generación cibernética de hoy, el **hurgar** en los **avisos** de la prensa y enviar solicitudes de trabajo por correo es una odiosa tarea que **pertenece** al pasado.

*to dig*
*ads*

*belongs*

Quien quiera tener hoy éxito en la búsqueda de un cambio en la vida **no tiene más que encender** su computadora y consultar el Internet. «Internet es la mejor forma de hallar un empleo, especialmente para aquellos que posean una cierta habilidad técnica. Hay allí buenos consejos para todos los campos de trabajo», dice Joel Oleson, especialista en Internet en Utah.

*only has to turn on*

*realize*
*to get the ball rolling*

Quienes buscan trabajo **se dan cuenta** rápidamente de que el usar el Internet es sólo el primer paso para **echar la bola a rodar.** Si tiene usted estudios y experiencia, su nombre y su currículum pasarán, sin que usted lo sepa, de mano en mano por el Internet. Y más pronto de lo que usted se imagina, tendrá más de una tentadora oferta de trabajo bajo la forma de email en su **pantalla.** En el Internet abundan las ofertas en ciertas categorías de empleos, en especial en alta tecnología, informática y computación, además de servicios, educación y **mercadeo.** Pero eso se **ampliará** tan rápido como evoluciona la «red». Aparte de los grupos de noticias Usenet, otra fuente de búsqueda de trabajo son los llamados «motores de búsqueda» de la Red, como Yahoo o InfoSeek.

*screen*

*marketing / will be expanded*

### ¿Entendiste bien?

**C. Ideas principales** Responde a las siguientes preguntas.

1. **¿Sí o no?**

   __sí__ Es relativamente fácil encontrar trabajos en el Internet.

   __sí__ La práctica tradicional de enviar solicitudes de trabajo por correo está desapareciendo.

   __sí__ En la red hay muchas oportunidades de trabajo en diferentes campos.

   __sí__ Se puede usar un motor de búsqueda como Yahoo para encontrar un trabajo.

   __no__ Los materiales que se envían por Internet son siempre privados y secretos.

2. ¿En qué campos abundan las ofertas de trabajo en el Internet?

3. Según el autor, ¿quiénes se benefician más de las ofertas de trabajo en el Internet? ¿Por qué?

**Answers C:** 2. en los campos tecnológicos, la educación, los servicios y el mercadeo 3. las personas con más habilidad técnica, porque tienen más acceso a estas tecnologías

**D. Actividad de extensión** Consulta el Internet para investigar cuáles son las oportunidades de trabajo que hay en tu campo en este momento. Presenta en clase ejemplos de los trabajos que ofrecen (dónde, cuánto dinero ofrecen, qué requisitos tienen, etc.).

# Mis antecedentes y expectativas laborales

## I. Vocabulario: La hoja de vida

**Un arquitecto** Busca la siguiente información en la hoja de vida de Juan Fernando.

1. ¿Cuál es su profesión?
2. ¿De dónde es él?
3. ¿Cuántos años tiene?
4. ¿Dónde estudió?
5. ¿Cuántos años de experiencia tiene?
6. Además de la arquitectura, ¿qué otras aptitudes tiene Juan Fernando?

---

### JUAN FERNANDO LENIS TAMAYO
a r q u i t e c t o

#### DATOS PERSONALES

**Nombre:** Juan Fernando Lenis Tamayo
**Lugar y fecha de nacimiento:** Caracas, 29 de enero de 1968
**Dirección:** Edificio Torre Las Mercedes, Avenida la Estancia, Chuao
**Teléfonos:** 993.4156 - 993.3880 Fax: 993.6289
**Correo electrónico:** jflenis@latino.net.ve
**Matrícula profesional:** 257670-2423 Caracas, Venezuela

#### ESTUDIOS REALIZADOS

**Primarios:** Colegio San Francisco de Asís, Caracas, Venezuela
**Secundarios:** Lycée Claude Bernard, París, Francia
**Universitarios:** Universidad Central de Venezuela, Caracas Facultad de Arquitectura y Urbanismo
**Fecha de grado:** 12 de septiembre de 2000

#### EXPERIENCIA LABORAL

**R.B.M. ARQUITECTOS (Jorge Rueda Borda y Esteban Morales Díaz)**
**Octubre a diciembre de 2000:** Participación en el concurso para el diseño de la Policlínica Metropolitana

**MELÉNDEZ-MELÉNDEZ ARQUITECTOS LTDA. (Isaías Meléndez e hijos) Enero a diciembre de 2001:** Diseño de edificio multifamiliar de 53 apartamentos en Sabana Grande, Caracas (6000 m2)

**L.T.S. ARQUITECTOS LTDA. (Felipe Serpa-Gutiérrez y Juan Fernando Lenis Tamayo) Febrero de 2002 a la actualidad:** Diseño, dirección arquitectónica y promoción de 17 proyectos en las ciudades de Valencia y Caracas

#### IDIOMAS Y OTROS

**Idiomas:** español, inglés, francés
**Programas de computación:** Autocard 13, Office 98, Windows, Corel Draw

**Marzo de 2006**

---

## Vocabulario práctico

la carta de presentación *cover letter*
los datos personales *personal information*
la entrevista *interview*
los estudios realizados *studies completed*
la experiencia laboral *work experience*
la fecha de grado *graduation date*
la matrícula/licencia profesional *professional license*
solicitar trabajo *to apply for a job*
la solicitud *application*

## ■ Asimilación

**8-22 Todo en orden** Ana está preparando su hoja de vida. ¿Dónde debe escribir la siguiente información? Para cada punto, indica la letra de la categoría a la que corresponde.

___d___ 1. inglés e italiano
___a___ 2. Valencia, 2 de mayo de 1978
___c___ 3. Orquesta Filarmónica Nacional
___b___ 4. Universidad Central de Venezuela, Escuela de Artes
___a___ 5. Ana Mercedes López Vallejo

a. datos personales
b. estudios realizados
c. experiencia laboral
d. idiomas y otros

**Script 8-23:** Me llamo Efraín Meneses Gómez. Nací el 15 de febrero de 1975 en Maracay, Estado de Aragua. Soy egresado de la Facultad de Derecho de la Universidad Católica Andrés Bello de Caracas. Hace dos años que trabajo en la firma Domínguez-Serna Asociados, en Maracay. Hablo inglés y un poco de francés.

CD2–17  **8-23 Efraín Meneses Gómez** Completa las oraciones con la información que vas a escuchar.

1. Datos personales: Nació el _____ en _____.
2. Estudios realizados:
3. Experiencia laboral:
4. Idiomas y otros:

### ESTRATEGIAS PARA LA COMPRENSIÓN

**Note-taking** If you are unable to understand a word, write it down the way it sounds and continue listening. Later you can compare notes with a classmate.

**Answers 8-23:** 15 de febrero de 1975 en Maracay; Facultad de Derecho de la Universidad Católica Andrés Bello de Caracas; dos años en la firma Domínguez-Serna Asociados; habla inglés y un poco de francés

## ◾ Aplicaciones

**8-24 Preguntas y respuestas** Preparen las preguntas que hay que hacer para averiguar los siguientes datos.

---

### DATOS PERSONALES

Nombre: *¿Cómo se llama Ud.?*
Lugar y fecha de nacimiento: _____
Domicilio: _____
Teléfonos: _____
Correo electrónico: _____

### ESTUDIOS

Primarios: _____
Secundarios: _____
Universitarios: _____
Fecha de grado: _____

### OTROS ANTECEDENTES

Experiencia laboral: _____
Idiomas: _____
Programas de computación: _____

---

**REMEMBER**

The formal **usted** is commonly used for business transactions.

**REMEMBER**

**¿Cuál...?** asks for a specific fact: **¿Cuál es la dirección? La dirección es calle Minerva No 23.**

**¿Qué...?** asks for a definition: **¿Qué es la dirección? La dirección es el lugar exacto donde vives.**

**8-25 Entrevista** Completa la hoja de vida de tu compañero(a) usando las preguntas que preparaste en el ejercicio anterior.

After students finish this activity, have each student save his/her own résumé. Later in the chapter students will be refining their résumés and writing job letters.

---

### DATOS PERSONALES

Nombre: _____
Lugar y fecha de nacimiento: _____
Domicilio: _____
Teléfonos: _____
Correo electrónico: _____

### ESTUDIOS REALIZADOS

Primarios: _____
Secundarios: _____
Universitarios: _____
Fecha de grado: _____

### EXPERIENCIA LABORAL

_____
_____

### IDIOMAS Y OTROS

Idiomas: _____
Programas de computación: _____

---

**8-26 Una carta de presentación** Pongan en orden las siguientes oraciones para formar la carta de presentación.

   2    Me dirijo a Uds. para solicitar un puesto como abogado en su firma.

   3    Terminé mis estudios de leyes en 1995 y me gradué con honores.

   9    Atentamente,

   5    Como pueden comprobar por mis referencias, me caracterizo por ser dedicado y creativo.

   7    Puedo hacer una contribución importante a su compañía.

   1    Estimados señores:

   4    Desde entonces, he trabajado en dos de las principales oficinas de abogados de esta ciudad.

   8    Sírvanse comunicarse conmigo en caso de que deseen más información.

   6    Me adapto muy bien a cualquier situación y trabajo bien en equipo.

## ■ Integración

**8-27 Una entrevista de trabajo** Representa la siguiente situación con un(a) compañero(a).

| **Jefe(a) de personal** *(Human Resources Manager / Personnel Director)* | **Aspirante** |
|---|---|
| Tu compañía está buscando un(a) candidato(a) para ocupar un puesto muy importante. Entrevista al / a la siguiente candidato(a) para saber si es la persona adecuada.<br>■ Averigua sus datos personales.<br>■ Averigua sus antecedentes académicos y laborales.<br>■ Trata de determinar algunas de sus cualidades personales. | Tú deseas un trabajo en esta compañía. Responde a las preguntas del / de la jefe(a) de personal acerca de tus datos personales, así como tus antecedentes académicos y laborales. Recuerda que sus preguntas también van dirigidas a *(are intended to)* determinar tus cualidades personales. ¡Trata de dar una buena impresión! |

**8-28 Mi solicitud de empleo** Prepara tu hoja de vida y una carta de presentación para solicitar un empleo.

1. Saca la hoja de vida que preparaste con tu compañero(a) al principio de este tema (página 321).
2. Repasa la lista de cualidades laborales y elabora un poco más la sección de «experiencia laboral».
3. Saca el bosquejo de la carta que preparaste en el **Tema 1.**
4. Elabora el bosquejo para escribir un primer borrador *(draft)*.

# II. Funciones y estructuras: Influencing others with formal commands

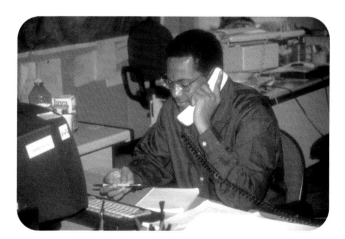

—Imprenta Robles, buenos días.

—Quisiera solicitar trabajo en la imprenta. ¿Qué debo hacer?

—**Venga** a nuestras oficinas y **llene** una solicitud. Si lo desea, **envíe** su currículum por fax.

—Muchas gracias. Voy a ir en persona.

One of the ways to get others to do what we want them to do is by using direct commands like *Come in, Don't call again!*, and *Please, sit down.* When giving direct commands to others in Spanish you must keep in mind the distinction between formal and informal commands. Formal commands are those you would give to people you would refer to as **usted** whereas informal commands are those you would give to people you would refer to as **tú.** The plural form of the **usted** command, however, may be used in both formal and informal contexts.

To give an *affirmative* command, (1) drop the **-o** from the **yo** form of the present tense and (2) add **-e/-en** if the verb is an **-ar** verb and **-a/-an** if it is an **-er** or **-ir** verb.

Students will learn about informal commands in **Capítulo 10, Tema 1.**

**REMEMBER**

Use **tú** with relatives, friends and people your age or younger. Use **usted** with people who are older than you or whom you do not know.

| VERB | llenar | leer | venir |
|---|---|---|---|
| **yo** present tense form | lleno | leo | vengo |
| (1) | llen- | le- | veng- |
| (2) | llene (Ud.) | lea (Ud.) | venga (Ud.) |
|  | llenen (Uds.) | lean (Uds.) | vengan (Uds.) |

Sra. Asencio, **traiga** su licencia profesional, por favor.

Señores, **esperen** su turno.

*Mrs. Asencio, please **bring** your professional license.*

*Gentlemen, **wait** for your turn.*

To make a *negative* command simply place **no** before the verb.

Por favor, **no entren** todavía.

Doña Luisa, **no firme** ese formulario.

*Please, **do not enter** yet.*

*Mrs. Luisa, **do not sign** that form.*

In some contexts, using these command forms may be considered rude by the interlocutor, especially if this person is an authority figure with more status than the speaker. To soften the imperative, make sure to add the expression **por favor.**

Verbs that end in **-car, -gar,** and **-zar** in their infinitive form have a spelling change in order to maintain the pronunciation of the letters **c, g,** and **z.**

| -car: c → qu | -gar: g → gu | -zar: z → c |
|---|---|---|
| bus**car** | pa**gar** | empe**zar** (ie) |
| bus**que** (Ud.) | pa**gue** (Ud.) | empie**ce** (Ud.) |
| bus**quen** (Uds.) | pa**guen** (Uds.) | empie**cen** (Uds.) |

The verbs **dar, ir, saber,** and **ser** have irregular formal command forms.

| dar | ir | saber | ser |
|---|---|---|---|
| dé (Ud.) | vaya (Ud.) | sepa (Ud.) | sea (Ud.) |
| den (Uds.) | vayan (Uds.) | sepan (Uds.) | sean (Uds.) |

## ■ Asimilación

**8-29 ¿Apropiado o inapropiado?** Indica si consideras apropiado o inapropiado decirle las siguientes cosas a tu profesor(a). Escribe los números de las oraciones en la categoría correcta. Cuando termines, compara las respuestas con las de un(a) compañero(a). ¿Piensan de la misma forma?

Por favor,...

1. explique eso otra vez.
2. venga a clase en bañador.
3. no dé clase hoy.
4. salga del salón durante el examen.
5. repita esta palabra.
6. lea nuestro periódico en Internet.
7. devuelva las tareas a tiempo.
8. diga qué significa esa frase.
9. no hable español.
10. acepte los trabajos dos semanas después.

Mandatos apropiados:
   1, 5, 6, 8

Mandatos inapropiados:
   2, 3, 4, 7, 9, 10

CD2-18 **8-30 Dos anuncios** Primero, familiarízate con los siguientes anuncios. Luego, escucha las oraciones e indica si se asocian con el anuncio A o con el anuncio B.

**No más papel...**

IC Recorder ICD-30
(tamaño actual)

**Digitalice sus ideas**

**SONY**®

**Ahorre tiempo y aproveche su viaje.**

**OAG**

E-mail: oaglatam@oag.com • Internet: www.oag.com

**Anuncio A**                              **Anuncio B**

1. __B__   2. __A__   3. __A__   4. __A__   5. __B__   6. __B__

## ■ Aplicaciones

**8-31 En una agencia de empleo** Imaginen que trabajan en una agencia de empleo y que les dan consejos a las personas que se presentan. Seleccionen un verbo lógico para formar una oración que le podrían decir a un cliente. Escríbanlo en la forma de mandato formal singular.

MODELO    (presentar / mover / comprar) su matrícula profesional
          *Presente su matrícula profesional.*

1. (leer / incluir / llamar) la fecha de grado en la solicitud   Incluya
2. (salir / poner / llegar) temprano a la entrevista   Llegue
3. (escuchar / dirigir / escribir) sus datos personales aquí   Escriba
4. (mostrar / sacar / saber) evidencia de su experiencia laboral   Muestre
5. (dar / tener / comenzar) paciencia y va a conseguir trabajo   Tenga
6. (ir / solicitar / contribuir) a la oficina número tres, por favor   Vaya
7. (practicar / viajar / entretener) antes de la entrevista   Practique
8. (alcanzar / buscar / contra) una solicitud en la próxima ventanilla   Busque

**8-32 Consejos y reacciones** Escriban un mandato afirmativo lógico y un mandato negativo lógico para cada situación. Usen verbos diferentes. ¡Sean creativos!

| SITUACIÓN | MANDATO AFIRMATIVO | MANDATO NEGATIVO |
|---|---|---|
| 1 | | |
| 2 | | |
| 3 | | |

1. La Sra. Echevarría siempre gasta mucho dinero cuando va de compras y nunca paga las cuentas a tiempo. Si continúa, su crédito se va a afectar.
2. Daniel y Berta no son muy dedicados. Salen todas las noches y no hacen las tareas de sus clases. Es posible que fracasen en todas sus clases este semestre.
3. Los Beltrán no son muy buenos vecinos. Llegan muy tarde a la casa y hacen demasiado ruido. Además, tiran la basura frente a la casa, tienen un perro muy agresivo y no mantienen su propiedad en buenas condiciones.

**8-33 Entre compañeros** Escriban una lista de cinco mandatos para el (la) profesor(a) y cinco mandatos para dos estudiantes de la clase. Cuando les toque su turno, léanlos. ¡El (La) profesor(a) y sus dos compañeros de clase tienen que hacer lo que Uds. les digan!

MODELOS  *Profesor(a), diga la fecha de su cumpleaños.*
*Joe y Kate, corran por el salón de clase.*

### ▦ Integración

**8-34 Falta de comunicación** Imaginen que Uds. son los padres o hermanos mayores de cinco niños muy activos. Esta noche van a salir al teatro y los van a dejar con un(a) niñero(a). Díganles a los niños las cosas que quieren que hagan y que no hagan. ¡OJO! Uds. tienen opiniones diferentes sobre cómo criar a sus hijos o hermanos y se contradicen constantemente.

**8-35 Con el (la) Rector(a)** *(president)* **de la universidad** Imagina que el (la) rector(a) de tu universidad te ha pedido que trabajes como su asesor(a) personal. Él/Ella quiere saber qué cosas te gustan y no te gustan de su administración. Prepara una lista de las cosas que le vas a decir en una reunión la próxima semana. Incluye mandatos formales afirmativos y negativos. Dale una copia a tu profesor(a) para que te dé su opinión.

## III. Funciones y estructuras: Using pronouns and formal commands

### Conéctese a
# INTERNET

**La conexión sin límite.**

En INTERNET vía **InfoMundo** usted encontrará:

- Velocidad hasta 56 K.
- Consumo sin límite por el mismo cargo fijo mensual.
- Contratos a un año prorrogables.
- Centro de Atención al Cliente permanente.
- Capacitación en centros especializados sin costo adicional.
- Software de navegación incluido en el costo inicial.

Conéctese vía InfoMundo a un mundo sin fronteras... INTERNET.

### Otra solución InfoMundo.

Ahora vía InfoMundo y por un reducido cargo fijo mensual, conéctese a INTERNET 24 horas al día... SIN LÍMITE DE TIEMPO.

### CONÉCTESE YA

---

# Grábese esta marca de memoria.

Así sea un apellido que usted necesite recordar o un plan completo de negocios que requiera almacenar, IML le ofrece una gran selección de medios de almacenamiento de memoria de absoluta confiabilidad. Contamos con diskettes de doble, alta y extra densidad en colores vibrantes, formateados en IBM y APPLE y sin formatear. Datacartridges, mini-cartridges, cartuchos de 4mm. y 8mm, Disco MO (Magnet Optical), CD-R y CD-Rom, para que usted escoja de acuerdo a su necesidad. Por eso, grábese esta marca de memoria: IML

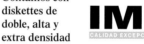

**IML** CALIDAD EXCEPCIONAL

---

Do you notice anything different in the command forms of the verbs at the top of these ads? If you said that they have pronouns attached to them, you are correct! In fact, reflexive, direct object, and indirect object pronouns are attached to the affirmative command form of the verb.

| | |
|---|---|
| REFLEXIVE: | Cálme**se**, Sra. Vega. *(Calm down, Mrs. Vega.)* |
| | Páren**se**, señores. *(Stand up, gentlemen.)* |
| DIRECT OBJECT: | Tráiga**la**, por favor. *(Bring **it**, please.)* |
| | Póngan**los** ahí. *(Put **them** there.)* |
| INDIRECT OBJECT: | Díga**le** que no puedo. *(Tell **him** that I can't.)* |
| | Den**me** las cartas. *(Give **me** the letters.)* |

Notice that you must place an accent mark on the vowel with the stress when you use affirmative commands with pronouns and there are more than two syllables.

In the case of negative commands, the pronouns are placed between **no** and the verb.

| | |
|---|---|
| REFLEXIVE: | No **se** preocupe. *(Do not worry.)* |
| | No **se** pongan ansiosos. *(Do not get anxious.)* |
| DIRECT OBJECT: | No **las** entregue. *(Do not hand **them** in.)* |
| | No **lo** compren. *(Do not buy **it**.)* |
| INDIRECT OBJECT: | ¡No **me** diga! *(You're kidding [me]!)* |
| | ¡No **me** mientan! *(Don't lie to **me**!)* |

## Asimilación

**8-36 ¿Qué dice... ?** Para contestar las siguientes preguntas, selecciona la alternativa más lógica. Al terminar, compara tus respuestas con las de un(a) compañero(a). ¿Están de acuerdo?

¿Qué dice...

_c_ 1. un profesor?      _d_ 4. una abogada?

_f_ 2. un mesero?       _b_ 5. un arquitecto?

_a_ 3. una recepcionista?   _e_ 6. una ama de casa?

a. Siéntense, por favor. El doctor los va a atender enseguida *(soon)*.
b. Consígame los planos del edificio de la avenida Bolívar.
c. ¿Las composiciones? Escríbanlas en la computadora.
d. ¡Váyase de mi oficina! ¡Yo no defiendo a criminales!
e. ¿Los paquetes? Pónganlos sobre la mesa del comedor. Gracias.
f. Llévales las bebidas a los señores de la mesa diez.

Script 8-37: 1. ¿Escribo mi nombre completo en la solicitud? 2. ¿Le traigo flores el día de su cumpleaños? 3. ¿La invito a almorzar hoy, señorita? 4. ¿Mando dos referencias personales? 5. ¿Me visto bien para la entrevista? 6. ¿Incluyo la matrícula profesional en el expediente?

CD2–19 **8-37 ¿Sí o no?** Es un día como todos en la agencia de empleos donde trabajas. A ésta vienen personas muy simpáticas, pero también personas muy imprudentes. Responde de manera lógica a las preguntas que vas a escuchar.

1. a. Sí, escríbalo.          b. No, no lo escriba.
2. a. Sí, tráigame flores.     b. No, no me traiga flores.
3. a. Sí, invíteme.           b. No, no me invite.
4. a. Sí, mándelas.           b. No, no las mande.
5. a. Sí, vístase bien.        b. No, no se vista bien.
6. a. Sí, inclúyala.          b. No, no la incluya.

## Aplicaciones

Answers 8-38: *Answers may vary*: 1. No se siente en el escritorio del entrevistador. Siéntese... 2. Inclúyala con la solicitud. 3. Vístase bien para la entrevista. 4. No los dé. Dé datos ciertos. 5. No las diga. / No le diga mentiras. Diga la verdad. / Dígale la verdad. 6. No lo saque durante la entrevista. (Saque... / Déjelo en el bolso.) 7. No los ponga en la carta de presentación. Póngalos en la hoja de vida. 8. No se vaya sin decir «gracias». / decirlo. (Váyase después de decir «gracias» / Dígalo.)

**8-38 Recomendaciones** Usen la siguiente información para escribir una serie de recomendaciones para una persona que está buscando trabajo. Si dicen que **no** a algo, den una alternativa. Usen pronombres en sus respuestas.

MODELO    no escribir la fecha de nacimiento en la carta de presentación
*No la escriba en la carta de presentación. Escríbala en la hoja de vida.*

1. no sentarse en el escritorio del entrevistador
2. incluir una carta de recomendación con la solicitud
3. vestirse bien para la entrevista
4. no dar datos falsos sobre la experiencia laboral
5. no decir mentiras al entrevistador
6. no sacar el maquillaje durante la entrevista
7. no poner los datos personales en la carta de presentación
8. no irse sin decir «gracias» luego de la entrevista

**8-39 ¿Qué hago con... ?** Túrnense para hacer y responder a las preguntas usando las claves.

MODELO  las cartas / no mandar / corregir
E1: *¿Qué hago con las cartas?*
E2: *No las mande. Corríjalas.*

1. estos documentos / organizar
2. los papeles / poner en el escritorio
3. esta hoja de vida / no archivar / dejar en la mesa
4. las computadoras / apagar
5. mis correcciones / no escribir en el margen / escribir en otro papel
6. estos libros / llevar a la sala de reuniones
7. las fotocopias / no distribuir / contar
8. mi almuerzo / meter en el refrigerador

**8-40 Antes de una entrevista** Escriban una lista de recomendaciones sobre lo que las personas deben hacer y no deben hacer antes y durante una entrevista de trabajo. Usen los verbos de la lista.

MODELO  levantarse:  *No se levanten tarde. / Levántense temprano.*

OPCIONES:  bañarse  ponerse perfume  desayunarse  peinarse maquillarse  llegar...  saludar  despedirse  conversar estar...  ponerse ropa...  irse...  ponerse (adjetivo)

## ■ Integración

**8-41 Conseguir un buen empleo** Representa la siguiente situación con dos compañeros(as).

**Consejero(a) estudiantil**

Tú eres consejero(a) estudiantil y estás hablando con dos estudiantes que quieren saber qué deben hacer y qué no deben hacer para asegurarse de conseguir un buen empleo cuando se gradúen. Escúchalos(las) y dales las recomendaciones pertinentes.

**Estudiantes preocupados(as)**

Tu amigo(a) y tú están preocupados(as) y están hablando con un(a) consejero(a) estudiantil. Uds. quieren saber qué deben hacer y qué no deben hacer para conseguir un buen empleo cuando se gradúen de la universidad. Explíquenle su preocupación y pídanle un consejo.

**8-42 Un volante** *(flier)* Como quedaste tan satisfecho(a) después de hablar con el (la) consejero(a) de la actividad 8-41, decidiste preparar un volante informativo para los estudiantes de tu universidad. Incluye las cosas que los estudiantes deben hacer y no deben hacer para conseguir un buen trabajo después de graduarse. Cuando termines, dale una copia a un(a) compañero(a) para que te dé su opinión.

## IV. Vídeo: El secreto de Sofía

### ■ Preparación

**A. ¡Secretos, secretos!** Sofía tiene un secreto que está a punto de ser revelado. Antes de ver el vídeo, piensen en lo que ya saben de Sofía (qué tipo de persona es, qué le interesa, etc.) y completen las oraciones.

■ Creemos que el secreto de Sofía es que ella...

■ Es posible que ése sea su secreto porque...

Ahora, presenten su opinión a la clase. Un(a) voluntario(a) debe escribir las ideas de cada grupo en la pizarra. ¡Veamos si algún grupo adivinó correctamente el secreto de Sofía!

### ■ ¿Entendiste bien?

**ESTRATEGIA DE COMPRENSIÓN**

*Scanning* Concentrate on identifying the information requested in **Paso 1** of activity B.

Activity B, Paso 1: Play the first part of the video segment (approximate duration: 2:50), stopping the CD after Sofia says, "No. Yo sé que no va a ser fácil. Pero eso es lo que quiero hacer, ¡y lo voy a intentar!"

**B. Sofía revela su secreto** Esta actividad se divide en dos pasos. Primero vas a contestar algunas preguntas específicas sobre lo que pasa en el segmento. Luego vas a adivinar y a seguir viendo el segmento para averiguar si tenías razón o no.

**Paso 1:** Lee las siguientes preguntas y luego mira el vídeo para poder contestarlas.

1. Al principio Sofía le mintió a Javier sobre lo que leía en el periódico. Le dijo que...
   a. leía su horóscopo.
   b. leía los resultados de la lotería.
   c. leía los anuncios.

2. ¿Qué hacía Sofía *de verdad* cuando Javier la asustó?
   a. Leía su horóscopo.
   b. Leía los resultados de la lotería.
   c. Leía los anuncios.

3. Completa la siguiente información sobre el plan de Sofía:

Sofía le confesó a Javier que leía el periódico porque buscaba un
___apartamento___. Le contó su plan de quedarse a vivir en
___Puerto Rico___ después de que termine el mes del proyecto.
También le dijo que fue algo que pensó antes de venir, desde que
estaba en ___España___. Luego, Sofía reveló la razón principal
de su decisión: quiere _escribir un libro_.

4. ¿Dónde ha pensado Sofía buscar trabajo? ¿Haciendo qué? en la universidad; dando clases
de literatura o de gramática

**Paso 2:** Compara tus respuestas al **Paso 1** con las de un(a) compañero(a).
Luego, contesten las siguientes preguntas sobre el trabajo de Sofía
antes de ver la conclusión del segmento.

**Activity B, Paso 2:** After giving
students time to answer the
questions, play the final part of the
segment (approximate duration:
50 seconds).

1. ¿Creen que Sofía ha conseguido el tipo de trabajo que quería?
¿Por qué sí o no?
2. ¿Dónde creen que trabaja Sofía? ¿Por qué?
3. Basándose en su respuesta a la pregunta 2, den ejemplos de por lo
menos cinco actividades que creen que Sofía ha hecho en su trabajo.

**C. Nuestros sueños en la vida** Todos tenemos aspiraciones y sueños personales y profesionales que queremos realizar *(fulfill)*. Pueden ser cosas
fáciles o difíciles de conseguir; por ejemplo, vivir en otro país, aprender
un idioma, practicar un deporte, graduarse, conseguir un trabajo, tener
un carro y una casa propios, etc. En esta actividad vas a pensar en un
sueño tuyo y luego vas a compartirlo con tus compañeros(as) de clase.

**Paso 1: Mi sueño** ¿Cuál es tu sueño? Puede ser algo que ahora mismo
estás intentado realizar o algo que ya has realizado. Contesta las preguntas
correspondientes.

### OPCIÓN A: Un sueño que estás tratando de realizar

- ¿Le has revelado tu sueño a alguien, por ejemplo, a un(a) amigo(a)
o a un miembro de tu familia? ¿Por qué sí o por qué no? Si has
respondido que sí, ¿cómo reaccionó esa persona? ¿Te ha apoyado
*(supported)?* ¿Te ha ofrecido ayuda para alcanzar tu sueño?

- ¿Qué has hecho para realizar tu sueño? Sé específico(a). Piensa en tus
acciones y en el tiempo que ha sido necesario para realizar cada acción.

### OPCIÓN B: Un sueño que ya has realizado

- ¿Fue un secreto tu sueño o lo compartiste con un(a) amigo(a) o
miembro de tu familia? ¿Por qué?

- ¿Qué hiciste para realizar tu sueño? Sé específico(a). Piensa en cada
acción que hiciste y en el tiempo que te llevó hacer cada acción.

- ¿Cómo te sentiste al realizar tu sueño?

**Paso 2: Nuestros sueños** Trabajando en grupos, túrnense para hacerle
preguntas a cada miembro del grupo sobre su sueño.

**D. Enfoque comunitario** Un sueño común que casi todos los inmigrantes
tienen es conseguir un empleo en el país al que se han mudado. Entrevista a un(a) inmigrante que viva en tu comunidad. Pregúntale cómo
consiguió su empleo, si está contento(a) con su trabajo y con su forma de
vida, y qué actividades hace cada día. Presenta un informe oral en clase.

# El nuevo empleo

## I. Vocabulario: Las tareas de oficina

atender (ie) al público

asistir a reuniones

preparar informes

imprimir expedientes

(enviar/recibir) un fax

(hacer/recibir) llamadas telefónicas

los altavoces/parlantes

la pantalla

la página web

el teclado

el disquete

la computadora portátil

el ratón

## Vocabulario práctico

el archivo *file*

el correo electrónico *e-mail*

**Verbos**

abrir un programa *to open a program*

cerrar [ie] / abandonar un programa *to close / to quit a program*

consultar un motor de búsqueda *to use a search engine*

encender [ie] / apagar la computadora *to turn on / to turn off the computer*

enviar un mensaje electrónico *to send an e-mail*

guardar un documento *to save a document*

hacer clic / oprimir / cliquear *to click*

imprimir un documento *to print a document*

insertar el disco *to insert the CD*

instalar un programa *to install a program*

navegar el (la) Internet *to surf the net*

revisar el buzón/correo *to check the mailbox*

## ■ Asimilación

**8-43 ¿En qué orden?** Indica el orden lógico de las siguientes actividades. Al terminar, compara tus respuestas con las de un(a) compañero(a). ¿Están de acuerdo?

___6___ apagar la computadora     ___4___ imprimir el documento deseado

___1___ encender la computadora     ___3___ consultar un motor de búsqueda

___2___ abrir el programa de navegación     ___5___ cerrar el programa de navegación

2-20 **8-44 Instrucciones** Tu jefe ha tenido problemas con su vuelo y te ha dejado un mensaje en el contestador. Indica qué cosas debes hacer, según sus indicaciones.

_____ Atender a unos clientes     __X__ Preparar un informe

__X__ Asistir a una reunión     _____ Imprimir un informe

__X__ Buscar unos documentos     __X__ Enviar un fax

**Script 8-44:** Le habla el Dr. Rojas. Estoy todavía en el aeropuerto de Medellín y me temo que no voy a poder volar hoy a Bogotá debido al mal tiempo. Por favor, busque los documentos para la reunión de vendedores en el archivo de mi oficina y asista a la reunión a las tres de la tarde en la sala de reuniones. Después prepare un informe sobre los resultados de la reunión. Ah, y envíeme una copia por fax aquí al Hotel Intercontinental cuanto antes. El teléfono es 541-2234. Gracias.

## ■ Aplicaciones

**8-45 Tareas** Completa el párrafo con la palabra más apropiada.

**OPCIONES:**    hacer unas llamadas    imprimir    preparar un informe asistir

Tengo mucho que hacer hoy. Primero tengo que ___preparar un informe___ para presentarlo esta tarde en la reunión de inversionistas y luego tengo que ___imprimir___ quince copias para todos los asistentes. Al mediodía tengo que ___asistir___ a un almuerzo de negocios con mi jefe y en la tarde debo ___hacer unas llamadas___ a varios clientes en la capital. Va a ser un día muy largo.

**8-46 Experiencia** Ustedes trabajan en una compañía multinacional y necesitan un(a) nuevo(a) secretario(a). Preparen por lo menos cinco preguntas para evaluar la experiencia de los aspirantes.

> MODELO   *¿Ha preparado Ud. un informe alguna vez? ¿Ha enviado un fax?*

This activity serves as preparation for the **Integración** task 8-48 below.

### EN TU COMUNIDAD

You may wish to interview several people who have recently changed careers to find out about the things that motivated them to do so. In addition, try to find out if the interviewees are happy with the career change and if they foresee a positive professional future. In class, use the information you gathered to discuss trends in your community.

**8-47 Entrevista** Hazle las siguientes preguntas a un(a) compañero(a) y prepara un breve informe sobre sus respuestas.

1. ¿Te interesan las computadoras?
2. ¿Qué tipo de computadora tienes?
3. ¿Con qué frecuencia la usas? ¿Para qué la usas?
4. ¿Cuáles son tus programas favoritos? (¿Procesador de textos? ¿Procesador de datos? ¿Navegador? ¿Otros?)
5. En tu opinión, ¿qué es lo mejor de las computadoras? ¿Y lo peor?

### ■ Integración

**8-48 Entrevista de trabajo** Representa la siguiente situación con un(a) compañero(a).

| Entrevistador(a) | Aspirante |
|---|---|
| Usted trabaja para una compañía multinacional y tiene que contratar a un(a) asistente de oficina. Esta persona debe poder hablar español y tiene que ser capaz de desempeñar diferentes tareas de oficina (como hacer y recibir llamadas, preparar informes, usar la computadora, etc.). Entreviste a este(a) aspirante y determine si debe ser contratado(a) para ese puesto. | Usted necesita un trabajo y sabe que esta compañía multinacional busca un(a) asistente de oficina. Convenza al / a la entrevistador(a) de que Ud. puede desempeñar muy bien las diferentes tareas que se requieren (hacer y recibir llamadas, preparar informes, usar la computadora, etc.). |

### SUGERENCIAS

Usen las preguntas de las actividades 8-46 y 8-47 como guía.

**8-49 Carta de presentación** Amplía la carta de presentación que preparaste en el **Tema 2** de este capítulo para incluir tus habilidades con respecto a tareas de oficina y computación.

## II. Funciones y estructuras: Avoiding stating who or what is performing an action with the passive *se*

Para buscar información en el Internet, **se enciende** la computadora, **se consulta** un motor de búsqueda y **se escriben** las palabras clave.

In Spanish, when you do not want to (or cannot) specify who or what is performing an action, you may use a passive **se** construction. This construction consists of the pronoun **se** followed by the third-person form of the verb. It translates as *is/are + -ed* or as a generic *they* in English.

<table>
<tr><td>Aquí se contesta el teléfono rápidamente.</td><td>Here the phone is answered quickly. (they answer the phone quickly)</td></tr>
<tr><td>Y se preparan informes diariamente.</td><td>And reports are prepared daily. (they prepare reports daily)</td></tr>
</table>

This *they* is considered generic because it does not refer to anybody or anything in particular, as in the sentence: *On TV **they** said that it is going to rain tomorrow.*

As you may have noticed, the number of the verb (singular or plural) is determined by the number of the noun that follows, which is actually the subject of the sentence.

| **se** + | { verb in the third person singular | + | singular noun } |
|---|---|---|---|
| | { verb in the third person plural | + | plural noun } |

The passive **se** is often used to talk about activities that are performed on a regular basis and activities that are associated with specific places.

<table>
<tr><td>En Japón se fabrican muchas computadoras.</td><td>In Japan they make a lot of computers.</td></tr>
<tr><td>En esta tienda se vende lo mejor en tecnología.</td><td>In this store they sell the best in technology.</td></tr>
</table>

Here is a list of expressions with **se.**

| | |
|---|---|
| se incluye(n)... | . . . *is/are included* |
| se necesita(n)... | . . . *is/are necessary* |
| se recomienda(n)... | . . . *is/are recommended* |
| se require(n)... | . . . *is/are required* |
| se vende(n)... | . . . *is/are sold* |

The verbs in these expressions are used in the third-person singular when they are followed by an infinitive: **Se recomienda leer las instrucciones.** *(Reading the instructions is recommended.)*

■ **Asimilación**

**8-50 ¿Qué se hace?** Usa números para poner en orden las oraciones de cada grupo. Cuando termines, compara tus respuestas con las de un(a) compañero(a). ¿Están de acuerdo?

1. Para guardar un documento...
   - _1_ se selecciona «guardar» del menú
   - _3_ se oprime «guardar»
   - _2_ se da un nombre al documento

2. Para enviar un mensaje electrónico...
   - _3_ se oprime «enviar»
   - _2_ se escribe el mensaje
   - _1_ se entra al buzón personal

3. Para imprimir un documento...
   - _2_ se especifican las páginas que se van a imprimir
   - _1_ se selecciona «imprimir» del menú
   - _3_ se oprime «imprimir»

**Script 8-51:** No me gusta CD2–21 mucho mi trabajo. El sueldo es bueno, pero se hace demasiado. Por ejemplo, temprano en la mañana se reciben las llamadas y se envían las cartas de las citas. Luego, antes del mediodía, se archiva la información importante, se asiste a reuniones y, si hay tiempo, se organizan las oficinas. Por la tarde se hace mucho más porque es cuando el público viene y hay que atenderlo. Además se imprimen los documentos para el día siguiente y se hace el mantenimiento de las computadoras. ¡Es agotador!

**8-51 En el nuevo empleo** Escucha la descripción que da Pablo de su nuevo empleo y escribe cada actividad en la categoría correcta.

**OPCIONES:** imprimir los documentos    enviar las cartas
archivar la información    organizar las oficinas
asistir a reuniones    atender al público    recibir las llamadas
hacer el mantenimiento de las computadoras

| Temprano en la mañana | Antes del mediodía | Por la tarde |
|---|---|---|
| recibir llamadas, enviar las cartas | archivar la información, asistir a reuniones, organizar las oficinas | atender al público, imprimir los documentos, hacer el mantenimiento de las computadoras |

■ **Aplicaciones**

**8-52 En diferentes lugares** Digan qué se hace en los siguientes lugares.

**MODELO**    En una biblioteca _se leen libros y revistas, y se estudia._

1. En un restaurante...
2. En una iglesia...
3. En una oficina de correos...
4. En una plaza...
5. En la clase de español...
6. En una tienda de ropa...
7. En un museo...
8. En un aeropuerto...

**8-53 Productos internacionales** Indiquen qué se produce o se fabrica en los siguientes países.

MODELO    Alemania: *En Alemania se fabrican carros de muy buena calidad.*

1. Venezuela    3. Italia      5. Francia      7. Chile
2. Rusia        4. Holanda     6. Sudáfrica    8. Estados Unidos

SUGERENCIAS

Pueden buscar información en el Internet antes de hacer esta actividad.

**8-54 En casa**

**Paso 1:** Escribe por lo menos tres actividades que se hacen en tu casa en los siguientes días.

| Los sábados | Los domingos | Los miércoles |
| --- | --- | --- |
|  |  |  |

**Paso 2:** Compara tu información con la de dos compañeros y prepara un informe breve.

MODELO    *En nuestras casas se... y se... los sábados. En la casa de... también se..., pero en mi casa se... los... y en la casa de... se... los...*

### ■ Integración

**8-55 ¡Por fin!** ¡Tu compañero(a) y tú ya saben todo lo que hay que saber para obtener un buen empleo! Hagan un recuento *(summary)* de todos los pasos que se deben seguir. Incorporen el vocabulario de este capítulo e indiquen qué se recomienda, qué se necesita y qué se requiere.

SUGERENCIAS

Utilicen las frases conectoras que ya conocen: **primero, segundo, tercero, además/ también, por otro lado, por ejemplo** y **finalmente/por fin.**

**8-56 Ahora, ¡por escrito!** Haz un repaso escrito de la información que tu compañero(a) y tú mencionaron en la actividad 8-55. Al terminar, dale una copia a tu compañero(a) para que te dé ideas. Organiza tu repaso siguiendo el siguiente esquema:

- En una carta de presentación se incluye(n):
- En una hoja de vida se incluye(n):
- Para obtener un buen empleo se requiere(n):
- Para obtener un buen empleo se recomienda(n):

## III. Funciones y estructuras: Avoiding repetition using double object pronouns

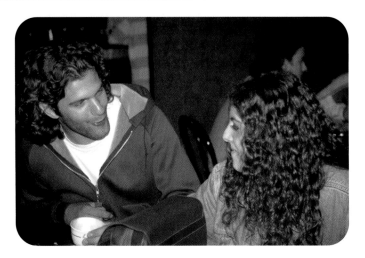

> MANOLO: ¡Coral, felicidades por el nuevo empleo!
> CORAL: ¡Gracias! **Me lo** ofrecieron el lunes.
> MANOLO: Me alegro. Voy a decír**selo** a Felipe.

**REMEMBER**

Think of the mnemonic **I-D** (**I** = indirect, **D** = direct).

When both direct and indirect object pronouns are used in a sentence, the indirect object pronoun always precedes the direct object pronoun. No other word may break the unity of these two pronouns.

| | |
|---|---|
| ¿La computadora? **Te la** voy a encender ahora mismo. | *The computer? I am going to turn **it** on **for you** right now.* |
| ¿El documento? Guárda**melo,** por favor. | *The document? Save **it for me,** please.* |

When the indirect object pronouns **le** and **les** are used before the direct object pronouns **lo, la, los** or **las,** the indirect object pronoun changes to **se.** Remember that a phrase introduced by the preposition **a** can be used to specify the referent of **se.**

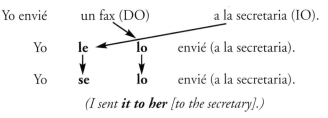

Yo envié     un fax (DO)          a la secretaria (IO).

Yo   **le** ← **lo**   envié (a la secretaria).

Yo   **se**   **lo**   envié (a la secretaria).

*(I sent **it to her** [to the secretary].)*

Indirect and direct object pronouns are placed:

- before conjugated verbs (but after negative words like **no** and **nunca**):

  **Me lo** <u>contaron</u> ayer.   *They told (**it to**) **me** yesterday.*
  **Se las** <u>quiero</u> comprar a ella. *I want to buy **them for her.***
  ¿Ellos nunca **te la** <u>entregaron</u>? *They never delivered **it to you**?*

- attached to infinitives and past participles in verb phrases:

  Vamos a <u>arreglár</u>**telo**  *We are going to fix **it for you***
   mañana.       *tomorrow.*
  Están <u>preparándo</u>**melas**  *They are preparing **them for***
   ahora.        *me now.*

- attached to affirmative commands:

  Sra. López, <u>dé</u>**melos,** por  *Mrs. López, give **them to me**,*
   favor.        *please.*
  Chicos, <u>póngan</u>**selo** ahí.  *Guys, put **it** there **for him.***

- between **no** and the verb in negative commands:

  <u>No</u> **me la** <u>expliques</u> todavía. *Do not explain **it to me** yet.*
  Señores, <u>no</u> **se lo** <u>instalen</u> *Gentlemen, do not install **it for***
   hoy.         *him today.*

### Asimilación

**8-57 Publicidad** ¿Puedes encontrar el verbo con pronombre de objeto indirecto y objeto directo en el anuncio? ¿A qué se refieren estos pronombres? Contesta estas preguntas y compara tus respuestas con las de un(a) compañero(a). ¿Han respondido lo mismo?

Answers 8-57: The verb is **se lo quita** (se = Ud., lo = el fuego de la acidez).

Script 8-58: 1. ¿Qué va a hacer Nelda con los papeles? 2. ¿Cuándo le vas a traer la impresora a Beto? 3. ¿Qué quieres hacer con el disquete? 4. ¿Qué están haciendo ustedes con las solicitudes? 5. ¿Le envío los mensajes al licenciado Pastrana?

CD2–22  **8-58 Preguntas y respuestas** Escucha las preguntas y selecciona las respuestas más lógicas.

1. (a.) Te los va a archivar.
   b. Me la va a archivar.
2. a. Voy a traértela hoy.
   (b.) Voy a traérsela hoy.
3. a. Quiero devolvérsela.
   (b.) Quiero devolvérselo.
4. (a.) Estamos organizándotelas.
   b. Estamos organizándoselo.
5. (a.) No se los envíes todavía.
   b. No me los envíes todavía.

■ **Aplicaciones**

Answers 8-59: 1. ...Sí, la Sra. Padró se las devolvió. 2. ...Sí, el contable me los dio. 3. ...Sí, Lola se la entregó. 4. ...Sí, se lo instalé. 5. ...Sí, Pedro te los guardó (en la computadora). 6. ...Sí, Rosa y yo se los enviamos. 7. ...Sí, Saúl se los atendió. 8. ...Sí, el mensajero me las llevó (a la oficina de correos).

**8-59 Ayer en la oficina** Ayer ocurrieron cosas que normalmente no ocurren en la oficina. Uno(a) de Uds. faltó al trabajo *(took the day off)* y el (la) otro(a) lo está poniendo al día *(giving you an update)*. Túrnense para ser la persona que faltó.

MODELO    E1: *Gabriela nos trajo el desayuno a todos los empleados.*
          E2: *¿Qué?*
          E1: *Sí, Gabriela nos lo trajo.*

1. La Sra. Padró les devolvió las evaluaciones a las secretarias.
2. El contable me dio los informes.
3. Lola le entregó su renuncia al director.
4. Le instalé el monitor nuevo a mi compañero.
5. Pedro te guardó los documentos en la computadora.
6. Rosa y yo le enviamos los faxes a Esteban.
7. Saúl le atendió los clientes al Sr. García.
8. El mensajero me llevó las cartas a la oficina de correos.

**8-60 Hoy en la oficina** Ahora, túrnense para hacer y responder preguntas sobre las personas que se están encargando de hacer diferentes actividades en este momento en la oficina. Miren el dibujo y usen los verbos de la lista.

MODELO    E1: *¿Y las copias del Sr. Feliciano?*
           E2: *José se las está haciendo. / José está sacándoselas.*

OPCIONES:   preparar  hacer  dar  instalar  buscar  enviar

1. ¿Y el informe de la Sra. Salazar?
2. ¿Y el monitor de Leonor y Beatriz?
3. ¿Y la computadora de Eulalia?
4. ¿Y los expedientes del Lic. Balboa?
5. ¿Y el fax del Lic. Guzmán y del Lic. Rubio?

**Answers 8-60:** 1. Sonia se lo está preparando. / Sonia está preparándoselo. 2. Pepe se lo está dando. / Pepe está dándoselo. 3. Mercedes se la está instalando. / Mercedes está instalándosela. 4. Sergio se los está buscando. / Sergio está buscándoselos. 5. Doña Inés se lo está enviando. / Doña Inés está enviándoselo.

**8-61 Mañana en la oficina** Tu compañero(a) y tú son muy organizados y quieren saber exactamente qué deben hacer mañana en la oficina. Túrnense para hacer y responder a preguntas usando las claves.

> MODELO   E1: *¿Qué hago con estos sobres?* (mandar / a Héctor)
> E2: *Mándeselos a Héctor.*

1. ¿Qué hago con esta impresora? (dejar / a mí / ahí)
2. ¿Y con estas solicitudes? (<u>no</u> llevar / al Sr. Rodríguez – llevar / a la Srta. Ochoteco)
3. ¿Qué hago con el informe del personal? (<u>no</u> imprimir / a mí – guardar en la computadora / a mí)
4. ¿Y qué hago con los mensajes del Sr. Torres? (revisar / a él)
5. ¿Y el programa nuevo? (instalar / a nosostros)
6. ¿Qué hago con los discos? (<u>no</u> sacar de aquí / a mí – poner en el escritorio / a Ángel)

### ■ Integración

**8-62 Pertenencias** *(Belongings)* Individualmente, hagan una lista de los cinco objetos más preciados *(most valued)* que tienen y otra lista de cinco cosas que tienen y de las que quieren deshacerse *(want to give away)*. Cuando terminen, intercambien papeles. Luego, túrnense para hacer y responder a preguntas sobre quién les dio las cosas más preciadas y a quién les van a dar las cosas de las que se quieren deshacer.

> MODELOS   E1: *Los aretes de oro, ¿te los dio/regaló tu madre?*
> E2: *No, me los dio/regaló mi abuelo.*
> E1: *La mesa de noche, ¿se la vas a dar a tu hermana menor?*
> E2: *No, voy a dársela a mi prima.*

 **8-63 Carta de presentación** En parejas, revisen las cartas de presentación que han venido preparando en este capítulo. ¿Necesitan usar pronombres para evitar repeticiones innecesarias? Identifiquen las frases que se pueden mejorar y hagan las debidas correcciones en casa. Entréguenle una copia al / a la profesor(a) en la próxima clase.

# IV. Lectura: «Mi amigo»

## ■ Antes de leer

**A. Para conversar** Contesten las siguientes preguntas.

1. ¿Qué es una «disculpa» o una «excusa»?
2. ¿En qué circunstancias se usan las disculpas? Indiquen las más apropiadas.

   ____ cuando no se quiere hacer algo

   ____ cuando no se puede hacer algo

   ____ cuando se tienen otros compromisos (obligaciones)

   ____ otras circunstancias: _____

3. ¿Consideran que las excusas o disculpas son buenas o malas? Expliquen por qué.

**B. Vocabulario y conceptos** Las siguientes palabras son importantes para la comprensión de la lectura. Para cada palabra, indiquen la letra de la definición apropiada.

| | | |
|---|---|---|
| _e_ 1. obstáculo | a. cosas útiles o indispensables |
| _d_ 2. interferencias | b. pagar, sostener |
| _c_ 3. faltar | c. no tener, necesitar |
| _a_ 4. necesidades | d. problemas, intromisiones |
| _b_ 5. mantener | e. impedimento, dificultad |

## ■ A leer

### Germán Cuervo

Germán Cuervo es un pintor y cuentista nacido en Cali, Colombia, en 1950. Es autor de varios libros de cuentos y novelas, entre ellos *Los indios que mató John Wayne* (1985), *Historias de amor, salsa y dolor* (1990) y *El mar* (1994).

### «Mi amigo»

Mi amigo quería ser escritor, pero no podía hacerlo porque no tenía máquina de escribir. Al fin consiguió una. Aún así, no pudo comenzar, pues le hacía falta una habitación privada. **Al cabo de** dos días pudo saltar ese obstáculo, pero en aquella nueva habitación había mucho ruido e interferencias. Fue **preciso**, entonces, **conseguir** una casa. **Tomando prestado** de aquí y allá, con ayuda de su familia, mi amigo pudo conseguir una casa solitaria y **retirada** para poder comenzar su trabajo de escritura.

*after*

*necesario / to find*
*Borrowing*

*distant*

Al cabo de un tiempo me lo encontré en la calle muy deprimido y le pregunté qué le pasaba. «Ya tengo máquina de escribir, un cuarto y una casa —me dijo— sin embargo, no puedo hacerlo. Algo muy importante me hace falta para poder escribir; me hace falta una mujer. Necesito compañía». **Dicho y hecho,** mi amigo se puso en aquel **empeño** y **a la vuelta** de los días tenía una mujer cálida y buena que lo acompañaba en su difícil trabajo de la escritura. Ahora solamente le faltaba ponerse a hacerlo; sin embargo, no lo hizo, pues si ya tenía máquina, cuarto, casa retirada y mujer, le hacía falta, **por añadidura lógica,** un auto. Se puso entonces en ese empeño consiguiendo un trabajo que le **devengaba** el dinero suficiente para mantener esa cadena de necesidades. La última vez que lo encontré le pregunté si estaba escribiendo.

«No —me contestó—. Si ya tengo máquina de escribir, cuarto, casa, mujer, carro y trabajo, para qué me voy a poner a escribir. Ahora estoy viendo cómo conseguir un betamax».

*Said and done*
*endeavor / at the end of, after*

*after all*
*daba*

■ **¿Entendiste bien?**

**C. ¿En qué orden sucedieron los hechos?** Ordenen los siguientes eventos de la historia.

<u> 5 </u>   Su amigo consiguió un auto.

<u> 6 </u>   Su amigo consiguió un trabajo.

<u> 4 </u>   Su amigo consiguió una esposa.

<u> 3 </u>   Su amigo consiguió una casa tranquila.

<u> 1 </u>   Su amigo consiguió una máquina de escribir.

<u> 2 </u>   Su amigo consiguió una habitación privada.

**D. Para conversar** ¿Por qué creen Uds. que este hombre nunca pudo ser escritor?

*Encourage discussion and debate of possible reasons (fear, lack of talent, lack of resources, lack of guidance, lack of training, etc.).*

**E. Enfoque lingüístico** Clasifiquen los verbos que se usan en la lectura.

| Pretérito (narración de eventos pasados) | Imperfecto (descripciones, acciones habituales en el pasado) |
|---|---|
| consiguió, pudo, fue, encontré, pregunté, se puso, hizo, contestó | quería, podía, tenía, hacía (falta), había, pasaba, acompañaba |

**REMEMBER**

• The preterite tense is used to narrate completed past events.

• The imperfect tense is used to provide background descriptions and to talk about habitual or ongoing actions in the past.

**F. Enfoque comunitario** Entrevisten a algún (alguna) artista o profesional de habla hispana acerca de qué obstáculos encontró mientras estaba comenzando a practicar su arte o profesión. Pregúntenle cómo superó *(overcame)* esos obstáculos. Después, presenten una breve biografía de esa persona a la clase.

## Los anuncios clasificados — *Classified ads*

la buena presencia — *good personal appearance*

la facilidad de expresión — *ease of expression, ability to speak*

la hoja de vida / el currículum — *résumé*

el técnico — *technician*

el trabajador no calificado — *unqualified worker*

## Verbos para hablar de buscar trabajo

arreglar/reparar — *to fix*

colaborar — *to collaborate*

cuidar — *to care for, to watch over*

defender (ie) — *to defend*

encargarse de + *verb* — *to be responsible for doing something*

entretener (ie) — *to entertain*

manejar — *to operate, to handle*

presentarse — *to present oneself, to appear*

solicitar — *to request*

## La hoja de vida — *Résumé*

la carta de presentación — *cover letter*

los datos personales — *personal information*

la entrevista — *interview*

los estudios realizados — *studies completed*

la experiencia laboral — *work experience*

la fecha de grado — *graduation date*

la matrícula/licencia profesional — *professional license*

solicitar trabajo — *to apply for a job*

la solicitud — *application*

## Las tareas de oficina — *Office duties*

atender (ie) al público — *to deal with customers*

asistir a reuniones — *to attend meetings*

preparar informes — *to prepare reports*

imprimir expedientes — *to print files*

enviar/recibir un fax — *to send/receive a fax*

hacer/recibir llamadas telefónicas — *to make/receive phone calls*

## Las computadoras/ los ordenadores — *Computers*

el archivo — *file*

el CD — *CD-ROM*

la computadora portátil — *laptop computer*

el correo electrónico — *e-mail*

la impresora — *printer*

la pantalla — *screen*

los parlantes/altavoces — *speakers*

el ratón — *mouse*

el teclado — *keyboard*

## Verbos para hablar de las computadoras

abrir un programa — *to open a program*

cerrar (ie) / abandonar un programa — *to close / to quit a program*

consultar un motor de búsqueda — *to use a search engine*

encender (ie) / apagar la computadora — *to turn on / to turn off the computer*

enviar un mensaje electrónico — *to send an e-mail*

guardar un documento — *to save a document*

hacer clic/oprimir/ cliquear — *to click*

imprimir un documento — *to print a document*

insertar el disco — *to insert the CD*

instalar un programa — *to install a program*

navegar el (la) Internet — *to surf the net*

revisar el buzón — *to check the mailbox*

## Funciones y estructuras

Expresiones de tiempo que se usan con el pretérito perfecto, pp. 313

Expresiones con **se,** p. 327

# Puesta en acción

| **SITUACIÓN:** | La empresa multinacional para la que trabajas te ha anunciado que tiene planes de trasladarte a Caracas, Venezuela, para abrir una nueva oficina regional. |
| --- | --- |
| **MISIÓN:** | Coordinar la mudanza, organizar tu nueva casa y establecer la nueva oficina regional de tu compañía en Venezuela. |
| **DESTREZAS:** | Planificar un viaje internacional de negocios, ir a una entrevista y escribir una carta y un mensaje electrónico de negocios. |

## 1. La mudanza

**A. La mudanza a Venezuela** Lee el siguiente mensaje electrónico y luego contesta las preguntas.

| Enviar | Direcciones | Archivos adjuntos | Ver. ortografía | Guardar | Cancelar |

| Para | John Smith |
| De | Miguel Fernández, gerente general |
| Fecha | 15 de agosto de 2006 |

**Asunto:** Traslado   **Prioridad:** Normal

Normal   12

La presente es para informarle que Ud. ha sido escogido para encargarse de la nueva oficina regional de esta compañía en la ciudad de Caracas, Venezuela. Haga todos los arreglos pertinentes para estar en Sudamérica el 1º del mes entrante. Diríjase a nuestra división financiera para coordinar el pago de su mudanza.

¡Buena suerte!

- ¿Qué te dice el gerente general de la compañía?
- ¿Cuándo comienza la nueva asignación?
- ¿Quién va a pagar la mudanza?

**B. ¿Qué tengo que hacer?** Preparen una lista de los preparativos que necesitan hacer para el viaje.

*Prioritizing* Determine essential elements for successful planning.

| Llamar a... | Ir a... | Obtener... |
| --- | --- | --- |
|  |  |  |

**C. En la agencia de viajes** Representa la siguiente situación con un(a) compañero(a).

| **Empleado(a) trasladado(a)** | **Agente de viajes** |
| --- | --- |
| Tu compañía te va a trasladar a Caracas, Venezuela, y necesitas hacer los preparativos para el viaje. Habla con tu agente de viajes para hacer los arreglos necesarios. | Uno(a) de tus clientes ha sido trasladado(a) a Caracas, Venezuela, por su compañía. Ayúdale a hacer los arreglos correspondientes. Tu cliente necesita: |
| ■ compra los boletos de avión, | ■ boletos de avión, |
| ■ haz las reservaciones en un buen hotel de Caracas y | ■ reservaciones en un buen hotel e |
| ■ pide información general sobre Venezuela, tal como: lugares para visitar, cosas que hay que saber, el clima, la ropa que se debe llevar, etc. | ■ información general sobre Venezuela. |

**D. Dinero** Ahora, completa esta carta para concretar los aspectos financieros de tu traslado. Escribe **por** o **para**.

Miami, 20 de agosto de 2006

Señores:
Banco Central de Venezuela

Me mudo ____para____ Venezuela el mes entrante y necesito saber qué debo hacer ____para____ transferir mi dinero electrónicamente desde mi banco en los Estados Unidos. ____Para____ mí es muy importante tener acceso fácil e inmediato a mi dinero. Además, ____por____ favor, díganme qué documentos exigen ____para____ abrir una cuenta corriente y qué servicios especiales tienen ____para____ sus clientes.

Muchísimas gracias ____por____ su gentil ayuda.

Atentamente,

_____

**E. En busca de una casa** Ahora, escribe una carta a la inmobiliaria Sabana Grande en Caracas con una descripción de tu casa ideal. (Usa la carta anterior como guía.) Asegúrate de incluir la siguiente información:

- ubicación
- número de habitaciones
- tipo de vecindario
- precio

## 2. La organización de la nueva oficina regional

**F. Prioridades** Lo primero que necesitas es un(a) asistente. Escribe el anuncio clasificado correspondiente. (Usa los anuncios clasificados de la actividad de **Asimilación 8.1,** pág. 307, como modelo.)

**G. Datos sobre los aspirantes** Túrnense para hacer y responder a preguntas sobre la información de los aspirantes al puesto de asistente.

**SUGERENCIAS**

Pueden hacer preguntas como las siguientes:
**¿Cómo se llama la persona que... ?**
**¿Qué estudió la persona que... ?**
**¿Cuántos años de experiencia tiene... ?**
**¿Qué ha hecho... ?**
**¿Qué es lo que le gusta del puesto a... ?**

**Estudiante 1**

| Nombre | Especialidad | Años de experiencia | Datos sobresalientes | Lo que le gusta del puesto |
|---|---|---|---|---|
| Celia Mercado | | 8 | | |
| | finanzas | | | el prestigio de la compañía |
| | | 12 | ha trabajado para la compañía | |
| Sonia Useche | ciencias secretariales | | ha terminado sus estudios de postgrado | la oportunidad de ascender |
| Julio Beltrán | | 3 | | |

**H. Entrevista de trabajo** Representa la siguiente situación con un(a) compañero(a).

| Jefe(a) | Aspirante |
|---|---|
| Vas a entrevistar a uno(a) de los aspirantes al puesto de asistente. Por medio de preguntas, determina si ésta es la persona con quien quieres trabajar. Averigua: <br>■ sus antecedentes académicos <br>■ sus antecedentes laborales <br>■ algunas de sus características personales | Tienes la gran oportunidad de trabajar en una compañía multinacional. Asegúrate de dar una buena impresión durante la entrevista. Habla de: <br>■ los estudios que has hecho <br>■ las experiencias laborales que has tenido <br>■ tus cualidades personales más sobresalientes |

**Estudiante 2**

| Nombre | Especialidad | Años de experiencia | Datos sobresalientes | Lo que le gusta del puesto |
|---|---|---|---|---|
| | administración de empresas | | ha vivido en el extranjero | la flexibilidad del horario |
| Arturo Mejías | | 10 | ha estudiado tres lenguas | |
| Demetrio Salas | economía | | | la oportunidad de quedarse en Venezuela |
| | | 2 | | |
| | relaciones públicas | | ha recibido premios por su trabajo | trabajar para esta compañía |

**Estudiante 2** must turn the book upside down.

**I. Instrucciones** Completen el siguiente mensaje electrónico con las tareas que debe hacer el (la) asistente el día de hoy.

a. Conversa con un(a) compañero(a) sobre las tareas más importantes que debe realizar este(a) asistente el primer día de trabajo.
b. Organiza las actividades en orden de prioridad.
c. Escribe los mandatos correspondientes.
d. Prepara un saludo y una despedida apropiados para este tipo de comunicación electrónica.

**CRITICAL THINKING SKILLS**

*Prioritizing* List the most important tasks a manager's new assistant might have to do.

## CORRECCIONES

Intercambia este primer borrador con otro(a) estudiante y respondan a las siguientes preguntas:

**Paso 1: Contenido.** ¿La carta incluye toda la información necesaria? Si no es así, ¿qué falta?

**Paso 2: Organización.** ¿Están claras las tareas y las prioridades? ¿El mensaje tiene un saludo y una despedida?

**Paso 3: Gramática.** ¿Los mandatos formales están bien formados?

**Para hacer en casa:**

**Paso 4: Revisión.** Revisa tu carta y entrégasela a tu profesor(a) el día de la próxima clase.

## Servicio comunitario

Contact your local school district and offer to provide one of the following services:

- Buddy system for students who recently moved to your area.
- Basic computer courses for students and their parents.
- Workshops on how to prepare a résumé and a cover letter for youngsters who wish to get a part-time or summer job.

| Enviar | Direcciones | Archivos adjuntos | Ver. ortografía | Guardar | Cancelar |

Para
De
Fecha

**Asunto:** **Prioridad:** Normal ▼

Normal ▼    12 ▼

_____:
Las siguientes son sus tareas para el día de hoy:

1.
2.
3.
4.
...

_____

# Guatemala, Honduras, El Salvador, Argentina y Uruguay

*Interacciones*

In this unit you will talk about relationships (friendship, love, and conflict), fitness, health, and leisure. Also, you will learn to make suggestions, express emotions, and talk about hypothetical situations. The readings will explore issues pertaining to relationships and leisure time activities. In turn, the videos will show you how South American people spend their free time. At the end of the unit, you will design a personal enrichment program for workers in a Spanish-speaking corporate setting. You will also be able to connect with your community by providing services at a local community center.

# Capítulo 9

9

# Acuerdos y desacuerdos

## In this chapter you will learn . . .

- how to describe different types of personal relationships (with friends, with coworkers, with spouses, etc.)
- how to make suggestions
- how to express emotions
- how to express doubt
- how to talk about hypothetical situations
- about interpersonal relationships in the Spanish-speaking world

## Para comenzar

Escoge la descripción más apropriada para cada fotografía:

- El futuro de El Salvador Foto 3
- La tradición indígena de Guatemala Foto 1
- La producción agrícola de Honduras Foto 2

| | **TEMA 1**<br>Las amistades | **TEMA 2**<br>Relaciones laborales | **TEMA 3**<br>Relaciones de pareja |
|---|---|---|---|
| **Vocabulario** | Un buen amigo | Los compañeros y los jefes | Amor, noviazgo y matrimonio |
| **Funciones y estructuras** | Giving advice with the subjunctive (regular verbs)<br>Giving advice with the subjunctive (irregular verbs) | Expressing wishes and requests<br>Expressing emotions and feelings | Expressing doubt and denial<br>Talking about hypothetical situations with the subjunctive |
| **Lecturas y vídeo** | Perspectivas: La timidez | Vídeo: ¿Algo más que una amistad? | Lectura: La hija del caníbal |

Foto 1

Foto 2

Foto 3

Transparencies A-16: Country Profiles: Guatemala, El Salvador; A-17: Country Profiles: Honduras, Nicaragua

# Enfoque

For more info, you may want to check the **Temas** site:
**http://temas.heinle.com**

**A. ¿Qué sabes ya de Guatemala?** Antes de ver el vídeo, decide si las siguientes oraciones son ciertas **(C)** o falsas **(F).** Después, compara tus respuestas con las de un(a) compañero(a) y corrijan las oraciones falsas.

___F___ 1. Guatemala es el país más al sur de Centroamérica.  *al norte*

___C___ 2. La mayoría de los guatemaltecos son mestizos, una combinación de lo indígena y lo europeo.

___F___ 3. El 40% de la población vive en la pobreza.  *60%*

___C___ 4. En Guatemala hubo una guerra que duró 36 años. Terminó formalmente en 1996, cuando el gobierno firmó un tratado *(treaty).*

___F___ 5. La base de la economía guatemalteca es el petróleo. *la agricultura: el café y la caña de azúcar*

**B. La ciudad de Antigua** Lee las oraciones que aparecen a continuación sobre la ciudad de Antigua. Mientras ves el vídeo, marca con una **X** las oraciones que escuches. Después, compara tus respuestas con las de un(a) compañero(a).

_____ 1. Antigua se encuentra en el Valle de Pancho, a sólo 45 minutos de la actual capital.

___X___ 2. Fundada en 1543, Antigua es la capital colonial más antigua de Centroamérica.

___X___ 3. Por los frecuentes terremotos, no hay edificios altos en la ciudad.

___X___ 4. La Casa Popenoe es un buen ejemplo de las elegantes casas coloniales construidas en el siglo XVIII.

_____ 5. En las discotecas y en los bares, los guatemaltecos y los visitantes de Antigua disfrutan de un ambiente cosmopolita.

**C. Tiempo libre en Antigua** A continuación hay una lista de actividades y excursiones que se pueden hacer en la ciudad de Antigua. Cada miembro del grupo debe escoger **una** de las opciones y explicarles a los otros miembros por qué le parece interesante.

1. **Pasear en bicicleta** Recorran en bicicleta los sitios más destacados de Antigua y de sus alrededores.
2. **Conocer la arquitectura de estilo barroco** Visiten el Palacio de los Capitanes Generales, el ayuntamiento, la catedral, las iglesias y monasterios de las Capuchinas, Santa Clara y La Merced, y vean la arquitectura de la época colonial.
3. **Ver una plantación de café** Hagan un recorrido por una plantación de café, infórmense sobre el proceso de cultivo del café y vean aves, lagartijas e insectos nativos de la región.
4. **Ir de compras** Descubran las tiendas especializadas en artesanía, muñecos de cerámica de Sacatepéquez, vajillas (platos, tazas y vasos) decoradas con palabras en lengua maya, artículos de jade y trajes típicos de los pueblos indígenas.

# Las amistades

## I. Vocabulario: Un(a) buen(a) amigo(a)...

**Se preocupa** por ti. Te **escucha** cuando tienes algún problema y te **da consejos** cuando los necesitas.

Es **leal.** Sabes que puedes contar con él porque siempre está dispuesto a **apoyarte.**

Es **honesta.** Siempre te dice la verdad y hasta te **corrige** si estás errada.

**Comparte** contigo los buenos y los malos momentos.

Te **acepta** tal y como eres y te **quiere** incondicionalmente.

### Vocabulario práctico

**Adjetivos**

confiable *trustworthy*
generoso *generous*
honesto *honest*
leal *loyal*
paciente *patient*

**Verbos**

aceptar *to accept*
apoyar *to support*
compartir *to share*

contar (ue) con *to count on*
corregir (i, i) *to correct*
dar consejos *to give advice*
estar dispuesto a... *to be ready (eager) to . . .*
fallar *to fail (not be there)*
juzgar *to judge*
preocuparse por *to worry about*
querer/amar *to love*

## ■ Asimilación

**9-1 ¿Eres un(a) buen(a) amigo(a)?** Toma la prueba y determina si cumples con los criterios para ser un(a) buen(a) amigo(a). Compara tus respuestas con las de algunos de tus compañeros. ¿Quién obtuvo el mayor puntaje?

_____ ¿Te preocupas mucho por tus amigos?

_____ ¿Eres leal?

_____ ¿Estás siempre dispuesto(a) a escuchar sus problemas?

_____ ¿Los corriges si están cometiendo algún error?

_____ ¿Los apoyas siempre en sus proyectos?

_____ ¿Compartes con ellos los buenos y los malos momentos?

_____ ¿Les das consejos cuando los necesitan?

_____ ¿Tratas de no fallarles nunca?

_____ ¿Eres paciente con ellos?

_____ ¿Los quieres incondicionalmente?

---

### Tabulación

**Entre 8 y 10 respuestas afirmativas**

¡Felicitaciones! Eres un(a) amigo(a) ideal.

**Entre 5 y 7 respuestas afirmativas**

Aunque a veces fallas, eres un(a) buen(a) amigo(a). Trata de corregir tus áreas débiles.

**Entre 0 y 4 respuestas afirmativas**

Tienes que hacer un gran esfuerzo por mejorar. Un(a) buen(a) amigo(a) es un tesoro que debemos apreciar y cultivar.

---

**9-2 Su mejor amiga** Vas a escuchar un párrafo acerca de una persona importante en la vida de la narradora. Anota su nombre y por lo menos **cuatro** razones por las que la narradora la considera su mejor amiga.

Nombre de su mejor amiga:  Susan

Razones por las que la considera su mejor amiga:

1. ...   3. ...
2. ...   4. ...

## ■ Aplicaciones

**9-3 ¿Cómo es?** Cada uno(a) debe describir una de las siguientes características. El (La) compañero(a) debe escuchar con atención y adivinar de qué característica se trata. **¡OJO!** Sólo tienen dos oportunidades para adivinar.

**OPCIONES:**  confiable   generoso   honesto   leal   paciente   simpático

MODELO   E1: _Una persona que no se enoja fácilmente, que es tolerante..._
   E2: _¿Paciente?_
   E1: _¡Correcto!_

---

You may want to ask your students to react to the survey. For instance, you can ask them:

■ Are the included items adequate indicators of a good friend? (**¿Les parece que están todas las categorías necesarias en este cuestionario?**)

■ If not, which ones would you delete or include? (**Si no es así, ¿cuáles eliminarían o incluirían Uds.?**)

Script 9-2: ¿Quién es mi mejor amiga? Pues sin lugar a dudas que se trata de mi compañera Susan. Ella siempre está dispuesta a escucharme cuando tengo problemas y a darme consejos cuando los necesito. De hecho, me gusta cuando me corrige y me hace ver los errores que estoy cometiendo. Ella siempre comparte conmigo los momentos buenos y los malos, y ha sido siempre muy leal y fiel. Susan nunca me falla.

### ESTRATEGIAS PARA LA COMPRENSIÓN

**Selective Listening** Do not try to understand every word. Concentrate on recognizing familiar words and expressions related to the topic of conversation (in this case, friendship).

Answers 9-2: Razones: está dispuesta a escuchar, da consejos, la corrige, le hace ver sus errores, comparte los buenos y los malos momentos, es muy leal y fiel, nunca le falla.

**9-4 ¿Quién es tu mejor amigo(a)?** Prepara preguntas para averiguar quién es el (la) mejor amigo(a) de uno(a) de tus compañeros y por qué. Haz la entrevista, toma notas y, al terminar, cuéntale a la clase lo que averiguaste.

**SUGERENCIAS**

¿Cómo se llama tu mejor amigo(a)? ¿Por qué lo/la consideras tu mejor amigo(a)? Cuéntame alguna experiencia que haya consolidado la amistad entre ustedes.

**9-5 Todos podemos mejorar** Acabas de encontrar este artículo en una revista española. ¿Cuál de sus consejos te gustaría aplicar a tu vida?

MODELO    *De ahora en adelante* (From now on), *voy a tratar de **sonreír** un poco más.*

# CÓMO HACER AMIGOS

1. Hable con las personas que lo rodean. No hay nada más agradable que un saludo entusiasta.

2. Sonría. Se necesita mover 65 músculos para hacer mala cara y sólo 15 para sonreír.

3. Llame a las personas por su nombre. No hay música más dulce a los oídos que escuchar el propio nombre.

4. Sea amigable y cooperador. Para tener amigos hay que ser un buen amigo.

5. Sea cordial. Hable y actúe como si cada cosa que hiciera le causara un gran placer.

*to like (a person)*

6. Interésese genuinamente por los demás. Todos le pueden llegar a **caer bien,** si se esfuerza.

*moderate*

7. Sea generoso en elogiar y **parco** en criticar.

*take into account*

8. **Tome muy en cuenta** los sentimientos de los demás. Le será grandemente reconocido.

9. Tome en cuenta las opiniones de los demás. Hay tres puntos de vista en cada controversia: el suyo, el del otro y... el correcto.

10. Esté atento a prestar un servicio. Lo que más cuenta en esta vida es lo que hacemos por los demás.

## Integración

**9-6 Cómo hacer amigos** Representa la siguiente situación con un(a) compañero(a).

---

**Una persona muy popular**

Tú eres una persona muy popular en esta universidad y tienes muchos amigos. Tu compañero(a), sin embargo, es nuevo(a) y no conoce a nadie. Contesta sus preguntas y ofrécele algunos consejos prácticos *(tips)*.

---

**El (La) solitario(a)**

Eres nuevo(a) en esta universidad y todavía no tienes muchos amigos. Tu compañero(a), por el contrario, es una persona muy popular y quiere darte algunos consejos para hacer amigos aquí.

Pregúntale...

- qué debes y qué no debes hacer para hacer nuevos amigos en esta universidad
- a qué lugares debes ir y
- en qué actividades debes participar para conocer a más personas.

---

**REMEMBER**

To give formal commands, you drop the **-o** from the **yo** form of the present tense and add **-e/-en** for **-ar** verbs and **-a/-an** for **-er** and **-ir** verbs.

**MODELO** estudiar

**Estudie** sus lecciones con tiempo.
No **estudie** a último momento.

---

**9-7 ¿Cómo hacer amigos en los Estados Unidos?** Imagínense que son consejeros de estudiantes extranjeros. En parejas, preparen un documento con sugerencias prácticas sobre cómo hacer amigos en este país.

This activity recycles formal commands. If necessary, take some time to go over and/or expand on the **Remember** student annotation.

1. Intercambien ideas (¿Qué hacer? ¿Qué no hacer? ¿Adónde ir para hacer amigos en este país? etc.).
2. Preparen una lista de actividades y luego decidan en qué orden van a presentar la información.
3. Preparen el primer borrador de su lista de sugerencias. (Recuerden usar los mandatos formales.)
4. Traigan el primer borrador de su composición a la próxima clase para hacer las revisiones necesarias.
5. Revisen su composición y entréguensela a su profesor(a) para que les sugiera más correcciones.

---

**Correcciones**

Intercambien composiciones y comenten los siguientes aspectos.

**Paso 1: Contenido.** ¿Tiene toda la información necesaria? ¿Qué falta? ¿Qué sobra? *(What is not necessary?)*

**Paso 2: Organización.** ¿La presentación está organizada de una manera lógica? ¿Qué cambios son necesarios?

**Paso 3: Gramática.** Subraya los mandatos formales y asegúrate de que estén correctamente conjugados.

---

## II. Funciones y estructuras: Giving advice with the subjunctive (regular verbs)

ESTELA: Hola, doña Tere. Soy Estela.

DOÑA TERE: ¿Qué te pasa, Estela? ¿Por qué estás llorando?

ESTELA: Tuve una discusión muy fuerte con mi amiga Penélope y...

DOÑA TERE: Mira, es importante que **tomes** las cosas con calma. Todas las relaciones tienen sus altibajos *(ups and downs)*. Te recomiendo que la **invites** a un café y que **hables** con ella. Ya verás que todo se resuelve. ¡Anímate, mujer!

ESTELA: Bueno... No sé si vaya a resultar bien, pero lo voy a intentar.

Up until now, all the verb tenses you have studied belong to the indicative mode. Generally speaking, the indicative mode is associated with objectivity. However, there is another mode that is associated with subjectivity: the subjunctive mode. For instance, in the above conversation, the verbs in bold refer to doña Tere's personal opinion about what Estela should do to solve the problem she has with her friend Penélope. These verbs are used in the subjunctive mode because doña Tere has a subjective perspective about what should be done.

The subjunctive is used in sentences with a main clause and a subordinate clause (with more than one subject). Consider the following examples (the subjects are underlined):

MAIN CLAUSE | SUBORDINATE CLAUSE

<u>Jorge</u> recomienda      que (<u>nosotros</u>) **apoyemos** a Lila.
*<u>Jorge</u> recommends*      *(that) we **support** Lila.*

Es necesario      que (<u>tú</u>) **estés** dispuesta a cambiar.
*It is necessary*      *for <u>you</u> to **be** willing to change.*

One of the uses of the subjunctive mode is to give advice. Here is a list of verbs and impersonal expressions used for this purpose.

When there is only one subject or when the statement applies to the speaker, the verb in the subordinate clause is used in the infinitive.

Students will learn more about this use of the infinitive in **Capítulo 10.**

Although the use of *that* is optional in English, the use of **que** is obligatory in Spanish.

| VERBS | | IMPERSONAL EXPRESSIONS | |
|---|---|---|---|
| aconsejar | *to advise* | es aconsejable que... | *it is advisable that . . .* |
| recomendar (ie) | *to recommend* | es bueno que... | *it is good that . . .* |
| sugerir (ie, i) | *to suggest* | es importante que... | *it is important that . . .* |
| | | es justo que... | *it is fitting that . . .* |
| | | es mejor que... | *it is better that . . .* |
| | | es necesario que... | *it is necessary that . . .* |
| | | es preferible que... | *it is preferable that . . .* |
| | | es urgente que... | *it is urgent that . . .* |

The present subjunctive of regular verbs is formed by dropping the **-ar**, **-er**, or **-ir** from the infinitive and adding the following endings. Notice that **-er** and **-ir** verbs share the same set of endings and that the **yo** and **él/ella/Ud.** forms are the same.

You are already familiarized with the **él/ella/Ud.** and **ellos(as)/Uds.** forms because they are just like the command forms you learned in **Capítulo 8, Tema 2.**

| ENDINGS | -ar VERBS<br>hablar | ENDINGS | -er/-ir VERBS<br>comer | vivir |
|---------|---------|---------|---------|---------|
| e | hable | a | coma | viva |
| es | hables | as | comas | vivas |
| e | hable | a | coma | viva |
| emos | hablemos | amos | comamos | vivamos |
| éis | habléis | áis | comáis | viváis |
| en | hablen | an | coman | vivan |

## ■ Asimilación

**9-8 Relaciones amistosas sanas** *(healthy)* ¿Qué le recomendarías a una persona para mantener relaciones amistosas sanas? Escoge las alternativas más lógicas y, al terminar, compara tus respuestas con las de un(a) compañero(a). ¿Están de acuerdo acerca de cómo se debe tratar a los amigos?

1. Le recomiendo que...
   - a. respete sus opiniones.
   - b. los visite todos los días.
   - c. no los llame por teléfono.

2. Es preferible que nunca...
   - a. coman juntos en restaurantes.
   - b. hablen de sus preferencias personales.
   - c. compartan secretos de otras personas.

3. Le sugiero que...
   - a. no esté dispuesto(a) a ayudar.
   - b. no escuche a sus amigos.
   - c. no les falle cuando lo/la necesiten.

4. Es importante que...
   - a. confíe en sus amigos.
   - b. dude de la integridad de sus amigos.
   - c. trabaje con estas personas.

**9-9 ¿Típico o atípico?** Escucha los consejos que los padres le dan a un adolescente e indica si son consejos típicos (**T**) o atípicos (**A**).

1. _T_
2. _A_
3. _A_
4. _T_
5. _T_
6. _T_
7. _A_
8. _A_

**Script 9-9:** 1. Creo que es mejor que estudies antes de casarte. 2. Te aconsejo que gastes todo el dinero en ropa. 3. No te recomiendo que descanses antes de estudiar para tus exámenes. 4. Es justo que limpies tu habitación por lo menos una vez por semana. 5. Es urgente que llames para decir que vas a regresar tarde a la casa. 6. Te sugiero que desayunes todos los días. 7. No es importante que aceptes las reglas de esta casa. 8. No es necesario que respetes a tus padres.

## ■ Aplicaciones

**9-10 Una situación delicada** El siguiente diálogo es la continuación de la conversación de doña Tere y Estela. Completen las oraciones con la forma correcta de los verbos de la lista para saber qué ocurrió. **¡OJO!** Hay un verbo adicional.

**OPCIONES:** comprender   insistir   arreglar   aceptar   participar   tratar

> DOÑA TERE: ¡No digas eso, Estela! Si quieres mantener la amistad con Penélope, es muy importante que ___insistas___ en verla. Te aconsejo que ___arregles___ esta situación antes de que sea tarde.
>
> ESTELA: Eso es lo que quiero, ¡pero ella es tan terca!
>
> DOÑA TERE: Pues es necesario que cada una ___comprenda___ el punto de vista de la otra y que las dos ___traten___ de buscar una solución. ¡Son muchos años de amistad!
>
> ESTELA: Es cierto... ¿Y Ud. cree que es posible que ella ___acepte___ mi invitación para hablar?
>
> DOÑA TERE: No sé, pero sólo hay una forma de saberlo. ¡Llámala ahora mismo!
>
> ESTELA: Está bien. La voy a llamar. Hasta luego y gracias, doña Tere.
>
> DOÑA TERE: Buena suerte. Hablamos luego.

**9-11 ¿Qué aconseja el (la) profesor(a)?** Hagan una lista de algunas de las cosas que su profesor(a) les aconseja para salir bien en la clase de español. Pueden usar los verbos de la lista.

**OPCIONES:** estudiar   leer   viajar   tratar de   comprar
hablar   asistir a

**MODELO** *El (La) profesor(a) nos aconseja que repasemos los apuntes todos los días.*

### EN TU COMUNIDAD

Try to find out what professors in other disciplines recommend to their students in order to be succesful. Present your findings and discuss them in groups.

**9-12 Lo que me gusta y lo que no me gusta**

**Paso 1:** Piensa en los consejos que otras personas te han dado recientemente. Luego, completa la tabla con los consejos que te han gustado y los que *no* te han gustado.

### SUGERENCIAS

Usa expresiones como **...me aconseja/recomienda/sugiere que...** y **...dice que es mejor/necesario/importante/... que...**

| CONSEJOS QUE TE HAN GUSTADO | CONSEJOS QUE *NO* TE HAN GUSTADO |
|---|---|
| | |

**Paso 2:** Compara tu tabla con la tabla de un(a) compañero(a). ¿Descubriste algo nuevo sobre su personalidad? Prepara un informe breve.

## ■ Integración

 **9-13 Una persona tímida** Representa la siguiente situación con un(a) compañero(a).

**SUGERENCIAS**

Para dar consejos, puedes usar estas expresiones y preguntas:

| | |
|---|---|
| **¿Me puede ayudar?** | *Can you help me?* |
| **Necesito su ayuda.** | *I need your help.* |
| **¿Qué piensa de...?** | *What do you think about . . .?* |
| **Quisiera saber su opinión con respecto a...** | *I would like to know your opinion about . . .* |

| Persona tímida | Consejero(a) |
|---|---|
| Imagínate que eres una persona muy tímida a la que se le hace muy difícil hacer amistades. Quieres ser un poco más sociable y decides visitar a tu consejero(a) para que te ayude a modificar este rasgo de tu personalidad. Descríbele tu problema y escucha su opinión profesional. | Imagínate que eres consejero(a) en esta universidad. Un(a) estudiante tiene un problema serio de timidez que le impide hacer amistades y ha decidido venir a tu oficina a buscar tu ayuda profesional. Escucha la descripción de su problema y dale tu opinión. |

**9-14 Consejo electrónico** Lee el siguiente mensaje de correo electrónico y luego escribe una respuesta con tus consejos.

**SUGERENCIAS**

Aquí tienes expresiones útiles para alentar:

| | |
|---|---|
| **¡Anímate!** | *Cheer up!* |
| **¡No te preocupes!** | *Don't worry!* |
| **¡Todo va a salir bien!** | *Everything's going to be fine!* |

**Para:** (Tu nombre)
**De:** Andrés Guzmán

Hola. ¿Cómo estás? ¿Recuerdas que estaba buscando trabajo? ¡Pues ya conseguí! Pero tengo un problema. Es que el trabajo es en los Estados Unidos y no estoy seguro de si debo aceptarlo o no. Sé que es una excelente oportunidad profesional para mí, pero aquí en El Salvador tengo a todos mis amigos y a toda mi familia. Soy una persona que se adapta fácilmente a situaciones nuevas, pero éste sería *(would be)* un cambio muy drástico. ¡No sé qué hacer! ¿Qué me recomiendas?

## III. Funciones y estructuras: Giving advice with the subjunctive (irregular verbs)

ROLANDO: Beatriz, mi hijo es un chico muy solitario. No tiene amigos en la escuela y siempre está solo. ¿Qué me recomiendas?

BEATRIZ: Bueno, pues te recomiendo que le **busques** ayuda profesional. Es importante que él **conozca** a chicos de su edad y que se **sienta** cómodo con ellos. Es mejor que **resuelvas** este pequeño problema ahora, ¿no crees?

In the previous grammar section you learned how to form the present subjunctive tense and used it to give advice. You will now learn about irregular verbs in this tense.

In general, if a verb is irregular in the **yo** form of the present indicative, it is irregular in the entire present subjunctive conjugation. To conjugate these verbs, simply drop the **-o** of the **yo** form and add the appropriate endings. Consider the following chart.

| VERB | **yo** FORM | STEM | PRESENT SUBJUNCTIVE |
|---|---|---|---|
| **conocer** | conozco | conozc- | conozca, conozcas, ... |
| **decir** | digo | dig- | diga, digas, ... |
| **hacer** | hago | hag- | haga, hagas, ... |
| **oír** | oigo | oig- | oiga, oigas, ... |
| **poner** | pongo | pong- | ponga, pongas, ... |
| **salir** | salgo | salg- | salga, salgas, ... |
| **tener** | tengo | teng- | tenga, tengas, ... |
| **traer** | traigo | traig- | traiga, traigas, ... |
| **venir** | vengo | veng- | venga, vengas, ... |
| **ver** | veo | ve- | vea, veas, ... |

Es mejor que **tengan** paciencia.    *It is better that you **have** patience.*
Ella aconseja que **digamos** todo.    *She advises us **to say** everything.*

There are two exceptions to this rule:

- **-ar** and **-er** verbs with **e→ie** and **o→ue** stem changes: the changes do not affect the **nosotros** and **vosotros** forms.

  pensar (ie): **pie**nse, **pie**nses, **pie**nse, pensemos, penséis, **pie**nsen
  poder (ue): **pue**da, **pue**das, **pue**da, podamos, podáis, **pue**dan

- **-ir** verbs with **e→i, e→ie,** and **o→ue** stem changes: they also show a change in the **nosotros** and **vosotros** forms (the same change that appears in the present participle).

  pedir (i, i): p**i**da, p**i**das, p**i**da, p**i**damos, p**i**dáis, p**i**dan

  sentir (ie, i): s**ie**nta, s**ie**ntas, s**ie**nta, s**i**ntamos, s**i**ntáis, s**ie**ntan

  dormir (ue, u): d**ue**rma, d**ue**rmas, d**ue**rma, d**u**rmamos, d**u**rmáis, d**ue**rman

Verbs that end in **-car, -gar, -guar,** and **-zar** are irregular in the present subjunctive. They undergo orthographic changes in order to maintain the sound of the letters **c, g, g + u,** and **z.** These changes affect all the forms of the verb.

| | | |
|---|---|---|
| **-car: c → qu** | tocar | to**qu**e, to**qu**es, … |
| **-gar: g → gu** | pagar | pa**gu**e, pa**gu**es, … |
| **-ger/-gir: g → j** | corregir | corri**j**a, corri**j**as, … |
| **-guar: gu → gü*** | averiguar | averi**gü**e, averi**gü**es, … |
| **-zar: z → c** | empezar | empie**c**e, empie**c**es, … |

✱The two dots over the letter **u** are called **diéresis.** They are used to indicate that this letter *does* sound, unlike in **pague, pagues,** etc.

Finally, there is a small group of verbs that show various irregularities.

| | | | |
|---|---|---|---|
| **dar** | dé, des, dé,… | **ir** | vaya, vayas, vaya,… |
| **estar** | esté, estés, esté,… | **saber** | sepa, sepas, sepa,… |
| **haber** | haya, hayas, haya,… | **ser** | sea, seas, sea,… |

### ▇ Asimilación

**9-15 A tu mejor amigo(a)** Indica si le recomiendas a una persona hacer las siguientes cosas para mantener una buena relación con su mejor amigo(a). Escribe **sí** o **no.** Al terminar, compara las respuestas con las de un(a) compañero(a). ¿Piensan igual?

  <u>no</u>  Le recomiendo que le diga mentiras.

  <u>sí</u>  Le aconsejo que sea honesto con él/ella.

  <u>no</u>  No es bueno que piense en sus sentimientos antes de hablar.

  <u>no</u>  Es importante que le dé dinero siempre.

  <u>sí</u>  Le sugiero que conozca sus gustos.

  <u>no</u>  Pienso que es necesario que su amigo sepa todo sobre Ud.

  <u>no</u>  Es preferible que le pida favores con frecuencia.

  <u>no</u>  No le recomiendo que escuchen el mismo tipo de música.

2-26 **9-16 En la oficina** Escucha las instrucciones que les da el Lic. Viera a sus empleados. Marca con una **X** las frases que escuches.

| | | | |
|---|---|---|---|
| <u>X</u> | volver a redactar una carta | ___ | tener la agenda al día |
| ___ | hacer llamadas telefónicas temprano | <u>X</u> | no ser agresivos con el Lic. Ortiz |
| <u>X</u> | buscar los documentos | ___ | entender la propuesta del Sr. Hernández |
| <u>X</u> | analizar el caso de los Roldán | <u>X</u> | entregar corregidos unos documentos |

**Script 9-16:** Asunción, le aconsejo que busque los documentos que le di ayer. Es muy importante que me los entregue corregidos esta tarde. José y Pilar, es necesario que vayan a la oficina de la Lic. González y que analicen el caso de los Roldán con ella. Ella y yo tenemos una reunión mañana. Aníbal, te sugiero que vuelvas a redactar la carta para la Sra. Suárez. Además, es aconsejable que Nelda y tú piensen en una estrategia para el caso del Sr. Hernández. Finalmente, Nelda y Milton, les recomiendo que no sean agresivos con el Lic. Ortiz. Es mejor que él crea que va a ganar el caso. Bueno, a trabajar, y que tengan un día muy productivo. Voy a estar en mi oficina.

■ **Aplicaciones**

**9-17 Situaciones** Completen las oraciones con los verbos de la lista.
**¡OJO!** Cada grupo tiene un verbo adicional.

dar   haber   hacer   ir

1. Para estar en forma, te recomiendo que ___hagas___ ejercicios tres
veces por semana. Además, te sugiero que ___vayas___ a la oficina
de un experto en nutrición para que él/ella te ___dé___ ideas
sobre cómo puedes balancear tu dieta.

empezar   pagar   utilizar   tener

2. Si quieren tener un buen crédito, les aconsejamos (a Uds.) que
___paguen___ sus cuentas a tiempo. Es muy importante que
___tengan___ cuidado cuando usan sus tarjetas de crédito. Es mejor
que las ___utilicen___ sólo en caso de emergencia.

comenzar   ver   estar   morir

3. Para sacar buenas notas en la clase de español, la profesora nos
recomienda que (nosotros) ___comencemos___ a estudiar varios días
antes de las pruebas y que ___veamos___ programas de televisión en
español. Ella también nos dice que es bueno que ___estemos___
atentos en clase.

**9-18 Le aconsejamos que...** ¿Qué les aconsejan Uds. a las siguientes
personas? Den dos consejos por persona. ¡Sean creativos!

> MODELO    al / a la profesor(a)
> *Le aconsejamos que duerma más y que empiece la clase media
> hora más tarde.*

1. al presidente de los Estados Unidos
2. a un(a) cantante famoso(a)
3. a un(a) deportista famoso(a)
4. a un(a) estudiante de la clase
5. a los estudiantes de esta universidad
6. a nadie

**9-19 Lo que debes y no debes hacer** Imagínense que todo el mundo viene para pedirles consejos porque Uds. saben de todo. Túrnense para dar un consejo afirmativo y uno negativo para cada caso. Usen diferentes expresiones como: (**Te sugiero que..., Te recomiendo que..., Es necesario que..., Es mejor que...,** etc.).

MODELO
E1: *No tengo muchos amigos.*
E2: *Te aconsejo que hables con los estudiantes de la universidad y que no te quedes en la residencia estudiantil en tu tiempo libre.*

1. Siempre estoy cansado(a).
2. No me gusta la comida de la cafetería.
3. Soy un poco tímido(a).
4. Nunca termino los trabajos a tiempo.
5. Llego tarde a mis clases todos los días.
6. Necesito ganar más dinero.
7. No sé hablar español muy bien.
8. Me encantan los países centroamericanos.

## Integración

**9-20 La 1ª (primera) opinión de los expertos** Representa la siguiente situación con un(a) compañero(a).

**Estudiante A**

Escoge uno de los siguientes temas y pídele sugerencias a tu compañero(a):

- Cómo preparar un plato que nunca has preparado.
- Cómo conseguir un buen trabajo.

Tu compañero(a) también te va a pedir sugerencias sobre un tema específico. Debes estar preparado(a) para dar tu opinión de experto(a).

**Estudiante B**

Escoge uno de los siguientes temas y pídele sugerencias a tu compañero(a):

- Cómo perder peso y mejorar la salud.
- Cómo tener una vida estudiantil exitosa *(successful)* y fructífera.

Tu compañero(a) también te va a pedir sugerencias sobre un tema específico. Debes estar preparado(a) para dar tu opinión de experto(a).

### SUGERENCIAS

Para organizar tus ideas, puedes usar las siguientes expresiones: **en primer lugar** *(first of all)*, **en segundo lugar** *(second of all)*, **además** *(also)*, **por otro lado** *(on the other hand)*, **por el contrario** *(on the contrary)*, **sin embargo** *(however)*, and **por fin** *(finally)*.

**9-21 La 2ª (segunda) opinión de los expertos** Ahora, haz un resumen de lo que sugieres para hacer las cosas que ni tu compañero(a) ni tú escogieron en la actividad 9-20. Sigue las sugerencias que se dieron para esa actividad. Cuando termines, dale una copia de tu resumen a tu profesor(a) para que te dé su opinión.

## IV. Perspectivas: La timidez

### ■ Antes de leer

**A. Para conversar** Responde a las preguntas y luego comparte tus respuestas con otros compañeros.

1. ¿En qué situaciones te pones nervioso(a)? (Indica todas las que correspondan.)

_____ cuando estoy con gente que no conozco

_____ cuando tengo que hablar en público

_____ en una cita

_____ en una entrevista de trabajo

_____ en otra(s) situación (situaciones): _____

2. ¿Qué haces cuando te pones nervioso(a)?

_____ Me pongo rojo(a) y a veces sudo *(sweat).*

_____ Trato de salir de la situación rápidamente.

_____ Otra(s) estrategia(s): _____

**B. Vocabulario y conceptos** Para cada palabra de la izquierda, escriban la letra de su definición. Consulten el diccionario si es necesario.

<u>f</u> 1. superar

<u>c</u> 2. huir

<u>a</u> 3. perder el control

<u>e</u> 4. seguridad en sí mismo

<u>b</u> 5. afrontar

<u>d</u> 6. truco

a. no tener el dominio de una situación

b. hacer frente, manejar directamente

c. escapar, evitar

d. estrategia, procedimiento ingenioso

e. confianza, no dudar de las capacidades

f. vencer, terminar

### ■ A leer

Lee el siguiente artículo sobre estrategias para superar la timidez.

### Cómo superar el miedo

Para superar cualquier tipo de ansiedad social debemos aprender lo que los expertos denominan «estrategias de exposición», que básicamente consisten en no huir a la primera ocurrencia de cambio de las situaciones que nos provocan **temor.** Los sicólogos recomiendan elaborar un plan de ataque para poner en práctica en cada una de las situaciones que nos hacen perder el control.

*fear*

*Miedo a llamar la atención.* Aprende a ser espontáneo. Para perder la rigidez, acostúmbrate a **transgredir** tus propias normas una vez a la semana. Por ejemplo, ponte ropa más **llamativa,** cambia el corte de pelo o ve al trabajo en bicicleta. Hacer pequeñas **locuras** te ayudará a sentir más seguridad en ti mismo y a perder el miedo a llamar la atención.

*to break*
*attractive*
*silly things*

*Miedo al ridículo.* Cuando la timidez **esconde** un grave problema de autoestima, conviene dejar a un lado los pensamientos negativos acerca de tus **supuestos** defectos físicos o psíquicos. Aprende a **reírte** de ti mismo.

*hides*

*assumed / to laugh*

*Temor a sentir la soledad en lugares públicos.* Acostúmbrate a salir solo una o dos veces por semana, así te obligarás a afrontar tú mismo cualquier situación que **surja,** sin **escudarte ni esconderte en acompañantes.** Actividades como ir al cine o a ver una exposición son una forma de entrenamiento para superar el miedo a enfrentarte a la gente. Una vez que hayas superado esto, puedes realizar otra serie de actividades como ir de compras, tomar café o ir a comer a un restaurante, en las que tendrás que hablar con **desconocidos,** y que te ayudarán a ver las relaciones con **extraños** con más naturalidad.

*surfaces, appears / to hide behind*
*companions*

*strangers*
*strangers*

*Quedarse en blanco.* Piensa que la mayoría de las conversaciones empiezan con temas más bien superficiales y que puedes iniciar la charla con una simple pregunta. De esta forma, llamarás la atención de la otra persona y le demostrarás que también tienes interés por hablar y dar tu opinión.

*Miedo a hablar en público.* Se denomina «miedo escénico» y un truco efectivo para **vencerlo** es ser el primero en empezar una conversación.

*to overcome it*

*Incomodidad con grupos.* Lo ideal para recuperar la simpatía de tus colegas o para introducirte en un grupo del que estás excluido es empezar centrándote en una sola persona, que te ayudará a que los demás te vean con mejores ojos.

*Eludir a los vecinos **por miedo.*** Simplemente empieza mostrándoles una sonrisa amable o sosteniéndoles la puerta del ascensor en lugar de **cerrársela en las narices.** Después, limítate a responder a lo que ellos te pregunten.

*out of fear*

*to shut it in their faces*

## ¿Entendiste bien?

ESTRATEGIA DE LECTURA

*Scanning* Look for terms that refer to social behavior and social context.

**C. Resumen** Completen el siguiente cuadro con sus propias palabras.

| Miedo a... | Estrategia para superarlo |
|---|---|
| Los grupos | Centrarse en una sola persona. |
| Los vecinos | Sonreír, ser amable, responder a sus preguntas. |
| La soledad en sitios públicos | Salir solo de vez en cuando. |
| Hablar en público | Ser el primero en empezar la conversación. |
| Llamar la atención | Ser espontáneo, ponerse ropa llamativa, hacer pequeñas locuras. |

**D. Enfoque lingüístico** Según el contexto, ¿qué creen que significan las siguientes declaraciones?

1. «Debemos aprender lo que los expertos denominan... "estrategias de exposición", que básicamente consisten en no huir **a la primera ocurrencia de cambio** de las situaciones que nos provocan temor».
   a. con dinero local
   b. rápidamente
   c. lo ideal, lo mejor

2. «Cuando la timidez esconde un grave problema de autoestima, conviene **dejar a un lado** los pensamientos negativos».
   a. abandonar, olvidar
   b. decir, explicar
   c. recordar, repetir

3. «Lo ideal... es empezar centrándote en una sola persona, que te ayudará a que los demás **te vean con mejores ojos**».
   a. poder ver bien
   b. aceptar, apreciar
   c. observar con atención

To expedite the activity, you may want to divide the class into seven groups and assign each group one of the categories in the reading.

**E. Actividad de extensión: Más estrategias para superar la timidez** ¿Qué otras estrategias se pueden usar para superar estas situaciones de timidez? Preséntenle sus recomendaciones al resto de la clase.

# Relaciones laborales

## I. Vocabulario: Los compañeros y los jefes

**ilrn**

### Vocabulario práctico

**Adjetivos**

accesible *accessible*
agresivo *aggressive*
buen(a) compañero(a) *good colleague*
competente *competent*
creativo *creative*
cumplidor *reliable, trustworthy*
eficiente *efficient*
firme *firm*
honesto *honest*
leal *loyal*
puntual *punctual*
respetuoso *respectful*
responsable *responsible*
seguro de sí mismo *confident*
trabajador *hard working*

**Sustantivos**

el buen sentido del humor *good sense of humor*

**Verbos**

amar el trabajo *to love one's work*
delegar parte del poder *to delegate power*
promover (ue) un ambiente positivo de trabajo *to promote a positive working environment*
respetar a los empleados *to respect the employees*
saber escuchar *to know how to listen*
tener metas *to have goals*
tomar riesgos/arriesgarse *to take risks*

Marta es una mujer **segura de sí misma.**

González tiene un gran **sentido del humor.**

### ■ Asimilación

**9-22 Comportamientos** Indica qué término describe mejor los siguientes comportamientos. Al terminar, compara tus respuestas con las de un(a) compañero(a).

1. Un compañero que habla fuerte y que no tiene miedo de expresar sus ideas.
   a. tímido      b. trabajador      c. seguro de sí mismo

2. Un compañero que va a la oficina todos los días, aún los fines de semana.
   a. puntual      b. trabajador      c. seguro de sí mismo

3. Un compañero que siempre está de buen ánimo y se ofrece a ayudar a los demás.
   a. agresivo      b. puntual      c. buen compañero

4. Un compañero que siempre quiere ser el número uno y que hace todo lo posible para lograrlo.
   a. que tiene metas      b. honesto      c. respetuoso

5. Un compañero que nunca llega tarde a una reunión y que siempre entrega sus informes a tiempo.
   a. agresivo      b. tímido      c. cumplidor/puntual

Nuestro jefe es muy **accesible.** Sabe escuchar.

Alicia es la mujer más **competente** que conozco.

CD2–27

**9-23 La nueva asistente de la profesora** Vas a escuchar la descripción de una asistente. Anota las **dos** características por las que obtuvo el puesto y las **tres** cualidades que reveló en los primeros tres meses de trabajo.

Nombre de la asistente:   Jennifer

Características que reveló en la entrevista:   responsable y eficiente

Cualidades en los primeros tres meses:   puntual, dinámica y trabajadora

### ■ Aplicaciones

**9-24 Necesitamos...** Imagínense que tienen que entrevistar a varios candidatos para diferentes trabajos. Indiquen las características que desean en cada caso. **¡OJO!** ¡Sólo pueden escoger **dos** características para cada ocupación!

| Para... | Necesitamos un candidato... |
| --- | --- |
| cuidar a unos niños | responsable, competente |
| manejar una empresa | |
| vender productos por teléfono | |
| diseñar materiales de multimedia | |
| organizar recepciones y fiestas | |
| hacer investigaciones científicas | |

**9-25 ¿Qué es más importante?** Clasifica las siguientes características de un buen jefe o una buena jefa en orden de importancia (1 = más importante, 6 = menos importante). Luego, compara tus respuestas con las de un(a) compañero(a). ¿Están de acuerdo?

____ saber escuchar ____ respetar a los empleados

____ ser creativo(a) ____ ser firme

____ saber delegar poder ____ amar el trabajo

**9-26 ¿Buen(a) o mal(a) compañero(a)?** Preparen cinco preguntas para determinar si alguien tiene las cualidades indicadas. Después, hagan y respondan a las preguntas que han preparado.

MODELO   ser cumplidor(a)
E1: *¿Entrega Ud. sus trabajos a tiempo?*
E2: *Desde luego. Yo soy muy cumplidor(a).*

1. tener buen sentido del humor
2. ser responsable
3. ser agresivo(a)
4. ser seguro(a) de sí mismo(a)
5. ser honesto

## ■ Integración

**9-27 En busca del candidato ideal** Representa la siguiente situación con un(a) compañero(a).

### Entrevistador(a)

Estás buscando un(a) nuevo(a) asistente para tu oficina. Es fundamental que esta persona se lleve bien con los jefes y los otros empleados.

Entrevista a este(a) aspirante y decide si es un(a) buen(a) candidato(a) para el puesto.

- Salúdalo(la).
- Averigua sus antecedentes.
- Hazle preguntas para saber cómo se relaciona con otras personas.
- Termina la conversación indicando cuándo vas a tomar una decisión.

### Candidato(a)

Necesitas un trabajo y esta compañía te ha dado una entrevista. Presenta tus antecedentes personales y demuestra que eres el (la) mejor candidato(a). **¡OJO!** Esta empresa busca una persona que se lleve muy bien con sus jefes y compañeros.

- Saluda al / a la entrevistador(a).
- Presenta tus antecedentes.
- Demuestra que te relacionas muy bien con otras personas.
- Averigua cuándo puedes saber cuál fue la decisión.

**9-28 Consejos** Tu amiga Alejandra tiene problemas en su trabajo y te ha mandado el siguiente mensaje electrónico. Respóndele con algunos consejos prácticos.

*This activity recycles the use of the subjunctive for advice.*

**Fecha:** 15 de mayo
**De:** Alejandra Macías
**Re:** Problemas

¿Cómo estás? Gracias por tu última carta y por tus consejos. Tú siempre tienes muy buenas ideas. Como te conté en mi último mensaje, empecé a trabajar como supervisora en esta compañía hace tres meses. Desafortunadamente, las cosas no andan muy bien *(not going very well)*. Tengo demasiadas responsabilidades y mucha presión. Lo peor es que los empleados no están muy contentos conmigo. ¿Qué crees que debo hacer?

## II. Funciones y estructuras: Expressing wishes and requests

Espero que el nuevo empleado **llegue** temprano hoy.
Quiero que Sonia y Elías **escuchen** bien a la Sra. Ferrer.
Prohíbo que Velázquez y Bazán **discutan** el nuevo proyecto.

Some of these verbs would be considered stronger than others. For example, the use of **insistir (en)**, **exigir, mandar,** and **prohibir** would be considered less polite and courteous and more of an expression of power.

The subjunctive mode is also used when the verb of the main clause expresses a wish or a request. Here is a list of verbs that trigger this use of the subjunctive.

| | |
|---|---|
| desear *to wish, to want* | pedir (i, i) *to ask for, to request* |
| esperar *to hope, to expect* | permitir *to allow, to permit* |
| exigir *to demand* | preferir (ie, i) *to prefer* |
| insistir (en) *to insist (on)* | prohibir *to forbid, to prohibit* |
| mandar *to order* | querer *to want* |
| necesitar *to need* | rogar (ue) *to beg* |

El jefe **quiere** que nosotros **seamos** buenos compañeros.

*The boss **wants** us **to be** good colleagues.*

También **insiste en** que yo **tenga** más sentido del humor.

*He also **insists on** me **having** a better sense of humor.*

As explained in **Tema 1,** the infinitive (and not the subjunctive mode) is used when the subjects of the verbs in both the main clause and the subordinate clause are the same. Consider these two examples.

Néstor **espera venir** hoy. (Néstor is the subject of both **esperar** and **venir.**)

Néstor **espera** que Silvia **venga** hoy. (Néstor is the subject of **esperar** and Silvia is the subject of **venir.**)

The expression **ojalá que** *(I hope)* is also used to talk about wishes. It is considered more informal and is always used with the subjunctive mode (never with an infinitive).

¡**Ojalá que** la nueva secretaria **sea** más competente!

*I hope the new secretary is more competent!*

## ■ Asimilación

**9-29 ¿Quién lo dice?** Lee las siguientes oraciones e indica si las dice un(a) jefe(a) (**J**) o un(a) empleado(a) (**E**). Cuando termines, compara tus respuestas con las de un(a) compañero(a). ¿Cuántas respuestas tienen en común?

_E_ 1. Espero que nos aumenten el sueldo.

_J_ 2. No permito que las secretarias trabajen menos de ocho horas diarias.

_J_ 3. Quiero que Rivera sea más puntual.

_J_ 4. Insisto en que la gente asuma riesgos en mi compañía.

_E_ 5. Ojalá que los supervisores sean respetuosos.

_E_ 6. Deseo que mis colegas sepan escuchar.

_J_ 7. Espero que el nuevo mensajero sea cumplidor.

_J_ 8. Exijo que en la oficina haya un ambiente de respeto mutuo.

**Answers 9-29:** *Answers may vary.*

D2-28

**9-30 ¿Qué se va a hacer hoy?** La Sra. Martínez no va a trabajar hoy y dejó un mensaje en el contestador de su secretaria. Escucha el mensaje y empareja las siguientes oraciones.

La Sra. Martínez...

_b_ 1. desea que Carlos...    a. termine el informe de gastos.

_d_ 2. quiere que Eleonora...    b. dirija la discusión sobre un proyecto.

_e_ 3. prefiere que Vidal...    c. le informe si hay problemas.

_c_ 4. pide que Claudia...    d. llame al técnico de computadoras.

_a_ 5. espera que Luis...    e. no asista a la reunión.

**Script 9-30:** Hola, Claudia. Soy la Sra. Martínez. No puedo ir al trabajo hoy porque no me siento bien, pero necesito que les des unos mensajes a ciertas personas. Quiero que Eleonora llame al técnico de computadoras. Mi impresora no funciona bien. También espero que Luis termine el informe de gastos para esta tarde. Además, deseo que Carlos dirija la discusión sobre el proyecto de mercadeo. Y prefiero que Vidal no asista a esta reunión, por favor. Finalmente, te pido que me informes si hay algún problema. Muchas gracias, Claudia. Hasta luego.

## ■ Aplicaciones

**9-31 ¡Todavía no!** Imagínense que Uds. son supervisores(as) en una compañía y están preocupados(as) porque algunos empleados todavía no han hecho ciertas cosas o no han demostrado tener ciertas cualidades. Lean las claves y escriban una reacción. Usen diferentes expresiones como: **Esperamos que..., Insistimos en que..., Preferimos que...,** etc.

> **MODELO**    Estefanía no ha archivado los contratos.
> *Esperamos que Estefanía archive los contratos.*

1. Marcos y Rebeca no han atendido bien al público últimamente.
2. Don Ángel no ha enviado el fax todavía.
3. Zelma no ha instalado el programa nuevo en nuestra computadora.
4. Juan y Rigoberto no han puesto los monitores en el sótano.
5. La Sra. López no ha sabido responder apropiadamente a las preguntas de Miguel.
6. Gustavo no es una persona segura de sí misma.
7. Los empleados de limpieza no han recogido las cajas todavía.
8. Mirna y Santiago no les han dicho todo a los auditores.

**Answers 9-31:** *Answers will vary:* 1. ...que Marcos y Rebeca atiendan bien al público. 2. ...que don Ángel envíe el fax. 3. ...que Zelma instale el programa nuevo en nuestra computadora. 4. ...que Juan y Rigoberto pongan los monitores en el sótano. 5. ...que la Sra. López sepa responder apropiadamente a las preguntas de Miguel. 6. ...que Gustavo sea una persona más segura de sí misma. 7. ...que los empleados de limpieza recojan las cajas. 8. ...que Mirna y Santiago les digan todo a los auditores.

**9-32 Profesores(as) por un día** Imagínense que su profesor(a) no puede venir a clase hoy y les pide que lo/la substituyan. Escriban por lo menos seis cosas que **esperan, quieren, prefieren,** etc. que la clase haga. ¡Sean creativos(as)!

> MODELO  *Queremos que Uds. hablen solamente en español.*
> *Esperamos que Cindy no se duerma en clase hoy.*

**9-33 Padres e hijos**

**Paso 1:** ¿Cuáles son algunas de las cosas que tus padres esperan de ti y de tus hermanos? Haz una lista de cinco cosas.

> MODELO  *Mis padres esperan que nosotros saquemos buenas notas.*

**Paso 2:** Compara tu lista con las de dos compañeros(as). ¿Qué tienen en común? Prepara un informe y compártelo con la clase.

■ **Integración**

**SUGERENCIAS**

Pueden hablar de los siguientes temas: **la política, la educación, la economía, los problemas de la vida urbana, los problemas de la vida rural, la salud, la alimentación, el trabajo, los valores** y **la amistad.**

You may ask the following questions:
**¿Qué opinas de...?**
*What is your opinion about . . .?*
**¿Qué esperas de...?**
*What do you hope/expect from . . .?*
**¿Te preocupa(n)...?**
*Are you concerned about . . .?*

**9-34 El mundo del futuro** ¿Qué esperan del mundo del futuro? ¿Qué cosas deben cambiar? ¿Qué cosas les preocupan? Saquen unos minutos para pensar en estas preguntas y respóndanlas usando diferentes expresiones como: **Ruego que..., Deseo que..., No quiero que...,** etc.

**9-35 En el trabajo** En el **Capítulo 8** tuviste la oportunidad de preparar tu hoja de vida y tu carta de presentación. ¿Has tenido la oportunidad de pensar en lo que realmente esperas de tu futuro empleo, de tu futuro jefe y de tus futuros compañeros de trabajo? Piensa en esto y escribe un breve informe. Cuando termines, dale una copia a tu profesor(a) para que te dé su opinión.

# III. Funciones y estructuras: Expressing emotion and feelings

**Diego:** **Me alegra mucho** que **quieras** continuar tus estudios, Nuria.

**Nuria:** Ay, gracias. Yo también **estoy muy contenta de** que en esta empresa nos **permitan** combinar el trabajo y los estudios.

**Antonio:** Así es. Pero **es una lástima** que no **haya** más personas que **aprovechen** esta oportunidad, ¿no?

**César:** Sí, **siento** que **sea** así, ¡pero las cosas van a cambiar! ¡Yo también voy a continuar mis estudios!

So far you have learned how to use the subjunctive mode to give advice and to talk about wishes and requests. Another use of this verb mode is to talk about emotions and feelings. Here is a list of useful verbs and impersonal expressions you can use with this purpose.

| Verbs | Impersonal expressions |
|---|---|
| agradar* *to like* | es un abuso que... *it is an abuse that . . .* |
| alegrarse (de) *to be glad* | es bueno que... *it is good that . . .* |
| doler (ue)* *to be hurt* | es curioso que... *it is odd that . . .* |
| estar contento(a) (de) *to be happy* | es extraño que... *it is strange that . . .* |
| estar furioso (de) *to be angry* | es impresionante que... *it is impressive that . . .* |
| gustar* *to be pleased* | es increíble que... *it is incredible that . . .* |
| molestar* *to be bothered* | es una lástima que... *it is a shame that . . .* |
| parecer fantástico* *to consider great* | es malo que... *it is bad that . . .* |
| parecer terrible* *to consider terrible* | es una pena que... *it is a pity that . . .* |
| parecer triste* *to consider sad* | es raro que... *it is unusual that . . .* |
| sentir *to feel, to lament* | es ridículo que... *it is ridiculous that . . .* |
| temer *to fear* | es terrible que... *it is terrible that . . .* |
| tener miedo *to be afraid* | |

*These verbs are used with indirect object pronouns (**me, te, le, nos, os, les**).

Nos **molesta** que Álvarez **sea** tan descortés.

**Es ridículo** que no nos **den** un aumento.

*The fact that Álvarez **is** so impolite **bothers** us.*

*It is ridiculous that they are not giving us a raise.*

The adjectives and nouns in the impersonal expressions can also be used in exclamations with **qué.**

| | |
|---|---|
| **¡Qué pena** que la Sra. Díaz no **promueva** un ambiente positivo! | **What a pity** that Mrs. Díaz does not **promote** a positive environment! |
| **¡Qué terrible** que no se **respeten** nuestros derechos! | **How terrible** that they do not **respect** our rights! |

Just as with the verbs used to give advice and to express wishes and requests, when the subject of the verbs in the main clause and in the subordinate clause are the same, the verb form used is the infinitive. The same applies to cases in which an impersonal expression is used in a generic sense (which would apply to the speaker as well).

| | |
|---|---|
| **Estoy contento** de **trabajar** aquí. | *I am glad to work* here. |
| <u>Ella</u> **dice** que **es magnífico poder** aprender tanto de Ud. | *She says (that) it is great to be able to learn so much from you.* |

## ■ Asimilación

**9-36 En esta universidad** Escoge los comentarios que puede hacer un(a) estudiante típico(a) de esta universidad. Al terminar, compara tus respuestas con las de un(a) compañero(a). ¿Están de acuerdo en todo?

_____ Es una lástima que haya tan pocas computadoras en el laboratorio de lengua.

_____ Estoy contento(a) de que mis profesores sean tan accesibles.

_____ Me parece terrible que no ofrezcan más clases de español.

_____ Temo que el estudiante típico no se gradúe en cuatro años.

_____ Es impresionante que construyan tantos edificios modernos.

_____ Es curioso que la comida de la cafetería sea buena.

_____ Es bueno que en la biblioteca haya muchas colecciones interesantes y útiles.

_____ Me parece fantástico que los estudiantes siempre encuentren estacionamiento enseguida.

**Script 9-37:** En mis clases de español, me agrada que los estudiantes lleguen diez minutos antes. CD2-29 Me gusta tomar asistencia inmediatamente y no tolero las tardanzas. Me molesta mucho que mis estudiantes me interrumpan para hacer preguntas y no me gusta para nada que traigan comida al salón de clase. ¡Es una falta de respeto total! Además, me molesta muchísimo que me traten de «tú». A mí se me trata de «usted» porque soy una persona mayor y con autoridad. Tampoco me gusta que los estudiantes no se interesen en la gramática. ¡La gramática es la base de todo! Me agrada que ellos sepan conjugar los verbos en todas sus formas. ¡Como en los viejos tiempos!

**9-37 Un profesor muy chapado a la antigua** *(old-fashioned)* Escucha al profesor Olmedo hablar de las cosas que le agradan y las cosas que le molestan. Luego, completa las siguientes oraciones.

Al Prof. Olmedo le agrada que sus estudiantes...

- lleguen a clase... diez minutos antes
- lo traten con el pronombre... usted
- sepan... conjugar los verbos en todas sus formas

Pero le molesta que sus estudiantes...

- lo interrumpan... para hacer preguntas
- traigan... comida al salón de clase
- no se interesen en... la gramática

## ■ Aplicaciones

**9-38 Tu nuevo empleo** Acabas de conseguir un nuevo empleo y tu nuevo jefe te ha enviado una lista de detalles sobre las condiciones de trabajo. Túrnense para leer los distintos puntos y para reaccionar usando las expresiones que estudiaron para reflejar emoción y sentimientos.

> **MODELO** E1: *Luis y tú van a compartir la oficina.*
> E2: *Me parece terrible que Luis y yo tengamos que compartir la oficina.*

1. Todo el mundo debe escribir varios informes semanales.
2. El sueldo es bastante alto.
3. Ningún empleado puede almorzar fuera de la oficina.
4. Nosotros pagamos por todos los viajes de negocio.
5. Todos los supervisores deben obtener un doctorado en su área.
6. Hay un mes completo de vacaciones durante el verano.
7. Te daremos un bono por cada nuevo cliente que consigas.
8. Yo decido cómo te debes vestir.

**9-39 Cinco minutos antes de la fiesta** Imagínense que Uds. van a dar una fiesta en su apartamento y faltan cinco minutos para que lleguen los primeros invitados. Algunas cosas están saliendo bien, pero otras no. Lean las claves y escriban una reacción apropiada.

> **MODELO** Lisa / saber preparar bebidas muy buenas
> *Me parece fantástico que Lisa sepa preparar bebidas muy buenas.*

1. el apartamento / estar completamente limpio
2. haber mucho espacio para entretener a los invitados
3. Sara y Josefa / no tener buena música
4. los entremeses / ser variados
5. Bernardo / querer ver a Elisa para reclamarle varias cosas
6. Leo y Diana / no venir porque tenían otro compromiso
7. tener permiso de los dueños del edificio para festejar hasta muy tarde
8. Ernesto / traer a quince personas que no conocemos

**9-40 En la clase de español** Hagan una lista de las cosas positivas y negativas de la clase de español. Luego, compártanla con la clase. ¿Saben cómo va a reaccionar el (la) profesor(a)?

> **MODELO** *Nos alegra que el libro explique bien las estructuras.*
> *¡Es bueno que tengamos que hablar sólo en español!*

## ■ Integración

**9-41 Diferencia de opiniones** Representa la siguiente situación con un(a) compañero(a).

### Estudiante preocupado(a)

Imagínate que acabas de cuestionarle a un profesor la nota que recibiste en un examen. Es obvio que él y tú tienen diferentes opiniones en cuanto a tu desempeño *(performance)* en este examen y quieres resolver la situación. Como estás muy preocupado(a), decides hablar con uno(a) de tus mejores amigos(as). Cuéntale qué pasó, dile cómo te sientes y pídele su consejo.

### Un(a) buen(a) amigo(a)

Uno(a) de tus mejores amigos(as) está pasando por un momento difícil y necesita tu ayuda y tu apoyo. Él/Ella acaba de cuestionarle a un profesor la nota que sacó en un examen, pero no logró resolver la situación. Pregúntale qué le pasa, ofrécele tu ayuda y dale algunos consejos prácticos.

### SUGERENCIAS

Para pedir consejo, usa las siguientes expresiones:

| | |
|---|---|
| **¿Qué piensas/ opinas de esto?** | *What do you think about this?* |
| **¿Qué te parece?** | *What do you think?* |
| **¿Qué harías tú?** | *What would you do?* |
| **¿Qué crees que debo hacer?** | *What do you think I should do?* |
| **¿Qué me sugieres?** | *What do you suggest?* |

**9-42 Andrés Guzmán** Termina la carta que le escribiste a Andrés Guzmán en la actividad 9-14 del **Tema 1** (pág. 361). Incorpora expresiones que reflejen tus sentimientos y tu opinión sobre la oferta de trabajo que él recibió y expresiones que reflejen tus deseos.

MODELO    *Me alegra mucho que puedas venir a los Estados Unidos, pero... Espero que tu familia y tus amigos te apoyen...*

### SUGERENCIAS

Para saber cómo se siente tu amigo(a), usa las siguientes expresiones y preguntas:

| | |
|---|---|
| **¿Qué te pasa/ sucede?** | *What is the matter?* |
| **Te veo triste/ preocupado(a).** | *You seem sad/ worried.* |
| **¿Todo bien?** | *Is everything okay?* |

El Salvador

Los Estados Unidos

# IV. Vídeo: ¿Algo más que una amistad?

## ■ Preparación

**A. Haciendo amigos** Hasta ahora han visto la llegada de los compañeros a Puerto Rico, algunas de las excursiones que han hecho juntos y muchas conversaciones que han tenido sobre varios temas. Basándose en lo que ya han visto y lo que ahora conocen sobre cada persona, contesten las siguientes preguntas.

1. Ya Uds. leyeron el artículo titulado «Cómo hacer amigos» (pág. 356). ¿Creen que los compañeros han seguido los diez consejos? ¿Por qué sí o por qué no?
2. ¿Hay alguien en particular que Uds. creen que no se ha hecho amigo(a) de los demás compañeros? ¿Qué le recomendarían a esa persona para cultivar una relación más amistosa con sus compañeros? Usen expresiones como **Le recomendamos que..., Es preferible que..., Le aconsejamos que..., Es mejor que...**, etc.
3. A veces, la amistad puede convertirse en algo más. ¿Creen que existe la posibilidad de una relación romántica entre algunos de los compañeros? ¿Entre quiénes? ¿Por qué?

> **ESTRATEGIA DE COMPRENSIÓN**
>
> ***Global comprehension and contextual clues*** Listen to get an overall understanding of each person in this context. In addition, use all the visual contextual clues (facial expressions and gestures) available to better understand the different emotions that each person feels during the conversation.

## ■ ¿Entendiste bien?

**B. Las relaciones son complicadas** Mira el vídeo y trata simplemente de identificar el tema general de la conversación y cómo se sienten las personas que hablan.

1. Valeria y Antonio están hablando de...
   a. sus relaciones amorosas actuales.
   (b.) sus relaciones amorosas ya terminadas.
2. Indica cuáles de las siguientes emociones experimentan Valeria y Antonio en el segmento del vídeo. Escribe **V** para Valeria, **A** para Antonio y **AM** para ambos.

   ____ aburrido(a)          ____ enojado(a)
   ____ cansado(a)           ____ feliz
   ____ celoso(a) *(jealous)*  ____ nervioso(a)
   ____ enfermo(a)           ____ curioso(a)

Compara tus respuestas con las de un(a) compañero(a).

*Answers B2: This is interpretative, so what is most important is that the students can justify their answers. Suggested answers are: Valeria: enojada, curisosa, feliz/nerviosa (at the end of the segment); Antonio: aburrido (perhaps, at the beginning of the segment), curioso, nervioso/feliz*

3. Ahora vas a ver el vídeo por segunda vez. Lee las siguientes oraciones y ponlas en orden según lo que sucede en el vídeo.

___3___ Antonio le preguntó a Valeria si estaba bien.

___2___ Valeria acusó a Antonio de estar espiándola y se enfadó con él.

___6___ Antonio le contó a Valeria lo que pasó entre Raquel, su ex-novia, y Rubén, su mejor amigo.

___7___ Antonio le preguntó a Valeria si quería hacer algo con él por la noche.

___5___ Valeria insistió en que nunca engañó a César y en que por eso no tenía por qué estar tan celoso.

___1___ Mientras hablaba por teléfono con César, Valeria se enfadó con él.

___4___ Valeria le explicó a Antonio por qué ella y César habían terminado *(had broken up)* su relación.

**C. En nuestra opinión...** Todos tenemos opiniones y experiencias personales que podemos usar para darles consejos a otras personas. ¿Qué opinan de lo que acaban de ver en el vídeo y qué consejos les darían a Valeria y a Antonio? Usen las siguientes preguntas para iniciar su conversación, pero no se limiten a ellas solamente. Compartan sus opiniones y experiencias y prepárense para presentarle sus conclusiones a la clase.

1. Valeria y Antonio quedaron en salir por la noche, pero no hicieron planes específicos sobre qué iban a hacer. ¿Qué les sugieren que hagan (ir a un café, cenar juntos, dar un paseo, ver una película, etc.)?

2. ¿Creen que ellos deben empezar una relación amorosa mientras están en Puerto Rico? ¿Por qué sí o por qué no?

3. ¿Es bueno o malo que las amistades se conviertan en relaciones amorosas?

4. ¿Qué creen que va a pasar entre Valeria y Antonio al final del mes, cuando tengan que volver a sus respectivos países?

**D. Enfoque comunitario** Visita tu tienda de vídeos favorita e investiga qué películas de España y Latinoamérica tienen disponibles. Escoge una que te parezca interesante y, mientras la ves, concéntrate en las relaciones entre los personajes (amistad, amor, conflicto, etc.). Escribe un breve resumen de la película en el que expliques qué tipos de relaciones había y finalmente tu opinión sobre la película diciendo si te gustó, si se la recomendarías a tus compañeros de clase, etc. Debes estar preparado(a) para presentarle tu resumen y tu opinión a la clase.

# Relaciones de pareja

## I. Vocabulario: amor, noviazgo y matrimonio

El señor y la señora González llevan 25 años de **casados.**

Juan y Marta se acaban de **separar,** pero todavía son buenos amigos.

Carmín y Augusto son **novios.**

### El estado civil *Marital Status*

**Adjetivos**

casado *married*
comprometido *engaged*
divorciado *divorced*
soltero *single*
viudo *widower*

**Verbos**

casarse (por la Iglesia / por lo civil) *to get married (religious/civil ceremony)*

divorciarse *to get divorced*
enamorarse *to fall in love*
estar comprometido *to be engaged*
salir juntos *to go out, to date*
separarse *to get separated*
ser fiel/infiel *to be faithful/ unfaithful*
ser novios *to be dating, going out*
vivir juntos *to live together*

Transparency E-4: La boda

Juan y Ángela **son novios** desde hace más de un año.
*Juan and Ángela **have been dating** for over a year.*

La hermana de Juan **está comprometida** con un muchacho hondureño.
*Juan's sister **is engaged** to a guy from Honduras.*

El sacerdote los **declaró** marido y mujer.
*The priest **declared** them husband and wife.*

Doña Matilde es **viuda** y su hermano David es **divorciado.**
*Doña Matilde is **a widow** and her brother David is **divorced.***

## ■ Asimilación

**9-43 Primero...** Organicen las siguientes etapas de las relaciones de pareja en un orden lógico.

<u> 3 </u> comprometidos      <u> 6 </u> divorciados

<u> 2 </u> novios      <u> 1 </u> amigos

<u> 5 </u> separados      <u> 4 </u> casados

**Script 9-44:** ¿Quieres saber más de mi familia? Pues bueno, mi hermano Pedro está casado con Alicia y mi hermana Patricia, la menor, está ahora saliendo con Fernando Sandoval, ¿lo recuerdas? Pero, anda, no parece que sea algo muy serio, ¿sabes? La verdad es que ella es muy joven todavía. Bueno, mi primo Juan, el que vive en Guatemala, es divorciado y ahora vive con la tía Estela, que es viuda. Ah, ¿mis padres? Pues ellos ya llevan casi cuarenta años de casados.

**CD2–30**

**9-44 Estado civil** Escucha la descripción de la familia de Ana María y anota el estado civil de las siguientes personas.

Pedro y Alicia: <u>están casados</u>      Sus padres: <u>están casados</u>

Patricia y Fernando: <u>están saliendo</u>      Tía Estela: <u>es viuda</u>

Juan: <u>es divorciado</u>

## ■ Aplicaciones

**9-45 Opiniones** Completa las oraciones con la palabra más apropiada. Al terminar, compara tus respuestas con las de un(a) compañero(a). Puedes usar las palabras más de una vez.

OPCIONES:   enamorarse   ser fiel   vivir juntos   se casan por lo civil
marido   amantes   matrimonio   separados   divorciarse
novios

1. Es imposible <u>enamorarse</u> a primera vista. El amor requiere tiempo.
2. Es mejor ser <u>novios</u> por varios años antes de casarse.
3. Las parejas que sólo <u>se casan por lo civil</u> usualmente se separan muy pronto.
4. El <u>marido</u> debe tener la última palabra en la casa.
5. Las parejas que no se comprenden deben <u>divorciarse</u>.
6. Las mujeres no deben tolerar que sus esposos tengan <u>amantes</u>.
7. <u>Vivir juntos</u> sin estar casados es inmoral e inaceptable. Las parejas deben contraer matrimonio antes de cohabitar.
8. Los <u>novios</u> deben pensarlo muy bien antes de formalizar su relación.
9. El <u>matrimonio</u> es lo más importante en la vida de una persona.
10. Los hijos de padres <u>separados</u> siempre tienen muchos problemas psicológicos.

You may also want to read the instructions to activity 9-46 at this point, so that students realize that they are to react critically to the following statements about love and relationships.

**CRITICAL THINKING SKILLS**

*Making Personal Value Judgments* Determine whether or not the statements in activity 9-45 agree with your own value system.

**9-46 ¿Qué opinas tú?** Reacciona de una manera crítica a las oraciones de la actividad 9-45. Si no estás de acuerdo con algunas, vuelve a escribirlas para que reflejen mejor tu modo de pensar *(way of thinking)*.

MODELO     *No creo que las parejas que sólo se casan por lo civil se separen pronto. Todo depende de las personas y de su compromiso.*

**9-47 Entrevista** Hazle las siguientes preguntas a un(a) compañero(a) y presenta a la clase un resumen de sus respuestas.

1. ¿Estás saliendo con alguien en especial? Si no es así, ¿por qué? ¿Qué tipo de persona te gustaría tener como pareja *(as a partner)*?
2. Si tienes pareja, ¿qué es lo que más te gusta de esa persona?
3. ¿Qué crees que se necesita para tener éxito en una relación de pareja?

## ■ Integración

**9-48 ¿Matrimonio?** Representa la siguiente situación con un(a) compañero(a).

| ¡Quiero casarme ya! | ¡Piénsalo! |
|---|---|
| Tú estás muy enamorado(a) y quieres casarte de inmediato. Tu amigo(a) es muy inteligente y quiere darte buenos consejos. | Tu amigo(a) parece estar muy enamorado(a) y quiere casarse de inmediato. Tú sabes de los problemas que se pueden presentar cuando se toma este tipo de decisión a la ligera *(lightly)*. |
| 1. Describe tu noviazgo, contestando preguntas como: ¿Quién es el (la) afortunado(a)? ¿Por qué estás tan enamorado(a)? etc. | 1. Averigua más acerca de su noviazgo: ¿Quién es el (la) afortunado(a)? ¿Por qué están tan enamorados? etc. |
| 2. Habla de tus planes de matrimonio, indicando cuándo, cómo, dónde, etc. va a tener lugar *(going to take place)*. | 2. Pregúntale acerca de sus planes de matrimonio para saber cuándo, cómo, dónde, etc. va a tener lugar. |
| 3. Pídele su opinión. | 3. Dale tu opinión al respecto. ¿Piensas tú que es una buena idea? ¿Qué crees que deben tener en cuenta antes de tomar esa decisión? etc. |

### 9-49 Problemas de pareja

**Paso 1:** En los Estados Unidos hay una tasa *(rate)* de divorcio de aproximadamente el 50%. ¿A qué creen que se debe esto? En grupos, preparen una lista de factores que ponen en peligro los matrimonios en este país.

**Paso 2:** Ahora, lee el siguiente artículo y escribe tu reacción personal. Usa las siguientes preguntas como guía.

1. ¿Estás de acuerdo con las ideas presentadas en el artículo?
2. ¿Qué factores de riesgo tienes, o cuáles te preocupan más?
3. ¿Qué pueden hacer las parejas para evitar la influencia negativa de cada uno de estos factores?

# Parejas en alto riesgo

Aunque en muchas ocasiones las parejas se rompen por **hechos puntuales,** algunos factores te pueden **poner en riesgo** más fácilmente:

*specific reasons*
*put at risk*

■ *Vivir en una ciudad.* En la ciudad existe un mayor riesgo de separación que en las zonas rurales, ya que hay más oportunidades de conocer gente —especialmente cuando los dos trabajan. Además, la presión familiar y social es mayor.

■ *La juventud.* Los jóvenes tienen mayor predisposición a la ruptura porque la mayoría de ellos no considera difícil volver a encontrar una nueva pareja.

■ *Antecedentes familiares.* Los hijos de padres divorciados pueden tener más tendencia a la separación porque la ven como un acontecimiento más normal.

*to take on*
*to face*
*will entail*

■ *Las personas arriesgadas.* Quienes están acostumbrados a **asumir** riesgos en su vida sienten menos miedo a **afrontar** lo que **acarreará** la ruptura.

■ *La promiscuidad.* Cuando los miembros de la pareja han tenido muchas relaciones amorosas gratificantes antes de casarse, existe más posibilidad de que haya ruptura porque ven como una liberación el poner fin a una relación infeliz.

■ *Mujeres de mayor nivel cultural y profesional.* Aceptan con más facilidad el divorcio, mientras que las que no trabajan o no tienen ingresos suficientes tienden a **temerle.** En cambio, algunos hombres que tienen estatus profesional alto **rehúsan** el divorcio por temor a las consecuencias negativas que pueda tener en su imagen profesional.

*to be afraid of it*
*refuse*

■ *Las parejas con hijos.* En contra de la creencia popular de que los hijos unen al matrimonio, la mayoría de los expertos, así como las estadísticas, confirman que los niños contribuyen a menudo a romper el equilibrio del hogar y la **convivencia.**

*life together*

## II. Funciones y estructuras: Expressing doubt and denial

SOL: ¿Supiste que Raúl y Lucía están saliendo juntos?

CHARO: ¡No! **Dudo** que **sean** novios... ¡Raúl sale con Tatiana!

SOL: ¡Pues créelo!

CHARO: Mmm... **Es posible** que sólo **sean** muy buenos amigos, ¿no?

SOL: ¡Charo, no lo creo! A otro con ese cuento.

The use of the subjunctive mode is also triggered by the use of verbs and impersonal expressions that convey the idea of doubt or denial. Here is a list of some of those verbs and expressions.

| Verbs | Impersonal expressions |
|---|---|
| dudar *to doubt* | es dudoso que... *it is doubtful that . . .* |
| negar (ie) *to deny* | es imposible que... *it is impossible that . . .* |
| no creer *to disbelieve* | es improbable que... *it is not likely that . . .* |
| no estar seguro(a) (de) *to be unsure (of)* | es posible que... *it is possible that . . .* |
| no pensar *to not think* | es probable que... *it is likely that . . .* |
| | no es cierto que... *it is not certain that . . .* |
| | no es seguro que... *it is not sure that . . .* |
| | no es verdad que... *it is not true that . . .* |

The affirmative counterpart of some of these verbs and expressions (**creer, estar seguro[a], pensar, es cierto que..., es seguro que...,** and **es verdad que...**) are usually followed by verbs in the indicative mode because they do not express doubt or denial.

Mi hermana **niega** que su novio y ella **estén** comprometidos.

*My sister **denies** that her boyfriend and she **are** engaged.*

¡**Es imposible** que **vivamos** juntos antes de casarnos!

*It is not possible for us to **live** together before getting married!*

Once again, if the subject of the verb in the main and subordinate clauses is the same, use the infinitive form of verb. The same applies when the impersonal expression is used to refer to people in general.

Paco **no cree poder** asistir a la boda.

*Paco **does not think** he **can** attend the wedding.*

¿**Es posible enamorarse** a primera vista?

*Is it possible to **fall in love** at first sight?*

## Asimilación

**9-50 ¿Duda o certeza?** Escoge la forma verbal correcta. Al terminar, compara tus respuestas con las de un(a) compañero(a). ¿Están de acuerdo?

1. Es verdad que mis padres (van a divorciarse / vayan a divorciarse) pronto.
2. No estamos seguros de que el Sr. Juárez (es / sea) viudo.
3. Es improbable que mi hermano y mi cuñada se (separan / separen).
4. ¿Piensas que esa chica (está / esté) comprometida?
5. Celia duda que Lalo y ella se (casan / casen) sólo por lo civil.
6. Estoy seguro de que ellos (viven / vivan) juntos.
7. ¿Es cierto que Betty y el Sr. Pérez (son / sean) novios?
8. La Sra. Cruz niega que su hija (está / esté) separada.

Script 9-51: 1. ¿Dudas que CD2–31 te cases algún día? 2. ¿Es probable que vivas con una persona antes de casarte? 3. ¿No piensas que el divorcio sea una buena alternativa en algunos casos? 4. ¿Niegas que le seas infiel a tu pareja? 5. ¿No es verdad que estás comprometido(a)?

**9-51 Preguntas personales** Escucha las preguntas y contéstalas en oraciones completas. En algunos casos es posible usar diferentes expresiones como: (**Creo que...**, **Pienso...**, **Estoy seguro[a] ...**, etc.).

1. ...       4. ...
2. ...       5. ...
3. ...

## Aplicaciones

**9-52 ¡Mentiras y más mentiras!** Túrnense para leer y reaccionar a las siguientes oraciones. Usen diferentes expresiones.

MODELO   E1: *Me caso la próxima semana.*
E2: *Dudo que te cases la próxima semana.*

1. Soy una persona divorciada.
2. Mi novio(a) tiene sesenta años.
3. Mi hermana y un atleta famoso salen juntos.
4. No creo en el matrimonio.
5. El (La) profesor(a) es soltero(a).
6. El presidente y su esposa se van a separar en menos de un mes.
7. Me encuentro con mi novio(a) en el parque todas las tardes.
8. Las bodas están pasadas de moda *(out of style)*.

**9-53 ¿Conocen bien al (a la) profesor(a)?** De acuerdo con lo que saben de su profesor(a) y de sus hábitos, ¿qué cosas dudan y niegan que vayan a pasar en la próxima clase? Usen diferentes expresiones. Cuando terminen, compartan las oraciones con él/ella para ver si está de acuerdo.

MODELO   *No creemos que el (la) profesor(a) no dé tarea.*
*Es imposible que él/ella llegue tarde.*

**9-54 En los próximos días**

**Paso 1:** Piensa en las cosas que tienes que hacer y las cosas que no vas a poder hacer en los próximos días. Luego, completa las siguientes oraciones.

*No es seguro que...*     *Dudo que...*     *No creo que...*

*Es posible que...*     *Es increíble que...*

**Paso 2:** Compara tus oraciones con las de dos compañeros(as) y prepara un breve informe. Al terminar, léeselo al resto de la clase.

MODELO     *No es seguro que yo visite a mi novio. Tampoco es seguro que Vicky vaya hoy a la biblioteca y que Richard lave toda su ropa. Por otro lado,...*

## ■ Integración

**9-55 ¿Cierto o falso?** Individualmente, preparen una lista de diez datos ciertos y diez datos falsos sobre su vida (no deben estar en orden). Luego, túrnense para leer esos datos y reaccionar según el caso. Si crees que el dato que ha leído tu compañero(a) es falso, debes explicar por qué. Al final, ¿quién conoce mejor al / a la otro(a)?

MODELO     E1: *Mis padres viven en otro estado.*
E2: *Sí, creo que tus padres viven en otro estado.*
E1: *¡Correcto!*
E2: *Mi hermano tiene novia y esposa.*
E1: *¡Dudo que tu hermano tenga novia y esposa porque eso es ser infiel!*
E2: *Mmm...*

**9-56 Inseguridades** Escríbele una carta a tu profesor(a) sobre algunas de las inseguridades académicas y profesionales que tienes. Usa diferentes expresiones de duda y negación. Antes de entregarle la carta, dale una copia a un(a) compañero(a) para que la corrija según los siguientes criterios:

- **Contenido:** ¿Es convincente? ¿Las ideas son claras?
- **Organización:** ¿La secuencia de ideas es lógica? ¿Sigue la estructura de una carta?
- **Vocabulario:** ¿La selección de vocabulario es efectiva? ¿Usa diferentes expresiones de duda y negación?
- **Gramática:** ¿Usa el subjuntivo correctamente? ¿Hay errores de concordancia *(agreement)* entre sustantivos y adjetivos o entre sujetos y verbos?

### SUGERENCIAS

Los datos pueden ser sobre: **las materias que toman, su familia** (personalidad, características físicas, etc.), **su casa, la comida, los gustos** (deportes, pasatiempos, etc.), **su pueblo o su ciudad, su trabajo, sus relaciones,** etc.

## III. Funciones y estructuras: Talking about hypothetical situations with the subjunctive

CARLA: Elena, me acabo de enterar de que te casas. ¡Felicidades!

ELENA: Gracias, Carla. Estoy súper feliz. ¿Y cuándo te casas tú?

CARLA: No sé... ¡Primero tengo que encontrar un hombre que **sea** guapo y simpático como tu Alberto. Pero dime, ¿dónde va a ser la recepción?

ELENA: Todavía no sabemos. Estamos buscando un lugar que **tenga** cabida para muchas personas y que no **esté** lejos.

The subjunctive mode is used in adjectival clauses that describe a non-specific antecedent (a person, a place, or an object). For example, in the previous dialogue, Carla is looking for a man with certain qualities, but this person may or may not exist. Elena, on the other hand, is looking for a reception hall with certain characteristics, but she has not found it yet. Compare the following examples.

| SPECIFIC AND DEFINITE ANTECEDENTS → indicative | NON-SPECIFIC AND INDEFINITE ANTECEDENTS → subjunctive |
|---|---|
| Hay una persona que me **atrae**. | No hay nadie que me **atraiga**. |
| Conozco un restaurante donde **sirven** comida guatemalteca. | Busco un restaurante donde **sirvan** comida guatemalteca. |
| Veo algo que me **llama** la atención. | No veo nada que me **llame** la atención. |

When **nadie** and **nada** are followed by an adjectival clause, it must contain a verb in the subjunctive because these pronouns always refer to non-specific entities.

The subjunctive is also used in questions with **algo** or **alguien** and an adjectival clause. The answer has a verb in the indicative mode if the antecedent is specific.

¿Hay **(algo/alguien)** que te **interese**?

*Is there **(anything/anybody)** that **interests** you?*

Sí, (eso/esa persona) me **interesa** mucho.

*Yes, (that/that person) **interests** me a lot.*

BUT

No, no hay (nada/nadie) que me **interese**.

*No, (nothing/nobody) **interests** me.*

## ■ Asimilación

**9-57 En mi familia...** Escoge las alternativas que se apliquen a tu familia y luego compara tus respuestas con las de un(a) compañero(a). ¿Tienen familias semejantes o diferentes?

En mi familia hay alguien que...
____ está divorciado.
____ está comprometido.
____ es viudo.
____ está separado.
____ vive con su pareja sin casarse.
____ tiene novio(a).
____ se casa este año.
____ no cree en el matrimonio.

En mi familia no hay nadie que...
____ esté divorciado.
____ esté comprometido.
____ sea viudo.
____ esté separado.
____ viva con su pareja sin casarse.
____ tenga novio(a).
____ se case este año.
____ no crea en el matrimonio.

**Script 9-58:** Busco una chica que sea joven, simpática y atractiva; idealmente, que tenga pelo largo... No sé, pero me fascinan las mujeres que tienen el pelo largo. ¡Ah! Y que tenga una carrera bien definida. Eso sí, tiene que ser una chica a quien le guste el deporte. A mí me encantan los deportes al aire libre y me gustaría compartir esta afición con mi futura esposa.

**9-58 ¿Cuál es la mejor candidata?** Esteban Salcedo está buscando su media naranja *(his better half)*. Escucha la descripción que hace de la mujer de sus sueños. Luego, observa las fotos, lee las descripciones de las candidatas y escoge la que consideres más apropiada para él.

1.

Soy estudiante de ingeniería. Me gusta leer y jugar al tenis.

2.

Soy abogada. Me encanta el deporte y hago ejercicios aeróbicos todos los días.

3.

Soy estudiante de medicina. No tengo mucho tiempo libre, pero me gusta ir de vez en cuando a conciertos.

**MODELO**   *Pues pienso que la mejor candidata es la número... porque...*

## ■ Aplicaciones

**9-59 Preferencias** Completen las siguientes oraciones de forma lógica.

**MODELO**   Queremos un trabajo que *nos permita ganar mucho dinero.*

1. Necesitamos un carro que...
2. Buscamos un(a) profesor(a) que...
3. Queremos viajar a un país donde...
4. El sábado vamos a ir a un lugar que...
5. En esta universidad no hay nada que...
6. No nos gusta hablar con personas que...
7. Nos encanta llevar ropa que...
8. La pareja ideal es una persona que...
9. Entre nuestros amigos no hay nadie que...
10. No conocemos a nadie que...

**EN TU COMUNIDAD**

Interview at least five of your friends and family members about the personality traits they look for in a partner. In class, share your findings with other classmates and present brief oral reports.

**9-60 En la clase de español** Escribe por lo menos seis preguntas sobre tus compañeros de clase. Luego, hazle las preguntas a un(a) compañero(a). ¿Están de acuerdo?

> MODELO  E1: *¿En la clase hay alguien que fume?*
> E2: *No, no hay nadie que fume.* or *Sí, hay alguien que fuma— Francine.*
> E1: *¡Claro que sí! ¡Francine fuma!* or *¡Estoy de acuerdo!*

1. ... 3. ... 5. ...
2. ... 4. ... 6. ...

**9-61 Donde vivimos** Túrnense para hacer y responder a preguntas sobre las ciudades o los pueblos donde viven. Pueden hacer preguntas adicionales para saber más detalles. Al final, ¿les gusta el lugar donde viven o prefieren el lugar donde vive el (la) otro(a) estudiante?

> MODELO  E1: *¿Hay un restaurante donde sirvan buenas ensaladas?*
> E2: *Sí, se llama Demetrio's Café.*
> E1: *¿Tienen ensalada de mariscos?*
> E1: *Creo que sí. ¿Y en tu ciudad hay algún centro comercial que sea grande?*
> E2: ...

■ **Integración**

**9-62 Aspiraciones para el futuro** Explícale a tu compañero(a) algunas de tus aspiraciones para el futuro. ¡Debes estar preparado(a) para sus preguntas!

**9-63 Clasificados** Imagínate que eres el (la) gerente de personal de una empresa y que tienes que contratar una secretaria, un mensajero y un contable. Escribe las descripciones de las personas que buscas y dale una copia a tu profesor(a). Usa el siguiente anuncio como modelo.

**SUGERENCIAS**

Pueden hablar sobre **la pareja ideal, el trabajo ideal, la casa de sus sueños, la familia ideal,** y **el tipo de persona que quieren ser.**

> Distrito escolar con más de 20.000 estudiantes busca profesor(a) de matemáticas que tenga por lo menos cinco años de experiencia. Se prefiere un(a) candidato(a) al (a la) que le guste trabajar con niños de escuela primaria y que esté familiarizado(a) con las técnicas de enseñanza más innovadoras. Llame a la Dra. Talavera. (718) 555-1234.

# IV. Lectura: El desamor

## ■ Antes de leer

**A. Para conversar** ¿Por qué se aburren algunas personas en su matrimonio? Preparen una lista de los factores que pueden acabar con el entusiasmo de una pareja con respecto a su matrimonio.

**B. Vocabulario y conceptos** Para cada palabra, indiquen la letra de la definición que corresponda.

<u>b</u> 1. rutina      a. tolerar, resistir, aceptar

<u>d</u> 2. manera de ser      b. costumbre, algo que hacemos de

<u>f</u> 3. ausencia               manera habitual

<u>a</u> 4. soportar      c. que no tiene solución

<u>e</u> 5. irritar      d. personalidad

<u>c</u> 6. irremediable      e. enojar, molestar

                               f. no estar presente

## ■ A leer

**ESTRATEGIA DE LECTURA**

**Getting the Gist** You do not have to understand every word. Concentrate on identifying the main points of the story and answering the comprehension questions that follow it.

### Rosa Montero

Rosa Montero es una de las más sobresalientes *(outstanding)* escritoras españolas contemporáneas. Nació en Madrid, donde estudió periodismo y sicología. Desde 1976 trabaja en el diario *El País*. En 1980 ganó el Premio Nacional de Periodismo y en 1997 el Premio Primavera de Novela por su obra *La hija del caníbal*. Entre sus novelas más destacadas *(prominent)* se encuentran: *Crónicas del desamor, La función Delta, Te trataré como una reina* y *Bella oscura*.

### La hija del caníbal (fragmento)

De manera que cogí un taxi y me fui a casa, y cuando comprobé lo que ya sabía, esto es, que Ramón tampoco estaba allí, me acerqué a la **comisaría** a presentar denuncia. Me hicieron multitud de preguntas, todas **desagradables:** que cómo nos llevábamos él y yo, que si Ramón tenía amantes, que si tenía enemigos, que si habíamos discutido, que si estaba nervioso, que si tomaba drogas, que si había cambiado últimamente de manera de ser. Y, aunque **fingí** una seguridad **ultrajada** al contestarles, el cuestionario me hizo advertir lo poco que me fijaba en mi marido, lo mal que conocía las respuestas, la inmensa ignorancia con que la rutina **cubre** al otro.

Pero esa noche, en la cama, aturdida por lo incomprensible de las cosas, me sorprendió sentir un dolor que hacía tiempo que no experimentaba: el dolor de la ausencia de Ramón. A fin de cuentas llevábamos diez años viviendo juntos, durmiendo juntos, soportando nuestros **ronquidos** y nuestras **toses,** los calores de agosto, los pies tan congelados en invierno.

*police station*

*unpleasant*

*pretended / insulted*

*covers*

*snores*
*coughs*

*pondering*

*to rub (imperfect tense) / bald spot / daily routine / ties / love, affection*

*uneasy / empty*

No le amaba, incluso me irritaba, llevaba mucho tiempo **planteándome** la posibilidad de separarme, pero él era el único que me esperaba cuando yo volvía de viaje y yo era la única que sabía que él se **frotaba** monoxidil todas las mañanas en la **calva**. La **cotidianeidad** tiene estos **lazos**, el **entrañamiento** del aire que se respira a dos, del sudor que se mezcla, la ternura animal de lo irremediable.

Así es que aquella noche, insomne y **desasosegada** en la cama **vacía**, comprendí que tenía que buscarlo y encontrarlo, que no podría descansar hasta saber qué le había ocurrido. Ramón era mi responsabilidad, no por ser mi hombre, sino mi costumbre.

## ■ ¿Entendiste bien?

**C. Ideas principales** Respondan a las siguientes preguntas.

1. ¿Cómo se llama el esposo de la narradora?
   a. Juan    b. Ramón    c. Pedro
2. ¿Cuánto tiempo llevan de casados?
   a. un año    b. cinco años    c. diez años
3. ¿Adónde fue la narradora cuando descubrió que su esposo no estaba en casa?
   a. a su trabajo    b. a la comisaría    c. al aeropuerto
4. ¿Qué descubrió ella en este lugar?
   a. que no conocía muy bien a su marido
   b. que amaba mucho a su esposo
   c. que necesitaba unas vacaciones
   d. que su marido tenía una amante
5. ¿Ama la narradora a su esposo?
   a. sí    b. no    c. tal vez
6. Menciona por lo menos tres cosas que tiene la narradora en común con su marido en este momento.

**ESTRATEGIA DE LECTURA**

**Scanning** Keep in mind the context of marriage as you scan the text for the following information.

**CRITICAL THINKING SKILLS**

**Analyzing and Inferring** Consider the protagonist's statements in order to determine what her true feelings may be.

Answer C: 6. *Three of the following:* dormir juntos, ronquidos, toses, calores en agosto, pies fríos en invierno

**ESTRATEGIA DE LECTURA**

**Guessing from Context** Consider the entire text as well as each sentence as you try to guess the meaning of the different sentences.

**D. Enfoque lingüístico** Basándote en el contexto, ¿cuál es el significado de las siguientes palabras?

1. «De manera que cogí un taxi y me fui a casa, y cuando comprobé lo que ya sabía, esto es, que Ramón tampoco estaba allí, me acerqué a la comisaría a presentar **denuncia**.»
   a. denounce    b. denial    c. report
2. «El cuestionario me hizo advertir lo poco que me **fijaba** en mi marido, lo mal que conocía las respuestas, la inmensa ignorancia con que la rutina cubre al otro.»
   a. fight    b. notice    c. find
3. «Pero esa noche, en la cama, **aturdida** por lo incomprensible de las cosas, me sorprendió sentir un dolor que hacía tiempo que no experimentaba: el dolor de la ausencia de Ramón.»
   a. confused    b. helpless    c. ashamed

**CRITICAL THINKING SKILLS**

**Making Associations and Creating** Consider the protagonist's circumstances as you think of recommendations.

**E. Actividad de extensión** ¿Qué creen que debe hacer esta mujer para revitalizar su matrimonio? Comenten qué recomendaciones le darían *(you would give)* a la protagonista si tuvieran *(if you had)* la oportunidad de hablar con ella sobre este asunto *(matter)*.

## Buenos amigos — *Good friends*

### Adjetivos

| | |
|---|---|
| confiable | *trustworthy* |
| generoso | *generous* |
| honesto | *honest* |
| leal | *loyal* |
| paciente | *patient* |

### Verbos

| | |
|---|---|
| aceptar | *to accept* |
| apoyar | *to support* |
| compartir | *to share* |
| contar (ue) con | *to count on* |
| corregir (i, i) | *to correct* |
| dar consejos | *to give advice* |
| estar dispuesto a... | *to be ready (eager) to . . .* |
| fallarle | *to fail (not be there)* |
| juzgar | *to judge* |
| preocuparse por | *to worry about* |
| querer/amar | *to love* |

## Los compañeros y los jefes — *Co-workers and bosses*

### Adjetivos

| | |
|---|---|
| accesible | *accessible* |
| agresivo | *aggressive* |
| buen compañero | *good colleague* |
| competente | *competent* |
| creativo | *creative* |
| cumplidor | *reliable* |
| eficiente | *efficient* |
| firme | *firm* |
| honesto | *honest* |
| leal | *loyal* |
| puntual | *punctual* |
| responsable | *responsible* |
| respetuoso | *respectful* |
| seguro de sí mismo | *confident* |
| tímido | *shy* |
| trabajador | *hard working* |

### Sustantivos

| | |
|---|---|
| el buen sentido del humor | *good sense of humor* |

## Verbos

| | |
|---|---|
| amar el trabajo | *to love one's work* |
| delegar parte del poder | *to delegate power* |
| promover (ue) un ambiente positivo de trabajo | *to promote a positive working environment* |
| respetar a los empleados | *to respect the employees* |
| saber escuchar | *to know how to listen* |
| ser creativo | *to be creative* |
| tener metas | *to have goals* |
| tomar riesgos/arriesgarse | *to take risks* |

## El estado civil — *Marital Status*

### Adjetivos

| | |
|---|---|
| casado | *married* |
| comprometido | *engaged* |
| divorciado | *divorced* |
| soltero | *single* |
| viudo | *widower* |

### Verbos

| | |
|---|---|
| casarse por la iglesia/ por lo civil | *to get married in a religious/civil ceremony* |
| divorciarse | *to get divorced* |
| enamorarse | *to fall in love* |
| estar comprometido | *to be engaged* |
| salir juntos | *to go out, to date* |
| separarse | *to get separated* |
| ser fiel/infiel | *to be faithful/unfaithful* |
| ser novios | *to be dating, going out* |
| vivir juntos | *to live together* |

## Funciones y estructuras

Verbos y expresiones impersonales para dar consejos, pp. 358, 362

Verbos para expresar deseos y peticiones, p. 372

Verbos y expresiones impersonales para expresar emociones y sentimientos, p. 375

Verbos y expresiones impersonales para expresar duda, p. 385

# ¿Qué quieres hacer?

**Para comenzar**

Contesta las siguientes preguntas.

■ ¿Qué actividades crees que se pueden hacer en estas regiones de Argentina y Uruguay?

■ ¿Cuál de estas regiones te gustaría visitar?

**In this chapter you will learn . . .**

■ how to talk about different leisure-time activities

■ how to talk about health and fitness issues

■ how to give informal commands

■ how to talk about future events

■ about outdoor activities and cultural events in Uruguay and Argentina

| | **TEMA 1**<br>A mantenernos en forma | **TEMA 2**<br>La diversión en la ciudad | **TEMA 3**<br>Panorama cultural |
|---|---|---|---|
| **Vocabulario** | La buena salud y las enfermedades | Los deportes urbanos | Las bellas artes |
| **Funciones y estructuras** | Giving suggestions and instructions (review of formal commands and advice)<br>Giving instructions with informal commands | Expressing opinion and emotion (review of the subjunctive)<br>Expressing purpose, stipulation, or future time frame with the subjunctive in adverbial clauses | Giving directives and advice (review of formal and informal commands and introduction of **nosotros** commands)<br>Talking about the future with the future tense |
| **Lecturas y vídeo** | Perspectivas: Una buena figura | Vídeo: Un desastre en la cocina | Lectura: El túnel |

Las cataratas del Iguazú tienen una altura de más de 250 pies y son una maravilla natural que marca la frontera entre Argentina y Brasil.

La Avenida 9 de Julio y el Obelisco, en pleno centro de la ciudad de Buenos Aires.

Montevideo, capital y centro urbano más importante de Uruguay.

# Enfoque

Transparencies A-8: Country Profiles: Argentina; A-9: Country Profiles: Paraguay, Uruguay

## A. ¿Qué sabes ya de Argentina?

Antes de ver el vídeo, empareja cada frase de la columna A con una frase lógica de la columna B. Después, compara tus respuestas con las de un(a) compañero(a).

| **A** | **B** |
|---|---|
| _c_ 1. el clima | a. altamente urbanizado |
| _b_ 2. los rioplatenses | b. de carácter abierto, generosos y amables |
| _e_ 3. las historias de gauchos | c. templado y agradable a lo largo del año |
| _d_ 4. una población | d. de inmigrantes provenientes de diversas partes del mundo |
| _a_ 5. un país | e. diversas e interesantes |

## B. Uruguay, urbano y rural

Lee las oraciones sobre Uruguay. Mientras ves el vídeo, marca con una **X** las oraciones que escuches. Luego, mientras compara tus respuestas con las de un(a) compañero(a).

1. Cerca de la mitad de la población vive en...
   - a. la zona fronteriza con Argentina.
   - (b.) la ciudad de Montevideo.
   - c. los poblados de Durazno, Florida y Artigas.

2. Uruguay es conocido internacionalmente por...
   - (a.) la calidad de las carnes que exporta.
   - b. el desfile de Llamadas, el principal espectáculo del Carnaval.
   - c. el mate, una infusión aromática.

3. ¿Con qué otro país comparte Uruguay el gran símbolo cultural del gaucho?
   - a. Brasil
   - b. Paraguay
   - (c.) Argentina

4. ¿Cuál de las siguientes oraciones sobre la ciudad de Colonia del Sacramento *no* es verdad?
   - a. Fue nombrada patrimonio cultural de la humanidad por la UNESCO.
   - (b.) Es el lugar donde nació el escritor Eduardo Galeano.
   - c. Fue una región disputada por España y Portugal.

## C. ¿Qué quieren hacer en Uruguay?

Busquen en el Internet artículos sobre los tipos de turismo que pueden hacer en Uruguay. Luego, decidan qué tipo de turismo sería más adecuado para su grupo, según los intereses personales de los miembros. Prepárense para presentarle lo que decidieron a la clase y las razones por las cuales escogieron ese tipo de turismo para su grupo.

For more info, you may want to check the **Temas** site:
**http://temas.heinle.com**

# A mantenernos en forma

## I. Vocabulario: La buena salud y las enfermedades

**iLrn**

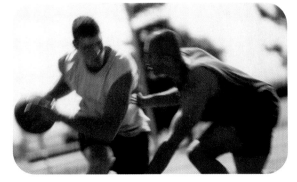

Además de **distraer,** el ejercicio sirve para **mantener un buen estado de salud** y para **combatir el estrés.**

Los ejercicios aeróbicos y de estiramiento son importantes para **mejorar** nuestra **elasticidad** y **resistencia.**

Para una buena **nutrición** es mejor evitar las **grasas animales** y los **productos refinados.**

Transparencies K-2: Las enfermedades, K-3: La nutrición; K-4: Una visita al médico; K-5: Los consejos del médico

### Vocabulario práctico

**Las ventajas del ejercicio físico**

aumentar nuestra fuerza *to augment our strength*

bajar de/perder peso *to lose weight*

ganar/subir de peso *to gain weight*

mantenerse en forma/en buen estado de salud *to keep fit/in good health*

**Es importante...**

dejar de fumar *to quit/stop smoking*

hacer estiramiento *to stretch*

hacer un poco de calentamiento *to do some warm-up exercises*

**Nutrición**

la fibra *fiber*

los minerales *minerals*

la proteína *protein*

las vitaminas *vitamins*

Este niño tiene **fiebre** y un poco de **tos.** También **le duele la cabeza.** Él tiene un **resfriado.**

Su mamá piensa darle unas **pastillas** o un **jarabe.**

Este chico tuvo un accidente. El médico le tomó una **radiografía** y le puso un **yeso** en el brazo.

## Vocabulario práctico

**Problemas médicos (Medical problems)**

la alergia *allergy*

la gripe/la influenza *flu*

los parásitos intestinales *intestinal parasites*

**Verbos**

doler (ue) *to ache, to hurt*

enfermarse *to get sick*

sentirse (ie, i) mal/mejor *to feel ill/better*

tener tos *to have a cough*

**Síntomas (Symptoms)**

la congestión *congestion*

el mareo *dizziness*

**Ayudas terapéuticas y diagnósticas (Therapeutical and Diagnostic Aids)**

el antibiótico *antibiotic*

el botiquín de primeros auxilios *first-aid kit*

la curita *Band-Aid*

el descanso *rest*

la inyección *shot, injection*

la receta *prescription*

You may point out to students that **distraer** is conjugated like **traer** and **mantenerse** like **tener.**

## ■ Asimilación

**10-1 ¿Bueno o malo?** Indica si las siguientes actividades son buenas o malas para la salud. Al terminar, compara tus respuestas con las de otros estudiantes. ¿Están todos de acuerdo?

1. hacer ejercicio aeróbico   bueno
2. llevar una vida sedentaria   malo
3. consumir comidas ricas en grasas animales   malo
4. escoger alimentos ricos en vitaminas y minerales   bueno
5. hacer ejercicios de calentamiento y estiramiento   bueno
6. dejar de fumar y de consumir alcohol   bueno
7. dormir cuatro horas o menos cada día   malo

CD2-34

Script 10-2: 1. Son unos medicamentos que vienen en trozos
pequeños (casi siempre redondos),
que se toman por lo general acom-
pañados de agua u otro líquido.
2. Una medicina en forma líquida.
Usualmente se toma por cucharadas.
3. Es una imagen de los huesos que
se toma con una cámara especial.
Es muy útil en casos de fracturas o
lesiones internas. 4. Son unos
medicamentos que sirven específicamente para combatir infecciones.

**10-2 Identifícalo** Vas a escuchar la descripción de varios tipos de ayudas terapéuticas y diagnósticas. ¿Puedes identificar los diferentes tipos? Indica el número de la descripción junto al tipo de ayuda que corresponda.

   _1_    unas pastillas     ____   un yeso

   _3_    una radiografía     _4_   unos antibióticos

   _2_    un jarabe     ____   una inyección

### ■ Aplicaciones

**10-3 ¿Qué haces?** Completa el cuadro con tu información personal. (Menciona por lo menos dos cosas por cada categoría.) Al terminar, compara tus respuestas con las de otros estudiantes. ¿Tienen algo en común?

**EN TU COMUNIDAD**

Find out about home remedies different people use. Gather information about remedies associated with various cultures, countries, and ethnic groups. Then, discuss this information in groups of three and choose the most interesting or nontradi- tional remedy of the group.

| ¿Qué haces para... | |
|---|---|
| mantenerte en forma? | |
| combatir el estrés? | |
| mejorar tu nutrición? | |
| aumentar tu energía? | |
| distraerte? | |

This activity recycles the use of verbs like **gustar** (**doler, molestar,** etc.).

This activity targets two very common ailments of travelers. If you prefer, you may add (or substitute) other medical conditions that may be more relevant to your group.

**10-4 Síntomas** Imagínense que están de vacaciones en un país de habla hispana y que necesitan atención médica. Preparen una descripción escrita de los síntomas asociados con cada una de las siguientes situaciones.

| Parásitos intestinales | Una caída |
|---|---|
| *Me duele el estómago.* | *Me duele la espalda.* |

This activity recycles the use of the subjunctive for advice.

**REMEMBER**

When giving advice, remember that the verb in the subordinate clause goes in the subjunctive.
**Te sugiero que *estudies* mucho.
Te recomiendo que *hagas* deporte.**

**10-5 ¿Qué debe hacer?** Denle la recomendación más apropiada a cada individuo.

MODELO     un joven turista que se cayó practicando esquí
         *Bueno, a este joven le recomendamos que se haga una radiografía. También es importante que tome unos analgésicos y que descanse lo más posible.*

     1. una chica que comió demasiado y tiene dolor de estómago
     2. una señora a quien le duele mucho la cabeza
     3. un señor que se encuentra muy tenso y preocupado
     4. unos niños que están resfriados
     5. una mujer que sufre de alergias

## ■ Integración

**10-6 En la farmacia** Representa la siguiente situación con un(a) compañero(a).

### Turista

Estás de vacaciones en Argentina y desde hace dos días tienes problemas digestivos. (¡Parece que comiste demasiado asado *[grilled beef]*!) Ve a una farmacia y pídele ayuda a un(a) farmacéutico(a).

1. Salúdalo(la) formalmente.
2. Explícale tus síntomas.
3. Pídele un remedio.
4. Pregúntale cómo prevenir este tipo de problema en el futuro.

### Farmacéutico(a)

Tú tienes una farmacia en el centro de Buenos Aires. Atiende a este(a) cliente(a) estadounidense. (¡Pobre! Se ve muy enfermo[a].)

1. Salúdalo(la) formalmente.
2. Pregúntale qué le pasa.
3. Dile qué remedios debe tomar.
4. Explícale las maneras de prevenir estos problemas en el futuro.

### SUGERENCIAS

Para evitar *(To avoid)* los problemas digestivos, algunas sugerencias son:

■ comer en lugares limpios *(clean)*
■ tomar siempre agua embotellada *(bottled water)*
■ no comer alimentos crudos *(raw)*
■ evitar las frutas sin pelar *(not peeled)*
■ pedir bebidas sin hielo *(without ice)*

**10-7 Para mantenerse en forma** En grupos, preparen una campaña para motivar a otros estudiantes a mantenerse en forma. Denles recomendaciones y consejos específicos.

MODELO    *Para mantenerse en forma es importante que Uds. le presten atención a su dieta. También es preciso que hagan más ejercicio y que no fumen...*

This activity recycles the use of the subjunctive for advice and formal commands. To facilitate the completion of the activity, it would be a good idea to break it into steps.

Step 1: Brainstorming of ideas.

Step 2: Selecting and organizing the information to be included in the campaign.

Step 3: Checking the completeness and accuracy of the text.

## II. Funciones y estructuras: Giving suggestions and instructions (review of formal commands and advice)

SRA. NARVÁEZ: ¿Qué recomienda, doctor?

DOCTOR: Bueno, **dele** comida sin grasa por unos días para controlar la irritación estomacal. También le **sugiero** que **compre** estas pastillas por si *(in case)* el dolor continúa.

SRA. NARVÁEZ: Muchas gracias, doctor. ¿Algo más?

DOCTOR: Sí. **Es necesario que** el niño **descanse** y que **tome** mucho líquido porque está un poco deshidratado.

In **Capítulo 8, Tema 2,** you learned how to give formal commands to people to whom you would refer as **usted** and **ustedes.** The verb forms of these commands are the same as the third-person singular and third-person plural forms of the present subjunctive.

| | |
|---|---|
| Doña Graciela, **consuma** más fibra y proteína en su dieta. | *Mrs. Graciela, **eat** more fiber and protein in your diet.* |
| Sr. Alvarado, **no compre** tantos productos refinados. | *Mr. Alvarado, **do not buy** so many refined products.* |

**REMEMBER**

Indirect object pronouns are placed before direct object pronouns. Also, remember that **le** and **les** change to **se** before the direct object pronouns **lo, la, los,** and **las.**

As you may remember, reflexive (**me, te, se, nos, os, se**), indirect object (**me, te, le, nos, os, les**), and direct object pronouns (**me, te, lo/la, nos, os, los/las**) are attached to the affirmative command and are placed between **no** and the verb in negative commands.

| | |
|---|---|
| Por favor, **deme** un jarabe para la tos. | *Please **give me** a cough syrup.* |
| Demetrio, **no se ponga** nervioso. Va a mejorarse pronto. | *Demetrio, **do not get (become)** nervous. You are going to get better soon.* |
| ¿Las pastillas? **No se las tomen** con el estómago vacío. | *The pills? **Do not take them** on an empty stomach.* |

In **Capítulo 9, Tema 1,** you learned how to use verbs and impersonal expressions that allow you to give suggestions and instructions in a more polite and less direct manner. Here is a list of useful expressions.

**REMEMBER**

Using the formal command of the verb may be interpreted as rude and impolite in certain cases.

| VERBS | IMPERSONAL EXPRESSIONS | |
|---|---|---|
| aconsejar *to advise* | es aconsejable que... | *it is advisable that . . .* |
| recomendar (ie) *to recommend* | es bueno que... | *it is good that . . .* |
| sugerir (ie, i) *to suggest* | es importante que... | *it is important that . . .* |
| | es justo que... | *it is fitting that . . .* |
| | es mejor que... | *it is better that . . .* |
| | es necesario que... | *it is necessary that . . .* |
| | es preferible que... | *it is preferable that . . .* |
| | es urgente que... | *it is urgent that . . .* |

| | |
|---|---|
| Les **sugiero** que **dejen** de fumar inmediatamente. | *I **suggest** that you **quit** smoking immediately.* |
| **Es preferible que haga** un poco de calentamiento primero. | *It is preferable that you **do** some warm-up exercises first.* |

## ▨ Asimilación

**10-8 Para mantenerse en buen estado de salud** Indica si las siguientes recomendaciones para mantenerse en buen estado de salud son lógicas **(L)** o ilógicas **(I).** Cuando termines, compara tus respuestas con las de un(a) compañero(a). ¿Hay algo en lo que no están de acuerdo?

   _I_   Aumenten su nivel de estrés.

   _L_   Tomen una aspirina diaria.

   _I_   Suban de peso.

   _I_   Consuman muchas grasas animales.

   _L_   Manténganse en forma.

   _I_   No duerman más de cinco horas por día.

   _I_   Eviten las vitaminas y los minerales.

   _L_   Promuevan su bienestar emocional.

**10-9 En la radio** Imagínate que estás escuchando tu programa de consejos favorito. Escucha las sugerencias y escoge las alternativas que mejor completen las siguientes oraciones.

1. El especialista dice que uno no debe preocuparse por las presiones...
   a. de la familia.    (b.) de la vida moderna.    c. del dinero.

2. También piensa que hay que sacar tiempo para...
   (a.) cuidar de nuestro interior.    b. reducir el estrés.
   c. hacer cosas divertidas.

3. Él está en contra de *(against)*...
   (a.) no disfrutar de la vida.    b. tomar muchas medicinas.
   c. comer descontroladamente.

4. En general, uno de los problemas principales que el especialista menciona es...
   a. las emociones.    (b.) el trabajo.    c. nuestra voz interior.

**Script 10-9:** Mi querido amigo, no se olvide de usted mismo *(yourself)*. Saque tiempo para meditar y para cuidar de su interior, de sus emociones. No trabaje tanto, no se preocupe por las presiones de la vida moderna. Préstele atención a la voz interna que le pide descansar y alcanzar su bienestar. Piénselo. ¿Es necesario que Ud. deje de pasar tiempo con su familia por ganar más dinero? ¿Es aconsejable que Ud. pierda la oportunidad de disfrutar de las cosas hermosas de la vida por tener más cosas materiales? Eche esas ideas a un lado; comience a concentrarse en su felicidad y en su salud. ¡Todavía está a tiempo!

## ▨ Aplicaciones

**10-10 ¡Las cosas cambian!** La Sra. Martínez y el Sr. Pereira quieren que Uds. les den consejos prácticos para tener una buena salud. ¡Ahora son los adultos los que quieren que los más jóvenes les den consejos! Usen los verbos entre paréntesis.

**Answers 10-10:** 1. tenga; 2. no sufra, póngase; 3. gane; 4. no espere; 1. incremente; 2. reduzca, no coma; 3. manténgase; 4. siéntase

Sra. Martínez,...

1. (tener) un botiquín de primeros auxilios para las emergencias.
2. (no sufrir) de gripe. (ponerse) una inyección contra la influenza todos los años.
3. (ganar) un poco de peso porque está muy delgada.
4. (no esperar) para ver al doctor si se siente mal.

Sr. Pereira,...

1. (incrementar) su actividad física.
2. si quiere sentirse mejor, (reducir) el estrés y (no comer) muchos productos con azúcar.
3. (mantenerse) en forma.
4. (sentirse) mejor haciendo cosas que le gusten.

**10-11 Consejos prácticos** Piensen en por lo menos ocho recomendaciones que les pueden dar a otros estudiantes de su universidad para salir bien en las clases.

> MODELO  *Estudien todos los días. Les aconsejamos que no salgan si tienen un examen al día siguiente. Es importante que vayan preparados a clase.*

SUGERENCIAS

Se usan los siguientes verbos en recetas: **añadir** *(to add)*, **batir** *(to shake)*, **calentar** *(to heat)*, **cortar** *(to cut)*, **echar** *(to put, to pour)*, **hervir** *(to boil)*, **mezclar** *(to mix)*, y **remover** *(to stir)*.

**10-12 Una receta saludable** Piensen en un plato saludable que le quieran recomendar al / a la profesor(a) y hagan una lista de los pasos que debe seguir para prepararlo. Asegúrense de incluir comentarios sobre cosas que no debe hacer y otras recomendaciones que debe seguir para que la receta quede bien.

## ■ Integración

**10-13 Una consulta completa** En grupos de tres estudiantes, imagínense que el Sr. Carmelo Feliciano está reunido con un(a) sicólogo(a), con un(a) nutricionista y con un(a) entrenador(a) porque quiere cambiar su estilo de vida y mejorar su salud. Lean lo que él les dice y aconséjenle de acuerdo con la profesión que escojan.

> SR. FELICIANO:  «Tengo sesenta años y siento que no estoy en buen estado de salud. Tengo unas cuantas libras de sobrepeso, fumo y mi dieta es un desastre. No hago ningún tipo de ejercicio, como pueden ver. Además de esto, quiero mejorar mi actitud hacia la vida porque, aunque tengo todo el tiempo del mundo —soy jubilado—, no hago nada interesante. ¿Qué me aconsejan? ¡Quiero vivir muchos años más!»

SUGERENCIAS

Para dar consejos, puedes usar los verbos **aconsejar, recomendar,** y **sugerir** y las expresiones **es necesario/recomendable/ urgente que…**

| El (La) sicólogo(a) | El (La) nutricionista | El (La) entrenador(a) |
|---|---|---|
| ¿Qué le puedes aconsejar al Sr. Feliciano para tener una actitud más positiva hacia la vida? ¿Qué tipo de actividades le puedes recomendar? ¿Qué cosas debe modificar? | ¿Qué le aconsejas al Sr. Feliciano para bajar de peso? ¿Qué cosas debe hacer para sentirse físicamente mejor? ¿Qué dieta le sugieres y qué pasos debe seguir para alcanzar esta meta? | ¿Qué plan de actividad física le recomiendas a una persona de sesenta años que no es muy activa? ¿Qué cosas debe hacer para tener éxito y para lograr mejores resultados? |

**10-14 Un afiche** *(poster)* Usen la información de la actividad 10-13 para hacer un afiche con una lista de las cosas que se deben y las que no se deben hacer para tener una vida saludable. Cuando esté listo, preséntenselo al resto de la clase.

## III. Funciones y estructuras: Giving instructions with informal commands

¡Hombre! ¿Qué haces aquí? **¡No vayas** a clase hoy! **Visita** a tu médico o **toma** alguna medicina. ¡**Anda, vete** a casa! **Llámame** si necesitas algo.

You are already familiar with the **usted** and **ustedes** (formal) command forms. You will now learn how to give commands in the **tú** (informal) form.

Affirmative **tú** verb commands have the same form as the **él, ella,** and **usted** present indicative form. Pronouns are attached to the end of the conjugated verb.

Elena, **descansa.** Te ves mal.

Cheo, **dame** la medicina para la tos.

**Vístete.** Vamos a hacer aeróbicos.

*Elena, rest. You look bad.*

*Cheo, give me the cough medicine.*

*Get dressed. We are going to do aerobics.*

> Notice that, when adding a pronoun to a command form, a written accent mark is necessary if the stress is on the third-to-the-last syllable. Compare **dame** (the stress is in on the second-to-the-last syllable) and **vístete** (the stress is on the third-to-the-last syllable).

Some verbs have irregular **tú** affirmative command forms (that is, they do not coincide with the **él, ella,** and **usted** present indicative verb form). Here is a list of some of those verbs.

| decir | di | salir | sal |
|-------|------|-------|-----|
| hacer | haz | ser | sé |
| ir | ve | tener | ten |
| mantener | mantén | venir | ven |
| poner | pon | | |

**Haz** los ejercicios tres veces y después **ve** al cuarto de sauna.

**Ponte** los tenis si quieres estar cómoda.

*Do three repetitions and then go to the sauna room.*

*Put on your sneakers if you want to be comfortable.*

To give a negative **tú** command, use **no** or **nunca** and the **tú** present subjunctive verb form. As in the case of formal commands, pronouns are placed between **no** or **nunca** and the verb.

**Nunca tomes** riesgos innecesarios.

Sofía, **no les des** tanta importancia a esas cosas.

¡Por favor, **no te preocupes**!

*Never take unnecessary risks.*

*Sofía, do not give so much importance to those things.*

*Please, do not worry!*

## ■ Asimilación

**10-15 Antes de practicar un deporte** Lee las siguientes recomendaciones para las personas que quieren practicar un deporte e identifica todos los mandatos en la forma **tú**.

1. (Consulta) a tu médico para asegurarte de que estás en buena condición física. (Dile) qué deporte quieres practicar y (pregúntale) si hay algún riesgo.

2. (Busca) toda la información posible sobre el deporte que escogiste. (Decide) qué equipo especial se necesita y (cómpralo) en una tienda especializada.

Script 10-16: Chicos, tengo que trabajar unas horas en la oficina y necesito que hagan varias cosas. Rosa, ordena tu cuarto y haz el almuerzo. Antonio, lava el carro de tu padre y recoge a Fermín de la práctica de béisbol a las dos de la tarde. ¡No te olvides! Pedrito, corta el césped y saca la basura. ¡Y no traigas a nadie a la casa! Ya sabes que me gusta estar ahí cuando vienen tus amigos. Y tú, Clarisa, pasea al perro por el parque y ayuda a Rosa a preparar el almuerzo. Yo regreso a eso de las cuatro de la tarde y los voy a llevar al cine. ¡Pórtense bien! ¡Adiós!

CD2-36

**10-16 Delegando responsabilidades** Escucha las instrucciones que les da la Sra. Lafuente a sus hijos e indica si las oraciones que siguen son ciertas (**C**) o falsas (**F**).

___C___ 1. La Sra. Lafuente quiere que Rosa haga el almuerzo.

___F___ 2. Antonio tiene que lavar el carro de su madre.

___C___ 3. A la Sra. Lafuente no le gusta que Pedrito traiga a sus amigos si ella no está en casa.

___F___ 4. Clarisa es responsable de hacer una sola tarea.

## ■ Aplicaciones

**10-17 ¿Qué debo hacer?** Lean el siguiente diálogo entre Sandra y Perla sobre cómo mantenerse en forma. Completen las oraciones con la forma **tú** del mandato de los verbos de la lista. **¡OJO!** Deben usar pronombres de objeto directo y de objeto indirecto en algunos casos.

ir    tomar    hablar    ser    disminuir

SANDRA:   Perla, quiero mantenerme en forma y no sé por dónde empezar.

PERLA:   _____Ve_____ a un gimnasio por lo menos tres veces por semana. El ejercicio cardiovascular es buenísimo y vas a ver que funciona.

SANDRA:   Lo he pensado, ¡pero es que soy tan perezosa para eso!

PERLA:   ¡Lo sé! Mira, conozco a un entrenador que trabaja en el gimnasio de la calle San Martín. __Háblale__ a él sobre tu problema y te va a ayudar. Es todo un profesional del ejercicio y del fisiculturismo.

SANDRA:   Está bien. También voy a pedirle que me ayude a modificar mis hábitos alimenticios.

PERLA:   Yo te puedo ayudar con eso. Para empezar, __disminuye__ la cantidad de calorías que consumes. Y los refrescos con azúcar, no __los tomes__. El agua es mucho mejor.

SANDRA:   Bueno, no sé cómo comenzar. Ya vamos a ver cómo me va.

PERLA:   ¡No __seas__ pesimista, mujer! Yo te voy a apoyar.

**10-18 ¡A actuar!** Escriban mandatos afirmativos y negativos para algunos compañeros de la clase. Cuando les toque el turno (*When your turn comes*), den los mandatos. Si la persona reacciona al recibir un mandato negativo, ésta pierde (*loses*). ¡Sean originales!

**MODELO**   *Cristina, corre por el salón. | Alberto, no le toques el pelo a Cinthia.*

**10-19 ¿Qué hago para...?** Túrnense y dense recomendaciones para lograr las siguientes cosas. Pueden usar los verbos sugeridos y otros verbos lógicos.

MODELO obtener una buena nota en la clase de español (estudiar, practicar, repasar, hablar inglés, prestar atención)
E1: *¿Qué hago para obtener una buena nota en la clase de español?*
E2: *Estudia todos los días, practica con tus compañeros, repasa los apuntes, no hables inglés en clase y préstale atención al / a la profesor(a).*

1. conseguir un buen trabajo (preparar, escribir, buscar, leer, considerar)
2. prepararme para una cita (bañarse, ponerse, comprar, maquillarse/afeitarse)
3. mantenerme en forma (ir, practicar, hacer, comer, fumar)
4. preparar unos espaguetis (comprar, conseguir, hervir, servir)
5. tener la mente sana (ir, salir, evitar, distraerse, reducir)
6. prepararme para una mudanza (comprar, llamar, reservar, empacar, hacer)

## ■ Integración

**10-20 Una nueva vida** Representa la siguiente situación con un(a) compañero(a).

This activity recycles vocabulary that is introduced in previous chapters. You may want to do a brainstorming exercise first.

### ¡Me mudo!

Te vas a mudar para una ciudad grande de los Estados Unidos por motivos de trabajo y no sabes qué hacer ni qué esperar. Explícale tu situación a un(a) amigo(a) y pídele sugerencias. Pregúntale acerca de:

■ los servicios básicos de tu nuevo apartamento
■ cómo hacer nuevos amigos
■ qué hacer para dar una buena impresión en tu trabajo
■ las oportunidades de crecimiento profesional y personal

### ¡Mi amigo(a) se muda!

Uno(a) de tus mejores amigos(as) se muda para una ciudad grande de los Estados Unidos porque consiguió un trabajo excelente ahí. Ahora está muy abrumado(a) *(overwhelmed)* porque no sabe qué debe hacer para prepararse para este cambio tan importante. Escúchalo(la) y dale tus sugerencias acerca de las cosas que te pregunte.

### SUGERENCIAS

Para responder negativamente a algo que diga tu compañero(a), puedes decir:

| | |
|---|---|
| **No sé.** | *I don't know.* |
| **Creo que no.** | *I don't think so.* |
| **No estoy seguro(a).** | *I am not sure.* |
| **No estoy de acuerdo.** | *I don't agree.* |

### SUGERENCIAS

Para introducir una nueva idea, puedes decir:

| | |
|---|---|
| **¡Ya sé!** | *I know!* |
| **¡Ya lo entiendo!** | *I got it!* |
| **Tengo una idea.** | *I have an idea.* |

**10-21 Direcciones** Uno de los usos más comunes de los mandatos es dar direcciones para ir de un lugar a otro. Imagínate que un estudiante de primer año que no conoce bien la universidad te pide direcciones para llegar a tres lugares diferentes. Escribe estas direcciones. Cuando termines, dale una copia a un(a) compañero(a) para que las revise. Usa las siguientes expresiones:

| | |
|---|---|
| ■ **doblar a la derecha/izquierda** | *to turn right/left* |
| ■ **seguir derecho** | *to go straight* |
| ■ **bajar** | *to go down* |
| ■ **subir** | *to go up* |
| ■ **cruzar** | *to cross* |

### SUGERENCIAS

Los lugares de interés pueden ser **la biblioteca, la librería, el centro de estudiantes, la oficina de admisiones, la oficina del Registrador** *(Registrar's office)*, **y el edificio de la Facultad** *(School/Department)* **de Biología/ Humanidades/...**

## IV. Perspectivas: Una buena figura

### ■ Antes de leer

**A. Para conversar** Contesten las siguientes preguntas.

1. ¿Eres miembro de un gimnasio? Si es así, ¿cuánto cuesta tu membresía *(membership)* por mes?
2. ¿Te parece que el costo de las membresías de los gimnasios es alto o bajo? Explica por qué.
3. ¿Qué servicios ofrece tu gimnasio?
4. ¿Con qué frecuencia vas?
5. ¿Hay horas, días o meses en que hay demasiada gente en el gimnasio? Si es así, explica qué horas/días/meses son y por qué crees que va tanta gente.

### ■ A leer

### La floreciente industria del cuerpo

*arrival*

Se cumple con exactitud matemática: con la **llegada** del buen tiempo, la gente comienza a hacer más ejercicio físico. Los clubes, las plazas de deportes y la **rambla** de Montevideo se llenan, en esta época del año, de nuevos aficionados que quieren ponerse **al día** con toda la actividad física que no hicieron durante los meses anteriores.

*boardwalk*

*up-to-date*

*members*

Como consecuencia de ello, aumenta en un promedio del 25% el número de **socios** en los gimnasios, en parte gracias a los planes que ofrecen estos centros. A causa de ello, las instituciones crean más grupos y se multiplican las horas de clases.

*counterpart*

Pero la proliferación de gimnasios tiene su **contrapartida.** No hay controles oficiales sobre los nuevos centros y los más antiguos, incluso con varias décadas de funcionamiento, son los primeros en advertir este aspecto negativo.

*La cultura del cuerpo perfecto*

*linked*

*season*

*to unveil, unrobe*

En esta época del año es habitual que la gente se preocupe por realizar alguna actividad física. La proximidad del verano aparece **ligada** con el hecho de ir a la playa y con la exposición del cuerpo. En esta **estación,** todos empezamos a hacer una evaluación de nuestro cuerpo y tendemos a pensar que no estamos presentables para **descubrirnos** frente a los demás. Este sentimiento existió siempre; no se trata de un fenómeno reciente.

De todas maneras, creo que hay dos factores vinculados con la **comunicación mediática** que influyen en gran forma en nuestros comportamientos.

*mass media*

El primero está asociado con el tipo de belleza física **que se venera** hoy en día. Esta belleza ha consistido en perder unos cuantos kilos, sobre todo en estos últimos años. Los medios nos imponen un modelo de mujer **escuálida.** Esto hace que la gente se compare y tienda a imitar a estas mujeres.

*that is revered*

*emaciated*

El segundo es que, en respuesta a esta tendencia, empiezan a aparecer una serie de servicios ligados al **afán** de conseguir una buena figura. Los mismos van desde gimnasios y dietas, hasta médicos especialistas.

*urge*

Los hombres y las mujeres no sienten la misma presión. Los estímulos **se han volcado** fundamentalmente sobre el mercado femenino. Nuestra cultura hace del cuerpo femenino un valor fundamental. Al varón se le permite ser un poco menos atractivo, mientras que la mujer debe cumplir con ciertos cánones de belleza.

*have been focused*

Estamos viviendo un redescubrimiento de la **corporalidad.** Antes la gente **se cubría** más que ahora. Tener un buen cuerpo genera **confianza,** prestigio y oportunidades. Hay un culto al cuerpo ágil, **liviano** y bien formado que se asocia, a la vez, con la **búsqueda** de la eterna juventud. Ésta constituye una preocupación que **desvela** a hombres y mujeres por igual.

*related to the body*
*to cover oneself (imperfect tense) /*
*confidence, trust / light*
*search*
*keeps awake*

Los uruguayos, en general, todavía nos permitimos ciertas libertades. Podemos presentarnos «**menos producidos**» ante los demás. De todas maneras, la preocupación por el cuerpo la estamos sintiendo cada vez más.

*less worked, less developed*

## ¿Entendiste bien?

**B. Ideas principales** Contesten las siguientes preguntas.

1. ¿Cuál es la época en que va más gente a los gimnasios en Uruguay? ¿Por qué?
2. ¿Cuál es el problema con la proliferación de gimnasios en este país sudamericano?
3. ¿Cuáles son los dos factores que explican el mayor interés que existe hoy en día en hacer ejercicio?
4. Según el artículo, ¿quiénes tienen más presión social por lucir un cuerpo «perfecto»?
5. ¿Cuál es el ideal físico de los uruguayos?

**C. Detalles importantes** Lean las siguientes oraciones e indiquen si son ciertas (**C**) o falsas (**F**).

   F   1. El frío motiva a los uruguayos a ir al gimnasio.

   C   2. Con el aumento de interés en el ejercicio, ha aumentado el número de gimnasios.

   F   3. El gobierno tiene controles muy estrictos sobre estos negocios.

   C   4. Los medios de comunicación son responsables de este interés en la industria del cuerpo.

   F   5. Los uruguayos están obsesionados por alcanzar la perfección física.

**D. Debate** ¿Es la situación en Uruguay semejante o diferente a la de los Estados Unidos? Expliquen su respuesta.

**E. Actividad de extensión** Imagínense que están en Montevideo y que van a abrir un nuevo gimnasio. Preparen el anuncio comercial para atraer y motivar a más clientes.

# La diversión en la ciudad

## I. Vocabulario: Los deportes urbanos

**Patinaje en línea:** Los patines tienen tres o cuatro ruedas alineadas en una hilera única —cinco en las pruebas de velocidad. Es un deporte de moda tanto en Estados Unidos como en Europa. Equipo: patines, coderas, rodilleras y casco.

**Ciclismo:** Es una manera muy divertida de mantenerse en forma. Las modalidades más importantes practicables en la ciudad son: ciclismo en carretera, «citybike» y BMX acrobático. Equipo: una bicicleta de carreras, de «mountainbike» o de «citybike» y un casco.

**Squash:** Se practica en una cancha cerrada o un frontón, entre dos jugadores que usan raquetas para golpear una pelota antes de que toque dos veces el suelo. Equipo: una raqueta de squash, pelotas y unas gafas protectoras.

**Los bolos:** Se practica en una cancha especial, usualmente automatizada. Equipo: una bola, bolos y unas zapatillas livianas.

**La escalada libre:** Se practica en gimnasios provistos de paredes especiales. Equipo: arnés.

Transparencies G-6: Deportes (1); G-8: Deportes (2)

## Vocabulario práctico

**Equipo** *Equipment*

al cubierto/bajo techo
  *indoors*
el arnés *harness*
la bicicleta *bicycle*
la cancha *court*
el casco *helmet*
la codera *elbow pad*
la cuerda *rope*
las gafas protectoras *goggles*
el juego/el set *set*

la pelota/la bola *ball*
la raqueta *racket*
la rodillera *knee pad*

**Habilidades** *Skills*

escalar *to climb*
golpear *to hit*
halar/jalar *to pull*
pedalear *to pedal*
tirar *to throw*

■ **Asimilación**

**10-22 Opiniones y preferencias** Clasifica los deportes urbanos de acuerdo con las siguientes categorías. Luego, compara tus respuestas con las de otros compañeros. ¿En qué están todos de acuerdo?

OPCIONES: el squash   el patinaje en línea   la escalada libre
los bolos   el ciclismo

| Difícil | Peligroso (Dangerous) | Interesante | Costoso | Aburrido |
|---------|----------------------|-------------|---------|----------|
|         |                      |             |         |          |

CD2-37

**10-23 Identifícalo** Vas a escuchar la descripción de tres deportes urbanos. ¿Puedes identificarlos? Indica el número de la descripción que corresponda a cada deporte.

____ el squash   ____ el ciclismo   __2__ los bolos

__3__ la escalada libre   __1__ el patinaje en línea

■ **Aplicaciones**

**10-24 Adivina** Menciona un lugar o un objeto relacionado con un deporte urbano. Tu compañero(a) debe adivinar de qué deporte se trata. Luego, intercambien papeles. **¡OJO!** ¡Sólo tienen dos oportunidades para adivinar!

MODELO   E1: *Casco.*
         E2: *Patinaje en línea.*
         E1: *Ése no, otro.*
         E2: *¿Ciclismo?*
         E1: *¡Correcto!*

**Script 10-23:** 1. Se trata de un deporte que hoy en día se practica por todas partes (por las calles, en los parques, y hasta en los centros comerciales). A mucha gente le gusta escuchar música con los auriculares de su radio portátil mientras practica este deporte. 2. Éste es un deporte que se juega en un espacio cerrado. Si no tienes los zapatos reglamentarios, los puedes alquilar en el mismo establecimiento. Es frecuente ver equipos de vecinos o compañeros de trabajo que juegan campeonatos muy divertidos. 3. Para practicar este deporte se necesita fuerza, concentración y disciplina. Aunque se puede practicar al aire libre, hoy en día abundan los rocódromos en gimnasios y otros establecimientos deportivos. Si le tienes miedo a las alturas, es mejor que escojas otro deporte para mantenerte en forma.

**10-25 ¿Qué deporte?** Indiquen el deporte más apropiado para cada individuo y expliquen su elección.

MODELO   una joven que está en forma, pero que está aburrida con sus clases de aeróbicos
*Bueno, creemos que esta joven debe practicar la escalada libre porque es un deporte ideal para personas en buena condición física.*

1. una señora casada que tiene dos hijos pequeños
2. un joven a quien le encantan la velocidad y las emociones fuertes
3. una chica universitaria que quiere perder peso
4. un hombre de negocios muy competitivo
5. una pareja de recién casados

**10-26 Entrevista** Hazle las siguientes preguntas a un(a) compañero(a) y comparte sus respuestas con el resto de la clase.

1. ¿Practicas algún deporte urbano?
2. ¿Cuáles de los deportes mencionados en este capítulo te gustaría aprender?
3. ¿Cuál(es) no te interesa(n)? ¿Por qué?
4. ¿Qué ventajas y qué inconvenientes tienen los deportes urbanos?

■ **Integración**

**10-27 Aburridos** Representa la siguiente situación con un(a) compañero(a).

| El (La) amante de la naturaleza | El (La) deportista urbano(a) |
|---|---|
| Hoy no tienes nada que hacer y te encuentras aburrido(a). Llama a tu amigo(a) para ver qué se le ocurre hacer. Importante: Trata de convencer a tu amigo(a) de hacer alguna actividad al aire libre.<br>1. Saluda a tu amigo(a).<br>2. Pregúntale qué está haciendo.<br>3. Si está libre, invítalo(la) a hacer alguna actividad al aire libre.<br>4. Explícale las ventajas de las actividades al aire libre y los inconvenientes de los deportes urbanos. | Hoy no tienes nada que hacer y te encuentras aburrido(a). Tu amigo(a) te llama para ver qué quieres hacer. Importante: Trata de convencer a tu amigo(a) de acompañarte a practicar tu deporte urbano favorito.<br>1. Saluda a tu amigo(a).<br>2. Dile que estás libre hoy.<br>3. Trata de convencerlo(la) de acompañarte a practicar tu deporte urbano favorito.<br>4. Explícale las ventajas de los deportes urbanos y los inconvenientes de las actividades al aire libre. |

**10-28 El deporte ideal para Ud. es...** En parejas, preparen un cuestionario para determinar el tipo de deporte que más le conviene *(is best for)* a una persona de acuerdo con sus preferencias y posibilidades. Por ejemplo: ¿Cuánto tiempo libre tiene? ¿Le gustan las actividades al aire libre? ¿Tiene Ud. bicicleta? etc. Al terminar, háganle esas preguntas a otra pareja, analicen sus respuestas y presenten sus recomendaciones.

MODELO   *A John le recomendamos que practique... porque... Por otra parte, a Jennifer le recomendamos... porque...*

SUGERENCIAS

Para persuadir a alguien de hacer algo diferente, puedes decir:

¿Sabes qué?   *You know what?*
**En realidad no me gusta...**   *I don't really like to . . .*
**Mira, ¿por qué no...?**   *Look, why don't we . . . ?*
**¿Qué te parece si...?**   *How about . . . ?*

SUGERENCIAS

Usa los siguientes conectores en tu informe:

**por otra parte** *on the other hand*
**sin embargo** *however*
**en cambio** *on the other hand*
**también** *also*
**de la misma manera** *by the same token*
**igualmente** *in the same way*

This activity recycles the use of the subjunctive for advice. To facilitate the completion of the activity, it would be a good idea to break it into steps.
Step 1: In pairs, develop the questionnaire.
Step 2: Conduct the interview. (One pair of students interviews another pair.)
Step 3: Analyze the findings. (Students go back to their original group, reflect on the other group's responses, and draft their suggestions following the model provided.)
Step 4: In a group plenary, a spokesperson for each of the groups presents the group's suggestions. After each presentation, you may want to ask students to react to the advice received: **¿Qué te parecen esas ideas? ¿Habías considerado esta alternativa alguna vez? ¿Piensas tratar de seguir sus recomendaciones?** etc.

## II. Funciones y estructuras: Expressing opinion and emotion (review of the subjunctive)

DIEGO: Pilar, **me alegra que hayas** decidido practicar ciclismo. Es un buen deporte para nosotros los que vivimos en la ciudad.

PILAR: Sí, hace tiempo que quería hacerlo, pero como no tenía bicicleta...

DIEGO: Claro. Y también **es bueno que tengas** un casco. Ya sabes: la seguridad ante todo.

PILAR: Así es. ¡Yo no montaría en bicicleta sin casco por estas avenidas ni loca!

As you learned in **Capítulo 9, Tema 2,** expressions of opinion and emotion like the ones Diego used in the conversation above trigger the use of the subjunctive mode. Here is a complete list of the verbs and impersonal expressions you learned in the previous chapter.

| VERBS | | IMPERSONAL EXPRESSIONS | |
|---|---|---|---|
| agradar* | to like | es un abuso que... | it is an abuse that . . . |
| alegrarse (de) | to be glad | es bueno que... | it is good that . . . |
| doler* (ue) | to be hurt | es curioso que... | it is odd that . . . |
| estar contento(a) (de) | to be happy | es extraño que... | it is strange that . . . |
| estar furioso (de) | to be angry | es impresionante que... | it is impressive |
| gustar* | to be pleased | | that . . . |
| molestar* | to be bothered | es increíble que... | it is incredible that . . . |
| parecer fantástico* | to consider great | es una lástima que... | it is a shame that . . . |
| parecer terrible* | to consider terrible | es malo que... | it is bad that . . . |
| parecer triste* | to consider sad | es una pena que... | it is a pity that . . . |
| sentir | to feel, to lament | es raro que... | it is unusual that . . . |
| temer | to fear | es ridículo que... | it is ridiculous that . . . |
| tener miedo | to be afraid | es terrible que... | it is terrible that . . . |

*Remember: These verbs are used with indirect object pronouns.

**Es raro que** Sergio y Leo, dos personas tan cuidadosas, no **usen** rodilleras.

*It is unusual that Sergio and Leo, two very careful people, do not **use** knee pads.*

A mi novio le **parece fantástico** que a mí me **guste** el patinaje en línea.

*My boyfriend **thinks it is great** that I **like** in-line skating.*

## ■ Asimilación

**10-29 Opiniones** Completa las siguientes oraciones de forma lógica. Al terminar, compara tus respuestas con las de un(a) compañero(a). ¿Tienen las mismas opiniones?

1. Es una pena que ustedes (lleven / (no lleven)) gafas protectoras.
2. ¡Estoy contenta de que nosotros ((juguemos) / no juguemos) a los bolos en familia los sábados!
3. Marla, es extraño que (traigas / (no traigas)) la raqueta si sabes que vamos a jugar.
4. Es ridículo que ellos ((quieran) / no quieran) jugar béisbol con una pelota de golf.
5. Temo que Fernando (pueda / (no pueda)) venir a la práctica hoy porque está enfermo.
6. Jaime, ¿te gusta que tu hijo ((escale) / no escale) esas paredes tan altas siendo tan pequeño?

**10-30 La Casa del Deporte** Escucha el anuncio de radio de La Casa del Deporte, una tienda de equipo deportivo, e indica si las oraciones que siguen son ciertas **(C)** o falsas **(F).**

  __F__ 1. En esta ciudad hay muy pocas personas que practican deportes.
  __C__ 2. En La Casa del Deporte hay una buena selección de cascos y rodilleras.
  __F__ 3. También tienen una buena selección de cuerdas y gafas protectoras.
  __F__ 4. Los empleados de esta tienda pueden ayudar al cliente a escoger una buena cancha para jugar.
  __F__ 5. Parece que La Casa del Deporte es una tienda pequeña.

## ■ Aplicaciones

**10-31 Es bueno que...** Completen la tabla con dos cosas que recomiendan para practicar cada uno de los siguientes deportes.

| el patinaje en línea | el ciclismo |
|---|---|
| *Es bueno que...* | *Es bueno que...* |
| **los bolos** | **la escalada libre** |
| *Es bueno que...* | *Es bueno que...* |

**Script 10-30:** Si usted es uno de los muchos deportistas en nuestra ciudad, es mejor que preste atención. En La Casa del Deporte nos alegramos de que más y más personas hayan descubierto las ventajas *(advantages/benefits)* de tener una vida activa, pero queremos que lo hagan de forma segura. Por eso, si usted es amante del patinaje en línea o del ciclismo, es recomendable que use un casco, coderas y rodilleras. Nadie tiene una mejor selección que La Casa del Deporte. Además, si le gusta el squash o el tenis, ¡nos parece increíble que usted no tenga una de las mejores raquetas del mercado! Y en La Casa del Deporte le ayudamos a escoger la que mejor se adapte a sus necesidades. ¿Y qué de los amantes del béisbol, básquetbol, vóleibol y golf? ¡Es una lástima que no jueguen con una pelota de calidad, como las que tenemos en La Casa del Deporte! ¿Qué está esperando? Visítenos en el número 46 de la calle Ortega y se convencerá. La Casa del Deporte: para el deportista que lo quiere todo.

### EN TU COMUNIDAD

Find out if there are any laws related to safety while practicing certain sports in your community. Discuss your findings in groups and present an oral report in class.

**10-32 ¿Qué piensan?** Túrnense para leer las siguientes oraciones y reaccionar de forma lógica.

> MODELO E1: *Mis amigos piensan que jugar a los bolos es aburrido.*
> E2: *Es una pena que tus amigos piensen que jugar a los bolos es aburrido. A mí me gusta mucho jugar a los bolos.*

1. La cancha de tenis de mi barrio es grande.
2. Quiero practicar algún deporte, pero no tengo tiempo.
3. Los hijos de mis vecinos no usan casco cuando montan en bicicleta.
4. Voy a comprar una nueva raqueta de squash.
5. Tengo que dejar de hacer escalada libre porque me duele mucho una rodilla.
6. No puedo ir al partido de béisbol esta noche porque tengo que estudiar.
7. Estas gafas protectoras sirven para practicar cualquier deporte.
8. Quiero ir con ustedes, pero mis patines están dañados *(broken: they don't work).*

**10-33 Eventos recientes** *(current events)* ¿Qué cosas han pasado últimamente en el mundo de la política, el cine, el arte, la ciencia y la educación? ¿Qué piensan Uds. sobre estas cosas? Escriban por lo menos seis oraciones para expresar sus opiniones y sus sentimientos.

> MODELO *Nos alegra que... esté embarazada.*
> *Es terrible que el senador... diga que...*

## ■ Integración

**10-34 ¡Un momento!** Representa la siguiente situación con un(a) compañero(a).

### SUGERENCIAS

Las siguientes expresiones pueden ayudarte a convencer a tu entrenador(a):

| | |
|---|---|
| **¡Estoy seguro(a)!** | *I am sure!* |
| **¡Tengo lo que se necesita!** | *I have what it takes!* |
| **¡Soy muy bueno(a) para...!** | *I am very good at . . . !* |
| **¡Estoy en excelente condición física para...!** | *I am in excellent physical condition to . . . !* |

**Un(a) deportista que tiene demasiadas metas**

Eres una persona que quiere poder practicar la mayor cantidad de deportes posible. Habla con un(a) entrenador(a) y trata de convencerlo(la) de que tienes las cualidades necesarias para lograr esta meta.

**Un(a) entrenador(a) realista**

Eres un(a) entrenador(a) y una de las personas con quien trabajas quiere practicar muchos deportes diferentes. Como eres muy realista, prefieres que esta persona aprenda deporte por deporte *(one sport at a time)*. Escucha lo que te dice y exprésale tu opinión y lo que sientes al respecto.

### SUGERENCIAS

Puedes usar las siguientes expresiones para convencer a tu cliente de que debe hacer las cosas de a poco:

| | |
|---|---|
| **Un momento!** | *One moment!* |
| **¡Con calma!** | *Take it easy!* |
| **¡Piénsalo bien!** | *Think about it!* |
| **¡No estoy de acuerdo!** | *I don't agree!* |

**10-35 Una carta para tu supervisor(a)** Imagínate que eres el (la) entrenador(a) de la actividad 10-34. Como esta persona no quedó completamente convencida de que debe tomar las cosas con calma y temes que se queje *(complains),* has decidido escribirle una carta a tu supervisor(a) para explicarle la situación. Usa los verbos y las frases para expresar emoción y opinión que ya sabes. Cuando termines, dale una copia a tu profesor(a) para que la corrija.

## III. Funciones y estructuras: Expressing purpose, stipulation, or future time frame with the present subjunctive in adverbial clauses

> **¡Gran apertura!**
>
> GIMNASIO HÉRCULES
>
> Con el equipo más avanzado **para que pierda** peso y **desarrolle** un cuerpo espectacular en corto tiempo.
>
> Oferta introductoria de sólo $75 por mes.
>
> **¡Cuando vea** los resultados, va a quedar convencido(a)! **¡En caso de que no esté** satisfecho(a), le devolveremos su dinero!

The subjunctive mode is required in subordinate clauses that are introduced by certain conjunctions. These conjunctions can be grouped in three categories.

As with other expressions that trigger the use of the subjunctive mode, when the subject of the main clause and the subordinate clause is the same these expressions are followed by an infinitive (with some exceptions that you will learn about in **Capítulo 11, Tema 2**).

■ conjunctions that express purpose or reason

| **a fin de que** *in order that, so that* | **para que** *in order that, so that* |
| --- | --- |

Voy a pasar por tu casa a las diez **para que vayamos** a patinar.
Decidí acompañarte **a fin de que** no **regreses** sola esta noche.

*I will stop by your house at ten **so that we can go** skating.*
*I decided to go with you **so that you** do not **come back** alone tonight.*

■ conjunctions that express stipulation

| **a menos que** *unless* **con tal de que** *provided that* | **en caso de que** *in case that, in the event that* |
| --- | --- |

Ella va a llegar al gimnasio a eso de las cinco **a menos que ocurra** algo en la oficina.
Llámame **en caso de que vayan** a jugar a los bolos esta tarde.

*She is going to get to the gym at around five **unless** something **happens** at the office.*
*Call me **in case that you go** bowling this afternoon.*

■ adverbs and conjunctions that express future time frame

| **antes (de) que** *before* **cuando** *when* **después (de) que** *after* | **en cuanto** *as soon as* **hasta que** *until* **mientras (que)** *while* |
| --- | --- |

**Cuando salgas** de tu casa, trae los cascos y las coderas.
Vamos a construir una cancha bajo techo **en cuanto tengamos** el dinero.

***When you leave*** *home, bring the helmets and the elbow pads.*
*We are going to build an indoor court **as soon as we have** the money.*

## ■ Asimilación

**10-36 ¿Cuándo?** Empareja las frases de la izquierda con las de la derecha. Cuando termines, compara tus respuestas con las de un(a) compañero(a). ¿Crees que debes cambiar algo?

_c_ 1. No voy a poder estudiar...

_e_ 2. Vamos a ver televisión...

_a_ 3. No puedes usar la bicicleta...

_d_ 4. Dice que va a leer...

_b_ 5. Te aviso...

_f_ 6. Vamos a jugar...

a. antes de que yo la pague.

b. en cuanto tenga la información.

c. mientras estés escuchando música.

d. hasta que lo entienda todo.

e. después de que tú limpies la sala.

f. cuando abran la cancha.

CD2-39 **10-37 Preguntas** Escucha las preguntas y escoge la respuesta más lógica.

Script 10-37: 1. ¿Por qué tienes un botiquín de primeros auxilios? 2. ¿Para qué haces calentamiento? 3. ¿Por qué el entrenador les exige tanto? 4. ¿Vas a dejar de fumar? 5. ¿Cuándo te vas a sentir mejor? 6. ¿Vas a llegar temprano a la práctica?

1. En caso de que...
   a. haya una emergencia.   b. tenga que ir al doctor.
2. Para que...
   a. los músculos se relajen.   b. no me dé alergia.
3. A fin de que nosotros...
   a. subamos un poco de peso.   b. nos mantengamos en forma.
4. Cuando...
   a. me ponga un yeso.   b. compre los parches (patches)
5. En cuanto...
   a. tome una pastilla.   b. me duela el estómago.
6. Sí, a menos que...
   a. aumente mi elasticidad.   b. me despierte tarde.

## ■ Aplicaciones

Answers 10-38: 1. ...a menos que su madre se lo recuerde. 2. ...después de que su novia salga del trabajo. 3. ...antes de que la oferta termine el jueves. 4. ...a fin de que ustedes lo puedan usar. 5. ...en caso de que decidamos ir a un restaurante después de la práctica. 6. ...cuando no quiera jugar más. 7. ...hasta que cierren el gimnasio. 8. ...para que ella pierda peso rápidamente.

**10-38 Propósitos y condiciones** Unan los siguientes pares de oraciones y usen las conjunciones entre paréntesis. Hagan los cambios que sean necesarios.

MODELO   Ernesto lleva a sus hijos. Sus hijos juegan a los bolos también. (para que)
*Ernesto lleva a sus hijos para que jueguen a los bolos también.*

1. Patricia nunca trae el casco. Su madre se lo recuerda. (a menos que)
2. Andrés puede jugar. Su novia sale del trabajo. (después de que)
3. Quiero comprar la bicicleta. La oferta termina el jueves. (antes de que)
4. Vamos a traer el equipo. Ustedes lo pueden usar. (a fin de que)
5. Traje un cambio de ropa. Decidimos ir a un restaurante después de patinar. (en caso de que)
6. Te presto la raqueta. No quiero jugar más. (cuando)
7. Carmen y Tomás van a hacer aeróbicos. Cierran el gimnasio. (hasta que)
8. José motiva a su hermana. Ella pierde peso rápidamente. (para que)

**10-39 Los estudios**

**Paso 1:** Completa las siguientes oraciones de una manera lógica.

1. Mis padres quieren que termine mis estudios para que yo...
2. Voy a tener un buen promedio general este semestre a menos que...
3. Quiero graduarme antes de que...
4. Es posible que tome menos cursos el próximo semestre en caso de que...
5. Pienso tomar cursos de español hasta que...
6. Siempre saco buenas notas con tal de que...
7. Voy a seguir estudiando hasta que...
8. En cuanto..., espero comprar una casa grande y un carro nuevo.

**Paso 2:** Compara tus respuestas con las de un(a) compañero(a). Prepara un informe breve y preséntalo en clase.

> **MODELO** *Mis padres quieren que termine mis estudios para que yo pueda ganar mucho dinero, pero los padres de Danielle quieren que ella termine para que sea una abogada excelente.*

**10-40 Causa y efecto** Combinen elementos de las siguientes columnas para formar oraciones lógicas. Pueden usar otros verbos y expresiones.

> **MODELO** los padres   trabajar...   para que...
> *Los padres trabajan muchas horas para que sus hijos vivan bien.*

| los padres | | |
| el (la) profesor(a) | trabajar... | |
| la gente | estudiar... | |
| los niños | establecer... | |
| los atletas | + decidir... | + para que... |
| los artistas | asignar... | |
| el gobierno | comportarse... | |
| | respetar... | |

### ■ Integración

**10-41 Metas y perspectivas** Túrnense para hacer y responder a las siguientes preguntas. Al terminar, preparen un informe breve y preséntenselo a la clase.

1. ¿Piensas hacer un postgrado? ¿Cuándo? ¿En qué disciplina?
2. ¿Esperas independizarte pronto? ¿Por qué o para qué? ¿Cuándo?
3. ¿Piensas abrir tu propia empresa? ¿Cuándo? ¿Para qué?
4. ¿Vas a perfeccionar tus conocimientos *(knowledge)* de español? ¿Por qué? ¿Cuándo? ¿Cómo?
5. ¿Piensas casarte? ¿Cuándo? ¿Con quién?
6. ¿Quieres tener hijos? ¿Cuándo? ¿Cuántos?

**10-42 Analizando mi comportamiento** Saca unos minutos para analizar tu comportamiento. ¿Siempre haces algunas cosas antes o después de que ocurren otras? ¿Haces ciertas cosas para obtener una reacción específica de los demás? ¿Y haces algo esperando otra cosa a cambio? Escribe un breve resumen sobre este tema y preséntaselo a tu profesor(a).

> **MODELO** *Creo que, desafortunadamente, les hago favores a mis amigos con tal de que ellos después me ayuden a mí. Pero también hago muchas cosas para que ellos se sientan bien, como...*

## IV. Vídeo: Un desastre en la cocina

### ■ Preparación

**A. La comida y la salud** Todos sabemos que la buena nutrición es importantísima para la salud. Entrevista a un(a) compañero(a) sobre los siguientes aspectos de sus hábitos alimenticios:

- si se preocupa por comer saludablemente o no
- si sabe cocinar
  - ¿Le gusta cocinar? ¿Por qué sí o no?
  - ¿Sigue las instrucciones de las recetas o cocina más bien sin seguirlas?
- qué tipos de comida come diariamente
- si le gustaría cambiar algo respecto a su dieta

### ■ ¿Entendiste bien?

**ESTRATEGIA DE COMPRENSIÓN**

**Selective listening** Concentrate on the specific information required in order to complete the exercises below.

This activity recycles vocabulary related to food. You may want to do a brainstorming exercise first or provide a word bank. You may also ask students to review this vocabulary as part of the previous lesson's homework.

**B. ¡Ay, qué complicado es cocinar!** Mira a Valeria mientras se embarca en una aventura culinaria y completa la siguiente información que Alejandra le da para ayudarla a preparar la receta.

#### *Cómo se preparan los chiles rellenos al horno...*

**Paso 1:** Empecemos con los ingredientes y las cantidades. Valeria, vas a necesitar:

____seis____ chiles poblanos (asados, pelados y desvenados), una taza y media de ____arroz____ blanco guisado, una taza de ____crema____, tres cebollitas de cambray, media cucharadita de ____sal____, una taza de caldillo de jitomate, ____queso____ añejo al gusto...

**Paso 2:** Ahora, hablemos de la preparación. Sigue los siguientes pasos con precisión.

- Rellena los ____chiles____ con el ____arroz____.
- Colócalos en un platón refractario *(heat-resistant)*.
- Licúa la ____crema____, las cebollitas y la ____sal____.
- Baña los chiles con el caldillo de jitomate.
- Échales *(Pour)* la crema por encima.
- Espolvorea *(Sprinkle)* el ____queso____ añejo.
- Pon todo en el horno por ____diez____ minutos a ____190____ grados centígrados.

Compara tus respuestas con las de un(a) compañero(a).

**Paso 3:** Ahora, miren el vídeo de nuevo y contesten las siguientes preguntas.

1. Valeria le admite a Alejandra que no le gusta cocinar para nada. Entonces ¿por qué quería preparar este plato?
2. Alejandra habla de la diferencia entre los nombres de alimentos en diferentes países hispanos.
   - ¿Qué ejemplo específico da? ¿Cómo se llama ese alimento en su país?
   - ¿Conocen más ejemplos? Hagan una lista.
3. ¿Cómo le queda la cena a Valeria? ¿Cómo reaccionan los demás compañeros?

**Answers B, Paso 3:** 1. quería sorprender a Antonio con una cena; quería cocinar un plato típico mexicano. 2. el tomate, que se llama jitomate en Colombia 3. fatal/todo un desastre (se le quemaron los chiles, el queso estaba muy salado, le echó mucho picante a la salsa); a pesar de eso, los compañeros fueron corteses e incluso Antonio se comió un chile relleno

**C. Mi plato favorito** Piensa en tu plato favorito y luego escoge una de las opciones siguientes (dependiendo de si sabes cocinar o no).

**Opción 1: Los sabios de la cocina.** Si sabes cocinar tu plato favorito, descríbele a tu compañero(a) cómo se prepara. Empieza con la lista de ingredientes y cantidades y luego los pasos específicos que hay que seguir. No te olvides de usar mandatos informales (**tú**) para darle a tu compañero(a) las instrucciones. Él/Ella debe apuntar toda la información que le des.

**Opción 2: Los perdidos en la cocina.** Si eres como Valeria (o sea, un desastre en la cocina), pídele ayuda a tu compañero(a). Dile cuál es tu plato favorito y deja que él/ella intente explicarte cómo se prepara. Pídele a tu compañero(a) que te diga todos los ingredientes y cantidades necesarios y apunta esa información. Luego, pregúntale acerca de cómo se prepara el plato paso por paso y apunta todo lo que te diga.

**D. Enfoque comunitario** Investiga acerca de qué servicios alimenticios ofrece tu universidad. ¿Hay una amplia oferta de diferentes tipos de comidas de países distintos? Y para una buena nutrición, ¿hay opciones que permitan seguir una dieta equilibrada y sana? Prepara un breve informe en español en el cual presentes tus conclusiones y recomendaciones para mejorar los servicios alimenticios. Debes estar preparado(a) para presentar tu informe en clase.

# Panorama cultural

## I. Vocabulario: Las bellas artes

Los artistas de la escuela **neoclásica** producen obras donde predomina el orden y **la proporción.**

Los impresionistas juegan con los efectos de la **luz y la perspectiva.**

Los cubistas usan **formas abstractas** para **representar** la realidad.

Los artistas de **la escuela Pop** utilizan imágenes de **la cultura masiva.**

### Vocabulario práctico

**El arte**

el (la) artista *artist*
la cultura masiva *mass culture*
el dibujo *drawing*
la escena *scene*
el (la) escultor(a) *sculptor*
la escultura *sculpture*
la exposición *exposition*
la fotografía *photography*
la galería de arte *art gallery*
la imagen *image*
la luz *light*
el movimiento *movement/school*
la muestra *sample, show*
la obra *work*

la obra maestra *masterpiece*
el paisaje *landscape*
el pintor *painter*
la pintura/el cuadro *painting*
la proporción *proportion*
la sala *room*
la técnica *technique*

**Verbos**

presentar *to present*
producir *to produce*
representar *to represent*
usar *to use*
utilizar *to make use*

## ■ Asimilación

**10-43 Unas exposiciones de arte** Completa las frases con información de la guía cultural.

---

### Guía cultural - Buenos Aires

En el **Museo Nacional de Buenos Aires (MNBA)** una muestra inolvidable, sin par, de un clásico atemporal: Henry Moore. Integrada por 53 esculturas y 72 dibujos. Organizó el British Council y la Fundación Henry Moore.

En el **Centro Cultural Recoleta (CCR)** expondrá **Manuel Cancel** sus típicos y apaisados paisajes ovales, expuestos anteriormente en la Galería Art House.

En el CCR una muestra que abarca desde el año 1983 a 1996 del gran artista **Miguel Barceló,** cuya vida transcurre entre París, Mallorca y Mali, expone hasta el 14 de diciembre 50 trabajos sobresalientes que despiertan enorme interés en el público asistente.

En el CCR expone **Joaquín Molina** «Paraísos custodiados», 20 trabajos con el laberinto como eje.

En la **Galería Benzacar** expuso sus recientes pinturas **Rogelio Polesello.** Después de la muestra «Brasil, nuevas propuestas».

En la **Art House** se realizó una muestra fuera de serie, «Calzar el arte», el zapato como un objeto de arte y como objeto de uso. Organización, selección de artistas, catálogo y montaje de Silvia de Ambrosini.

---

## ■ ¿Entendiste bien?

1. Hay una exposición de escultura en _____el MNBA_____ .
2. _____ es un pintor argentino.
3. La muestra que se presenta en Art House se llama ___Calzar el arte___ y trata sobre ___zapatos___ .

**Answer** 2. Manuel Cancel/Joaquín Molina/Rogelio Polesello

### EN TU COMUNIDAD

Visit a local museum and report on the art being exhibited in a particular section. You can do this in groups (invite your classmates!) or individually.

CD2-40  **10-44 ¿De qué pintura se trata?** Vas a escuchar la descripción de una pintura. Indica la imagen que corresponde a la descripción.

**Script 10-44:** Esta pintura representa a una mujer, pero no lo hace de una manera realista o directa. En esta obra, el artista no juega con la luz, ni utiliza las imágenes de la cultura masiva. Por el contrario, el artista usa solamente formas geométricas para representar la imagen femenina de una manera abstracta. Se trata, sin lugar a dudas, de una pintura cubista.

Pintura A ____      Pintura B _X_      Pintura C ____

## ■ Aplicaciones

**10-45 Las actividades del MNBA** Completa la siguiente reseña con las palabras de la lista. Al terminar, compara tus respuestas con las de un(a) compañero(a).

OPCIONES:   artista   exposición   pinturas   muestra   salas

En el Museo Nacional de Buenos Aires se acaba de inaugurar una ___exposición___ excepcional. Se trata de una ___muestra___ de la pintura del famoso pintor Pablo Picasso. En cinco ___salas___ se presentan más de 50 de sus obras del período de 1930 a 1950. La mayoría de las ___pinturas___ expuestas son de la escuela cubista. El museo está presentando también un documental sobre la vida del ___artista___.

As homework, you may want to ask your students to research information about several of the artists or schools in the **Sugerencias** box.

**10-46 ¿A qué (o a quién) me refiero?** Describe a un artista, una escuela de arte o una obra maestra. Tus compañeros deben adivinar de qué (o de quién) se trata.

MODELO   E1: *Fue un pintor y escultor italiano muy famoso. Pintó la cúpula de la Capilla Sixtina. Algunas de sus esculturas más conocidas son el David y La Piedad.*
E2: *¿Miguel Ángel?*
E1: *¡Así es!*

### SUGERENCIAS

Aquí tienes una lista de algunos de los movimientos y artistas más famosos de la historia.

**Renacimiento:** Leonardo da Vinci, Rafael, Miguel Ángel
**Barroco:** Diego Velázquez, Peter Paul Rubens
**Impresionismo:** Edouard Manet, Edgar Degas, Claude Monet, Pierre Renoir, Paul Cezanne, Vincent van Gogh
**Cubismo:** Pablo Picasso, Georges Bracques, Juan Gris
**Surrealismo:** Salvador Dalí, Joan Miró, René Magritte, Frida Kahlo, Remedios Varo
**Arte Pop:** Andy Warhol

**10-47 Entrevista** Hazle las siguientes preguntas a un(a) compañero(a) y presenta un resumen de sus respuestas.

1. ¿Te gusta tener cuadros en las paredes de tu casa o de tu cuarto? ¿Por qué?
2. Sí es así, describe algunas de las pinturas que tienes. Específicamente, di qué tienen en común estas obras, tales como los temas, los colores, los estilos, los artistas, etc., y dónde están expuestas en tu casa.
3. ¿Te gusta el trabajo de algún artista en particular? Si es así, ¿quién es y qué tipo de obras hace?

## ■ Integración

**10-48 Amantes del arte** Representa la siguiente situación con un(a) compañero(a).

### Amante del arte

Estás en Buenos Aires y has convencido a un(a) amigo(a) de pasar por el Centro Cultural Recoleta. Desgraciadamente, a tu amigo(a) no le gusta mucho el arte y, evidentemente, está muy aburrido(a).

1. Háblale acerca de estos dos cuadros y ayúdale a apreciar su mérito artístico.
2. Trata de convencerlo(a) de que se quede en la galería para ver el resto de la exposición.

### El arte no es mi punto fuerte

Estás de visita en Buenos Aires y tu amigo(a) te ha convencido de entrar a una exposición de arte en el Centro Cultural Recoleta. A ti no te interesa mucho la pintura y estás un poco aburrido(a).

1. Explícale que en realidad no te gusta mucho el arte y que estás aburrido(a).
2. Trata de convencer a tu amigo(a) de que vaya contigo a otra parte lo más pronto posible.

### SUGERENCIAS

Para expresar que estás aburrido(a), y que quieres hacer algo diferente, di:

**¿No crees que ya hemos visto suficientes cuadros?** *Don't you think we have seen enough paintings?*

**¿Por qué no vamos a...?** *Why don't we go to . . . ?*

**Quiero irme de esta galería ya.** *I want to leave this gallery right now.*

«Mundo», Alejandro Xul Solar

«Años de temor», Roberto Matta

**10-49 Actividades culturales** Investiga qué exposiciones hay en tu universidad o en tu ciudad en este momento. Visita la galería de arte que corresponda a tus intereses y lleva a clase una breve reseña de la exposición que tuviste la oportunidad de ver. Incluye la siguiente información:

- nombre del / de la artista
- número de pinturas (o esculturas)
- técnicas o estilos utilizados
- temas o escenas típicos
- opinión personal (si te gustó la exposición o no, y por qué)

## II. Funciones y estructuras: Giving directives and advice (review of formal and informal commands and introduction of *nosotros* commands)

El Museo del Prado (Madrid)

—Chicos, ya llegamos al Museo del Prado. **¡Disfrutemos** de las obras de Goya, Velázquez y El Greco! **No nos perdamos** porque el museo es grandísimo. ¡Ah! ¡Y **no comamos** nada ni **tomemos** fotos! ¡Por favor! ¿Estamos listos? Pues, **¡entremos!**

You already know how to give affirmative and negative commands in the **usted, ustedes,** and **tú** forms. As you may recall, the form of these commands coincides with the verb forms of the present subjunctive, with the exception of affirmative **tú** commands, which coincide with the third-person singular present indicative verb forms.

USTED: **(No) Ponga** la escultura en el estante.
*(Don't) Put the sculpture on the shelf.*
USTEDES: **(No) Apliquen** esta técnica.
*(Don't) Apply this technique.*
TÚ: **(No hables) Habla** con el artista.
*(Don't) Speak with the artist.*

The present subjunctive **nosotros** form can also be used to give directives and advice that applies to the speaker. It is the equivalent of the *Let's . . .* English expression. Negative commands are formed by placing **no** before the verb.

**¡Produzcamos** una obra maestra, amigos!
***Let's produce** a masterpiece, friends!*
Colegas, **no utilicemos** estas brochas.
*Colleagues, **let's not use** these brushes.*

Just like with **usted, ustedes,** and **tú** commands, indirect and direct object pronouns are attached to the verb in **nosotros** affirmative commands and are placed between **no** and the verb in **nosotros** negative commands.

Notice that the verb takes a written accent mark when the pronoun is attached to it.

### REMEMBER

The indirect object pronoun goes before the direct object pronoun and **le** and **les** change to **se** before **lo, la, los,** or **las.**

**Presentémosle** esta pintura al dueño de la galería.
***Let's present** this painting to the gallery owner **(to him).***
**No se la llevemos** todavía.
***Let's not bring it to him** yet.*
**Busquémoselos** ahora mismo.
***Let's find it for her** right now.*

In the affirmative command form of reflexive verbs, the final **-s** of the present subjunctive **nosotros** form is dropped before attaching the reflexive pronoun **nos.** This change does not affect the negative form.

**Sentémonos** (*not* **sentémosnos**) a admirar esta obra.

*Let's sit down to admire this work.*

**No nos vistamos** formalmente para ir a la exposición.

*Let's not dress formally to go to the exposition.*

The same thing happens if the **nosotros** affirmative command has the pronouns **se** + **lo/la/los/las** attached to it: **Busquémoselos** ahora mismo. **Let's find it for her** right now.

## ■ Asimilación

**10-50 Una fotografía espectacular** Imagínate que tu amigo(a) y tú son fotógrafos y quieren llegar a exponer una de sus fotografías en una galería famosa. Pon las siguientes oraciones en orden lógico. Cuando termines, compara el orden con el de un(a) compañero(a). ¿Crees que tienes que hacer cambios?

The answers to activity 10-50 may vary slightly.

_5_ Hablemos con el (la) director(a) de una galería de arte.

_3_ No vayamos a la tienda de equipo fotográfico de la calle Viamonte.

_1_ Pensemos en una idea original para la fotografía.

_6_ No nos pongamos nerviosos cuando hablemos con él o ella.

_2_ Compremos el equipo que necesitamos.

_8_ Celebremos nuestro triunfo.

_4_ Trabajemos todos los días hasta tener la fotografía perfecta.

_7_ Expongámosla hasta que se venda.

2-41 **10-51 ¿Para quién es la orden?** Escucha a Cecilia Pereira, una profesora de arte, mientras les da indicaciones a ciertas personas. Luego, indica quién debe hacer las siguientes actividades. Presta atención a las formas verbales.

Script 10-51: Buenas tardes a todos. Disculpen la tardanza. Carla y Efraín, comiencen a trabajar en el estudio. Por favor, no muevan los dibujos de los estudiantes nocturnos. Rigoberto, búscame el catálogo de pinturas que está sobre mi escritorio y dile a Serena que voy a llegar tarde a la reunión. Sr. Beltrán, mucho gusto de verlo. Por favor, pase a mi oficina. Voy a estar con Ud. en unos minutos. Y no se preocupe. Le tengo una pintura que le va a fascinar. Leonor, vamos a hablar con Esmeralda un momento. Quiero que la ayudes con un informe que tengo que presentar mañana.

**OPCIONES:** 1 = su asistente (tú)
2 = un comprador *(buyer)* de alta sociedad (Ud.)
3 = dos estudiantes (Uds.)
4 = Cecilia Pereira y su secretaria (nosotras)

1. no preocuparse _2_
2. no mover los dibujos de los estudiantes nocturnos _3_
3. pasar a la oficina _2_
4. buscar el catálogo de pinturas _1_
5. irse a hablar con Esmeralda _4_
6. comenzar a trabajar en el estudio _3_
7. decirle a Serena que Cecilia Pereira va a llegar tarde a la reunión _1_

## Aplicaciones

**10-52 ¡Sí! ¡No!** Túrnense para leer y reaccionar a las siguientes oraciones. Deben decir lo opuesto y proveer detalles. **¡OJO!** Usen pronombres siempre que sea posible.

MODELO     E1: *Estudiemos en la biblioteca.*
               E2: *¡No! No estudiemos en la biblioteca. No me gusta estudiar ahí. Prefiero estudiar en un café.*

1. Digámosle al / a la profesor(a) que queremos un examen mañana.
2. No nos pongamos ropa cómoda para venir a la universidad.
3. No traduzcamos las instrucciones del español al inglés.
4. ¿Las clases? Tomémoslas los lunes, miércoles y viernes.
5. Empecemos a escribir la siguiente composición.
6. ¿El libro de español? No se lo prestemos a nadie.
7. Comámonos una ensalada en la cafetería de la universidad.

**10-53 ¿Qué hacemos?** Escriban un mandato afirmativo y un mandato negativo lógicos para cada situación. ¡Sean creativos!

MODELO     Hoy es sábado. Son las ocho de la noche y estamos aburridos. *¡No abramos los libros por nada en el mundo! ¡Vayamos a algún lugar divertido en la ciudad!*

1. Queremos conseguir un buen trabajo cuando nos graduemos.
2. Nuestro apartamento está muy sucio y tenemos visita esta noche.
3. Vamos a mudarnos en una semana y no tenemos nada listo.
4. Comimos demasiado y nos sentimos enfermos.
5. Nos preocupa la contaminación del medio ambiente.
6. Estamos en una tienda que tiene una oferta especial de una hora.
7. Nos interesa perder peso y mejorar nuestro estado de salud.

### SUGERENCIAS

Para formar oraciones lógicas, puedes usar los siguientes verbos: **(no) ponerse, bañarse, (no) vestirse, afeitarse, peinarse, maquillarse, arreglarse, (no) comprar, (no) recoger, (no) sentirse, (no) llevar** y **(no) comer.**

**10-54 Una cita doble** *(double date)* Imagínense que van a salir a una cita esta noche y quieren impresionar a sus respectivas parejas. ¿Qué cosas deben y no deben hacer? Escriban por lo menos ocho oraciones. (Importante: Traten de trabajar con una persona del mismo sexo.)

### SUGERENCIAS

Puedes usar algunas de estas frases: **un hotel de (cuatro/cinco) estrellas, una habitación con vista al mar/a las montañas/a la ciudad, ropa deportiva/casual/formal, museos, galerías, parques, monumentos nacionales** y **playas.**

## Integración

**10-55 De vacaciones** Representa la siguiente situación con un(a) compañero(a).

| **El (La) flexible** | **El (La) inflexible** |
|---|---|
| Tu amigo(a) y tú están planificando sus próximas vacaciones juntos(as). Sugiérele alternativas diferentes en cuanto al *(regarding)* destino turístico adonde van a ir, el hotel donde se van a quedar, la ropa que van a llevar y los lugares que van a visitar. | Tu amigo(a) y tú están planificando sus próximas vacaciones juntos(as). Lamentablemente, no estás de acuerdo con ninguna de las cosas que él/ella sugiere. Reacciona a las cosas que dice y propón *(propose)* alternativas diferentes. |

### SUGERENCIAS

Para mostrarte en desacuerdo, puedes usar estas expresiones:

**¡Estás loco(a)!** *Are you crazy!*
**¡No estoy de acuerdo!** *I don't agree!*
**¡No me parece una buena idea!** *I don't think that's a good idea.*
**¡Por supuesto que no!** *Of course not!)*

**10-56 Una causa noble** Prepara un afiche para animar *(encourage)* a tus compañeros de clase a involucrarse en una causa con la que te sientes identificado(a). Usa mandatos afirmativos y negativos con la forma de **nosotros.** Cuando lo tengas listo, muéstraselo a un(a) compañero(a) para que te dé su opinión y luego muéstraselo a la clase. ¿Qué reacción tienen tus compañeros?

## III. Funciones y estructuras: Talking about the future with the future tense

> El Museo Nacional de Bellas Artes le extiende la más cordial invitación a una recepción que **se llevará** a cabo el sábado, 15 de mayo a las 18 horas, en la Sala Picasso del museo. Ud. y un invitado **podrán** admirar algunas de las pinturas del renombrado pintor argentino Fernando Cánovas, tales como *Pájaro de acero, Libertad* y *Final del viaje*. El aclamado pintor nos **honrará** con su presencia. ¡Los esperamos!

So far you have used expressions like **ir** + **a** + infinitive and **esperar** + infinitive to talk about actions that will take place in the future. Spanish also has a simple future tense form that is used primarily in written and formal speech. This tense is formed by attaching directly to the infinitive the same set of endings for **-ar, -er,** and **-ir** verbs.

| ENDINGS | **-ar** VERBS | **-er** VERBS | **-ir** VERBS |
|---|---|---|---|
| **é** | tomar**é** | leer**é** | vivir**é** |
| **ás** | tomar**ás** | leer**ás** | vivir**ás** |
| **á** | tomar**á** | leer**á** | vivir**á** |
| **emos** | tomar**emos** | leer**emos** | vivir**emos** |
| **éis** | tomar**éis** | leer**éis** | vivir**éis** |
| **án** | tomar**án** | leer**án** | vivir**án** |

| | |
|---|---|
| Cuando revele las fotografías, **pasaré** por tu casa. | *When I get the pictures developed, I **will stop** by your house.* |
| ¿Uds. **irán** a la exposición esta noche? | ***Will you go** to the exposition tonight?* |

Some verbs undergo changes in their infinitive form when conjugated in the future tense. They can be grouped in three categories:

■ the shortened-stem group

| INFINITIVE | FUTURE TENSE STEM | CONJUGATION |
|---|---|---|
| decir | **dir-** | **dir**é, **dir**ás, **dir**á, **dir**emos, **dir**éis, **dir**án |
| hacer | **har-** | **har**é, **har**ás, **har**á, **har**emos, **har**éis, **har**án |

| | |
|---|---|
| La artista **hará** una presentación especial de su trabajo. | *The artist **will make** a special presentation of her work.* |
| ¿Qué crees que **dirán** los críticos? | *What do you think the critics **will say**?* |

■ the dropped -**e** group

| INFINITIVE | FUTURE TENSE STEM | CONJUGATION |
|---|---|---|
| caber | **cabr-** | **cabré, cabrás, cabrá, cabremos, cabréis, cabrán** |
| haber | **habr-** | **habré, habrás, habrá, habremos, habréis, habrán** |
| poder | **podr-** | **podré, podrás, podrá, podremos, podréis, podrán** |
| querer | **querr-** | **querré, querrás, querrá, querremos, querréis, querrán** |
| saber | **sabr-** | **sabré, sabrás, sabrá, sabremos, sabréis, sabrán** |

El domingo **habrá** una feria de pintores locales.
¿Piensas que Vicente **querrá** ir conmigo?

*There will be a fair of local painters on Sunday.*
*Do you think Vicente will want to go with me?*

■ the -**dr**- substitution group

| INFINITIVE | FUTURE TENSE STEM | CONJUGATION |
|---|---|---|
| poner | **pondr-** | **pondré, pondrás, pondrá, pondremos, pondréis, pondrán** |
| salir | **saldr-** | **saldré, saldrás, saldrá, saldremos, saldréis, saldrán** |
| tener | **tendr-** | **tendré, tendrás, tendrá, tendremos, tendréis, tendrán** |
| valer | **valdr-** | **valdré, valdrás, valdrá, valdremos, valdréis, valdrán** |
| venir | **vendr-** | **vendré, vendrás, vendrá, vendremos, vendréis, vendrán** |

Julia **tendrá** tiempo para terminar la obra esta noche.
Hernán y yo **vendremos** a verla mañana.

*Julia will have time to finish her work tonight.*
*Hernán and I will come to see it tomorrow.*

## ■ Asimilación

**10-57 ¿Qué harás mañana?** Piensa en las cosas que harás mañana y escoge las oraciones que sean ciertas. Al terminar, compara tus respuestas con las de un(a) compañero(a). ¿Van a hacer las mismas actividades?

____ Estudiaré.      ____ Trabajaré.

____ Cenaré en mi restaurante      ____ No haré nada.
favorito.      ____ Me quedaré en casa.

____ Practicaré algún deporte.      ____ Saldré con algunos amigos.

____ Iré al cine.      ____ Tendré que limpiar mi

____ Vendré a la universidad.      habitación.

**10-58 El futuro de un artista** Escucha los planes para el futuro que tiene este artista e indica si las siguientes oraciones son ciertas (**C**) o falsas (**F**).

  _F_  1. El artista expondrá sus pinturas en la galería de su colega.

  _C_  2. Según él, ganará mucho dinero.

  _C_  3. Expondrá sus obras en el museo de su pueblo.

  _F_  4. Se mudará a un país tropical.

  _F_  5. Desafortunadamente, nadie conocerá su nombre.

  _C_  6. En su opinión, él será famoso.

*2-42*

**Script 10-58:** Tengo muchos planes para el futuro. En un año tendré suficientes pinturas como para abrir mi propia galería. Podré vender algunas de ellas y ganaré mucho dinero. Luego haré una exposición en el museo de mi pueblo y el público podrá admirar mi talento. Si todo sale bien, me mudaré a una ciudad grande, donde seguiré trabajando y mi nombre saldrá en todos los periódicos. ¡Voy a ser famoso! Todo el sacrificio de estos años valdrá la pena.

## ■ Aplicaciones

**10-59 En la oficina** Imagínense que Uds. trabajan en una oficina donde todo se sabe. Túrnense para hacer y responder a preguntas sobre lo que los siguientes empleados harán este fin de semana.

**Answers 10-59:** 1. ...vendrán a la oficina. 2. ...pondrá cortinas nuevas en su casa. 3. ...tendrá una fiesta íntima en su apartamento. 4. ...se divertirán paseando por la ciudad. 5. ...se cortará el pelo. 6. ...saldrán a hacer compras. 7. ...irán a la cancha de tenis. 8. ...leerá la nueva novela de García Márquez.

MODELO    Eleuterio – irse para el campo
E1: *¿Qué hará Eleuterio este fin de semana?*
E2: *Eleuterio se irá para el campo.*

1. Diego y Matilde – venir a la oficina a terminar el informe
2. doña Petra – poner cortinas nuevas en su casa
3. Dalia – tener una fiesta íntima en su apartamento
4. Nora y su familia – divertirse paseando por la ciudad
5. Norberto – cortarse el pelo
6. Igor y su esposa – salir a hacer compras
7. don Ricardo y Josué – ir a la cancha de tenis
8. Maribel – leer la nueva novela de García Márquez

**10-60 Predicciones** ¿Cómo será la vida en veinticinco años? Hagan predicciones sobre los siguientes temas.

MODELO    el transporte
*Dentro de veinticinco años, todos los carros serán eléctricos.*

1. la alimentación      6. la educación
2. la economía      7. la ecología
3. el entretenimiento      8. el arte
4. las comunicaciones      9. la política
5. la salud      10. el deporte

**10-61 Nuestros planes para el futuro**

**Paso 1:** Haz una lista de seis cosas que estás seguro(a) que harás en el futuro.

1. ...                    4. ...
2. ...                    5. ...
3. ...                    6. ...

**Paso 2:** Convierte las oraciones del **Paso 1** en preguntas y entrevista a dos compañeros(as). Si responden negativamente, trata de hacer otras preguntas que se relacionen con el tema, tales como el trabajo, la vida personal, las aspiraciones académicas, etc. Apunta sus respuestas y prepara un resumen.

MODELO    *Yo tendré mi propio negocio de bienes raíces. En cambio, Sasha tendrá su propio estudio de contabilidad y Johnny será médico. Por otro lado. Johnny y yo...*

■ **Integración**

**10-62 Videntes** *(Psychics)* Representa la siguiente situación con un(a) compañero(a).

**SUGERENCIAS**

Para mostrar sorpresa o desacuerdo, puedes usar las siguientes expresiones:

| | |
|---|---|
| **¡No puede ser!** | *It can't be!* |
| **¡No lo puedo creer!** | *I cannot believe it!* |
| **¡Eso es increíble!** | *That's incredible!* |
| **¿De verdad?** | *Really?* |
| **¡Eso es maravilloso!** | *That's marvelous!* |
| **¡Qué estupendo!** | *How great!* |

**El (La) preocupado(a)**

Eres una persona que se preocupa mucho por el futuro. Un(a) amigo(a) te recomendó llamar a la línea directa de un(a) vidente y has decidido hacerlo. Responde a sus preguntas y prepárate para hacerle preguntas acerca de cosas que te interesen.

**El (La) vidente**

Tienes poderes síquicos y aceptas consultas telefónicas. Responde a la llamada de este(a) cliente(a) y predice su futuro. Además, responde a las preguntas que te haga.

**SUGERENCIAS**

Haz lo siguiente:

■ Averigua sus datos personales: nombre, fecha de nacimiento, signo del zodiaco, etc.
■ Haz predicciones sobre su vida romántica.
■ Dile cómo va a ser su futuro profesional y financiero.
■ Predice acerca de su vida personal: sobre su familia, sus hijos, etc.

**10-63 Preguntas para mi profesor(a)** Aunque conoces bastante bien a tu profesor(a), quieres saber un poco más sobre sus planes. Haz una lista de por lo menos diez preguntas que quieres que él/ella responda y entrégasela. ¿Cómo piensas que va a responder?

## IV. Lectura: *El túnel*

### ■ Antes de leer

**A. Para conversar** Responde a las siguientes preguntas y luego comenta tus respuestas con otros compañeros.

1. ¿Crees que existe el amor a primera vista? ¿Por qué sí o por qué no?
2. ¿Cuál sería el lugar más apropiado para conocer a tu pareja ideal? Escoge un lugar y explica por qué.

____ en un estadio

____ por la calle

____ en una fiesta

____ en una galería de arte

____ en un teatro

____ en un salón de clase

____ en otro lugar

**B. Vocabulario y conceptos** Emparejen cada palabra con su definición. (Consulten el diccionario si es necesario.)

___a___ 1. la escena
___d___ 2. la soledad
___b___ 3. esencial
___c___ 4. la ansiedad
___e___ 5. vacilar

a. subdivisión de una obra dramática, evento o espectáculo digno de prestarle atención *(pay attention)*

b. lo más importante, algo indispensable

c. inquietud que se experimenta ante un peligro real o imaginario

d. se experimenta al sentirse alejado *(detached/alienated)* o separado del resto del mundo

e. dudar, no saber qué hacer

**C. Aplicación** Ahora, completen las oraciones con las palabras que acaban de identificar en la actividad anterior.

1. Para apreciar mejor esta exposición es __esencial__ leer un poco sobre la historia del arte.
2. __Vacilo__ en exponer mis pinturas porque tengo miedo de los críticos.
3. Muchos pintores prefieren la __soledad__ para concentrarse más en sus creaciones.
4. La complejidad de esa obra se debe a que no contiene una, sino varias __escenas__ .
5. La __ansiedad__ del personaje de esta pintura es evidente en la expresión de la cara.

■ **A leer**

### Ernesto Sábato

Nació en la provincia de Buenos Aires en 1911. Hizo un doctorado en física y tomó cursos de filosofía en la Universidad de La Plata, pero abandonó las ciencias en 1945 para dedicarse a la literatura. Su producción tiene un tono existencialista y trata el tema de la angustia *(anguish)* del ser humano frente a la sociedad y la vida. Las novelas más famosas de este escritor son *El túnel* (1948), *Sobre héroes y tumbas* (1961) y *Abaddón, el exterminador* (1974). Su preocupación por la situación política y por los derechos humanos en su país lo llevó a presidir la Comisión Nacional sobre la Desaparición de Personas *(National Commission on Disappeared Persons)* y a escribir el libro *Nunca más* sobre los efectos de la guerra sucia durante la dictadura militar (1976–1983) en Argentina. En 1984, recibió el prestigioso Premio Cervantes de literatura.

### *El túnel* (fragmento)

En el Salón de Primavera de 1946 presenté un cuadro llamado *Maternidad*. Era por el estilo de muchos otros anteriores: como dicen los críticos en su **insoportable** dialecto, era sólido, estaba bien arquitecturado. Tenía, en fin, los **atributos** que esos **charlatanes** encontraban siempre en mis **telas,** incluyendo «cierta cosa profundamente intelectual». Pero arriba, a la izquierda, a través de una ventanita, se veía una escena pequeña y remota: una playa solitaria y una mujer que miraba el mar. Era una mujer que miraba como esperando algo, quizá algún llamado **apagado** y distante. La escena **sugería,** en mi opinión, una soledad ansiosa y absoluta.

Nadie **se fijó en** esta escena: **pasaban la mirada por encima,** como por algo secundario, probablemente decorativo. Con excepción de una sola persona, nadie pareció comprender que esa escena constituía algo esencial. Fue el día de la inauguración. Una muchacha desconocida estuvo mucho tiempo **delante** de mi cuadro sin dar importancia, en apariencia, a la gran mujer **en primer plano,** la mujer que miraba jugar al niño. En cambio, miró **fijamente** la escena de la ventana y mientras lo hacía tuve la seguridad de que estaba **aislada** del mundo entero: no vio ni oyó a la gente que pasaba o se **detenía** frente a mi tela.

La observé todo el tiempo con ansiedad. Después desapareció en la **multitud,** mientras yo **vacilaba** entre un miedo invencible y un angustioso deseo de llamarla.

¿Miedo de qué? Quizá, algo así como miedo de jugar todo el dinero de que se dispone en la vida a un solo número. Sin embargo, cuando

*intolerable*

*qualities*
*charlatans*
*paintings*

*muffled / suggested*

*noticed / glanced over it*

*in front*
*foreground*
*attentively*
*isolated*
*stopped*

*crowd / hesitated*

desapareció, me sentí irritado, infeliz, pensando que podría no verla más, perdida entre los millones de habitantes anónimos de Buenos Aires. Esa noche volví a casa nervioso, descontento, triste.

Hasta que **se clausuró** el salón, fui todos los días y **me colocaba** suficientemente cerca para reconocer a las personas que se detenían frente a mi cuadro. Pero no volvió a **aparecer.**

Durante los meses que siguieron, sólo pensé en ella, en la posibilidad de volver a verla. Y en cierto modo, sólo pinté para ella. Fue como si la pequeña escena de la ventana empezara a crecer y a invadir toda la tela y toda mi obra.

*closed / found myself*

*to turn up, show up*

## ■ ¿Entendiste bien?

**D. ¿Qué pasó?** Organiza los siguientes eventos de acuerdo con la historia. Al terminar, compara tus respuestas con las de un(a) compañero(a).

<u> 4 </u> El artista regresó a su casa nervioso y triste.

<u> 2 </u> Una muchacha observó con interés la escena de la ventanita.

<u> 6 </u> La exposición fue clausurada.

<u> 5 </u> El artista fue a la exposición todos los días esperando el regreso de la muchacha.

<u> 1 </u> Se abrió la exposición del artista en el Salón de Primavera.

<u> 7 </u> El artista empezó a trabajar con la obsesión de ver a la muchacha.

<u> 3 </u> La muchacha desapareció en la multitud.

**E. Puntos clave** Realicen las siguientes actividades.

1. Hagan un dibujo de la obra *Maternidad* basándose en la descripción que hace el narrador de la misma.
2. Expliquen por qué se obsesionó el artista con esa muchacha.

**F. Los personajes** Aunque el narrador no nos da muchos detalles acerca de los personajes, nos deja ver a través de sus acciones algunas de sus características más sobresalientes. Lean de nuevo el texto y traten de «leer entre líneas» *(read between the lines)* para concretar en palabras la imagen que nos quiere presentar el autor de estos personajes.

|  | Características |
|---|---|
| **Narrador** | solo, obsesivo, sensible, arrogante |
| **La muchacha** | joven, educada, sensible |

**G. Enfoque lingüístico** Para narrar la historia, el autor usó las diferentes formas del pasado. Busquen ejemplos de cada una de estas formas.

**H. Actividad de extensión** Escriban el final de esta historia. (¿Creen Uds. que al fin se encontraron el artista y la muchacha? ¿Piensan que se hicieron amigos? ¿Que se casaron? O por el contrario, ¿piensan que ellos nunca más se volvieron a ver?)

### CRITICAL THINKING SKILLS

*Inferring and Classifying* What do the characters' actions tell us about their personalities?

Activity G recycles the use of the preterite and imperfect.

### REMEMBER

1. The preterite tense is used to refer to completed past events.
2. The imperfect tense is used to refer to:
   ■ habitual past actions (things one used to do)
   ■ ongoing states or conditions in the past
   ■ the background of past events (time, weather, location, etc.)
   ■ physical or psychological characteristics of something or someone in the past
   ■ actions in progress at a given point in the past

# Vocabulario

**El ejercicio físico**
bajar de/perder peso — *to lose weight*
distraer — *to entertain, to amuse*
evitar — *to avoid*
ganar/subir de peso — *to gain weight*
aumentar nuestra elasticidad y resistencia — *to increase our flexibility and resistance*
mantenerse en forma/en buen estado de salud — *to keep fit/in good health*
reducir/combatir el estrés — *to reduce/combat stress*

**Es importante...**
dejar de fumar — *to quit, stop smoking*
hacer estiramiento — *to stretch*
hacer un poco de calentamiento — *to do some warm-up exercises*

**Nutrición**
la fibra — *fiber*
las grasas animales — *animal fat*
los minerales — *minerals*
los productos refinados — *refined products*
la proteína — *protein*
las vitaminas — *vitamins*

**Problemas médicos**
la alergia — *allergy*
la gripe/la influenza — *flu*
los parásitos intestinales — *intestinal parasites*
el resfriado — *cold*

**Verbos**
doler (ue) — *to ache, to hurt*
enfermarse — *to get sick*
sentirse (ie, i) mal/mejor — *to feel ill/better*
tener tos — *to have a cough*

**Síntomas**
la congestión — *congestion*
el dolor de cabeza — *headache*
la fiebre — *fever*
el mareo — *dizziness*
la tos — *cough*

**Ayudas terapeúticas y diagnósticas**
el antibiótico — *antibiotic*
el botiquín de primeros auxilios — *first-aid kit*
la curita — *Band-Aid*

el descanso — *rest*
el jarabe — *cough syrup*
la pastilla — *pill*
la radiografía — *x-ray*
la receta — *prescription*
el yeso — *cast*

**Deportes urbanos**
los bolos — *bowling*
el ciclismo — *bike riding*
la escalada libre — *rock climbing*
el patinaje en línea — *in-line skating*

**Equipo**
al cubierto/bajo techo — *indoors*
el arnés — *harness*
la bicicleta — *bicycle*
la cancha — *court*
el casco — *helmet*
la codera — *elbow pad*
la cuerda — *rope*
las gafas protectoras — *goggles*
el juego/el set — *set*
la pelota/la bola — *ball*
la raqueta — *racket*
la rodillera — *knee pad*

**Habilidades** — *Skills*
escalar — *to climb*
golpear — *to hit*
halar/jalar — *to pull*
pedalear — *to pedal*
tirar — *to throw*

**El arte**
el artista — *artist*
la cultura masiva — *mass culture*
el dibujo — *drawing*
la escena — *scene*
el escultor — *sculptor*
la escultura — *sculpture*
la exposición — *exposition*
la fotografía — *photography*
la galería de arte — *art gallery*
la imagen — *image*
la luz — *light*
el movimiento — *movement/school*
la muestra — *sample, show*
la obra — *work*

| la obra maestra | *masterpiece* |
| el paisaje | *landscape* |
| el pintor | *painter* |
| la pintura/el cuadro | *painting* |
| la proporción | *proportion* |
| la sala | *room* |
| la técnica | *technique* |

## Verbos

| presentar | *to present* |
| producir | *to produce* |
| representar | *to represent* |
| usar | *to use* |
| utilizar | *to make use* |

## Funciones y estructuras

Expresiones adverbiales y conjunciones que se usan con verbos en el modo subjuntivo, pp. 400, 412

# Puesta en acción

| | |
|---|---|
| **SITUACIÓN:** | La empresa multinacional en la que trabajas requiere un nuevo programa de desarrollo personal para todos sus empleados. |
| **MISIÓN:** | Diseñar el programa de desarrollo personal para la empresa y desarrollar los mecanismos para diseminar la información entre los empleados de habla hispana. |
| **DESTREZAS:** | Diseñar un programa de desarrollo personal para los empleados de una empresa multinacional, diseñar una campaña de promoción e informar a los empleados sobre los servicios disponibles mediante este programa. |

**A. La campaña** *(campaign)* Lee el siguiente mensaje electrónico.

| Enviar | Direcciones | Archivos adjuntos | Ver. ortografía | Guardar | Cancelar |
|---|---|---|---|---|---|

**Para:** John Smith
**De:** Miguel Fernández, gerente general
**Fecha:** 1º de noviembre de 2006

**Asunto:** Programas de bienestar para los empleados     **Prioridad:** Normal ▼

Normal ▼     12 ▼

Nuestra compañía debe distinguirse por el énfasis en desarrollar sus recursos humanos. Es por esto que necesitamos que su división diseñe un nuevo programa de bienestar para los empleados de esta empresa. El programa debe incluir actividades recreativas, culturales y de crecimiento personal para las horas de descanso y para los días libres de nuestros empleados. Presenten su propuesta a más tardar el 30 de este mes y especifiquen las actividades que piensan promover, el costo de las mismas y cómo piensan estimular la participación del personal.

**B. ¿Entendiste bien?** Contesta las siguientes preguntas sobre el mensaje anterior.

    a. ¿Qué quiere el gerente general de la compañía?
    b. ¿Para cuándo debe estar lista la campaña?
    c. ¿Qué características debe tener esta campaña?

**C. ¿Qué actividades podemos organizar?** Preparen una lista de posibles actividades deportivas, culturales y de crecimiento personal para los empleados de la empresa.

| Actividades deportivas (actividades físicas para mantenerse en forma o divertirse) | Actividades culturales (actividades de recreación, información o capacitación) | Actividades de crecimiento personal (actividades dirigidas al bienestar personal y familiar de los empleados) |
|---|---|---|
| | | |

**D. La decisión** Reúnanse con otra pareja de estudiantes y comenten las ideas que generaron en la actividad anterior. Los objetivos son:

    a. escoger la mejor actividad para cada una de las categorías y
    b. determinar los requisitos y materiales necesarios para cada actividad.

CRITICAL THINKING SKILLS

***Prioritizing*** Choose the most effective and practical possibilities.

| | Para las horas de descanso de los empleados | Para los fines de semana |
|---|---|---|
| Las mejores actividades deportivas | 1. | 1. |
| Requisitos y materiales | | |
| Las mejores actividades culturales | 2. | 2. |
| Requisitos y materiales | | |
| Las mejores actividades de crecimiento personal | 3. | 3. |
| Requisitos y materiales | | |

**E. Justificaciones** Completen el siguiente informe preliminar para comunicar sus ideas a la administración.

    Actividades deportivas

    a. Para los descansos, recomendamos que los empleados _____ para que _____.
    b. Para los fines de semana, sugerimos que los empleados _____ a fin de que _____.

Actividades culturales

a. Durante los descansos, esperamos que los empleados _____ para que _____.

b. Para los fines de semana, recomendamos que los empleados _____ a fin de que _____.

Actividades de crecimiento personal

a. Para los descansos, recomendamos que los empleados _____ para que _____.

b. Para los fines de semana, sugerimos que los empleados _____ a fin de que _____.

**F. Inscripciones** Ahora, piensen en los pasos o procedimientos *(procedures)* que deben seguir los empleados de la compañía para participar en los diferentes programas que han diseñado. ¿Necesitan una evaluación médica? ¿Tienen que tomar exámenes de aptitud? ¿Deben llenar algún formulario? Escriban la lista de los pasos que se deben seguir.

MODELO     *Primero, hazte un examen médico.*
*Segundo, toma un examen de aptitud.*
*Tercero, llena este formulario,* etc.

**G. Consejería** Representa la siguiente situación con un(a) compañero(a).

| **Empleado(a)** | **Jefe(a) de personal** |
|---|---|
| Has oído rumores acerca de los programas deportivos, culturales y de crecimiento personal que piensa ofrecer la empresa y te gustaría tener más información al respecto. | Los empleados ya se han enterado de los programas que va a ofrecer tu compañía. Ayuda a este(a) empleado(a) a escoger el programa que más le conviene. |
| ■ Saluda al / a la jefe(a) de personal. | ■ Dale la bienvenida. |
| ■ Pregúntale acerca de estos programas de bienestar. | ■ Explícale los programas y determina cuál es el tipo de actividad que más le conviene. |
| ■ Averigua cuáles son los requisitos y materiales necesarios para cada uno de estos programas. | ■ Infórmale acerca de los requisitos y materiales que necesita para participar en el programa que le recomendaste. |

**H. Campaña publicitaria** Para informarles a todos los empleados de la compañía sobre los nuevos programas de bienestar, es necesario organizar una campaña publicitaria. Diseñen los volantes e incluyan lo siguiente:

- una lista de los datos de cada programa (actividades, fechas, horas, etc.)
- una breve explicación de la importancia de cada programa, con frases y oraciones motivadoras
- una lista de requisitos y materiales necesarios
- los pasos que deben seguir para inscribirse (instrucciones precisas de cómo se participa en los programas)

Sigan los siguientes pasos:

a. Decidan cómo está el diseño del volante y la manera como lo harán más interesante y atractivo.
b. Organicen y distribuyan en la página el contenido del volante (dónde van a ir los títulos, los datos, las frases descriptivas, los requisitos, los materiales, los gráficos, etc.).
c. Preparen cada una de las secciones (datos, instrucciones, motivación, etc.).
d. Incluyan el material visual necesario (imágenes, gráficos, etc.).

**I. Dos empleados interesados** Dos empleados de la compañía ya les enviaron una nota para informarles que están interesados en participar en los programas de bienestar. Primero, lean individualmente las notas que les corresponden. Luego, túrnense para hacer y responder a preguntas y completen la planilla.

**CORRECCIONES**

Intercambien el primer borrador de su volante con otro grupo y respondan a las siguientes preguntas.

**Paso 1: Contenido.** ¿El volante incluye toda la información necesaria? Si no es así, ¿qué falta?

**Paso 2: Organización.** ¿La información de los programas (fechas, requisitos, etc.) está clara? ¿La distribución de la información es clara, efectiva y visualmente atractiva?

**Paso 3: Gramática.** ¿Hay algún problema con el uso del subjuntivo en los mandatos y las recomendaciones?

**Para hacer en casa:**

**Paso 4: Correcciones.** Revisen su volante y entréguenselo al / a la profesor(a) el día de la próxima clase.

## Estudiante 1

5 de diciembre de 2006

Estimado(a) jefe(a) de personal:

Le escribo esta nota para informarle que me interesa participar en los nuevos programas de bienestar de la compañía. En particular, mi esposa, mis dos hijos y yo quisiéramos participar en las actividades deportivas. Me parece que para nosotros sería más conveniente hacer esto los fines de semana. Para mí no es posible hacerlo en mis horas de descanso y quiero que mi familia participe. También les quisiera sugerir que inviten a los supervisores de la compañía para que podamos conocerlos mejor.

Cordialmente,
Nelson Estrada Millán

| Nombre del / de la empleado(a) | |
| --- | --- |
| Programa que le interesa | |
| Participantes | |
| Razón por la que le interesa | |
| Sugerencias | |

**Estudiante 2** must turn the book
upside down.

# Servicio comunitario

Visit a community service center in
your area and offer to provide and/
or organize one of the following
services:

- Workshops on how to cultivate
  healthy relationships.
- Workout sessions.
- Art classes.

**Estudiante 2**

7 de diciembre de 2006

Estimado(a) jefe(a) de personal:

El propósito de esta comunicación es felicitarlo(a) por la implementación del programa de bienestar. Creo que es una estupenda idea. Personalmente me gustaría participar en el programa de crecimiento personal porque es importante que tengamos buena salud mental para poder hacer nuestro trabajo eficientemente. Quisiera participar en este programa durante las horas de descanso con mis compañeros de la oficina de contabilidad. Sería muy bueno que nos permitieran llevar nuestro almuerzo y así aprovechar el tiempo. ¿Qué opina Ud.?

Saludos,
Catalina Chacón Paz

| Nombre del / de la empleado(a) | |
| --- | --- |
| Programa que le interesa | |
| Participantes | |
| Razón por la que le interesa | |
| Sugerencias | |

# Unidad 6

## Chile, Paraguay y los Estados Unidos

In this unit you will talk about your hopes for and concerns about the future. Also, you will learn how to make hypotheses and conjectures. The readings will examine the impact of technological developments on the Spanish-speaking world and, more specifically, the current dynamics of social change in Paraguay and Chile. At the end of the unit you will explore the history, present situation, and future perspectives of Hispanics in the U.S. You will also have a chance to connect with your community by creating a program that will enhance and improve people's quality of life.

## Expectativas

# Capítulo 11

# Mirando hacia el futuro

## Para comenzar

Indica qué foto le corresponde a cada descripción.

- El Parque Vicente Pérez Rosales es el primer parque nacional de Chile. Foto 2
- Vista aérea de la ciudad de Asunción, la capital de Paraguay. Foto 3
- El árido desierto de Atacama se encuentra en el norte del país, entre la cordillera de los Andes y el Océano Pacífico. Foto 1

## In this chapter you will learn . . .

- how to make hypothetical statements
- how to express conjecture
- about the impact of technological development in the Spanish-speaking world
- about social change in the Spanish-speaking world

| | TEMA 1<br>Proyectos personales | TEMA 2<br>Un futuro tecnificado | TEMA 3<br>Utopías |
|---|---|---|---|
| Vocabulario | Mis aspiraciones | Las comodidades de la era electrónica | Un mundo mejor |
| Funciones y estructuras | Talking about aspirations (review of the future tense)<br>Expressing conjecture and probability with the conditional tense | Expressing opinion, emotion, wishes, doubt, stipulation, purpose and future time frame with the subjunctive and the infinitive<br>Talking about the past using the imperfect subjunctive (regular verbs) | Talking about the past using the imperfect subjunctive (irregular verbs)<br>Expressing condition (si clauses) |
| Lecturas y vídeo | Perspectivas: Las claves de la ilusión | Vídeo: Aspiraciones y planes para el futuro | Lectura: El albergue de las mujeres tristes |

Foto 1

Foto 2

Foto 3

# Enfoque

Transparencies A-9: Country Profiles: Paraguay, Uruguay; A-13: Country Profiles: Bolivia, Chile

**A. ¿Qué sabes ya de Chile?** Antes de ver el vídeo, completa el siguiente párrafo sobre la economía de Chile.

El foco de la economía de Chile está en la explotación de __minerales__, incluyendo el cobre, los nitratos y el hierro. Sólo el cobre, del que Chile es el mayor productor mundial, representa el 50% del total de las __exportaciones__ a otros países. La economía de Chile es una de las más fuertes y estables de toda __Sudamérica__, con un ingreso per cápita de 12.500 dólares. La moneda del país es el __peso__.

Compara tus respuestas con las de otro(a) compañero(a).

**B. La política de Chile** Una categoría que no viste en la primera actividad es la política. Mientras ves el vídeo, pon en orden los siguientes eventos políticos de Chile.

 __3__  el gobierno socialista de Salvador Allende

 __5__  Patricio Alwyn lidera el país como presidente, pero no como jefe del ejército

 __2__  la etapa reformista del presidente Eduardo Frey

 __1__  la fundación de las ciudades de Santiago, Concepción y Valdivia por el español Pedro de Valdivia

 __6__  Ricardo Lagos es electo presidente del país

 __4__  la dictadura militar de Augusto Pinochet

For more info, you may want to check the **Temas** site: **http://temas.heinle.com**

**C. Mirando hacia el futuro** Reúnanse en grupos de tres o cuatro estudiantes. Luego, lean el siguiente dato demográfico de Chile y contesten la pregunta.

> Los chilenos viven concentrados en grandes ciudades; siete de cada diez chilenos se hallan en las siguientes grandes urbes y sus alrededores: Santiago, Valparaíso y Concepción. En Santiago se concentra el 40% de la población total de Chile; es una de las áreas metropolitanas más pobladas de América Latina con cerca de 6 millones de personas. Las proyecciones demográficas indican que las futuras generaciones de chilenos vivirán en grandes ciudades. Actualmente hay más de 15.5 millones de habitantes y la población se duplicará en 50 años.

¿Qué opinan de esta proyección demográfica? ¿Es buena o mala?

# Proyectos personales

## I. Vocabulario: Mis aspiraciones

Mi **ilusión** es llegar a ser rico. Sé que voy a **hacer realidad** algún día mi **sueño** porque tengo mucha **constancia** y **disciplina**.

Lo que deseo es tener una familia unida y feliz. A pesar de los **retos**, sé que lo voy a **lograr**. Voy a **poner de mi parte** para **alcanzar** esta **meta**.

### Vocabulario práctico

| | |
|---|---|
| la ilusión *dream, illusion* | lograr *to achieve* |
| la meta *goal* | llegar a ser *to become* |
| el reto / el desafío *challenge* | tener constancia *to be constant, to persist* |
| el sueño *dream* | |
| alcanzar *to reach* | tener disciplina *to be disciplined* |
| aspirar a *to aspire to* | tener éxito *to be successful* |
| enfrentar *to face; to confront* | tener paciencia *to be patient* |
| hacer realidad *to make come true* | tener suerte *to be lucky* |

**11-1 Mis metas personales** Indica todas las metas que te correspondan. Luego, compara tus respuestas con las de un(a) compañero(a). ¿Tienen algunos sueños en común?

____ Sueño con ser rico(a).

____ Mi ilusión es vivir en otro país.

____ Aspiro a ser famoso(a).

____ Aspiro a conseguir un buen trabajo.

____ Quiero viajar por todo el mundo.

____ Mi sueño es tener un romance con...

____ Deseo tener una familia.

____ Otra(s) meta(s):

**Script 11-2:** Sí, cuando era pequeño, quería ser policía o científico. Me gustaba la idea de ser policía porque quería ayudar a otra gente, y bueno, porque admiraba mucho a mi tío Francisco, que era oficial de policía. También quería ser piloto, **CD2-44** porque me gustaba la idea de viajar por todo el mundo, y me imaginaba lo divertido que sería manejar esos aviones. Hoy en día soy profesor de español y mi ilusión es hacer que mis estudiantes aprendan bien la lengua de Cervantes. Como tengo dos niños, también quiero que mis hijos se eduquen y tengan mucho éxito en sus actividades en el futuro.

**11-2 Aspiraciones** Toma nota de la información que vas a escuchar para completar la siguiente tabla.

| Cuando era pequeño(a)... | Ahora... |
|---|---|
| quería ser policía o científico, quería ayudar a otra gente, admiraba a su tío Francisco, quería ser piloto, le gustaba viajar, imaginaba lo divertido que sería manejar aviones | es profesor de español, su ilusión es hacer que los estudiantes aprendan bien, quiere que sus hijos se eduquen y que tengan éxito en el futuro |

## ■ Aplicaciones

**11-3 ¿Quién es?** Túrnense para hablar de las metas y aspiraciones de personajes históricos.

> MODELO E1: *Quería ser un cantante original. Su sueño era la existencia de la paz y del amor en el mundo.*
> E2: *¿John Lennon?*
> E1: *¡Correcto!*

**11-4 ¿Qué tengo que hacer?** Túrnense para indicar lo que tiene que hacer la otra persona para alcanzar sus metas. Usen por lo menos uno de los verbos de la lista en todas sus respuestas.

> OPCIONES: tener constancia    tener disciplina    tener paciencia
> hacer realidad    tener éxito

> MODELO E1: *¡Quiero graduarme pronto!*
> E2: *Tienes que tener paciencia y aprobar todas tus asignaturas.*

1. ¡Quiero viajar por todo el mundo!
2. ¡Quiero ser millonario(a)!
3. ¡Quiero ser muy famoso(a)!
4. ¡Quiero ser feliz!
5. ¡Quiero hablar español fluidamente!
6. ¡Quiero tener éxito en mi carrera!

**11-5 Entrevista** Túrnense para hacerse las siguientes preguntas con un(a) compañero(a). Tomen nota y preséntenle un informe de sus respuestas al resto de la clase.

1. ¿Qué tan importante es tu carrera para ti? (¿muy importante? ¿más o menos importante? ¿poco importante?)
2. ¿Qué metas concretas tienes con respecto a tu carrera? (¿Quieres prepararte mejor para encontrar un trabajo o quieres llegar a ser rico, famoso?)
3. ¿Cuáles son los mayores retos que enfrentas en este momento? (¿tiempo? ¿dinero? ¿paciencia?)

> MODELO *Para mi compañera, su carrera es muy importante. Su meta es...*

## ■ Integración

**11-6 Las preocupaciones de los padres** Representa la siguiente situación con un(a) compañero(a).

| Padre/Madre preocupado(a) | Hijo(a) desmotivado(a) |
|---|---|
| Tu hijo(a) ha llegado a casa con calificaciones *(grades)* muy deficientes. <br> 1. Averigua qué pasó. <br> 2. Habla con tu hijo(a) sobre sus metas. <br> 3. Háblale a tu hijo(a) acerca de la importancia de la educación para lograr esas metas. | Las cosas no van muy bien en la universidad. Es hora *(It's time)* de llevar a casa tus calificaciones y de seguro vas a recibir un regaño *(reprimand)*. <br> 1. Explícale a tu padre/madre lo que pasó. <br> 2. Habla de tus metas para el futuro. <br> 3. Responde a sus consejos. |

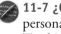

**11-7 ¿Cuáles son tus metas?** Escribe un ensayo acerca de tus metas personales y lo que estás haciendo en este momento para alcanzarlas. También, menciona lo que tienes que hacer en el futuro inmediato para asegurar el éxito de tus planes.

## II. Funciones y estructuras: Talking about aspirations (review of the future tense)

Para alcanzar mi sueño de ser la mejor abogada del mundo, **tendré** disciplina y paciencia, **estudiaré** mucho y **enfrentaré** todos los obstáculos que encuentre en mi camino. ¡Sé que lo **lograré**!

In **Capítulo 10, Tema 3,** you learned how to use the future tense. This tense is formed by adding the same set of endings to the infinitive form of -**ar**, -**er**, and -**ir** verbs.

| | |
|---|---|
| ¿Crees que Lina y Josefa **llegarán** a ser ricas algún día? | *Do you think Lina and Josefa **will become** rich someday?* |
| Estoy seguro de que Alana y yo **seremos** muy buenas atletas. | *I am sure that Alana and I **will be** very good athletes.* |

As you may remember, the infinitive form of a number of verbs undergoes changes in the future tense. These verbs were grouped in three categories:

1. the shortened stem group (**decir → dir-** and **hacer → har-**),

2. the dropped-**e**-group (**caber → cabr-, haber → habr-, poder → podr-, querer → querr-,** and **saber → sabr-**), and

3. the -**dr**- substitution group (**poner → pondr-, salir → saldr-, tener → tendr-, valer → valdr-,** and **venir → vendr-**).

| | |
|---|---|
| **Haré** lo que sea necesario para alcanzar mi meta. | *I **will do** whatever is necessary to reach my goal.* |
| Ella **sabrá** enfrentar todos los retos. | *She **will know** how to face all the challenges.* |
| El éxito **vendrá** a su debido momento. | *Success **will come** at the right moment.* |

## ■ Asimilación

**11-8 Para tener éxito en mi carrera...** Piensa en la carrera que has elegido y en las cosas que tendrás que hacer para ser una persona exitosa en ese campo. Luego, lee las siguientes oraciones e indica si se aplican o no a tu situación. Al terminar, compara tus respuestas con las de un(a) compañero(a). ¿Tienen retos semejantes o diferentes?

Tendré que...

____ invertir mucho dinero.
____ hacer estudios de postgrado.
____ tener mi propia oficina.
____ contratar a varios asistentes.
____ sacrificar mi vida personal y familiar.

No tendré que...

____ depender de nadie.
____ viajar frecuentemente.
____ estar disponible las veinticuatro horas del día.
____ hacer trabajo en casa.
____ tener un jefe o supervisor.

**11-9 Actitudes** Escucha lo que dicen Simón, Melinda y Beto sobre sus aspiraciones personales y profesionales y decide si tienen una buena actitud o no. Debes justificar tu opinión.

Simón: sí / no
Razones:

Melinda: sí / no
Razones:

Beto: sí / no
Razones:

## ■ Aplicaciones

**11-10 De otra forma** Vuelvan a escribir las siguientes oraciones usando verbos en el futuro.

MODELO  Minerva y yo vamos a salir del seminario de auto-mejoramiento a las dos.
*Minerva y yo saldremos del seminario de auto-mejoramiento a las dos.*

1. Voy a querer hacer estudios de postgrado cuando me gradúe.
2. A Andrés se le van a presentar muchas oportunidades en la vida profesional.
3. Sé que vas a triunfar porque tienes mucha constancia.
4. ¿Uds. van a asistir a la charla sobre disciplina personal?
5. Mauricio y yo vamos a ser grandes hombres de negocios.
6. Mi hermana va a poder ingresar en la universidad que quiera.
7. Voy a poner todo mi empeño para que mi sueño se haga realidad.
8. Nuestros consejeros nos van a decir cómo vencer estos problemas.

**Script 11-9:**
Lograré mis metas con mucho esfuerzo y dedicación. Sueño con ser médico y tendré que ser muy constante y disciplinado. Sé que las cosas no serán fáciles y que habrá muchos desafíos, pero confío en mi talento.

Mi ilusión es ser una actriz famosa. Estudiaré arte dramático y me prepararé profesionalmente porque el campo de la actuación es muy competitivo. Tendré que ser muy paciente y perseverante, pero valdrá la pena. Ésta es mi pasión y lucharé hasta que mi sueño se haga realidad.

No me interesa ni estudiar ni luchar por nada. Como me gustan las cosas caras y la buena vida, me casaré con una mujer rica que me mantenga. Si no la consigo, ¡viviré con mi familia y dependeré de ellos! Después de todo, para eso son las relaciones familiares.

**REMEMBER**

The expression **ir** + **a** + *infinitive* is used to talk about actions that will take place in the future: **Yo *voy a estudiar* (= *estudiaré*) por tres horas.**

**Answers 11-10:** 1. Querré... 2. Se le presentarán... 3. ...triunfarás... 4. ...asistirán... 5. ...seremos... 6. ...podrá... 7. Pondré... 8. ...nos dirán...

**11-11 Planificando el futuro** Hagan una lista de las cosas que harán para garantizar que Uds. tendrán éxito en los siguientes aspectos de la vida en el futuro. Usen la forma **nosotros(as)** de los verbos.

| El aspecto sentimental | El aspecto familiar |
|---|---|
| El aspecto profesional | El aspecto social |

**11-12 Oye, fulano(a),...** En parejas, escriban preguntas para hacerles a por lo menos seis compañeros de la clase para saber qué harán o qué esperan hacer en el futuro. Déjense llevar por lo que ya saben de estas personas. Luego, háganles las preguntas.

MODELO    *Nancy, ¿tendrás paciencia cuando seas profesora de un colegio? Robert y Sheila, ¿lograrán su sueño de ser biólogos?*

■ **Integración**

**11-13 Personas importantes del futuro** ¿Qué personas jóvenes prometen ser aún más importantes e influyentes en el futuro? Individualmente, piensen en una de estas personas, describan las cosas que él/ella logrará y expliquen por qué piensan que será tan importante.

**SUGERENCIAS**

Pueden hablar de un actor o actriz, de un(a) cantante, de un político o hasta de un(a) compañero(a) de clase.

**11-14 Una carta de agradecimiento** Imagínate que quieres escribir una carta a una persona que siempre ha creído en ti y que te ha dado ánimo para seguir adelante en la vida. Sigue los pasos que se mencionan a continuación y, al terminar, intercambia cartas con un(a) compañero(a) de clase para que se hagan correcciones.

**Paso 1: Planificación:** Haz una lista de ejemplos que demuestre que la persona a quien le escribes la carta te ha apoyado, y otra lista de las cosas que harás para no defraudarla *(disappoint him/her)*.

**Paso 2: La carta:** Empieza la carta con un saludo cordial. Luego dale las gracias a esta persona y menciona las razones que apuntaste en el **Paso 1.** Además, incluye la lista de cosas que harás para no defraudarla y para demostrarle que has alcanzado tus metas. Finalmente, escribe una despedida cordial.

**Paso 3: Revisión:** Lee la carta y determina si está completa, si las ideas están bien organizadas y si necesitas usar palabras y frases conectoras (**por eso, por lo tanto, además, por el contrario, en conclusión,** etc.).

**CORRECCIÓN**

Al intercambiar cartas, usen las siguientes ideas para hacer sus correcciones:
**Contenido:** ¿Las ideas están bien presentadas? ¿Faltan detalles que apoyen alguna de las ideas?
**Organización:** ¿La carta sigue un orden lógico? ¿Incluye un saludo y una despedida?
**Gramática:** ¿Los verbos están bien conjugados? ¿Usó el futuro correctamente? ¿Hay concordancia de género y número entre los sustantivos y los adjetivos?

## III. Funciones y estructuras: Expressing conjecture and probability with the conditional tense

| | |
|---|---|
| ENTREVISTADORA: | Señor, con su permiso. ¿Le puedo hacer algunas preguntas para una encuesta? |
| DIONISIO RUIZ: | Claro, pero sea breve porque tengo poco tiempo. |
| ENTREVISTADORA: | Muchas gracias. ¿Le **gustaría** tener más dinero o piensa que gana lo suficiente para ser feliz? |
| DIONISIO RUIZ: | ¡Por supuesto que me **gustaría** tener más dinero! Así **podría** viajar más y mi familia **tendría** todo lo que necesita. ¡Y no **trabajaría** tanto, como ahora! |
| ENTREVISTADORA: | ¿Y cree que ellos lo **querrían** más a Ud.? |
| DIONISIO RUIZ: | Eso no. Ellos me quieren como soy. El tener más dinero no **cambiaría** nada... ¡Pero algunas cosas **serían** más fáciles! |

The highlighted verbs in the previous conversation are conjugated in the conditional tense. This tense is the equivalent of the *would* + verb English expression used to talk about actions that *would* happen if certain conditions existed.

| | |
|---|---|
| Si tuviera suerte, me **ganaría** la lotería. | *If I had luck, I **would win** the lottery.* |
| ¿Te **sentirías** más satisfecha con tu vida si fueras más exitosa? | *Would you feel more satisfied with your life if you were more successful?* |

Students will learn about sentences with the conjunction **si** in **Tema 3.**

Just like the future tense, the conditional is formed by attaching identical sets of endings to the infinitive of the verb.

| ENDINGS | -ar VERBS | -er VERBS | -ir VERBS |
|---|---|---|---|
| -ía | lograría | comería | viviría |
| -ías | lograrías | comerías | vivirías |
| -ía | lograría | comería | viviría |
| -íamos | lograríamos | comeríamos | viviríamos |
| -íais | lograríais | comeríais | viviríais |
| -ían | lograrían | comerían | vivirían |

Notice that the **yo** and **él/ella/usted** forms are the same.

The verbs that show irregularities in the stem in the future tense (**decir, tener, salir,** etc.) show the same irregularities in the conditional tense.

| | |
|---|---|
| En este trabajo **tendría** un mejor salario y **podría** ascender rápidamente. | *In this job **I would have** a better salary and **would be able** to get promoted quickly.* |
| ¿Qué **harías** en esta situación? ¿Se lo **dirías** a tu jefe? | *What **would you do** in a situation like this? **Would you tell** your boss?* |

### REMEMBER

There are three types of irregularities. They were presented in the previous **Funciones y estructuras** section (p. 448).

The conditional is also used to express politeness when making requests or giving suggestions.

| | |
|---|---|
| Sra. Peralta, Ud. **debería** ser más cuidadosa y astuta. | *Mrs. Peralta, you **should** be more careful and astute.* |
| ¿**Podrías** ayudarme a escribir mi hoja de vida? | ***Could** you help me write my résumé?* |

The following expressions are often used with the conditional tense.

| **probablemente** *probably* | **quizás** *maybe* | **tal vez** *maybe* |
|---|---|---|

| | |
|---|---|
| Si no estuviera casado, **tal vez volvería** a estudiar en la universidad | *If I were not married, **maybe I would go back** to college.* |
| Con más dinero en el banco, **quizás** me **jubilaría** ahora mismo. | *With more money in the bank, **maybe I would retire** right now.* |

### ■ Asimilación

**11-15 Si fuera** *(If he/she were)* **presidente(a) de los Estados Unidos...** Lee las siguientes oraciones y complétalas con el nombre de una persona famosa que haría esa actividad si fuera presidente(a) de los Estados Unidos. Cuando termines, compara tus respuestas con las de un(a) compañero(a). ¿Quién formó las oraciones más originales?

...llevaría al país a la bancarrota *(bankrupcy)*.

...tendría fiestas en la Casa Blanca todos los días.

...no se preocuparía por nada.

...establecería la capital del país en Hollywood.

...le traería mucho prestigio al gobierno.

...sería el (la) mejor presidente(a) de la historia del país.

...nos obligaría a aceptar a más de una primera dama.

...no tendría una buena relación con los senadores y congresistas.

CD2-46

Script 11-16: Si pudiera empezar mi vida de nuevo, no trabajaría en el campo de los negocios. Creo que viviría en las montañas, en una casa de madera, y pasaría el tiempo pescando y disfrutando de la naturaleza. Por otro lado, no sería tan trabajador y les dedicaría más tiempo a mi esposa y a mis hijos. Definitivamente, tampoco me concentraría tanto en el dinero. También viajaría más a menudo y tendría la oportunidad de hacer algunas cosas que me gustan, como pintar y esquiar.

**11-16 Una vida diferente** Escucha la descripción que da el Sr. Miranda, administrador de una empresa de computación, sobre cómo sería su vida si pudiera empezar de nuevo. Luego, indica si las oraciones que siguen son ciertas **(C)** o falsas **(F)**.

___C___ 1. El Sr. Miranda no sería administrador de una empresa.

___C___ 2. Él viviría en un área rural, no en un área urbana.

___C___ 3. Podemos deducir que este señor no pasa mucho tiempo con su familia.

___F___ 4. A él no le gusta viajar muy a menudo.

___C___ 5. Si pudiera, él pintaría y esquiaría en su tiempo libre.

## ■ Aplicaciones

**11-17 ¿Adónde vamos?** Lee el diálogo entre David y Victoria y complétalo con la forma correcta del condicional de los verbos de la lista.

**OPCIONES:**    tener   gastar   sugerir   ser   visitar   divertirse
                pasar   gustar

DAVID:   Victoria, ¿vamos a ir a Chile o a Paraguay durante las vacaciones de primavera?

VICTORIA:   Si fuéramos a Chile, el precio _____sería_____ más bajo.

DAVID:   No, creo que en Paraguay nosotros _____gastaríamos_____ menos dinero.

VICTORIA:   Tienes razón, porque en Chile (nosotros) _____tendríamos_____ que ir a Valparaíso.

DAVID:   Pero, por otro lado, en Paraguay (nosotros) _____visitaríamos_____ otros lugares igualmente interesantes y bonitos.

VICTORIA:   David, escúchame. Creo que yo lo _____pasaría_____ mejor en Chile. ¿Vas conmigo o no?

DAVID:   ¡Tranquila!

VICTORIA:   Me _____gustaría_____ que fueras conmigo porque (nosotros) _____nos divertiríamos_____ muchísimo, pero es obvio que tenemos gustos diferentes.

DAVID:   Tienes razón. Te _____sugeriría_____ que esperáramos unos días y que habláramos del asunto. ¿De acuerdo?

VICTORIA:   ¡De acuerdo!

**11-18 ¿Qué harías... ?** Túrnense para hacer y responder a preguntas usando la información dada.

MODELO    en el puesto *(position)* de rector(a) de la universidad
         E1: *¿Qué harías en el puesto de rector(a) de la universidad?*
         E2: *Yo mejoraría las instalaciones* (facilities) *de la universidad y cambiaría el menú de la cafetería.*

1. con cinco millones de dólares
2. con treinta años más de edad
3. en tu fiesta ideal
4. en las vacaciones ideales
5. en el puesto del / de la presidente(a) del país
6. para obtener un trabajo perfecto
7. para conseguir una casa perfecta
8. para perder peso

**11-19 Profesores(as) por un mes** Imagínense que tienen la oportunidad de ser profesores(as) de español por un mes. ¿Qué harían y qué no harían? Escriban por lo menos ocho oraciones originales.

MODELO    *Nosotros nunca daríamos exámenes y haríamos fiestas en clase.*

### ■ Integración

**11-20 Hombres y mujeres** ¿Alguna vez han pensado en qué harían si fueran personas del sexo opuesto?

- ¿Qué cosas cambiarían?
- ¿Y qué cosas harían de una manera diferente?

En parejas, intercambien opiniones sobre este asunto. ¡Aprovechen esta oportunidad para demostrarle a los (las) estudiantes del sexo opuesto que Uds. sí los/las conocen bien!

For activity **11-20**, try to pair off female students with male students.

### SUGERENCIAS

- Las mujeres pueden usar algunos de estos verbos y expresiones: **comprender, atender, apoyar, (no) trabajar, (no) mirar la televisión, (no) vestirse, escuchar, salir** y **(no) ponerse.**
- Los hombres pueden usar algunos de estos verbos y expresiones: **(no) maquillarse, (no) quejarse, (no) hablar, (no) vestirse, interesarse, compartir, (no) decir** y **(no) ponerse.**

**11-21 Desde mi punto de vista** Imagínate que uno(a) de tus mejores amigos(as) no tiene muchas aspiraciones para su futuro. ¿Qué le recomendarías? Escríbele una breve nota para motivarlo(la) a ser más positivo(a). Y para que no lo tome tan personalmente, usa la forma **yo** de los verbos. Cuando termines, dale una copia a tu profesor(a) para que te dé su opinión. ¿Tienes que cambiar algo? ¿Tienes que ser más persuasivo(a) y convincente?

## IV. Perspectivas: Cómo convertir los sueños en una realidad

### ■ Antes de leer

**A. Para conversar** En grupos de tres o cuatro estudiantes, respondan a las siguientes preguntas.

1. ¿Es bueno o malo soñar despierto *(to daydream)*? Expliquen por qué.

2. ¿Pueden los sueños convertirse en realidad? ¿Cómo? Den ejemplos.

**B. Vocabulario y conceptos** Las siguientes palabras son importantes para comprender el texto. Para cada palabra, busca la letra que corresponda a su definición. (Consulten el diccionario si es necesario.)

| | | |
|---|---|---|
| _d_ 1. la clave | a. convertirse en una realidad |
| _f_ 2. un fracaso | b. objetivo, que no se basa en ilusiones |
| _b_ 3. realista | c. la suerte |
| _a_ 4. cumplir | d. la idea importante |
| _c_ 5. el azar | e. pronto, en un futuro cercano |
| _e_ 6. a corto plazo | f. algo que tuvo malos resultados, que no tuvo éxito |

**C. Aplicación** Ahora, completen las oraciones con las palabras que acaban de aprender en la actividad anterior.

1. En un juego de lotería, el factor más importante es el _____azar_____.

2. Muchas personas le tienen miedo al _____fracaso_____, pero en realidad puede ser algo positivo.

3. Las fantasías son buenas, pero es mejor tener metas _____realistas_____ para no tener desilusiones.

4. Mi abuelo dice que la _____clave_____ para tener éxito en la vida es ser honesto.

5. En el futuro quiero ser médico, pero por ahora, una de mis metas _____a corto plazo_____ es salir bien en el examen de esta tarde.

6. Sé que voy a _____cumplir_____ todas mis metas porque tengo mucha disciplina.

■ **A leer**

Lee rápidamente el siguiente artículo y responde a las preguntas que siguen.

## Las claves de la ilusión [dreaming]

Aunque soñar despierto es muy positivo, lo cierto es que de la ilusión no se puede vivir. Por eso, todos los expertos **coinciden** en que si queremos convertir nuestros sueños en realidad, debemos **poner mucho de nuestra parte** y no olvidar una serie de puntos concretos.

agree

to make a big effort

*Aceptar los fracasos.* Muchos de los sueños que tenemos no se cumplen, pero esto no quiere decir que seamos unos fracasados. Es necesario aprender a mantener viva la ilusión, a aceptar que no hemos conseguido algo y a buscar siempre una salida positiva.

*Planificar para conseguir los objetivos.* Uno de los secretos para conseguir nuestras metas es planificar nuestra actuación. Y uno de los mejores **trucos,** según algunos sicólogos, es escribir estas metas.

tricks

*Tener metas realistas.* Es necesario soñar con cosas que no sean imposibles de conseguir. «Las personas que tienen expectativas demasiado desproporcionadas a la realidad terminan **cayendo** en una continua desilusión, porque es muy difícil que todos sus sueños se cumplan», explica el sociólogo Armando de Miguel.

falling

*Saber adaptarse a los **vaivenes.*** «La capacidad de adaptarse al **medio,** a lo que se tiene delante, es una **señal** de salud mental», comenta Héctor González. Es importante aceptar los **imprevistos** e ir variando los objetivos si la realidad nos dice que no podemos cumplirlos.

fluctuations / environment
sign
surprises

***Fijarse** objetivos a corto plazo.* Aunque está muy bien tener expectativas **a largo plazo,** si queremos que se cumplan es necesario que tengamos también objetivos a corto plazo, como **etapas** sucesivas hacia la **consecución** de esas metas finales. Por ejemplo, si lo que esperamos es aprobar una carrera, debemos **plantearnos** aprobar primero asignatura por asignatura, luego curso por curso...

Set
long term
stages
obtaining
to consider

*Tener objetivos personales.* «Es importante ilusionarse con cosas que realmente signifiquen algo para nosotros, que no nos llamen la atención sólo **por el simple hecho** de que están de moda o son populares en nuestro **entorno** inmediato», explica el sicólogo Pedro Rodríguez.

just because
social group

■ ¿Entendiste bien?

D. Ideas generales Con un(a) compañero(a), respondan a las siguientes
preguntas.

1. ¿Cuál es la idea principal del texto?
2. ¿Cuántos consejos presenta?
3. ¿Quiénes son los expertos citados como fuentes *(cited as sources)*?

E. ¿Sí o no? Ahora lee de nuevo el texto e indica si las siguientes oraciones
corresponden a las ideas que presenta este artículo.

  _sí_ 1. Debemos tener siempre una actitud positiva a pesar de *(in
       spite of)* los fracasos.
  _no_ 2. Para lograr nuestras metas no es necesario elaborar un plan de
       acción.
  _sí_ 3. Para alcanzar nuestras metas, tenemos que ser flexibles.
  _no_ 4. Todas nuestras metas deben ser a largo plazo.
  _sí_ 5. Nuestras metas deben ser originales.

F. Actividad de extensión Después de leer el artículo, ¿qué le dirían a una
persona que quiere tener mucho éxito en su profesión y también tener
una familia unida y feliz? Escriban por lo menos cinco recomendaciones.

   MODELO    *Para lograr tus metas, es importante que...*

# Un futuro tecnificado

## I. Vocabulario: Las comodidades de la era electrónica

⊗ **¿Qué es esto?** Busquen en el dibujo cada uno de los artículos indicados.

| | |
|---|---|
| la alarma | la videograbadora |
| el horno microondas | el calentador/la caldera de agua |
| la antena parabólica | el equipo de sonido / el estéreo |
| la lavaplatos / el lavavajillas | la lavadora |
| el sistema de riego automático | el contestador |
| la cafetera automática | la secadora |
| el aire acondicionado | el fax |
| el televisor | la nevera / el refrigerador |
| la puerta automática | la computadora / el ordenador |

Tell students to try to do the activity without the use of their dictionaries. (Many of these words are cognates or have already been used in previous chapters.) The idea is to allow them to activate this vocabulary, providing help only when no group is able to find the correct answer.

### Instrucciones de uso

**Conecte** la unidad y **préndala** con el control remoto.
*Plug in* the unit and *turn it on* with the remote control.

**Apague** y **desconecte** el equipo después de cada uso.
*Turn off* and *unplug* the equipment after each use.

**Presione** el botón de encendido y use el teclado del control remoto para **programar** la máquina.
*Push* the "on" button and use the keyboard on your remote control to *program* the machine.

**Inserte** el disco compacto en la ranura.
*Insert* the compact disk in the slot.

**Hale** la perilla para activarla.
*Pull* the knob to activate it.

## Vocabulario práctico

apagado *off*
encendido *on*
No funciona. *It doesn't work. / It's broken.*

digitar *to key in*
halar *to pull*
presionar/oprimir/pulsar *to push, to hit*

### ■ Asimilación

**11-22 ¿Lo tienes?** Indica si tienes, quieres o no necesitas los siguientes aparatos. Luego, compara tus respuestas con las de un(a) compañero(a). ¿Tienen mucho o poco en común?

| Aparato | Lo tengo | Me gustaría tenerlo | No lo necesito |
|---|---|---|---|
| una antena parabólica | | | |
| un sistema de aire acondicionado | | | |
| una lavadora | | | |
| una secadora | | | |
| un horno microondas | | | |
| una lavaplatos | | | |
| una cafetera automática | | | |
| una videograbadora | | | |
| un equipo de sonido | | | |
| un contestador | | | |
| una computadora | | | |

-47 **11-23 ¿Qué aparato es?** Escucha las siguientes instrucciones de uso. ¿A qué aparato se refiere cada una? Escoge la respuesta más apropiada.

1. lavadora, contestador, videograbadora
2. computadora, cafetera, alarma
3. calentador, aire acondicionado, antena parabólica
4. contestador, computadora, alarma
5. equipo de sonido, lavadora, aire acondicionado

Script 11-23: 1. Oprima el botón para escuchar los mensajes. Si no desea borrarlos, oprima el botón que dice "Guardar". 2. Guarde con frecuencia los archivos que esté usando. Para esto, puede insertar su disco en la ranura correspondiente. 3. Mueva la perilla para escoger la temperatura deseada. La opción "Normal" le proporcionará agua a una temperatura promedio de 40 grados centígrados. 4. Para programar el equipo, digite la clave y oprima la tecla de "Activar". Después de 30 segundos escuchará una señal que indica que su residencia está segura. 5. Conecte la unidad a una fuente de energía de 120 voltios y oprima el botón de Encendido. Escoja el nivel de volumen, y con la ayuda de su control remoto, oprima la función deseada. Antes de operar la radio, debe instalar la antena correspondiente.

## Aplicaciones

### 11-24 Manual de instrucciones

**Paso 1:** Ordenen las siguientes instrucciones para operar una máquina lavadora.

  <u>1</u>  Prepare los artículos para el lavado.

  <u>3</u>  Ponga la carga *(load)* de lavado en la lavadora.

  <u>2</u>  Añada el detergente.

  <u>4</u>  No sobrecargue *(overload)* la lavadora.

  <u>5</u>  Presione la perilla para iniciar el ciclo.

  <u>6</u>  Retire los artículos al terminar el ciclo.

**Paso 2:** Escojan otro aparato de uso doméstico y escriban las instrucciones de uso correspondientes.

### 11-25 Publicidad

Imagínense que tienen que vender los siguientes productos. Escriban los anuncios comerciales correspondientes.

    a. videograbadora        b. lavadora        c. fax

### 11-26 ¿Cómo van a ser las casas en el año 3000?

Con un(a) compañero(a), piensen en las características de los hogares del futuro y diseñen su versión de la casa típica del año 3000.

## Integración

### 11-27 ¿Qué es lo más importante?

Formen grupos de tres estudiantes. Cada uno(a) va a leer una de las siguientes noticias sobre avances tecnológicos y va a informarle al resto del grupo acerca de sus ideas más importantes. Al terminar, decidan cuál es la información más importante y expliquen por qué.

*will become dominant since*

*states*

*place of business*

### Noticias tecnológicas

«Hoy el comercio electrónico es residual en la Red, sobre todo por las limitaciones en cuestión de seguridad, aunque en un futuro **se impondrá, ya que** se está avanzando en este terreno», **sostiene** Enrique García, de la UCE. Las ventajas pasan por la comodidad y por la reducción de precios, ya que tener una página «Web» es más barato que un **local.** Pero la principal desventaja es que no se ha conseguido que la seguridad en las transacciones económicas sea la adecuada, aunque se están desarrollando protocolos para encriptar los números de las tarjetas de crédito de los clientes.

## ¿La energía del futuro?

La fusión nuclear es un proceso similar al que se produce en el núcleo del sol, el cual genera luz y calor. Ésta podría ser una de las principales **fuentes** de energía del futuro, ya que se trata de un proceso limpio que no produce gases contaminantes ni lluvia ácida. De hecho, todos los elementos químicos que se emplean son **inocuos** para el ser humano y el medio ambiente. Hay reservas para mil años de **litio,** metal necesario para producir el **tritio, a su vez** esencial para la fusión.

*sources*

*harmless*
*lithium*
*trithium / in turn*

## ¿Qué utilidad tendrá la estación «Alfa» para la humanidad?

La colaboración internacional ha sido la **pieza clave** para la construcción de la nueva estación. En ella se podrán investigar nuevos medicamentos, observar los cambios climáticos y saber si el hombre podrá viajar algún día a **Marte.** La estación internacional —la estructura más grande **jamás** construida en el espacio, con 110 metros de largo— **pesará** 405 **toneladas, se desplazará** a 29.000 km/h y dará una **vuelta** completa a la Tierra cada noventa minutos. Tendrá seis módulos que servirán de laboratorio, dos que **se destinarán** a viviendas —donde residirán hasta siete astronautas— y otros siete serán utilizados como almacén. **Se prevé** que esté en operación durante al menos diez años.

*key piece*

*Mars*

*ever*
*will weigh*
*tons / will move*
*turn*

*will dedicate*
*It is foreseen*

**11-28 Opiniones** Hazte las siguientes preguntas y presenta un informe escrito con tus conclusiones.

a. ¿Qué opinas de la tecnología? ¿Te parece algo positivo o negativo?
b. ¿Cuál de los siguientes avances del siglo XX consideras que fue el más importante? ¿Por qué?
  - el avión
  - la penicilina
  - la computadora
  - los satélites artificiales
  - los transbordadores espaciales *(space shuttles)*
  - la clonación genética
  - el Internet
c. Si pudieras diseñar un nuevo aparato para hacer la vida humana más cómoda, ¿qué aparato sería? (Describe las funciones y características que **tendría** este aparato.)

### EN TU COMUNIDAD

Conduct an Internet search to find out if cellular phones, computers and wireless Internet connections are as readily available in Spanish-speaking countries such as Chile and Paraguay as in the United States. (You may choose other countries.) Also, find out how much these products and services cost. When you have all the necessary information, prepare a written report.

### SUGERENCIAS

Para ponerle un nombre *(To give it a name)* a tu invento, puedes usar uno de los siguientes modelos: **para lavar platos: una lavaplatos, para contestar las llamadas: un contestador.** Algunos verbos útiles son **tener, poder, ser, resolver, ayudar, hacer, reemplazar, simplificar, preparar, decidir, curar.**

## II. Funciones y estructuras: Expressing opinion, emotion, wishes, doubt, stipulation, purpose and future time frame with the subjunctive and the infinitive

DORIS: **Quiero conseguir** una casa con alarma, sistema de riego automático y un calentador de agua nuevo.

IRMA: Mmm... **Dudo que** la **consigas. Es imposible encontrar** una casa así en este vecindario.

DORIS: Te aseguro que la voy a conseguir **antes de casarme.**

IRMA: **Me parece fantástico que seas** tan optimista, pero recuerda que *yo* soy la agente de bienes raíces.

DORIS: Irma, **para lograr** algo **es aconsejable ser** positivo.

You have already studied the use of the subjunctive mode with verbs and impersonal expressions that convey:

- Opinion and advice

  **Es necesario que desenchufes** los enseres antes de salir.

  *It is necessary for you to unplug the appliances before leaving.*

- Wishes and requests

  **Prefiero que uses** la secadora por la mañana.

  *I prefer for you to use the dryer in the morning.*

- Emotions and feelings

  **Es increíble que** este apartamento **tenga** tantas comodidades.

  *It is incredible that this apartment has so many comforts.*

- Doubt

  **No estoy segura de que** el horno microondas **funcione** bien.

  *I am not sure that the microwave oven works well.*

You have also studied the use of this mode with conjunctions of stipulation, purpose, and future time frame.

Compraré el aire acondicionado **para que durmamos** cómodamente.

*I will buy the air conditioner so that we sleep comfortably.*

When the subject of one of these verbs is the same as the subject of the verb in the subordinate clause, the verb in the latter is used in the infinitive form. Compare the following pairs of sentences. (The subjects are underlined.)

SUBJUNCTIVE: (<u>Yo</u>) Espero que <u>Ana</u> **compre** la videograbadora.

INFINITIVE: (<u>Yo</u>) Espero **comprar** la videograbadora.

The other use of the subjunctive (in adjectival clauses that refer to hypothetical antecedents) is not included in this discussion because the infinitive form of the verb is never used in this context.
**Queremos una casa que *tenga* puertas automáticas.**

Notice that **que** is omitted when the main verb, the impersonal expression, or the conjunction is followed by an infinitive.

Similarly, personal expressions are followed by an infinitive when the speaker is making a generic statement that applies to people in general, including himself or herself. This is also useful when the speaker wants to make a comment that affects the listener but in an indirect and polite manner. Compare these pairs of sentences.

SUBJUNCTIVE: Es ridículo que ellos no **sepan** programar una computadora.

INFINITIVE: Es ridículo no **saber** programar una computadora.

The only conjunctions that can be used with the infinitive form of the verb are **con tal de** and **en caso de** (stipulation); **a fin de** and **para** (purpose); and **antes de, después de,** and **hasta** (future time frame).

SUBJUNCTIVE: Zelma limpia la casa a fin de que su madre **se sienta** bien.

INFINITIVE: Zelma limpia la casa a fin de **sentirse** bien.

### ■ Asimilación

**11-29 Vivir bien hoy en día** Lee las siguientes oraciones e indica si estás de acuerdo o no. Cuando termines, compara las respuestas con las de un(a) compañero(a). ¿Están de acuerdo? ¿Por qué?

Para vivir bien hoy día...

_____ es necesario tener un horno microondas.

_____ no es importante tener una secadora.

_____ no es aconsejable usar una lavaplatos.

_____ es recomendable comprar una antena parabólica.

_____ es mejor regar las plantas con un sistema de riego automático.

_____ es preciso pagar las cuentas por computadora.

_____ es imposible estar en ciertos (certain) lugares sin aire acondicionado.

_____ es posible informarnos solamente a través de la televisión.

**11-30 Los recién casados** Escucha el diálogo entre Estrella y Héctor, unos recién casados, y escoge las alternativas que mejor completen las siguientes oraciones.

1. Héctor piensa arreglar el calentador cuando...
   a. termine el partido.     b. Estrella se bañe.
   c. Estrella se vaya al trabajo.
2. Dadas las condiciones, Estrella dice que es imposible...
   a. descansar.     b. ir a trabajar.     c. bañarse.
3. Héctor duda que el agua...
   a. esté caliente.     b. esté fría.     c. no esté helada.
4. Estrella no puede creer que Héctor...
   a. duerma tanto.     b. no sea cooperador.
   c. no quiera trabajar.
5. Cuando Estrella se lleva el control remoto, Héctor dice que...
   a. no es imprescindible.     b. no es justo.
   c. no es importante.

Although **cuando, en cuanto,** and **mientras** cannot be used with infinitives, they can be used with verbs in the indicative mode if the action of the subordinate clause does not refer to the future. The same applies to **antes de, después de,** and **hasta.**
Conecto la cafetera _cuando_ mi madre desconecta el radio.
Me iba de casa _en cuanto_ terminaba de enviar los faxes.
Elena me acompañaba _hasta que yo_ estaba lista.

Script 11-30:
Estrella: ¡Héctor, todavía no has arreglado el calentador de agua! ¿Qué estás esperando?
Héctor: No te preocupes, mi amor. Lo arreglaré cuando termine el partido de fútbol americano.
Estrella: Pero, Héctor, tengo que bañarme antes de ir al trabajo. Sabes que es imposible bañarse sin agua caliente. ¿Qué quieres que haga?
Héctor: Estrella, dudo que el agua esté tan helada. ¿No crees que me merezco descansar un rato? Además, es temprano.
Estrella: Es increíble que seas tan poco cooperador. [_Playfully._] Estoy segura de que reaccionarías inmediatamente si me llevara el control remoto, ¿verdad? ¡Pues me lo llevo!
Héctor: [_Playfully._] ¡No, Estrella! ¡No seas así! No es justo que una mujer deje a su querido esposo sin el control remoto. ¡Dámelo, por favor!
Estrella: No. Primero, al sótano a arreglar el calentador de agua.
Héctor: Está bien. ¡Tú ganas!

## ■ Aplicaciones

**11-31 En un almacén** Lean el diálogo entre Marcos y el empleado de un almacén y decidan si el verbo debe usarse en el infinitivo o en el subjuntivo. Si debe usarse en el subjuntivo, conjúguenlo correctamente.

EMPLEADO: Buenas tardes, señor. ¿En qué puedo ayudarlo?

MARCOS: Hola. Estoy buscando un horno de microondas que no (costar) mucho y que (ser) de buena calidad.

EMPLEADO: Tenemos una amplia selección. Le recomiendo que (comprar) un modelo que (usar) poca electricidad, como éste.

MARCOS: Me parece bien. Creo que es importante (economizar) como sea, ¿no?

EMPLEADO: Estoy de acuerdo. ¿Y para Ud. es necesario (tener) un microondas con plato giratorio *(rotating)*?

MARCOS: Mmm... Sí. Quiero un horno que (distribuir) uniformemente el calor. ¿Tiene garantía?

EMPLEADO: De un año. Y, si lo desea, puede comprar un servicio de por vida que (cubrir) el arreglo de cualquier tipo de desperfecto.

MARCOS: Eso me interesa. Me lo llevo.

EMPLEADO: ¡Perfecto! Pues pase por aquella caja registradora para (pagar).

*[Cinco minutos después.]*

EMPLEADO: Hasta luego, señor. Espero que Ud. y su familia (disfrutar) del horno de microondas.

MARCOS: Gracias por todo. Hasta luego.

**11-32 Planes futuros**

**Paso 1:** Usa las claves para formar oraciones sobre tus planes para el futuro. Usa las conjunciones que se proveen. Puedes añadir la información que creas necesaria.

MODELO    trabajar / para (que) / mi familia
*Trabajaré como dentista para sentirme productivo(a) y para que mi familia tenga lo que necesite.*

1. casarme / después de (que) / mi futuro(a) esposo(a)

2. comprar / antes de (que) / mis futuros hijos

3. ahorrar / en caso de (que) / mis padres o mis hermanos

4. tener / con tal de (que) / alguien

5. ir / hasta (que) / mi mejor amigo(a)

6. ser / para (que) / todo el mundo

**Paso 2:** Compara las respuestas del **Paso 1** con las respuestas de un(a) compañero(a) de clase. ¿Cuáles de sus planes te parecen más interesantes, curiosos o extraños? Escoge tres de sus respuestas y escribe un breve informe.

MODELO      *Me parece interesante que Nelson vaya a trabajar para ganar mucho dinero y para que su madre tenga la casa de sus sueños. Además, me parece curioso que él...*

**11-33 Consejos** Preparen una lista de ocho consejos que quieren darles a sus hijos cuando sean adolescentes.

MODELO      *Les sugiero que estudien antes de pensar en el matrimonio. Es importante respetar a toda la gente.*

### ■ Integración

**11-34 Las prioridades de la vida** Representa la siguiente situación con un(a) compañero(a).

| **El (La) ambicioso(a)** *(greedy)* | **El (La) práctico(a)** |
|---|---|
| Eres una persona demasiado ambiciosa que sólo piensa en las cosas materiales que quieres conseguir. Háblale a tu amigo(a) de algunas de estas cosas y pídele su opinión. ¡Debes estar preparado(a) para su reacción y para defender tu punto de vista sobre las prioridades de la vida! | Uno(a) de tus amigos(as) sólo habla de las cosas materiales que quiere en su vida. Ya estás cansado(a) de esto y vas a aprovechar la oportunidad para darle tu opinión. Explícale cuáles son las prioridades de la vida y defiende tu punto de vista. |

**SUGERENCIAS**

Para expresar desacuerdo, puedes usar algunas de las siguientes expresiones:
**No pienso de la misma manera.**
*I don't think the same way.*
**Tengo una opinión diferente.**
*I have a different opinion.*
**No estoy de acuerdo.**
*I don't agree.*
**Es tu opinión, no la mía.**
*That's your opinion, not mine.*

**11-35 Para alcanzar la felicidad** De acuerdo con tu experiencia, ¿qué cosas son importantes, necesarias, imposibles, etc., para alcanzar la felicidad en la vida? Como a veces es mejor escribir las ideas, haz una lista de por lo menos diez cosas que no quieres olvidar en momentos difíciles.

**SUGERENCIAS**

Usa algunos de los verbos y expresiones impersonales que ya sabes para dar consejos, expresar emociones, duda y deseos, tales como: **aconsejar, recomendar, no creer, esperar, querer, es importante, es preciso, es increíble, es triste, es mejor**, etc.

### III. Funciones y estructuras: Talking about the past using the imperfect subjunctive

¿Qué pasó ayer en la oficina?

El jefe me **dijo** que **enviara** este fax inmediatamente.

A los empleados no les **gustó** que la compañía les **pagara** menos este mes.

El jefe nos dijo que **era necesario** que **nos quedáramos** en la oficina **hasta** que **termináramos** de revisar todos los datos.

The subjunctive mode also has an imperfect tense. This tense is formed by dropping the **-ron** ending of the **ellos(as)/ustedes** preterite conjugation of the verb and adding the endings that follow to the remaining stem.

The **yo** and **él/ella/usted** endings are identical.

The **nosotros** form of the imperfect subjunctive takes a written accent mark on the third-to-last syllable.

| ENDINGS | **-ar** VERBS<br>**tomaron → toma-** | **-er** VERBS<br>**comieron → comie-** | **-ir** VERBS<br>**vivieron → vivie-** |
|---|---|---|---|
| -ra | toma**ra** | comie**ra** | vivie**ra** |
| -ras | toma**ras** | comie**ras** | vivie**ras** |
| -ra | toma**ra** | comie**ra** | vivie**ra** |
| -ramos | tom**áramos** | comi**éramos** | vivi**éramos** |
| -rais | toma**rais** | comie**rais** | vivie**rais** |
| -ran | toma**ran** | comie**ran** | vivie**ran** |

The imperfect subjunctive is used in the same contexts in which the present subjunctive is used. The difference is that the imperfect subjunctive is used when the verb in the main clause is in the past tense (the preterite or the imperfect indicative).

- advice and suggestions

  Mi colega me **sugirió** que **buscara** otro trabajo.

  *My colleague **suggested looking for** another job.*

- wishes

  **Queríamos** que el jefe **escuchara** nuestras quejas.

  *We **wanted** the boss **to listen** to our complaints.*

- emotion

  **Me alegré** mucho de que te **invitaran** a dar una charla.

  *I **was** very **glad** to hear that they **invited** you to give a talk.*

- doubt and denial

  Ella nunca **dudó** que yo **terminara** el informe a tiempo.

  *She never **doubted** that I **would finish** the report on time.*

- hypothetical situations and antecedents

  La empresa **necesitaba** un abogado que nos **defendiera** en este caso.

  *The company **needed** a lawyer that **would defend** us in this case.*

- conjunctions of stipulation

  Nosotros **sabíamos** que la junta no aprobaría el proyecto <u>a menos que</u> **presentáramos** evidencia.

  *We **knew** that the board would not approve the project <u>unless</u> **we presented** evidence.*

- conjunctions of purpose

  **Llamé** a mi secretaria <u>para</u> pedirle que **sacara** las copias del documento.

  *I **called** my secretary to ask her **to make** copies of the document.*

- conjunctions that indicate future time frame

  **Tuvimos** que irnos <u>antes de que</u> **empezara** la reunión.

  *We **had** to leave <u>before</u> the meeting **started**.*

## ■ Asimilación

**11-36 ¿Ocurrió o no?** Primero, empareja cada frase de la izquierda con una frase lógica de la derecha. Después, indica si esas acciones ocurrieron o no en la clase de español la última vez que se reunieron los estudiantes. Al terminar, compara tus respuestas con las de un(a) compañero(a). ¿Quién tiene mejor memoria?

El (La) profesor(a) de español...

<u>b</u>   prohibió que habláramos...

<u>a</u>   nos pidió que empezáramos...

<u>e</u>   dijo que era importante que estudiáramos...

<u>f</u>   prometió que daría una fiesta cuando terminara...

<u>d</u>   dijo que era imposible que todos sacáramos...

<u>c</u>   confesó que no había estudiantes que trabajaran...

a. a estudiar para el examen.

b. inglés en clase.

c. más que nosotros.

d. una A en la clase.

e. todos los días.

f. el semestre.

2-49   **11-37 La niñez** Escucha lo que dice Emma de su niñez y escoge las alternativas que mejor completen las oraciones que siguen.

1. A ella le gustaba que su padres la llevaran a la casa de sus abuelos los...

   a. viernes.        b. sábados.        (c.) domingos.

2. Le gustaba que ellos la recibieran con...

   a. sorpresas.        (b.) regalos.        c. muchos besos.

3. Para los abuelos, era muy importante que la familia... lo más posible.

   (a.) compartiera        b. comiera        c. disfrutara

4. No volvían a casa hasta que todos hablaran...

   a. del amor familiar.        (b.) de la semana anterior.        c. de la niñez.

**Script 11-37:** En mi niñez, me gustaba mucho que mis padres nos llevaran a mis hermanos y a mí a la casa de mis abuelos los domingos. Nos encantaba que ellos nos recibieran con regalos y que nos permitieran hacer lo que queríamos. Para eso son los abuelos, ¿verdad? Para ellos era muy importante que la familia compartiera todo lo que fuera posible y que sus nietos disfrutaran del amor y del calor de su hogar. No regresábamos a casa hasta que comíamos juntos y pasábamos un rato hablando de lo que había ocurrido *(had taken place)* la semana anterior. Tuve una niñez muy especial.

■ **Aplicaciones**

**11-38 Una encuesta** A continuación se presenta un artículo sobre las expectativas de los estudiantes antes de ingresar en la universidad. Usa la información para saber si tu compañero(a) era un(a) estudiante típico(a) o no.

MODELO   E1: *¿Esperabas que los profesores incorporaran tecnología en sus cursos?*
E2: *Sí, esperaba que ellos incorporaran tecnología, pero no con tanta frecuencia.*

---

# Los estudiantes universitarios del futuro

De acuerdo con una encuesta informal que se realizó en tres escuelas secundarias de esta ciudad, los estudiantes universitarios del futuro...

■ esperan que los profesores incorporen tecnología en sus cursos

■ están interesados en asistir a universidades que ofrezcan programas interdisciplinarios

■ quieren tomar cursos que les permitan trabajar por la noche

■ creen que es necesario hacer una práctica cuando completen la mayoría de los requisitos curriculares

■ recomiendan que la administración responda a los reclamos de los estudiantes

■ insisten en que el estacionamiento no les cueste nada

■ no creen que sus padres acepten que vivan en una residencia estudiantil

■ piensan que es dudoso que las computadoras reemplacen a los profesores

---

**11-39 Compañeros(as) de apartamento** Imagínense que Uds. son compañeros(as) de apartamento y quieren saber por qué o para qué compraron ciertas cosas. Túrnense para hacer y responder a las preguntas.

MODELO  el horno de microondas
E1: *¿Para qué compraste el horno de microondas?*
E2: *Lo compré para que cocináramos más rápidamente.*

**Verbos útiles:** grabar   ver   secar   recibir   bañarse   vivir   proteger
ahorrar   divertirse   lavar

**Expresiones útiles:** más rápidamente   más efectivamente
más seguramente   más económicamente

1. la secadora
2. la antena parabólica
3. el lavavajillas
4. el aire acondicionado
5. el contestador
6. la alarma
7. la videograbadora
8. el calentador de agua

**11-40 Cuando tenía como diez años...** Piensen en su vida cuando tenían diez años y formen oraciones con elementos de las dos columnas. Terminen las oraciones de forma lógica y original.

MODELO  nosotros + (no) querer que...
*Nosotros no queríamos que nuestros amigos usaran nuestros juguetes.*

nosotros
nuestros padres
los profesores
nuestros amigos
nuestros hermanos
...

+

(no) querer que...
(no) insistir en que...
(no) pensar que era importante que...
(no) pedir que...
(no) esperar que...
(no) pensar que era posible que...
negar que...
desear que...
...

+ ...

### ■ Integración

**11-41 Entrevista** Individualmente, escriban diez preguntas para saber cómo era su compañero(a) cuando era niño(a). Luego, entrevístense y tomen notas.

**11-42 Comparaciones** Usa la información que recopilaste en la actividad 11-41 para compararte con tu compañero(a) cuando eran niños(as). Cuando termines, dale una copia a él/ella para que te dé su opinión.

MODELO  *Creo que... y yo éramos semejantes/diferentes cuando éramos niños(as).*
*En primer lugar, nosotros...*

**SUGERENCIAS**

Pueden usar las siguientes expresiones como modelo para hacer las preguntas:
**¿Te molestaba que... ?**
**¿Te parecía (interesante/triste/curioso/...) que... ?**
**¿Le(s) decías a... que... ?**
**¿Siempre dudabas que... ?**
**¿Sentías que... ?**
**¿Creías que era (imposible/increíble/...) que... ?**
**¿Te alegrabas de que... ?**
**¿(Querían tus padres que estudiaras/jugaras...) hasta... ?**

**SUGERENCIAS**

Usa los conectores que ya sabes para hacer esta comparación:
**de igual forma** *similarly*
**por otro lado** *on the other hand*
**sin embargo** *however*
**además** *in addition*
**también** *also*
**por el contrario** *on the contrary*
**por ejemplo** *for example*
**en conclusión** *in conclusion*

## IV. Vídeo: Aspiraciones y planes para el futuro

### ■ Preparación

**A.** **¿Qué quieren hacer?** En el vídeo, los compañeros van a hablar sobre sus aspiraciones y planes para el futuro. Basándose en lo que ya saben de cada compañero(a), adivinen qué quieren hacer Alejandra, Javier y Sofía. Escriban el nombre correcto al lado de cada descripción.

1. «Viajaré al extranjero y viviré en otro país. Tendré mi propia agencia de ecoturismo y deportes de aventura.» _____Javier_____

2. «Cuando regrese a mi país, montaré una exposición de fotografía en el Museo de Arte.» _____Alejandra_____

3. «Terminaré de escribir mi libro aquí en Puerto Rico y luego regresaré a mi país.» _____Sofía_____

En las oraciones anteriores no estaban incluidas ni las aspiraciones de Valeria ni las de Antonio. ¿Qué planes creen que tienen ellos?

Valeria:
Antonio:

**ESTRATEGIA DE COMPRENSIÓN**

**Listening for Details** As you match the video and do the following listening comprehension activities, keep in mind that you are listening for recognition of specific pieces of information about the roommates' aspirations and future plans.

### ■ ¿Entendiste bien?

**B.** **El sueño de Javier** Mientras ves el vídeo, completa el diagrama de la página 469 con las ideas y preguntas que tiene Javier sobre cómo hacer realidad su sueño.

**¿QUÉ?**

Mi sueño es _tener mi propia agencia de ecoturismo y deportes de aventura_

**DUDAS PARA RESOLVER**

- ¿Cuánto cuesta un boleto de San Juan a Belice o Tegucigalpa?
- ¿Dónde compro los boletos?
- En _Costa Rica_, ¿qué es mejor, viajar por carretera o por _avión_?
  ¿Cuánto cuesta alquilar un _carro_?
- ¿Cuál es el medio de transporte más conveniente para unir los países de Centroamérica?

**¿DÓNDE?**

Aún no sé dónde me gustaría hacerlo, pero estoy considerando: las playas de _Costa Rica_ o _Belice_ o las Islas Roatán en _Honduras_.

**PASOS QUE HAY QUE SEGUIR**

1. Tomar un avión a _Centroamérica_.
2. Visitar Belice, Honduras y Costa Rica.
3. En Costa Rica, recorrer la costa del _Pacífico_ en bicicleta.
4. Tomar un avión a _Cuzco_ y de allí un tren a Macchu Picchu.

Compara tus respuestas con las de un(a) compañero(a).

**C. Decisiones, decisiones** Al final del episodio, Valeria le dijo a Antonio: «Déjame pensarlo...». Es una decisión difícil y seguramente le vendrían bien algunos consejos. En grupos, piensen qué pasaría si Valeria decidiera decirle a Antonio que sí. ¿Qué ventajas y desventajas tendría el dar una respuesta afirmativa? Luego, piensen qué pasaría si Valeria decidiera decirle que no. De nuevo, ¿qué ventajas y desventajas tendría esto? Finalmente, lleguen a una conclusión basada en sus razonamientos y completen la siguiente oración afirmativa o negativamente.

*Si fuéramos Valeria, nosotros (no) aceptaríamos la propuesta de Antonio porque...*

**D. Enfoque comunitario** Entrevista a algún (alguna) estudiante extranjero(a) de tu universidad para averiguar sus planes y sueños para el futuro. Graba *(Tape)* tu conversación y lleva la cinta a la clase. Asegúrate de incluir las siguientes preguntas en tu entrevista.

1. ¿Te gustaría quedarte a vivir en los Estados Unidos? ¿Por qué sí o por qué no?
2. En cualquiera de los casos *(In either case)*, ¿dónde te gustaría vivir y qué te gustaría hacer?

# Utopías

## I. Vocabulario: Un mundo mejor

—Me gustaría que hubiera menos violencia.

—Sí, deberíamos **respetar** más la vida y ser más tolerantes.

—Tenemos que hacer algo para **proteger** a las **especies en vías de extinción,** ¿no crees?

—De acuerdo. Es nuestra obligación **preservar** el **medio ambiente** para las próximas generaciones.

—¡Es terrible ver cuánta gente en el mundo sufre de **hambre** y vive en la más absoluta **miseria!**

—¿Qué te parece si **nos vinculamos** con algún grupo de **caridad** o **beneficencia**?

—Nadie debería conducir **embriagado.**

—Sí. El gobierno debería **invertir** más en campañas educativas para evitar estas tragedias.

### Vocabulario práctico

la caridad / la beneficencia *charity*
los derechos humanos *human rights*
la discriminación *discrimination*
las especies en vías de extinción *endangered species*
la guerra *war*
el hambre *hunger*
la indiferencia *indifference*
la investigación *research*
el medio ambiente *the environment*
la miseria *extreme poverty*
el odio *hate*
el respeto *respect*

la solidaridad *solidarity*
la violencia *violence*

embriagado/borracho *drunk*
tolerante *tolerant*

consumir *to consume*
evitar *to avoid*
invertir (ie, i) *to invest*
pasar hambre *to go hungry*
preservar *to preserve*
proteger *to protect*
respetar *to respect*
salvar *to save*
vincularse *to get involved*

## ■ Asimilación

**11-43 ¿Problema o solución?** Usa la tabla para clasificar las siguientes palabras.

la contaminación    la investigación    la violencia    la solidaridad
la guerra    el hambre    la tolerancia    las enfermedades    el respeto
la justicia    la discriminación    la indiferencia

| Problemas | Soluciones |
|---|---|
| la contaminación, la violencia, la guerra, el hambre, las enfermedades, la discriminación, la indiferencia | la investigación, la solidaridad, la tolerancia, el respeto, la justicia |

02-50    **11-44 Causa y efecto** Vas a escuchar una serie de situaciones y problemas que nos afectan hoy en día. Para cada una, identifica su causa más probable.

   _3_   No existe una distribución justa de la riqueza.

   _5/2_   No somos tolerantes.

   _2/5_   No respetamos la vida.

   _4_   Alguna gente irresponsable conduce embriagada.

   _1_   Abusamos de los combustibles fósiles.

Script 11-44: 1. Hay polución ambiental. 2. Hay violencia y terrorismo. 3. Hay hambre en el mundo. 4. Hay muchos accidentes de tránsito. 5. Hay discordias y odios.

## ■ Aplicaciones

**11-45 Adivina** Túrnense para definir diferentes palabras del vocabulario. El (La) compañero(a) tiene sólo dos oportunidades para adivinar.

MODELO    E1: *Es un problema que existe en muchas partes del mundo.*
*Ocurre cuando la gente no tiene qué comer. La gente que*
*tiene este problema se pone* (becomes) *muy delgada*
(skinny) *y enferma porque no tiene una nutrición*
*adecuada.*
E2: *¿El hambre?*
E1: *¡Correcto!*

**11-46 ¿Qué podemos hacer?** Completa las oraciones de una manera lógica usando el presente del subjuntivo.

1. Para erradicar la violencia, es necesario que...
2. Para salvar las especies en vías de extinción, es importante que...
3. Para terminar con el narcotráfico, es urgente que...
4. Para evitar la proliferación del crimen, es mejor que...
5. Para reducir los efectos de la contaminación, es preciso que...

**11-47 Preocupaciones** Respondan a las siguientes preguntas y preparen un informe.

a. ¿Cuál de los siguientes problemas es el más grave en este momento?

_____ el terrorismo

_____ la corrupción

_____ la guerra

_____ la contaminación del medio ambiente

_____ el hambre

_____ otro:

b. ¿Qué podríamos hacer nosotros como estudiantes universitarios para ayudar a resolver ese problema? (Den algunos ejemplos concretos.)

## ■ Integración

**11-48 Las noticias** Representa la siguiente situación con un(a) compañero(a).

| **Estudiante A** | **Estudiante B** |
| --- | --- |
| Acabas de ver las noticias y estás muy preocupado(a) por la proliferación de actos de violencia y terrorismo en todo el mundo. Comenta tus preocupaciones con tu amigo(a) y traten juntos de ver si es posible hacer algo para cambiar esta situación. | Acabas de ver un informe del programa «60 Minutos» sobre la corrupción y estás muy preocupado(a) por la pérdida de valores morales en el mundo. Comenta tus preocupaciones con tu amigo(a) y traten juntos de ver si es posible hacer algo para cambiar esta situación. |

**11-49 Utopía** ¿Cómo serían las noticias si viviéramos en un mundo perfecto? Tomen el periódico local y vuelvan a escribir los titulares de la primera página para que reflejen esa utopía.

## II. Funciones y estructuras: Talking about the past using the imperfect subjunctive (irregular verbs)

«Esperábamos que el conflicto **estuviera** resuelto, pero las partes no han podido llegar a un acuerdo. No creíamos que el asunto **fuera** tan complicado. **Quisiéramos** que el pueblo **tuviera** un poco más de paciencia y que **hiciera** lo posible por comprender que esta situación es delicada.»

In **Tema 2** you learned how to use the imperfect subjunctive when the verb or the impersonal expression that conveys an opinion, a wish, an emotion or doubt is in the past tense. You also used verbs in this tense to describe hypothetical antecedents and to talk about stipulation, purpose and future time frame when the verb in the main clause is in the past tense.

A nosotros no nos gustó que el Sr. Rojas no **evitara** la violencia.

*We did not like that Mr. Rojas did not **avoid** violence.*

Íbamos a dictar una ley que **protegiera** el medio ambiente.

*We were going to issue a law that **would protect** the environment.*

Since the imperfect subjunctive is formed from the **ellos(as)/ustedes** preterite conjugation of the verb, all verbs that are irregular in the preterite are also irregular in the imperfect subjunctive. Here is a summary of the most common irregularities.

■ verbs that take an **i**

| INFINITIVE | PRETERITE | IMPERFECT SUBJUNCTIVE |
|---|---|---|
| decir | di̱jeron | **dijera, dijeras, dijera, dijéramos, dijerais, dijeran** |
| hacer | hi̱cieron | **hiciera, hicieras, hiciera, hiciéramos, hicierais, hicieran** |
| pedir | pi̱dieron | **pidiera, pidieras, pidiera, pidiéramos, pidierais, pidieran** |
| querer | qui̱sieron | **quisiera, quisieras, quisiera, quisiéramos, quisierais, quisieran** |
| sentir | si̱ntieron | **sintiera, sintieras, sintiera, sintiéramos, sintierais, sintieran** |
| venir | vi̱nieron | **viniera, vinieras, viniera, viniéramos, vinierais, vinieran** |

This summary only includes verbs that are used frequently. You may review the chapters and **Temas** that present irregular verbs in the preterite tense to find other verbs that are irregular in the imperfect subjunctive.

### REMEMBER

To form the imperfect subjunctive, drop **-ron** from the **ellos(as)/ustedes** form of the preterite and add the endings **-ra, -ras, -ra, -ramos, -rais,** and **-ran**: beber → bebieron → bebie- → bebiera, bebieras, bebiera, bebiéramos, bebierais, bebieran.

■ verbs that take a **u**

| INFINITIVE | PRETERITE | IMPERFECT SUBJUNCTIVE |
|---|---|---|
| dormir | durmieron | **durmiera, durmieras, durmiera, durmiéramos, durmierais, durmieran** |
| estar | estuvieron | **estuviera, estuvieras, estuviera, estuviéramos, estuvierais, estuvieran** |
| haber | hubieron | **hubiera, hubieras, hubiera, hubiéramos, hubierais, hubieran** |
| morir | murieron | **muriera, murieras, muriera, muriéramos, murierais, murieran** |
| poder | pudieron | **pudiera, pudieras, pudiera, pudiéramos, pudierais, pudieran** |
| poner | pusieron | **pusiera, pusieras, pusiera, pusiéramos, pusierais, pusieran** |
| saber | supieron | **supiera, supieras, supiera, supiéramos, supierais, supieran** |
| tener | tuvieron | **tuviera, tuvieras, tuviera, tuviéramos, tuvierais, tuvieran** |

■ verbs that take a **y**

| INFINITIVE | PRETERITE | IMPERFECT SUBJUNCTIVE |
|---|---|---|
| caer | cayeron | **cayera, cayeras, cayera, cayéramos, cayerais, cayeran** |
| creer | creyeron | **creyera, creyeras, creyera, creyéramos, creyerais, creyeran** |
| leer | leyeron | **leyera, leyeras, leyera, leyéramos, leyerais, leyeran** |
| oír | oyeron | **oyera, oyeras, oyera, oyéramos, oyerais, oyeran** |

■ other irregular verbs

| INFINITIVE | PRETERITE | IMPERFECT SUBJUNCTIVE |
|---|---|---|
| dar | dieron | **diera, dieras, diera, diéramos, dierais, dieran** |
| ir / ser | fueron | **fuera, fueras, fuera, fuéramos, fuerais, fueran** |

The imperfect subjunctive conjugation of the verb **querer** is used to be polite when making requests.

| | |
|---|---|
| Señor presidente, **quisiera** que Ud. hablara del problema de la discriminación en este país. | *Mr. President, **I would like** for you to talk about the discrimination problem in this country.* |

## Asimilación

**11-50 La opinión y los deseos de los padres** Lee las siguientes oraciones y escoge las alternativas que se apliquen a ti. Al terminar, compara tus respuestas con las respuestas de un(a) compañero(a). ¿Sus padres tenían las mismas opiniones y los mismos deseos?

Mi padres esperaban que yo fuera...

_____ doctor(a).

_____ ingeniero(a).

_____ profesor(a).

_____ abogado(a).

_____ sicólogo(a).

_____ otra profesión: _____

Ellos querían que yo tuviera...

_____ más paciencia.

_____ más responsabilidades.

_____ más dedicación a los estudios.

_____ más disciplina.

_____ más auto-estima.

_____ otra cualidad: _____

A ellos nunca les gustaba que yo les pidiera...

_____ dinero.

_____ más privacidad.

_____ permiso para regresar tarde.

_____ el carro.

_____ más libertad.

_____ otra cosa: _____

**11-51 Un mensaje telefónico** Marla faltó a la clase de francés hoy y su amigo César le dejó un mensaje en el contestador. Escucha el mensaje e indica si las siguientes oraciones son ciertas **(C)** o falsas **(F).**

__F__ 1. César quería que Marla supiera qué hizo Martín en la clase hoy.

__F__ 2. El profesor pidió que hicieran las actividades del cuaderno de ejercicios.

__C__ 3. Él también dijo que esperaba que pudieran terminar el diálogo.

__F__ 4. César quisiera que Marla fuera a su oficina para terminar el trabajo.

__F__ 5. Él quisiera reunirse con Marla esta noche.

**Script 11-51:** Hola, Marla, Soy César. Mira, quería que supieras qué pasó en la clase de francés hoy. El profesor nos pidió que hiciéramos las actividades del manual de laboratorio. También nos dijo que leyéramos la información de la página sesenta y que esperaba que pudiéramos terminar de escribir el diálogo sobre la visita al restaurante. Como estamos trabajando juntos en esto, quisiera que vinieras a mi casa para terminarlo. Quisiera que me dijeras si puedes venir esta tarde. Bueno, llámame cuando puedas. Un beso. Chao.

## ■ Aplicaciones

**11-52 Problemas mundiales** Uds. trabajan para el periódico de la universidad y tienen que preparar un informe sobre las cosas que dijeron los panelistas de una charla sobre problemas mundiales.

Algunos de los verbos que se usan en artículos periodísticos para citar *(quote)* a otras personas son **decir, señalar, expresar, apuntar, afirmar** y **manifestar**.

Answers 11-52: 1. ...que no podemos aceptar que tantos niños tuvieran hambre en el mundo. 2. ...que quería que la ONU y la UNESCO hicieran algo con relación al problema de la violencia. 3. ...que le parecía muy triste que los oficiales gubernamentales no creyeran en los resultados de estos informes. 4. ...que... no pensaban que la guerra fuera la mejor alternativa. 5. ...que no teníamos que hacer que las agencias pusieran más recursos a disposición de los científicos. 6. ...que iba a luchar hasta que pudiéramos salvar las especies en vías de extinción!

MODELO    Dr. Fernández: «Es lamentable que todavía haya tanta miseria en el mundo.»
*El Dr. Fernández dijo que era lamentable que todavía hubiera tanta miseria en el mundo.*

1. Dra. Zapata: «No podemos aceptar que tantos niños tengan hambre en el mundo.»
2. Sr. Palermo: «Quiero que la ONU y la UNESCO hagan algo con relación al problema de la violencia.»
3. Dr. Acosta: «Me parece muy triste que los oficiales gubernamentales no crean en los resultados de estos informes.»
4. Sra. Linares: «Los investigadores no piensan que la guerra sea la mejor alternativa.»
5. Dra. Jiménez: «Tenemos que hacer que las agencias pongan más recursos a disposición de los científicos.»
6. Dr. Bermúdez: «¡Voy a luchar hasta que podamos salvar las especies en vías de extinción!»

**11-53 Mini-situaciones** Completen las siguientes mini-situaciones con la forma correcta del imperfecto de subjuntivo de los verbos que se proveen. **¡OJO!** Hay un verbo adicional en cada grupo.

*dormirse    ser    poner    oír*

1. Me gustaría que mis nietos _____se durmieran_____ más temprano y que no _____oyeran_____ esa música tan ruidosa. Así podría estar más tranquila cuando voy a visitar a mi hija y podríamos compartir más. ¡Es que son tan inquietos! Sería fantástico si los niños _____fueran_____ como los niños de antes: respetuosos y obedientes.

*leer    estar    poder    querer*

2. Delia, (yo) _____quisiera_____ que (tú) _____pudieras_____ venir conmigo al concierto, pero entiendo que no tienes dinero para el boleto. Me da mucha pena que (tú) _____estuvieras_____ tan ilusionada y que ahora no vayas. Bueno, ¿qué tal si te presto los cien dólares y me pagas cuando cobres?

*dar    ir    sentir    pedir*

3. Mis amigos Pablo y Margarita querían estudiar en una universidad que les _____diera_____ la oportunidad de tomar cursos nocturnos y sabatinos; por eso no quisieron estudiar en ésta. Yo les recomendé que se trasladaran *(transfer)* cuando (ellos) _____sintieran_____ que no tienen que trabajar tanto para pagar la matrícula. También les sugerí que _____fueran_____ a la oficina de ayuda económica para ver si consiguen una beca.

**11-54 Entrevista** Túrnense para hacer y responder a las siguientes preguntas sobre la niñez. Cuando terminen, preparen un informe breve y preséntenselo al resto de la clase.

1. ¿Qué cosas querían tus padres que tú leyeras cuando eras niño(a)? ¿Y qué tipo de música querían que oyeras?
2. ¿Tus padres esperaban que tú fueras de cierta manera cuando eras niño(a)? Explica tu respuesta.
3. En cuanto a los quehaceres del hogar, ¿qué cosas se suponía que tú hicieras?
4. ¿Tus padres querían que compitieras en algún deporte? ¿En cuál(es)?
5. ¿Tus padres se alegraban de que supieras hacer ciertas cosas? ¿Cuáles?
6. ¿Alguna vez tus padres se enojaron porque tú dijeras una tontería o una grosería? Explica tu respuesta.

## ▧ Integración

**11-55 Los críticos** Escojan una película reciente y hablen de sus aspectos positivos y negativos. Pueden hablar del trabajo de los actores, de la trama, de la cinematografía y de los efectos especiales. Al final, ¿quién es más convincente?

MODELO  *Yo esperaba que la película... fuera más... y que la actuación de... tuviera más... en la trama. Sin embargo, me sorprendió que... pudiera...*

**11-56 Una carta a un(a) funcionario(a) público(a)** ¿Hay algún(a) funcionario(a) público(a) con cuyo *(whose)* trabajo no estés de acuerdo? Escríbele una carta y menciona las cosas que esperabas y que querías que él/ella hiciera durante su término como funcionario(a) público(a). Cuando termines, intercambia cartas con un(a) compañero(a) y corríjanlas siguiendo las siguientes pautas *(guidelines)*.

**Contenido:** ¿La carta es convincente? ¿Se proveen ejemplos que apoyen las ideas? ¿Hay algo más que se pueda incluir?

**Organización:** ¿La organización es efectiva? ¿La carta sigue un orden lógico? ¿Sigue la estructura tradicional de una carta (fecha, saludo, cuerpo y despedida)?

**Gramática:** ¿En la carta se usan las formas verbales de **usted** (formal)? ¿Se usan el modo indicativo y el modo subjuntivo correctamente? ¿Los verbos en el imperfecto de subjuntivo están conjugados correctamente?

**SUGERENCIAS**

Pueden usar las siguientes expresiones: **esperaba que..., quería que..., pienso que era (importante/necesario/preciso/...) que..., sería mejor si... (dijera/estuviera/fuera/pudiera/tuviera)...,** etc.

**SUGERENCIAS**

Recuerda usar los conectores que conoces:
**por otro lado** *on the other hand*
**sin embargo** *however*
**además** *in addition*
**por el contrario** *on the contrary*
**por ejemplo** *for example*
**en conclusión** *in conclusion*

TEMA 3

## III. Funciones y estructuras: Expressing condition (*si* clauses)

Escoge las frases que completen lógicamente la siguiente oración:

Si **protegiéramos** el medio ambiente,...

❏ el aire que respiramos **sería** más puro.
❏ **respetaríamos** los derechos humanos.
❏ los seres humanos no **pasarían** hambre.
❏ **habría** menos indiferencia.

❏ ciertas especies **tendrían** un lugar donde vivir.
❏ todo el mundo **se beneficiaría.**

In the previous exercise you were asked to indicate what *would* happen if we protected the environment. In the resulting sentences, the condition under which something else would happen (**protegiéramos**) is expressed in the imperfect subjunctive and is introduced by the conjunction **si** *(if)*. The actions that would occur given this condition (**el aire <u>sería</u> más puro, ciertas especies <u>tendrían</u> un lugar donde vivir,** and **todo el mundo <u>se beneficiaría</u>**) are expressed in the conditional tense. These sentences are called *contrary-to-fact sentences* because they refer to hypothetical situations.

Si **te vincularas** con una causa como la lucha contra el cáncer, **ayudarías** a mucha gente.

*If **you got involved** with a cause like the fight against cancer, **you would help** a lot of people.*

Si el gobierno **actuara** preventivamente, **evitaría** muchos problemas.

*If the government **acted** preventively, **it would avoid** many problems.*

When the condition under which something else would happen already exists or is likely to exist, use verbs in the indicative mode.

Si **tengo** tiempo, **llevo** comida a los albergues de mi ciudad.

*If **I have** time, **I bring** food to the shelters in my city.*

Si Ud. **ve** la miseria que existe en esos países, **querrá** hacer algo al respecto.

*If you **see** the extreme poverty that exists in those countries, **you will want** to do something about it.*

## ■ Asimilación

**11-57 Acciones problables e hipótesis** Indica si la persona que dice las siguientes oraciones piensa que las condiciones y los resultados de éstas son probables (**P**) o si sólo representan una hipótesis (**H**). Cuando termines, compara tus respuestas con las de un(a) compañero(a) y decide si están de acuerdo.

   _H_   1. «Si tuviera menos que hacer, me iría de vacaciones.»

   _H_   2. «Si me ganara la lotería, les compraría una casa nueva a mis padres.»

   _P_   3. «Si salgo temprano hoy, pasaré por la casa de Hilda.»

   _P_   4. «Si mejoro mi promedio general (*GPA*), hago estudios de postgrado.»

   _H_   5. «Si al profesor no le importaran sus estudiantes, les diría que no hicieran la tarea.»

   _P_   6. «Si como algún marisco, me enfermo inmediatamente.»

   _H_   7. «Si pudiera estar en otro lugar, estaría en Chile.»

   _H_   8. «Si hiciera mejor tiempo, podríamos ir a la playa.»

CD2-52

**11-58 Deducciones** Escucha lo que respondió Mariana cuando se le preguntó qué haría si tuviera más tiempo y escribe por lo menos cinco cosas que se pueden deducir sobre ella.

> MODELO    *Ella no hace ejercicio con frecuencia.*

1. ...
2. ...
3. ...

4. ...
5. ...

## ■ Aplicaciones

**11-59 Condiciones**

**Paso 1:** Completa las siguientes oraciones de forma lógica.

> MODELO    Si pudiera cambiar de especialización, *estudiaría teatro.*
>                    *Si tuviera mucha hambre,* me comería cuatro hamburguesas.

1. Si no fuera estudiante de esta universidad, _____.
2. _____, viviría en Europa.
3. Si tuviera millones de dólares en el banco, _____.
4. _____, sería el hombre / la mujer más feliz del mundo.
5. Si me dieran la oportunidad, _____.
6. _____, me daría mucho miedo.

**Paso 2:** Hazle preguntas a tu compañero(a) para averiguar cómo completó las oraciones del **Paso 1** y prepara un informe.

> MODELO    ¿Qué harías si pudieras cambiar de especialización?
>                 ¿Bajo qué circunstancias te comerías cuatro hamburguesas?

**Script 11-58:** Bueno, creo que si tuviera más tiempo, podría hacer ejercicio con más frecuencia y también podría disfrutar más de mi casa y de mis cosas. Por otro lado, iría al cine y a la peluquería más a menudo y pasaría más tiempo con mi familia. Mmm... Pienso que también completaría mis estudios universitarios y, al terminarlos, ganaría más dinero. ¡Eso sería muy bueno! Por último, me imagino que sería una persona más serena porque tendría más tiempo para *mí* [*emphatically*] y no me preocuparía tanto por las cosas triviales de la vida.

**Answers: 11-58:** *Answers may vary:* Minerva no disfruta de su casa ni de sus cosas, no va al cine ni a la peluquería a menudo, no pasa mucho tiempo con su familia, no ha completado sus estudios universitarios, no es una persona serena, no tiene mucho tiempo para ella y se preocupa mucho por las cosas triviales de la vida.

### SUGERENCIAS

Empieza la pregunta con **¿Qué harías...** si se da la cláusula con **si** (#1, #3 y #5) y con **¿Bajo qué circunstancias...** (*Under what condition . . .*) si no se da (#2, #4 y #6).

**11-60 Situaciones hipotéticas** Indiquen bajo qué circunstancias harían las siguientes cosas.

> MODELO   dejar la universidad
> *Nosotros(as) dejaríamos la universidad si nuestras familias tuvieran problemas económicos.*

1. ser presidente(a) de los Estados Unidos
2. mentirle al / a la profesor(a)
3. trabajar gratis *(for free)*
4. olvidar nuestros principios morales
5. invertir en la bolsa de valores *(stock market)*
6. arriesgar *(to risk)* la vida
7. mudarse a otro país
8. aprender más español

**11-61 Preguntas** Escriban por lo menos seis preguntas hipotéticas para seis compañeros(as) diferentes.

> MODELO   *Jessica, si te enfermeras, ¿dejarías de fumar?*

1. ...
2. ...
3. ...
4. ...
5. ...
6. ...

## ■ Integración

**11-62 El (La) próximo(a) asesor(a)** *(advisor)* **presidencial** Representa la siguiente situación con un(a) compañero(a).

**SUGERENCIAS**

Usa las siguientes expresiones para inspirarle confianza al / a la entrevistador(a):
**Por supuesto.** *Of course.*
**Sin lugar a duda.** *Without a doubt.*
**Seguramente.** *For sure.*
**De hecho,...** *In fact, . . .*

**SUGERENCIAS**

Puedes usar algunos conectores que sirven para introducir ideas conflictivas o diferentes:
**sin embargo** *however*
**por otro lado** *on the other hand*
**por el contrario** *on the contrary*
**además de esto** *besides this*

**SUGERENCIAS**

Usa los siguientes criterios para revisar el ensayo de tu compañero(a):
**Contenido:** ¿Hay algo más que se pueda decir? ¿Qué?
**Organización:** ¿La organización es efectiva? ¿El ensayo sigue un orden lógico? ¿Sigue la estructura tradicional de un ensayo (introducción, cuerpo y conclusión)?
**Gramática:** ¿Se usa el modo indicativo y el modo subjuntivo correctamente? ¿Los verbos en el imperfecto de subjuntivo y el condicional están conjugados correctamente?

| El (La) candidato(a) | El (La) entrevistador(a) |
|---|---|
| Imagínate que tienes una entrevista para nada más y nada menos que el puesto de asesor(a) del / de la presidente(a) de los Estados Unidos sobre asuntos mundiales. Responde a las preguntas del / de la entrevistador(a) y demuéstrale que estás al tanto *(you are up-to-date)* de las cuestiones sobre los derechos humanos y sobre los problemas sociales en todo el mundo. | Tienes una responsabilidad muy grande. Tienes que entrevistar a un(a) candidato(a) para el puesto de asesor(a) del / de la presidente(a) de los Estados Unidos sobre asuntos mundiales. Hazle preguntas hipotéticas a esta persona para decidir si sería un(a) buen(a) asesor(a) o no. En tu opinión, esta persona debe ser inteligente y debe estar comprometida en la lucha por los derechos humanos y civiles, al igual en la lucha contra otros problemas del mundo de hoy. |

**11-63 Perfección** Imagínate cómo sería tu vida si tuvieras la familia y el trabajo perfectos. Escribe un ensayo corto en el que describas tu vida y dale una copia a un(a) compañero(a) de clase para que lo revise. Cuando hagas las correcciones que tu compañero(a) te sugiera, entrégale el ensayo a tu profesor(a).

## IV. Lectura: ¿Estamos listos para el cambio?

### ■ Antes de leer

**A. Para conversar** Contesten las siguientes preguntas en grupo.

1. ¿Cómo han cambiado las relaciones entre los hombres y las mujeres en los últimos 50 años en este país? (Consideren temas como el poder, las oportunidades, la independencia, etc. Den algunos ejemplos concretos.)

    MODELO   *Antes las mujeres no podían..., pero ahora sí pueden...*

2. ¿Cómo creen que serán las relaciones entre los hombres y las mujeres en el futuro?

**B. Vocabulario y conceptos**. Las siguientes son palabras y conceptos clave para la comprensión del texto. Escriban la letra de la definición de cada palabra.

__f__ 1. el albergue      a. enfermedad, dolencia, problema

__a__ 2. el mal      b. que se siente en peligro

__e__ 3. la autonomía      c. falta de afecto, alejamiento

__b__ 4. amenazado      d. despreciar, excluir

__d__ 5. rechazar      e. independencia

__c__ 6. el desamor      f. un tipo de hotel económico, un refugio

**C. Aplicación** Completen las oraciones con las palabras que aprendieron en la actividad anterior. **¡OJO!** ¡Asegúrense de conjugar los verbos cuando sea necesario!

1. La gripe es un ___mal___ frecuente durante los meses de invierno.
2. No me gusta esa medicina y por eso siempre la ___rechazo___.
3. Como no tengo mucho dinero, voy a pasar mis vacaciones en un ___albergue___.
4. La Sra. Díaz es muy independiente y defiende mucho su ___autonomía___.
5. Siempre me siento un poco ___amenazado___ cuando camino de noche por el centro.
6. El opuesto del amor es el ___desamor___.

■ **A leer**

## Marcela Serrano

Es una de las escritoras más leídas en este momento en Latinoamérica. Nació en Santiago de Chile y es licenciada en grabado *(engraving)* de la Universidad Católica. En 1991 publicó su primera novela *(Nosotras que nos queremos tanto),* la cual recibió el Premio Sor Juana Inés de la Cruz, otorgado *(granted)* a la mejor novela latinoamericana escrita por una mujer en 1994. Otras de sus obras son *Para que no me olvides* (1993), *Antigua vida mía* (1995), *El albergue de las mujeres tristes* (1997), *Nuestra señora de la soledad* (1999) y *Un mundo raro* (2000).

## El albergue de las mujeres tristes (fragmento)

—¿Y cómo se te ocurrió formar el Albergue? —pregunta Floreana mientras comienzan a escalar la **colina,** a la salida del pueblo.

*hill*

—Mi padre era un hombre muy rico y construyó un hotel en esta isla por puro **capricho,** antes de que estuviera de moda, cuando no existía en este país un concepto del turismo como negocio. Lo recibí de **herencia** a su muerte. Mis hermanos decidieron que yo era la única **chiflada** de la familia que podía **sacarle algún provecho.**

*whim*

*inheritance*
*crazy / to get some benefit from it*

—El lugar es estupendo y tiene una vista privilegiada. Si lo hubieras destinado a un hotel **común y corriente** habrías ganado mucha **plata.**

*average / money*

—No es tan cierto. Tendría clientes sólo en verano. ¿A quién se le ocurriría pasar aquí el invierno? Pero la verdad es que ni el **lucro** ni la hotelería me interesaban.

*profit*

Floreana **constata** el buen estado físico de Elena a través de la fluidez con que habla, **a pesar del esfuerzo** que significa subir la colina.

*establishes*
*in spite of the effort*

—¿Cuándo te vino la idea del Albergue, entonces?

—Cuando detecté un nuevo mal: las mujeres ya no eran las mismas, pero no todos los resultados del cambio las **beneficiaban.**

*to benefit (imperfect tense)*

—**¿O sea?**

*In other words?*

—O sea que, alcanzada su autonomía, se quedaron a **medio camino** entre el amor romántico y la desprotección.

*half way*

—¿Y eso es todo?

—**No deja de ser.** Los hombres se sienten **amenazados** por nuestra independencia, y esto da lugar al rechazo, a la impotencia... y así empieza un círculo vicioso bastante dramático.

*It is plenty / threatened*

—A este rechazo masculino siguen el **desconcierto** y el miedo femeninos; ¿es ésa la idea?

*confusion*

—Es que las mujeres viven esta **lejanía** como agresión, lo que a su vez produce más distancia en ellos. ¿Te das cuenta del resultado? Las mujeres **se vuelcan** más hacia adentro, se afirman en **lo propio...**

*distance*

*turn / one's own*

—**Se quema la cara de la luna.**

*The moon's face catches on fire.*

Elena la mira interrogante.

—¡Olvídalo! Es parte de la mitología del pueblo **yagán.**

*native group from Tierra del Fuego*

—Bueno, el resultado es **lisa y llanamente** el desamor —dice Elena categórica.

*plainly and simply*

—Pero lo que no me has respondido es qué te trajo hasta aquí.

—A ver... Todo comenzó cuando partió Fernandina. Abandoné el trabajo político y fui desarrollando **a fondo** mi profesión. Al trabajar a fondo con los problemas sicológicos y culturales de mis pacientes, fui descubriendo que para poder **sanarlas,** en este mundo tan complejo, no basta la actividad siquiátrica que yo podía **ejercer** en la ciudad, era necesario darle un carácter más sistemático al proceso de recuperación de las mujeres.

*thoroughly*

*to heal them*
*to practice one's profession*

—**¡Menuda tarea!** ¿Cómo se puede lograr?

*What a task!*

—Mis objetivos son modestos. Algo se logra permitiéndoles «socializar» sus **penurias,** contarse sus dramas individuales, los que créeme, siempre terminan siendo colectivos, y generando así una atmósfera de compañerismo.

*sadnesses*

—¿A condición de estar a más de mil kilómetros de Santiago?

—Ironías aparte, sí. El silencio es vital, Floreana. **Concebí** un lugar lejos del **mundanal ruido,** donde las que necesitan recuperar la paz puedan hacerlo para luego **reinsertarse...**

*came up with*
*mundane noise*
*reintegrate*

—**A fin de cuentas**, Elena, ¿qué es el Albergue? ¿Una terapia, una **casa de reposo,** un hotel entretenido, un resort ecológico? ¿Puedes definírmelo?

*At the end / sanatorium*

—El Albergue es lo que tú quieras que sea.

■ ¿Entendiste bien?

**D. Aspectos literarios** Contesten las siguientes preguntas sobre la lectura.

1. **Personajes** Describan a cada uno de los personajes que participan en este diálogo. (¿Quiénes son? ¿Qué hacen? etc.)

| Elena | |
|---|---|
| Floreana | |

2. **Espacio** ¿Dónde está el albergue? ¿Cómo es?
3. **Temas centrales:**
   a. ¿Quiénes van al albergue? ¿Por qué?
   b. Completa el diagrama del círculo vicioso del desamor del que habla Elena.

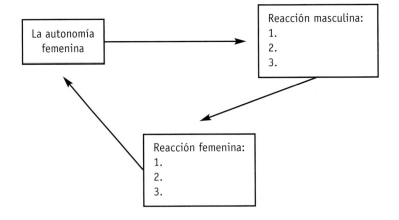

   c. ¿Cómo es el tratamiento que les ofrece Elena a las mujeres en su albergue?

**E. Enfoque lingüístico** El condicional se usa para hacer hipótesis y conjeturas (**trabajaría, vendería, escribiría,** etc.). ¿Puedes encontrar algunos ejemplos del uso de este tiempo verbal en el fragmento de la obra de Serrano?

**F. Actividad de extensión: Debate** ¿Existe en los Estados Unidos una situación de desamor similar a la que describe Elena? ¿Cómo podrían las mujeres latinoamericanas superar *(to overcome)* ese círculo vicioso?

# Vocabulario

| Las ilusiones | Dreams, illusions | Un mundo mejor | A better world |
|---|---|---|---|
| la meta | *goal* | la caridad / la beneficencia | *charity* |
| el reto / el desafío | *challenge* | los derechos humanos | *human rights* |
| el sueño | *dream* | la discriminación | *discrimination* |
| | | las especies en vías de | *endangered species* |
| alcanzar | *to reach* | extinción | |
| aspirar a | *to aspire to* | la guerra | *war* |
| enfrentar | *to face; to confront* | el hambre | *hunger* |
| hacer realidad | *to make come true* | la indiferencia | *indifference* |
| lograr | *to achieve* | la investigación | *research* |
| llegar a ser | *to become* | el medio ambiente | *the environment* |
| tener constancia | *to be constant, to persist* | la miseria | *extreme poverty* |
| tener disciplina | *to be disciplined* | el odio | *hate* |
| tener éxito | *to be successful* | el respeto | *respect* |
| tener paciencia | *to be patient* | la solidaridad | *solidarity* |
| tener suerte | *to be lucky* | la violencia | *violence* |

## Los aparatos electrónicos

| | | | |
|---|---|---|---|
| apagado | *off* | embriagado/borracho | *drunk* |
| encendido | *on* | tolerante | *tolerant* |
| No funciona. | *It doesn't work. / It's broken.* | | |
| | | consumir | *to consume* |
| apagar | *to turn off* | evitar | *to avoid* |
| conectar/enchufar | *to plug in* | invertir (ie, i) | *to invest* |
| desconectar/desenchufar | *to unplug* | pasar hambre | *to go hungry* |
| digitar | *to key in* | preservar | *to preserve* |
| halar | *to pull* | proteger | *to protect* |
| insertar | *to insert* | respetar | *to respect* |
| prender | *to turn on* | salvar | *to save* |
| presionar/oprimir/pulsar | *to push, to hit* | vincularse | *to get involved* |
| programar | *to program* | | |

# Capítulo 12

# La herencia hispana

## In this chapter you will . . .

- review how to narrate and describe in the past
- review how to give advice and directions
- review how to make predictions and hypotheses
- explore the history of Spanish-speaking peoples in the U.S. and learn about their present concerns and aspirations

## Para comenzar

Para cada foto, indica la descripción que le corresponda.

- En Nueva York hay una comunidad hispana muy activa.  Foto 2
- Por su clima y su proximidad al Caribe, Miami atrae a hispanohablantes.  Foto 1
- En Los Ángeles hay grandes comunidades de origen hispano que expresan con sus murales su historia y sus costumbres.  Foto 3

| | TEMA 1<br>Historia de la presencia hispana en los Estados Unidos | TEMA 2<br>Abriendo caminos | TEMA 3<br>Desafíos |
|---|---|---|---|
| Funciones y estructuras | Talking about the past with the preterite, the imperfect, and the present perfect (review) | Giving commands, advice, and opinions (review) | Indicating probability with the future and conditional tenses (review) |
| Lecturas y vídeo | Lectura: Los antecedentes (Partes 1 y 2) | Vídeo: Se les fue volando el mes | Lectura: Entró y se sentó |

Foto 1          Foto 2          Foto 3

# Enfoque

Transparency A-6: Country Profile: Los Estados Unidos

**A. ¿Qué sabes ya de los hispanos en los EE.UU.?** Seguro que conoces a muchos hispanos influyentes que contribuyen a la vida cultural, social e intelectual de los Estados Unidos. Haz una lista de cinco hispanos (deportistas, actores, músicos, políticos, escritores, educadores, etc.) y una breve descripción de cada uno.

Léele los nombres de las personas de tu lista a un(a) compañero(a) y averigua si sabe quién es cada persona.

**B. La presencia hispana en los EE.UU.** Mientras ves el vídeo, indica si las siguientes oraciones son ciertas (**C**) o falsas (**F**). Compara tus respuestas con las de otro(a) estudiante y corrijan las oraciones falsas.

   _C_ 1. Ya cerca de 36 millones de hispanohablantes viven en los Estados Unidos.

   _F_ 2. Hoy en día, San Antonio es la segunda ciudad salvadoreña en extensión del mundo.

   _C_ 3. En Los Ángeles, el 40% de la población es hispana, la mayoría de origen mexicano y centroamericano.

   _C_ 4. La Pequeña Habana, situada cerca del centro de Miami, es un buen ejemplo de cómo los latinos han sabido mantener sus costumbres y su estilo de vida.

**C. La herencia hispana en los EE.UU.** Desde el año 1987, la Fundación de los Premios de la Herencia Hispana (HHAF) en los Estados Unidos ha rendido homenaje a hispanos por su contribución a la comunidad hispana y a la vida cultural, social e intelectual de los Estados Unidos. En 2004, algunas de las personas premiadas fueron **Juan D. González, Narciso Rodríguez, Sandra Benítez** y **Gloria G. Rodríguez.** Escriban el nombre de la persona junto a su descripción.

   _Narciso Rodríguez_ 1. Este diseñador nacido en Nueva Jersey de padres de origen cubano ganó el premio de Visión.

   _Gloria G. Rodríguez_ 2. Esta educadora de origen mexicano recibió el premio de Educación por su trabajo a favor de los niños y de la educación.

   _Juan D. González_ 3. Este periodista puertorriqueño recibió el premio de Liderazgo por su activismo en asuntos laborales y de derechos civiles.

   _Sandra Benítez_ 4. Esta escritora, de madre puertorriqueña y de padre de Missouri, ganó el premio de Literatura. Se inspira en las experiencias que tuvo durante su niñez en México, El Salvador y Missouri.

For more info, you may want to check the **Temas** site:
http://temas.heinle.com

# Historia de la presencia hispana en los Estados Unidos

## I. Funciones y estructuras: Talking about the past with the preterite, the imperfect and the present perfect (Review)

Los hispanos **se han convertido** en el grupo minoritario de mayor representación en los Estados Unidos. A pesar de la fuerza de su presencia y de que muchos de ellos ya **hicieron** realidad su «sueño norteamericano», hay muchos otros hispanos que todavía luchan por tener una vida mejor en suelo estadounidense. Éstos trabajan día a día para alcanzar las metas que **se propusieron** cuando **vivían** en sus respectivos países.

The **preterite** tense is used to talk about:

- the beginning or the end of an action that took place in the past (**El término «hispano»** *empezó* **a usarse hace más de treinta años.**)
- actions that took place at specific moments in the past (usually accompanied by expressions such as **ayer, anoche, una vez, el lunes/mes/año pasado, la semana pasada,** etc.) (**Damaris** *vivió* **en Miami desde 1984 hasta 1990.**)
- actions that are perceived as completed (*Trabajamos* **diez horas diarias en el campo.**)
- a series of actions that were completed in the past (*Llegamos, nos dedicamos* **a luchar y** *logramos* **muchas cosas.**)

The endings for regular **-ar** verbs are **-é, -aste, -ó, -amos, -asteis,** and **-aron.** (**Mis padres** *emigraron* **de Cuba.**) For regular **-er** and **-ir** verbs, the endings are **-í, -iste, -ió, -imos, -isteis,** and **-ieron.** (**El Sr. Rivera** *salió* **de Honduras hace diez años.**)

Some of the most common irregular verbs in the preterite are **dar** (di, diste, dio, ...), **estar** (estuve, estuviste, estuvo, ...), **hacer** (hice, hiciste, hizo, ...), **ir/ser** (fui, fuiste, fue, ...) and **tener** (tuve, tuviste, tuvo, ...). (**Primero** *estuve* **en Houston y después** *me fui* **a Dallas.**)

The **imperfect** tense is used to talk about:

- habitual actions in the past (usually accompanied by the expressions **todos los lunes/días/años, siempre, frecuentemente,** etc.) (**Siempre** *pensaba* **en vivir aquí.**)
- descriptions (**Mi barrio** *tenía* **muchas calles estrechas.**)
- events that were in progress while other actions were taking place (**Mi esposa estudió en la universidad mientras yo** *trabajaba.*)

- descriptions of the participants who carry out the main events of a story (including age, physical appearance, conditions, and emotions) (*Éramos muy jóvenes* en aquel entonces.)

- background information of past events (including time and weather conditions) (**Cuando llegamos a Nueva York** *hacía* **un frío increíble.**)

The endings for regular -**ar** verbs in the imperfect are -**aba, -abas, -aba, -ábamos, -abais,** and -**aban.** (Leo *estudiaba* periodismo en su país.). For regular -**er** and -**ir** verbs, the endings are -**ía, -ías, -ía, -íamos, -íais,** and -**ían.** (Pero lo que *quería* era ser ingeniero.)

There are only three irregular verbs in the imperfect tense: **ir** (**iba, ibas, iba, ...**), **ser** (**era, eras, era, ...**), and **ver** (**veía, veías, veía, ...**). (Cuando *era* más chico, *iba* al mercado con mi abuela.)

The present perfect tense is used to talk about:

- actions that began in the past and have an effect in the present and perhaps in the immediate future (the equivalent of the English *has/have* + past participle). (**Todavía no** *han podido* **progresar.**)

The **present perfect** is formed with the present of **haber** (**he, has, ha, hemos, habéis,** and **han**) followed by the past participle of the main verb, which ends in -**ado** for -**ar** verbs and in -**ido** for -**er** and -**ir** verbs. (Yo *he progresado*, Mirta *ha tenido* éxito y Ángel *ha vivido* muy bien desde que terminó los estudios.)

Some of the most common verbs with irregular past participle forms are **decir** (**dicho**), **escribir** (**escrito**), **hacer** (**hecho**), and **poner** (**puesto**). (¿Alguna vez le *has escrito* una carta a algún funcionario público?)

> **REMEMBER**
>
> This tense is called **pretérito perfecto** in Spanish, not **presente perfecto**.

## ■ Asimilación

**12-1 Memorias** Indica si los verbos en negritas *(bold)* están conjugados en el pretérito, el imperfecto o el pretérito perfecto y explica por qué. Cuando termines, compara tus respuestas con las de un(a) compañero(a). ¿Están de acuerdo?

> MODELO  vine: *pretérito – el verbo se refiere a una acción que se completó hace quince años*

**Vine** a los Estados Unidos hace quince años, cuando **tenía** apenas cinco años. Mi mamá y yo **llegamos** a la ciudad de Nueva York, donde **vivían** mi tío Gustavo, su esposa Victoria y mis primos Nino y Adriana. Al principio no me **gustaba** para nada vivir aquí, pero poco a poco me **fui** acostumbrando y **he aceptado** que éste es mi país. Mi mamá **empezó** a trabajar muy pronto y, aunque siempre **estaba** muy cansada, **sacaba** tiempo para compartir conmigo y para asegurarse de que yo me **sentía** a gusto. Todavía es así, y se lo **he agradecido** toda la vida.

**12-2 Preguntas personales** Escucha las preguntas y contéstalas en oraciones completas. Presta atención a la forma de los verbos.

    1. ...        3. ...        5. ...

    2. ...        4. ...        6. ...

**Script 12-2:** 1. ¿Cuándo ingresaste en la universidad? 2. ¿Cómo te sentías el primer día de clases? 3. ¿Qué cursos tomaste el primer semestre? 4. En general, ¿cómo ha sido tu experiencia universitaria? 5. ¿Qué cosas hacías antes que ahora no haces por ser estudiante universitario? 6. ¿Has descubierto cosas nuevas acerca de ti desde que empezaste a estudiar aquí?

■ **Aplicaciones**

**12-3 Eventos negativos** Escribe la fecha de tres eventos negativos que has tenido en tu vida y provee los detalles que se piden. Al terminar, intercambia la información con un(a) compañero(a).

| Fecha | ¿Qué pasó? | ¿Dónde estabas? | ¿Con quién estabas? | ¿Cómo te ha afectado? |
|---|---|---|---|---|
| 6 de enero de 1995 | Me caí de una motocicleta y me rompí un brazo. | Estaba en un parque. | Estaba con mi hermano y con mi mejor amigo. | No he montado en motocicleta desde ese momento hasta ahora. |
| | | | | |

**12-4 Cuentos** (*Short stories*) Usen la información dada para inventar una historia relacionada con los dibujos que siguen. Pueden añadir detalles adicionales.

1. ser el día de la fiesta de graduación / Perla comprar un vestido / sentirse / entrar al salón / Diana tener el mismo vestido / preferir

2. Adalberto invitar a su novia / ir a un restaurante / pedir / pasarlo / llegar el mesero con la cuenta / darse cuenta / no tener / el restaurante no aceptar tarjetas de crédito / su novia estar

3. ser las tres / Doris estar tomando un examen / tener que salir bien / la profesora estar lista para irse / ella pedir más tiempo / la profesora ser muy estricta / Doris sentirse

**12-5 Esta mañana** Cuéntense qué hicieron esta mañana y cómo se sentían. Prepárense para hacerse preguntas mutuamente.

## ■ Integración

**12-6 La experiencia de un(a) inmigrante I** En parejas, entrevisten a una persona de origen extranjero (preferiblemente de origen hispano) para averiguar cómo era su vida antes de venir a este país y cómo fue el proceso de llegada *(arrival)* a los Estados Unidos y de adaptación a su nueva vida aquí. Tomen notas.

**12-7 La experiencia de un(a) inmigrante II** Usa la información que recopilaste en la actividad 12-6 para escribir las experiencias que has escuchado. Si tú fuiste el (la) entrevistado(a), escribe sobre tu propia experiencia. Cuando termines, intercambia composiciones con otro(a) estudiante y corríjanlas siguiendo los siguientes criterios.

| | |
|---|---|
| **Contenido:** | ¿Incluye toda la información que se menciona en la actividad 12-6 (la vida en su país de origen, el proceso de llegada a los Estados Unidos y el proceso de adaptación en este país)? ¿Se incluyen los detalles y ejemplos necesarios? ¿Se puede decir algo más? |
| **Organización:** | ¿La composición tiene la introducción, el cuerpo y la conclusión bien definidos? ¿Los párrafos están bien estructurados? ¿Las ideas siguen un orden lógico? |
| **Gramática:** | ¿Los verbos están bien conjugados en el pretérito y el imperfecto? ¿Se sigue la concordancia sustantivo-adjetivo y sujeto-verbo? |

**SUGERENCIAS**

Pueden usar algunas de la siguientes expresiones: **levantarse temprano/tarde, (no) desayunar, hacer buen/mal tiempo, estar cansado(a)/contento(a)/triste porque..., salir de la casa** y **llegar a la universidad.**

**EN TU COMUNIDAD**

Note that you will need the information that will be gathered in activity 12-6 in order to do activity 12-7.

**SUGERENCIAS**

Pueden hacer preguntas sobre la familia, la casa, los amigos y la vida en general en el país de origen. Además, acuérdense de *(remember to)* usar los siguientes conectores cuando sea posible: **primero, después, más tarde, luego, también** y **finalmente.**

## II. Lectura: La presencia hispana en los Estados Unidos

### ■ Antes de leer

**A. Un poco de historia** ¿Qué recuerdan de sus clases de historia? Traten de responder a las siguientes preguntas. (Más adelante van a tener la oportunidad de confirmar sus respuestas.)

1. ¿Cuándo llegaron los primeros hispanos a los Estados Unidos?
   a. en el Siglo XVI
   b. en el Siglo XIX
   c. en el Siglo XX

2. ¿Cuáles de las siguientes ciudades fueron fundadas por los españoles? Indica todas las que correspondan.
   a. Miami
   b. El Paso
   c. Santa Fe
   d. Los Ángeles
   e. Denver
   f. San Francisco

3. ¿Cómo se convirtió el estado de Texas en parte de los Estados Unidos?
   a. Fue comprado por los Estados Unidos después de la guerra con México.
   b. Fue ganado por los Estados Unidos a consecuencia de la guerra con México.
   c. Fue fundado por los Estados Unidos antes de la guerra con México.

4. ¿Qué otros territorios fueron anexados a los Estados Unidos después de 1836?
   a. California
   b. Nuevo México
   c. Colorado
   d. Arizona
   e. Utah
   f. Nevada

5. El fenómeno de la inmigración ilegal ha aumentado significativamente desde el año...
   a. 1902.
   b. 1929.
   c. 1965.
   d. 1975.

**B. Vocabulario y conceptos** Para cada palabra, indiquen la letra de la definición que corresponda. (Usen el diccionario si es necesario.)

_a_ 1. fundar
_d_ 2. despojar
_b_ 3. tratado
_c_ 4. la ciudadanía
_e_ 5. los braceros

    a. crear, establecer, iniciar
    b. convenio o acuerdo escrito entre dos gobiernos
    c. condición especial (con derechos y deberes) que tienen las personas de un país o nación
    d. quitar, robar, tomar sin permiso o sin derecho
    e. jornaleros, trabajadores agrícolas no calificados que se emplean por días

**C. Puesta en práctica** Ahora, completen las oraciones con las palabras del ejercicio anterior. **¡OJO!** ¡Tienen que conjugar los verbos y adaptar las palabras según el contexto! Al terminar, comparen sus respuestas con las de otro grupo.

1. Los españoles ___fundaron___ la misión de San Diego en 1769.
2. Los conquistadores ___despojaron___ del oro a muchos indígenas.
3. Con el ___Tratado___ Guadalupe-Hidalgo terminó la guerra entre México y los Estados Unidos.
4. En las granjas de California aún se emplean a muchos ___braceros___.
5. Los inmigrantes aspiran a obtener la ___ciudadanía___ estadounidense.

## ■ A leer

### Los antecedentes (primera parte)

#### Los primeros hispanos

La presencia hispana en Norteamérica no es un fenómeno reciente. **De hecho,** los primeros **asentamientos** europeos en lo que es hoy Estados Unidos **fueron establecidos** por los españoles. (El primero de ellos: San Agustín en la Florida, 1565.) De allí los conquistadores continuaron su labor de exploración y colonización hacia el oeste, fundando El Paso (Texas) en 1598, Santa Fe (Nuevo México) en 1609 y la misión de San Diego en 1769. Para el año de 1760, ya había más de 20.000 **colonos** españoles en Nuevo México y unos 25.000 en Texas.

«El Álamo, escenario de la guerra entre Estados Unidos y México en 1836»

#### Los mexicanos

México declaró su independencia del control español en el año de 1821. Por esta fecha, muchos **pobladores** anglosajones empezaron a mudarse a lo que es hoy en día el estado de Texas. En 1836, los nuevos colonos

*In fact*
*settlements*
*were established*

*settlers*

*inhabitants*

To facilitate the transition into the Intermediate Proficiency level, Chapter 12 provides receptive and productive tasks that encourage the recycling of familiar material and its use in more complex tasks. Point out to students that the different structure of this chapter is indeed a preview of the type of work they will be called upon to do in future language courses.

The following reading is a brief history of the main Hispanic groups in the U.S. (Mexican, Puerto Rican, and Cuban). To facilitate its presentation, the text has been divided into two parts: first the history of the Mexican-American group, and second, that of the Puerto Rican and Cuban communities. Comprehension and application tasks can be found at the end of each segment.

| | |
|---|---|
| *protected by* | |
| *to end (preterite) / signing* | |
| *was forced to yield* | |
| *to stipulate (preterite)* | |
| *time limit* | |
| *property* | |
| *non-English speakers* | |
| *in spite of the fact that* | |
| *revolt* | |
| *to flee* | |
| *due to* | |
| *decrease* | |
| *wave / made up from* | |
| *coming from / western* | |
| *includes* | |

proclamaron la independencia de su territorio y le dieron el nombre de República de Texas. En vista de que encontraron una débil reacción mexicana, y de que se encontraban **bajo el amparo** de la doctrina del *Destino Manifiesto,** los ejércitos norteamericanos invadieron México en 1846. La guerra entre los dos países **culminó** con la **firma** del Tratado Guadalupe-Hidalgo, según el cual México **se vio forzado a ceder** casi la mitad de su territorio a los Estados Unidos (incluyendo Texas, California, gran parte de Arizona y Nuevo México, partes de Colorado, Utah y Nevada). El tratado también **estipuló** que los habitantes de esos territorios tendrían **plazo** de un año para cambiar su nacionalidad. Así pues, en 1847, unos 75.000 mexicanos se convirtieron en ciudadanos de los Estados Unidos.

Aunque el Tratado Guadalupe-Hidalgo conservaba los derechos de **propiedad** de los mexicanos, no decía nada acerca de su lengua o su cultura. Entre 1850 y 1900 se aprobaron múltiples leyes de exclusión lingüística que limitaron sistemáticamente el acceso de los que **no eran angloparlantes** al voto, la justicia y la educación. Finalmente, en 1902 el Acta de Reclamación despojó a los hispanos de sus antiguas propiedades (excepto en Nuevo México). Ante condiciones tan adversas (y **a pesar de que** no existían todavía leyes de restricción migratoria), el flujo de mexicanos hacia los Estados Unidos durante la segunda mitad del siglo XIX fue muy limitado.

A principios del siglo XX en México, la dictadura de Porfirio Díaz (1877–1911) generó un gran descontento que terminó en una **revuelta** popular (La Revolución Mexicana, 1910–1917).

Muchos mexicanos decidieron entonces **huir** de la difícil situación en su país para establecerse en los Estados Unidos. (Aproximadamente un 30% de la población mexicana emigró hacia los Estados Unidos entre 1910 y 1930.)

Estos mexicanos fueron bienvenidos **debido a** la expansión económica y a las necesidades laborales de los Estados Unidos en ese momento. Aunque hubo un **descenso** migratorio durante los años de la depresión (1930–1940), la Segunda Guerra Mundial trajo consigo una segunda **oleada** de inmigración mexicana **compuesta** básicamente de trabajadores agrarios temporales o braceros (unos 350.000 mexicanos por año entre 1951 y 1964).

El constante y voluminoso flujo migratorio de mexicanos hacia los Estados Unidos durante el período de la posguerra llegó a su fin en 1965 cuando este país impuso por primera vez un límite a la inmigración de personas **provenientes** del hemisferio **occidental.** Tales restricciones se tradujeron eventualmente en el preocupante fenómeno de la inmigración ilegal que **abarca** en este momento a unos 5 millones de personas.

* Expansionist doctrine that dominated U.S. foreign policy during the nineteenth century.

## ¿Entendiste bien?

**D. ¿Correcto o no?** Revisen las respuestas que dieron a la actividad **Un poco de historia** de la sección **Antes de leer.**

**E. Cronología de la presencia mexicana en los Estados Unidos** Completen la gráfica con los eventos principales presentados en la sección «Los mexicanos».

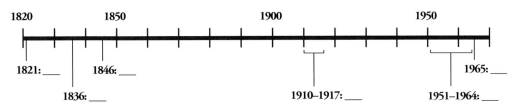

**Los mexicanos**

1820    1850    1900    1950

1821: ___    1846: ___                1965: ___

1836: ___        1910–1917: ___    1951–1964: ___

## Los antecedentes (segunda parte)

## Antes de leer

**F. Para conversar** ¿Saben Uds. de dónde son (o eran) las siguientes personalidades?

1. Desi Arnaz   Cuba
2. Benicio Del Toro   Puerto Rico
3. Gloria Estefan   Cuba
4. Andy García   Cuba
5. Geraldo Rivera   Puerto Rico

**G. Vocabulario y conceptos** Para cada palabra, indiquen la letra de la definición que corresponda. (Usen el diccionario si es necesario.)

__c__ 1. la conquista
__e__ 2. otorgar
__b__ 3. refugiado
__d__ 4. un enclave
__a__ 5. la represión

a. cuando se detiene un movimiento colectivo
b. persona que busca (o encuentra) asilo en otro país, debido a una guerra o a un problema político
c. proceso por el cual se gana o toma posesión de un territorio por medio de las armas
d. una región o territorio especial
e. dar, entregar

**H. Puesta en práctica** Ahora, completen las oraciones con las palabras de la actividad anterior. Al terminar, comparen sus respuestas con las de otro grupo.

1. Muchos pobladores indígenas de América murieron durante el período de la ___conquista___ .
2. En países donde no se respetan los derechos humanos hay mucha ___represión___ .
3. El barrio chino es un ___enclave___ de cultura asiática en la ciudad.
4. Los padres de mi amiga Liliana llegaron a este país como ___refugiados___ .
5. A este inmigrante le van a ___otorgar___ un préstamo especial para que compre su primera casa.

■ A leer

### El grupo puertorriqueño

Los puertorriqueños, como los mexicanos, se convirtieron en ciudadanos americanos **en virtud de** conquistas militares. Después de la guerra entre España y los Estados Unidos en 1898, Puerto Rico se convirtió en una posesión de los Estados Unidos en virtud del Tratado de París. Aunque en un principio no se les dio ciudadanía a todos los habitantes de la isla, el Acta Jones de 1917 no sólo les otorgó la ciudadanía estadounidense a todos los puertorriqueños, sino que también permitió el libre tránsito entre la isla y el continente. Ya para 1920, el número de puertorriqueños en ciudades como Nueva York era muy significativo.

*by virtue of*

### Los cubanos

Al igual que Puerto Rico, Cuba se convirtió en posesión de los Estados Unidos (EE.UU.) en 1898 después del Tratado de París, dando fin a trescientos ochenta y siete años de control español. A diferencia de Puerto Rico, Cuba **se mantuvo** como territorio estadounidense sólo por un corto tiempo, logrando su independencia en 1902. El gran **flujo** migratorio de cubanos hacia los EE.UU. **tuvo lugar** con la llegada de Fidel Castro al poder en 1959. Gran cantidad de profesionales y capitalistas buscaron refugio temporal en los Estados Unidos. La migración masiva fue detenida por Castro en 1973 y sólo hasta 1980 se les permitió la salida a 130.000 refugiados más hacia los EE.UU. (en la **controvertida** operación «Mariel», dada la inclusión en este grupo de un cierto porcentaje de **presidiarios** y de enfermos mentales). Hoy en día hay más de un millón de cubanos en los EE.UU., especialmente en la Florida, pero con enclaves importantes también en California, Illinois, Massachusetts, Nueva York y Nueva Jersey. Aunque muchos de los primeros refugiados pensaban volver a Cuba, la continuación del régimen socialista de Fidel Castro ha llevado a que muchos concluyan que no van a poder regresar y a que deben hacerse ciudadanos estadounidenses. Hoy en día, el grupo cubano es quizás el grupo hispano que mejor se ha integrado y que más éxito ha tenido en los Estados Unidos.

*remained*

*flow / took place*

*controversial*
*convicts*

### Otros grupos

En diferentes momentos de la historia, diferentes olas migratorias han llegado de otros países latinoamericanos como Nicaragua, Colombia, la República Dominicana, Guatemala, Honduras y El Salvador. Más de la mitad han llegado a los EE.UU. a partir de 1970 **debido a** la situación de violencia, guerra civil, pobreza o represión de su país de origen.

*due to*

■ **¿Entendiste bien?**

**I. Cronología de la presencia puertorriqueña y cubana en los Estados Unidos** Ahora, completen el cuadro con los eventos principales presentados en las secciones «El grupo puertorriqueño» y «Los cubanos».

### Los puertorriqueños y los cubanos

1890  1900  1910  1920  1930  1940  1950  1960  1970  1980  1990  2000

1902: ___          1959: ___      1980: ___

1898: ___   1917: ___          1973: ___

**J. Actividad de extensión** Entrevista a una persona de origen hispano-americano y averigua cuándo y por qué su familia se mudó a este país. Prepara un breve informe para presentar en clase.

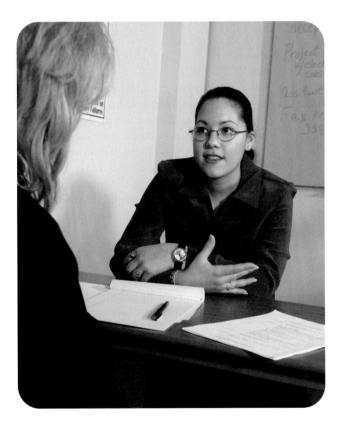

# Abriendo caminos

## I. Funciones y estructuras: Giving commands, advice and opinions (review)

OBRERO: Chico, no quiero trabajar más en construcción. Quisiera hacer otra cosa.

AMIGO: Mira, **no dejes** este trabajo hasta que tengas otro. **Esfuérzate** y **ten** paciencia. Ya verás que conseguirás lo que quieres. **Te recomiendo que leas** los anuncios clasificados con frecuencia y que les **digas** a tus amigos que quieres cambiar de trabajo para que te avisen si se enteran de algo.

Affirmative **tú** commands are formed with the third-person singular form of the present indicative: **Mi querida amiga,** *escribe* **la carta de presentación ahora mismo.**

Affirmative and negative commands in the **Ud., nosotros,** and **Uds.** forms are similar to the present subjunctive forms. The same applies to the negative commands in the **tú** form. (**Sr. Viera,** *firme* **aquí. Chicos,** *no entremos* **a la sala todavía. Carlos y Jimena,** *llamen* **a la Lic. Ortega. ¡Mario,** *no hables* **tanto!**)

The present subjunctive is formed by dropping the **-o** ending of the present indicative **yo** form of the verb and adding the endings **-e, -es, -e, -emos, -éis,** and **-en** for **-ar** verbs and the endings **-a, -as, -a, -amos, -áis,** and **-an** for **-er** and **-ir** verbs: **cantar → cante, cantes, cante, cantemos, cantéis, canten; beber → beba, bebas, beba, bebamos, bebáis, beban; vivir → viva, vivas, viva, vivamos, viváis, vivan.**

Some verbs have orthographic changes in the present subjunctive: **buscar → busque, busques, ...; llegar → llegue, llegues, ...; alcanzar → alcance, alcances, ...; producir → produzca, produzcas, ...,** etc.

Some of the most common irregular verbs in the present subjunctive are: **dar (dé, des, dé, ...), estar (esté, estés, esté, ...), ir (vaya, vayas, vaya, ...), saber (sepa, sepas, sepa, ...),** and **ser (sea, seas, sea, ...).**

The subjunctive is also used to give commands in a more indirect manner with verbs like **aconsejar, recomendar,** and **sugerir,** and with impersonal expressions like **es (mejor/peor/preferible/...) que...**

Les **recomiendo** que **piensen** en las consecuencias antes de actuar.
**Es mejor** que **hagas** un esfuerzo y **termines** los estudios.

Another use of the subjunctive is to give opinions with expressions of doubt, emotion, and wish; in adjectival clauses that describe hypothetical or nonexistent antecendents; and in adverbial clauses with **a fin de que, para que, con tal de que, antes de que, después de que, hasta que** and **cuando.**

**Siento que tengas** que sacrificarte tanto para poder ayudar a tu familia.
¿Te gustaría conocer a **alguien** que **comparta** tus mismos valores?
Voy a insistir **hasta que me escuchen.**

## ▨ Asimilación

**12-8 Los futuros estudiantes de español** ¿Cuáles de los siguientes consejos les darías a los futuros estudiantes de español? Compara tus respuestas con las de un(a) compañero(a) para saber si tienen opiniones semejantes.

____ Estudien la noche antes del examen.

____ Traten de hablar en español lo más que puedan.

____ Hagan los ejercicios del cuaderno de ejercicios con bastante anticipación.

____ No practiquen fuera del salón de clase.

____ No dejen el diccionario en la casa.

____ Escuchen con regularidad el disco compacto que acompaña el libro.

____ No tengan miedo de cometer errores en clase.

____ Estudien solamente el vocabulario, no la gramática.

____ No se preocupen por desarrollar las destrezas de escritura.

____ Si pueden, vayan a alguna comunidad donde se hable español para practicar.

2-55  **12-9 Propósitos y restricciones** Escucha las oraciones y complétalas de forma lógica desde tu punto de vista.

MODELO    ESCUCHAS: *Voy a estudiar en esta universidad hasta que...*
ESCRIBES: *tome todos los cursos y me gradúe.*

1. ...          4. ...
2. ...          5. ...
3. ...

**Script 12-9:** 1. Quiero tener mi propia casa cuando... 2. Voy a ser una persona ejemplar para que mi familia... 3. Tengo que tener cuidado con el dinero en caso de que... 4. No pienso jubilarme antes de que... 5. Me gustaría viajar por todo el mundo a fin de que...

## ▨ Aplicaciones

**12-10 Consejos** Mencionen por lo menos dos consejos que le darían a una persona que tiene los siguientes problemas. Usen mandatos formales.

1. No consigue trabajo.
2. Su hijo tiene problemas de salud
3. Extraña a sus familiares en su país.
4. Quiere encontrar a la persona de sus sueños.
5. Sufre de discriminación en su trabajo.
6. No sabe inglés.
7. Vive en un barrio donde hay mucha criminalidad.
8. Siente que su vida no tiene un propósito.

**12-11 La vida en los Estados Unidos** Imagínense que conocen a un(a) hispano(a) que llegó a los Estados Unidos hace poco tiempo y quiere informarse sobre diferentes aspectos de la vida en este país.

> MODELO   la educación
> *Los padres quieren que sus hijos asistan a la universidad y se eduquen. En este país es importante tener un título universitario para poder vivir bien.*

1. los empleos
2. el papel de la mujer en la sociedad
3. el papel del hombre en la sociedad
4. los servicios médicos
5. la familia
6. las oportunidades económicas
7. la compra de una casa
8. las responsabilidades cívicas

**12-12 ¿Qué recomiendan?** Miren los siguientes dibujos y denles consejos a estas personas. Usen expresiones impersonales y verbos en la forma de mandato.

MODELO  *No es aconsejable que maneje su auto. Llame a un amigo para que lo busque y espere. No tome más porque puede causarle problemas.*

**Vocabulario útil:** tener determinación, bajar de peso, hacer ejercicio, (no) comer...

**Vocabulario útil:** dejar de usar drogas, hablar con..., ser más responsables, buscar ayuda

**Vocabulario útil:** declarar tu amor, tener confianza en ti mismo, no esperar, ser arriesgado

## ▨ Integración

**12-13 Una carta** Lean la siguiente carta que un hispano de California envió a un periódico local y comenten qué cosas debe hacer para mejorar su situación.

*15 de noviembre de 2005*

*A todos los lectores del periódico El Latino:*

*Les escribe Miguel Talavera Pedraza para pedirles su consejo. Vivo en los Estados Unidos desde hace dos meses. Aunque tengo un buen trabajo ——soy ingeniero químico—— y me encanta vivir en esta ciudad, extraño mucho a mi familia. Desde aquí los puedo ayudar más y disfruto mucho de lo que este país tiene que ofrecer, pero me hace falta mi gente y estar en contacto directo con mi cultura. He conocido a muchas personas magníficas, pero no es lo mismo... Quisiera regresar a mi país, pero no quiero darme por vencido. ¿Qué debo hacer?*

*El confundido*

**EN TU COMUNIDAD**

Find out about the resources available in your community to address the legal, medical, and psychological needs of immigrants. Get in touch with one of these agencies, inquire about their services, and prepare an oral report.

**12-14 Una respuesta** Ahora, escríbele una carta a Miguel Talavera Pedraza, «el confundido» de la actividad 12-13, para darle tu apoyo y tus recomendaciones. Cuando termines, dale una copia a tu profesor(a) para que te dé su opinión.

## II. Vídeo: Se les fue volando el mes

### ■ Preparación

**A. Una retrospectiva** Ya que su estancia en Puerto Rico está casi por terminar, repasemos lo que les ha pasado a los compañeros. Ordenen cronológicamente los siguientes eventos en función de cuándo ocurrieron en el vídeo. Marquen el primer evento que ocurrió con el número **1** y el más reciente con el número **12.**

   8    Valeria estaba triste porque nadie se había acordado de su cumpleaños.

  12   Los compañeros expresaron sus aspiraciones y sus planes para el futuro.

   6    Todos menos Valeria hicieron esnórkeling.

   1    Cinco hispanos de distintos países viajaron a Puerto Rico para vivir juntos durante un mes.

   5    Alejandra le prestó a Sofía algunas de sus prendas de vestir.

  10   Antonio y Valeria hablaron sobre sus antiguas relaciones amorosas.

   2    Javier, Sofía, Valeria, Antonio y Alejandra se conocieron por primera vez. Se presentaron y hablaron de sus países de origen y de sus estudios universitarios.

   4    Los compañeros exploraron la ciudad de San Juan.

   7    Los compañeros aprendieron a bailar la bomba.

   9    Javier sugirió salir a cenar y los demás compañeros descubrieron que Sofía trabajaba de camarera.

   3    Mientras todos deshacían sus maletas, Alejandra le enseñaba a Sofía unas fotos de su familia.

  11   Valeria trató de preparar un plato mexicano: chiles rellenos al horno.

### ■ ¿Entendiste bien?

**B. El momento de decir adiós** Mientras ves el vídeo, indica con quién se asocian las siguientes oraciones. Usa la siguiente clave: **A** = Alejandra, **AN** = Antonio, **J** = Javier, **S** = Sofía.

  S   1. «Voy a extrañar a mis amigos y la casa y las montañas de Vista Alegre.»

  J   2. «Ellos cambiaron el destino de mi vida.»

 AN  3. «He vivido una experiencia inolvidable... Un mes en Puerto Rico con cuatro personas maravillosas.»

  S   4. «Pensaba que mi aventura en Puerto Rico apenas estaba por comenzar.»

  J   5. «Es increíble todo lo que se aprende al convivir con cuatro extraños en una misma casa.»

  A   6. «La verdad es que al principio fue como un reto, pero luego se convirtió en una diversión muy especial.»

**ESTRATEGIA DE COMPRENSIÓN**

*Scanning* Concentrate on identifying the information requested in activity B.

Ahora, mira el vídeo de nuevo y concéntrate en lo que dice Valeria, la que tiene la última palabra. Completa lo que dice.

«Al principio, cuando llegué a esta casa me sentía muy ___rara___. Todo era muy diferente para mí. Los muchachos me parecían ___aburridos___. Javier era como raro, ___solitario___. Siempre andaba despeinado. Sofi, con su libro todo el tiempo. Era como muy ___intelectual___. Alejandra, muy ___divertida___ para mi gusto, y Antonio siempre estaba ___bromeando___. Pero ahora, ahora no podré vivir sin ninguno de ellos. Nunca los podré olvidar. Javier me enseñó que todo lo que se quiere en la vida se puede conseguir. Sofi me mostró el mundo desde su punto de vista, su cultura, sus libros. ¿Alejandra? Alejandra me enseñó a sonreír. Siempre está alegre. ¿Y Antonio? Antonio le puso ilusión a mi vida.»

Compara tus respuestas con las de un(a) compañero(a).

**C. Las primeras impresiones** Valeria habló de la primera impresión que tuvo de cada compañero y de cómo, al conocerlos mejor durante el mes, llegó a apreciar mucho a cada uno de ellos. En grupos, discutan lo siguiente: *¿Podemos confiar en la primera impresión que nos dan las personas?* Usen las siguientes preguntas para iniciar su conversación y preparen una respuesta con argumentos sólidos para presentárselos a la clase.

- ¿En qué basamos nuestra primera impresión de una persona? ¿En sus características físicas, la ropa que lleva, el trabajo que tiene, lo que dice durante el primer encuentro, etc.?
- ¿Pueden dar algún ejemplo de una situación en la que su primera impresión sobre una persona fue acertada *(right)*? ¿Y equivocada *(wrong)*?

**D. Enfoque comunitario** Entrevista a algún (alguna) estudiante extranjero(a) sobre su primera impresión de vivir en otro país. Averigua si esas primeras impresiones han cambiado o no. Puedes enfocar la entrevista en un tema específico o preguntarle sobre sus impresiones generales con relación a varios temas. Algunos de estos temas pueden ser:

- la comunidad donde vive (la gente, las viviendas, los lugares de interés [parques, teatros, restaurantes, etc.], ...)
- la vida universitaria (las asignaturas, los profesores, los otros alumnos, las actividades...)

# Desafíos

## I. Funciones y estructuras: Indicating probability with the future and conditional tenses (review)

Mmm... No salí bien en este examen. ¿**Estudiaría** lo suficiente? ¿**Me confundiría** con algunas de las preguntas? **Hablaré** con la profesora y le **preguntaré.**

The future tense is used to:

■ make predictions

En veinte años todos los carros **funcionarán** con electricidad.

This is expressed in English with the verb *to wonder:* ¿**Quién *tocará* la puerta?** *I wonder who is knocking on the door.*

■ make conjectures about the present

¿Quién **será** ese hombre que está hablando con Federico?
*I wonder who that man talking with Federico is?*

The future is formed by simply adding the following endings to the infinitive: **-é, -ás, -á, -emos, -éis,** and **-án.**

The conditional tense is used to:

■ express wishes in a polite manner

Me **gustaría** que me ayudaras a conseguir otro empleo.

### REMEMBER

The verb that follows the conjunction **si** is conjugated in the imperfect subjunctive: **Si *fuéramos* más comprensivos, habría más tolerancia.**

■ hypothesize (usually in clauses with **si**)

En esa situación, yo no **me quedaría** con los brazos cruzados.

This is also expressed in English with the verb *to wonder.*

■ make conjectures about the past

¿Quién me **llamaría** mientras estaba en la biblioteca?
*I wonder who called me . . . ?*

These are some of the verbs with irregular stems in both the future and conditional tenses: **decir → dir-, hacer → har-, poder → podr-, poner → pondr-, salir → saldr-, tener → tendr-,** and **venir → vendr-.**

## ■ Asimilación

**12-15 ¿Quién(es)?** Piensa en las cosas que sabes de tus compañeros de clase. Luego, lee las siguientes oraciones y complétalas con los nombres de algunos(as) de ellos. Finalmente, compara tus respuestas con las de otro(a) estudiante. ¿Tienen opiniones semejantes o diferentes?

1. _____ será una excelente madre.
2. _____ y _____ tendrán su propio negocio.
3. _____ y _____ seguirán siendo muy buenos(as) amigos(as).
4. _____ se casará muy pronto.
5. _____ llegará a ser una persona famosa.
6. _____ y _____ se divertirán hasta el último momento de su vida.
7. _____ podrá viajar por todo el mundo.
8. _____ y _____ se postularán para puestos políticos.

**12-16 Hipótesis** Escucha las preguntas y contéstalas en oraciones completas.

1. ...
2. ...
3. ...
4. ...
5. ...

CD2-56

**Script 12-16:** 1. ¿Qué harías si tuvieras que dejar la universidad? 2. ¿Podrías hablar español bien si viajaras a un país hispano? 3. ¿En qué estado o ciudad te gustaría vivir cuando te gradúes? 4. ¿A quiénes nunca les dirías mentiras? 5. ¿Qué cosas nunca harías por dinero?

## ■ Aplicaciones

**12-17 Monolingüismo y bilingüismo**

**Paso 1:** ¿Qué pasaría si todos los estadounidenses fueran bilingües? Hagan una lista de por lo menos diez hipótesis.

MODELO    *Habría mejor comunicación entre la gente de diferentes culturas.*

**Paso 2:** ¿Y qué le pueden decir a una persona para convencerla de que el monolingüismo no es la mejor alternativa en un mundo global? Hagan una lista de por lo menos diez cosas que esta persona lograría si hablara más de un idioma.

MODELO    *Podrías comunicarte con personas de otros países.*

**VERBOS ÚTILES**

decir, comunicarse, hacer, llevarse, poder, tener, viajar

**VERBOS ÚTILES**

convivir *(to coexist)*, hacer, interactuar, salir, tener, comprender, hablar

**12-18 Planes** Túrnense para hacer y responder a las siguientes preguntas. Luego, preséntenle la información al resto de la clase. Usen el futuro y el condicional apropiadamente.

MODELO    E1: *Peter, ¿qué harás después de la clase?*
E2: *Almorzaré en la cafetería.*
E1: *Peter dijo que almorzaría en la cafetería después de la clase.*

1. ¿Qué harás al llegar a casa hoy?
2. ¿Qué harás después de cenar?
3. ¿Qué harás esta noche?
4. ¿Qué harás el próximo verano?
5. ¿Qué harás para alcanzar la felicidad en tu vida?
6. ¿Qué harás al graduarte de la universidad?
7. ¿Qué harás para combatir algún mal social?
8. ¿Qué harás para mejorar tus conocimientos de español?

**12-19 Especulaciones**

**Paso 1:** Imagínense que ayer Uds. vieron a las personas de los dibujos que siguen. Ahora están recordando lo que vieron y especulando sobre las características de esas personas y sobre lo que estaba ocurriendo. ¡Sean creativos!

**MODELO** *La señora tendría noventa años. Ella pensaría que era muy atractiva. Las demás personas estarían sorprendidas. Su perro se sentiría avergonzado.*

**Paso 2:** Ahora, imagínense que están caminando por la ciudad y ven a las siguientes personas. Como no las conocen ni saben lo que está ocurriendo, ¿qué preguntas de conjetura pueden hacer?

**MODELO** *¿Será un hippie? ¿Estará atrapado en el tiempo? ¿Pensará que es el año 1969? ¿Las demás personas creerán que está loco?*

### ■ Integración

**12-20 Tu comunidad** ¿Qué cosas positivas creen que ocurrirán en su comunidad? ¿Y qué cosas negativas ocurrirán? Conversen en parejas.

**12-21 Un tema de interés personal** Escoge un tema que te interese (la educación bilingüe, el desempleo, la lucha contra el SIDA, etc.) y averigua qué harán y qué harían los funcionarios públicos y las personas de tu comunidad con respecto a esto. Luego, escribe un informe y preséntalo en clase.

**SUGERENCIAS**

Pueden hablar de la educación, la economía, el sistema de salud, los ancianos, los niños, los hispanos, el transporte, la criminalidad y los valores morales.

**EN TU COMUNIDAD**

Note that you will need the information that will be gathered in activity 12-20 in order to complete activity 12-21.

## II. Lectura: «Entró y se sentó»

### Antes de leer

**A. Para conversar** Contesten las siguientes preguntas.

1. ¿Qué puede hacer un universitario para ayudar a su comunidad? (Si es posible, den ejemplos de cómo los diferentes miembros del grupo colaboran con causas de beneficencia.)
2. ¿Cómo piensan servir a sus comunidades después de graduarse?

**B. Vocabulario y conceptos** Para cada palabra, indiquen la letra de la definición que corresponda. (Usen el diccionario si es necesario.)

| | | |
|---|---|---|
| _c_ 1. ingrato | a. | conjunto de personas que tienen el mismo origen étnico |
| _a_ 2. la raza | | |
| _e_ 3. huelga | b. | dedicarse a algo |
| _b_ 4. comprometerse | c. | persona que nunca dice «gracias» |
| _d_ 5. el sistema | d. | la manera como son las cosas, las instituciones, la sociedad |
| | e. | lo que hacen los trabajadores cuando paran de trabajar como protesta |

**C. Aplicaciones** Ahora, completa las oraciones con las palabras del ejercicio anterior. Al terminar, compara tus respuestas con las de otro(a) compañero(a).

1. Si el ___sistema___ es injusto, hay que cambiarlo.

2. A nosotros nos preocupan mucho los problemas que enfrenta nuestra ___raza___ en este momento.

3. Los empleados están en ___huelga___ porque quieren mejores salarios.

4. Si quieres tener éxito en tu proyecto, tienes que ___comprometerte___ a trabajar con paciencia y dedicación.

5. Tienes que venir a visitarnos, no seas ___ingrato___.

In the following reading you will find many examples of Spanish slang (words and expressions used by people in informal situations). Although slang is widely used, keep in mind that it is considered to be outside standard polite use.

■ **A leer**

### Rosaura Sánchez

Nació en San Ángelo, Texas, una población pequeña a 160 millas de la frontera con México. Cursó estudios de literatura en la Universidad de Texas en Austin y hoy en día es profesora en la Universidad de California, San Diego. Rosaura Sánchez escribe en español no sólo porque es su lengua nativa, sino también porque quiere dar voz a la vida y las contradicciones de los chicanos. Ha escrito y editado libros de cuentos en español como *Requisa treinta y dos* y ha publicado varios de sus estudios socio-lingüísticos, entre ellos *Telling Identities: The California Testimonios* y *Chicano Discourse: Socio-Historic Perspectives*.

### Entró y se sentó

Entró y se sentó frente al enorme escritorio que le esperaba lleno de papeles y cartas.

*behaved* — Estaba furioso. Los estudiantes **se habían portado** como unos ingratos.

*Wretched bunch (insult) / right in my face / Wretched bunch (insult)* —**Bola de infelices,** venir a gritarme a mí **en mis narices** que soy un «Poverty Pimp». **Bola de desgraciados.** Como si no lo hiciera todo por ellos, por la raza, pues.

Llamó a Mary Lou, la secretaria, y le pidió que le trajera un café y un pan dulce de **canela.**

*cinnamon*

*nerve* —Y luego tienen el **descaro** de insultarme porque no me casé con una mexicana. Son bien cerrados, unos racistas de primera. Lo que pasa es que no se dan cuenta que yo acepté este puesto para ayudarlos, para animarlos a que continuaran su educación.

En ese momento sonó el teléfono. Era el Sr. White, el director universitario del departamento de educación. No, no habría más problemas. Él mismo hablaría con el principal Jones para resolver el *misunderstanding* problema. Era cosa de un **malentendido** que pronto se resolvería.

Mary Lou llegó con el café cuando terminó de hablar. Después de un **sorbo** de café, se puso a hacer el informe de gastos para el mes. Gasolina. *sip* Gastos de comida con visitantes importantes. Vuelo a Los Ángeles para la reunión de educadores en pro de la educación bilingüe. Motel.

—Para ellos yo sólo estoy aquí porque el sueldo es bueno. Si bien es verdad que pagan bien y que las oportunidades son muchas, también es verdad que los dolores de cabeza son diarios. Yo podría haberme dedicado a mi trabajo universitario y no haberme acordado de mi gente.

Se le permitía 22 dólares de gastos diarios y como había estado cinco días podía pedir 110 dólares. A eso **se agregaban** los gastos de taxi. Ahora querían que los **apoyara** en su huelga estudiantil. Pero eso ya era demasiado. Lo estaban comprometiendo.

*they added*
*support*

—Si supieran esos muchachos lo que he tenido que **sudar** yo para llegar aquí. Con esa **gritería** de que hay que cambiar el sistema no llegamos a ninguna parte. No se dan cuenta que lo que hay que hacer es estudiar para que el día de mañana puedan ser útiles a la sociedad.

*to sweat*
*loud protest*

De repente **se apagaron** las luces. Afuera comenzaba a **tronar** y la lluvia caía en torrentes. **Volteó** en su silla **rodante** y se acercó a la ventana. Primero vio los edificios grises universitarios que **se asemejaban** a los **recintos** de una prisión. Se oscureció más y más hasta que vio la **troca** perdida en la lluvia.

*went out / to thunder*
*He turned / with wheels*
*resembled*
*compounds / truck (slang)*

—Con este **aguacero** tendremos que parar un rato, hijo. Llegando a la **orilla** del **surco,** nos metemos debajo de la troca hasta que **escampe** un poco. **Pesó** el algodón pero no vació el **costal** arriba porque con la lluvia le estaba dando frío.

*downpour*
*edge / furrow / stops raining*
*He weighed / sack*

—Mira, hijo, si te vas a la escuela no sé cómo le vamos a hacer. Con lo que ganas de busboy y lo que hacemos los sábados **pizcando,** nos ayudamos bastante. Ya sabes que en mi trabajo no me pagan **gran cosa.**

*hand picking*
*a lot*

Sabía lo que era trabajar duro, de sol a sol, **sudando la gorda.** Entonces que **no me vengan a mí con cuentos,** señores. ¿Qué se han creído esos **babosos**? Después de tanto trabajo, tener que **lidiar** con estos **huevones.** Porque lo que pasa es que no quieren ponerse a trabajar, a estudiar como los **meros** hombres.

*working very hard*
*don't come to me with stories*
*stupid (insult) / to deal with*
*idiots (insult)*
*real (slang)*

—Mire, **apá,** le mandaré parte de mi préstamo federal cada mes. Verá que no me he de **desobligar** y ya estando en Austin, buscaré allá otro trabajito para poder ayudarles.

*papá (slang)*
*to forget about an obligation*

Éramos pocos los que estudiábamos entonces. Estos que tienen la **chiche** del gobierno no saben lo que es canela. Sólo sirven para quejarse de que no les dan más.

*breast, source of nourishment (slang)*

—Yo ya estoy muy viejo, hijo. Cuida a tu mami y a tus hermanos.

Seguía lloviendo y la electricidad no volvía. Afuera **relampagueó.**

*there was lightning*

El carro se les había parado en la esquina. El semáforo ya se había puesto verde pero el carro no **arrancaba.** Su papá salió, levantó el **capacete** y quitó el filtro. Mientras su papá ponía y quitaba la mano del carburador,

*started / hood*

él **pisaba** el acelerador. Atrás los autos **pitaban** y pitaban. Por la izquierda y la derecha **se deslizaban** los Cadillacs y los Oldsmobiles de los rancheros **airados** con el **estorbo** en **plena** calle Chadbourne. Su papá estaba **empapado** por la lluvia cuando por fin arrancó el carro. Ese día los **había maldecido** a todos, a todos los gringos de la tierra que los hacían **arrastrar** los costales de algodón por los surcos mientras los zapatos se les **hundían** en la tierra **arada**, a los gringos que les pagaban tan poco que sólo podían comprar aquellas **garraletas** que nunca arrancaban. Años después se había casado con una gringa. Y ahora después de tanto **afán**, querían que **se rifara el pellejo. Qu'esque** por la causa. Como si fuera tan fácil cambiar el sistema. No señores, que no contaran con él.

Volvió la electricidad y se puso a ver la correspondencia.

—Gracias a Dios que tengo mi oficina aquí en la Universidad, en el sexto piso de esta monstruosidad donde no tengo que ver a nadie. No más le digo a la secretaria que diga que no estoy, así puedo dedicarme al **papeleo** que siempre hay que atender.

Estos estudiantes del Cuerpo de Maestros van a tener que **sujetarse** a las reglas o si no, **pa'** fuera. Tiene uno que **ponerse duro,** porque si no, **se lo lleva la chingada.**

Alguna vez le contaré mi vida a esta gente... A ver... Bueno mañana no será. Tengo que ir a Washington a la reunión nacional de programas federales de educación para las minorías y luego... a ver... tengo que ir a San Antonio como consultante del programa bilingüe. Vale más llamar a Mary Lou para ver si me consiguió ya el pasaje de avión para mañana. Mary Lou... ah, si mmmhhhmmm, en el Hilton, del 8 al 10 de noviembre. Muy bien. Y ¿qué sabes del vuelo?... ¿Por Continental o American?...

Miró por la ventana y vio a su papá empapado en agua y lleno de grasa.

---

**Glossary (margin):**

to step on (imperfect tense) / to honk (imperfect tense) / to slide (imperfect tense) / upset / inconvenience / in the middle of / soaked / had cursed
to pull
to sink (imperfect tense) / plowed
useless vehicles

effort / to auction off his hide / Supposedly (slang)

paperwork

adhere to
para (slang) / to be tough
you are doomed

## ■ ¿Entendiste bien?

**D. La vida del profesor** Organicen los siguientes eventos del cuento de manera cronológica. Piensen en el orden real de los sucesos (no el orden en que se presentan en el cuento).

- \_\_2\_\_ El carro de su padre tuvo problemas mecánicos en la carretera.
- \_\_1\_\_ Su padre le pidió que no se fuera a estudiar a la universidad.
- \_\_3\_\_ Se graduó de la facultad de educación.
- \_\_5\_\_ Tuvo una discusión con los estudiantes latinos.
- \_\_6\_\_ Preparó un informe de gastos para su jefe.
- \_\_4\_\_ Fue a una convención de educación bilingüe.

**E. Estudio de personajes** Describan a los siguientes personajes de la historia. (Si es posible, indiquen cómo es su carácter, qué hacen y por qué son importantes en el cuento.)

| Personaje | Descripción |
|---|---|
| el profesor | |
| los estudiantes | |
| el padre del profesor | |
| la secretaria | |

**F. Preguntas y respuestas** Lean de nuevo la historia y contesten las siguientes preguntas.

1. ¿Qué esperaban los estudiantes del profesor? ¿Por qué lo insultan?
2. ¿Qué recuerdos le trae la lluvia al profesor? ¿Cómo fue su infancia?
3. ¿Cómo piensa el profesor que está ayudando a su comunidad?
4. ¿Por qué es tan importante para el profesor la imagen de su padre bajo la lluvia?
5. ¿Por qué crees que se llama este cuento «Entró y se sentó»?

**G. Enfoque comunitario** Averigua qué recursos hay en tu comunidad para ayudar y orientar a los inmigrantes. Si es posible, entrevista a una de las personas que trabaja allí para averiguar lo siguiente.

- ¿Por qué lo hace?
- ¿Qué es lo que más le gusta de su trabajo?
- ¿Cuáles son los problemas más graves que enfrenta?
- ¿Que anécdotas o experiencias significativas ha tenido en su trabajo?

**ESTRATEGIA DE LECTURA**

***Skimming*** Skim the text to establish the actual sequence of events.

The story has a number of flashbacks that may confuse some students. It is important to help them establish the basic facts of the story and how they actually would have been sequenced in real life. (You may even want to discuss why the facts of the story were organized the way they were.)

**Answers F:** *Answers will vary.* 1. Esperaban que los ayudara en su huelga. Lo insultaban por su falta de compromiso con la comunidad hispana en su universidad. 2. Le recuerda la humillación de su padre el día que se le descompuso el coche viejo que tenía, en plena calle Chadbourne. Su infancia fue pobre. 3. Él quiere ayudar a su comunidad animando a los estudiantes a continuar sus estudios desde su puesto como profesor universitario. 4. *There could be several interpretations.* Es un recuerdo de su deseo de salir de la pobreza. De no volver a la humillación que tuvo que pasar su padre por no tener dinero para comprar un mejor auto. 5. *Again, there could be several possible answers. The important thing is the quality of the explanation.* Indica que el profesor se ha asimilado a la cultura anglosajona (Entró), pero que su ingreso al «sistema» no lo ha llevado a hacer nada por su comunidad (Se sentó).

# Puesta en acción

| | |
|---|---|
| **SITUACIÓN:** | El Departamento de Relaciones Públicas de tu municipalidad, agencia gubernamental en la que trabajas, quiere saber qué opinan los ciudadanos sobre la calidad de vida y desea crear programas que ayuden a mejorarla. |
| **MISIÓN:** | Averiguar qué opinan los ciudadanos de tu municipalidad sobre diferentes temas de interés social, diseñar un programa que ayude a mejorar su calidad de vida y preparar una campaña publicitaria para diseminar la información relacionada con este programa. |
| **DESTREZAS:** | Recopilar datos mediante cuestionarios y entrevistas, diseñar un programa social que fomente el mejoramiento de la calidad de vida de los habitantes de tu municipalidad e informarles sobre este programa. |

**A. Un mensaje electrónico** Lee el mensaje que te envió la directora del Departamento de Relaciones Públicas y contesta las preguntas que siguen.

| Enviar | Direcciones | Archivos adjuntos | Ver. ortografía | Guardar | Cancelar |
|---|---|---|---|---|---|

| **Para:** | John Smith |
|---|---|
| **De:** | Leonor Alarcón Rivas, directora |
| **Fecha:** | 20 de enero del 2007 |

**Asunto:** La calidad de vida en nuestra municipalidad          **Prioridad:** Normal ▼

Normal ▼          12 ▼

Con el propósito de mejorar la calidad de vida de nuestros ciudadanos, el Departamento de Relaciones Públicas de esta municipalidad quisiera recopilar datos sobre lo que opinan los habitantes con relación a diferentes aspectos, como sus expectativas y aspiraciones, las comodidades del hogar y los problemas sociales. Por esta razón, quisiéramos que Ud. y sus asistentes se dieran a la tarea de preparar un cuestionario para distribuir entre todos los ciudadanos, y que entrevistaran a una muestra *(sample)* de la población. Además, nos gustaría que usaran la información que obtuvieran para diseñar un programa de mejoramiento comunitario. Sería ideal que éste incluyera seminarios y actividades culturales que integraran a todos los miembros de la comunidad. Esperamos que presente un informe sobre su investigación a finales del próximo mes y desearíamos que nos describiera el programa que piensa implementar a finales de marzo. Pueden contar con todos los recursos de nuestra oficina.

1. ¿Qué aspectos de la vida de los ciudadanos quiere la directora que investigues?
2. ¿Qué tipo de actividades debe incluir el programa de mejoramiento comunitario?
3. ¿Cuánto tiempo tienes disponible para recopilar los datos y diseñar el programa?

**B. Aprendiendo sobre el tema** Has decidido aprender un poco más sobre las cosas que le preocupan al ciudadano común antes de comenzar con tu proyecto, y encontraste información sobre dos estudios similares que se realizaron en comunidades vecinas *(neighboring)*. Primero, lean individualmente sus respectivos artículos. Luego, túrnense para hacer y responder a preguntas sobre estos estudios, y completen la planilla. Cuando terminen comenten en qué se diferencian estas dos comunidades y las personas que viven en ellas según los resultados de estos estudios.

**Estudiante 1**

Metas más importantes para los ciudadanos:

| | |
|---|---|
| 1. tener suerte para obtener un trabajo | 46% |
| 2. hacer realidad el sueño de tener una casa propia | 32% |
| 3. enfrentar sus problemas personales | 20% |

Importancia de tener los siguientes aparatos electrónicos en su casa:

| | |
|---|---|
| 1. lavadora y secadora | 37% |
| 2. televisor | 25% |
| 3. refrigerador | 21% |

Problemas sociales que más les preocupan:

| | |
|---|---|
| 1. la violencia | 58% |
| 2. la discriminación | 39% |
| 3. la miseria | 27% |

| Metas | % | Aparatos electrónicos más importantes | % | Problemas sociales que más les preocupan | % |
|---|---|---|---|---|---|
| alcanzar bienestar económico | | | 43 | | |
| | | | 34 | la guerra | |
| | 20 | | | las especies en vías de extinción | |

**Estudiante 2** must turn the book upside down.

| Metas | % | Aparatos electrónicos más importantes | % | Problemas sociales que más les preocupan | % |
|---|---|---|---|---|---|
| | 46 | | | la violencia | |
| | | televisor | | | 39 |
| enfrentar sus problemas personales | | | | | |

**Estudiante 2**

Metas más importantes para los ciudadanos:

1. alcanzar bienestar económico — 46%
2. tener éxito en el trabajo — 32%
3. enfrentar sus problemas personales — 20%

Importancia de tener los siguientes aparatos electrónicos en su casa:

1. computadora — 43%
2. puerta automática — 34%
3. cafetera automática — 30%

Problemas sociales que más les preocupan:

1. el hambre — 41%
2. la guerra — 35%
3. las especies en vías de extinción — 19%

### C. El cuestionario

**Paso 1:** En parejas, preparen una lista de los posibles temas que pueden incluir en el cuestionario.

**CRITICAL THINKING SKILLS**

*Prioritizing* Choose the topics that would allow you to find out more vital information about the citizens of your town or city.

| Expectativas y aspiraciones | Comodidades del hogar | Problemas sociales |
|---|---|---|
| | | |
| | | |

**Paso 2:** Compartan con otro grupo las ideas que generaron en la actividad anterior.
    a. comenten la importancia de cada tema y
    b. escojan un mínimo de cinco temas para cada categoría

**D. El diseño del cuestionario** Diseñen el cuestionario que se va a distribuir entre todas las personas de la comunidad. Incluyan un ítem para cada uno de los temas que seleccionaron en la actividad anterior. Presten atención a la forma verbal que utilizarán en las preguntas.

**E. Preguntas**

**Paso 1:** Escriban por lo menos seis preguntas que quisieran hacerles a las personas de su comunidad para saber un poco sobre las cosas que han hecho durante el pasado año. Usen el pretérito, el imperfecto y el pretérito perfecto correctamente.

MODELO *¿Ha alcanzado Ud. todos sus sueños? ¿Compró una computadora o un teléfono celular durante el pasado año? ¿Sentía que el problema de la guerra era justificable?*

**Paso 2:** Ahora, escriban por lo menos seis preguntas hipotéticas con **si.**

MODELO *Si usted tuviera el tiempo, ¿sería más activo(a) en la comunidad? ¿Usted se sentiría más feliz si viviera en un lugar con menos problemas de intolerancia?*

**F. Una entrevista** Representa la siguiente situación con un(a) compañero(a).

| **El (La) entrevistador(a)** | **El (La) entrevistado(a)** |
|---|---|
| Trabajas en el Departamento de Relaciones Públicas de tu comunidad. Como parte del proyecto de mejoramiento de la calidad de vida de los ciudadanos, vas a entrevistar a una de las personas que viven aquí. <br>■ Saluda a esta persona. <br>■ Explícale el propósito de este proyecto. <br>■ Hazle las preguntas que preparaste con un(a) compañero(a) en la actividad **E.** (Reacciona a las respuestas que te da esta persona con más preguntas pertinentes para obtener toda la información que puedas.) | Una de las personas que trabaja en el Departamento de Relaciones Públicas de tu comunidad quiere entrevistarte para obtener más información sobre la calidad de vida de los ciudadanos. <br>■ Saluda al / a la entrevistador(a). <br>■ Averigua cuál es el propósito de este proyecto. <br>■ Responde a sus preguntas. Provee todos los detalles que puedas. |

**G. La propuesta** Preparen una lista de las actividades culturales y seminarios que coordinarán para mejorar la calidad de vida de las personas de su comunidad. Además, preparen una lista de otras cosas que harían si tuvieran los recursos necesarios. Asegúrense de incluir eventos para personas de diferentes edades y culturas y con diferentes preferencias. Usen el futuro y el condicional correctamente.

**SUGERENCIAS**

Pueden consultar un motor de búsqueda para encontrar ideas sobre cómo estructurar un buen cuestionario.

At this point you may present samples of questionnaires that you have administered or filled out yourself.

**CRITICAL THINKING SKILLS**

***Evaluating*** Consider activities (seminars, meetings, orientation sessions, cultural events, etc.) that would help address some of the issues you included in the questionnaire and issues that personally interest you or affect you.

If the institution has the appropriate facilities and resources, you may want to ask students to actually create and publish the web site.

**H. Campaña publicitaria** Diseñen una página de Internet para informar a todas las personas de la municipalidad sobre los eventos que planificaron. Incluyan lo siguiente:

- un nombre original para el proyecto de mejoramiento de la calidad de vida,
- una descripción de todos los eventos y una explicación de cómo éstos ayudarán a la comunidad en general,
- la fecha, el lugar y la hora de cada evento y
- elementos visuales interesantes (gráficas, fotos, etc.)

Sigan los siguientes pasos.

a. Decidan cómo será el diseño de la página y cómo la van a hacer fácil de usar e informativa.
b. Organicen y distribuyan la información en diferentes ventanas. Pueden usar un papel diferente para representar cada ventana e incluir los enlaces *(links)*.
c. Decidan dónde van a ir los títulos, los datos, las descripciones, las gráficas, etc.

## Servicio comunitario

Contact someone at the public relations office of your local government and offer to do what is included in activities G and H. You may even take this a step further and actually coordinate the activities that your group suggested.

# Apéndices

# APÉNDICE A: Los verbos regulares

| Infinitive | Present Indicative | Imperfect | Preterite | Future | Conditional | Present Subjunctive | Past Subjunctive | Commands |
|---|---|---|---|---|---|---|---|---|
| hablar | hablo | hablaba | hablé | hablaré | hablaría | hable | hablara | habla (no hables) |
| to speak | hablas | hablabas | hablaste | hablarás | hablarías | hables | hablaras | hable |
| | habla | hablaba | habló | hablará | hablaría | hable | hablara | hablad (no habléis) |
| | hablamos | hablábamos | hablamos | hablaremos | hablaríamos | hablemos | habláramos | hablen |
| | habláis | hablabais | hablasteis | hablaréis | hablaríais | habléis | hablarais | |
| | hablan | hablaban | hablaron | hablarán | hablarían | hablen | hablaran | |
| aprender | aprendo | aprendía | aprendí | aprenderé | aprendería | aprenda | aprendiera | aprende (no aprendas) |
| to learn | aprendes | aprendías | aprendiste | aprenderás | aprenderías | aprendas | aprendieras | aprenda |
| | aprende | aprendía | aprendió | aprenderá | aprendería | aprenda | aprendiera | aprended (no aprendáis) |
| | aprendemos | aprendíamos | aprendimos | aprenderemos | aprenderíamos | aprendamos | aprendiéramos | aprendan |
| | aprendéis | aprendíais | aprendisteis | aprenderéis | aprenderíais | aprendáis | aprendierais | |
| | aprenden | aprendían | aprendieron | aprenderán | aprenderían | aprendan | aprendieran | |
| vivir | vivo | vivía | viví | viviré | viviría | viva | viviera | vive (no vivas) |
| to live | vives | vivías | viviste | vivirás | vivirías | vivas | vivieras | viva |
| | vive | vivía | vivió | vivirá | viviría | viva | viviera | vivid (no viváis) |
| | vivimos | vivíamos | vivimos | viviremos | viviríamos | vivamos | viviéramos | vivan |
| | vivís | vivíais | vivisteis | viviréis | viviríais | viváis | vivierais | |
| | viven | vivían | vivieron | vivirán | vivirían | vivan | vivieran | |

## Compound tenses

| | | | | |
|---|---|---|---|---|
| Present progressive | estoy estás está | estamos estáis están | hablando | aprendiendo | viviendo |
| Present perfect indicative | he has ha | hemos habéis han | hablado | aprendido | vivido |
| Present perfect subjunctive | haya hayas haya | hayamos hayáis hayan | hablado | aprendido | vivido |
| Past perfect indicative | había habías había | habíamos habíais habían | hablado | aprendido | vivido |

# APÉNDICE B· Los verbos con cambios en la raíz

| Infinitive / Present Participle / Past Participle | Present Indicative | Imperfect | Preterite | Future | Conditional | Present Subjunctive | Past Subjunctive | Commands |
|---|---|---|---|---|---|---|---|---|
| pensar *to think* **e → ie** pensando pensado | **pienso** **piensas** **piensa** pensamos pensáis **piensan** | pensaba pensabas pensaba pensábamos pensabais pensaban | pensé pensaste pensó pensamos pensasteis pensaron | pensaré pensarás pensará pensaremos pensaréis pensarán | pensaría pensarías pensaría pensaríamos pensaríais pensarían | **piense** **pienses** **piense** pensemos penséis **piensen** | pensara pensaras pensara pensáramos pensarais pensaran | **piensa** (**no pienses**) **piense** pensad (**no penséis**) **piensen** |
| acostarse *to go to bed* **o → ue** acostándose acostado | me **acuesto** te **acuestas** se **acuesta** nos acostamos os acostáis se **acuestan** | me acostaba te acostabas se acostaba nos acostábamos os acostabais se acostaban | me acosté te acostaste se acostó nos acostamos os acostasteis se acostaron | me acostaré te acostarás se acostará nos acostaremos os acostaréis se acostarán | me acostaría te acostarías se acostaría nos acostaríamos os acostaríais se acostarían | me **acueste** te **acuestes** se **acueste** nos acostemos os acostéis se **acuesten** | me acostara te acostaras se acostara nos acostáramos os acostarais se acostaran | acuéstate (**no te acuestes**) acuéstese acostaos (**no os acostéis**) acuéstense |
| sentir *to feel* **e → ie, i** **sintiendo** sentido | **siento** **sientes** **siente** sentimos sentís **sienten** | sentía sentías sentía sentíamos sentíais sentían | sentí sentiste **sintió** sentimos sentisteis **sintieron** | sentiré sentirás sentirá sentiremos sentiréis sentirán | sentiría sentirías sentiría sentiríamos sentiríais sentirían | **sienta** **sientas** **sienta** **sintamos** **sintáis** **sientan** | **sintiera** **sintieras** **sintiera** **sintiéramos** **sintierais** **sintieran** | **siente** (**no sientas**) **sienta** **sentaos** (**no sintáis**) **sientan** |
| pedir *to ask for* **e → i, i** **pidiendo** pedido | **pido** **pides** **pide** pedimos pedís **piden** | pedía pedías pedía pedíamos pedíais pedían | pedí pediste **pidió** pedimos pedisteis **pidieron** | pediré pedirás pedirá pediremos pediréis pedirán | pediría pedirías pediría pediríamos pediríais pedirían | **pida** **pidas** **pida** **pidamos** **pidáis** **pidan** | **pidiera** **pidieras** **pidiera** **pidiéramos** **pidierais** **pidieran** | **pide** (**no pidas**) **pida** **pedid** (**no pidáis**) **pidan** |
| dormir *to sleep* **o → ue, u** **durmiendo** dormido | **duermo** **duermes** **duerme** dormimos dormís **duermen** | dormía dormíais dormía dormíamos dormíais dormían | dormí dormiste **durmió** dormimos dormisteis **durmieron** | dormiré dormirás dormirá dormiremos dormiréis dormirán | dormiría dormirías dormiría dormiríamos dormiríais dormirían | **duerma** **duermas** **duerma** **durmamos** **durmáis** **duerman** | **durmiera** **durmieras** **durmiera** **durmiéramos** **durmierais** **durmieran** | **duerme** (**no duermas**) **duerma** **dormid** (**no durmáis**) **duerman** |

# APÉNDICE C: Los verbos con cambios de ortografía

| Infinitive / Present Participle / Past Participle | Present Indicative | Imperfect | Preterite | Future | Conditional | Present Subjunctive | Past Subjunctive | Commands |
|---|---|---|---|---|---|---|---|---|
| comenzar (e → ie) *to begin* z → c before e comenzando comenzado | comienzo comienzas comienza comenzamos comenzáis comienzan | comenzaba comenzabas comenzaba comenzábamos comenzabais comenzaban | **comencé** comenzaste comenzó comenzamos comenzasteis comenzaron | comenzaré comenzarás comenzará comenzaremos comenzaréis comenzarán | comenzaría comenzarías comenzaría comenzaríamos comenzaríais comenzarían | **comience comiences comience comencemos comencéis comiencen** | comenzara comenzaras comenzara comenzáramos comenzarais comenzaran | comienza (**no comiences**) **comience** comenzad (**no comencéis**) **comiencen** |
| conocer *to know* c → zc before a, o conociendo conocido | **conozco** conoces conoce conocemos conocéis conocen | conocía conocías conocía conocíamos conocíais conocían | conocí conociste conoció conocimos conocisteis conocieron | conoceré conocerás conocerá conoceremos conoceréis conocerán | conocería conocerías conocería conoceríamos conoceríais conocerían | **conozca conozcas conozca conozcamos conozcáis conozcan** | conociera conocieras conociera conociéramos conocierais conocieran | conoce (**no conozcas**) **conozca** conoced (**no conozcáis**) **conozcan** |
| construir *to build* i → y; y inserted before a, e, o construyendo construido | **construyo construyes construye** construimos construís **construyen** | construía construías construía construíamos construíais construían | construí construiste **construyó** construimos construisteis **construyeron** | construiré construirás construirá construiremos construiréis construirán | construiría construirías construiría construiríamos construiríais construirían | **construya construyas construya construyamos construyáis construyan** | **construyera construyeras construyera construyéramos construyerais construyeran** | **construye (no construyas) construya** construid (**no construyáis**) **construyan** |
| leer *to read* i → y; stressed i → í **leyendo** leído | leo lees lee leemos leéis leen | leía leías leía leíamos leíais leían | leí leíste **leyó** leímos leísteis **leyeron** | leeré leerás leerá leeremos leeréis **leyeron** | leería leerías leería leeríamos leeríais leerían | lea leas lea leamos leáis lean | **leyera leyeras leyera leyéramos leyerais leyeran** | lee (no leas) lea leed (no leáis) lean |

# APÉNDICE C: Los verbos con cambios de ortografía *(continued)*

| Infinitive Present Participle Past Participle | Present Indicative | Imperfect | Preterite | Future | Conditional | Present Subjunctive | Past Subjunctive | Commands |
|---|---|---|---|---|---|---|---|---|
| pagar | pago | pagaba | **pagué** | pagaré | pagaría | **pague** | pagara | paga **(no pagues)** |
| *to pay* | pagas | pagabas | pagaste | pagarás | pagarías | **pagues** | pagaras | **pague** |
| **g → gu** | paga | pagaba | pagó | pagará | pagaría | **pague** | pagara | pagad **(no** |
| **before e** | pagamos | pagábamos | pagamos | pagaremos | pagaríamos | **paguemos** | pagáramos | **paguéis)** |
| pagando | pagáis | pagabais | pagasteis | pagaréis | pagaríais | **paguéis** | pagarais | **paguen** |
| pagado | pagan | pagaban | pagaron | pagarán | pagarían | **paguen** | pagaran | |
| | | | | | | | | |
| **seguir** | **sigo** | seguía | seguí | seguiré | seguiría | **siga** | siguiera | sigue **(no sigas)** |
| **(e → i, i)** | sigues | seguías | seguiste | seguirás | seguirías | **sigas** | siguieras | **siga** |
| *to follow* | sigue | seguía | siguió | seguirá | seguiría | **siga** | siguiera | seguid **(no sigáis)** |
| **gu → g** | seguimos | seguíamos | seguimos | seguiremos | seguiríamos | **sigamos** | siguiéramos | **sigan** |
| **before a, o** | seguís | seguíais | seguisteis | seguiréis | seguiríais | **sigáis** | siguierais | |
| siguiendo | siguen | seguían | siguieron | seguirán | seguirían | **sigan** | siguieran | |
| seguido | | | | | | | | |
| | | | | | | | | |
| tocar | toco | tocaba | **toqué** | tocaré | tocaría | **toque** | tocara | toca **(no toques)** |
| *to play, to touch* | tocas | tocabas | tocaste | tocará | tocarías | **toques** | tocaras | **toque** |
| **c → qu** | toca | tocaba | tocó | tocarás | tocaría | **toque** | tocara | tocad **(no** |
| **before e** | tocamos | tocábamos | tocamos | tocaremos | tocaríamos | **toquemos** | tocáramos | **toquéis)** |
| tocando | tocáis | tocabais | tocasteis | tocaréis | tocaríais | **toquéis** | tocarais | **toquen** |
| tocado | tocan | tocaban | tocaron | tocarán | tocarían | **toquen** | tocaran | |

# APÉNDICE D: Los verbos irregulares

| Infinitive / Present Participle / Past Participle | Present Indicative | Imperfect | Preterite | Future | Conditional | Present Subjunctive | Past Subjunctive | Commands |
|---|---|---|---|---|---|---|---|---|
| andar<br>*to walk*<br>andando<br>andado | ando<br>andas<br>anda<br>andamos<br>andáis<br>andan | andaba<br>andabas<br>andaba<br>andábamos<br>andabais<br>andaban | **anduve**<br>**anduviste**<br>**anduvo**<br>**anduvimos**<br>**anduvisteis**<br>**anduvieron** | andaré<br>andarás<br>andará<br>andaremos<br>andaréis<br>andarán | andaría<br>andarías<br>andaría<br>andaríamos<br>andaríais<br>andarían | ande<br>andes<br>ande<br>andemos<br>andéis<br>anden | **anduviera**<br>**anduvieras**<br>**anduviera**<br>**anduviéramos**<br>**anduvierais**<br>**anduvieran** | anda (no andes)<br>ande<br>andad<br>(no andéis)<br>anden |
| *caer<br>*to fall*<br>**cayendo**<br>caído | **caigo**<br>caes<br>cae<br>caemos<br>caéis<br>caen | caía<br>caías<br>caía<br>caíamos<br>caíais<br>caían | caí<br>**caíste**<br>**cayó**<br>**caímos**<br>**caísteis**<br>**cayeron** | caeré<br>caerás<br>caerá<br>caeremos<br>caeréis<br>caerán | caería<br>caerías<br>caería<br>caeríamos<br>caeríais<br>caerían | **caiga**<br>**caigas**<br>**caiga**<br>**caigamos**<br>**caigáis**<br>**caigan** | cayera<br>cayeras<br>cayera<br>cayéramos<br>cayerais<br>cayeran | cae (no caigas)<br>**caiga**<br>caed (**no caigáis**)<br>**caigan** |
| *dar<br>*to give*<br>dando<br>dado | **doy**<br>das<br>da<br>damos<br>dais<br>dan | daba<br>dabas<br>daba<br>dábamos<br>dabais<br>daban | **di**<br>**diste**<br>**dio**<br>**dimos**<br>**disteis**<br>**dieron** | daré<br>darás<br>dará<br>daremos<br>daréis<br>darán | daría<br>darías<br>daría<br>daríamos<br>daríais<br>darían | **dé**<br>**des**<br>**dé**<br>**demos**<br>**deis**<br>**den** | diera<br>dieras<br>diera<br>diéramos<br>dierais<br>dieran | da (no des)<br>**dé**<br>dad (**no deis**)<br>den |
| *decir<br>*to say, tell*<br>**diciendo**<br>**dicho** | **digo**<br>**dices**<br>**dice**<br>decimos<br>decís<br>**dicen** | decía<br>decías<br>decía<br>decíamos<br>decíais<br>decían | **dije**<br>**dijiste**<br>**dijo**<br>**dijimos**<br>**dijisteis**<br>**dijeron** | **diré**<br>**dirás**<br>**dirá**<br>**diremos**<br>**diréis**<br>**dirán** | **diría**<br>**dirías**<br>**diría**<br>**diríamos**<br>**diríais**<br>**dirían** | diga<br>digas<br>diga<br>digamos<br>digáis<br>digan | dijera<br>dijeras<br>dijera<br>dijéramos<br>dijerais<br>dijeran | **di (no digas)**<br>**diga**<br>decid (**no digáis**)<br>**digan** |
| *estar<br>*to be*<br>estando<br>estado | **estoy**<br>**estás**<br>**está**<br>estamos<br>estáis<br>**están** | estaba<br>estabas<br>estaba<br>estábamos<br>estabais<br>estaban | **estuve**<br>**estuviste**<br>**estuvo**<br>**estuvimos**<br>**estuvisteis**<br>**estuvieron** | estaré<br>estarás<br>estará<br>estaremos<br>estaréis<br>estarán | estaría<br>estarías<br>estaría<br>estaríamos<br>estaríais<br>estarían | **esté**<br>**estés**<br>**esté**<br>**estemos**<br>**estéis**<br>**estén** | estuviera<br>estuvieras<br>estuviera<br>estuviéramos<br>estuvierais<br>estuvieran | **está (no estés)**<br>**esté**<br>estad (**no estéis**)<br>**estén** |

| Infinitive<br>Present Participle<br>Past Participle | Present Indicative | Imperfect | Preterite | Future | Conditional | Present Subjunctive | Past Subjunctive | Commands |
|---|---|---|---|---|---|---|---|---|
| haber<br>*to have*<br>habiendo<br>habido | **he**<br>**has**<br>**ha [hay]**<br>**hemos**<br>**habéis**<br>**han** | había<br>habías<br>había<br>habíamos<br>habíais<br>habían | **hube**<br>**hubiste**<br>**hubo**<br>**hubimos**<br>**hubisteis**<br>**hubieron** | **habré**<br>**habrás**<br>**habrá**<br>**habremos**<br>**habréis**<br>**habrán** | **habría**<br>**habrías**<br>**habría**<br>**habríamos**<br>**habríais**<br>**habrían** | **haya**<br>**hayas**<br>**haya**<br>**hayamos**<br>**hayáis**<br>**hayan** | hubiera<br>hubieras<br>hubiera<br>hubiéramos<br>hubierais<br>hubiéran | |
| ★hacer<br>*to make, do*<br>haciendo<br>**hecho** | **hago**<br>haces<br>hace<br>hacemos<br>hacéis<br>hacen | hacía<br>hacías<br>hacía<br>hacíamos<br>hacíais<br>hacían | **hice**<br>**hiciste**<br>**hizo**<br>**hicimos**<br>**hicisteis**<br>**hicieron** | **haré**<br>**harás**<br>**hará**<br>**haremos**<br>**haréis**<br>**harán** | **haría**<br>**harías**<br>**haría**<br>**haríamos**<br>**haríais**<br>**harían** | **haga**<br>**hagas**<br>**haga**<br>**hagamos**<br>**hagáis**<br>**hagan** | hiciera<br>hicieras<br>hiciera<br>hiciéramos<br>hiciérais<br>hicieran | haz (**no hagas**)<br>haga<br>haced (**no hagáis**)<br>hagan |
| ir<br>*to go*<br>**yendo**<br>ido | **voy**<br>**vas**<br>**va**<br>**vamos**<br>**vais**<br>**van** | **iba**<br>**ibas**<br>**iba**<br>**íbamos**<br>**ibais**<br>**iban** | **fui**<br>**fuiste**<br>**fue**<br>**fuimos**<br>**fuisteis**<br>**fueron** | iré<br>irás<br>irá<br>iremos<br>iréis<br>irán | iría<br>irías<br>iría<br>iríamos<br>iríais<br>irían | **vaya**<br>**vayas**<br>**vaya**<br>**vayamos**<br>**vayáis**<br>**vayan** | fuara<br>fueras<br>fuera<br>fuéramos<br>fuerais<br>fueran | ve (**no vayas**)<br>vaya<br>id (**no vayáis**)<br>vayan |
| ★oír<br>*to hear*<br>**oyendo**<br>**oído** | **oigo**<br>**oyes**<br>**oye**<br>**oímos**<br>oías<br>**oyen** | oía<br>oías<br>oía<br>oíamos<br>oíais<br>oían | oí<br>**oíste**<br>**oyó**<br>**oímos**<br>**oísteis**<br>**oyeron** | oiré<br>oirás<br>oirá<br>oiremos<br>oiréis<br>oirán | oiría<br>oirías<br>oiría<br>oiríamos<br>oiríais<br>oirían | **oiga**<br>**oigas**<br>**oiga**<br>**oigamos**<br>**oigáis**<br>**oigan** | **oyera**<br>**oyeras**<br>**oyera**<br>**oyéramos**<br>**oyerais**<br>**oyeran** | oye (**no oigas**)<br>**oiga**<br>oíd (**no oigáis**)<br>**oigan** |

# APÉNDICE D: Los verbos irregulares *(continued)*

| Infinitive / Present Participle / Past Participle | Present Indicative | Imperfect | Preterite | Future | Conditional | Present Subjunctive | Past Subjunctive | Commands |
|---|---|---|---|---|---|---|---|---|
| poder<br>(o → ue)<br>*can, to be able*<br>**pudiendo**<br>podido | **puedo**<br>**puedes**<br>**puede**<br>podemos<br>podéis<br>**pueden** | podía<br>podías<br>podía<br>podíamos<br>podíais<br>podían | **pude**<br>**pudiste**<br>**pudo**<br>**pudimos**<br>**pudisteis**<br>**pudieron** | **podré**<br>**podrás**<br>**podrá**<br>**podremos**<br>**podréis**<br>**podrán** | **podría**<br>**podrías**<br>**podría**<br>**podríamos**<br>**podríais**<br>**podrían** | **pueda**<br>**puedas**<br>**pueda**<br>podamos<br>podáis<br>**puedan** | **pudiera**<br>**pudieras**<br>**pudiera**<br>**pudiéramos**<br>**pudierais**<br>**pudieran** | |
| ★poner<br>*to place, put*<br>poniendo<br>**puesto** | **pongo**<br>pones<br>pone<br>ponemos<br>ponéis<br>ponen | ponía<br>ponías<br>ponía<br>poníamos<br>poníais<br>ponían | **puse**<br>**pusiste**<br>**puso**<br>**pusimos**<br>**pusisteis**<br>**pusieron** | **pondré**<br>**pondrás**<br>**pondrá**<br>**pondremos**<br>**pondréis**<br>**pondrán** | **pondría**<br>**pondrías**<br>**pondría**<br>**pondríamos**<br>**pondríais**<br>**pondrían** | **ponga**<br>**pongas**<br>**ponga**<br>**pongamos**<br>**pongáis**<br>**pongan** | **pusiera**<br>**pusieras**<br>**pusiera**<br>**pusiéramos**<br>**pusierais**<br>**pusieran** | **pon (no pongas)**<br>**ponga**<br>poned (no **pongáis)**<br>**pongan** |
| querer<br>(e → ie)<br>*to want, wish*<br>queriendo<br>querido | **quiero**<br>**quieres**<br>**quiere**<br>queremos<br>queréis<br>**quieren** | quería<br>querías<br>quería<br>queríamos<br>queríais<br>querían | **quise**<br>**quisiste**<br>**quiso**<br>**quisimos**<br>**quisisteis**<br>**quisieron** | **querré**<br>**querrás**<br>**querrá**<br>**querremos**<br>**querréis**<br>**querrán** | **querría**<br>**querrías**<br>**querría**<br>**querríamos**<br>**querríais**<br>**querrían** | **quiera**<br>**quieras**<br>**quiera**<br>queramos<br>queráis<br>**quieran** | **quisiera**<br>**quisieras**<br>**quisiera**<br>**quisiéramos**<br>**quisierais**<br>**quisieran** | **quiere (no quieras)**<br>**quiera**<br>quered (no queráis)<br>**quieran** |
| reír<br>*to laugh*<br>**riendo**<br>**reído** | **río**<br>**ríes**<br>**ríe**<br>**reímos**<br>reís<br>**ríen** | reía<br>reías<br>reía<br>reíamos<br>reíais<br>reían | reí<br>**reíste**<br>**rió**<br>**reímos**<br>**reísteis**<br>**rieron** | reiré<br>reirás<br>reirá<br>reiremos<br>reiréis<br>reirán | reiría<br>reirías<br>reiría<br>reiríamos<br>reiríais<br>reirían | **ría**<br>**rías**<br>**ría**<br>**riamos**<br>**riáis**<br>**rían** | **riera**<br>**rieras**<br>**riera**<br>**riéramos**<br>**rierais**<br>**rieran** | **ríe (no rías)**<br>**ría**<br>**reíd (no riáis)**<br>**rían** |

★Verbs with irregular *yo*-forms in the present indicative

| Infinitive / Present Participle / Past Participle | Present Indicative | Imperfect | Preterite | Future | Conditional | Present Subjunctive | Past Subjunctive | Commands |
|---|---|---|---|---|---|---|---|---|
| *saber | **sé** | sabía | **supe** | **sabré** | **sabría** | **sepa** | **supiera** | sabe (**no sepas**) |
| *to know* | sabes | sabías | **supiste** | **sabrás** | **sabrías** | **sepas** | **supieras** | **sepa** |
| sabiendo | sabe | sabía | **supo** | **sabrá** | **sabría** | **sepa** | **supiera** | sabed (**no sepáis**) |
| sabido | sabemos | sabíamos | **supimos** | **sabremos** | **sabríamos** | **sepamos** | **supiéramos** | **sepan** |
| | sabéis | sabíais | **supisteis** | **sabréis** | **sabríais** | **sepáis** | **supierais** | |
| | saben | sabían | **supieron** | **sabrán** | **sabrían** | **sepan** | **supieran** | |
| *salir | **salgo** | salía | salí | **saldré** | **saldría** | **salga** | saliera | sal (**no salgas**) |
| *to go out* | sales | salías | saliste | **saldrás** | **saldrías** | **salgas** | salieras | **salga** |
| saliendo | sale | salía | salió | **saldrá** | **saldría** | **salga** | saliera | salid (**no salgáis**) |
| salido | salimos | salíamos | salimos | **saldremos** | **saldríamos** | **salgamos** | saliéramos | **salgan** |
| | salís | salíais | salisteis | **saldréis** | **saldríais** | **salgáis** | salierais | |
| | salen | salían | salieron | **saldrán** | **saldrían** | **salgan** | salieran | |
| ser | **soy** | **era** | **fui** | seré | sería | **sea** | **fuera** | **sé (no seas)** |
| *to be* | **eres** | **eras** | **fuiste** | serás | serías | **seas** | **fueras** | **sea** |
| siendo | **es** | **era** | **fue** | será | sería | **sea** | **fuera** | sed (**no seáis**) |
| sido | **somos** | **éramos** | **fuimos** | seremos | seríamos | **seamos** | **fuéramos** | **sean** |
| | **sois** | **erais** | **fuisteis** | seréis | seríais | **seáis** | **fuerais** | |
| | **son** | **eran** | **fueron** | serán | serían | **sean** | **fueran** | |
| *tener | **tengo** | tenía | **tuve** | **tendré** | **tendría** | **tenga** | **tuviera** | ten (**no tengas**) |
| *to have* | **tienes** | tenías | **tuviste** | **tendrás** | **tendrías** | **tengas** | **tuvieras** | **tenga** |
| teniendo | **tiene** | tenía | **tuvo** | **tendrá** | **tendría** | **tenga** | **tuviera** | tened (**no tengáis**) |
| tenido | tenemos | teníamos | **tuvimos** | **tendremos** | **tendríamos** | **tengamos** | **tuviéramos** | **tengan** |
| | tenéis | teníais | **tuvisteis** | **tendréis** | **tendríais** | **tengáis** | **tuvierais** | |
| | **tienen** | tenían | **tuvieron** | **tendrán** | **tendrían** | **tengan** | **tuvieran** | |

*Verbs with irregular *yo*-forms in the present indicative

# APÉNDICE D: Los verbos irregulares *(continued)*

| Infinitive / Present Participle / Past Participle | Present Indicative | Imperfect | Preterite | Future | Conditional | Present Subjunctive | Past Subjunctive | Commands |
|---|---|---|---|---|---|---|---|---|
| traer *to bring* **trayendo** **traído** | **traigo** traes trae traemos traéis traen | traía traías traía traíamos traíais traían | **traje** **trajiste** **trajo** **trajimos** **trajisteis** **trajeron** | traeré traerás traerá traeremos traeréis traerán | traería traerías traería traeríamos traeríais traerían | **traiga** **traigas** **traiga** **traigamos** **traigáis** **traigan** | **trajera** **trajeras** **trajera** **trajéramos** **trajerais** **trajeran** | trae (**no traigas**) **traiga** traed (**no traigáis**) **traigan** |
| ★venir *to come* **viniendo** venido | **vengo** **vienes** **viene** venimos venís **vienen** | venía venías venía veníamos veníais venían | **vine** **viniste** **vino** **vinimos** **vinisteis** **vinieron** | **vendré** **vendrás** **vendrá** **vendremos** **vendréis** **vendrán** | **vendría** **vendrías** **vendría** **vendríamos** **vendríais** **vendrían** | **venga** **vengas** **venga** **vengamos** **vengáis** **vengan** | **viniera** **vinieras** **viniera** **viniéramos** **vinierais** **vinieran** | **ven (no vengas)** **venga** venid (**no vengáis**) **vengan** |
| ver *to see* viendo **visto** | **veo** ves ve vemos veis ven | **veía** **veías** **veía** **veíamos** **veíais** **veían** | **vi** **viste** **vio** **vimos** **visteis** **vieron** | veré verás verá veremos veréis verán | veía veías veía veíamos veíais verían | **vea** **veas** **vea** **veamos** **veáis** **vean** | viera vieras viera viéramos vierais vieran | ve (**no veas**) **vea** ved (**no veáis**) **vean** |

★Verbs with irregular *yo*-forms in the present indicative

# Glosario: español-inglés

## A

**a cuadros** plaid, checked
**a rayas** striped
**a fin de que** in order that, so that
**a la hora** on time
**a menos que** unless
**a pesar de** despite
**¿A qué hora?** (At) What time?
**A su servicio.** You are welcome.
**A sus órdenes.** You are welcome.
**a veces** sometimes
**abandonar un programa** to quit a program
**abdomen** *m.* abdomen
**abogado(a)** attorney
**abordar** to board
**Abran el libro en la página...** Open your books on page . . .
**abrigo** overcoat
**abril** April
**abrir** to open
**abuelo(a)** grandfather (grandmother)
**aburrido** *adj.* bored
**acabar de** + *infinitive* to have just (done something)
**acampar** to camp
**accesible** *adj.* accessible
**aceite** *m.* oil
**¿Aceptan tarjetas de crédito?** Do you take credit cards?
**aceptar** to accept
**acomodar** to accommodate, to arrange
**aconsejar** to advise
**acordarse (ue) de** to remember
**acrílico** acrylic
**activo** *adj.* active
**aderezo** dressing
**¡Adiós!** Good-bye!
**administración de empresas** *f.* business administration
**administrar** to manage, to administer
**aeróbicos** aerobics
**aeropuerto** airport
**africano** *adj.* African

**afuera** away, outside
**agencia de bienes raíces** real estate agency
**agosto** August
**agresivo** *adj.* aggressive
**agricultor(a)** farmer
**agua** water
**ahora** now
**ajo** garlic
**al cubierto** indoors
**al lado de** next to
**alcalde** *m.* mayor
**alcantarillado** sewage system
**alcanzar (c)** to reach
**alegrarse (de)** to be glad (about)
**alegre** *adj.* happy
**alegría** happiness
**alergia** allergy
**alfombra** carpet
**álgebra** algebra
**algo** something
**¿Algo más?** Anything else?
**algodón** *m.* cotton
**alguien** somebody, someone, anyone
**algún** any, some
**alimentar** to feed
**allí** there
**almacén** *m.* store
**almeja** clam
**almuerzo** lunch
**alojamiento** lodging
**alquilar** to rent
**altavoz** *m.* speaker
**alto** *adj.* high, tall
**ama de casa** housewife
**amable** *adj.* kind
**amar** to love
**amar el trabajo** to love one's work
**amarillo** *adj.* yellow
**amigable** *adj.* friendly
**amigo(a)** friend
**amistad** *f.* friendship
**amistoso** *adj.* friendly
**amor** *m.* love
**anaranjado** *adj.* orange
**aniversario** anniversary
**anoche** last night
**antes (de) que** before

**antibiótico** antibiotic
**anticipo** down payment
**antipático** *adj.* unfriendly
**antropología** anthropology
**anuncio clasificado** classified ad
**añorar** to long for
**apagado** *adj.* turned off
**apagar** to turn off
**aparcamiento** parking lot
**apellido** last name
**aperitivo** before-dinner drink
**apoyar** to support
**aprender** to learn
**aquél/aquélla** that one (over there)
**aquéllos(as)** those ones
**aquí** here
**Aquí tiene.** Here you are.
**árbitro** referee
**árbol** *m.* tree
**archivo** file
**arena** sand
**arete** *m.* earring
**argentino** *adj.* Argentinean
**armario** dresser
**arnés** *m.* harness
**arquitecto(a)** architect
**arreglar** to fix, to tidy up
**arriesgarse** to take risks
**arroz** *m.* rice
**arte** *m.* art
**arvejas** peas
**artista** *m., f.* artist
**asiático** *adj.* Asian
**asiento** seat
**asistir** to attend
**aspirar (a)** to aspire to; to vacuum
**atender (ie) al público** to deal with customers
**ático** attic
**atletismo** track and field
**atún** *m.* tuna
**aumentar** to increase
**avión** *m.* airplane
**ayudar** to help
**azúcar** *m., f.* sugar
**azul** *adj.* blue

## B

**baile** *m.* dance
**bajar de peso** to lose weight
**bajo** *adj.* low, short
**bajo techo** indoors
**baloncesto** basketball
**banana** banana
**banco** bank
**bañador** swimsuit
**baño** bathroom
**bar** *m.* bar
**barato** *adj.* cheap
**barra** bar
**barrio** neighborhood
**basura** garbage, trash
**basurero** garbage hauler
**bautizo** baptism
**beber** to drink
**béisbol** *m.* baseball
**beneficencia** charity
**biblioteca** library
**bicicleta** bicycle
**bien** well, good, fine, okay
**Bien, ¿y tú?** Fine, and you?
   (informal)
**Bien, ¿y Ud.?** Fine, and you?
   (formal)
**bienes raíces** *m.* real estate
**bienvenido** *adj.* welcome
**billete** *m.* airline ticket
**billetera** wallet
**biología** biology
**bistec** *m.* beef steak
**blanco** *adj.* white
**blusa** blouse
**boca** mouth
**bocadillo** sandwich
**boda** wedding
**bola** ball
**boleto** airline ticket
**bolígrafo** pen
**boliviano** *adj.* Bolivian
**bolos** bowling
**bombero** firefighter
**bonito** *adj.* pretty, beautiful
**borrador** *m.* eraser
**bota** boot
**botiquín de primeros auxilios**
   *m.* first-aid kit
**brazo** arm
**brócoli** *m.* broccoli
**bucear** to dive

**buena presencia** good personal ap-
   pearance
**¡Buenas noches!** Good evening!
**¡Buenas tardes!** Good afternoon!
**bueno** *adj.* good,
**¡Buenos días!** Good Morning!
**Busco...** I am looking for . . .

## C

**caballo** horse
**cabeza** head
**cable** *m.* cable
**cada** each, every
**café** *m.* coffee; *adj.* brown
**caja** box
**caja de cartón** cardboard box
**cajero automático** automatic teller
   machine (ATM)
**calcetín** *m.* sock
**cálculo** calculus
**calentamiento** warm-up
**calle** *f.* street
**cama** bed
**camarón** *m.* shrimp
**cambiar** to exchange
**cambio** change
**caminar** to walk
**camión de mudanzas** *m.* moving
   truck
**camisa** shirt
**camiseta** T-shirt
**campesino(a)** farmer
**campo** countryside (field)
**cancha** court
**cangrejo** crab
**cansado** *adj.* tired
**cantar** to sing
**cara** face
**cargar** to load
**caridad** *f.* charity
**carne** *f.* meat
**carro** car
**carta** menu
**carta de presentación** cover letter
**cartera** handbag
**casa** house
**casado** *adj.* married
**casarse por la iglesia/por lo civil** to
   get married in a religious /civil
   ceremony
**casco** helmet
**casi nunca** almost never

**casi siempre** almost always
**CD** *m.* CD-ROM
**cebolla** onion
**ceja** eyebrow
**cena** dinner
**centro** downtown
**centro comercial** mall
**cerca de** near
**cerdo** pig
**cereal** *m.* cereal
**cerrar (ie)** to close
**césped** *m.* grass, lawn
**chaleco** vest
**champiñón** *m.* mushroom
**chaqueta** jacket
**charlar por teléfono** to chat on the
   phone
**¡Chau!** Bye!
**cheque** *m.* check
**cheque de viajero** traveler's
   check
**chícharos** peas
**chileno** *adj.* Chilean
**chofer** *m., f.* driver
**chuleta (de cerdo)** (pork) chop
**ciclismo** bike riding
**cien** one hundred
**cien mil** 100.000
**cien mil uno/a** 100.001
**cien mil dos** 100.002
**ciencias naturales** natural sciences
**ciencias políticas** political science
**ciencias sociales** social sciences
**ciento uno/a** 101
**ciento dos** 102
**ciento tres** 103
**cine** *m.* movies; movie theater
**cinta** tape
**cintura** waist
**cinturón** *m.* belt
**cliquear** to click
**clóset** *m.* closet
**cocina** kitchen
**cocinar** to cook
**cocinero(a)** cook
**coche** *m.* car
**codera** elbow pad
**codo** elbow
**colaborar** to collaborate
**collar** *m.* necklace
**colombiano** *adj.* Colombian
**color naranja** *adj.* orange
**combatir** to combat

**comedor** *m.* dining room
**comer** to eat
**cómico** *adj.* funny
**comida** food, meal, lunch
**como** like, as
**¿Cómo?** How?, What?, Excuse me?
**¿Cómo está Ud.?** How are you? (formal)
**¿Cómo estás?** How are you? (informal)
**¿Cómo se dice... ?** How do you say . . . ?
**¿Cómo te va?** How are you? (informal)
**compañero(a)** colleague
**compañero(a) de trabajo** co-worker
**compartir** to share
**competente** *adj.* competent
**comprar** to buy
**comprender** to understand
**comprometido** *adj.* engaged
**computadora** computer
**computadora portátil** laptop computer
**comunicación** *f.* communication
**con** with
**¡Con gusto!** You are welcome!, With pleasure!
**con tal de que** provided that
**conectar** to plug in
**conexión a Internet** *f.* Internet connection
**confiable** *adj.* trustworthy
**congestión** *f.* traffic congestion; congestion
**conocer (zc)** to know; to meet
**consejo** advice
**conservar** to preserve
**construir** to build
**consumir** to consume
**contable** *m., f.* accountant
**contaminación** *f.* pollution
**contar (ue) con** to count on
**contento** *adj.* happy
**contestar** to answer
**contrato** contract
**copa** wine glass
**corazón** *m.* heart
**corbata** tie
**corregir (i, i)** to correct
**correo electrónico** e-mail
**correr** to run
**cortar** to cut

**cortina** curtain
**corto** *adj.* short
**cosecha** harvest
**cosechar** to harvest
**costarricense** *adj. m., f.* Costa Rican
**costo de la vida** cost of living
**cotización** *f.* price estimation
**creativo** *adj.* creative
**criar** to raise
**cuaderno** notebook
**cuaderno de ejercicios** workbook
**cuadra** city block
**cuadro** painting
**¿Cuál? ¿Cuáles?** Which? Which ones?
**cualquier** any, whatever
**¿Cuándo?** When?
**cuando** when
**¿Cuánto?** How much?
**¿Cuántos?** How many?
**cuatrocientos/as** 400
**cubano** *adj.* Cuban
**cubiertos** tableware
**cuchara** spoon
**cucharita** teaspoon
**cuchillo** knife
**cuello** neck
**cuenta** check
**cuerda** rope
**cuerpo** body
**cuero** leather
**cuidar** to care for, to watch over, to look after
**cultivar** to cultivate
**cultivo** crop
**cultura masiva** mass culture
**cumpleaños** birthday
**cumplidor** *adj.* reliable, trustworthy
**cuñado(a)** brother-in-law/sister in law
**cuota inicial** down payment
**curar** to heal
**curita** Band-Aid
**currículum** *m.* résumé

## D

**dar** to give
**datos personales** personal information
**de buen humor** funny
**de fantasía** costume (jewelry)
**de lunares/puntos** polka-dot

**¡De nada!** You are welcome!
**de un solo tono** solid color
**de maravilla** great
**débil** *adj.* weak
**dedo** finger
**dedo del pie** toe
**defender (ie)** to defend
**dejar** to leave, to quit, to stop, to let (allow)
**dejar de** to quit, to stop (doing something)
**delegar parte del poder** to delegate power
**delgado** *adj.* thin
**delincuencia (juvenil)** (youth) crime
**deporte** *m.* sport
**deprimido** *adj.* depressed
**derecho** law, right
**derechos humanos** human rights
**desafío** challenge
**desayuno** breakfast
**descanso** rest
**desconectar** to unplug
**desde** from, since
**desear** to want
**desempacar** to unpack
**desenchufar** to unplug
**despacio** slowly
**despedida** farewell
**despertador** *m.* alarm clock
**después (de) que** after
**detrás de** behind
**día** *m.* day
**dibujo** drawing
**diciembre** December
**diente** *m.* tooth
**diez mil** 10.000
**diez mil uno/a** 10.001
**diez mil dos** 10.002
**difícil** *adj.* difficult
**digitar** to key in
**diligente** *adj.* diligent
**dinero** money
**dirección** *f.* address
**disco** CD
**discriminación** *f.* discrimination
**diseño** design
**disgustado** *adj.* angry
**distraer** to entertain, to amuse
**divertido** *adj.* fun

**divorciado** *adj.* divorced
**divorciarse** to get divorced
**doctor(a) (Dr.[a])** doctor
**documento** document
**doler (ue)** to ache, to hurt
**dolor de cabeza** *m.* headache
**domicilio** address
**domingo** Sunday
**dominicano** *adj.* Dominican
**¿Dónde?** Where?
**¿Dónde está?** Where is?
**dorado** *adj.* gold
**dormitorio** bedroom
**doscientos/as** 200
**doscientos/as uno/a** 201
**doscientos/as dos** 202
**doscientos/as tres** 203
**dos millones** 2.000.000
**duro** *adj.* hard, difficult

# E

**echar de menos** to miss
**ecología** ecology
**ecólogo** ecologist
**economía** economy
**ecosistema** *m.* ecosystem
**ecuatoriano** *adj.* Ecuadorian
**edificio** building
**educación** *f.* education
**educación física** physical education
**efectivo** cash
**eficiente** *adj.* efficient
**egoísta** *adj.* selfish
**elasticidad** *f.* flexibility
**electricidad** *f.* electricity
**embalaje** *m.* packing
**embriagado** *adj.* drunk
**emocionado** *adj.* excited
**empacadores** *m.* packing staff
**empacar** to pack
**emparedado** sandwich
**empleado(a)** employee
**empleado(a) doméstico(a)** maid
**en** on, in, at
**en cambio** instead
**en caso (de) que** in case, in the event that
**en cuanto** as soon as
**¿En qué puedo servirle, señor?** How can I help you, sir?
**enamorarse** to fall in love
**Encantado(a).** Pleased to meet you.

**encantar** to love, to like something very much
**encargarse de + *verb*** to be responsible for doing something
**encender (ie)** to turn on
**encendido** *adj.* turned on
**enchufar** to plug in
**encima de** on, over, above
**enero** January
**enfermarse** to get sick
**enfermero(a)** nurse
**enfermo** *adj.* sick
**enfrentar** to face; to confront
**enfrente de** in front of
**enojado** *adj.* angry
**ensalada** salad
**enseñar** to teach
**entrada** appetizer
**entre** between
**entremés** *m.* appetizer
**entretener (ie)** to entertain
**entrevista** interview
**enviar** to send
**envolver (ue)** to wrap
**equipaje** *m.* luggage
**equipaje de mano** carry on luggage
**equipo** equipment; team
**es dudoso** it is doubtful
**¡Es fantástico!** It's wonderful!
**¡Es ideal!** It's wonderful!
**es importante** it is important
**es imposible** it is impossible
**es improbable** it is improbable (not likely)
**es justo** it is fitting
**¡Es maravilloso!** It's wonderful!
**es mejor** It is better
**es necesario** it is necessary
**¡Es perfecto!** It's wonderful!
**es posible** it is possible
**es preciso** it is necessary
**es probable** it is probable
**es urgente** it is urgent
**escalada libre** rock climbing
**escalar** to climb
**escalera** stairs
**escena** scene
**Escriban...** Write . . .
**escribir** to write
**escritorio** desk
**escuchar** to listen to
**escultor(a)** sculptor
**escultura** sculpture
**eso(a)** that one

**esos(as)** those (ones)
**espalda** back
**español** *adj.* Spanish
**espárrago** asparagus
**especialidad** *f.* major
**especie** *f.* species
**especie en vía de extinción** threatened species
**espejo** mirror
**esposo(a)** husband/wife
**esquí** *m.* ski
**esquiar** to ski
**esquiar en el agua** to water-ski
**esquina** street corner
**estación** *f.* season
**estación de policía** police station
**estación de trenes/autobús/metro** train/bus/subway station
**estacionamiento** parking lot
**estado civil** marital status
**estadounidense** *adj. m., f.* American (from the US)
**estampado** print
**Están/Son como para chuparse los dedos.** They are finger-licking good.
**¿Están listos para pedir?** Are you ready to order?
**estante** *m.* bookcase
**estar** to be
**estar dispuesto** to be ready (eager)
**estar (parcialmente) nublado** to be (partly) cloudy
**éste(a)** this one
**estéreo** stereo
**estimado** price estimation
**estiramiento** stretching
**estómago** stomach
**éstos(as)** these (ones)
**estrés** *m.* stress
**estricto** *adj.* strict
**estudiante** *m., f.* student
**estudios realizados** studies completed
**estufa** stove
**estúpido** *adj.* stupid
**europeo** *adj.* European
**evitar** to avoid
**expediente** *m.* file
**experiencia laboral** work experience
**exposición** *f.* exposition
**extinción** *f.* extinction
**extinguirse** to become extinct

**extrañar** to miss
**extrovertido** *adj.* extroverted

## F

**fácil** *adj.* easy
**facilidad de expresión** *f.* ease of
　expression, ability to speak
**falda** skirt
**fallarle** to fail (not be there)
**familia** family
**famoso** *adj.* famous
**farmacia** pharmacy
**fauna** fauna, wildlife
**fax** *m.* fax
**febrero** February
**fecha de nacimiento** date of birth
**fecha de grado** graduation date
**feliz** *adj.* happy
**feo** *adj.* ugly
**fibra** fiber
**fiebre** *f.* fever
**fiel** *adj.* faithful
**filete de res/salmón** *m.* beef/salmon
　filet
**filosofía** philosophy
**finalmente** *adv.* finally
**finca** farm
**firme** *adj.* firm
**fisioterapia** physical therapy
**flaco** *adj.* skinny
**flora** flora
**formulario** application form
**fotografía** photography
**fresa** strawberry
**frijoles** *m.* beans
**frito** *adj,* fried
**fruta** fruit
**fuerte** *adj.* strong
**fuerza** strength
**fumar** to smoke
**funcionario(a) público(a)** public
　official
**fútbol** *m.* soccer
**fútbol americano** football
**futuro** future

## G

**gafas protectoras** goggles
**galería de arte** art gallery
**galleta** cookie
**gallina** hen

**gambas** shrimp
**ganado** livestock
**ganar** to gain
**garaje** *m.* garage
**garganta** throat
**gas** *m.* natural gas
**gato** cat
**generoso** *adj.* generous
**geografía** geography
**geología** geology
**geometría** geometry
**gerente** *m.* manager
**gimnasia** gymnastics
**gimnasio** gymnasium
**golpear** to hit
**gordo** *adj* fat
**gorra** cap
**Gracias.** Thank you.
**gracioso** *adj.* funny
**graduación** *f.* graduation
**grande** *adj.* big
**grasa animal** animal fat
**gripe** *f.* flu
**gris** *adj.* gray
**guante** *m.* glove
**guapo** handsome
**guardamuebles** *m.* storage
**guardaparques** *m.* park ranger
**guardar** to store, to save,
**guatemalteco** *adj.* Guatamalan
**guerra** war
**gustar** to like, to please

## H

**habitación** *f.* bedroom
**hablar** to talk, to speak
**hacer** to do, to make
**hacer buen tiempo** to be good
　weather
**hacer calor** to be hot
**hacer clic** to click
**hacer estiramiento** to stretch
**hacer fresco** to be cool
**hacer frío** to be cold
**hacer la cama** to make the bed
**hacer mal tiempo** to be bad
　weather
**hacer realidad** to make come true
**hacer sol** to be sunny
**hacer surf** to surf
**hacer un poco de calentamiento** to
　do some warm-up exercises

**hacer un viaje** to take a trip
**hacer una pregunta** to ask a
　question
**hacer viento** to be windy
**halar** to pull
**hambre** *m.* hunger
**hamburguesa** hamburger
**hasta (que)** until
**¡Hasta la vista!** See you around!
**Hasta luego.** See you later.
**¡Hasta pronto!** See you soon!
**helado** ice cream
**hermanastro(a)** stepbrother/
　stepsister
**hermano(a)** brother/sister
**hijo(a)** son/daughter
**hipoteca** mortgage
**historia** history, story
**hogar** *m.* household, home
**hoja de vida** résumé
**¡Hola!** Hi! Hello!
**hombre de negocios** *m.* business-
　man
**hombro** shoulder
**hondureño** *adj.* Honduran
**honesto** *adj.* honest
**horno microóndas** microwave oven
**hospital** *m.* hospital
**hotel** *m.* hotel
**hueso** bone
**huevo** egg
**humanidades** *f.* humanities

## I

**idioma** *m.* language
**iglesia** church
**ilusión** *f.* dream, illusion
**imagen** *f.* image
**impermeable** *m.* raincoat
**impresora** printer
**imprimir** to print
**indiferencia** indifference
**individual** *m.* placemat
**infiel** *adj.* unfaithful
**influenza** flu
**informática** computer science
**informe** *m.* report
**ingeniería** engineering
**ingeniería multimedia** multimedia
　engineering
**ingeniero(a)** engineer
**inmobiliaria** real estate agency

**insertar** to insert
**instalar** to install
**inteligente** *adj.* intelligent
**invertir (ie, i)** to invest
**investigación** *f.* research
**investigar** to research, to investigate
**invierno** winter
**ir** to go
**irse** to leave
**isla** island

## J

**jalar** to pull
**jamón** *m.* ham
**jarabe** *m.* cough syrup
**jardín** *m.* garden
**jefe(a)** boss
**joven** *adj.* young
**jubilación** *f.* retirement
**judía verde** string bean
**juego** game, set
**jueves** *m.* Thursday
**jugador(a)** player
**jugar (ue)** to play
**jugo** juice
**julio** July
**junio** June
**juntos** together
**juzgar** to judge

## L

**lago** lake
**lámpara** lamp
**lana** wool
**langosta** lobster
**lápiz** *m.* pencil
**largo** *adj.* long
**lavandería** laundromat
**lavar** to wash
**lavar la ropa** to do laundry
**lavar los platos** to do the dishes
**leal** *adj.* loyal
**Lean...** Read . . .
**leche** *f.* milk
**lechuga** lettuce
**leer** to read
**legumbre** *f.* vegetable
**lejos de** far
**lengua** language
**lentes de sol** *m.* sunglasses

**levantamiento de pesas** weight lifting
**librería** bookstore
**libro** book
**licencia profesional** professional license
**licenciado(a)/Lic(a).** (for various professions) licensed
**limonada** lemonade
**limpiar** to clean
**liso** *adj.* straight, solid color
**listo** *adj.* smart, ready
**literatura** literature
**llamada telefónica** phone call
**llegar** to reach
**llegar a ser** to become
**llevar** to wear
**llover (ue)** to rain
**lograr** to achieve
**los...** on (day[s] of the week)
**lucha libre** wrestling
**lugar de interés** *m.* landmark
**lunes** *m.* Monday
**luz** *f.* light, electricity

## M

**madrastra** stepmother
**madre** *f.* mother
**maíz** *m.* corn
**maleta** suitcase
**maletín** *m.* briefcase
**malo** *adj.* bad, mean
**mamá** mother
**manejar** to operate, to handle, to drive, to manage
**mango** mango
**mano** *f.* hand
**manta** blanket
**mantel** *m.* tablecloth
**mantener (ie)** to maintain, to support
**mantenerse en buen estado de salud** to keep in good health
**mantenerse en forma** to keep fit
**mantequilla** butter
**manzana** apple; city block
**mar** *m.* sea
**maravilloso** *adj.* wonderful
**marcador** *m.* marker
**marcar** to label
**mareo** dizziness
**mariscos** seafood

**marrón** *adj.* brown
**martes** *m.* Tuesday
**marzo** March
**más** more
**Más despacio, por favor.** More slowly, please.
**más o menos** so so
**matemáticas** mathematics
**material sintético** *m.* synthetic material
**matrícula profesional** professional license
**matrimonio** wedding
**mayo** May
**mayor** *adj.* mature, older
**Me llamo...** My name is . . .
**¿Me podría traer... ?** Could you bring me . . . ?
**media** sock, stocking
**medicina** medicine
**médico(a)** doctor
**medio ambiente** environment
**mejillones** *m.* mussels
**mejor** better
**mejorar** to improve
**melón** *m.* melon
**menaje** *m.* household goods, belongings
**menor** *adj.* younger
**mensaje electrónico** *m.* e-mail
**mentir (ie, i)** to lie
**mermelada** jam, marmalade, jelly
**mes** *m.* month
**mesa** table
**mesa de centro (mesita)** coffee table
**mesa de noche/mesa de luz (mesita)** bedside table
**mesero(a)** waiter/waitress
**meta** goal
**metal** *m.* metal
**mexicano** *adj.* Mexican
**miel** *f.* honey
**mientras que** while, whereas
**miércoles** *m.* Wednesday
**mil** *m.* one thousand
**mil uno/a** 1.001
**mil dos** 1.002
**millón** *m.* one million
**mineral** *m.* mineral
**minifalda** mini-skirt
**mirar** to see, to look at, to watch
**miseria** extreme poverty
**mochila** backpack
**montaña** mountain

**montar a caballo** to horseback ride

**morado** *adj.* purple

**moreno** *adj.* dark-haired

**mostaza** mustard

**mostrar (ue)** to show

**motor de búsqueda** *m.* search engine

**movimiento** movement (school)

**Muchas gracias.** Many thanks.

**mucho** many, much

**Mucho gusto.** Pleased to meet you.

**mudanza** move

**mudarse** to move

**muebles** *m.* furniture

**muestra** sample, show

**mujer de negocios** *f.* businesswoman

**mundo** world

**museo** museum

**música** music

**Muy bien, gracias.** Very well, thank you.

**muy** very

## N

**nacimiento** birth

**nacionalidad** *f.* nationality

**nada** nothing

**nadar** to swim

**nadie** nobody

**naranja** orange

**nariz** *f.* nose

**natación** *f.* swimming

**naturalista** *m. f.* naturalist

**navegar el Internet (la red)** to surf the net

**negro** *adj.* black

**nervioso** *adj.* nervous

**nevar (ie)** to snow

**nevera** refrigerator

**ni... ni** neither . . . nor

**nicaragüense** *adj. m., f.* Nicaraguan

**nieto(a)** grandson/granddaughter

**No comprendo.** I do not understand.

**No funciona.** It doesn't work. / It is broken.

**nombre** *m.* name

**Nos vemos el lunes.** I'll see you on Monday.

**novecientos/as** 900

**novecientos mil** 900.000

**novecientos noventa y nueve mil** 999.000

**noviembre** November

**novio(a)** boyfriend, girlfriend, fiancé(e)

**nuevo** *adj.* new

**nunca** never

## O

**objeto** object

**obra** work

**obra maestra** masterpiece

**obrero(a)** construction worker

**ochocientos/as** 800

**octubre** October

**ocupado** *adj.* busy

**odio** hatred

**oficina de correos** post office

**oficina de turismo** tourist office

**oído** inner ear

**Ojalá.** I hope.

**ojo** eye

**olvidar** to forget

**oprimir** to push, to hit, to click

**ordenador** *m.* computer

**oreja** ear

**oro** gold

**otoño** fall

## P

**paciente** *adj.* patient

**padrastro** stepfather

**padre** *m.* father

**página** page

**paisaje** *m.* landscape

**palabra** word

**pan** *m.* bread

**pan tostado** toast

**pana** corduroy

**panameño** *adj.* Panamanian

**pantalla** screen

**pantalones** *m.* pants

**pantalones cortos** shorts

**papa** potato

**papas fritas** french fries

**para que** in order that, so that

**parada de autobús/tren/metro** bus/train/subway stop

**paraguayo** *adj.* Paraguayan

**paramédico(a)** paramedic

**parásitos intestinales** parasites

**parecer (zc)** to deem, to consider, to seem, to appear

**pared** *f.* wall

**pariente** *m., f.* relative

**parlante** speaker

**parque** *m.* park

**parqueadero** parking lot

**pasaporte** *m.* passport

**pasar hambre** to be hungry

**pasar tiempo libre/los ratos libres** to spend free time

**pasear** to take a short trip, to go for a walk

**pasillo** aisle

**pasta** pasta

**pastel** *m.* cake

**pastilla** pill

**patatas fritas** french fries

**patinaje (sobre hielo)** *m.* skating (ice skating)

**patinaje en línea** in-line skating

**pato** duck

**patria** homeland

**pavo** turkey

**pedalear** to pedal

**pedir (i, i)** to ask, request

**película** movie

**pelo** hair

**pelo blanco** gray hair

**pelo castaño** brown hair

**pelota** ball

**peluquería** barber shop, beauty parlor

**peluquero(a)** hairdresser

**pendiente** *m.* earring

**pequeño** *adj.* small

**pera** pear

**perder (ie)** to lose

**perezoso** *adj.* lazy

**periodismo** journalism

**periodista** *m., f.* journalist

**permitir** to allow, permit

**pero** but

**perro** dog

**pescado** fish (caught)

**peso** weight

**pez** *m.* fish (live)

**pie** *m.* foot

**piel** *f.* skin

**pierna** leg

**pimienta** pepper

**pintor(a)** painter

**pintura** painting

**piña** pineapple

**pizarra** blackboard, chalkboard
**pizza** pizza
**planos** blueprints
**planta baja** first floor
**plástico de burbujas** bubblewrap
**plata** silver
**plátano** plantain, banana
**plateado** *adj.* silver
**platillo** saucer
**plato** dish, plate
**plato principal** entrée (main course)
**playa** beach
**plaza** town square
**pobre** *adj.* poor
**poco: un poco** some, a little
**poder** *m.* power
**poder (ue)** to be able, to succeed
**policía** *m., f.* police, policeman(woman)
**policía vial (de tránsito)** traffic police
**poliéster** *m.* polyester
**pollo** chicken
**por** for, on
**por ciento** percent
**por cierto** for certain
**por ello** because of that
**por eso** because of that
**por esto** because of this
**por favor** please
**por fin** finally
**por la mañana** in the morning
**por la noche** at night
**por la tarde** in the afternoon
**por otro lado** on the other hand
**¿por qué?** why?
**Por supuesto.** Of course.
**postre** *m.* dessert
**pregunta** question
**prender** to turn on
**preocupado** *adj.* worried, preoccupied
**preocuparse** to worry about
**preparar** to prepare
**presentar** to present, to introduce
**presentarse** to present oneself, to appear
**preservar** to preserve
**presionar** to push, to hit
**préstamo** loan
**primavera** spring
**primer piso** *m.* second floor

**primo(a)** cousin
**producir** to produce
**producto refinado** refined product
**profesión** *f.* job
**profesional** *m., f.* professional
**profesor(a)** teacher
**programa** *m.* program
**programador(a) de computadoras** computer programmer
**programar** to program
**promover (ue)** to promote
**propiedad** *f.* property
**propina** tip
**proporción** *f.* proportion
**proteger** to protect
**proteína** protein
**puerco** pig, pork
**puerta** door
**puertorriqueño** *adj.* Puerto Rican
**pulcera** bracelet
**pulmón** *m.* lung
**pulsar** to push, to hit
**puntual** *adj.* punctual

## Q

**¿Qué?** What?
**¿Qué significa... ?** What does . . . mean?
**¿Qué tiempo hace?** What is the weather like?
**quehaceres** *m.* chores
**¿Quién?, ¿Quiénes?** Who?
**queso** cheese
**querer** to want, to love
**química** chemistry
**quinientos/as** five hundred

## R

**rábalo** bass
**radiografía** x-rays
**raqueta** racket
**rasgo** trait
**ratón** *m.* mouse
**recámara** bedroom
**recepción** *f.* reception desk
**receta** prescription
**recibir** to receive
**reciclar** to recycle
**recoger** to collect, to pick up
**recuerdo** memory
**recursos naturales** natural resources

**reducir (zc)** to reduce
**reforestar** to reforest
**refresco** soda
**refrigerador** *m.* refrigerator
**refugio natural (silvestre)** wildlife reserve
**regresar** to return
**regular** *adj.* regular, so so
**reloj** *m.* watch
**reparar** to fix, to repair
**repetir (i, i)** to repeat
**representar** to represent
**reserva biológica** biological reserve
**resfriado** cold
**resistencia** resistance
**respetar** to respect
**respeto** respect
**respetuoso** *adj.* respectful
**responder** to answer
**responsable** *adj.* responsible
**restaurante** *m.* restaurant
**reto** challenge
**reunión** *f.* meeting
**revisar el buzón** to check the mailbox
**revuelto** *adj.* scrambled
**rico** *adj.* rich
**riesgo** risk
**río** river
**rizado** *adj.* curly
**róbalo** bass
**rodilla** knee
**rodillera** knee pad
**rojo** *adj.* red
**ropa** clothes, laundry
**ropa interior** underwear
**rosado** *adj.* pink
**rubio** *adj* blond(e)
**ruido** noise

## S

**sábado** Saturday
**saber** to know (how)
**sacar** to get, to take out, to obtain
**sal** *f.* salt
**sala** (living) room
**sala de espera** boarding area
**salchicha** sausage (hot dog)
**salir (juntos)** to go out, to exit, to leave, (to date)
**salón de belleza** *m.* beauty parlor
**salón de clase** classroom

**salsa de tomate** tomato sauce
**salud** *f.* health
**saludo** greeting
**salvadoreño** *adj.* Salvadorian
**salvar** to save
**sandalia** sandal
**sandía** watermelon
**sándwich** *m.* sandwich
**sección de no fumar** *f.*
  non-smoking section
**seda** silk
**seguro de sí mismo** *adj.* confident
**seiscientos/as** 600
**selva** jungle
**semáforo** traffic light
**semana** week
**sembrar (ie)** to sow
**sentido del humor** sense of humor
**sentir (ie, i)** to feel, lament
**sentirse mal** to feel ill
**Señor (Sr.)** Sir, Mr.
**Señora (Sra.)** Madam, Mrs.
**Señorita (Srta.)** Miss
**separarse** to get separated
**septiembre** September
**ser** to be
**ser novios** to be dating/going out
**serio** *adj.* serious
**servicios públicos** utilities
**servicios sociales** social services
**servilleta** napkin
**set** *m.* set
**setecientos/as** 700
**sicología** psychology
**siempre** always
**silla** chair
**sillón** *m.* armchair
**simpático** *adj.* nice
**sobre** on, over, above
**sobrino(a)** nephew/niece
**sofá** *m.* sofa
**solicitar** to request
**solicitar trabajo** to apply for a job
**solicitud** *f.* application
**solidaridad** *f.* solidarity
**soltero** *adj.* single
**sombrero de sol** sun hat
**sopa** soup
**sótano** basement
**subir de peso** to gain weight
**suegro(a)** father-in-law/
  mother-in-law
**suelo** soil

**sueño** dream
**suéter** *m.* sweater
**supermercado** supermarket

## T

**también** also
**tampoco** neither, either
**tarea** homework, duty
**tarjeta de crédito** credit card
**tarjeta de embarque** boarding pass
**taza** cup
**té** *m.* tea
**techo** roof
**teclado** keyboard
**técnica** technique
**técnico** *m., f.* technician
**tejanos** blue jeans
**tela** fabric
**teléfono** telephone, phone number
**televisión** *f.* television, TV
**televisor** *m.* television set
**tenedor** *m.* fork
**Tenemos una reservación a nombre
  de...** We have a reservation. The
  name is . . .
**tener** to have
**tener calor** to be hot
**tener constancia** to be constant, to
  persist
**tener disciplina** to be disciplined
**tener éxito** to be successful
**tener frío** to be cold
**tener ganas de** to want, to have the
  desire (to do something)
**tener hambre** to be hungry
**tener miedo (de)** to be afraid (of )
**tener paciencia** to be patient
**tener prisa** to be in a hurry
**tener sed** to be thirsty
**tener sueño** to be sleepy
**tener suerte** to be lucky
**tenis** *m.* tennis
**teñido** *adj.* colored
**terminal internacional** *f.* international departures terminal
**terminar** to finish, to break up
**términos de financiamiento** credit
  terms
**ternera** veal
**tiempo** time; weather
**tienda** store
**tienda de ropa** clothing store

**tierra** land, earth, homeland
**tijeras** scissors
**tímido** *adj.* shy
**tintorería** dry cleaners
**tío(a)** uncle/aunt
**tirar** to throw
**título** title
**tiza** chalk
**tobillo** ankle
**tocino** bacon
**todos los días** every day
**tolerante** *adj.* tolerant
**tomar** to take, to drink
**tomate** *m.* tomato
**tonto** *adj.* foolish, dull
**toro** bull
**torta** cake
**tos** *f.* cough
**trabajador** *adj.* hardworking
**trabajador(a)** worker
**trabajador(a) no calificado(a)**
  unqualified worker
**trabajo social** social work
**traje** *m.* suit
**traje de baño** swimsuit
**transporte** *m.* transportation
**trasladarse** to relocate
**traslado** relocation, transfer
**tratar de** to try
**trescientos/as** 300
**triste** *adj.* sad
**trucha** trout

## U

**ubicación** *f.* location
**un millón** 1.000.000
**uña** fingernail
**uruguayo** *adj.* Uruguayan
**usar** to use, to wear
**útil** *adj.* useful
**utilizar (c)** to make use
**uva** grape

## V

**vaca** cow
**valle** *m.* valley
**vaqueros** blue jeans
**variedad** *f.* variety
**vaso** glass
**vegatales** *m.* vegetables
**vendedor(a)** salesperson

**vender** to sell
**venezolano** *adj.* Venezuelan
**venta** sale
**ventana, ventanilla** window
**ver** to see, to look
**ver televisión** to watch TV
**verano** summer
**verde** *adj.* green
**verduras** vegetables
**vestido** dress
**veterinario(a)** veterinary
**viajar** to travel
**vida** life
**viejo** *adj.* old
**viernes** *m.* Friday
**vinagre** *m.* vinegar

**vincularse** to get involved
**vino** wine
**violencia** violence
**vitamina** vitamin
**viuda** widow
**vivir** to live
**volcán** *m.* volcano
**voleibol** *m.* volleyball
**volver (ue)** to return
**Vuelva pronto.** Come back soon.

# Y

**y** and
**yeso** cast

# Z

**zanahoria** carrot
**zapatilla** slipper
**zapato** shoe
**zapato alto/de tacones** high heel shoe
**zapato de tenis** sneakers
**zumo** juice

# Glosario: inglés-español

## A

**a little** un poco
**abdomen** abdómen *m.*
   **ability to speak** facilidad de
     expresión *f.*
**above** sobre, encima de
**accept** aceptar
**accessible** accesible *adj.*
**accommodate** acomodar
**accountant** contable *m., f.*
**achieve** lograr
**acrylic** acrílico
**active** activo *adj.*
**address** dirección *f.,* domicilio
**administer** administrar
**advice** consejo
**advise** aconsejar
**aerobics** aeróbicos
**African** africano *adj.*
**after** después (de) que
**aggressive** agresivo *adj.*
**airline ticket** billete *m.,* boleto
**airplane** avión *m.*
**airport** aeropuerto
**aisle** pasillo
**alarm clock** despertador *m.*
**alergy** alergia
**algebra** álgebra
**allow** permitir
**almost always** casi siempre
**almost never** casi nunca
**also** también
**always** siempre
**American** (from the US) estadounidense *adj.*
**amuse** distraer
**and** y
**angry** disgustado, enojado *adj.*
**animal fat** grasa animal
**ankle** tobillo
**answer** contestar, responder
**anthropology** antropología
**antibiotic** antibiótico
**any** algún, cualquier
**anyone** alguien
**Anything else?** ¿Algo más?
**appear** parecer (zc), presentarse
**appetizer** entrada, entremés *m.*
**apple** manzana

**application** solicitud *f.*
**application form** formulario
**apply for a job** solicitar trabajo
**April** abril
**architect** arquitecto(a)
**Are you ready to order?** ¿Está listo
   para pedir?
**Argentinean** argentino *adj.*
**arm** brazo
**armchair** sillón *m.*
**arrange** acomodar
**art** arte *m.*
**art gallery** galería de arte
**artist** artista *m., f.*
**as** como
**as soon as** en cuanto
**Asian** asiático *adj.*
**ask** pedir (i, i)
**ask a question** hacer una pregunta
**asparagus** espárrago
**aspire to** aspirar a
**at** en
**at night** por la noche
**attend** asistir
**attic** ático
**attorney** abogado(a)
**August** agosto
**aunt** tía
**automatic teller machine (ATM)**
   cajero automático
**avoid** evitar
**away** afuera

## B

**back** espalda
**backpack** mochila
**bacon** tocino
**bald** calvo *adj.*
**ball** bola, pelota
**banana** banana
**Band-Aid** curita
**bank** banco
**baptism** bautizo
**bar** bar *m.*
**bar** barra
**barber shop** peluquería
**bass** rábalo
**baseball** béisbol *m.*
**basement** sótano

**basketball** baloncesto
**bathroom** baño
**be** ser; estar
**be able** poder
**be afraid (of )** tener miedo (de)
**be bad weather** hacer mal tiempo
**be cold** tener frío, hacer frío
**be constant** tener constancia
**be cool** hacer fresco
**be dating/going out** ser novios
**be disciplined** tener disciplina
**be glad (about)** alegrarse (de)
**be good weather** hacer buen tiempo
**be hot** tener calor, hacer calor
**be hungry** tener hambre, pasar
   hambre
**be in a hurry** tener prisa
**be lucky** tener suerte
**be (partly) cloudy** estar (parcialmente) nublado
**be patient** tener paciencia
**be ready (eager)** estar dispuesto
**be responsible for (doing some-**
   **thing)** encargarse de + *verb*
**be sleepy** tener sueño
**be successful** tener éxito
**be sunny** hacer sol
**be thirsty** tener sed
**be windy** hacer veinto
**beach** playa
**beans** frijoles *m.*
**beautiful** bonito *adj.*
**beauty parlor** peluquería, salón de
   belleza *m.*
**because of that** por ello, por eso
**because of this** por esto
**become** llegar a ser
**become extinct** extinguirse
**bed** cama
**bedroom** dormitorio, habitación *f.,*
   recámara
**bedside table** mesa de noche/de luz
   (mesita)
**beef filet** filete de res *m.*
**beef steak** bistec *m.*
**before** antes (de) que
**before-dinner drink** aperitivo
**behind** detrás de
**belongings** menaje *m.*
**belt** cinturón *m.*

**better** mejor
**between** entre
**bicycle** bicicleta
**bike riding** ciclismo
**big** grande *adj.*
**biological reserve** reserva biológica
**biology** biología
**birth** nacimiento
**birthday** cumpleaños
**black** negro *adj.*
**black hair** pelo negro
**blanket** manta
**blond(e)** rubio *adj.*
**blond hair** pelo rubio
**blouse** blusa
**blue** azul *adj.*
**blue jeans** tejanos, vaqueros
**blueprints** planos
**board** abordar
**boarding area** sala de espera
**boarding pass** tarjeta de embarque
**body** cuerpo
**Bolivian** boliviano *adj.*
**bone** hueso
**book** libro
**bookcase** estante *m.*
**bookstore** librería
**boot** bota
**bored** aburrido *adj.*
**boss** jefe(a)
**bowling** bolos
**box** caja
**boyfriend** novio
**bracelet** pulsera
**bread** pan *m.*
**break (up)** terminar
**breakfast** desayuno
**briefcase** maletín *m.*
**broccoli** brócoli *m.*
**brother** hermano
**brother-in-law** cuñado
**brown** marrón, café *adj.*
**brown hair** pelo castaño
**bubblewrap** plástico de burbujas
**build** construir
**building** edificio
**bull** toro
**bus station** estación de autobús *f.*
**bus stop** parada de autobús
**business administration** administración de empresas *f.*
**businessman** hombre de negocios *m.*
**businesswoman** mujer de negocios *f.*
**busy** ocupado *adj.*

**but** pero
**butter** mantequilla
**button** botón *m.*
**buy** comprar
**Bye!** ¡Chau!

# C

**cable** cable *m.*
**cake** pastel *m.*, torta
**calculus** cálculo
**camp** acampar
**cap** gorra
**car** coche *m.*, carro
**cardboard box** caja de cartón
**care for** cuidar
**carpet** alfombra
**carrot** zanahoria
**carry-on luggage** equipaje de mano *m.*
**cash** efectivo
**cast** yeso
**cat** gato
**CD** disco
**CD-ROM** CD *m.*
**cereal** cereal *m.*
**chair** silla
**chalk** tiza
**chalkboard** pizarra
**challenge** desafío, reto
**change** cambio
**charity** beneficencia, caridad *f.*
**chat on the phone** charlar por teléfono
**cheap** barato *adj.*
**check** cheque *m.*
**check** *(bill)* cuenta
**check the mailbox** revisar el buzón
**checked** a cuadros *adj.*
**cheese** queso
**chemistry** química
**chicken** pollo
**Chilean** chileno *adj.*
**chores** quehaceres *m.*
**church** iglesia
**city block** cuadra, manzana
**clam** almeja
**classified ad** anuncio clasificado.
**classroom** salón de clase *m.*
**clean** limpiar
**click** cliquear, hacer clic, oprimir
**climb** escalar
**close** cerrar (ie)
**closet** clóset *m.*

**clothes** ropa
**clothing store** tienda de ropa
**coffee** café *m.*
**coffee table** mesa de centro (mesita)
**cold** resfriado
**collaborate** colaborar
**colleague** compañero(a)
**collect** recoger
**Colombian** colombiano *adj.*
**colored** teñido *adj.*
**combat** combatir
**Come back soon.** Vuelva pronto.
**communication** comunicación *f.*
**competent** competente *adj.*
**computer programmer** programador(a) de computadoras
**computer science** informática
**computer** computadora, ordenador *m.*
**confident** seguro de sí mismo *adj.*
**confront** enfrentar
**congestion** congestión *f.*
**consider** parecer (zc)
**construction worker** obrero(a)
**consume** consumir
**contract** contrato
**cook** cocinar
**cook** cocinero(a)
**cookie** galleta
**corduroy** pana
**corn** maíz *m.*
**correct** corregir (i, i)
**cost of living** costo de la vida
**Costa Rican** costarricense *adj. m., f.*
**costume (jewelry)** de fantasía
**cotton** algodón *m.*
**Could you bring me . . . ?** ¿Me podría traer...?
**cough syrup** jarabe *m.*
**cough** tos *f.*
**count on** contar con (ue)
**countryside** campo
**court** cancha
**cousin** primo(a)
**cover letter** carta de presentación
**cow** vaca
**co-worker** compañero(a) de trabajo
**crab** cangrejo
**creative** creativo *adj.*
**credit card** tarjeta de crédito
**credit terms** términos de financiamiento

**crime (youth)** delincuencia (juvenil)
**crop** cultivo
**Cuban** cubano *adj.*
**cultivate** cultivar
**cup** taza
**curly** rizado *adj.*
**curtain** cortina
**cut** cortar

## D

**dance** baile *m.*
**dark-haired** moreno *adj.*
**date of birth** fecha de nacimiento
**date** salir (juntos)
**daughter** hija
**day** día *m.*
**deal with customers** atender (ie) al público
**December** diciembre
**defend** defender (ie)
**delegate power** delegar parte del poder
**depressed** deprimido *adj.*
**design** diseño
**desk** escritorio
**dessert** postre *m.*
**develop** desarrollar
**difficult** duro, difícil *adj.*
**diligent** diligente *adj.*
**dining room** comedor *m.*
**dinner** cena
**discrimination** discriminación *f.*
**dish** plato
**dive** bucear
**divorced** divorciado *adj.*
**dizziness** mareo
**do** hacer
**do laundry** lavar la ropa
**do some warm-up exercises** hacer un poco de calentamiento
**do the dishes** lavar los platos
**Do you take credit cards?** ¿Aceptan tarjetas de crédito?
**doctor** doctor(a) (Dr.[a]), médico(a)
**document** documento
**dog** perro
**Dominican** dominicano *adj.*
**door** puerta
**down payment** cuota inicial, anticipo

**downtown** centro
**drawing** dibujo
**dream** ilusión *f.*, sueño
**dress** vestido
**dresser** armario
**dressing** aderezo
**drink** tomar, beber
**drive** manejar
**driver** chofer *m., f.*
**drunk** embriagado *adj.*
**dry cleaners** tintorería
**duck** pato
**dull** tonto *adj.*
**duty** tarea

## E

**each** cada
**ear** oreja
**earring** arete *m.*, pendiente *m.*
**earth** tierra
**ease of expression** facilidad de expresión *f.*
**easy** fácil *adj.*
**eat** comer
**ecologist** ecólogo
**ecology** ecología
**economy** economía
**ecosystem** ecosistema *m.*
**Ecuadorian** ecuatoriano *adj.*
**education** educación *f.*
**efficient** eficiente *adj.*
**either** tampoco
**elbow** codo
**elbow pad** codera
**electricity** electricidad *f.*, luz *f.*
**e-mail** mensaje electrónico *m.*
**employee** empleado(a)
**engaged** comprometido *adj.*
**engineer** ingeniero(a)
**engineering** ingeniería
**entertain** distraer, entretener (ie)
**entrée (main course)** plato principal
**environment** medio ambiente
**equipment** equipo
**eraser** borrador *m.*
**European** europeo *adj.*
**every** cada
**every day** todos los días
**exchange** cambio
**excited** emocionado *adj.*
**Excuse me?** ¿Cómo?
**exit** salir

**exposition** exposición *f.*
**extinction** extinción *f.*
**extroverted** extrovertido *adj.*
**eye** ojo
**eyebrow** ceja
**e-mail** correo electrónico

## F

**face** enfrentar
**face** cara
**fabric** tela
**fail (not be there)** fallarle
**faithful** fiel *adj.*
**fall** otoño
**fall in love** enamorarse
**family** familia
**famous** famoso *adj.*
**far** lejos de
**farewell** despedida
**farm** finca
**farmer** campesino(a), agricultor(a)
**fat** gordo *adj*
**father** padre *m.*
**father-in-law** suegro
**fauna** fauna
**fax** fax *m.*
**February** febrero
**feed** alimentar
**feel** sentir (ie, i)
**feel ill** sentirse mal
**fever** fiebre *f.*
**fiancé** novio
**fiancée** novia
**fiber** fibra
**field** campo
**file** expediente *m.*
**file** archivo
**finally** por fin, finalmente *adv.*
**fine** bien
**Fine, and you? (informal)** Bien, ¿y tú?
**Fine, and you? (formal)** Bien, ¿y Ud.?
**finger** dedo
**fingernail** uña
**finish** terminar
**firefighter** bombero(a)
**firm** firme *adj.*
**first floor** planta baja
**first-aid kit** botiquín de primeros auxilios *m.*
**fish (caught)** pescado
**fish (live)** pez *m.*

**five hundred** quinientos
**fix** arreglar, reparar
**flexibility** elasticidad *f.*
**flora** flora
**flu** gripe *f.*, influenza
**food** comida
**foolish** tonto *adj.*
**foot** pie *m.*
**football** fútbol americano *m.*
**for** por
**forget** olvidar
**fork** tenedor *m.*
**french fries** papas/patatas fritas
**Friday** viernes *m.*
**fried** frito *adj.*
**friend** amigo(a)
**friendly** amistoso, amigable *adj.*
**friendship** amistad *f.*
**from** desde
**fruit** fruta
**fun** divertido *adj.*
**funny** cómico, gracioso *adj.*, de buen humor
**furniture** muebles *m.*
**future** futuro

## G

**gain** ganar
**gain weight** subir de peso
**game** juego
**garage** garaje *m.*
**garbage** basura
**garbage hauler** basurero
**garden** jardín *m.*
**garlic** ajo
**generous** generoso *adj.*
**geography** geografía
**geology** geología
**geometry** geometría
**get** sacar
**get divorced** divorciarse
**get involved** vincularse
**get married in a religious/civil ceremany** casarse por la iglesia/por lo civil
**get separated** separarse
**get sick** enfermarse
**girlfriend** novia
**give** dar
**glass** vaso
**glove** guante *m.*
**go** ir
**go for a walk** pasear

**go out** salir
**goal** meta
**goggles** gafas protectoras
**gold** dorado *adj.*
**gold** oro
**good** bueno *adj.*
**Good afternoon!** ¡Buenas tardes!
**Good evening!** ¡Buenas noches!
**Good morning!** ¡Buenos días!
**Good-bye!** ¡Adiós!
**grandfather** abuelo
**grandmother** abuela
**grandson** nieto
**granddaughter** nieta
**graduation** graduación *f.*
**graduation date** fecha de grado
**grape** uva
**grass** césped *m.*
**gray** gris *adj.*
**gray hair** pelo blanco
**great** de maravilla
**green** verde *adj.*
**greeting** saludo
**Guatemalan** guatemalteco *adj.*
**gymnasium** gimnasio
**gymnastics** gimnasia

## H

**hair** pelo
**hair dresser** peluquero(a)
**ham** jamón *m.*
**hamburguer** hamburguesa
**hand** mano *f.*
**handbag** cartera
**handsome** guapo *adj.*
**happiness** alegría
**happy** alegre, feliz, contento *adj.*
**hard** duro *adj.*
**hardworking** trabajador(a) *adj.*
**harness** arnés *m.*
**harvest** cosecha
**harvest** cosechar
**hatred** odio
**have just (done something)** acabar de + *infinitive*
**head** cabeza
**headache** dolor de cabeza *m.*
**heal** curar
**health** salud *f.*
**heart** corazón *m.*
**helmet** casco
**help** ayudar

**hen** gallina
**here** aquí
**Here you are.** Aquí tiene.
**Hi!** ¡Hola!
**high** alto *adj.*
**high heel shoe** zapato alto/de tacones
**history** historia
**hit** golpear, pulsar
**home** hogar *m.*
**homeland** patria, tierra
**homework** tarea
**Honduran** hondureño *adj.*
**honest** honesto *adj.*
**honey** miel *f.*
**hope** esperar
**horror** horror *m.*
**horse** caballo
**hospital** hospital *m.*
**hotel** hotel *m.*
**house** casa
**household** hogar *m.*
**household goods** menaje *m.*
**housewife** ama de casa
**How?** ¿Cómo?
**How are you? (formal)** ¿Cómo está Ud.?
**How are you? (informal)** ¿Cómo estás?, ¿Cómo te va?
**How can I help you, sir?** ¿En qué puedo servirle, señor?
**How do you say . . . ?** ¿Cómo se dice... ?
**How many?** ¿Cuántos?
**How much?** ¿Cuánto?
**human rights** derechos humanos
**humanities** humanidades *f.*
**hunger** hambre *m.*
**hurt** doler (ue)
**husband** esposo

## I

**I am looking for . . .** Busco...
**I do not understand.** No comprendo.
**I'll see you on Monday.** Nos vemos el lunes.
**I hope.** Ojalá.
**ice cream** helado
**illusion** ilusión *f.*
**image** imagen *f.*
**improve** mejorar
**in** en
**in case** en caso (de) que

**in front of** enfrente de
**in order that** a fin de que, para que
**in the afternoon** por la tarde
**in the event that** en caso (de) que
**in the morning** por la mañana
**increase** aumentar
**indifference** indiferencia
**indoors** al cubierto, bajo techo
**in-line skating** patinaje en línea *m.*
**inner ear** oído
**insert** insertar
**install** instalar
**instead** en cambio
**intelligent** inteligente *adj.*
**international departures terminal**
    terminal internacional *f.*
**Internet connection** conexión a In-
    ternet *f.*
**interview** entrevista
**introduce** presentar
**invest** invertir (ie)
**investigate** investigar
**island** isla
**It doesn't work.** No funciona.
**It is wonderful!** ¡Es fantástico!, ¡Es
    ideal!, ¡Es maravilloso!, ¡Es perfecto!

## J

**jacket** chaqueta
**jam** mermelada
**January** enero
**jelly** mermelada
**job** profesión *f.*
**journalism** periodismo
**journalist** periodista *m., f.*
**judge** juzgar
**juice** jugo, zumo
**July** julio
**June** junio
**jungle** selva

## K

**keep** guardar
**keep fit** mantenerse en
    forma
**keep in good health** mantenerse en
    buen estado de salud
**key in** digitar
**keyboard** teclado
**kind** amable *adj.*
**kitchen** cocina
**knee** rodilla

**knee pad** rodillera
**knife** cuchillo
**know** conocer
**know (how)** saber

## L

**label** marcar
**lake** lago
**lamp** lámpara
**land** tierra
**landmark** lugar de interés *m.*
**landscape** paisaje *m.*
**language** lengua, idioma *m.*
**laptop computer** computadora
    portátil
**last name** apellido
**last night** anoche
**laundromat** lavandería
**laundry** ropa
**law** derecho
**lawn** césped *m.*
**lazy** perezoso *adj.*
**learn** aprender
**leather** cuero
**leave** salir, dejar, irse
**leg** pierna
**lemonade** limonada
**let (allow)** dejar
**lettuce** lechuga
**library** biblioteca
**lie** mentir (ie)
**life** vida
**light** luz *f.*
**like** como
**like** gustar
**like something very much** encantar
**listen to** escuchar
**literature** literatura
**live** vivir
**livestock** ganado
**living room** sala
**load** cargar
**loan** préstamo
**lobster** langosta
**location** ubicación *f.*
**lodging** alojamiento
**long** largo *adj.*
**long for** añorar
**look** ver
**look after** cuidar
**look at** mirar
**lose** perder (ie)
**lose weight** bajar de peso

**love** amor *m.*
**love (someone)** amar, querer
**love (something)** encantar
**love one's work** amar el trabajo
**low** bajo *adj.*
**loyal** leal *adj.*
**luggage** equipaje *f.*
**lunch** almuerzo, comida
**lung** pulmón *m.*

## M

**maid** empleado(a) doméstico(a)
**maintain** mantener
**major** especialidad *f.*
**make** hacer
**make come true** hacer realidad
**make the bed** hacer la cama
**make use** utilizar (c)
**mall** centro comercial
**manage** administrar, manejar
**mango** mango
**many** mucho
**Many thanks.** Muchas gracias.
**March** marzo
**marital status** estado civil
**marker** marcador *m.*
**marmalade** mermelada
**married** casado *adj.*
**mass culture** cultura masiva
**masterpiece** obra maestra
**mathematics** matemáticas
**mature** mayor *adj.*
**May** mayo
**mayor** alcalde *m.*
**meal** comida
**mean** malo *adj.*
**meat** carne *f.*
**medicine** medicina
**meet** conocer
**meeting** reunión *f.*
**melon** melón *m.*
**memory** recuerdo
**menu** carta
**metal** metal *m.*
**Mexican** mexicano *adj.*
**microwave oven** horno microóndas
**milk** leche *f.*
**mineral** mineral *m.*
**mini-skirt** minifalda
**mirror** espejo
**miss** echar de menos, extrañar
**Miss** Señorita (Srta.)
**Monday** lunes *m.*

**money** dinero
**month** mes *m.*
**more** más
**More slowly, please.** Más despacio, por favor.
**mortgage** hipoteca
**mother** mamá, madre *f.*
**mother-in-law** suegra
**mountain** montaña
**mouse** ratón (mouse) *m.*
**mouth** boca
**move** mudanza
**move** mudarse
**movement (school)** movimiento
**movie theater** cine *m.*
**movie** película
**movies** cine *m*
**moving truck** camión de mudanzas *m.*
**Mr., Sir** Señor (Sr.)
**Mrs., Madam** Señora (Sra.)
**much** mucho
**multimedia engineering** ingeniería multimedia
**museum** museo
**mushroom** champiñón *m.*
**music** música
**mussel** mejillón *m.*
**My name is . . .** Me llamo...

## N

**name** nombre *m.*
**napkin** servilleta
**nationality** nacionalidad *f.*
**natural gas** gas *m.*
**natural resources** recursos naturales
**natural sciences** ciencias naturales
**naturalist** naturalista *m., f.*
**near** cerca de
**neaklace** collar *m.*
**neck** cuello
**neighborhood** barrio
**neither** tampoco
**neither . . . nor** ni... ni
**nephew** sobrino
**nervous** nervioso *adj.*
**never** nunca
**next to** al lado de
**Nicaraguan** nicaragüense *adj. m., f.*
**nice** simpático *adj.*
**niece** sobrina
**nobody** nadie
**noise** ruido

**non-smoking section** sección de no fumar *f.*
**nose** naríz *f.*
**notebook** cuaderno
**nothing** nada
**November** noviembre
**now** ahora
**nurse** enfermero(a)

## O

**objects** objetos
**obtain** sacar
**ocean** océano
**October** octubre
**Of course.** Por supuesto.
**old** viejo *adj.*
**oil** aceite *m.*
**older** mayor *adj.*
**on** en, encima de, sobre
**on time** a la hora
**on the other hand** por otro lado
**one hundred** cien
**one million** millón *m.*
**one thousand** mil *m.*
**onion** cebolla
**open** abrir
**Open your books on page . . .** Abran el libro en la página...
**operate** actuar, manejar
**orange** anaranjado, color naranja *adj.*
**orange** naranja
**outside** afuera
**over** sobre, encima de
**overcoat** abrigo

## P

**pack** empacar
**packing** embalaje *m.*
**packing staff** empacadores *m., f.*
**page** página
**painter** pintor(a)
**painting** cuadro, pintura
**Panamanian** panameño *adj.*
**pants** pantalones *m.*
**Paraguayan** paraguayo *adj.*
**paramedic** paramédico(a)
**parasites** parásitos intestinales
**park ranger** guardaparques *m.*
**park** parque *m.*
**parking lot** aparcamiento, estacionamiento, parqueadero
**passport** pasaporte *m.*

**patient** paciente *adj.*
**pear** pera
**peas** arvejas, chícharos
**pedal** pedalear
**pen** bolígrafo
**pencil** lápiz *m.*
**pepper** pimienta
**percent** por ciento
**permit** permitir
**persist** tener constancia
**perseverance** constancia
**personal information** datos personales
**pharmacy** farmacia
**philosophy** filosofía
**phone call** llamada telefónica
**phone number** teléfono
**photography** fotografía
**physical education** educación física *f.*
**physical therapy** fisioterapia
**pick** picar
**pig** cerdo, puerco
**pill** pastilla
**pineapple** piña
**pizza** pizza
**pink** rosado *adj.*
**placemat** individual *m.*
**plaid** a cuadros
**plantain** plátano
**plate** plato
**play** jugar (ue)
**player** jugador(a)
**please** gustar
**please** por favor
**Pleased to meet you.** Encantado(a), Mucho gusto.
**plug in** conectar, enchufar
**police** policía
**police station** estación de policía *f.*
**policeman(woman)** policía *m., f.*
**political science** ciencias políticas
**polka-dot** de puntos, de lunares
**pollution** contaminación *f.*
**polyester** poliéster *m.*
**poor** pobre *adj.*
**pork** puerco
**(pork)chop** chuleta (de cerdo)
**post office** oficina de correos
**potato** papa
**power** poder *m.*
**preoccupied** preocupado *adj.*
**prepare** preparar
**prescription** receta

**present (oneself)** presentar(se)
**preserve** preservar, conservar
**pretty** bonito *adj,*
**price estimation** cotización *f.,* estimado
**print** imprimir
**print** estampado
**printer** impresora
**produce** producir
**professional** profesional *m., f.*
**professional license** licencia profesional, matrícula profesional
**program** programa *m.*
**program** programar
**promote** promover (ue)
**property** propiedad *f.*
**proportion** proporción *f.*
**protect** proteger
**protein** proteína
**provided that** con tal de que
**psychology** sicología
**public official** funcionario(a) público(a)
**Puerto Rican** puertorriqueño *adj.*
**pull** halar, jalar
**punctual** puntual *adj.*
**purple** morado *adj.*
**push** presionar, oprimir, pulsar

## Q

**question** pregunta
**quit** dejar de
**quit a program** abandonar un programa

## R

**racket** raqueta
**rain** llover (ue)
**raincoat** impermeable *m.*
**raise** criar
**reach** alcanzar (c), llegar
**read** leer
**Read . . .** Lean...
**ready** listo *adj.*
**real estate agency** inmobiliaria, agencia de bienes raíces
**receive** recibir
**recycle** reciclar
**red** rojo *adj.*
**red hair** pelo rojo
**reduce** reducir (zc)

**referee** árbitro
**refined product** producto refinado
**refrigerator** nevera, refrigerador *m.*
**regular** regular *adj.*
**relative** pariente *m., f.*
**reliable** cumplidor *adj.*
**relocate** trasladarse
**relocation** traslado
**remember** acordarse (ue) de
**rent** alquilar
**repair** reparar
**repeat** repetir (i, i)
**report** informe *m.*
**represent** representar
**request** pedir (i, i), solicitar
**research** investigación *f.*
**research** investigar
**resistance** resistencia
**respect** respetar
**respect** respeto
**respectful** respetuoso *adj.*
**responsible** responsable *adj.*
**rest** descanso
**restaurant** restaurante *m.*
**résumé** hoja de vida, currículum *m.*
**retirement** jubilación *f.*
**return** regresar, volver (ue)
**rice** arroz *m.*
**rich** rico *adj.*
**right** derecho
**risk** riesgo
**river** río
**rock climbing** escalada libre
**roof** techo
**rope** cuerda
**rude** grosero *adj.*
**run** correr

## S

**sad** triste *adj.*
**salad** ensalada
**sale** venta
**salesperson** vendedor(a)
**salmon filet** filete de salmón *m.*
**salt** sal *f.*
**Salvadorian** salvadoreño *adj.*
**sample** muestra
**sand** arena
**sandal** sandalia
**sandwich** bocadillo, emparedado, sándwich *m.*
**Saturday** sábado
**saucer** platillo

**sausage (hot dog)** salchicha
**save** salvar
**scene** escena
**scissors** tijeras
**scramble** revuelto *adj.*
**screen** pantalla
**sculptor** escultor(a)
**sculpture** escultura
**sea** mar *m.*
**seafood** mariscos
**search engine** motor de búsqueda *m.*
**season** estación *f.*
**seat** asiento
**second floor** primer piso *m.*
**see** mirar, ver
**See you around!** ¡Hasta la vista!
**See you later.** Hasta luego.
**See you soon!** ¡Hasta pronto!
**seem** parecer (zc)
**selfish** egoísta *adj.*
**sell** vender
**send** enviar
**sense of humor** sentido del humor
**September** septiembre
**serious** serio *adj.*
**set** set *m.,* juego
**sewage system** alcantarillado
**share** compartir
**shirt** camisa
**shoe** zapato
**short** corto, bajo *adj.*
**shorts** pantalones cortos *m.*
**shoulder** hombro
**show** mostrar (ue)
**shrimp** camarón *m.,* gamba
**shy** tímido *adj.*
**sick** enfermo *adj.*
**silver** plata
**silver** plateado *adj.*
**silk** seda
**since** desde
**sing** cantar
**sister** hermana
**sister-in-law** cuñada
**single** soltero *adj.*
**skating (ice skating)** patinaje (sobre hielo) *m.*
**ski** esquí *m.*
**ski** esquiar
**skin** piel *f.*
**skinny** flaco *adj.*
**skirt** falda

**slipper** zapatilla
**slowly** despacio
**small** pequeño *adj.*
**smart** listo *adj.*
**smoke** fumar
**sneakers** zapatos de tenis
**snow** nevar (ie)
**so so** más o menos, regular *adj.*
**so that** a fin de que, para que
**soccer** fútbol *m.*
**social services** servicios sociales
**social sciences** ciencias sociales
**social work** trabajo social
**sock** calcetín *m.*, media
**soda** refresco
**sofa** sofá *m.*
**soil** suelo
**solid color** de un solo tono, liso
**solidarity** solidaridad *f.*
**some** un poco, algún
**somebody** alguien
**someone** alguien
**something** algo
**sometimes** a veces
**son** hijo
**soup** sopa
**sow** sembrar (ie)
**Spanish** español *adj.*
**speak** hablar
**speaker** parlante *m.*, altavoz *m.*
**specialty** especialidad *f.*
**species** especie *f.*
**spend free time** pasar tiempo libre/los ratos libres
**spoon** cuchara
**sport** deporte *m.*
**spring** primavera
**stairs** escalera
**stepbrother** hermanastro
**stepfather** padrastro
**stepmother** madrastra
**stepsister** hemanastra
**stereo** estéreo
**stocking** media
**stomach** estómago
**stop (doing something)** dejar de
**storage** guardamuebles *m.*
**store** almacén *m.*,tienda
**store** guardar
**story** historia
**stove** estufa
**straight** liso *adj.*
**strawberry** fresa
**street** calle *f.*

**street corner** esquina
**strength** fuerza
**stress** estrés *m.*
**stretch** hacer estiramiento
**stretching** estiramiento
**strict** estricto *adj.*
**strike** huelga
**string bean** judía verde
**striped** a rayas
**strong** fuerte *adj.*
**student** estudiante *m., f.*
**studies completed** estudios realizados
**stupid** estúpido *adj.*
**subway station** estación de metro *f.*
**subway stop** parada de metro
**succeed** poder
**sugar** azúcar *m., f.*
**suit** traje *m.*
**suitcase** maleta
**summer** verano
**sun hat** sombrero de sol
**Sunday** domingo
**sunglasses** lentes de sol *m.*
**supermarket** supermercado
**support** apoyar
**support** mantener
**surf** hacer surf
**surf the net** navegar el Internet (la red)
**sweater** suéter *m.*
**swim** nadar
**swimming** natación *f.*
**swimsuit** bañador *m.*, traje de baño *m.*
**synthetic material** material sintético *m.*

# T

**table** mesa
**tablecloth** mantel *m.*
**tableware** cubiertos
**take** tomar
**take a short trip** pasear
**take a trip** hacer un viaje
**take out** sacar
**take risks** arriesgarse
**talk** hablar
**tall** alto *adj.*
**tape** cinta
**tea** té *m.*
**teach** enseñar
**teacher** profesor(a)

**team** equipo
**teaspoon** cucharita
**technician** técnico *m., f.*
**technique** técnica
**telecommunications** telecomunicaciones *f.*
**telephone** teléfono
**television** televisión *f.*
**television set** televisor *m.*
**tennis** tenis *m.*
**terrible** terrible *adj.*
**Thank you.** Gracias.
**that one (over there)** aquél (aquélla)
**that one** eso
**there** allí
**these (ones)** éstos(as)
**They are finger-licking good.** Están/Son como para chuparse los dedos.
**thin** delgado *adj.*
**this one** éste
**those** ésos(as)
**those (over there)** aquéllos
**threatened species** especie en vía de extinción *f.*
**throat** garganta
**throw** tirar
**Thursday** jueves *m.*
**tidy up** arreglar
**tie** corbata
**time** tiempo
**tip** propina
**tired** cansado *adj.*
**title** título
**toast** tostada
**toe** dedo del pie
**together** juntos
**tolerant** tolerante *adj.*
**tomato** tomate *m.*
**tomato sauce** salsa de tomate
**tooth** diente *m.*
**tourist office** oficina de turismo
**townsquare** plaza
**track and field** atletismo
**traffic congestion** congestión *f.*
**traffic light** semáforo
**traffic police** policia vial (de tránsito)
**train station** estación de trenes *f.*
**train stop** parada de trenes
**trait** rasgo
**transfer** traslado
**transportation** transporte *m., f.*
**trash** basura

**travel** viajar
**traveler's check** cheque de viajero *m.*
**tree** árbol *m.*
**trout** trucha
**trustworthy** confiable, cumplidor *adj.*
**try** querer, tratar de
**T-shirt** camiseta
**Tuesday** martes *m.*
**tuna** atún *m.*
**turkey** pavo
**turn off** apagar
**turn on** encender (ie), prender
**turned off** apagado
**turned on** encendido

## U

**ugly** feo *adj.*
**uncle** tío
**under** debajo de
**understand** comprender
**underwear** ropa interior
**unfaithful** infiel *adj.*
**unfriendly** antipático *adj.*
**unless** a menos que
**unpack** desempacar
**unplug** desconectar, desenchufar
**unqualified worker** trabajador(a) no calificado
**until** hasta (que)
**Uruguayan** uruguayo *adj.*
**use** usar
**useful** útil *adj.*
**utilities** servicios públicos

## V

**vacuum** aspirar
**valley** valle *m.*
**value** valor *m.*
**variety** variedad *f.*
**veal** ternera
**vegetable** verdura, legumbre *f.*, vegetal *m.*
**Venezuelan** venezolano *adj.*
**very** muy
**Very well, thank you.** Muy bien, gracias.
**vest** chaleco
**veterinary** veterinario(a)

**vinegar** vinagre
**violence** violencia
**violet** violeta *adj.*
**vitamin** vitamina
**volcano** volcán *m.*
**volleyball** voleibol *m.*

## W

**waist** cintura
**waiter/waitress** mesero(a)
**walk** caminar
**wall** pared *f.*
**wallet** billetera
**want** aspirar, desear, querer
**want (to do something)** tener ganas de
**war** guerra
**warehouse** bodega
**warm up** calentamiento
**wash** lavar
**watch** reloj *m.*
**watch** mirar
**watch over** cuidar
**watch TV** ver televisión
**water** agua
**watermelon** sandía
**water-ski** esquiar en el agua
**weak** débil *adj.*
**wear** usar, llevar
**weather** tiempo
**wedding** boda, matrimonio
**Wednesday** miércoles *m.*
**week** semana
**We have a reservation. The name is . . .** Tenemos una reservación a nombre de...
**weight** peso
**weight lifting** levantamiento de pesas
**welcome** bienvenido *adj.*
**well** bien
**What?** ¿Cómo?, ¿Qué?
**What does it mean?** ¿Qué significa?
**What is the weather like?** ¿Qué tiempo hace?
**(At) What time?** ¿A qué hora?
**whatever** cualquier
**when** cuando
**When?** ¿Cuándo?
**Where?** ¿Dónde?
**Where is?** ¿Dónde está?

**Where to?** ¿Adónde?
**whereas** mientras que
**Which?** ¿Cuál?
**Which ones?** ¿Cuáles?
**while** mientras (que)
**white** blanco *adj.*
**Who?** ¿Quién?, ¿Quiénes?
**Why?** ¿Por qué?
**widow** viuda
**wife** esposa
**wildlife reserve** refugio natural (silvestre)
**wildlife** fauna
**window** ventana, ventanilla
**wine** vino
**wine glass** copa
**winter** invierno
**with** con
**With pleasure!** ¡Con gusto!
**wonderful** maravilloso *adj.*
**wool** lana
**word** palabra
**work experience** experiencia laboral
**work** obra
**workbook** cuaderno de ejercicios
**worker** trabajador(a)
**world** mundo
**worried** preocupado
**worry about** preocuparse
**wrap** envolver (ue)
**wrestling** lucha libre
**write** escribir
**Write . . .** Escriban...

## X

**x-ray** radiografía

## Y

**yellow** amarillo *adj.*
**You are welcome!** ¡De nada!, ¡Con gusto!, A su servicio. A sus órdenes.
**young** joven *adj.*
**younger** menor *adj.*

## Z

**zero** cero

# Índice

## "Service-learning is education in action."
### Senator John Glenn

# **Temas** helps your students learn Spanish while they help their communities

Service-learning enriches education by engaging students in meaningful interactions and service to their schools and communities. At the same time, it benefits the community as a whole and helps break down the barriers that sometimes exist between colleges and universities and their surrounding communities. Students learn to apply their newly acquired and growing language skills as they solve real-world issues.

**Temas: Spanish for the Global Community** employs a unique and highly effective service-learning component to involve students in the community. Every chapter of **Temas** features service- and community-based learning activities that give students the opportunity to use their emerging linguistic abilities to effect change in the real world. These tasks put students in direct contact with their community, and help them develop awareness of their ability to make a difference—in school and beyond.

Throughout each chapter students will find *En tu comunidad* activities. These brief suggestions provide new ways for students to use what they're learning in new settings and in meaningful contexts.

> ### EN TU COMUNIDAD
> Research the topic of family constitution in your community or in your state. You may visit family agencies or other agencies that collect such data. Also, you can find out what the local government is doing to improve the quality of life of families. Then share the information with the class.

Each *Tema 2* ends with *Enfoque comunitario,* a very specific activity that requires students to interact with a Spanish-speaking individual or group in their own community. By moving the learning experience outside of the classroom and into the larger community, **Temas** helps students build partnerships that can bridge intergenerational, racial, and cultural gaps.

> **D. Enfoque comunitario** Get in touch with the office of international students in your school and interview one of their Spanish-speaking students. Ask him/her to describe his/her family and prepare for your instructor a brief summary of your findings in Spanish. If possible, invite the student to visit your class.

Each comprehensive *Puesta en acción* includes a *Servicio comunitario* section, which drives home the real-world focus of the entire program and requires interaction with Spanish speakers in the community.

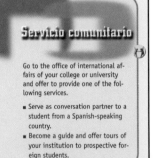

> ### Servicio comunitario
> Go to the office of international affairs of your college or university and offer to provide one of the following services.
> - Serve as conversation partner to a student from a Spanish-speaking country.
> - Become a guide and offer tours of your institution to prospective foreign students.

## Additional Resources

### Juntos: Community Partnerships in Spanish and Portuguese (Volume V)

*Josef Hellerbrandt, Jonathan Arries, and Lucía Varona* ■ 0-8384-6071-2

Published in association with the American Association of Teachers of Spanish and Portuguese, **Juntos** provides a concise overview and practical guide to establishing authentic learning partnerships through service- and community-based learning, promoting civic engagement.